BLMC 1100 & ⌐
Owners
Workshop
Manual

by J H Haynes
Member of the Guild of Motoring Writers

and B L Chalmers - Hunt
TEng (CEI), AMIMI, AMIRTE, AMVBRA

Models covered:
Austin America
Austin 1100 & 1300 Saloon & Estate Mk I, II & III
MG 1100 & 1300 Saloon Mk I & II
Morris 1100 & 1300 Saloon & Estate Mk I, II & III
Riley Kestrel Saloon Mk I & II
Vanden Plas Princess 1100 & 1300 Mk I & II
Vanden Plas Princess 1300 Mk III
Wolseley 1100 & 1300 Saloon Mk I & II
Wolseley 1300 Mk III

Covers manual and automatic transmission versions of the above.

ISBN 0 85696 260 0

2804/260

Printed in England (260 - 9C1)

HAYNES PUBLISHING GROUP
SPARKFORD YEOVIL SOMERSET ENGLAND
distributed in the USA by
HAYNES PUBLICATIONS INC
861 LAWRENCE DRIVE
NEWBURY PARK
CALIFORNIA 91320
USA

Acknowledgements

Thanks are due to BLMC Limited for their assistance in the supply of technical material, to Castrol Limited for advice on lubrication, and the Champion Sparking Plug Company supplied the illustrations showing the various spark plug conditions. The bodywork repair photographs used in this manual were provided by Lloyds Industries Limited who supply 'Turtle Wax', Dupli-color Holts', and other Holts range products.

Lastly, special thanks are due to all of those people at Sparkford who helped in the production of this manual. Particularly, Brian Horsfall and Les Brazier, who carried out the mechanical work and took the photographs respectively Rod Grainger who edited the text and Stanley Randolph who planned the layout of each page.

About this manual

This, the second edition of the Haynes BLMC 1100/1300 Owner's Workshop Manual, retains many elements of the original widely acclaimed, and very popular publication. It is a completely revised book containing details of most recent BLMC 1100/1300 models, and information on the modifications made to the range during its many years of production.

We like to think that the BLMC 1100/1300 manual has matured over the years, along with the BLMC 1100/1300, and that this manual like the car is even better than the original.

This is a manual for the do-it-yourself minded BLMC 1100/1300 motoring enthusiasts. It shows how to maintain these cars in first class condition, and how to carry out repairs when components become worn or break. By doing all maintenance and repair work themselves owners will gain three ways: they will know the job has been done properly; they will have had the satisfaction of doing the job themselves; and they will have saved garage labour charges which, although quite fair bearing in mind the high cost of capital equipment and skilled men, can be very high. Regular and careful maintenance is essential if maximum reliability and minimum wear are to be achieved.

The author has stripped, overhauled, and rebuilt all the major mechanical and electrical assemblies and most of the minor ones as well. Only through working in this way can solutions be found to the sort of problems facing private owners. Other hints and tips are also given which can only be obtained through practical experience.

The step-by-step photographic strip and rebuild sequences show how each of the major components was removed, taken apart, and rebuilt. In conjunction with the text and exploded illustrations this should make all the work quite clear - even to the novice who has never previously attempted the more complex job.

Manufacturers' official manuals are usually splendid publications which contain a wealth of technical information. Because they are issued primarily to help the manufacturers' authorised dealers and distributors they tend to be written in very technical language, and tend to skip details of certain jobs which are common knowledge to garage mechanics. *Haynes Owner's Workshop Manuals* are different as they are intended primarily to help the owner, and therefore contain details of all sorts of jobs not normally found in official manuals.

Owners who intend to do their own maintenance and repairs should have a reasonably comprehensive tool kit. Some jobs require special service tools, but in many instances it is possible to get round their use with a little care and ingenuity. For example a jubilee clip makes a most efficient and cheap piston ring compressor.

Throughout this manual ingenious ways of avoiding the use of special equipment and tools are shown. In some cases the proper tool must be used. Where this is the case the tool number and its correct use is included.

When a component malfunctions garage repairs are becoming more and more a case of replacing the defective item with an exchange rebuilt unit. This is excellent practice when a component is thoroughly worn out, but it is a waste of good money when overall the component is only half worn, and requires the replacement of but a single small item to effect a complete repair. As an example, a non-functioning dynamo can frequently be repaired quite satisfactorily just by fitting new brushes.

A further function of this manual is to show the owner how to examine malfunctioning parts; determine what is wrong; then how to make the repair.

Given the time, mechanical do-it-yourself aptitude, and a reasonable collection of tools this manual will show the enthusiastic owner how to maintain and repair his car really economically with minimum recourse to professional assistance and expensive tools and equipment.

Using the manual

The book is divided into twelve Chapters, each of which covers a logical sub-division of the vehicle. Each Chapter is divided into numbered Sections which are headed in **bold type** between horizontal lines. Each Section consists of serially numbered paragraphs.

There are two types of illustration:

Figures: These are numbered according to Chapter, and sequence of occurrence in that Chapter. Thus, 'Fig. 2.8' is the eighth illustration in Chapter 2. Every figure has an individual caption.

Photographs: The majority of the photographs in this manual form complete dismantling and reassembly sequences - and can be used, as such, with little reference to the text. If you are attempting a relatively major task for the first time, it may be better to use the text of the manual (which is more detailed), making occasional references to the relevant photographs. Photographic and textual sequences may vary slightly, so it is best to try to stick to one, or the other. Photographs which form a complete sequence are numbered serially. The remaining photographs have their reference numbers divided by a point (eg: 7.31). In this case the photograph number pinpoints the paragraph and Section number of the piece of text relevant to the photograph. Thus, the example quoted refers to paragraph 31/Section 7 of the Chapter in which the photograph occurs.

When the left or right-hand side of a car is mentioned it is as if one were looking in a forward direction of travel.

Although every care has been taken to ensure all the information in this manual is correct, no liability can be accepted by the authors or publishers for damage, loss, or injury caused by any errors in, or omissions from, the information given.

Contents

In addition each Chapter contains, where applicable: Specifications, General description and Fault diagnosis.

Glossary of terms

As this book has been written in England, it uses the appropriate English component names, phrases, and spelling. Some of these differ from those used in America. Normally, these cause no difficulty, but to make sure, a glossary is printed below. In ordering spare parts remember the parts list will probably use these words:

Glossary

English	American	English	American
Accelerator	Gas pedal	Leading shoe (of brake)	Primary shoe
Alternator	Generator (AC)	Locks	Latches
Anti-roll bar	Stabiliser or sway bar	Motorway	Freeway, turnpike etc.
Battery	Energizer	Number plate	Licence plate
Bonnet (engine cover)	Hood	Paraffin	Kerosene
Boot lid	Trunk lid	Petrol	Gasoline
Boot (luggage compartment)	Trunk	Petrol tank	Gas tank
Bottom gear	1st gear	'Pinking'	'Pinging'
Bulkhead	Firewall	Propellor shaft	Driveshaft
Camfollower or tappet	Valve lifter or tappet	Quarter light	Quarter window
Carburettor	Carburetor	Retread	Recap
Catch	Latch	Reverse	Back-up
Choke/venturi	Barrel	Rocker cover	Valve cover
Circlip	Snap ring	Roof rack	Car-top carrier
Clearance	Lash	Saloon	Sedan
Crownwheel	Ring gear (of differential)	Seized	Frozen
Disc (brake)	Rotor/disk	Side indicator lights	Side marker lights
Drop arm	Pitman arm	Side light	Parking light
Drop head coupe	Convertible	Silencer	Muffler
Dynamo	Generator (DC)	Spanner	Wrench
Earth (electrical)	Ground	Sill panel (beneath doors)	Rocker panel
Engineer's blue	Prussion blue	Split cotter (for valve spring cap)	Lock (for valve spring retainer)
Estate car	Station wagon	Split pin	Cotter pin
Exhaust manifold	Header	Steering arm	Spindle arm
Fast back (Coupe)	Hard top	Sump	Oil pan
Fault finding/diagnosis	Trouble shooting	Tab washer	Tang; lock
Float chamber	Float bowl	Tailgate	Liftgate
Free-play	Lash	Tappet	Valve lifter
Freewheel	Coast	Thrust bearing	Throw-out bearing
Gudgeon pin	Piston pin or wrist pin	Top gear	High
Gearchange	Shift	Trackrod (of steering)	Tie-rod (or connecting rod)
Gearbox	Transmission	Trailing shoe (of brake)	Secondary shoe
Halfshaft	Axle-shaft	Transmission	Whole drive line
Handbrake	Parking brake	Tyre	Tire
Hood	Soft top	Van	Panel wagon/van
Hot spot	Heat riser	Vice	Vise
Indicator	Turn signal	Wheel nut	Lug nut
Interior light	Dome lamp	Windscreen	Windshield
Layshaft (of gearbox)	Counter shaft	Wing/mudguard	Fender

Miscellaneous points

An "Oil seal" is fitted to components lubricated by grease!

A "Damper" is a "Shock absorber" it damps out bouncing, and absorbs shocks of bump impact. Both names are correct, and both are used haphazardly.

Note that British drum brakes are different from the Bendix type that is common in America, so different descriptive names result. The shoe end furthest from the hydraulic wheel cylinder is on a pivot; interconnection between the shoes as on Bendix brakes is most uncommon. Therefore the phrase "Primary" or "Secondary" shoe does not apply. A shoe is said to be Leading or Trailing. A "Leading" shoe is one on which a point on the drum, as it rotates forward, reaches the shoe at the end worked by the hydraulic cylinder before the anchor end. The opposite is a trailing shoe, and this one has no self servo from the wrapping effect of the rotating drum.

Buying spare parts
and vehicle identification numbers

Buying spare parts

Spare parts are available from many sources, for example: BLMC garages, other garages and accessory shops, and motor factors. Our advice regarding spare part sources is as follows:

Officially appointed BLMC garages - This is the best source of parts which are peculiar to your car and are otherwise not generally available (eg. complete cylinder heads, internal gearbox components, badges, interior trim etc). It is also the only place at which you should buy parts if your car is still under warranty; non-BLMC components may invalidate the warranty. To be sure of obtaining the correct parts it will always be necessary to give the storeman your car's engine and chassis number, and if possible, to take the 'old' part along for positive identification. Remember that many parts are available on a factory exchange scheme - any parts returned should always be clean! It obviously makes good sense to go straight to the specialists on your car for this type of part for they are best equipped to supply you.

Other garages and accessory shops - These are often very good places to buy materials and components needed for the maintenance of your car (eg. oil filters, spark plugs, bulbs, fan belts, oils and greases, touch-up paint, filler paste etc). They also sell general accessories, usually have convenient opening hours, charge lower prices and can often be found not far from home.

Motor factors - Good factors will stock all of the more important components which wear out relatively quickly (eg. clutch components, pistons, valves, exhaust systems, brake cylinders/pipes/hoses/seals/shoes and pads etc). Motor factors will often provide new or reconditioned components on a part exchange basis - this can save a considerable amount of money.

Vehicle identification numbers

When ordering spare parts it is essential to give full details of your car to the storeman. He will want to know the commission, car, and engine numbers. When ordering parts for the transmission unit or body it is also necessary to quote the transmission casing and body numbers.

Commission number: Stamped on a plate fixed on the bonnet locking platform.

Car number: Stamped on a metal plate fixed to the bonnet locking platform.

Engine number: Stamped on a metal plate fixed to the right-hand side of the cylinder block.

Transmission casing assembly: Stamped on a facing provided on the casing joint below the starter motor.

Body number: Stamped on a plate fixed to the right-hand wing valance.

Austin 1300 GT

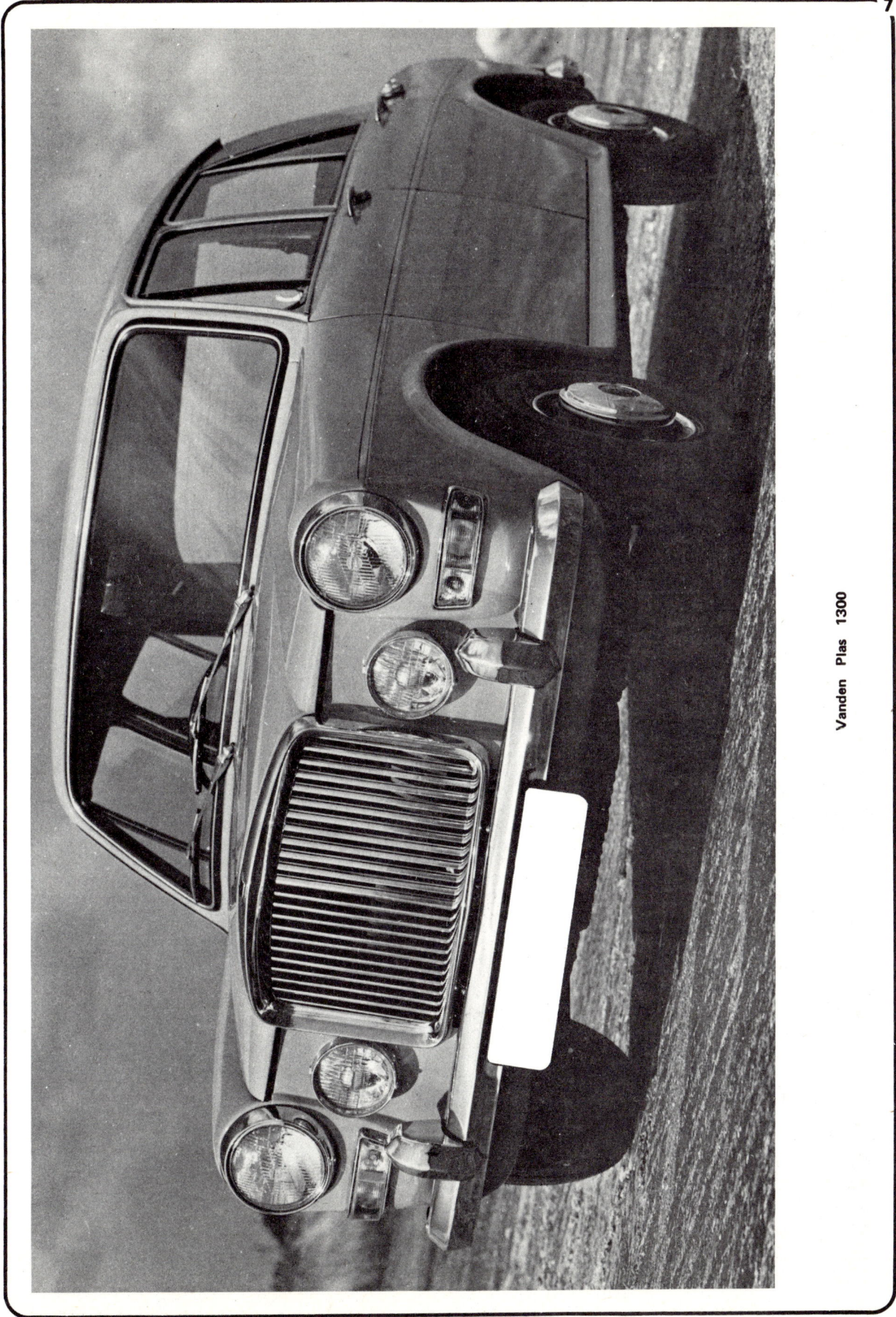

Vanden Plas 1300

Routine maintenance

The maintenance instructions listed are basically those recommended by the manufacturer. They are supplemented by additional maintenance tasks proven to be necessary.

The additional tasks are indicated by an asterisk (*) and are primarily of a preventative nature, in that they will assist in eliminating the unexpected failure of a component due to fair wear and tear.

When a new car is delivered the complete engine/transmission unit contains sufficient running-in oil for the running-in period. Providing the level is maintained between the low and high marks on the dipstick during this period, topping-up is unnecessary. At the first "Free Service", the running-in oil is drained and the sump replenished to the level of the high mark on the dipstick.

Important: Because of the US Federal regulations for exhaust emission several modifications have been made to the engine and ancillary equipment. This equipment should not be tampered with unless absolutely necessary. The car must then be taken to the local BLMC garage so that any adjustments necessary, as indicated by expensive electronic test equipment, may be made.

Weekly, before a long journey or every 250 miles (400 km)

1 Remove the dipstick and check the engine/transmission unit oil level which should be up to the 'MAX' mark. Top-up the oil with Castrol GTX. On no account allow the oil to fall below the 'MIN' mark on the dipstick. The distance between the 'MAX' and 'MIN' marks corresponds to approximately 2 pints. (1.14 litres).

2 Check the tyre pressures with an accurate gauge and adjust as necessary. As a safety precaution make sure that the tyre walls and treads are free of damage. Remember that the tyre tread must have a minimum of 1 millimetre depth across three quarters of the total width and around the whole circumference of the tyre.

3 Check the battery electrolyte level and top-up as necessary with distilled water. Make sure that the top of the battery is always kept clean and free of moisture.

4 Refill the windscreen washer bottle with soft water. Add an antifreeze satchet in cold weather to prevent freezing (do not use ordinary antifreeze). Check that the jets operate correctly.

5 Remove the wheel trims and check all wheel nuts for tightness but take care not to overtighten.

Every 3000 miles (5000 km) or 3 months

Complete the service items in the weekly service check plus:

1 Where the car is used for much town-work involving much stop/start driving; in very cold conditions; and in hot dusty conditions; run the engine until it has reached its normal working temperature. Then drain the oil from the sump/gearbox casing and wipe the magnetic drain plug clean. Refill with the correct amount of Castrol GTX (photo).

2 Jack-up the front of the car. Fill a grease gun with Castrol LM Grease or a similar multi-purpose grease and thoroughly lubricate the steering swivel knuckle joints. There are two grease nipples, one upper and one lower on each side (total 4) (photo).

3 Unscrew the tops of the carburettor/s dashpots and top up with Castrol GTX (photo).

4 Check the level of the hydraulic fluid in the clutch and brake master cylinder reservoir and top-up if the level has fallen to ¼ in. (6.5 mm), or more, below the bottom of the filler neck, with Castrol Girling Universal Brake and Clutch Fluid (photo).

5 Check the steering column clamp bolt for tightness.

6* Adjust the rear brakes, and on the front disc brakes inspect the friction pads for wear. Check the hoses and pipes for loose joints, or leaks or wear caused by the suspension or tyres rubbing

The sump drain plug

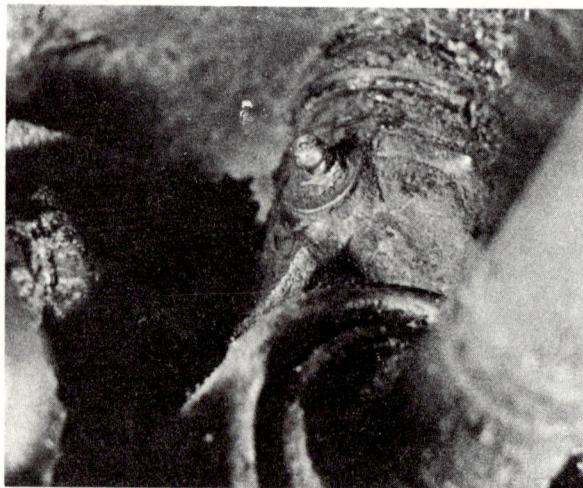

The upper right-hand steering swivel grease nipple

Topping-up the carburettor dashpot

The brake (left) and clutch (right) master cylinder reservoirs

When adjusting the fanbelt tension there are four bolts to be loosened at the dynamo attachment bolts. The 4th bolt (not visible) is behind the lower right-hand bolt.

against the flexible piping.

7* Carefully inspect the rubber boots over the CV joints for splits or tears and renew as necessary.

8* Wash the bodywork and chromium fittings and clean out the interior.

9 Remove the spark plugs, clean them and adjust the electrode gaps.

10* Check that all the lights are functioning correctly and replace blown bulbs as necessary.

11 Lubricate with engine oil and door hinges, bonnet lock operating mechanism, and the safety catch.

12 Lubricate the boot catch and hinges with engine oil.

13 Check the battery cell specific gravity readings, and clean the terminals.

14 Lubricate the dynamo rear bearing.

Note: If wished this task need only be performed once every 6,000 miles (10,000 km) but once every 3,000 miles (5,000 km) is to be preferred in the author's experience.

15 Examine the fan belt and adjust as necessary (photo).

16 Check the clearance at the clutch return stop and adjust as necessary.

17 Lubricate the carburettor controls.

Every 6,000 miles (10,000 km) or 6 months

Complete the service items in the 3000 mile service check plus:

1 Remove the SU carburettor suction chamber and piston; clean, reassemble and top-up the piston dampers with Castrol GTX.

2 Remove the oil filter, wash the bowl in petrol, and fit a new element and rubber seal. Refill the sump and filter with Castrol GTX.

3* Check the condition of the heater and cooling system hoses and replace as necessary.

4* Lubricate with engine oil the pivot point of the brake and clutch pedal shafts.

5* Check the fuel lines and the union joints for leaks and replace defective parts as necessary.

6 Remove and clean the filters in the carburettor/s and fuel pump where these are fitted.

7 Check and adjust the valve rocker clearances.

8 Remove the distributor cap, pull off the rotor arm and apply three drops of engine oil to the head of the large screw in the centre of the distributor.

9 Allow three drops of oil past the cam to the automatic timing mechanism.

10 Lubricate the four-sided cam by smearing a faint trace of grease over it.

11 Apply a tiny spot of oil to the moving contact breaker pivot pin. Any excess might get on the points and cause misfiring.

12 Check the condition of the contact breaker points. Clean and regap them, and if necessary fit a new set and check the timing and advance and retard mechanism.

13* Adjust the carburettor slow running and tune if necessary.

14* Examine the exhaust system for holes and leaks and replace defective components as necessary.

15* Wax polish the body and also the chromium plating. Force wax polish into any joints in the bodywork to help prevent rust formation.

16* Balance the front wheels to eliminate steering vibration as necessary.

17 Check and adjust the steering 'toe-in' of the front wheels.

18 Check the suspension nuts, and the steering nuts for tightness.

19* If wished, change over the tyres to equalise wear (not recommended for fabric belted radials) and inspect the walls for damage.

20 Lubricate the washer round the wheelbase spindle with several drops of glycerine.

Every 12,000 miles (20,000 km) or 12 months

Complete the service items in the 6000 mile service check plus:

1   Remove the carburettor float chamber, empty any sediment present, check the condition of the needle valve, clean and refit.

2   Remove the speedometer cable, clean, and lightly lubricate the inner cable with Castrol LM Grease or similar. When re-assembling the inner cable should be withdrawn approximately 8 in (203 mm) and the surface grease wiped off. This is so none will work its way into the speedometer head.

3*   Steam clean the underside of the body and clean the engine and engine compartment.

4   Remove the spark plugs, and fit new ones, correctly gapped.

5*   Inspect the ignition leads for cranks and perishing or damage and replace as necessary.

6*   Remove the brake drums, blow out the dust, and inspect the linings for wear.

7   Examine the dynamo brushes, replace them if worn, and clean the commutator.

8*   Renew the windscreen wiper blades.

9   Check the headlamp bulbs and renew them if slightly blackened or if the element sags.

10   On later models fitted with a crankcase closed circuit breather system, change the engine oil filler cap and clean the crankcase breather valve. All the metal parts can be washed in petrol. The diaphragm should be cleaned with detergent or methylated spirits.

11   Grease the one nipple on the gear change linkage with Castrol LM Grease or similar. The nipple is very inaccessible being between the bulkhead and engine and really requires a flexible hose. On no account give more than two strokes with the greasegun.

12   Lubricate the water pump. To do this unscrew the plug just behind the pulley wheel and grease sparingly with Castrol LM Grease. Replace the plug, If the pump squeaks a few tea-spoonfuls of hydraulic fluid in the cooling system will silence the carbon sealing ring.

13   Take out the air cleaner element by unscrewing the wing nut/s on top of the cleaner, and removing the cover and cleaner element. Clean out the inside of the air cleaner and fit a new cleaner element. Replace the cover and wing nut/s.

Every 24,000 miles (40,000 km) or 18 months

Complete the service items in the 6000 and 12000 mile service check as applicable plus:

1*   Check and adjust any loose play in the rack and pinion steering gear.

2*   Examine the ball joints and hub bearings for wear and replace as necessary.

3*   Examine the inner 'rubber' universal joints for wear and renew as necessary.

4*   Check the tightness of the battery earth lead on the body-work.

5*   Renew the condenser in the distributor.

6   Remove the starter motor, examine the brushes, and replace as necessary, and clean the commutator and starter drive.

7*   Test the cylinder compressions, and if necessary remove the cylinder head, decarbonise, grind the valve and fit new valve springs.

8   Drain the brake fluid from the hydraulic system. Renew all the rubber seals and flexible hoses. Examine the brake pistons and their bores for scratches and renew as necessary. Refill the system and bleed the brakes.

Other aspects of Routine Maintenance

1 Jacking up

Always chock a wheel on the opposite side in front as well as behind. The car's own jack has to be able to work when the car is very low with a flat tyre so it locates under the sill. Always ensure it is correctly positioned so the sill is not damaged

2 Wheel nuts

These should be cleaned and lightly smeared with grease as necessary during work, to keep them moving easily. If the nuts are stubborn to undo due to dirt and overtightening, it may be necessary to hold them by lowering the jack till the wheel rests on the ground. Normally if the wheel brace is used across the hub centre a foot or knee held against the tyre will prevent the wheel from turning, and so save the wheels and nuts from wear if the nuts are slackened with weight on the wheel. After replacing a wheel make a point later of rechecking the nuts again for tightness.

3 Safety

Whenever working, even partially, under the car, put an extra strong box or piece of timber underneath onto which the car will fall rather than onto you.

4 Cleanliness

Whenever you do any work allow time for cleaning. When something is in pieces or components removed to improve access to other areas, give an opportunity for a thorough clean. This cleanliness will allow you to cope with a crisis on the road without getting yourself dirty. During bigger jobs when you expect a bit of dirt it is less extreme and can be tolerated at least whilst removing a component. When an item is being taken to pieces there is less risk of ruinous grit finding its way inside. The act of cleaning focuses your attention onto parts and you are more likely to spot trouble. Dirt on the ignition parts is a common cause of poor starting. Large areas such as the engine compartment inner wings or bulkhead should be brushed thoroughly with a solvent like Gunk, allowed to soak and then very carefully hosed down. Water in the wrong places, particularly the carburettor or electrical components will do more harm than dirt. Use petrol or paraffin and a small paintbrush to clean the more inaccessible places.

5 Waste disposal

Old oil and cleaning paraffin must be destroyed. Although it makes a good base for a bonfire the practice is dangerous. It is also illegal to dispose of oil and paraffin down domestic drains. By buying your new engine oil in one gallon cans you can refill with old oil and take back to the local garage who have facilities for disposal.

6 Long journeys

Before taking the car on long journeys, particularly such trips as continental holidays, make sure that the car is given a thorough check in the form of the next service due, plus a full visual inspection well in advance so that any faults found can be rectified in time.

Terry Davey
© HAYNES
H.6106

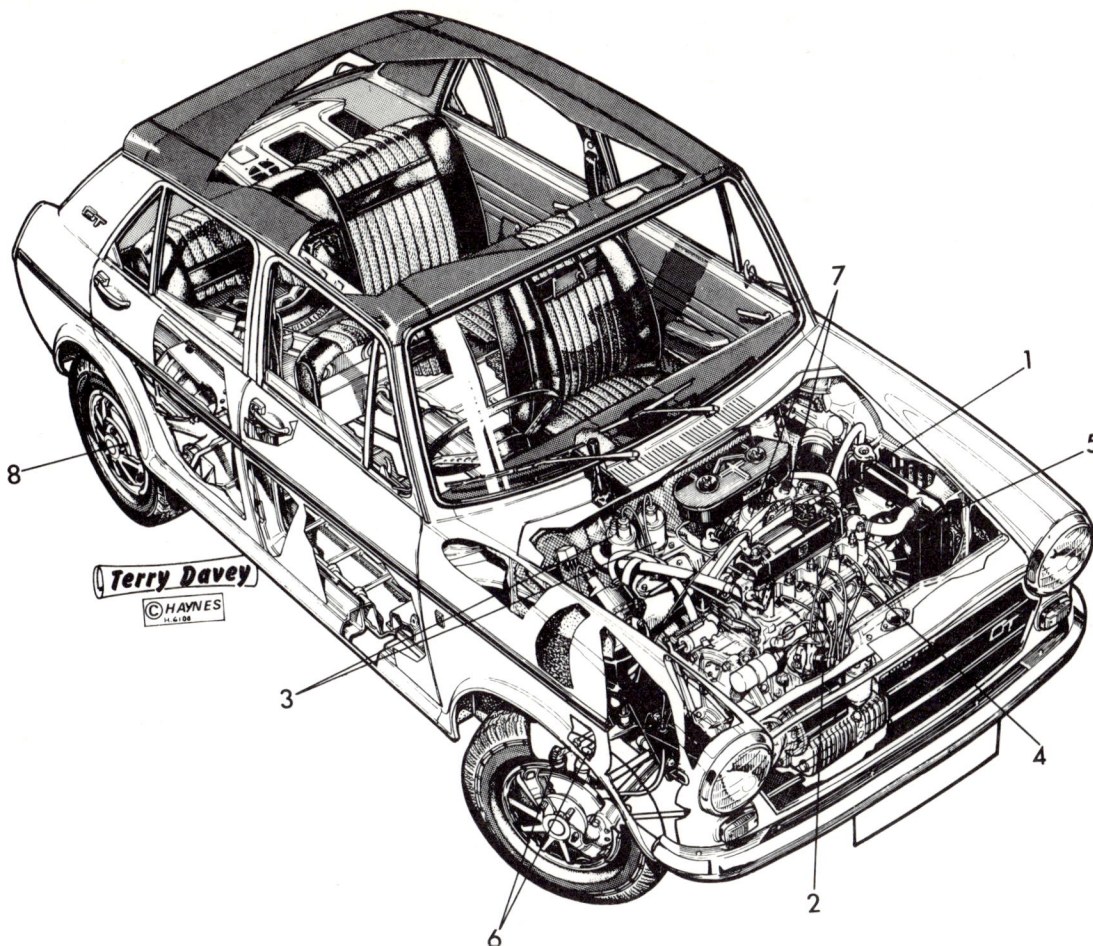

Recommended lubricants

Component		Lubricant
1	Engine/final drive/gearbox	Castrol GTX
2	Distributor	Castrol Everyman
3	Braking and clutch systems	Castrol Girling Universal Brake and Clutch Fluid
4	Dynamo end bush	Castrol GTX
5	Water pump	Castrol LM Grease
6	Steering - joint nipples	Castrol LM Grease
7	Carburettor dashpot	Castrol GTX
8	Rear wheel bearings	Castrol LM Grease
	Steering rack	Castrol Hypoy
	Handbrake cable	Castrol LM Grease
	Foot pedal bearings and handbrake linkages, door hinges, locks, throttle linkage, etc.	Castrol Everyman

Note: *The above are general recommendations. Lubrication requirements vary from territory-to-territory and depend on the vehicle usage. Consult the operators handbook supplied with the car.*

Tools and working facilities

Introduction

A selection of good tools is a fundamental requirement for anyone contemplating the maintenance and repair of a motor vehicle. For the owner who does not possess any, their purchase will prove a considerable expense, offsetting some of the savings made by doing-it-yourself. However, provided that the tools purchased are of good quality, they will last for many years and prove an extremely worthwhile investment.

To help the average owner to decide which tools are needed to carry out the various tasks detailed in this manual, we have compiled three lists of tools under the following headings: Maintenance and minor repair, Repair and overhaul, and Special. The newcomer to practical mechanics should start off with the 'Maintenance and minor repair' tool kit and confine himself to the simpler jobs around the vehicle. Then, as his confidence and experience grows, he can undertake more difficult tasks, buying extra tools as, and, when, they are needed. In this way, a 'Maintenance and minor repair' tool kit can be built-up into a 'Repair and overhaul' tool kit over a considerable period of time without any major cash outlays. The experienced do-it-yourselfer will have a tool kit good enough for most repair and overhaul procedures and will add tools from the 'Special' category when he feels the expense is justified by the amount of use these tools will be put to.

It is obviously not possible to cover the subject of tools fully here. For those who wish to learn more about tools and their use there is a book entitled 'How to Choose and Use Car Tools' available from the publishers of this manual.

Maintenance and minor repair tool kit

The tools given in this list should be considered as a minimum requirement if routine maintenance, servicing and minor repair operations are to be undertaken. We recommend the purchase of combination spanners (ring one end, open-ended the other); although more expensive than open-ended ones, they do give the advantages of both types of spanner.

Combination spanners - 7/16, 1/2, 9/16, 5/8, 11/16, 3/4, 13/16, 15/16, 1, 1 1/8 AF
Adjustable spanner - 9 inch
Engine sump/gearbox/rear axle drain plug key (where applicable)
Spark plug spanner (with rubber insert)
Spark plug gap adjustment tool
Set of feeler gauges
Brake adjuster spanner (where applicable)
Brake bleed nipple spanner
Screwdriver - 4 in. long x ¼ in dia. (plain)
Screwdriver - 4 in. long x ¼ in dia. (crosshead)
Combination pliers - 6 inch
Hacksaw, junior
Tyre pump
Tyre pressure gauge
Grease gun (where applicable)
Oil can
Fine emery cloth (1 sheet)
Wire brush (small)
Funnel (medium size)

Repair and overhaul tool kit

These tools are virtually essential for anyone undertaking any major repairs to a motor vehicle, and are additional to those given in the Basic list. Included in this list is a comprehensive set of sockets. Although these are expensive they will be found invaluable as they are so versatile - particularly if various drives are included in the set. We recommend the ½ in square-drive type, as this can be used with most proprietary torque wrenches. If you cannot afford a socket set, even bought piecemeal, then inexpensive tubular box spanners are a useful alternative.

The tools in this list will occasionally need to be supplemented by tools from the Special list.

Sockets (or box spanners) to cover range 7/16 to 1 1/8 AF
Reversible ratchet drive (for use with sockets)
Extension piece, 10 inch (for use with sockets)
Universal joint (for use with sockets)
Torque wrench (for use with sockets)
Mole wrench - 8 inch
Ball pein hammer
Soft-faced hammer, plastic or rubber
Screwdriver - 6 in long x 5/16 in (plain)
Screwdriver - 2 in long x 5/16 in square (plain)
Screwdriver - 1½ in long x ¼ in dia. (crosshead)
Screwdriver - 3 in long x 1/8 in dia. (electricians)
Pliers - electricians side cutters
Pliers - needle nosed
Pliers - circlip (internal and external)
Cold chisel - ½ inch
Scriber (this can be made by grinding the end of a broken hacksaw blade)
Scraper (this can be made by flattening and sharpening one end of a piece of copper pipe)
Centre punch
Pin punch
Hacksaw
Valve grinding tool
Steel rule/straight edge
Allen keys
Selection of files
Wire brush (large)
Axle stands
Jack (strong scissor or hydraulic type)

Special tools

The tools in this list are those which are not used regularly, are expensive to buy, or which need to be used in accordance with their manufacturers instructions. Unless relatively difficult mechanical jobs are undertaken frequently, it will not be economic to buy many of these tools. Where this is the case, you could consider clubbing together with friends (or a motorists club) to make a joint purchase, or borrowing the tools against a deposit from a local garage or tool hire specialist.

The following list contains only those special tools and instruments freely available to the public, and not those special tools produced by the vehicle manufacturer specifically for its dealer network. You will find occasional reference to these manufacturers special tools in the text of this manual. Generally, an alternative method of doing the job without the vehicle manufacturers special tool is given. However, sometimes there is no alternative to using them. Where this is the case and the relevant tool cannot be bought or borrowed you will have to entrust the work to a franchised garage.

Valve spring compressor
Piston ring compressor
Balljoint separator
Universal hub/bearing puller
Impact screwdriver
Micrometer and/or vernier gauge
Carburettor flow balancing device (where applicable)
Dial gauge
Stroboscopic timing light
Dwell angle meter/tachometer
Universal electrical multi-meter
Cylinder compression gauge
Lifting tackle
Trolley jack
Light with extension lead

Buying tools

For practically all tools, a tool factor is the best source since he will have a very comprehensive range compared with the average garage or accessory shop. Having said that, accessory shops often offer excellent quality tools at discount prices, so it pays to shop around.

Remember, you don't have to buy the most expensive items on the shelf, but it is always advisable to steer clear of the very cheap tools. There are plenty of good tools around, at reasonable prices, so ask the proprietor or manager of the shop for advice before making a purchase.

Care and maintenance of tools

Having purchased a reasonable tool kit, it is necessary to keep the tools in a clean and serviceable condition. After use, always wipe off any dirt, grease and metal particles using a clean, dry cloth, before putting the tools away. Never leave them lying around after they have been used. A simple tool rack on the garage or workshop wall, for items such as screwdrivers and pliers is a good idea. Store all normal spanners and sockets in a metal box. Any measuring instruments, gauges, meters, etc., must be carefully stored where they cannot be damaged or become rusty.

Take a little care when the tools are used. Hammer heads inevitably become marked and screwdrivers lose the keen edge on their blades from time-to-time. A little timely attention with an emery cloth or a file will soon restore items like this to a good serviceable finish.

Working facilities

Not to be forgotten when discussing tools, is the workshop itself. If anything more than routine maintenance is to be carried out, some form of suitable working area becomes essential.

It is appreciated that many an owner mechanic is forced by circumstances to remove the engine or similar item, without the benefit of a garage or workshop. Having done this, any repairs should always be done under the cover of a roof.

Wherever possible, any dismantling should be done on a clean flat workbench or table at a suitable working height.

Any workbench needs a vice: one with a jaw opening of 4 in (100 mm) is suitable for most jobs. As mentioned previously, some clean dry storage space is also required for tools, as well as the lubricants, cleaning fluids, touch-up paints and so on which soon become necessary.

Another item which may be required and which has a much more general usage, is an electric drill with a chuck capacity of at least 5/16 in (8 mm). This, together with a good range of twist drills, is virtually essential for fitting accessories such as wing mirrors and reversing lights

Last, but not least, always keep a supply of old newspapers and clean, lint-free rags available, and try to keep any working area as clean as possible.

Spanner jaw gap comparison table

Jaw gap (in.)	Spanner size
0.250	1/4 in. AF
0.275	7 mm AF
0.312	5/16 in. AF
0.315	8 mm AF
0.340	11/32 in. AF/1/8 in. Whitworth
0.354	9 mm AF
0.375	3/8 in. AF
0.393	10 mm AF
0.433	11 mm AF
0.437	7/16 in. AF
0.445	3/16 in. Whitworth 1/4 in. BSF
0.472	12 mm AF
0.500	1/2 in. AF
0.512	13 mm AF
0.525	1/4 in. Whitworth/5/16 in. BSF
0.551	14 mm AF
0.562	9/16 in. AF
0.590	15 mm AF
0.600	5/16 in. Whitworth/ 3/8 in. BSF
0.625	5/8 in. AF
0.629	16 mm AF
0.669	17 mm AF
0.687	11/16 in. AF
0.708	18 mm AF
0.710	3/8 in. Whitworth/ 7/16 in. BSF
0.748	19 mm AF
0.750	3/4 in. AF
0.812	13/16 in. AF
0.820	7/16 in. Whitworth/ 1/2 in. BSF
0.866	22 mm AF
0.875	7/8 in. AF
0.920	1/2 in. Whitworth/ 9.16 in. BSF
0.937	15/16 in. AF
0.944	24 mm AF
1.000	1 in. AF
1.010	9/16 in. Whitworth/ 5/8 in. BSF
1.023	26 mm AF
1.062	1 1/16 in. AF/27 mm AF
1.100	5/8 in. Whitworth/ 11/16 in. BSF
1.125	1 1/8 in. AF
1.181	30 mm AF
1.200	11/16 in. Whitworth/ 3/4 in. BSF
1.250	1 1/4 in. AF
1.259	32 mm AF
1.300	3/4 in. Whitworth/ 7/8 in. BSF
1.312	1 5/16 in. AF
1.390	13/16 in. Whitworth/ 15/16 in. BSF
1.417	36 mm AF
1.437	1 7/6 in. AF
1.480	7/8in. Whitworth/ 1 in. BSF
1.500	1 1/2 in. AF/ 15/16 in. Whitworth
1.574	40 mm AF 15/16 in. Whitworth
1.614	41 mm AF
1.625	1 5/8 in. AF
1.670	1 in. Whitworth/1 1/8 in. BSF
1.687	1 11/16 in. AF
1.811	46 mm AF
1.812	1 13/16 in. AF
1.860	1 1/8 in. Whitworth/ 1 1/4 in. BSF
1.875	1 7/8 in. AF
1.968	50 mm AF
2.000	2 in. AF
2.050	1 1/4 in. Whitworth/ 1 3/8 in. BSF
2.165	55 mm AF
2.362	60 mm AF

Chapter 1 Engine

Contents

Specifications

Engine specification and data - 1,098 cc type 10H, 10AMW, 10GR, 10V

Engine (general):

Type	4 cylinder, in-line, transversely mounted, ohv
Bore	2.543 in. (64.58 mm)
Stroke	3.296 in. (83.72 mm)
Cubic capacity	1.098 cc (67 cu in)
Compression ratio:	
Single carburettor	8.5 : 1 (7.5 : 1 available)
Twin carburettor	8.9 : 1 (8.1 : 1 available)
Oversize bore:	
Maximum	0.020 in. (0.508 mm)
Minimum	0.010 in. (0.254 mm)

Brake mean effective pressure:

High compression, single carburettor	135 lb/sq in. (9.5 kg/sq cm) at 2,500 r.p.m.
High compression, twin carburettor	138 lb/sq in. (9.7 kg/sq cm) at 2,750 r.p.m.
Low compression, single carburettor	128 lb/sq in. (9.0 kg/sq cm) at 3,000 r.p.m.
Low compression, twin carburettor	136 lb/sq in. (9.6 kg/sq cm) at 2,750 r.p.m.

Maximum torque:

High compression, single carburettor	60 lb f ft (8.30 kg fm) at 2,500 r.p.m.
High compression, twin carburettor	61 lb f ft (8.40 kg fm) at 2,750 r.p.m.
Low compression, single carburettor	57 lb f ft (7.85 kg fm) at 3,000 r.p.m.
Low compression, twin carburettor	60 lb f ft (8.30 kg fm) at 2,750 r.p.m.
Firing order	1 3 4 2
Location of No. 1 cylinder	Next to radiator
Engine mountings	3 point suspension on rubber mountings

Camshaft and camshaft bearings:

The camshaft is driven from the crankshaft by a single roller chain. The camshaft is supported by three renewable white metal lined shell bearings pressed into, and reamed in position in the block.

Camshaft bearing clearance	0.001 to 0.002 in. (0.0254 to 0.0508 mm)
Inside bearing diameter reamed when fitted:	
Front bearing	1.667 to 1.6675 in. (42.342 to 42.355 mm)
Centre bearing	1.6242 to 1.6247 in. (41.256 to 41.269 mm)
Rear bearing	1.3745 to 1.3750 in. (34.912 to 34.925 mm)
Endfloat	0.003 to 0.007 in. (0.076 to 0.178 mm)
Journal diameters:	
Front	1.6655 to 1.666 in. (42.304 to 42.316 mm)
Centre	1.62275 to 1.62325 in. (41.218 to 41.231 mm)
Rear	1.3725 to 1.3735 in. (34.862 to 34.887 mm)
Clearance	0.001 to 0.002 in. (0.025 to 0.051 mm)

Connecting rods and big-end bearings:

Length between centres	5.75 in. (14.605 cm)
Big-end bearings	Steel-backed, lead-indium lined
Side clearance	0.008 to 0.012 in. (0.203 to 0.305 mm)
Bearing internal diameter clearance	0.001 to 0.0025 in. (0.025 to 0.063 mm)

Crankshaft and main bearings:

Main journal diameter	1.7505 to 1.7510 in. (44.46 to 44.47 mm)
Minimum main journal regrind diameter	1.7105 in. (43.45 mm)
Crankpin journal diameter	1.6254 to 1.6259 in. (41.28 to 41.30 mm)
Minimum crankpin regrind diameter	1.5854 in. (40.27 mm)
Main bearings	White metal, steel-backed liners, 3 shell-type
Endfloat	0.002 to 0.003 in. (0.051 to 0.076 mm)
Side thrust	Taken by thrust washers located on either side of centre main bearing
Undersizes available	-0.010 in. (-0.254 mm), -0.020 in. (-0.508 mm) -0.030 in. (-0.762 mm), -0.040 in. (-1.02 mm)

Cylinder block:

Type	Cylinder cast integral with top half of crankcase
Water jackets	Full length

Cylinder head:

Type	Cast iron with vertical valves. Siamised inlet ports, 2
Combustion chamber capacity with valves fitted	24.5 c. c.

Gudgeon pin:

Type	Fully floating
Fit to piston	Hand push fit -0.0001 to 0.00035 in. (0.0025 to 0.009 mm)
Fit in connecting rod	Hand push fit -0.0001 to 0.0006 in. (0.0025 to 0.015 mm)
Diameter (outer)	0.6244 to 0.6246 in. (15.86 to 15.865 mm)

Lubrication system:

Type	Pressure feed. Pressure fed bearings: Main, camshaft and connecting rods. Reduced pressure to rocker shaft. Piston pin and cylinder wall lubrication - splash.
Oil filter	Full flow
Capacity of oil filter	1 pint (1.2 US pints - 0.57 litre)
Crankcase ventilation	Directed flow via road draught tube on left-hand side of engine (early models) Closed breathing system (later models)
Transmission casing/sump & filter capacity (manual)	8.5 pints (10.2 U.S. pints. - 4.83 litres)
Oil pump: Type	Eccentric rotor or vane

Oil pump relief pressure	60 lb/sq. in. (4.2 kg/cm^2)
Oil pressure:	
Normal	60 lbs/sq. in. (4.2 kg/cm^2)
Idling	15 lbs/sq. in. (1.05 kg/cm^2)
Relief valve spring:	
Free length	2.859 in. (72.63 mm)
Fitted length	2.156 in. (54.77 mm)

Pistons:

Type	Solid skirt, anodised aluminium alloy. 3 compression rings, 1 oil control ring
Clearance of piston:	
Top of skirt	0.0021 to 0.0037 in. (0.053 to 0.094 mm)
Bottom of skirt	0.0005 to 0.0011 in. (0.013 to 0.028 mm)
Piston oversizes available	+0.010 in. (+0.254 mm) +0.020 in. (+0.508 mm)

Piston rings:

Top compression ring	Plain internal champer (Chrome faced)
2nd & 3rd compression ring	Tapered
Fitted gap	0.007 to 0.012 in. (0.178 to 0.30 mm)
Groove clearance	0.0015 to 0.0035 in. (0.038 to 0.089 mm)
Oil control ring (early models)	Slotted scraper
Clearance in groove	0.0015 to 0.0035 in. (0.038 to 0.089 mm)
Oil control ring (later models)	Duaflex 61
Rails fitted gap	0.012 - 0.028 in. (0.30 - 0.78 mm)
Side springs fitted gap	0.100 - 0.150 in. (2.5 - 3.75 mm)

Tappets (cam followers):

Type	Barrel
Length	1.505 in. (38.23 mm)
Diameter	0.8120 in. (20.62 mm)

Valves:

Head diameter:	
Inlet	1.151 to 1.156 in. (29.23 to 29.36 mm)
Exhaust	1.000 to 1.005 in. (25.40 to 25.53 mm)
Later twin carburettor engines: Inlet	1.213 to 1.218 in. (30.81 to 30.94 mm)
Valve lift	0.312 in. (7.925 mm)
Seat angle	Inlet & Exhaust: 45°
Valve clearance	0.012 in. (.305 mm)
Stem diameter:	
Inlet	0.2793 to 0.2798 in. (7.094 to 7.107 mm)
Exhaust	0.2788 to 0.2793 in. (7.081 to 7.094 mm)
Valve stem to guide clearance:	
Inlet	0.0015 to 0.0025 in. (.038 to .063 mm)
Exhaust	0.002 to 0.003 in. (0.051 to 0.076 mm)
Valve rocker bush bore (reamed)	0.5630 to 0.5635 in. (14.30 to 14.31 mm)

Valve guides:

Length (Inlet & Exhaust)	1.531 in. (38.89 mm)
Diameter (Inlet & Exhaust):	
Outside	0.4695 to 0.470 in. (11.92 to 11.94 mm)
Inside	0.2813 to 0.2818 in. (7.145 to 7.177 mm)
Fitted height above head	19/32 in. (15.1 mm)

Valve timing:

Inlet valve:	
Opens	5° btdc
Closes	45° abdc
Exhaust valve:	
Opens	51° bbdc
Closes	21° atdc
Valve timing marks	Dimples on crankshaft and camshaft sprockets. Marks on flywheel
Chain pitch & No. of pitches	3/8 in. (9.52 mm) 52 pitches
Valve rocker clearance: timing	0.029 in. (0.74 mm)

Valve springs:

	Single valve springs	Double valve springs	
Type	Single valve springs	Double valve springs	
Number of coils	4½	Inner: 6½	Outer: 4½
Free-length (Inlet & Exhaust)	1.750 in. (44.45 mm)	Inner: 1.672 in.	Outer: 1.750 in.
Valve spring pressure with valves open	85 lb.	Inner: 30 lb	Outer: 88 lb
Valve spring pressure with valves closed	52.5 lb	Inner: 18 lb	Outer: 52 lb

Engine Specification and data - 1275 cc Type 12G and 12H

Engine (general):

Number of cylinders	4
Bore	2.78 in. (70.61 mm)
Stroke	3.2 in. (81.28 mm)
Capacity	1274.86 cc (77.8 cu in)
Firing order	1, 3, 4, 2.
Valve operation	Overhead by pushrod

Compression ratio:

HC	8.8 : 1 or 9.75 : 1
LC *(alternative to 8.8 : 1 CR only)*	8 : 1

Compression pressure:

8.8 : 1 CR engines	155 to 180 lb/sq in. (10.9 to 12.7 kg/cm^2) at 300 to 400 r.p.m.
9.75 : 1 CR engines	185 to 210 lb/sq in. (13 to 14.75 kg/cm^2) at 335 to 485 r.p.m.

BMEP :

8.8 : 1 CR Single carburetter application	134 lb/sq in. (9.4 kg/cm^2) at 2,500 r.p.m.
8.8 : 1 CR Twin-carburetter application	136 lb/sq in. (9.6 kg/cm^2) at 3,000 r.p.m.
9.75 : 1 CR Twin-carburetter application	143 lb/sq in. (10.05 kg/cm^2) at 3,250 r. p. m.

Torque:

8.8 : 1 CR Single-carburetter application	69 lb ft (9.54 kg m) at 2,500 r.p.m.
8.8 : 1 CR Twin-carburetter application	70.5 lb ft (9.75 kg m) at 3,000 r.p.m.
9.75 : 1 CR Twin-carburetter application	74 lb ft (10.23 kg m) at 3,250 r.p.m.

Oversize bore:

1st	0.010 in. (0.25 mm)
Maximum	0.020 in. (0.51 mm)

Crankshaft

Main journal diameter	2.0005 to 2.0010 in. (50.81 to 50.82 mm)

Crankpin journal diameter:

12H engines	1.7504 to 1.7509 in. (44.45 to 44.47 mm)
12G engines	1.6254 to 1.626 in. (41.28 to 41.29 mm)
Crankshaft end-thrust	Taken in thrust washers at centre main bearing
Crankshaft endfloat	0.002 to 0.003 in. (0.05 to 0.07 mm)

Main bearings:

Number and type	Three thin-wall; split shells copper-lead-indium
Material	VP3, lead-indium at NFM/3B
Length	0.975 to 0.985 in. (24.76 to 25.02 mm)
Diametrical clearance	0.001 to 0.0027 in. (0.025 to 0.07 mm)
Undersizes	0.020 in. (0.51 mm) and (0.40 in. (1.02 mm)

Connecting rods:

Type	Horizontally split big-end, plain small end
Length between the centres	5.748 to 5.752 in. (145.1 to 146 mm)

Big-end bearings:

Type	Thin-wall; steel-backed, copper-lead-indium plated
Length	0.840 to 0.850 in. (21.33 to 21.59 mm)
Diametrical clearance	0.001 to 0.0025 in. (0.02 to 0.06 mm)
Endfloat of crankpin	0.006 to 0.010 in. (0.15 to 0.25 mm)

Pistons

Type	Aluminium, solid skirt, dished crown.

Clearance in cylinder:

Top of skirt	0.0029 to 0.0037 in. (0.07 to 0.09 mm)
Bottom of skirt	0.0015 to 0.0021 in. (0.04 to 0.05 mm)
Number of rings	4 (3 compression, 1 oil control)

Width of ring grooves:

Top, second, third	0.0484 to 0.0494 in. (1.23 to 1.26 mm)
Oil control	0.1578 to 0.1588 in. (4.01 to 4.03 mm)
Gudgeon pin bore	0.8125 to 0.8129 in. (20.64 to 20.65 mm)

Piston rings

Compression - type:

Top	Internally chamfered chrome
2nd and 3rd	Tapered cast iron

Compression - width:

Top	0.0615 to 0.0625 in. (1.57 to 1.60 mm)
2nd and 3rd	0.0615 to 0.0625 in. (1.57 to 1.60 mm)

Compression - fitted gap:

Top	0.011 to 0.016 in. (0.28 to 0.41 mm)
2nd and 3rd	0.008 to 0.013 in. (0.20 to 0.33 mm)

Compression - ring to groove clearance:

Top	...	...	...	...	...	...	...	0.0015 to 0.0035 in. (0.04 to 0.09 mm)
2nd and 3rd	...	...	...	...	...	...	...	0.0015 to 0.0035 in. (0.04 to 0.09 mm)

Oil control

Type (early): - fitted gap:	...	...	...	...	...	...	...	Duaflex 61
Rails	...	...	...	...	...	...	...	0.012 to 0.028 in. (0.30 to 0.78 mm)
Side spring	...	...	...	...	...	...	...	0.100 to 0.150 in. (2.54 to 3.75 mm)
Type (later):	...	...	...	...	...	...	...	Apex
Width of rails	...	...	...	...	...	...	...	0.100 to 0.106 in. (2.54 to 2.69 mm)
Thickness of rails	...	...	...	...	...	...	...	0.0235 to 0.025 in. (0.6 to 0.63 mm)
Fitted gap	...	...	...	...	...	...	...	0.010 to 0.40 in. (0.25 to 1.02 mm)

Gudgeon pins

Type	...	...	...	...	...	...	...	Pressed in connecting rod
Fit in piston	...	...	...	...	...	...	...	Hand push fit
Diameter (outer)	...	...	...	...	...	...	...	0.8123 to 0.8125 in. (20.63 to 20.64 mm)
Fit to connecting rod	...	...	...	...	...	...	...	0.0008 to 0.0015 in. (0.02 to 0.04 mm) interference

Camshaft

Journal diameter:

Front	...	...	...	...	...	...	...	1.6655 to 1.6660 in. (42.304 to 42.316 mm)
Centre	...	...	...	...	...	...	...	1.62275 to 1.6233 in. (41.218 to 41.231 mm)
Rear	...	...	...	...	...	...	...	1.37275 to 1.37350 in. (34.866 to 34.889 mm)

Bearing liner inside diameter:
Unreamed after fitting:

Front	...	...	...	...	...	...	...	1.652 in. (41.98 mm)
Centre	...	...	...	...	...	...	...	1.61 in. (40.89 mm)
Rear	...	...	...	...	...	...	...	1.36 in. (34.52 mm)

Reamed after fitting:

Front	...	...	...	...	...	...	...	1.667 to 1.6675 in. (42.34 to 42.35 mm)
Centre	...	...	...	...	...	...	...	1.62425 to 1.62475 in. (41.25 to 41.37 mm)
Rear	...	...	...	...	...	...	...	1.3745 to 1.3750 in. (34.91 to 34.92 mm)
Bearings: Type	...	...	...	...	...	...	...	White-metal-lined, steel-backed
Diametrical clearance	...	...	...	...	...	...	...	0.001 to 0.002 in. (0.02 to 0.05 mm)
End-thrust	...	...	...	...	...	...	...	Taken on locating plate
Endfloat	...	...	...	...	...	...	...	0.003 to 0.007 in. (0.07 to 0.18 mm)
Cam lift	...	...	...	...	...	...	...	0.318 in. (8.07 mm)
Drive	...	...	...	...	...	...	...	Duflex chain and gear from crankshaft
Timing chain	...	...	...	...	...	...	...	3/8 in. (9.52 mm) Pitch x52 pitches

Tappets (cam followers):

Type	...	...	...	...	...	...	...	Bucket
Outside diameter	...	...	...	...	...	...	...	0.81125 to 0.81175 in. (20.60 to 20.62 mm)
Length	...	...	...	...	...	...	...	1.445 to 1.505 in. (37.97 to 38.23 mm)

Rocker gear:

Rocker shaft: Diameter	...	...	...	...	...	...	...	0.5616 to 0.5625 in. (14.26 to 14.29 mm)

Rocker arm:

Bore	...	...	...	...	...	...	...	0.686 to 0.687 in. (17.45 mm)
Bush inside diameter	...	...	...	...	...	...	...	0.5630 to 0.5635 in. (14.3 to 14.31 mm)

Valves

Seat angle: Inlet and exhaust		...	...	...	...	...	...	45°

Head diameter:

Inlet (8.8 : 1 CR engines)		...	...	...	...	...	...	1.307 to 1.312 in. (33.2 to 33.21 mm)
Inlet (9.75 : 1 CR engines)		...	...	...	...	...	...	1.401 to 1.406 in. (35.59 to 35.71 mm)
Exhaust	...	...	...	...	...	...	...	1.1515 to 1.1565 in. (29.24 to 29.37 mm)

Stem diameter:

Inlet	...	...	...	...	...	...	...	0.2793 to 0.2798 in. (7.09 to 7.11 mm)
Exhaust	...	...	...	...	...	...	...	0.2788 to 0.2793 in. (7.08 to 7.09 mm)
Stem to guide clearance (Inlet and exhaust)			...	...	...	...		0.0015 to 0.0025 in. (0.04 to 0.08 mm)
Valve lift (Inlet and exhaust)		...	...	...	...	...		0.318 in. (8.07 mm)

Valve guides:

Length:

Inlet	...	...	...	...	...	...	...	1.6875 in. (42.87 mm)
Exhaust	...	...	...	...	...	...	...	1.8437 in. (46.83 mm)

Fitted height above seat:

Exhaust	...	...	...	...	...	...	...	0.540 in. (13.72 mm)
Inlet	...	...	...	...	...	...	...	0.540 in. (13.72 mm)

Valve springs:

12H Engines (8.8 : 1 CR)

Free-length	1.95 in. (49.13 mm)
Fitted length	1.383 in. (35.13 mm)
Length at top of lift	1.065 in. (27.05 mm)
Load at fitted length	79.5 lb. (36.03 kg)
Load at top of lift	124 lb. (56.3 kg)
No. of working coils	4½

12H Engines (9.75 : 1 CR)

	Outer	Inner
Free-length	1.740 in. (44.20 mm)	1.705 in. (43.31 mm)
Fitted length	1.383 in. (35.12 mm)	1.270 in. (32.26 mm)
Length at top of lift	1.065 in. (27.05 mm)	0.952 in. (24.18 mm)
Load at fitted length	50 lb. (22.7 kg)	26 lb. (11.8 kg)
Load at top of lift	94 lb. (42.6 kg)	46 lb. (20.9 kg)

12G Engines

	Outer	Inner
Free-length	1.828 in. (46.42 mm)	1.703 in. (43.259 mm)
Fitted length	1.383 in. (35.13 mm)	1.270 in. (32.258 mm)
Length at top of lift	1.065 in. (27.05 mm)	0.952 in. (24.18 mm)
Load at fitted length	51 lb. (23.1 kg)	25 lb. (11.3 kg)
Load at top of lift	87 lb. (39.5 kg)	44 lb. (20 kg)
Valve crash speed	6,750 rpm	

Valve timing

Timing marks	Dimples on timing gears
Rocker clearance (cold)	0.012 in. (0.305 mm)
Inlet valve:	
Opens	5° btdc
Closes	45° bbdc
Exhaust valve:	
Opens	51° bbdc
Closes	21° atdc

Oil pump:

Type	Internal gear, splined drive from camshaft
Oil pressure relief valve	60 lb/sq in. (4.2 kg/cm^2)
Relief valve spring:	
Free-length	2.86 in. (72.64 mm)
Fitted length	2.156 in. (54.77 mm)
Load at fitted length	13 to 14 lb (5.90 to 6.35 kg)

Oil filter:

Type (All models except later Austin America)...	Fall flow, renewable-element, pressure differential switch (early models)
Later Austin America	Full flow, renewable cartridge
Capacity	1 pint (1.2 US pints, 0.57 litre)

Engine specification and data - 1100 and 1300 Automatics

Important: The information given in this Section is only applicable to 1100 and 1300 Automatics. For other information refer to the specifications and data applicable to the engine type

1098 cc

Type:	10H, 10AG
Compression ratio	8.9 : 1
Combustion chamber volume	28.3 cc (1.73 cu in)
Engine idle speed	650 rpm
bhp	56 at 5500 rpm
Torque	61 lb f ft (8.44 kg f m) at 2000 rpm
Valves: inlet valve head diameter	1.219 to 1.224 in. (30.96 to 31.10 mm)
Oil pump: Type	Hobourn Eaton
Oil filter: Type	Full flow
Capacity	1 pint (1.2 US pints 0.57 litre)
Oil pressure:	
Normal	60 lb/sq in. (4.22 kg/cm^2)
Idle	15 lb/sq in. (1.05 kg/cm^2)

1275 cc

Refer to the 1275 cc engine specifications and data

Capacity:	
Transmission casing (including filter)	13 pints (7.38 litres, 16 US pints)
Refill capacity (approx)	9 pints (5 litres, 11 US pints)

Torque wrench settings:

							lb f ft	Kg f m
1098 cc engine (manual)								
Cylinder head stud nuts:								
1100 Mk I and Mk II cars	...	...	...	...	...	...	35 to 40	4.8 to 5.5
1100 Mk III cars	...	...	...	...	...	...	50	6.9
Connecting rod big-end bolts	...	...	...	...	...	...	35 to 38	4.8 to 5.3
Main bearing bolts	...	...	...	...	...	...	60 to 65	8.3 to 10
Flywheel centre-bolt	...	...	...	...	...	...	110 to 115	15.2 to 15.9
Rocker bracket nuts	...	...	...	...	...	...	22 to 25	3 to 3.5
Cylinder side covers ...	...	...	...	...	...	...	2	0.28
Second type - (deep pressed cover)	...	...	...	...	...	3 to 4	0.4 to 0.55
Timing cover - (¼ in. UNF bolt)	...	...	...	...	...	...	4 to 6	0.55 to 0.8
Timing cover - (5/16 in. UNF bolt)	...	...	...	...	...	10 to 14	1.4 to 1.9
Water pump ...	...	...	...	...	...	...	14 to 18	1.9 to 2.5
Water outlet elbow ...	...	...	...	...	...	...	6 to 9	0.8 to 1.2
Oil filter (renewable element) centre bolt		...	...	...	...	12 to 16	1.7 to 2.2
Filter head nuts ...	...	...	...	...	...	...	12 to 16	1.7 to 2.2
Oil pump ...	...	...	...	...	...	...	6 to 9	0.8 to 1.2
Manifold to cylinder head ...	...	...	...	...	...	12 to 16	1.7 to 2.2
Rocker cover ...	...	...	...	...	...	...	3 to 4	0.4 to 0.55
Crankshaft pulley nut ...	...	...	...	...	...	70 to 80	9.6 to 11
Sump drain plug ...	...	...	...	...	...	...	25 max	3.5 max
Flywheel housing bolts and stud nuts	...	...	...	...	18	2.5
Distributor clamp bolts:								
Fixed nut type ...	...	...	...	...	...	...	50 lb f in.	0.58 kg fm
Fixed bolt type ...	...	...	...	...	...	...	27 to 32 lb f in.	0.3 to 0.37 kg f m
Transmission case to crankcase	...	...	...	...	...	6	0.8

1275 cc engines (manual)

as 1098 cc engine with following exceptions:

							lb f ft	Kg f m
Cylinder head stud nuts	...	...	...	...	...	...	48 to 52	6.65 to 7.2
Cylinder head: additional bolt (9.75 : 1 CR engines only)				...	25	3.46
Connecting rod bolt nuts ...	...	...	...	...	...	35 to 38 oiled	4.85 to 5.25 oiled
Oil filter (cartridge type) ...	...	...	...	...	...	4	0.55

1098 and 1275 cc (automatic transmission)

see Specifications, Chapter 6

---

1 General description

The 1100/1300 engine is of the four cylinder overhead valve type, fitted with one or two carburettors depending on the model and year of manufacture. The engine is supported in its subframe by rubber mountings which reduce both noise and vibrations.

Two valves per cylinder are mounted vertically in the cast iron cylinder head and run in pressed-in valve guides. They are operated by rocker arms and pushrods from the camshaft which is located at the base of the cylinder bores in the left-hand side of the engine (viewed from the flywheel end).

The cylinder head has all five inlet and exhaust ports on the left-hand side. Cylinders 1 and 2 share a siamised inlet port and also cylinders 3 and 4.

Cylinders 1 and 4 have individual exhaust ports and cylinders 2 and 3 share a siamised exhaust port.

The cylinder block and the upper half of the crankcase are cast together. The bottom half of the crankcase consists of a combined transmission casing and oil sump.

The pistons are made from anodised aluminium alloy and unlike some other 'A' series engines all models have solid skirts. Three compression rings and a slotted oil control ring are fitted on all models. The gudgeon pin is not retained in the little end of the connecting rod by a pinch bolt, as on early 'A' series models, but is of the fully floating type. A circlip at each end of the hole in the piston retains the gudgeon pin in place. Renewable white metal, lead-indium, or lead-tin big-end bearings are fitted.

At the front of the engine a single row chain drives the camshaft, via the camshaft and crankshaft chain wheels. On all models the chain is tensioned by two rubber rings either side of the gearwheel teeth. The camshaft is supported by three steel-backed white metal bearings. If these are replaced it is necessary to ream the bearings in position.

The overhead valves are operated by means of rocker arms mounted on the rocker shaft running along the top of the cylinder head. The rocker arms are activated by pushrods and tappets which in turn rise and fall in accordance with the cams on the camshaft. The valves are held closed by small powerful springs, double valve springs being fitted to some models.

The statically and dynamically balanced forged steel crankshaft is supported by three renewable main bearings. Crankshaft endfloat is controlled by four semi-circular thrust washers, two of which are located on either side of the centre main bearing.

The centrifugal water pump and radiator cooling fan are driven together with the dynamo or alternator from the crankshaft pulley wheel by a rubber/fabric belt. The distributor is mounted towards the rear of the right-hand side of the cylinder block and advances and retards the ignition timing by mechanical and vacuum means. The distributor is driven at half crankshaft speed by a short shaft and skew gear from a skew gear on the camshaft. The oil pump is driven from the rear of the camshaft.

During the long production run of these engines several modifications have been made, not only because of the process of continued development but also to adapt the unit when automatic transmission is fitted. Where these occur full information will be found in the following text.

---

2 Major operations possible with engine in place

Not very many major operations can be carried out on the 1100/1300 engine with it in-situ because it is not possible to drop the sump as can be done with most cars. The following operations *are* possible however:

1 Removal and replacement of the cylinder head assembly.

2   Removal and replacement of the timing chain and gears.
3   Removal and replacement of the clutch/flywheel.
4   Removal and replacement of the engine mountings.

3   Major operations requiring engine removal

The following major operations can be carried out with the engine out of the body frame and on the bench or floor:
1   Removal and replacement of the main bearings.
2   Removal and replacement of the crankshaft.
3   Removal and replacement of the oil pump.
4   Removal and replacement of the big-end bearings.
5   Removal and replacement of the pistons and connecting rods.
6   Removal and replacement of the camshaft.

4   Methods of engine removal

There are two methods of engine removal. The engine can either be removed from under the car complete with subframe, or the engine can be lifted out through the bonnet aperture.

In either instance the engine is removed complete with the transmission, and also the radiator.

It is easier to lift the engine/transmission assembly out of the engine compartment with the aid of a suitable block and pulley than to separate the subframe from the body, and lift the body up, using the rear wheels as a pivot. This is because the Hydrolastic suspension has to be depressurised and evacuated if the subframe is removed. The subframe comprises the frame itself, the wheels, brakes, driveshafts, hubs and suspension.

In either case it is necessary to raise and support the front of the car so that it can be worked on from underneath, or the car placed over an inspection pit.

5   Engine/transmission unit (manual transmission) - removal

The engines on all 1100/1300 models can be removed by the system detailed below. Where slight variations occur between one model and another, these are detailed at the end of this Section.

Practical experience has proved that the engine can be removed easily in about 4½ hours (less with experience) by adhering to the following sequence of operations:
1   Turn on the water drain taps found at the bottom of the radiator and on the side of the cylinder block. On later models a drain plug is fitted to the cylinder block and it may be found there is no tap or plug at the base of the radiator.
2   Disconnect and remove the battery and battery tray from the engine compartment.
3   With a suitable container in position unscrew the drain plug from the rear end of the transmission casing (under the clutch bellhousing) and drain off the oil. When the oil is drained screw the plug back in tightly to ensure it is not mislaid. If the engine, gearbox, or differential is to be stripped down, remove the oil filter and empty away the oil.
4   Remove the bonnet by undoing the two set bolts and spring washers from each of the bonnet hinges on the bonnet side of the hinge. Carefully lift the bonnet off and place it somewhere safe where it will not be scratched or damaged.
5   Jack-up each side of the car in turn placing supporting blocks under each side of the frame. Alternatively place the car over a pit or on ramps.
6   Disconnect the inlet and outlet water hoses to the heater/demister unit (where fitted) by undoing the securing clips on the valve at the rear of the cylinder head and the return pipe running parallel to the left-hand side of the block.
7   Release the heater control operating cable from the regulating valve at the rear of the cylinder head.
8   Pull the leads off the spark plugs, snap back the distributor

cap securing clips, undo the HT lead to the centre of the cap, and lift off the distributor cap. If left in place it is easily broken when the engine is removed.
9   Remove the windscreen washer bottle and the bottle carrier on models where they are fitted on the wing valance.
10 Pull off the breather hose from the pipe on the rocker cover, loosen the butterfly nut which holds the air cleaner in place, and remove the air cleaner.
11 Free the cooling system overflow hose from its connection to the radiator and from the clip on the cowling.
12 Disconnect the choke linkage and the throttle cable at the carburettor end.
13 Undo the small nut which holds the distributor vacuum advance pipe to the carburettor, and also the union nut which secures the fuel pipe in place.
14 Undo the two nuts which hold the carburettor in place and lift the carburettor away together with the metal plate.
15 Unscrew the bolts which hold the exhaust pipe clamp in place so separating the exhaust pipe from the exhaust manifold.
16 From underneath the car remove the bolt on the transmission casing which holds the exhaust pipe in place and then tie the pipe to the bulkhead to keep it out of the way.
17 *Early models:*
a) From inside the car release the rubber boot from the base of the gearlever, and through this hole undo the two set bolts on the gearlever retaining plate. Pull the gearlever away and place on one side.
b) Undo the two bolts which hold the gearlever remote control housing extension to the tunnel in the floor. Then from underneath the car undo the four lower bolts (two each side) which hold the remote control housing extension to the differential casing, and lift the extension away.
18 *Later models,* with floor mounted remote control:
a) Using a suitable diameter parallel pin pinch remove the roll pin securing the selector rod sleeve to the selector shaft at the rear of the transmission unit.
b) Undo and remove the nut, bolt and washers securing the remote control stabiliser to the transmission unit.
19 When a tie-rod is fitted to the engine this should next be detached from the engine (Fig. 1.1).
20 Disconnect the low tension lead to the distributor and the leads from the dynamo, starter motor, water temperature gauge (where fitted) and oil pressure warning bulb.
21 Disconnect the oil pressure pipe to the oil pressure gauge (where fitted) by loosening the retaining clip on the rubber connector pipe, and then pulling the pipe off.
22 Undo the bolt which holds the earth lead to the clutch cover.
23 In the case of models fitted with a tachometer either remove the reduction drive and cable from the rear of the dynamo or remove the drive cable from the timing gear cover. N. B. Modified cars might make use of electronic tachometers. If this is the case check the wiring and disconnect as appropriate.

Fig. 1.1. Exploded view of engine tie-rod components (Sec. 5)

Engine and transmission removal sequence (early models). Photographs 1 to 24

1 Step one is to drain water by opening two taps; at base of radiator and at bulkhead side of block. Then drain oil after removing drain plug

2 Remove bonnet, giving better access to engine after undoing the two nuts and bolts which hold each hinge to the bonnet. Also release support strut

3 Disconnect battery terminals and undo the two nuts from the battery retaining strap. Lift battery from engine compartment. Remove battery carrier

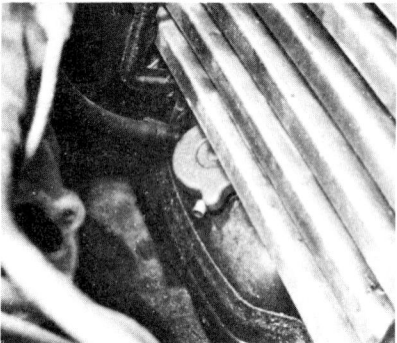

4 Release the overflow pipe to the expander tank at the radiator neck end. Shown above are the tank and pipe (the engine has been removed for clarity)

5 Undo the knurled nut which holds the speedometer cable to the transmission casing

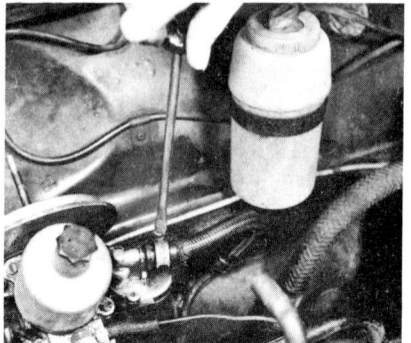

6 Next the clip on the carburettor fuel intake pipe must be slackened and the pipe removed from the float chamber

7 The bottom nut on the carburettor flange is rather difficult to get at and undo. A good tip is to use a normal open ended spanner cut in half

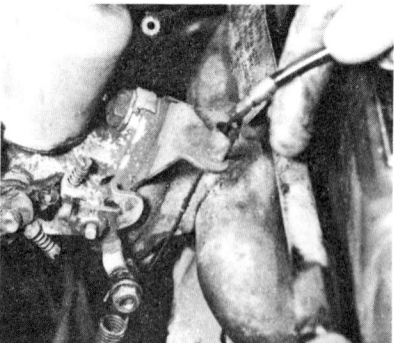

8 Next the accelerator cable connection, together with the choke cable and vacuum pipe must be freed from the carburettor

9 With both nuts removed from the studs on the inlet manifold the carburettor can be removed and placed on one side

10 The next step is to undo the two nuts and bolts from the clamp which holds the exhaust pipe to the exhaust manifold

11 Undo four bolts holding remote control extension to the transmission casing and undo the two front mounting bolts

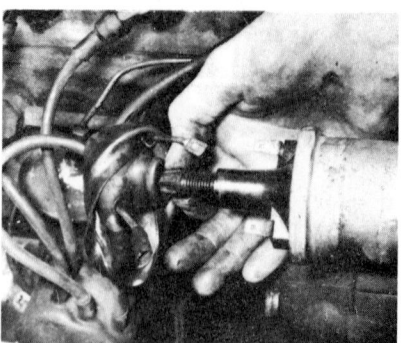

12 Remove the three leads from the coil and unscrew the two nuts and washers holding the two cables to rear of dynamo

13 Then remove the clutch return spring from the clutch operating lever with the aid of a pair of pliers

14 Remove the two bolts holding the clutch operating cylinder to the flywheel casing. On no account push clutch pedal after the operating cylinder is disconnected

15 Pull the HT leads off the spark plugs, spring back the two clips which hold the distributor cap in place, and remove the cap to prevent it getting damaged

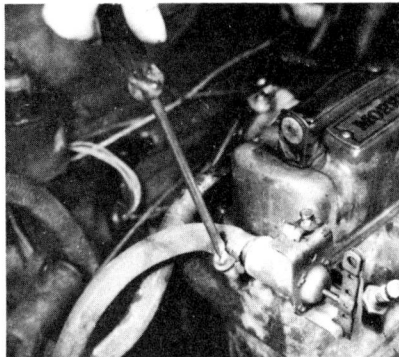

16 Undo clips holding heater hoses to the take off points on cylinder head (shown) and the bottom radiator hose. Undo the starter motor cable from starter motor

17 Jack up front of car, place load spreaders (bits of plank) behind front wheel arches and fit supports. NEVER work under the car with only the jack supporting it

18 Undo the two nuts from each of the three engine mountings (one on each side or one under the timing case), and one under the clutch housing

19 Release the exhaust pipe where it is held to the lug on the gearbox extension by undoing the nut and bolt

20 Two of the bolts holding the front engine mounting to the subframe should have been removed previously (photo 11). Now swing the mounting to one side

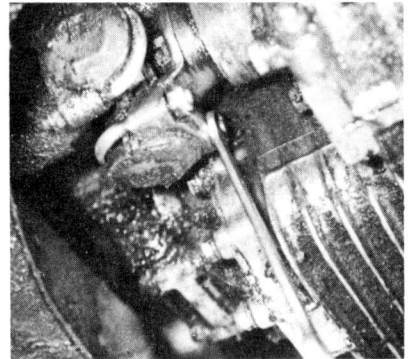

21 Undo the four inner nuts from the two 'U' bolts on each of the rubber universal joints. Leave the nuts on the drive shaft flange 'U' bolts in place

22 With the aid of a screwdriver lever out the two 'U' bolts which hold the rubber joint to the final drive flanges

23 Place a sling aound the engine/ transmission unit, or attach lifting hooks to the cylinder head as shown

24 Carefully hoist the engine out of the car, complete with radiator, ensuring that all cables are out of the way

25 Removal of bonnet hinge securing nuts, bolts and washers

26 Lifting away bonnet

27 Removal of engine weathershield

28 Disconnecting battery terminals

29 Releasing battery clamp

30 Lifting away battery

31 Removal of battery support tray

32 Cylinder block drain plug

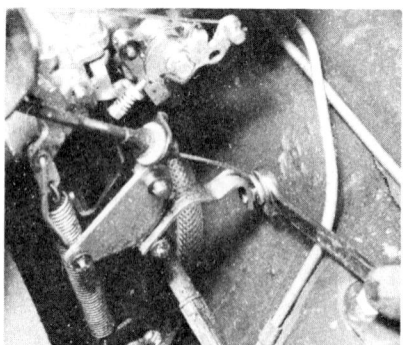

33 Releasing throttle inner cable

34 The choke control cable must next be detached

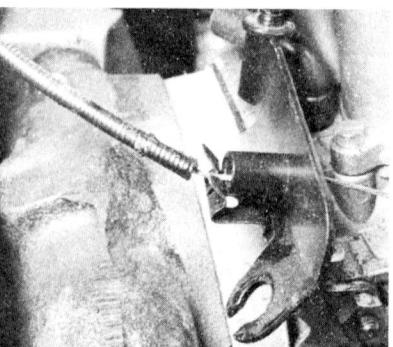

35 Draw choke control cable through support bracket

36 Detach crankcase ventilation hose from carburettor

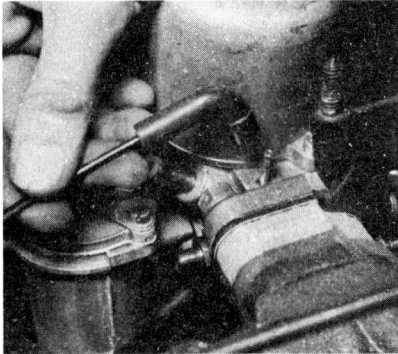

37 Detach vacuum advance pipe from carburettor body

38 Slacken hose clip and remove fuel hose from float chamber

39 With the air cleaner removed the carburettor can be lifted away from the inlet manifold

40 Slacken the fuel outlet hose clip on the mechanical pump

41 Detach fuel outlet hose

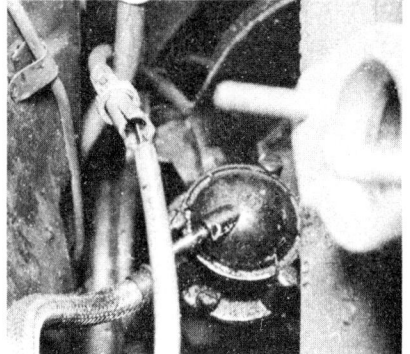

42 Part the speedometer drive cable connection

43 Detach flexible hose from main fuel line

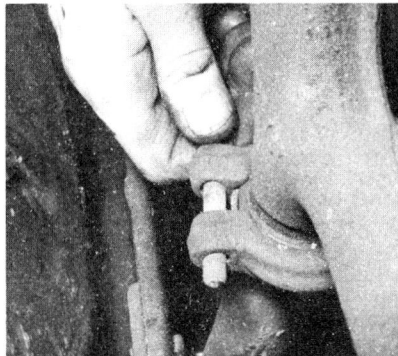

44 Remove the exhaust manifold to down-pipe clamp

45 Remove the distributor cap complete with HT leads

46 Detach temperature sender unit Lucas connector

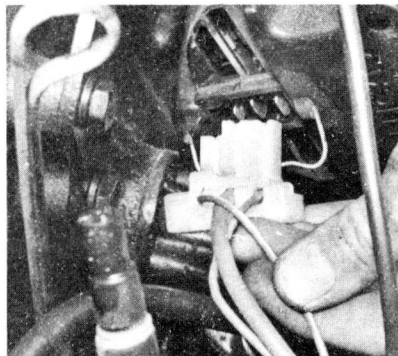

47 Detach alternator multi pin connector

48 Note cable connections to coil and also oil pressure switch and detach

49 Terminal connections on coil are of different widths

50 Release the engine earth cable

51 Detach starter motor heavy duty cable

52 Detach control cable from heater tap

53 Slacken hose clip and detach hose from heater tap

54 Slacken hose clip and detach hose from crankcase breather unit

55 Remove flywheel housing ventilation unit

56 Detach clutch withdrawal arm return spring

57 Remove clutch slave cylinder. Do not disconnect hydraulic hose

58 Release clip and detach spill pipe

59 Slacken engine tie-rod to body mounted bracket securing nut and bolt

60 Release engine tie-rod bracket from cylinder block

61 Move the rod upwards out of the way of the engine

62 If not already done, drain the engine/transmission unit oil

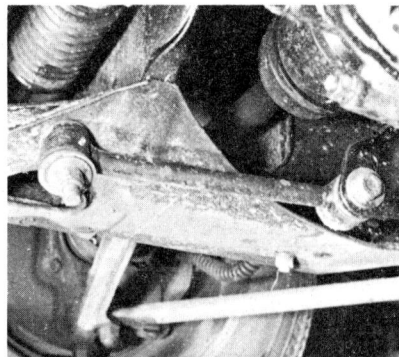
63 On some models there is tie-rod between the transmission unit and subframe

64 Remove the tie-rod to transmission unit mounting bracket securing nuts, bolt and washer and move tie-rod out of the way

65 Detach the exhaust downpipe from the rear of the transmission unit

66 Release exhaust system intermediate clamp

67 Slacken exhaust pipe rear mounting

68 The swivel tab assembly must now be detached from one side

69 The floor mounted remote control assembly

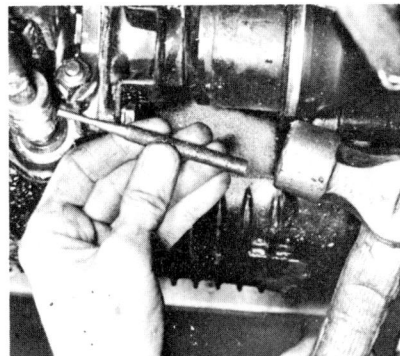
70 Using parallel pin punch, drift out roll pin from selector rod sleeve

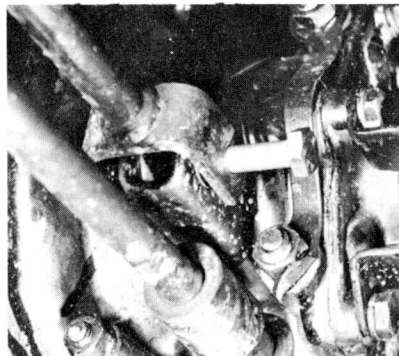
71 Remove remote control stabilizer rod to transmission unit securing nut, bolt and washers

72 Stabilizer rod yoke with bolt removed

73 Mounting above driveshaft constant velocity joint must next be released

74 Using a large screwdriver to release driveshaft constant velocity joint ...

75 ... whilst a tapered bar is 'shocked' against the constant velocity joint to release it from the transmission unit

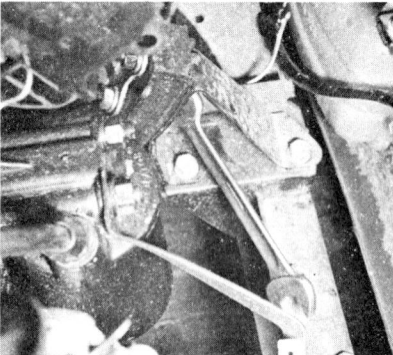

76 Releasing front engine mounting from bracket

77 Releasing bracket from subframe

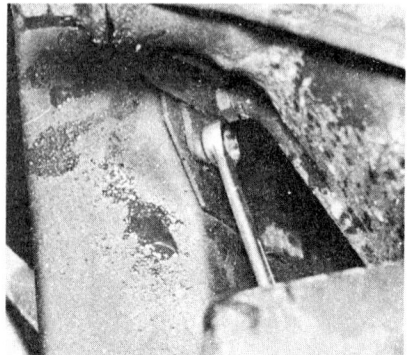

78 Using a ring spanner to hold the nut whilst the bracket securing bolt is removed

79 Take the weight of the engine/transmission unit from the mountings

80 Lift away the front mounting

81 Commence lifting ensuring all cables, hoses and controls are well out of the way

82 Detaching driveshaft constant velocity joint from final drive

83 Continue lifting the engine/transmission unit ...

84 ... until it is clear of the engine compartment

85 Engine/transmission unit being lowered to the ground

86 Left-hand view of engine compartment

87 Right-hand view of engine compartment

24 Undo the two bolts holding the clutch slave cylinder to the flywheel housing, detach the tension spring, and remove the pushrod from the slave cylinder. Tie the clutch slave cylinder back out of the way. **On no account depress the clutch pedal after this has been done.**

25 *Earlier models:* Disconnect the differential flexible drive flanges from the drive shafts by undoing the nuts from the two 'U' bolts on each side facing out which hold the rubber coupling to the drive shaft sliding joint onto the drive shaft, taking care not to damage the flexible rubber boot. Some later models are fitted with roller bearing universal joints. Mark the flanges so they are replaced in the correct relative position and undo the four retaining nuts from each joint. Pull away each joint from the flanges.

26 *Later models,* with drive shaft inner constant velocity joint mounted on transmission unit. Refer to Chapter 11, and remove the right-hand front suspension swivel hub.

27 On models fitted with the starter motor solenoid switch mounted on a bracket on the flywheel housing, remove the switch and cables by undoing the two screws which hold the bracket in place. On some models the coil is fitted in this position and should be removed in the same way as the solenoid switch.

28 Remove the bolts securing the horn in place and disconnect the electrical wires at the snap connectors. Place the horn on one side.

29 To make the engine easier to lift, the starter motor, dynamo or alternator and cylinder head can be removed if wished.

30 The engine can be removed either by a sling placed round each end of the transmission casing, or by special lifting hooks available from most BLMC garages. There are five cylinder head studs on the front of the cylinder head. If lifting hooks are being used remove the nuts and washers from studs two and four, position the hooks over the studs and tighten down the securing nuts.

31 With lifting tackle connected to the lifting hooks or with slings round the engine as previously described, take the weight of the engine/transmission unit.

32 Undo the two nuts which secure the left-hand engine mounting bracket to the bearer plate and the bolts holding the right-hand bracket to the engine and subframe. Also remove the two bolts which hold the rear mounting under the clutch housing to the subframe.

33 *Early models:* The engine/transmission unit can now be lifted out. Tilt it slightly backwards as it comes up to allow the differential projection to clear the body. Ensure that the drive shaft flexible couplings, the engine tie-rod, and the clutch slave cylinder are clear.

34 *Later models:* It is now necessary to detach the drive shaft (full information will be found in Chapter 7) using either the special tool or suitable levers.

35 When the engine is halfway out disconnect the speedometer cable from the transmission casing. This is much easier than disconnecting it from the rear of the speedometer. **Do not forget**

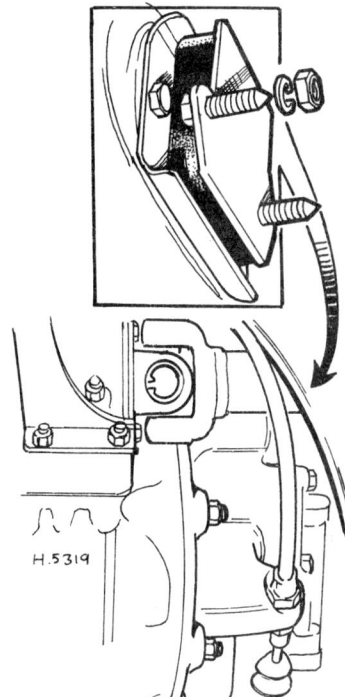
H.5319

Fig. 1.2. Location of converter housing mounting as seen from under the car (Sec. 5)

to reconnect it when the engine is replaced.

36 On certain later models a crankcase closed circuit breathing system is fitted. The purpose of the system is to ensure that crankcase fumes are absorbed by the engine. Fumes are collected from the tappet chamber by a pipe and fed through a special non-return valve into the inlet manifold. The unit is removed by undoing the front tappet chest cover retaining bolt and the nut and securing bolt on the top of the inlet manifold.

37 On models which have been modified for full exhaust emission control as required in the USA there are several pipes, cables and controls that will have to be detached before the engine/transmission unit can be removed. The location will depend on the degree of modification: relevant information will be found in Chapter 3.

6 **Engine/transmission unit (automatic transmission) - removal**

The sequence for removal of the engine/automatic transmission unit is, in principle, basically identical to that for the manual transmission. However, there are several differences and to assist the reader a summary of the necessary operations is given in this Section.

1 Disconnect and remove the battery and battery tray.
2 Remove the bonnet.
3 Remove the bellcrank lever guard or (early models) pull back the rubber boot. Disconnect the selector cable yoke from the bellcrank lever.
4 Slacken the yoke clamp nut and remove the yoke, nut, rubber ferrules and sleeve.
5 Remove the cable front adjustment nut from the outer cable and move the cable clear of the transmission.
6 Remove the selector cable to body clip and tie the cable back out of the way.
7 Remove the exhaust pipe steady bracket from the transmission case. Note that one nut has a locking tab.
8 Raise the front of the car until the wheels are free and remove the driveshaft flange securing nuts.
9 If fitted, disconnect the additional engine steady rod from its anchor plate.
10 Remove the rear engine mounting to subframe securing nuts.
11 Drain the cooling system, as described in Chapter 2.
12 Disconnect the heater hoses and water control valve cable.
13 Disconnect the split type speedometer drive cable.
14 Disconnect the earth lead from the body. Also, disconnect the electrical leads from the ignition coil, starter motor, dynamo or alternator, temperature sender unit, and oil pressure switch. Remove the distributor cap.
15 Refer to Chapter 3, and remove the air cleaner. Also disconnect the choke and throttle control cables and the fuel feed pipe.
16 Disconnect the control cable from the heater control valve and then detach the water hoses from the valve and return pipe (where fitted).
17 Disconnect the stabilizer bar from the cylinder block.
18 Remove the crankcase breather and then remove the nuts that secure the two front engine mountings.
19 Remove the exhaust pipe manifold to downpipe clamp.
20 Detach the radiator to expansion chamber spill hose from the radiator cowling.
21 Suitably sling the engine using ropes or chains and an overhead hoist.
22 Lift the engine vertically and by a sufficient amount to release the driveshafts from the driving flanges and then remove the complete unit from the engine compartment.

7 Engine/transmission unit (manual transmission) - removal with subframe

The engine transmission unit can be removed from under the body; the body being lifted at the front by three or four strong men and then wheeled away; or the body can be lifted at the front with a block and tackle and subframe and engine/transmission unit wheeled out from underneath by two men. The engine/transmission unit is removed together with the subframe, which together weigh about 430 lb.

It is essential to have the hydrolastic system depressurised at your local BLMC agent before work commences. Providing the speed is kept below 30 mph, the car can be driven several miles without any damage to the suspension units.
1 Presuming that the engine is to be separated from the transmission casing after removal, turn on the water drain taps found at the bottom of the radiator and on the side of the cylinder block.

On later models a drain plug is fitted to the cylinder block and it may be found there is no tap or plug at the base of the radiator.
2 Disconnect the battery by removing the earth lead.
3 With a container, capable of holding no less than 1¼ Imp. gallons, in position, unscrew the drain plug from the rear end of the transmission casing (under the clutch bellhousing), and drain off the oil. When the oil has all drained screw back the plug tightly to ensure it is not mislaid. Remove the hubcaps and loosen the front wheel nuts.

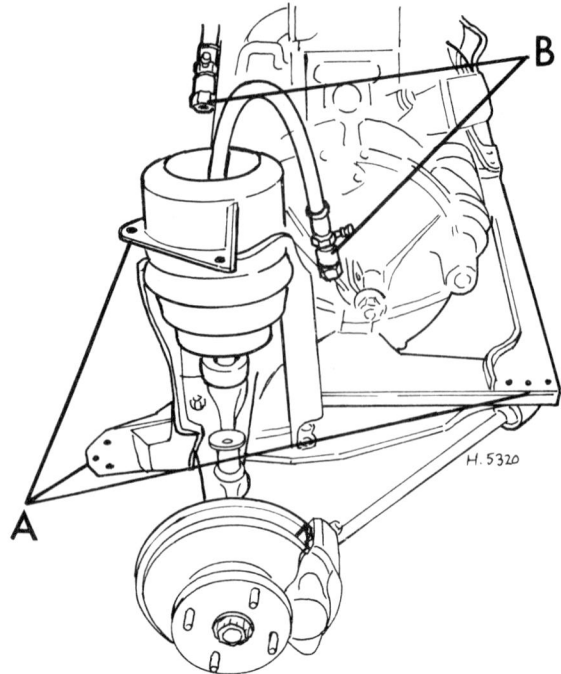

Fig. 1.3. The engine and subframe can be removed from the car as a unit after disconnecting the hydrolastic hoses 'B' and removing the nuts and bolts from the positions 'A' from each side of the car (Sec. 7)

4 Remove the bonnet by undoing the two set bolts and spring washers from each of the two bonnet hinges on the bonnet side of the hinge. Carefully lift the bonnet off and place it somewhere safe where it will not be scratched or damaged. Jack-up the front of the car so as to be able to work underneath it and to later remove the front wheels.
5 Disconnect the inlet and outlet water hoses to the heater/demister unit (where fitted) by undoing the securing clips. Release the heater control operating cable from the regulating valve at the rear of the cylinder head.
6 Pull the leads off the spark plugs, snap back the distributor cap securing clips, undo the HT lead to the centre of the cap, and lift off the distributor cap. If left in place it is easily broken when the engine is removed.
7 Pull off the breather hose from the pipe on the rocker cover, loosen the nut which holds the air cleaner to the air intake pipe, and remove the air cleaner.
8 Undo the small nut which holds the distributor vacuum advance pipe to the carburettor, and also the union nut which secures the fuel pipe in place.
9 Disconnect the choke linkage and the throttle cable at the carburettor end, undo the two nuts which hold the carburettor in place and lift the carburettor away together with the metal plate.
10 Unscrew the bolts from the clamp which holds the exhaust manifold to the exhaust pipe.
11 From underneath the car remove the bolt on the transmission casing which holds the exhaust pipe in place. Also undo the two attachments on the rear subframe which support the rear of the exhaust system and lower the exhaust pipe and silencer to the ground.
12 Free the cooling system overflow hose from its connection to the radiator and from the clip on the cowling.
13 *Early models:*
a) From inside the car release the rubber boot from the floor at the base of the gearlever. This leaves an aperture through which the two set bolts retaining the gearlever retaining plate can be undone. Pull the gearlever out and place it on one

side.

b) Undo the two bolts which hold the gearlever remote control housing extension to the underside of the tunnel in the floor.

14 *Later models:* with floor mounted remote control.

a) Using a suitable diameter parallel pin punch remove the roll pin securing the selector rod sleeve to the selector shaft at the rear of the transmission unit.

b) Undo and remove the nut, bolt and washers securing the remote control stabiliser to the transmission unit.

15 Remove the horn.

16 Free the engine tie-rod from the cylinder block and pull the rod back against the bulkhead out of the way, on models where it is fitted.

17 Disconnect the low tension lead to the distributor and the leads from the dynamo, starter motor, water temperature gauge (where fitted), oil pressure warning bulb, and the stop light switch.

18 Disconnect the oil pressure pipe from the oil pressure gauge (where fitted) by loosening the retaining clip on the rubber connector pipe, and then pull the pipe off.

19 Undo the bolt which holds the earth lead to the clutch cover.

20 In the case of models fitted with a tachometer either remove the reduction drive and cable from the rear of the dynamo; or remove the drive cable from the timing gear cover. N.B. Some modified cars might use a electronic tachometer. If this is the case check the wiring and disconnect as appropriate.

21 Undo the two bolts holding the clutch slave cylinder to the flywheel housing, detach the tension spring and remove the pushrod from the slave cylinder. Tie the clutch slave cylinder back out of the way. **On no account press the clutch pedal after the slave cylinder has been removed.**

22 On models fitted with the starter motor solenoid switch mounted on a bracket on the flywheel housing, remove the switch and cables by undoing the two screws which hold the bracket in place.

23 Undo the two front brake hoses from the hydraulic brake pipe and block the holes by covering them with masking tape. This will help eliminate the accidental entry of dirt.

24 The car should have already been jacked-up and the wheel nuts loosened. Remove the wheelnuts and take off each of the front wheels.

25 Knock back the locking tabs from the nuts (some models use self-locking nuts) on the ball joints at the end of the steering tie-rods, remove the nuts, and free the ball pins from the steering arm by impact hammering. (Use two hammers opposite each other on the sides of the eye of each steering arm).

26 It is now necessary to disconnect the hydrolastic suspension hose from the suspension fluid pipes on the front bulkhead after the system has been depressurised by releasing the interconnecting pipe valve. **Note:** The system will need evacuating, re-pressuring, and trimming, which involves the use of specialised equipment only found at officially approved BLMC garages, after the subframe has been replaced. Seal the open ends of the pipes and the hoses with masking tape to prevent the entry of dirt.

27 Replace the front wheels and lower the car to the ground. Place suitable blocks underneath the transmission casing to support the engine.

28 Undo the 14 nuts and bolts which hold the subframe to the body. There are three mounting points on each side. On the front of each side of the subframe are two bolts; there are a further two bolts on each suspension unit tower; and three bolts at the rear of each side of the subframe. Take off the subframe tower mounting brackets from each side of the bulkhead. Make sure they are marked so they can be replaced in their original positions.

29 Finally carefully lift the body up to clear the engine, taking care that the radiator matrix is not damaged, and that no wires or cables get caught between the body and the engine/transmission assembly.

30 Wheel the bodyshell away from the engine, or the subframe away from the bodyshell, whichever is most convenient.

8 Engine/transmission unit - removal from subframe

Removal of the engine from the subframe is fairly straightforward and should take about 20 minutes. The engine/transmission unit can be lifted either by a block and tackle, or three strong men. If all the ancillaries such as the starter motor, dynamo, exhaust and inlet manifolding, etc., are removed, then two men can lift the unit.

1 Place supports under each of the subframe sidemembers. Remove the radiator after undoing the hose clips, and the bolts holding the top and bottom brackets in place.

2 *Earlier models:*

a) Separate the drive shafts from the differential flanges by undoing the four outside nuts on the two 'U' bolts on each side of the differential. Pull the two 'U' bolts clear. Do not touch the nuts on the other two 'U' bolts. Some later models are fitted with roller bearing universal joints. Mark the flanges and adjacent universal joints so each can be replaced in its original position.

b) The drive shaft flange can then be pushed into the drive shaft so separating the flexible coupling from the drive shaft flange.

3 *Later models,* with driveshaft inner constant velocity joint mounted on transmission unit. Refer to Chapter 11, and remove the right-hand front suspension swivel hub.

4 Undo the bolts which hold each of the three engine mountings to the subframe.

5 *Early models:* Lift the engine/transmission unit out using a sling, block and pulley or three men, as already indicated.

6 *Later models:* It is now necessary to detach the driveshafts, (full information will be found in Chapter 7) using either the special tool or suitable levers. Lift the engine/transmission unit out using a sling, block and pulley or three men, as already indicated.

7 *Automatic transmission:* The sequence is basically identical to that for manual transmission models. The driveshaft flanges must be separated by undoing and removing the securing nuts and washers. Contract the driveshaft and then remove the unit from the subframe.

9 Separating engine from manual transmission - flywheel and clutch removal

Before the engine can be stripped right down it is essential to separate the transmission casing from the cylinder block. Until this is done it is not possible to remove the pistons, connecting rods, or crankshaft. Before the transmission casing/sump can be removed it is necessary to take off the clutch, flywheel, and flywheel housing. The clutch and flywheel are best removed together because of their unusual construction.

1 Remove the clutch cover, as described in Chapter Five.

2 Remove the clutch thrust plate by undoing the three nuts which hold it to the spring pressure plate.

3 Before removing the flywheel it is most important to turn the crankshaft so that the mark ¼ on the flywheel periphery is at tdc. If this is done the 'C' washer which holds the primary gear in place cannot drop. If this is not done and the washer drops serious damage can be caused to the flywheel oil seal.

4 The flywheel is held in position on the tapered end of the crankshaft by a single centre retaining bolt which will have been tightened to a torque of 110 to 115 lb f ft (15.2 to 15.9 Kg fm). Knock back the tab on the lock washer, and if a spanner large enough to undo the retaining bolt is not available, then chisel it round three or four times using a suitable cold chisel on the ends of the flats.

5 To pull the flywheel off the taper on the end of the crankshaft will involve the use of a special puller. This is BLMC service tool '18G 304' which is used with adapter '18G 304 M' (coil spring clutch) or '18GN' (diaphragm spring clutch). It is hardly worthwhile making up this tool as it involves drilling and cutting steel at least 0.5 in (12.70 mm) thick. It is far better to borrow

this tool from your friendly BLMC garage.

6 To operate the puller screw the three studs into the three tapped holes in the flywheel. Place the puller plate over the studs and then screw the nuts onto the studs keeping the plate parallel with the flywheel. Screw in the short centre screw and tighten till the flywheel breaks free from the crankshaft. If it proves very difficult to break the flywheel from the taper, tap the centre bolt with a hammer while the bolt is tightened down hard. This will jar the flywheel loose.

7 As soon as the taper had been broken remove the puller tool, unscrew the retaining bolt and take off the flywheel.

10 Separating engine from manual transmission - flywheel housing removal

With the flywheel and clutch removed the flywheel housing (which is effectively the engine end plate) can be separated from the transmission casing/engine as follows:

1 Knock back the tabs on the lock washers inside the housing.
2 Undo and remove the nine nuts from the studs on the transmission casing.
3 Undo and remove the six bolts from the cylinder block. Note the positions from which the shorter bolts are removed.
4 The housing can now be carefully pulled off. The flywheel housing oil seal should always be renewed when the housing is removed. If for any reason this is not possible, then wrap tinfoil or adhesive tape round the primary gear splines before pulling off the housing, so that the splines do not damage the oil seal.
5 To separate the engine from the transmission casing undo and remove the 14 bolts and washers. Carefully lift the engine from the transmission unit and place to one side suitably supported on blocks.

11 Separating engine from automatic transmission

1 With the engine/transmission unit removed from the car first remove the radiator mounting bracket from the transmission case.
2 Remove the starter motor and distance piece.
3 Remove the converter cover.
4 If not already done, drain the transmission unit.
5 Knock back the lockwasher on the converter centre bolt. Hold the converter by inserting a screwdriver through the hole in the converter housing.
6 Using a large socket remove the centre bolt.
7 Knock back the locking tabs and remove the three equally spaced set screws from the centre of the converter.
8 Make sure that the slot in the end of the crankshaft is horizontal and using service tool '18G 1086' remove the converter. (Fig. 1.5).
9 Remove the service tool and refit the three screws.
10 Remove the low pressure valve from the converter housing. Note that later produced valves are fitted with a screwed plug. This replaces a welch plug which **must not** be removed.
11 Using service tool '18G 1088' fitted onto the converter output gear undo and remove the input gear self locking nut. (Fig 1.6).
12 Disconnect the transverse rod from the bellcrank assembly, remove the nut that secures the bellcrank to its pivot and withdraw the bellcrank.
13 Knock back the locking washer that secures the bellcrank pivot. Undo and remove the pivot.
14 Fit the nylon protector sleeve service tool '18G 1098' over the converter output gear. Alternatively, wrap some thin tape over the gear.
15 Undo and remove the nuts and set screws that secure the converter housing to the transmission and lift away the housing.
16 Remove the converter oil outlet pipe from the housing.
17 Carefully lever the main oil feed pipe from the transmission

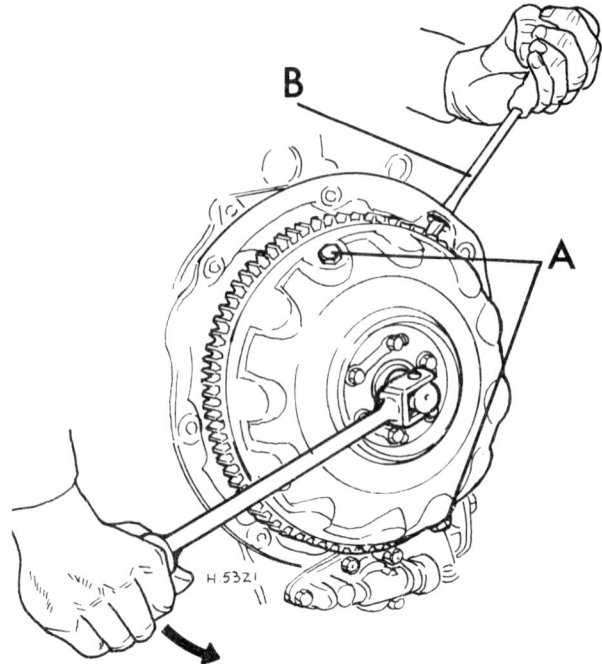

Fig. 1.4. Removal of converter centre-bolt (Sec. 11)

A   Converter drain plugs   B   Screwdriver

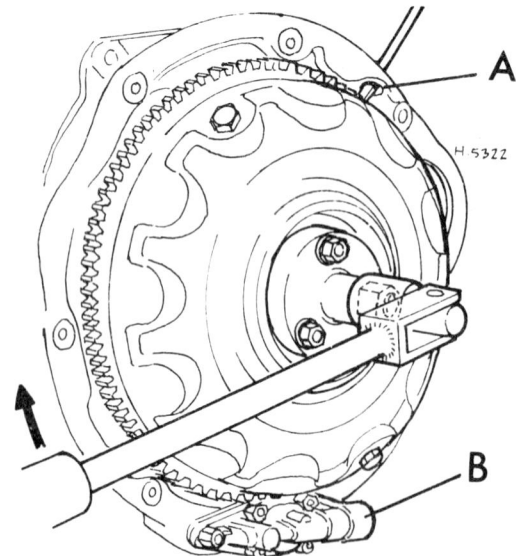

Fig. 1.5. Removal of converter using service tool '18G 1086' (Sec. 11)

Note: A A screwdriver is used to lock converter
          B Low pressure valve

and oil pump (Fig. 1.7).
18 Remove the idler gear, thrust-washers and the converter output gear assembly.
19 Disconnect the governor control rod at the carburettor.
20 Remove the oil filter assembly and then disconnect the engine oil feed pipe together with its rubber seal and spring washer. The last two items are on early units only.
21 Undo and remove the nuts and set screws that secure the engine to the transmission unit.
22 Using suitable lifting equipment carefully lift the engine from the top of the transmission unit.

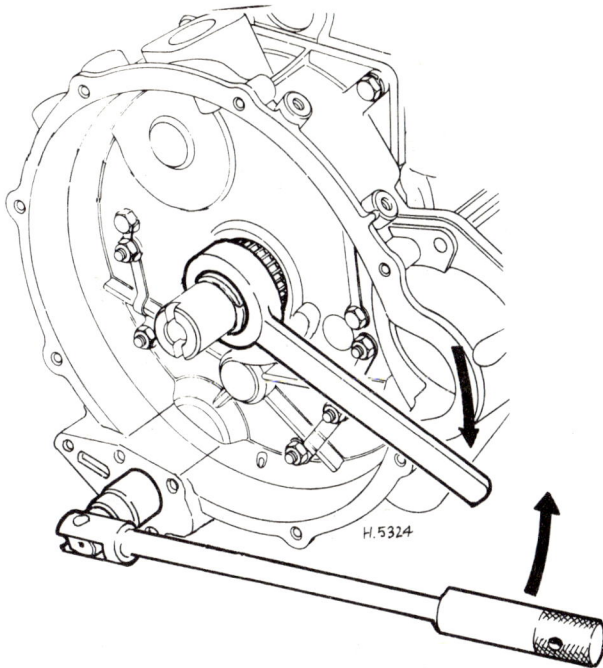

Fig. 1.6. Use of service tool '18G 1088' to hold converter output gear when removing input gear nut (Sec. 11)

Fig. 1.7. Engine oil feed pipe (1), adaptor (2) with internal 'O' ring oil seal (3) (Sec. 11)
Inset shows early type pipe assembly

12 Dismantling the engine - general

It is best to mount the engine on a dismantling stand, but as this is frequently not available, then the engine should be stood on a strong bench at a comfortable working height. Failing this, it can be stripped down on the floor. During the dismantling process the greatest care should be taken to keep the exposed parts free from dirt. As an aid to achieving this aim, thoroughly clean down the outside of the engine, removing all traces of oil and congealed dirt. A good grease solvent such as 'Gunk' will make the job much easier, as, after the solvent has been applied and allowed to stand for a time, a vigorous jet of water will wash off the solvent and all the grease and dirt. If the dirt is thick and deeply embedded, work the solvent into it with a wire brush.

Finally wipe down the exterior of the engine with a clean rag and only then, when it is finally quite free from dirt, should the dismantling process begin. As the engine is stripped, clean each part in a bath of paraffin or petrol. Never immerse parts with oilways in paraffin (ie. the crankshaft) but to clean, wipe down carefully with a petrol damaged rag. Oilways can be cleaned out with pipe cleaners. If an air line is present all parts can be blown dry and the oilways blown through as an added precaution.

A good way of cleaning black greasy nuts, bolts, and washers, and similar small components, is to wash them in a special tin. Place the parts to be cleaned in the tin and then dip it into a paraffin filled container. Shake the tin around so as to allow the paraffin to clean the parts. When the parts are clean lift the tin out allowing the paraffin to drain. You will not have had to grope around at the bottom of the paraffin container and none of the parts will be lost.

Re-use of old engine gaskets is a false economy and can give rise to oil and water leaks, if nothing worse. To avoid the possibility of trouble after the engine has been reassembled always use new gaskets throughout. Do not throw away the old gaskets as it sometimes happens that an immediate replacement cannot be found and the old gasket is then very useful as a template. Hang up the old gaskets as they are removed on a suitable hook or nail.

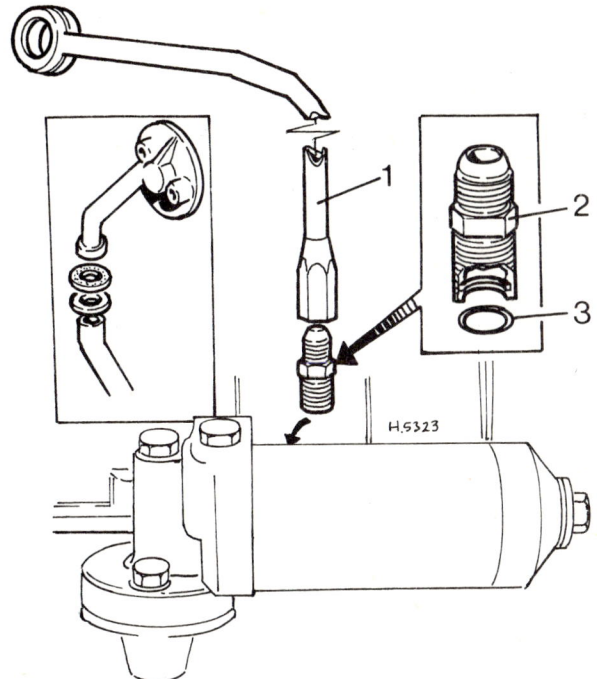

To strip the engine it is best to work from the top down. The transmission case provides a firm base on which the engine can be supported in an upright position. When the transmission case/sump has to be removed the engine should be lifted up off the transmission casing.

Wherever possible, replace nuts and bolts and washers finger-tight from the original stud, bolt, or hole from which they were removed. This helps avoid later loss and muddle. If they cannot be replaced then lay them out in such a fashion that it is clear from where they were removed, or keep them in clearly labelled boxes, tins or polythene bags.

13 Removing ancillary engine components

Before basic engine dismantling begins it is necessary to strip it of ancillary components and these are as follows:
Dynamo or alternator
Distributor
Thermostat
Oil filter assembly and pipe
Inlet manifold and carburettor/s
Exhaust manifold
Mechanical fuel pump

It is possible to strip all these items with the engine in the car if it is merely the individual items that require attention. Presuming the engine to be out of the car or on the bench, proceed as follows:

1 Slacken off the dynamo or alternator retaining bolts and remove the unit with its support brackets.

2 To remove the distributor first disconnect the manifold vacuum advance/retard pipe which leads from the small securing clip at the front of the cylinder head. Unscrew the clamp bolt at the base of the distributor and lift the distributor away from its base plate and drive shaft.

3 Remove the thermostat cover by releasing the three nuts and spring washers which hold it in position and then remove the gasket and lift out the thermostat unit.

4 Unscrew the bolts on the oil pipe leading from the filter to

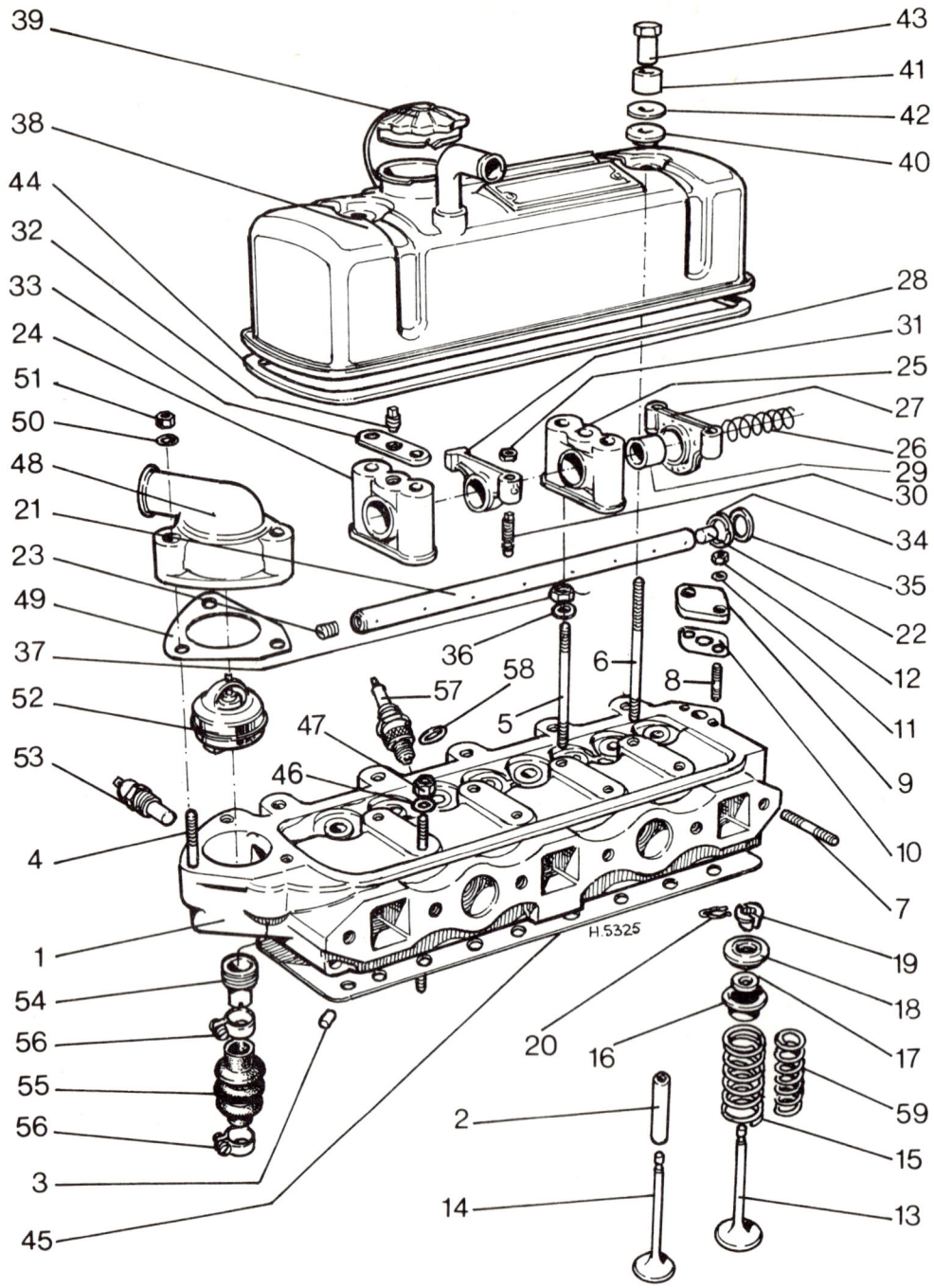

Fig. 1.8. Exploded view of cylinder head

1	Cylinder head	16	Guide shroud	30	Tappet adjusting screw	45	Cylinder head joint
2	Valve guide	17	Packing ring	31	Locknut	46	Washer
3	Plug	18	Spring cup	32	Locating screw	47	Nut
4	Water outlet elbow stud	19	Valve cotter	33	Bracket plate	48	Water outlet elbow
5	Rocker bracket stud - short	20	Circlip	34	Double - coil washer	49	Elbow joint
6	Rocker bracket stud - long	21	Rocker shaft	35	Washer	50	Washer
7	Manifold stud	22	Rocker shaft plug	36	Washer	51	Nut
8	Stud	23	Rocker shaft plug -	37	Nut	52	Thermostat
9	Cover plate		screwed	38	Valve rocker cover	53	Thermal transmitter
10	Cover joint	24	Rocker bracket - tapped	39	Oil filler cap	54	By-pass adaptor
11	Washer	25	Rocker bracket	40	Rubber bush	55	Rubber connection
12	Nut	26	Spacing spring	41	Distance piece	56	Clip
13	Inlet valve	27	Valve rocker - pressed type	42	Cup washer	57	Sparking plug
14	Exhaust valve	28	Valve rocker - forged type	43	Nut	58	Gasket
15	Outer spring	29	Rocker bush - forged type	44	Cover joint	59	Inner spring - twin - carburettor application

the block and remove the pipe. Mask over the hole left in the block with masking tape or block it with a clean piece of rag.

5   Remove the oil filter assembly by unscrewing the two retaining bolts which hold it to the block. The right-hand side of the engine is now stripped of all ancillary equipment

6   Inlet manifold and carburettors. Moving to the left-hand side of the engine, remove the inlet manifold complete with carburettor/s (if this item has not already been removed) by unscrewing the brass nuts and washers holding both the inlet and exhaust manifolds to the cylinder head. The engine is now stripped of all ancillary components and is ready for major dismantling to begin.

14 Cylinder head removal - engine on bench

Remove cylinder head in the following manner:

1   Release the clips on the small bypass hose between the water pump and the cylinder head and remove the hose. This may prove very difficult, and providing a replacement hose is available the hose can be cut away. Pull off the HT leads from the spark plugs and remove the plugs.

2   Unscrew the two rocker cover bolts and lift the rocker cover and gasket away.

3   Unscrew the rocker pedestal nuts (four) and the nine main cylinder head nuts half a turn at a time in the order shown in the Fig. 1.9 to avoid distortion of the head. When all the nuts are no longer under tension they may be screwed off the cylinder head one at a time.

4   Remove the rocker assembly complete, and place it on one side.

5   Remove the push rods, keeping them in the relative order in which they were removed. The easiest way to do this is to push them through a sheet of thick paper or thin card in the correct sequence.

6   The cylinder head can now be removed by lifting upwards. If the head is jammed, try to rock it to break the seal. Under no circumstances try to prise it apart from the block with a screwdriver or cold chisel as damage may be done to the faces of the head or block. If the head will not free readily, turn the engine over by the flywheel as the compression in the cylinders will often break the cylinder head joint. If this fails to work, strike the head sharply with a plastic or wooden headed hammer, or with a metal hammer with an interposed piece of wood to cushion the blows. Under no circumstances hit the head directly with a metal hammer as this may cause the iron casting to

fracture. Several sharp taps with the hammer at the same time pulling upwards should free the head. Lift the head off squarely and place on one side.

15 Cylinder head removal - engine in car

To remove the cylinder head with the engine still in the car proceed as follows:

1   Disconnect the battery by removing the lead from the positive terminal. Remove the engine front cover (later models only).

2   Drain the water by turning the taps at the base of the radiator, and at the bottom left-hand corner of the cylinder block. In some cases plugs are used instead of taps.

3   Loosen the clip at the thermostat housing end on the top water hose, and pull the hose from the thermostat housing outlet pipe.

4   Undo the three bolts holding the radiator support bracket to the cylinder head.

5   Free the distributor vacuum advance pipe from its mountings on the front of the thermostat housing.

6   Undo the clamp which holds the exhaust manifold to the down pipe.

7   Remove the carburettor/s and exhaust and inlet manifolds by undoing the retaining nuts and washers. Lift away the manifolds and carburettor/s complete.

8   Remove the small water pump to cylinder head by-pass hose.

9   Remove the heater/demister unit outlet hose by releasing the clip securing it to the cylinder head (on cars with heater/demister units).

The procedure is not the same as for removing the cylinder head when on the bench. One tip worth noting is that should the cylinder head refuse to free easily, the battery can be reconnected and the engine turned over on the solenoid switch. Under no circumstances turn the ignition on where an SU electrical fuel pump is fitted unless the wire to the pump is disconnected, and ensure that the distributor cap is removed to prevent the engine firing.

16 Valves - removal

1   The valves can be removed from the cylinder head as follows. With a pair of pliers remove the spring circlips holding the two halves of the split tapered collets together. Compress each spring

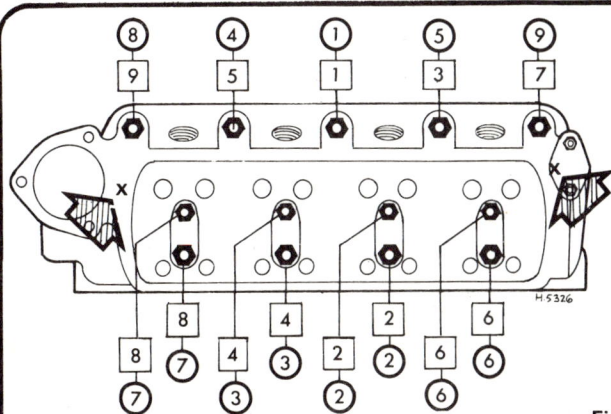

Fig. 1.9. Correct order of slackening and tightening cylinder head nuts (Secs. 14 and 61)

Figures shown thus ③ refer to 1275 cc engines.
Figures shown thus ③ refer to all other engines.
Arrows show additional bolt and nut fitted to 9.75 : 1 compression ratio 1275 cc engine. These are tightened last of all to the specified torque.

in turn with a valve spring compressor until the two halves of the collets can be removed. Release the compressor and remove the spring (or springs), shroud, and valve.

2 If, when the valve spring compressor is screwed down, the valve spring retaining cap refuses to free and expose the split collet, do not continue to screw down on the compressor as there is a likelihood of damaging it. Gently tap the top of the tool directly over the cap with a light hammer. This will free the cap. To prevent the compressor jumping off the valve spring retaining cap when it is tapped, hold the compressor firmly in position with one hand.

3 Slide the rubber oil control seal off the top of each valve stem and then drop out each valve through the combustion chamber. The 1275cc valve oil seal arrangement is shown in Fig 1.11.

4 It is essential that the valves are kept in their correct sequence unless they are so badly .worn that they are to be renewed. If they are going to be kept and used again, place them in a sheet of card having eight holes numbered 1 to 8 corresponding with the relative positions the valves were in when fitted. Also keep the valve springs, washers, etc., in the correct order.

17 Valve guides - removal

If it is wished to remove the valve guides they can be removed from the cylinder head in the following manner. Place the cylinder head with the gasket face on the bench and with a suitable hard steel punch drift the guides out of the cylinder head.

18 Rocker assembly - dismantling

To dismantle the rocker assembly, release the rocker shaft locating screw, remove the split pins, flat washers, and spring washers from each end of the shaft and slide from the shaft the pedestals, rocker arms, and rocker spacing springs.

19 Timing cover, gears and chain - removal

The timing cover, gears, and chain can be removed with the engine in the car provided the radiator and fan belt are removed. (For radiator and fan belt removal see Chapter 2). The procedure for removing the timing cover, gears and chain is otherwise the same irrespective of whether the engine is in the car or on the bench, and is as follows:

1 Bend back the locking tab of the crankshaft pulley locking washer under the crankshaft pulley retaining bolt, prising it back with a cold chisel or screwdriver through the radiator grille in the wing if the engine is still in the car. With a large spanner remove the bolt and locking washer. This bolt is sometimes very difficult to shift and hitting the free end of the spanner with a heavy hammer is sometimes the only way to start it. If the engine is still in the car, put the car in top gear and apply the handbrake hard to prevent the engine from turning.

2 Placing two large screwdrivers behind the camshaft pulley wheel at 180° to each other, carefully lever the wheel off. It is preferable to use a proper pulley extractor if this is available, but large screwdrivers or tyre levers are quite suitable, providing care is taken not to damage the pulley flange.

3 Remove the woodruff key from the crankshaft nose with a pair of pliers and note how the channel in the pulley is designed to fit over it. Place the woodruff key in a glass jar as it is a very small part and can easily be mislaid.

4 Unscrew the bolts holding the timing cover to the block. Note that four of the bolts are larger than the others, and that each bolt makes use of a large flat washer as well as a spring washer.

5 Take off the timing cover and gasket.

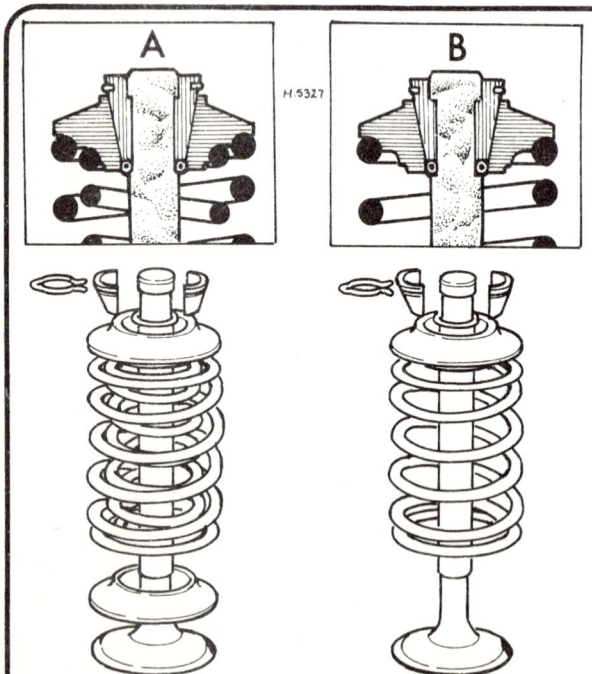

Fig. 1.10. Component parts of valve assembly (early type) (Sec. 16)

A Double valve spring
B Single valve spring
Inset shows correct location of valve seat at bottom of cotter groove

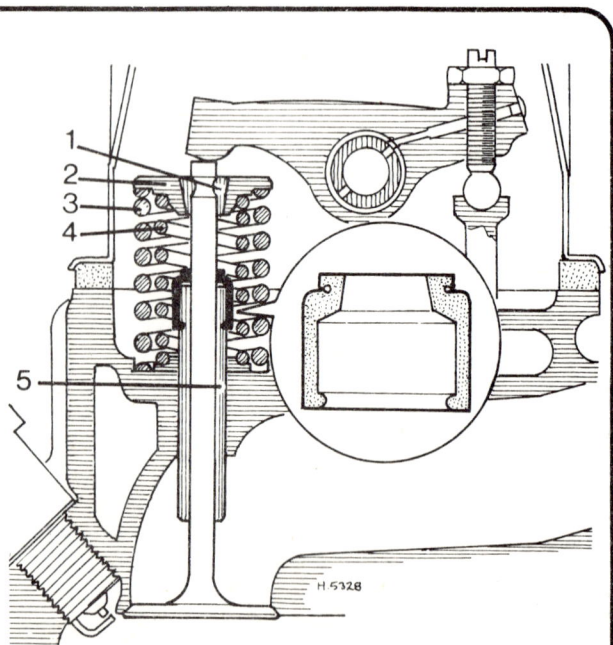

Fig. 1.11. Cross sectional view of 1275 cc valve components (Sec. 16)

1 Split cotters
2 Retaining cup
3 Outer spring
4 Inner spring (12G and 9.75 : 1 c.r. engines)
5 Valve guide

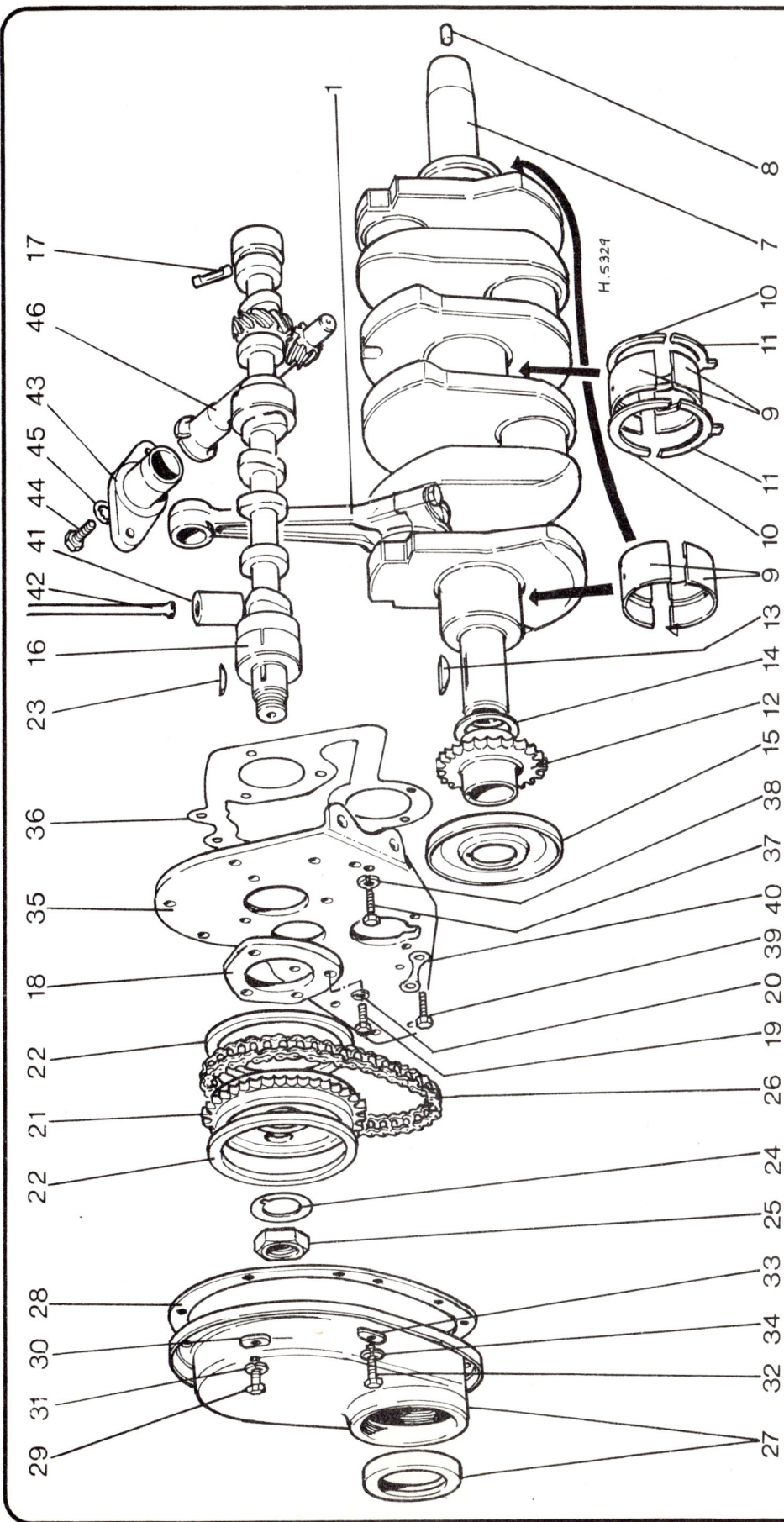

Fig. 1.12. Exploded view of engine internal components

1	Connecting rod	
7	Crankshaft	
8	Plug	
9	Crankshaft main bearing	
10	Main bearing thrust washer - upper	
11	Main bearing thrust washer - lower	
12	Crankshaft gear	
13	Key	
14	Washer	
15	Oil thrower	
16	Camshaft	
17	Pump driving pin	
18	Camshaft locating plate	
19	Screw	
20	Washer	
21	Camshaft gear	
22	Tensioner ring	
23	Gear key	
24	Lock washer	
25	Nut	
26	Timing chain	
27	Timing chain cover and seal	
28	Cover joint	
29	Cover screw	
30	Washer	
31	Washer	
32	Screw	
33	Washer	
34	Washer	
35	Mounting plate	
36	Plate joint	
37	Screw	
38	Washer	
39	Screw	
40	Lock washer	
41	Tappet	
42	Pushrod	
43	Distributor housing	
44	Screw	
45	Washer	
46	Drive spindle	

H.5329

6 With the timing cover off, take off the oil thrower. Note that the concave side faces forward.

7 Bend back the locking tab on the washer under the camshaft retaining nut and unscrew the nut noting how the locking washer locating tag fits in the camshaft gearwheel keyway.

8 To remove the camshaft and crankshaft timing wheels complete with chain, ease each wheel forward a little at a time, levering behind each gearwheel in turn with two large screwdrivers at 180° to each other. If the gearwheels are locked solid then it will be necessary to use a proper gearwheel and pulley extractor. With both gearwheels off, remove the woodruff keys from the crankshaft and camshaft with a pair of pliers and place them in the jar for safe keeping. Note the number of very thin packing washers behind the crankshaft gearwheel and remove them very carefully.

20 Camshaft - removal

The camshaft can be removed only with the engine on the bench. The timing cover, gears and chain, must be removed as detailed in Section 19. It is also necessary to remove the distributor drive gear as described in Section 21. With the drive gear out of the way, proceed in the following manner:

1 Remove the three bolts and spring washers which hold the camshaft locating plate to the block. The bolts are normally covered by the camshaft gearwheel.

2 Remove the tappets through the side cover apertures (early models) or using a magnet if it is not possible in invert the engine. Keep in order for correct refitment.

3 Remove the plate. The camshaft can now be withdrawn. Take great care to remove the camshaft gently, and in particular ensure that the cam peaks do not damage the camshaft bearings as the shaft is pulled forward.

21 Distributor drive - removal

To remove the distributor drive with the transmission casing still in position it is first necessary to remove one of the tappet cover bolts when the covers are fitted. Later 1275cc engines do not have them. With the distributor and the distributor clamp plate already removed, this is achieved as follows:

1 Unscrew the single retaining bolt and lock washer to release the distributor housing.

2 With the distributor housing removed, with the casing still in position, screw into the end of the distributor drive shaft a 5/16 in. UNF bolt. A tappet cover bolt is ideal for this purpose. The drive shaft can then be lifted out, the shaft being turned slightly in the process to free the shaft skew gear from the camshaft skew gear.

3 If the gear casing has already been removed then it is a simple matter to push the drive shaft out from inside the crankcase.

22 Pistons, connecting rods, and big-ends bearings - removal

The pistons, and connecting rods can be removed with the engine on the bench. Proceed as for removing the cylinder head with the engine on the bench. The piston and connecting rods are drawn up out of the top of the cylinder bores.

1 Undo the 10 set bolts and the two nuts holding the transmission casing to the cylinder block, taking care to note the positions from which the shorter bolts are removed.

2 With an assistant lift the engine away from the transmission casing, or alternatively, use a block and tackle.

3 Knock back with a cold chisel the locking tabs on the big-end retaining bolts, and remove the bolts and locking tabs (early models). On later models special nuts are fitted instead of tab washers and conventional nuts.

4 Remove the big-end caps one at a time, taking care to keep them in the right order and the correct way round. Also ensure that the shell bearings are also kept with their correct connecting rods and caps, unless they are to be renewed. Normally, the numbers 1 to 4 are stamped on adjacent sides of the big-end caps and connecting rods, indicating which cap fits on which rod and which way round the cap fits. If no numbers or lines can be found then with a sharp screwdriver scratch mating marks across the joint from the rod to the cap. One line for connecting rod No. 1, two for connecting rod No. 2, and so on. This will ensure there is no confusion later as it is most important that the caps go back in the correct position on the connecting rods from which they were removed.

5 If the big-end caps are difficult to remove they may be gently tapped with a soft hammer.

6 To remove the shell bearings, press the bearing opposite the groove in both the connecting rod, and the connecting rod caps and the bearings will slide out easily.

7 Withdraw the pistons and connecting rods upwards and ensure they are kept in the correct order for replacement in the same bore. Refit the connecting rod caps and bearings to the rods if the bearings do not require renewal to minimise the risk of getting the caps and rods muddled.

23 Gudgeon pins - removal

Fully floating gudgeon pins are fitted to all 1100 models. They are retained in position by circlips which fit into recesses in the pistons at each end of the hole for the gudgeon pin. To extract the pin, remove the circlip from the end of the gudgeon pin hole and push the pin out. Make sure that the pins are kept with the pistons from which they were removed as they must be replaced the same way round in the same piston.

If the little end bush is worn, the gudgeon pin will rock in it. The manufacturers advise that on no account should the gudgeon pin or little end bush be renewed separately. If renewal is necessary then the connecting rod/little end bush, and the piston/gudgeon pin should be renewed as a complete assembly. In the author's experience it is quite safe to renew the piston and gudgeon pin together and fit them to an existing connecting rod, providing the pin slips through the little end easily, and does not rock in it. Reputable manufacturers of pistons such as Hepolite can supply suitable piston and gudgeon pin assemblies.

On 1300 models a press type gudgeon pin is used and requires a special BLMC tool number '18G1150' with adaptor '18G1150A' to remove and replace the pin. This tool is shown in Fig. 1.13 and must be used in the following manner:

1 Securely hold the hexagonal body in a firm vice and screw back the large nut until it is flush with the end of the main centre screw. Well lubricate the screw and large nut as they have to withstand a high loading. Now push the centre screw in until the nut touches the thrust race.

2 Fit the adaptors number '18G1150A' onto the main centre screw with the piston ring cut-away positioned uppermost. Then slide the parallel sleeve with the groove end first onto the centre screw.

3 Fit the piston with the 'FRONT' or 'V' mark on towards the adaptor on the centre screw. This is important because the gudgeon pin bore is offset and irreparable damage will result if fitted the wrong way round. Next fit the remover/replacer bush on the centre screw with the flange towards the gudgeon pin.

4 Screw the stop nut onto the main centre screw and adjust it until approximately 0.032 inch (0.8 mm) endplay ('A' in Fig 1.13) exists, and lock the stop nut securely with the lock screws. Now check that the remover/replacer bush and parallel sleeve are positioned correctly in the bore on both sides of the piston. Also check that the curved face of the adaptor is clean and slide the piston onto the tool so it fits into the curved face of the adaptor with the piston rings over the cut-away.

5 Screw the large nut up to the thrust race and holding the lockscrew turn the large nut with a ring spanner or long socket until the gudgeon pin is withdrawn from the piston.

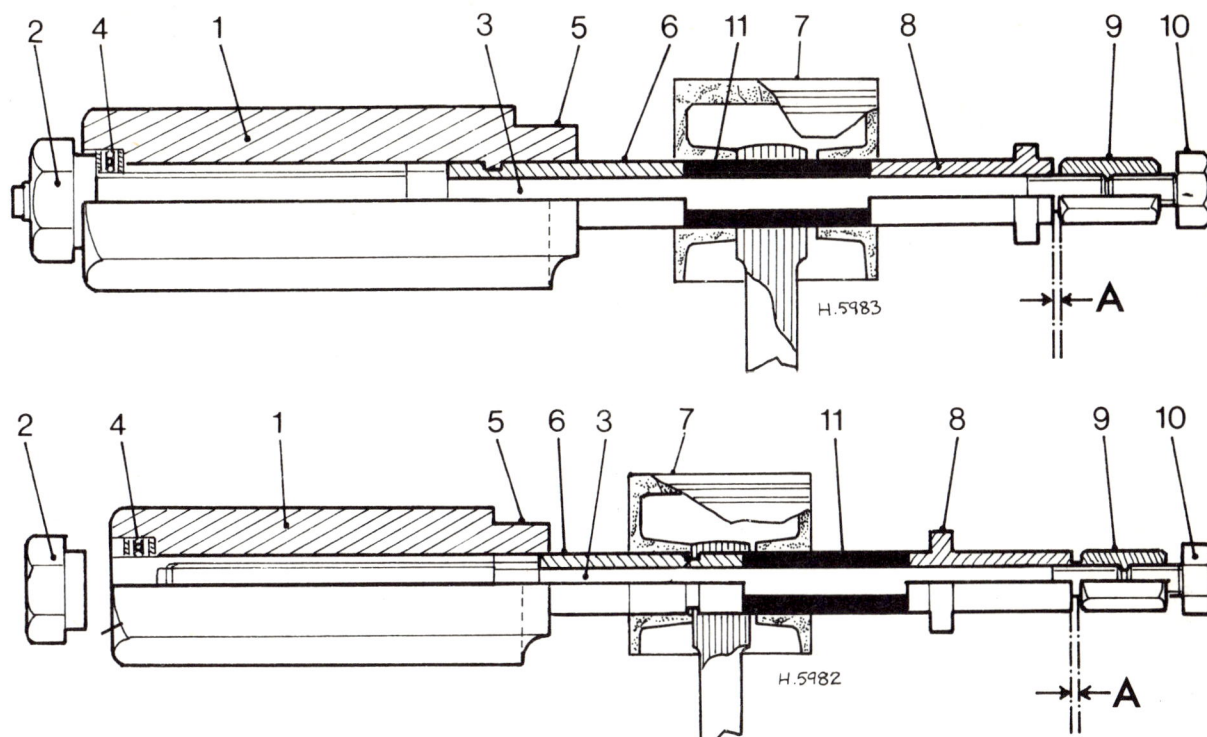

Fig. 1.13. Using service tool '18G 1150' to remove (upper illustration) and refit (lower illustration) gudgeon pin (Secs. 23 and 48)

1 Hexagon body	4 Thrust race	7 Piston	10 Lock screw
2 Large nut	5 Adaptor	8 Service tool bush	11 Gudgeon pin
3 Centre screw	6 Parallel sleeve	9 Stop nut	Dimension A = 1/32 in
			(0.8 mm)

24 Piston rings - removal

To remove the piston rings, slide them carefully over the top of the piston, taking care not to scratch the aluminium alloy. Never slide them off the bottom of the piston skirt. It is very easy to break the piston rings if they are pulled off roughly so this operation should be done with extreme caution. It is helpful to make use of an old hacksaw blade, or better still, an old 0.020 in (0.5 mm) feeler gauge. Lift one end of the piston ring to be removed out of its groove and insert the end of the feeler gauge under it. Turn the feeler gauge slowly round the piston and as the ring comes out of its groove apply slight upward pressure so that it rests on the land above. It can then be eased off the piston using the feeler gauge to stop it slipping into any empty grooves if it is any but the top piston ring that is being removed.

25 Crankshaft and main bearings - removal

Removal of the crankshaft can only be attempted with the engine on the bench.

Drain the engine oil, remove the timing gears and remove the transmission casing and the big-end bearings, flywheel and flywheel housing as has already been described.

1 Release the locking tabs from the six bolts which hold the three main bearing caps in place.

2 Unscrew the bolts and remove them together with the locking plates, (early models). On later models special bolts are used and locking plates are not required.

3 Remove the two bolts which hold the front main bearing cap against the engine front plate.

4 Remove the main bearing caps and the bottom half of each bearing shell, taking care to keep the bearing shells in the right caps.

5 When removing the centre bearing cap, note the bottom semi-circular halves of the thrust washers one half lying on each side of the main bearing. Lay them with the centre bearing along the correct side.

6 Slightly rotate the crankshaft to free the upper halves of the bearing shells and thrust washers which should now be extracted and placed over the correct bearing cap.

7 Remove the crankshaft by lifting it away from the crankcase.

26 Lubrication system - general description

A forced feed system of lubrication is fitted with oil circulated round the engine from the transmission casing/sump. The level of engine in the sump is indicated on the dipstick which is fitted on the right-hand side of the engine. It is marked to indicate the optimum level which is the maximum mark. The level of oil in the sump, ideally, should not be above or below this line. Oil is replenished via the filter cap on the front of the rocker cover.

The oil in the transmission casing/sump is also used to lubricate the gearbox and differential, the total capacity including the filter being 8½ Imp. pints.

The oil pump is mounted at the end of the crankcase and is driven by the camshaft. Two different types of oil pump have been fitted at different times. There are either the Hobourn Eaton or the Concentric (Engineering) Ltd. concentric rotor type. All are of the non-draining variety to allow rapid pressure build-up when starting the engine after it has been standing for some time.

Oil is drawn from the sump through a gauze screen in the oil strainer and is sucked up the pick-up pipe and drawn into the oil pump. From the oil pump it is forced under pressure along a gallery on the right-hand side of the engine, and through drillings to the big-end, main and camshaft bearings. A small hole in each connecting rod allows a jet of oil to lubricate the cylinder wall with each revolution.

From the camshaft front bearing oil is fed through drilled passages in the cylinder block and head to the front rocker pedestal where it enters the hollow rocker shaft. Holes drilled in the shaft allow for the lubrication of the rocker arms, and the valve stems and pushrod ends. This oil is at a reduced pressure to the oil delivered to the crankshaft bearings. Oil from the front camshaft bearing also lubricates the timing gears and the timing chain. Oil returns to the sump by various passages, the tappets being lubricated by oil returning via the pushrod drillings in the block.

On all models a full flow oil filter is fitted, and all oil passes through this filter before it reaches the main oil gallery. The oil is passed directly from the oil pump across the block to an external pipe on the right-hand side of the engine which feeds into the filter head.

27 Oil filter - removal and replacement

Manual transmission - renewable element type

1 The full flow oil filter fitted to engines is located underneath the dynamo on the side of the engine facing the front of the car. It is removed by unscrewing the long centre bolt which holds the filter bowl in place. With the bolt released carefully lift away the filter bowl which contains the filter and will also be full of oil. It is helpful to have a large basin under the filter body to catch the amount which is bound to spill (Fig. 1.15).

2 Throw the old filter element away and thoroughly clean down the filter bowl, the bolts and associated parts with petrol and when perfectly clean wipe dry with a non-fluffy rag.

3 A rubber sealing ring is located in a groove round the head of the oil filter and forms an effective leak-proof joint between the filter head and the filter bowl. A new rubber sealing ring is supplied with each new filter element.

4 Carefully prise out the old sealing ring from the locating groove. If the ring has become hard and is difficult to move take care not to damage the sides of the sealing ring groove.

5 With the old ring removed, fit the new ring in the groove at four equidistant points and press it home a segment at a time. Do not insert the ring at just one point and work round the groove pressing it home as, using this method, it is easy to stretch the ring and be left with a small loop of rubber which will not fit into the locating groove.

6 Reassemble the oil filter assembly by first passing up the bolt through the hole in the bottom of the bowl, with a steel washer under the bolts head and a rubber or felt washer on top of the steel washer and next to the filter bowl.

7 Slip the spring over the bolt inside the bowl, then the other steel washer, the remaining rubber or felt washer and lastly the filter seating plate with the concave face downwards. Slip in a new filter element and with the bolt pressed hard up against the filter bowl body (to avoid leakage) three quarter fill the bowl with engine oil.

8 Offer up the bowl to the rubber sealing ring and before finally tightening down the centre bolt, check that the lip of the filter bowl is resting squarely on the rubber sealing ring and is not offset and off the ring. If the bowl is not seating properly, rotate it until it is. Run the engine and check the bowl for leaks.

Manual transmission - disposable cartridge type

On later cars a disposable cartridge type of oil filter is fitted. To renew the oil filter, unscrew the old cartridge from the filter head and throw it away.

Smear the new seal with a little engine oil and fit it into its groove in the new cartridge. Screw the new cartridge onto the filter head and tighten hand-tight. Start the engine and check for leaks.

Automatic transmission - renewable element type

The sequence for renewal is basically identical to that for the manual transmission, but the following additional points should be noted:

a) Slacken the ignition coil mounting bracket clamp bolt and place a container under the filter.

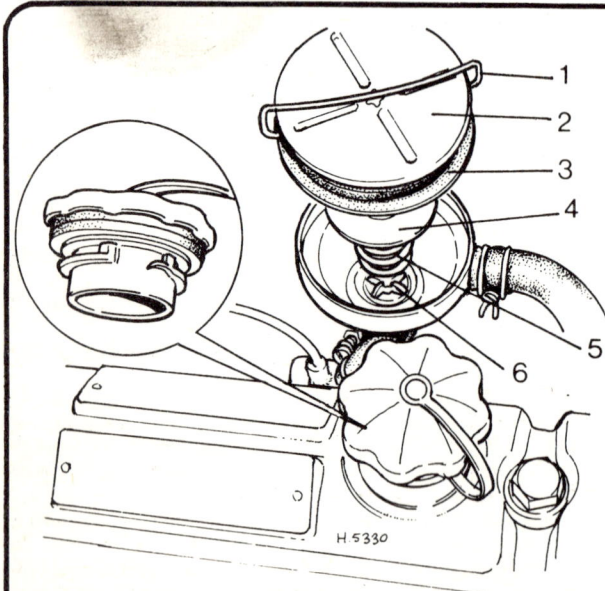

Fig. 1.14. Exploded view of closed circuit breather control valve (Sec. 26)

1 Spring clip	4 Metering needle
2 Cover	5 Spring
3 Diaphragm	6 Cruciform guides

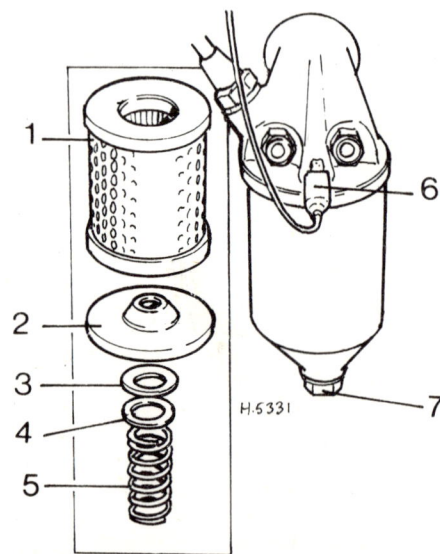

Fig. 1.15. Engine oil filter (renewable element type) (Sec. 27)

1 Filter element	5 Spring
2 Seating plate	6 Warning light switch
3 Seating washer	7 Filter retaining bolt
4 Steel washer	

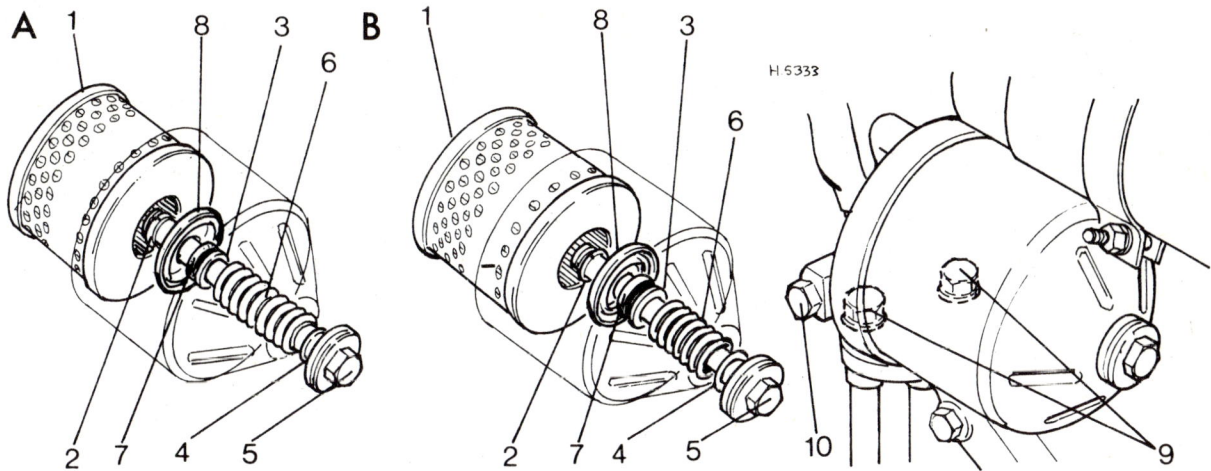

Fig. 1.16. Engine/automatic transmission oil filter components (Sec. 27)

1 Filter element	4 Sealing ring	7 Sealing washer	9 Filter head retaining bolts
2 Circlip	5 Centre bolt	8 Sealing plate	10 Oil pressure check plug
3 Steel washer	6 Spring		

A 1st type (short element (1) and long spring (6))
B 2nd type (longer element (1) and shorter spring (6))

b) Using a socket and extension inserted through a hole in the engine mounting plate, remove the bowl and element assembly (Fig. 1.16).
c) Refitting is the reverse sequence to removal. Do not overtighten the central retaining bolt.

Automatic transmission - disposable cartridge type

The sequence for renewal is identical to that for the manual transmission. If the cartridge is tight it can be removed with a spanner.

28 Oil pressure relief valve - removal and replacement

1 To prevent excessive oil pressure - for example when the engine is cold - an oil pressure relief valve is built into the right-hand side of the engine at the rear just below the oil pressure unit take-off point. (photo 179)
2 The relief valve is identified externally by a large domed hexagon nut. To dismantle the unit unscrew the nut and remove it, complete with the two fibre or copper sealing washers. The relief spring and the relief spring cup can then be easily extracted.
3 In position, the metal cup fits over the opposite end of the relief valve spring resting in the dome of the hexagon nut, and bears against a machining in the block. When the oil pressure exceeds 60 lb/sq.in. the cup is forced off its seat and the oil by-passes it and returns via a drilling directly to the sump.
4 Check the tension of the spring by measuring its length. If it is shorter than 2 7/8 in. (47.5 mm) it should be replaced with a new spring. Reassembly of the relief valve unit is a reversal of the above procedure.

29 Engine mountings - removal and replacement

The engine/transmission assembly is supported on three engine mountings. Two are located at the front of the engine, one either side, and the other under the clutch cover to which it is attached (right-hand mounting).

Should the mountings be worn or broken they can be replaced with the engine in place.

Place a jack under the same end of the transmission casing from which the engine mounting is to be removed and take the weight of the engine. **Note:** Use a block of wood interposed

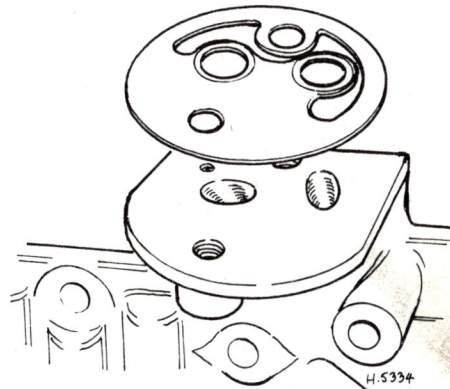

Fig. 1.17. Correct location of later type filter head/front cover joint washer (Sec. 27)

between the transmission casing and the jack to spread the load on the transmission case.

If the mounting under the clutch housing is to be removed proceed as follows:
1 Undo the engine tie-rod, and undo the two nuts and bolts on the exhaust manifold to exhaust pipe clamp.
2 Release the exhaust pipe mounting lug from its attachment point on the gearlever extension by undoing the securing nut and bolt.
3 Undo and remove the two nuts, bolts and spring washers which hold the engine mountings to the subframe sidemember.
4 Undo and remove the two bolts which hold the mounting block to the clutch housing.
5 Jack-up the engine just enough to be able to remove the engine mounting. While operating the jack frequently check that the fan blades are not fouling or damaging the radiator core.
6 Replacement is a straight reversal of the above sequence.

If the front mountings are to be removed proceed as below:
7 Undo the engine tie-rod (where fitted), and undo the two nuts and bolts on the exhaust manifold to exhaust pipe clamp.
8 Release the exhaust pipe mounting lug from its attachment point on the gearbox extension by undoing the securing nut and

bolt.

9   Undo and remove the nuts holding the engine mountings to the engine bearer plate, right-hand mounting bracket, and the left-hand subframes.

10   Jack-up the engine just enough to remove the engine mounting blocks. While operating the jack make sure the rear mounting block does not become too unnaturally distorted.

11   Replacement is a straight reversal of the above sequence.

30 Oil pump - removal and dismantling

Oil pump removal is an operation which can only be carried out with the engine out of the car. Prior to removing the pump it is necessary to remove the clutch, flywheel, and flywheel housing. The oil pump engages via a lip and slot with the rear of the camshaft from which it is directly driven.

1   Bend back the locking tabs on the three securing bolts which hold the pump on the block.

2   Unscrew the bolts and remove them complete with washers.

3   The oil pump cover can now be removed, complete with drive shaft and inner rotor.

4   To dismantle the Hobourn Eaton pump, merely unscrew the screw holding the pump end plate in position.

5   The Concentric (Engineering) Ltd. pump must not be dismantled and if suspect must be exchanged for a rebuilt unit.

Before engine No. '194195', only the Hobourn Eaton concentric rotor pump was used. After this engine, either the Hobourn Eaton or the Burman rotary vane type may be fitted. Check the rotor endfloat and lobe clearance of the Hobourn Eaton pump as follows:

1   Fit the rotors to the pump body and place a straight edged steel rule across the pump body joint face. With a feeler gauge measure the clearance between the rotors and the underside of the steel rule. If the gap is more than 0.005 in (0.127 mm) remove the two locating dowels, and carefully lap the pump body joint face till the gap is only .001 in.

2   Measure the gap between the rotor lobes when they are in the positions shown in Fig. 1.18. If the gap is more than 0.006 in (0.152 mm) new rotors must be fitted.

A modified Hobourn Eaton oil pump was fitted to later engines and is fully interchangeable with the earlier type. The later type can be recognised by the words 'Hobourn Eaton' round the cover flange as opposed to round the cover centre. The new pump is identified by Part No. '2A 692' and is fully interchangeable with the old pump, identified by Part No. '2A 341'.

Automatic transmission models: the pump may be removed once the converter and converter housing have been removed. It is retained by screws which should be removed enabling the pump to be lifted away. The dismantling and checking procedure is identical to that for the Hobourn Eaton type (Fig. 1.20).

31 Engine: examination and renovation - general

With the engine stripped down and all parts thoroughly cleaned, it is now time to examine everything for wear. The following items should be checked and where necessary renewed or renovated as described in subsequent Sections.

32 Crankshaft - examination and renovation

Examine the crankpin and main journal surfaces for signs of scoring or scratches. Check the ovality of the crankpins at different positions with a micrometer. If more than 0.001 in. out of round, the crankpins will have to be reground. It will also have to be reground if there are any scores or scratches present. Also check the journals in the same fashion. On highly tuned engines the centre main bearing has been known to break up. This is not always immediately apparent, but slight vibration in

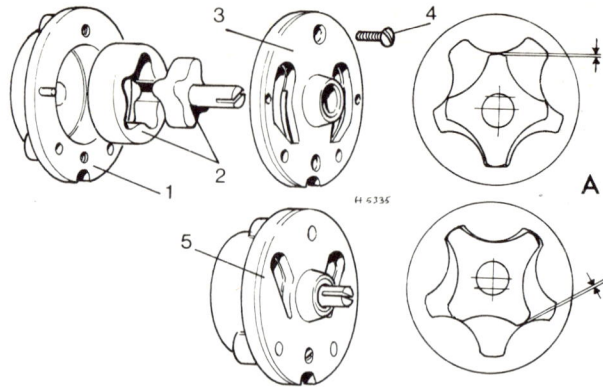

Fig. 1.18. Two types of oil pump which may be fitted to manual transmission models (Sec. 30)

Hobourn-Eaton
1   Body
2   Shaft and rotor
3   Cover
4   Screw - cover to body

Concentric (Engineering) Ltd
5   Pump (serviced as an assembly only)

A indicates the lobe positions for checking the clearance

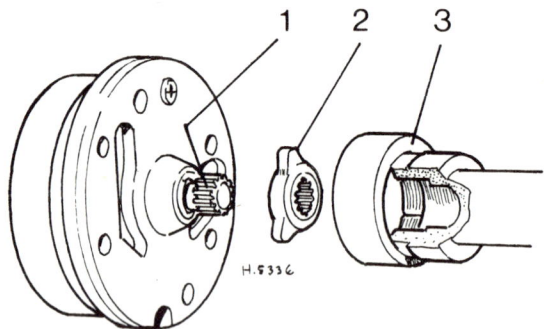

Fig. 1.19. Oil pump drive showing the correct position for the early type driving flange (Sec. 30)

1   Oil pump drive shaft   3   Camshaft
2   Driving flange

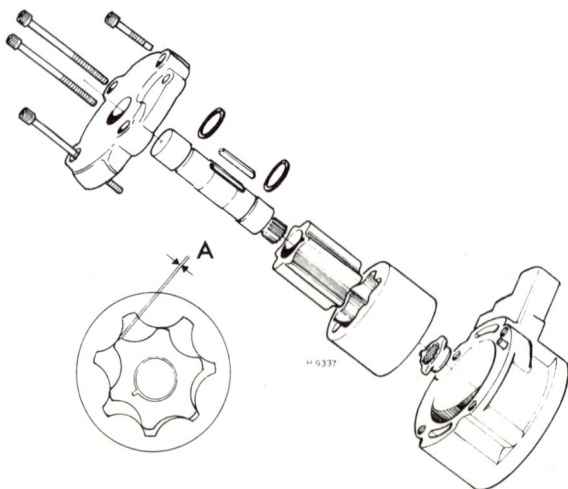

Fig. 1.20. Oil pump components (automatic transmission models) (Sec. 30)

A   Lobe clearance check position

an otherwise normally smooth engine and a very slight drop in oil pressure under normal conditions are clues. If the centre main bearing is suspected of failure it should be immediately investigated by dropping the transmission casing and removing the centre main bearing cap. Failure to do this will result in a badly scored centre main journal.

If it is necessary to regrind the crankshaft and fit new bearings an engineering works will be able to decide how much metal to grind off and supply the correct undersize bearing shells to fit.

33 Big-end and main bearings - examination and renovation

1 Big-end bearing failure is accompanied by a noisy knocking from the crankcase, and a slight drop in oil pressure. Main bearing failure is accompanied by vibration which can be quite severe as the engine speed rises and falls and a drop in oil pressure.

2 Bearings which have not broken up, but are badly worn will give rise to low oil pressure and some vibration. Inspect the big-ends, main bearings, and thrust washers for signs of general wear, scoring, pitting and scratches. The bearings should be mat grey in colour. With lead-indium bearings should a trace of copper colour be noticed the bearings are badly worn as the lead bearing material has worn away to expose the indium underlay. Renew the bearings if they are in this condition or if there is any sign of scoring or pitting.

3 The main and big-end bearing undersizes available are designed to correspond with the regrind sizes, ie., 0.010 bearings are correct for a crankshaft reground 0.010 undersize. The bearings are in fact, slightly more than the stated undersize as running clearances have been allowed for during their manufacture.

4 Very long engine life can be achieved by changing big-end bearings at intervals of 30,000 miles (48,000 Km) and main bearings at intervals of 60,000 miles (96,000 Km), irrespective of bearing wear. Normally, crankshaft wear is infinitesimal and regular changes of bearings will ensure mileage of up to 120,000 miles (192,000 Km) before crankshaft regrinding becomes necessary. Crankshafts normally have to be reground because of scoring caused by bearing failure.

5 Once dismantled only refit new bearing shells. It is false economy to replace old bearings even if they have only been in use for a short while.

34 Cylinder bores - examination and renovation

1 The cylinder bores must be examined for taper, ovality, scoring and scratches. Start by carefully examining the top of the cylinder bores. If they are at all worn a very slight ridge will be found on the thrust side. This marks the top of the piston ring travel. The owner will have a good indication of the bore wear prior to dismantling the engine, or removing the cylinder head. Excessive oil consumption accompanied by blue smoke from the exhaust is a sure sign of worn cylinder bores and piston rings.

2 Measure the bore diameter just under the ridge with a micrometer and compare it with the diameter at the bottom of the bore, which is not subject to wear. If the difference between the two measurements is more than .006 in. then it will be necessary to fit special piston rings or to have the cylinders rebored and fit oversize pistons and rings. If no micrometer is available remove the rings from a piston and place the piston in each bore in turn about 0.75 in (19mm) below the top of the bore. If an 0.010 inch (0.254 mm) feeler gauge can be slid between the piston and the cylinder wall on the thrust side of the bore then remedial action must be taken. Oversize pistons are available in the following sizes:

+ 0.010 inch (0.254 mm)
+ 0.020 inch (0.508 mm)

3 These are accurately machined to just below these measurements so as to provide correct running clearances in bores bored out to the exact oversize dimensions.

4 If the bores are slightly worn but not so badly worn as to justify reboring, then special oil control rings, or pistons and rings can be fitted which will restore compression and stop the engine burning oil.

5 If extreme cases it is possible to have cylinder liners fitted.

35 Pistons and piston rings - examination and renovation

1 If the old pistons are to be refitted, carefully remove the piston rings and then thoroughly clean them. Take particular care to clean out the piston ring grooves. At the same time do not scratch the aluminium in any way. If new rings are to be fitted to the old pistons then the top ring should be stepped so as to clear the ridge left above the previous top ring. If a normal but oversize new ring is fitted, it will hit the ridge and break, because the new ring will not have worn in the same way as the old, which will have worn in unison with the ridge.

2 Before fitting the rings on the pistons each should be inserted approximately 3 in. (76 mm) down the cylinder bore and the gap measured with a feeler gauge. This should be between 0.006 in. and 0.010 in (0.1524 and 0.254 mm). It is essential that the gap should be measured at the bottom of the ring travel, as if it is measured at the top of a worn bore and gives a perfect fit, it could easily seize at the bottom. If the ring gap is too small rub down the ends of the ring with a very fine file until the gap, when fitted, is correct. To keep the rings square in the bore for measurement, line each up in turn by inserting an old piston in the bore upside down, and use the piston to push the ring down about 3 in. (76 mm). Remove the piston and measure the piston ring gap.

3 When fitting new pistons and rings to a rebored engine the piston ring gap can be measured at the top of the bore as the bore will now not taper. It is not necessary to measure the side clearance in the piston ring grooves with the rings fitted as the groove dimensions are accurately machined during manufacture. When fitting new oil control rings to old pistons it may be necessary to have the grooves widened by machining to accept the new wider rings. In this instance the manufacturers representative will make this quite clear and will supply the address to which the pistons must be sent for machining.

4 When new pistons are fitted, take great care to fit the exact size best suited to the particular bore of your engine. BLMC go one stage further than merely specifying one size of piston for all standard bores. Because of very slight differences in cylinder machining during production it is necessary to select just the right piston for the bore. Five different sizes are available for the standard bore as well as the four oversize dimensions already shown.

5 Examination of the cylinder block face will show adjacent to each bore a small diamond shaped box with a number stamped

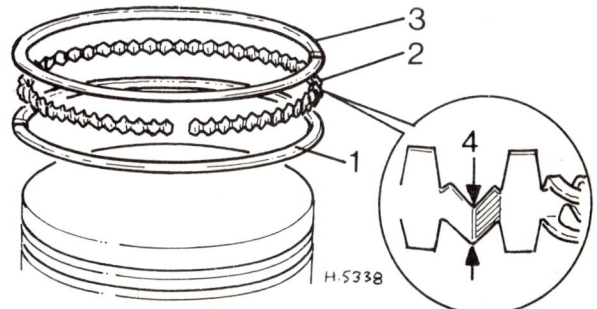

Fig. 1.21. Alternative oil control ring (Secs. 35 and 49)

1 *Bottom rail of oil control ring*
2 *Expander of oil control ring*
3 *Top rail of oil control ring*
4 *Expander ends correctly butting*

in the metal. Careful examination of the piston crown will show a matching diamond and number. These are the standard piston sizes and will be the same for all four bores. If standard pistons are to be refitted or standard low compression pistons changed to standard high compression pistons, then it is essential that only pistons with the same number in the diamond are used. With larger pistons, the amount oversize is stamped in an ellipse in the piston crown.

6 On engines with tapered second and third compression rings, the top narrow side of the ring is marked with a 'T'. Always fit this side uppermost and carefully examine all rings for this mark before fitting.

7 Before obtaining new piston rings obtain the relevant information from the Specifications at the beginning of this Chapter. If possible take the old rings along to the supplier. This is particularly applicable to the oil control rings.

36 Camshaft and camshaft bearings - examination and renovation

Carefully examine the camshaft bearings for wear. **Note:** On early engines only the front camshaft bearing is renewable. If the bearings are obviously worn or pitted or the metal underlay is showing through, then they must be renewed. This is an operation for your local BLMC garage or the local engineering works as it demands the use of specialised equipment. The bearings are removed with a special drift after which new bearings are pressed in, care being taken to ensure the oil holes line up with those in the block. With a special tool the bearings are then reamed in position.

2 The camshaft itself should show no sign of wear, but, if very slight scoring on the cams is noticed, the score marks can be removed by very gently rubbing down with very fine emery cloth. The greatest care should be taken to keep the cam profiles smooth.

37 Valves and valve seats - examination and renovation

1 Examine the heads of the valves for pitting and burning, especially the heads of the exhaust valves. The valve seatings should be examined at the same time. If the pitting on valve and seat is very slight the marks can be removed by grinding the seats and valves together with coarse, and then fine, valve grinding paste. Where bad pitting has occurred to the valve seats it will be necessary to recut them and fit new valves. If the valve seats are so worn that they cannot be recut, then it will be necessary to fit new valve seat inserts. These latter two jobs should be entrusted to the local BLMC garage or engineering works. In practice it is very seldom that the seats are so badly worn that they require renewal. Normally, it is the valve that is too badly worn for replacement, and the owner can easily purchase a new set of valves and match them to the seats by valve grinding.

2 Valve grinding is carried out as follows:
    Place the cylinder head upside down on a bench, with a block of wood at each end to give clearance for the valve stems. Alternatively place the head at 45° to a wall with the combustion chambers facing away from the wall.

3 Smear a trace of coarse carborundum paste on the seat face and apply a suction grinder tool to the valve head. With a semi-rotary motion, grind the valve head to its seat, lifting the valve occasionally to redistribute the grinding paste. When a dull matt even surface finish is produced on both the valve seat and the valve, then wipe off the paste and repeat the process with fine carborundum paste, lifting and turning the valve to redistribute the paste as before. A light spring placed under the valve head will greatly ease this operation. When a smooth unbroken ring of light grey matt finish is produced, on both valve and valve seat faces, the grinding operation is completed.

4 Scrape away all carbon from the valve head and the valve stem. Carefully clean away every trace of grinding compound,

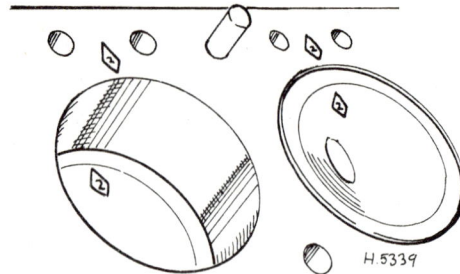

Fig. 1.22. If renewing standard size pistons ensure the grade number in the diamond on the block corresponds to the grade number in the diamond on the piston crown (Sec. 35)

taking great care to leave none in the ports or in the valve guides. Clean the valves and valve seats with a paraffin soaked rag then with a clean rag, and finally, if an air line is available, blow the valves, valve guides and valve ports clean.

38 Timing gears and chain - examination and renovation

Examine the teeth on both the crankshaft gear wheel and the camshaft gearwheel for wear. Each tooth forms an inverted 'V' with the gearwheel periphery, and if worn the side of each tooth under tension will be slightly concave in shape when compared with the other side of the tooth, ie., one side of the inverted 'V' will be concave when compared with the other. If any sign of wear is present the gearwheels must be renewed.

Examine the links of the chain for side slackness and renew the chain if any slackness is noticeable when compared with a new chain. It is a sensible precaution to renew the chain at about 30,000 miles (48,000 km) and at a lesser mileage if the engine is stripped down for a major overhaul. The actual rollers on a very badly worn chain may be slightly grooved.

39 Rockers and rocker shaft - examination and renovation

1 Remove the threaded plug with a screwdriver from the end of the rocker shaft and thoroughly clean out the shaft. As it acts as the oil passage for the valve gear, clean out the oil holes and make sure they are quite clear. Check the shaft for straightness by rolling it on the bench. It is most unlikely that it will deviate from normal, but, if it does, then a judicious attempt must be made to straighten it. If this is not successful purchase a new shaft. The surface of the shaft should be free from any worn ridges caused by the rocker arms. If any wear is present, renew the shaft. Wear is only likely to have occurred if the rocker shaft oil holes have become blocked.

2 Check the rocker arms for wear of the rocker bushes, for wear at the rocker arm face which bears on the valve stem, and for wear of the adjusting ball ended screws. Wear in the rocker arm bush can be checked by gripping the rocker arm tip and holding the rocker arm in place on the shaft, noting if there is any lateral rocker arm shake. If shake is present, and the arm is very loose on the shaft, remedial action must be taken. Pressed steel valve rockers cannot be renovated by renewal of the rocker arm bush. It is necessary to fit new rocker arms. Forged rocker arms which have worn bushes may be taken to your local BLMC garage or engineering works to have the old bush drawn out and a new bush fitted. Forged rockers and pressed steel rockers are interchangeable in sets of eight, but, where one or two pressed steel rockers only require renewal it is not advised to replace them with the forged type.

3 Check the top of the rocker arm where it bears on the valve head for cracking or serious wear on the case hardening. If none is present reuse the rocker arm. Check the lower half of the ball on the end of the rocker arm adjusting screw. On high performance 1100/1300 engines wear on the ball and top of the pushrod is easily noted by the unworn 'pip' which fits in the small central

oil hole on the ball. The larger this 'pip' the more wear has taken place to both the ball and the pushrod. Check the pushrods for straightness by rolling them on the bench. Renew any that are bent.

40 Tappets - examination and renovation

Examine the bearing surface of the tappets which lie on the camshaft. Any indentation in this surface or any cracks indicate serious wear and the tappets should be renewed. Thoroughly clean them out, removing all traces of sludge. It is most unlikely that the sides of the tappets will prove worn, but, if they are a very loose fit in their bores and can readily be rocked, they should be exchanged for new units. It is very unusual to find any wear in the tappets, and any wear present is likely to occur only at very high mileages.

41 Flywheel starter ring gear - examination and renovation

If the teeth on the flywheel starter ring are badly worn, or if some are missing, then it will be necessary to remove the ring. This is achieved by splitting the ring with a cold chisel. The greatest care should be taken not to damage the flywheel during this process.

To fit a new ring, heat it gently and evenly with an oxy-acetylene flame until a temperature of approximately 350° C (662° F) is reached. (This is indicated by a light metallic blue surface colour). With the ring at this temperature, fit it to the flywheel with the front of the teeth facing the flywheel register. The ring should be tapped gently down onto its register and left to cool naturally when the contraction of the metal on cooling will ensure that it is a secure and permanent fit. Great care must be taken not to overheat the ring, as if this happens the temper of the ring will be lost.

Alternatively, your local BLMC garage or local engineering works may have a suitable oven in which the flywheel can be heated. The normal domestic oven will only give a temperature of about 250 ° C (482° F) at the very most and, although it may just be possible to fit the ring with it at this temperature, it is unlikely and no great force should have to be used.

42 Oil pump - examination and renovation

It is unlikely that the oil pump will be worn, but, if the engine is fully stripped down it is only sensible to check the pump for wear. With the Hobourn Eaton pump dismantled check the rotor internally and also the drive shaft lobes for any signs of excessive wear or scoring, as described in Section 30. If wear is found, renew the worn components.

Also examine the inside faces of the pump body in which the rotors turn for signs of scoring. The outside of the rotors should be examined in the same way. If excessive scoring is found then the pump body must be renewed.

The Concentric Engineering pump, if suspect, cannot be dismantled and should be exchanged for a reconditioned unit.

43 Cylinder head - decarbonisation

1   This can be carried out with the engine either in or out of the car. With the cylinder head off carefully remove with a wire brush and blunt scraper all traces of carbon deposits from the combustion spaces and the ports. The valve head stems and valve guides should also be freed from any carbon deposits. Wash the combustion spaces and ports down with petrol and scrape the cylinder head surface free of any foreign matter with the side of a steel rule, or a similar article.
2   Clean the pistons and top of the cylinder bores. If the pistons

are still in the block then it is essential that great care is taken to ensure that no carbon gets into the cylinder bores as this could scratch the cylinder walls or cause damage to the pistons and rings. To ensure this does not happen, first turn the crankshaft so that two of the pistons are at the top of their bores. Stuff rag into the other two bores or seal them off with paper and masking tape. The waterways should also be covered with small pieces of masking tape to prevent particles of carbon entering the cooling system and damaging the water pump.
3   There are two schools of thought as to how much carbon should be removed from the piston crown. One school recommends that a ring of carbon should be left round the edge of the piston and on the cylinder wall as an aid to low oil consumption. Although this is probably true for early engines with worn bores, on later engines the second school recommends that for effective decarbonisation all traces of carbon should be removed.
4   If all traces of carbon are to be removed, press a little grease into the gap between the cylinder walls and the two pistons which are to be worked on. With a blunt scraper carefully scrape away the carbon from the piston crown, taking great care not to scratch the aluminium. Also scrape away the carbon from the surrounding lip of the cylinder wall. When all carbon has been removed, scrape away the grease which will now be contaminated with carbon particles, taking care not to press any into the bores. To assist prevention of carbon built-up the piston crown can be polished with a metal polish such as Brasso. Remove the rags or masking tape from the other two cylinders and turn the crankshaft so that the two pistons which were at the bottom are now at the top. Place rag or masking tape in the cylinders which have been decarbonised and proceed as before.
5   If a ring of carbon is going to be left round the piston then this can be helped by inserting an old piston ring into the top of the bore to rest on the piston and ensure that carbon is not accidentally removed. Check that there are no particles of carbon in the cylinder bores. Decarbonising is now complete.

44 Valve guides - examination and renovation

Examine the valve guides internally for wear. If the valves are a very loose fit in the guides and there is the slightest suspicion of lateral rocking, then new guides will have to be fitted. If the valve guides have been removed compare them internally by visual inspection with a new guide as well as testing them for rocking with the valves.

45 Engine reassembly - general

1   To ensure maximum life with minimum trouble from a rebuilt engine, not only must everything be correctly assembled, but everything must be spotlessly clean, all the oilways must be clear, locking washers and spring washers must always be fitted where indicated and all bearing and other working surfaces must

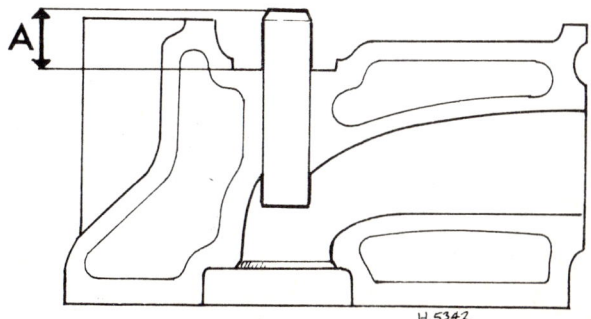

Fig. 1.23. Correct fitting dimension for valve guide (Sec. 44)

A = 0.5938 in (15.08 mm)

be thoroughly lubricated during assembly. Before assembly begins renew any bolts or studs the threads of which are in any way damaged, and whenever possible use new spring washers.

2 Apart from your normal tools, a supply of clean rag, an oil can filled with engine oil (an empty plastic detergent bottle thoroughly cleaned and washed out, will invariably do just as well), a new supply of assorted spring washers, a set of new gaskets, and preferably a torque wrench, should be collected together.

46 Crankshaft - replacement

Ensure that the crankcase is thoroughly clean and that all oilways are clear. A thin twist drill is useful for cleaning them out. If possible, blow them out with compressed air. Treat the crankshaft in the same fashion, and then inject engine oil into the crankshaft oilways.

Commence work on rebuilding the engine by replacing the crankshaft and main bearings:

1 If the old main bearing shells are to be replaced, (a false economy unless they are virtually as new), fit the three upper halves of the main bearing shells to their locations in the crankcase, after wiping the locations clean.

2 **Note:** At the back of each bearing is a tab which engages in locating grooves in either the crankcase or the main bearing cap housings.

3 If new bearings are being fitted, carefully clean away all traces of the protectuve grease with which they are coated.

4 With the three upper bearing shells securely in place, wipe the lower bearing cap housings and fit the three lower shell bearings to their caps ensuring that the right shell goes into the right cap if the old bearings are being refitted.

5 Wipe the recesses either side of the centre main bearings which locate the upper halves of the thrust washers.

6 Generously lubricate the crankshaft journals and the upper and lower main bearing shells and carefully place the crankshaft in position.

7 Introduce the upper halves of the thrust washers (the halves without tabs) into their grooves either side of the centre main bearing, rotating the crankshaft in the direction towards the main bearing tabs (so that the main bearing shells do not slide out). At the same time feed the thrust washers into their locations with their oil grooves outwards away from the bearing.

8 Ensure that all six tubular locating dowels are firmly in place, one on each side of the upper halves of the three main bearings, and then fit the main bearing caps in position ensuring they locate properly on the dowels. The mating surfaces must be spotlessly clean or the caps will not seat properly.

9 When replacing the centre main bearing cap, ensure the thrust washers, generously lubricated, are fitted with their oil grooves facing outwards, and the locating tab of each washer is in the slot in the bearing cap.

10 Replace the one-piece locking tabs over the main bearing caps and replace the main bearing cap bolts screwing them up finger-tight.

11 Test the crankshaft for freedom of rotation. Should it be very stiff to turn or possess high spots a most careful inspection must be made, preferably by a qualified mechanic with a micrometer to get to the root of the trouble. It is very seldom that any trouble of this nature will be experienced when fitting the crankshaft.

12 Tighten the main bearing bolts to a torque of 60 - 65 lb f ft 8.3 - 10 kg fm) and turn up the locking tabs (when fitted) with a cold chisel.

47 Oil pump - reassembly and replacement

1 The oil pump must be fitted before the flywheel housing on all models.

2 To reassemble the Hobourn Eaton oil pump replace the outer rotor, inner rotor and drive shaft in the pump body and secure the end cover in place with the screw.

3 The oil pump cover is accurately located on the pump body by two dowels. Ensure these are in place before fitting the pump together. It has been known for the dowels to be forgotten after the joint face of the pump body has been lapped.

4 To replace either the Hobourn or the Concentric (Engineering) Ltd. oil pump to the crankcase, fill the pump being fitted with engine oil, correctly place the paper gasket in position on the pump body flange, ensuring that the gasket does not cover the inlet or exhaust ports, and firmly bolt the pump unit to the crankcase using a spring washer under the head of each bolt, which should be tightened to a torque of 9 lb f ft (1.2 kg fm).

5 Because of the dispostion of the bolt holes it is impossible to fit the oil pump the wrong way round. Always use a new gasket.

6 Note that on 1275 engines a driving flange which fits on three splines in the end of the camshaft is used, to drive the pump. Make sure it is not forgotten.

48 Pistons and connecting rods - reassembly

1100 models

If the same pistons are being used, then they must be mated to the same connecting rod with the same gudgeon pin. If new pistons are being fitted it does not matter which connecting rod they are used with, but, the gudgeon pins should be fitted on the basis of selective assembly.

This involves trying each of the pins in each of the pistons in turn and fitting them to the ones they fit best as described below.

Because aluminium alloy, when hot has a greater co-efficient of expansion than steel, the gudgeon pin may be a very tight fit in the piston when it is cold. Damage will result if the pin is forced into the piston. It must be a hand push fit. If more force than this is needed then a different pin must be tried.

Lay the correct piston adjacent to each connecting rod and remember that the same rod and piston must go back into the same bore. If new pistons are being used it is only necessary to ensure that the right connecting rod is placed in each bore.

To assemble the pistons to the connecting rods proceed as follows:

1 Fit a gudgeon pin circlip in position at one end of the gudgeon pin hole in the piston.

2 Locate the connecting rod in the piston with the marking 'FRONT' on the piston crown towards the front of the engine, and the connecting rod caps towards the camshaft side of the engine.

3 Slide the gudgeon pin in through the hole in the piston and through the connecting rod little end until it rests against the previously fitted circlip. **Note:** The pin should be a push fit.

4 Fit the second circlip in position. Repeat this procedure for all four pistons and connecting rods.

1300 models

If the same pistons are being used, then they must be mated to the same connecting rod with the same gudgeon pin. If new pistons it does not matter which connecting rod they are used with, but the gudgeon pins are **not to be interchanged**. As the gudgeon pin is a press fit a special BLMC tool '18G1150' with adaptors '18G1150A' is required to fit the gudgeon pin as shown in Fig. 1.13 and should be used as follows:

1 Unscrew the large nut and withdraw the centre screw from the body a few inches. Well lubricate the screw thread and correctly locate the piston support adaptor.

2 Carefully slide the parallel sleeve with the groove end last onto the centre screw up as far as the shoulder. Lubricate the gudgeon pin and its bores in the connecting rod and piston with a graphited oil.

3 Fit the connecting rod and piston, side marked 'Front' or 'V' to the tool with the connecting rod entered on the sleeve up the

groove. Fit the gudgeon pin into the piston bore up to the connecting rod. Next fit the remover/replacer bush flange end towards the gudgeon pin.

4 Screw the stop nut onto the centre screw and adjust the nut to give a 0.032 inch (0.8 mm) end play. 'B' as shown in Fig. 1.13. Lock the nut securely with the lock screw. Ensure that the curved face of the adaptor is clean and slide the piston on the tool so that it fits into the curved face of the adaptor with the piston rings over the adaptor cut-away.

5 Screw the large nut up the thrust race. Adjust the torque wrench to a setting of 16 lb fft (2.2 kg fm) if of the 'click' type which will represent the minimum load for an acceptable fit. Use the torque wrench previously set on the large nut, and a ring spanner on the lock screw. Pull the gudgeon pin into the piston until the flange of the remover/replacer bush is 0.032 inch (0.8 mm) from the piston skirt. It is critically important that the flange is NOT allowed to contact the piston. Finally withdraw the BLMC service tool.

6 Should the torque wrench not 'click' or reach 16 lb fft (2.2 kg fm) throughout the pull, the fit of the gudgeon pin in the connecting rod is not within limits; the parts must be renewed.

7 Ensure that the piston pivots freely on the gudgeon pin and is free to slide sideways. Should stiffness exist wash the assembly in paraffin, lubricate the gudgeon pin with graphited oil and recheck. Again if stiffness exists dismantle the assembly and check for signs of ingrained dirt or damage.

8 On early type fully floating gudgeon pins make sure the little end bush in the connecting rod is lined up through the oilway orifice. Then heat the piston in boiling water and push the gudgeon pin through the piston, little end bush and out into the other side of the piston. Use circlip pliers to fit in the circlips at each end of the gudgeon pin. Be gentle at all times - use no force.

49 Piston rings - replacement

1 Check that the piston ring grooves and oilways are thoroughly clean and unblocked. Piston rings must always be fitted over the head of the piston and never from the bottom. The easiest method to use when fitting rings is to wrap a 0.020 feeler gauge round the top of the piston and place the rings one at a time, starting with the bottom oil control ring, over the feeler gauge.

2 The feeler gauge, complete with ring, can then be slid down the piston over the other piston ring grooves until the correct groove is reached. The piston ring is then slid gently off the feeler gauge into the groove.

3 An alternative method is to fit the rings by holding them slightly open with the thumbs and both of your index fingers. This method requires a steady hand and great care as it is easy to open the ring too much and break it.

4 The special oil control ring requires a special fitting procedure. First fit the bottom rail of the oil control ring to the piston and position it below the bottom groove. Refit the oil control expander into the bottom groove and move the bottom oil control ring rail up into the bottom groove. Fit the top oil control rail into the bottom groove.

5 Inspect the ends of the expander are butting not overlapping as shown in the inset in Fig. 1.21.

50 Pistons and connecting rods - replacement

The pistons, complete with connecting rods, can be fitted to the cylinder bores in the following sequence:

1 With a wad of clean rag wipe the cylinder bores clean.

2 The pistons, complete with connecting rods, are fitted to their bores from above.

3 As each piston is inserted into its bore ensure that it is the correct piston/connecting rod assembly for that particular bore, that the connecting rod is the right way round, and that the front of the piston is towards the front of the bore, ie., towards the front of the engine.

4 The piston will only slide into the bore as far as the oil control ring. It is then necessary to compress the piston rings in a clamp and to gently tap the piston into the cylinder bore with a wooden or plastic hammer. If a proper piston ring clamp is not available then a suitable diameter jubilee clip does the job very well.

51 Connecting rods to crankshaft - reassembly

As the big-ends on the connecting rods are offset it will be obvious if they have been inserted the wrong way round as they will not fit over the crankpins. The centre two connecting rods should be fitted with the offset part of the rods adjacent, and the connecting rods at each extremity of the engine should have the offset part of the rods facing outwards.

1 Wipe the connecting rod half of the big-end bearing cap and the underside of the shell bearing clean, and fit the shell bearing in position with its locating tongue engaged with the corresponding groove in the connecting rod.

2 If the old bearings are nearly new and are being refitted then ensure they are replaced in their correct locations on the correct rods.

3 Generously lubricate the crankpin journals with engine oil, and turn the crankshaft so that the crankpin is in the most advantageous position for the connecting rod to be drawn onto it.

4 Wipe the connecting rod bearing cap and back of the shell bearing clean and fit the shell bearing in position ensuring that the locating tongue at the back of the bearing engages with the locating groove in connecting rod cap.

5 Generously lubricate the shell bearing and offer up the connecting rod bearing cap to the connecting rod.

6 Fit the connecting rod bolts with the one-piece locking tab under them and tighten the bolts with a torque spanner to 35-38 lb f ft (4.8-5.3 kg fm). With a cold chisel knock up the locking tabs against the bolt head. On later models, special nuts are used and lockwashers are not required. The torque wrench setting should be obtained with the nut threads oiled and not dry.

7 When all the connecting rods have been fitted, rotate the crankshaft to check that everything is free, and that there are no high spots causing binding.

52 Flywheel housing oil seal - removal and replacement

1 If the sharp edges of the oil seal in the flywheel housing are at all damaged it is a simple matter to carefully prise it out. Keep it on one side to assist with the replacement of the new seal.

2 The new seal goes into position from the flywheel side of the flywheel housing. Ensure it enters the housing tensioning spring

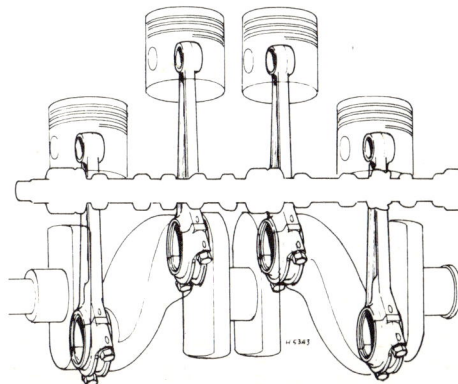

Fig. 1.24. Correct assembly of connecting rods and pistons to crankshaft (Sec. 51)

side first. Keep the oil seal square in the housing, and use the old seal to protect the new one as it is tapped or pressed gently into position.

53 Engine replacement on transmission (manual transmission) - flywheel housing

Carefully scrape away all traces of the old gaskets from the crankcase to transmission case joint and the engine/transmission to flywheel housing joints. **Note:** If it has been necessary to fit new transfer gears then it is essential to check the endfloat of the idler gear in the transmission casing before proceeding any further. See Chapter 6.

1 Fit a new front bearing cork oil seal and position the crankcase to transmission casing gaskets carefully. Ensure the 'O' ring on the top transmission casing flange is in place.

2 Lower the engine onto the transmission casing and ensure the cork oil seal and the gaskets do not slip.

3 Replace and tighten down the set bolts and nuts which hold the transmission casing to the engine. Use a torque of 6 lb f ft (0.8 kg fm).

4 Ensure that the primary gear thrust washer is fitted next to the crankshaft with its bevelled edge against the crankshaft flange. Replace the 'C' washer which locks the primary gear in place. Measure the primary gear endfloat which should be between 0.003 and 0.006 in (0.0762 and 0.1524 mm). If this is incorrect, measure the gap without the thrust washer in position. The width of the gap will determine the washer that should be used to give the ideal clearance of 0.0045 in (0.12 mm).

Gap width	Washer thickness
0.1295 to 0.1315 in.	0.125 to 0.127 in.
(3.27 to 3.34 mm.)	(3.17 to 3.22 mm.)
0.1315 to 0.1335 in.	0.127 to 0.129 in.
(3.34 to 3.39 mm.)	(3.22 to 3.27 mm.)
0.1335 to 0.1345 in.	0.129 to 0.131 in.
(3.39 to 3.42 mm.)	(3.27 to 3.32 mm.)

On older models it is important that the self lubricating bearing in the primary gear is in good condition. Check it by trying to rock the gear laterally when fitted. Any discernible movement indicates considerable wear.

5 Before fitting the flywheel housing make sure that a new flywheel housing oil seal has been fitted, and cover the splines of the crankshaft primary gear with the special thin sleeve used by BLMC garages (BLMC special tool No. '18G570'). Alternatively wrap a piece of tinfoil, or waxed paper tightly over the splines so no damage will be done to the oil seal by the sharp edges on the splines. Lubricate the seal prior to refitting the housing.

6 Fit a new gasket in position on the end of the engine/transmission casing. **Note** the cut out on the outer edge. This is to allow a measurement to be taken with a feeler gauge when the housing bolts/nuts have been fully tightened down. This is to check that the gasket has compressed to the correct thickness of 0.030 in. (0.762 mm).

7 Carefully fit the housing in position. If the small roller bearing on the outer end of the first motion shaft will not enter the housing, on no account try to force the housing on. Turn the bearing a quarter of a turn and try again. The rollers can be held in position with grease if wished. The second or third attempts are invariably successful.

8 Fit new locking tabs, and tighten down the nuts and six bolts evenly to a torque of 18 lb f ft (2.49 kg fm). Make certain that the correct short bolt is fitted in the top right-hand position. Too long a bolt may damage the main oil gallery in the cylinder block.

54 Flywheel - replacement

1 Turn the crankshaft so that pistons 1 and 4 are at tdc and the

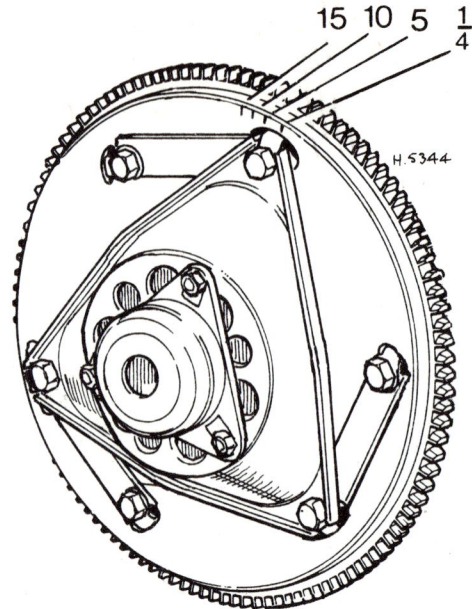

Fig. 1.25. Flywheel and clutch assembly (Sec. 54)
15°, 10° and 5° BTDC and 1/4 TDC marks shown

grooves in the sides of the crankshaft are vertical.

2 Check that the curved portion of the 'C' washer which holds the primary gear in place is at the top of the crankshaft, and that the sides of the washer fit in the crankshaft grooves.

3 Carefully clean the mating tapers in the flywheel and on the end of the crankshaft and make quite certain there are no traces of oil, grease, or dirt present. It is best to clean the tapers with petrol and then wipe dry with a clean rag.

4 Replace the flywheel on the end of the crankshaft with the ¼ tdc markings at the top and then replace the driving washer which positively locates the flywheel.

5 Fit a new lockwasher under the head of the flywheel securing bolt. Insert the bolt in the centre of the flywheel and tighten it to 110 to 115 lb f ft (15.2 to 15.9 kg fm).

6 Tap down the side of the lockwasher against the driving plate, and tap up the other side of the washer against the retaining bolt head.

7 Fit the thrust plate. Use new tab washers under the head of the nuts. Tighten the nuts down firmly and knock up the tabs of the washers. **Note:** On models with diaphragm clutches the thrust plate is held by a circular retaining spring.

55 Engine replacement on transmission - automatic transmission

For full information, refer to Chapter 6.

56 Camshaft - replacement

With the transmission casing in position the engine can be stood upright and the following operations, including camshaft replacement, will be found easier with the engine in this position.

Wipe the camshaft bearing journals clean and lubricate them generously with engine oil.

Insert the camshaft into the crankcase gently, taking care not to damage the camshaft bearings with the cams.

With the camshaft inserted into the block as far as it will go, rotate it slightly to ensure the slot in the oil pump drive has mated with the camshaft flange. If it has not yet mated the camshaft will go a further 0.25 in (6.35 mm) into the block as the flange and slot line up.

Replace the camshaft locating plate and tighten down the three retaining bolts and washers.

57 Timing gears, chain and cover - replacement

Before reassembly begins check that the packing washers are in place on the crankshaft nose. If new gearwheels are being fitted it may be necessary to fit additional washers (see paragraph 6). These washers ensure that the crankshaft gearwheel lines up correctly with the camshaft gearwheel.

1 Replace the woodruff keys in their respective slots in the crankshaft and camshaft and ensure that they are fully seated. If their edges are burred they must be cleaned with a fine file.

2 Lay the camshaft gearwheels on a clean surface so that the two timing dots are adjacent to each other. Slip the timing chain over them and pull the gearwheels back into mesh with the chain so that the timing dots, although further apart are still adjacent to each other.

3 Rotate the crankshaft so that the woodruff key is at top dead centre. (The engine should be standing upright on its transmission casing).

4 Rotate the camshaft so that when viewed from the front the woodruff key is at the two o'clock position.

5 Fit the timing chain and gearwheel assembly onto the camshaft and crankshaft, keeping the timing marks adjacent. If the camshaft and crankshaft have been positioned accurately it will be found that the keyways on the gearwheels will match the position of the keys, although it may be necessary to rotate the camshaft a fraction to ensure accurate lining-up of the camshaft gearwheel.

6 Press the gearwheels into position on the crankshaft and camshaft as far as they will go. **Note:** If new gearwheels are being fitted they should be checked for alignment before being finally fitted to the engine. Place the gearwheels in position without the timing chain and place the straight edge of a steel rule from the side of the camshaft gearteeth to the crankshaft gearwheel, and measure the gap between the steel rule and the gearwheel. If a gap exists a suitable number of packing washers must be placed on the crankshaft nose to bring the crankshaft gearwheel onto the same plane as the camshaft gearwheel (Fig. 1.26).

7 Fit the oil thrower to the crankshaft with the concave side forward.

8 Fit the locking washer to the camshaft gearwheel with its locating tab in the gearwheel keyway.

9 Screw on the camshaft gearwheel retaining nut and tighten securely.

10 Bend up the locking tab of the locking washer to hold the camshaft retaining nut securely.

11 Generously oil the chain and gearwheels.

12 Ensure the interior of the timing cover and the timing cover flange is clean. Examine the condition of the timing cover oil seal and replace it if damaged or worn. Then, with a new gasket in position, fit the timing cover to the block.

13 Screw in the timing cover retaining bolts with the flat washer next to the cover flange and under the spring washer. The ¼ in. bolts should be tightened with a torque spanner to 6 lb f ft (0.83 kg fm), and the 5/16 in. bolts to 14 lb f ft. (1.94 kg fm).

14 Fit the crankshaft pulley to the nose of the crankshaft ensuring that the keyway engages with the Woodruff key.

15 Fit the crankshaft retaining bolt locking washer in position and screw on the crankshaft pulley retaining bolt. Tighten to a torque of 70 lb f ft (9.68 kg fm).

58 Valves and valve springs - reassembly

To refit the valves and valve springs to the cylinder head, proceed as follows:

1 Rest the cylinder head on its side, or if the manifold studs are still fitted, with the side facing the cylinder block downwards.

2 Fit each valve and valve spring in turn, wiping down and

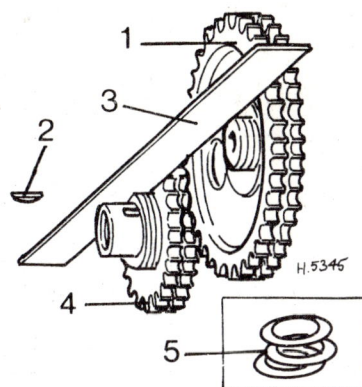

Fig. 1.26. Timing gear alignment (Sec. 57)

1 Camshaft gear
2 Woodruff key
3 Straight edge
4 Crankshaft gear
5 Inset: shims

lubricating each valve stem as it is inserted into the same valve guide from which it was removed.

3 As each valve is inserted slip the oil control rubber ring into place just under the bottom of the cotter groove. If this rubber ring is omitted, no harm will come to the valves and guides though the oil consumption will increase.

4 Move the cylinder head towards the edge of the work bench if it is facing downwards and slide it partially over the edge of the bench so as to fit the bottom half of the valve spring compressor to the valve head.

5 Slip the valve spring, shroud and cap over the valve stem.

6 With the base of the valve compressor on the valve head compress the valve spring until the cotters can be slipped into place in the valve grooves. Gently release the compressor and fit the circlip in position in the grooves in the cotters.

7 Repeat this procedure until all eight valves and valve springs are fitted.

59 Rocker shaft - reassembly

To reassemble the rocker shaft fit the split pin, flat washer, and spring washer at the rear end of the shaft and then slide on the rocker arms, rocker shaft pedestals, and spacing springs in the same order in which they were removed.

With the front pedestal in position, screw in the rocker shaft locating screw and slip the locating plate into position. Finally, fit to the front of the shaft the spring washer, plain washer, and split pin, in that order.

60 Tappets and pushrods - replacement

Generously lubricate the tappets internally and externally and insert them in the bores from which they were removed through the tappet chest.

With the cylinder head in position fit the pushrods in the same order in which they were removed. Ensure that they locate properly in the stems of the tappets, and lubricate the pushrod ends before fitment.

61 Cylinder head - replacement

After checking that both the cylinder block and cylinder head mating faces are perfectly clean, generously lubricate each cylinder with engine oil.

1 Always use a new cylinder head gasket as the old gasket will be compressed and not capable of giving a good seal. It is also easier at this stage to refit the small hose from the water pump to the cylinder head.

2 Never smear grease on either side of the gasket as when the

88 After removing the flywheel casing, by undoing the casing to crankcase bolts the crankcase is separated from the gearbox casing

89 Thoroughly clean the engine externally before dismantling. Remove the rocker cover, tappet chest covers, rocker gear and pushrods. Lift off the head

90 The crankshaft fan belt pulley wheel can be gently eased off after the retaining bolt has been removed

91 The crankshaft can be prevented from turning by placing a length of wood such as a hammer handle between the crankshaft and the side of the block

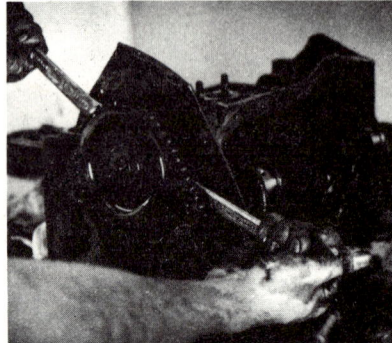

92 The gearwheels can be removed by levering with spanners or broad screwdrivers (shown). Move each wheel a little, in turn, so as not to strain the chain

93 The next step is to thoroughly clean the block internally. Check that the oilways are clear, and remove all traces of old gaskets

94 The camshaft is inserted from the front of the block. Make sure the peaks of the cams do not damage the white metal bearings

95 A vane-type oil pump may be found on a few very early models. 1 Pump body, 2 Vanes and rotor, 3 Cover plate, 4 Securing bolts and lockwashers

96 The vanes and rotor seat in the recess in the cover. They should be fitted first to the pump body

97 Ensure a new gasket is positioned between the pump and block. The slot in the rotor engages a lip in the camshaft

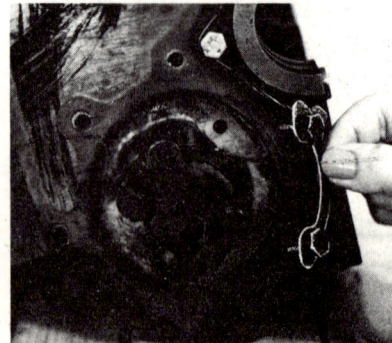

98 With the pump in place, fit the securing bolts and remember to turn up the tabs on the lockwasher

99 The pump is now securely fitted and the next step is to carefully examine the reciprocating components

100 Carefully examine the rings for wear. In this instance replacement of the complete piston is essential as the top ring has completely broken up

101 Measure the wear in the cylinder bore with a micrometer. Your local engineering works will be able to do this for you

102 If the bores are badly worn they must be rebored

103 A few very early models used clamped little ends. Ensure the cut-out in the gudgeon pin aligns with the hole for the little end bolt. 95% of models use circlips

104 When tightening the little end pinch bolt (where fitted) prevent the piston from turning by inserting a metal rod into the hollow bore of the gudgeon pin

105 In this illustration the rods are correctly fitted to the pistons with the offsets the right way round

106 This timing chain is badly worn. Note how it deflects inwards when pressed. If in good condition it should deflect not more than approx. ¼ in.

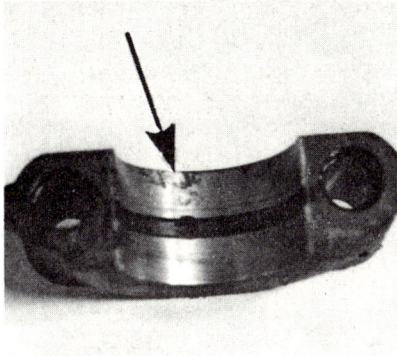

107 Examine the shell bearings for wear. This one is in dreadful condition. The surface is worn and has actually started to break up

108 If a bearing begins to disintegrate it will soon mark the crankshaft. The ridges on the journals can be easily seen and also felt with a fingernail

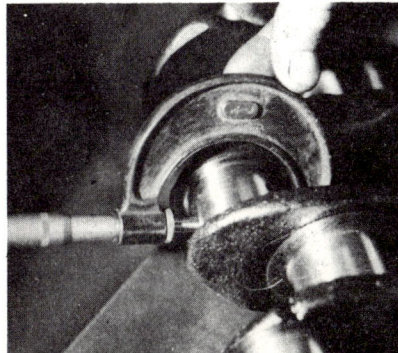

109 Check diameter of the crankshaft journals with a micrometer. If they are oval the crank must be reground

110 Check the flywheel starter ring for badly worn teeth. Renew ring if necessary

111 If the block is to be rebored and crank reground it is a false economy not to renew the front timing chain cover oil seal

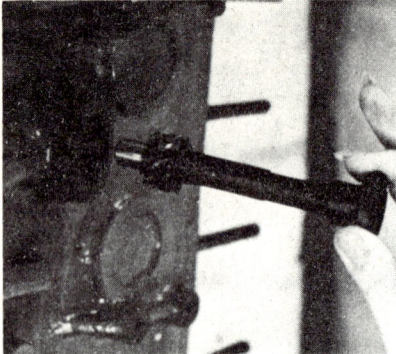

112 The next step is to fit the distributor drive. This can be inserted and removed by hand providing the sump is off

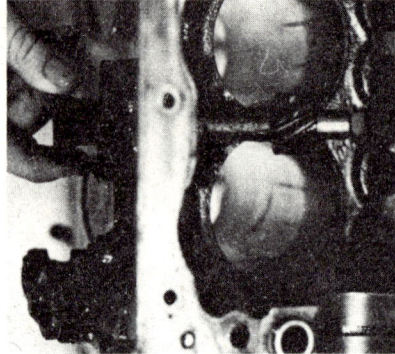

113 The lower end of the drive fits into a recess in the block and the skew gear meshes with a similar gear on the camshaft

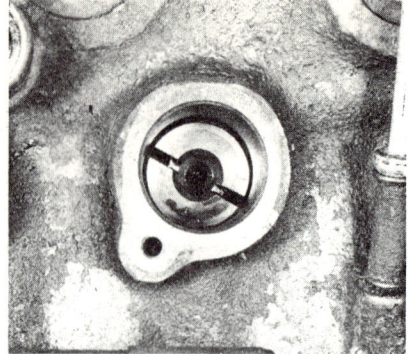

114 The drive head should initially be in this position to allow for rotation when fitted. NOTE. The larger segment should be on top

115 With the drive fully home the slots should be in the 'twenty to two' position

116 Next the distributor drive retaining plate is placed in position with the recessed hole lining up with the threaded hole in the flange on the block

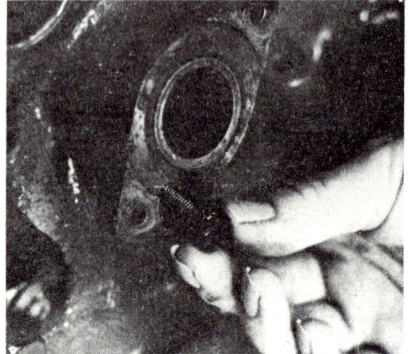

117 Screw in the retaining bolt and lockwasher to secure the plate

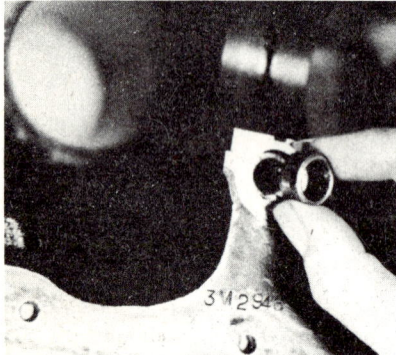

118 Before fitting the main bearings and crankshaft make sure the bearing cap locating dowels are in place

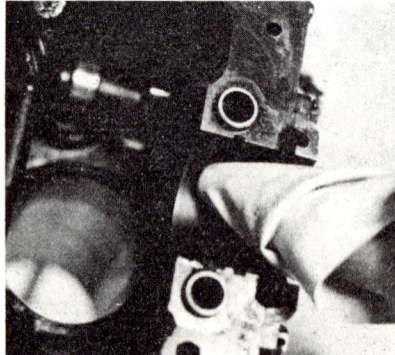

119 Thoroughly clean the bearing housings and the oilways in the block

120 The shell bearing on the left is worn and scored. Compare it with the condition of the new bearing on the right! Renew the bearing if worn

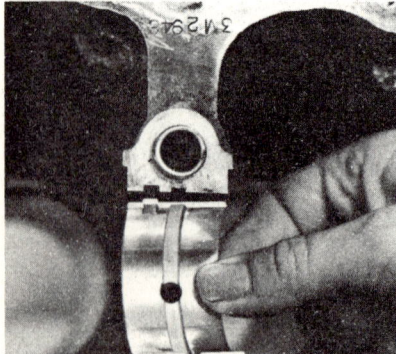

121 Fit the main bearings so that the lip on each shell engages with the machined slot in each bearing housing

122 Lubricate the new shells generously with SAE 20/30 engine oil. A plastic detergent bottle makes a handy oil can

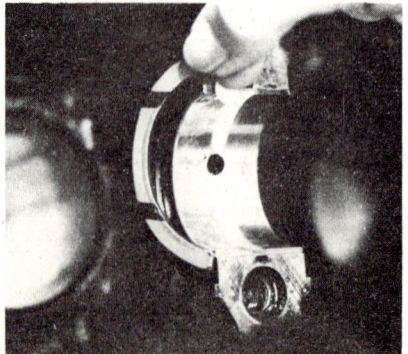

123 Place a thrust washer, grooves outwards, on either side of the centre main bearing housing with a dab of oil

124 Check that everything is scrupulously clean. Lubricate the main journals with engine oil before fitting the crankshaft to the crankcase

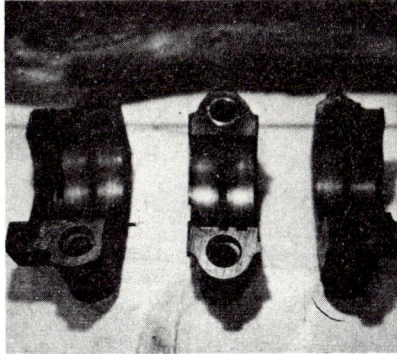

125 The three main bearing caps are each different. The one on the right is fitted at the front, and the other two at the middle and rear, respectively

126 Thoroughly clean the main bearing cap and fit the shell bearing so the notch lies in the groove in the cap

127 With the shell bearing in place in the centre main bearing cap, fit the lower halves of the thrust washer, grooves facing outwards

128 With the main bearing caps fitted check the endfloat between the thrust washers and the crank with a feeler gauge. .003 in endfloat is correct

129 Tighten all six main bearing bolts to a torque wrench setting of 60 lb f ft (8.2 kg f m)

130 Lock the bolts by knocking up the locking tabs

131 If the original crankshaft is being fitted check the washers are in place on the crankshaft nose. They ensure the gearwheels lie in the same plane

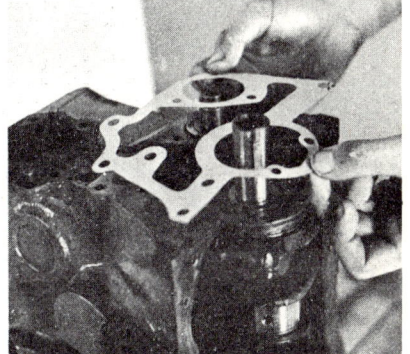

132 The next step is to thoroughly clean the face of the block and fit a new front end plate gasket

133 The front end plate must be carefully cleaned and then fitted to the block

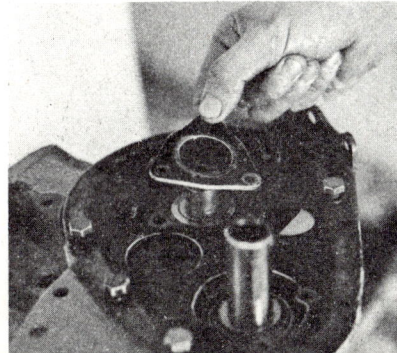

134 With the front endplate in place the camshaft retaining plate can be fitted

135 Fit the locking tab to the endplate as shown, and fit the two bolts. Turn up the tabs on the locking plate

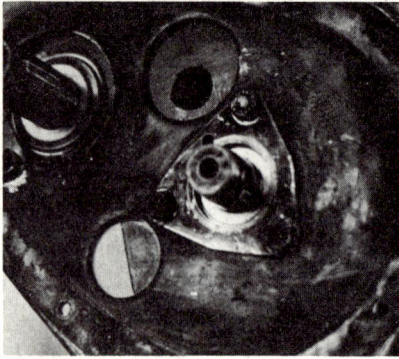

136 Fit and tighten down the three camshaft retaining plate bolts. Remember to fit spring washers

137 When refitting the chain round the gearwheels and to the engine, the two 'dots' must be adjacent on an imaginary line passing through each wheel centre

138 With the engine on its side, set the crankshaft and camshaft so the Woodruff keys are at 2 o'clock and 4 o'clock respectively

139 Next, place the camshaft locking washer with its tag in the gearwheel keyway. Then fit the securing nut

140 Tighten the camshaft gearwheel nut, holding the crankshaft stationary with a spanner as shown. Ensure plenty of rag is between the spanner and the crankshaft

141 The gearwheels and timing chain are now in place and correctly positioned

142 Next bend back the camshaft locking washer to lock the camshaft gearwheel nut in place

143 The flange on the timing gear case must be carefully cleaned and scraped and a new gasket laid on the front end-plate

144 Place the oil thrower, concave side down, on the nose of the crankshaft. Remember to position the thrower so it fits over the crankshaft key

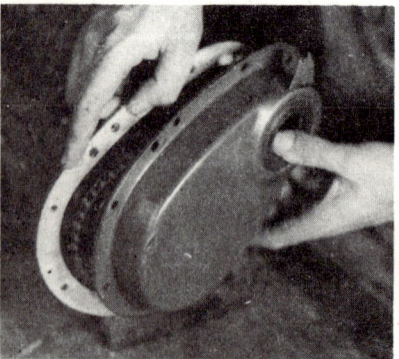

145 Replace the timing chain cover and tighten the retaining bolts and washers. Smear the edge of the oil seal with oil

146 Next fit the crankshaft pulley wheel. The wheel will only fit in one position with the key entering the pulley groove

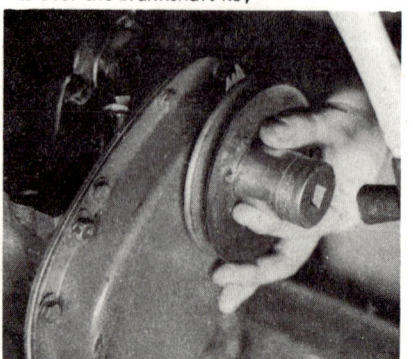

147 Although correctly lined up, when a new oil seal has been fitted it is often necessary to drive the wheel into place

148 With the crankshaft pulley wheel in place fit the lockwasher so the tab locks into the pulley wheel groove

149 Next screw in the pulley wheel bolt. This is the largest bolt on the engine and it may be necessary to borrow a socket

150 Hold the crankshaft from turning by inserting a square section bar or similar in the slot at the flywheel end. Then tighten the bolt to a torque of 70 lb/ft

151 When the bolt is correctly tightened knock up the lockwasher against one of the flats on the bolt

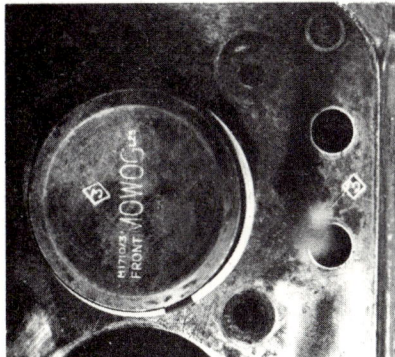

152 Each piston is clearly marked 'FRONT' Fit it this way round. The '3' in the diamond stamped on the block and piston crown indicates the grade of piston fitted

153 Measure each piston ring gap in turn, with a feeler gauge, with the rings fitted in the bore. The gap should be .007 to .012 in

154 Cylinder head studs can be removed and replaced by locking together on a stud two cylinder head nuts and then turning the stud out (or in)

155 When compressing the piston rings there is no need to use an expensive piston ring compressor. A jubilee clip is just as good

156 When all the pistons have been returned to the same bores from which they were removed, the connecting rods can be attached to the crankshaft

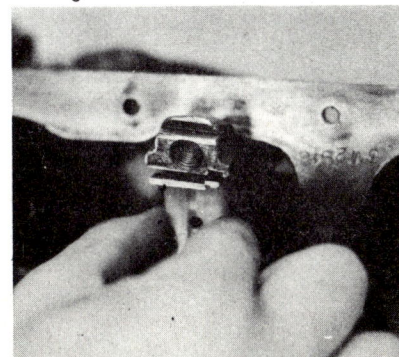

157 Connecting rod big end caps must be clean. Bearing shells can then be fitted with the lips in the groove in the rods

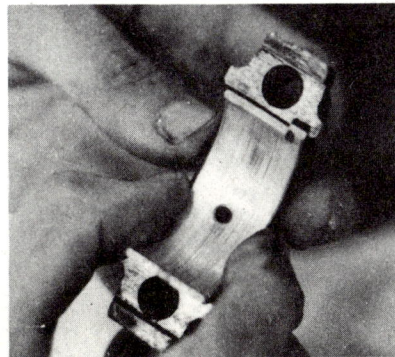

158 Fit the big end cap bearing shell in the same way ensuring you replace the cap to its original connecting rod

159 The next step is to tighten the big end bolts to a torque of 35 lb/ft and then knock up the tab on the locking washer

160 Turn the crankshaft over with the aid of a screwdriver as shown to make sure there are no tight spots

161 Carefully clean the thermostat housing cover. It is liable to corrode and should be renewed if suspect

162 Examine the teeth on the flywheel starter ring. If worn the ring must be cut off and a new gear ring heated and shrunk on

163 Carefully examine the clutch pressure plate. If the surface is ridged or there are minute cracks present the plate must be renewed

164 The next step is to fit the valves and valve springs to the cylinder head. Start by fitting the valve guide shroud in place

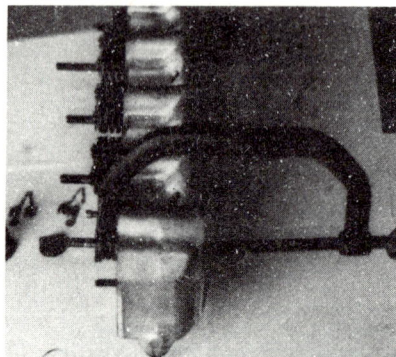

165 Next fit each valve, oil seal, and valve spring. Compress the spring with a compressor and make sure the head of the compressor does not slip

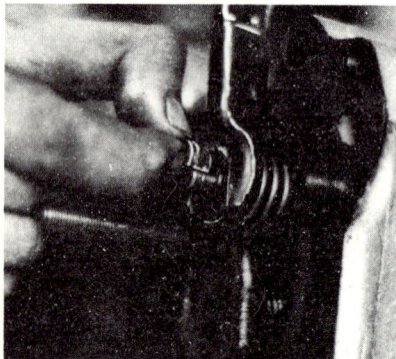

166 Now fit the split collets. A trace of grease will help hold them to the valve stem recess. This job calls for care as the items are small and easily dropped

167 Slacken off the spring compressor until the collets are firmly held by the valve spring cup. Fit a circlip to the collets to make sure they stay together

168 This is what the completed built-up valve and valve spring assembly should look like

169 Thoroughly clean the face of the block and cylinder head. Fit a new head gasket with the side marked 'top' upwards

170 The cylinder head can now be fitted. Keep the head and block parallel so the head does not bind on the studs

171 Make sure the oil holes in the tappets are clear, and replace them through the tappet chest apertures

172 Next fit the push rods with the mushroom shaped end fed into the block first. Make sure the push rods seat properly in the tappets

173 Next reassemble the rocker gear on the rocker shaft and fit to the cylinder head. Make sure that the oil holes are clear in the rocker shaft

174 Make sure that the rocker pedestal locking plate is fitted before replacing the rocker pedestal and cylinder head nuts

175 The cylinder head and rocker bracket washers and nuts are now fitted. Tighten the cylinder head nuts to a torque of 40 lb/ft in the order shown

176 Set the valve clearance to 0.012 in (0.305 mm) by unlocking the nut and screwing the tappet adjusting screw up or down until the arm just nips the blade

177 Clean the thermostat housing flange and then fit a new gasket in place

178 Then fit the thermostat and thermostat cover and replace the spring washer and do up the three nuts

179 The oil pressure relief valve fits into the threaded hole on the right-hand side of the engine at the rear

180 The next step is to clean the tappet chest flanges and refit the tappet chest covers using a new cork gasket. Tighten the bolts to 2 lb/ft

181 Ensure the hole at the rear of the cylinder head is covered by the heater take off (or flat plate) and fit a new gasket

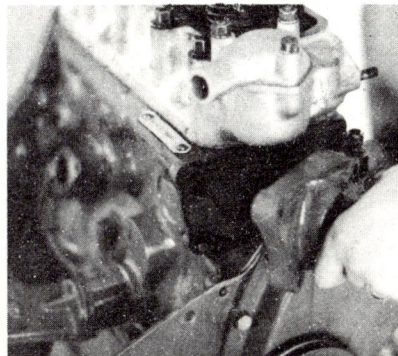

182 Fit the water pump to the front of the engine. Making sure mating surfaces are clean and a new gasket is fitted

183 Fit the by-pass hose and the pump. It is difficult to fit the hose after the pump is installed (cont. on page 132, pic. 87)

engine heats up the grease will melt and may allow compression leaks to develop. The author does not like using gasket cement as if a new gasket is used and the head and block faces are true there should be no requirement for it. (The most successful racing engines never use gasket cement.).

3 The cylinder head gasket is marked 'FRONT' and 'TOP' and should be fitted in position according to the markings.

4 With the gasket in position carefully lower the cylinder head onto the cylinder block.

5 With the head in position fit the cylinder head nuts and washers finger tight to the five cylinder head holding down studs, which remain outside the rocker cover. It is not possible to fit the remaining nuts to the studs inside the rocker cover until the rocker assembly is in position.

6 Fit the pushrods as detailed in Section 60.

7 The rocker shaft assembly can now be lowered over its eight locating studs. Take care that the rocker arms are the right way round. Lubricate the ball joints, and insert the rocker arm ball joints in the pushrod cups.
Note: Failure to place the ball joints in the cups can result in the ball joints seating on the edge of a pushrod or outside it when the head and rocker assembly is pulled down tight.

8 Fit the four rocker pedestal nuts and washers, and then the four cylinder head stud nuts and washers which also serve to hold down the rocker pedestals. Pull the nuts down evenly, but without tightening them right up.

9 When all is in position, the nine cylinder head nuts and the four rocker pedestal nuts can be tightened down in the order shown in Fig. 1.9.
   Turn the nuts a quarter of a turn a time and tighten the four rocker pedestal nuts to 25 lb f ft (3.5 kg fm) and the nine cylinder head nuts to the recommended torque wrench setting given in Specifications. Note that on 1275cc engines with 9.75:1 compression ratio the bolt has a separate torque wrench setting.
   Note: The rocker arm/valve adjustments must now be made as explained in the following Section. After the car has done about 250 miles (400 km) it will be found that the gasket has settled slightly and the cylinder head nuts can be tightened still further. This will upset the rocker arm/valve adjustment already made, so the rocker cover must be removed and the clearances reset.

62 Rocker arm/valve clearances - adjustment

1 The valve adjustments should be made with the engine cold. The importance of correct rocker arm/valve stem clearances cannot be overstressed as they vitally affect the performance of the engine. If the clearances are set too open, the efficiency of the engine is reduced as the valves open late and close earlier than was intended. If, on the other hand the clearances are set too close there is a danger that the stems will expand upon heating and not allow the valves to close properly which will cause burning of the valve head and seat and possible warping. If the engine is in the car access to the rockers is by removing the two holding down studs from the rocker cover, and then lifting the rocker cover and gasket away.

2 It is important that the clearance is set when the tappet of the valve being adjusted is on the heel of the cam, (ie., opposite the peak). This can be ensured by carrying out the adjustments in the following order (which also avoids turning the crankshaft more than necessary).

Valve fully open		Check & Adjust	
Valve No.	8	Valve No.	1
" "	6	" "	3
" "	4	" "	5
" "	7	" "	2
" "	1	" "	8
" "	3	" "	6
" "	5	" "	4
" "	2	" "	7

3 The correct valve clearance of 0.012 in (0.305 mm) is obtained by slackening the hexagon locknut with a spanner while holding the ball pin against rotation with the screwdriver (photo 176). Then, still pressing down with the screwdriver, insert a feeler gauge in the gap between the valve stem head and the rocker arm and adjust the ball pin until the feeler gauge will just move in and out without nipping. Then, still holding the ball pin in the correct position, tighten the locknut. An alternative method is to set the gaps with the engine running, and although this may be faster it is no more reliable.

63 Distributor and distributor drive - replacement

   It is important to set the distributor drive correctly as otherwise the ignition timing will be totally incorrect. It is possible to set the distributor drive in apparently the right position, but, in fact, 180° out, by omitting to select the correct cylinder which must not only be at tdc but must also be on its firing stroke with both valves closed. The distributor drive should therefore not be fitted until the cylinder head is in position and the valves can be observed. Alternatively, if the timing cover has not been replaced, the distributor drive can be replaced when the dots on the timing wheels are adjacent to each other.

1 Rotate the crankshaft so that No. 1 piston is at tdc and on its firing stroke (the dots in the timing gears will be adjacent to each other). When No. 1 piston is at tdc the inlet valve on No. 4 cylinder is just opening and the exhaust valve closing.

2 When the marks '1/4' on the flywheel are at tdc, then Nos. 1 and 4 pistons are at tdc.

3 Screw the tappet cover bolt into the head of the distributor drive (any 5/16 in. UNF. bolt will do if it is not less than 3 in. (76.2 mm) long).

4 Hold the distributor drive so that the larger segment is at the top and the right-hand side of the slot is just below horizontal. Insert the drive into its housing. As the gear on the end of the drive meshes with the skew gear on the camshaft the drive will turn anti-clockwise. When it is fully home, the upper part of the slot should be in the two o'clock position.

5 Remove the tappet cover bolt from the driveshaft.

6 Replace the distributor housing and lock it in position with the single bolt and lockwasher.

7 The distributor can now be replaced and the two securing bolts and spring washers which hold the distributor clamping plate to the distributor housing tightened. If the clamp bolt on the clamping plate was not previously loosened and the distributor body was not turned in the clamping plate, then the ignition timing will be as previously. If the clamping bolt has been loosened, then it will be necessary to retime the ignition as shown in Chapter 4.

64 Final assembly

   The rocker cover can now be fitted, using a new cork gasket. Fit the two tappet cover plates, using new gaskets, and tighten the tappet chest bolts to the recommended torque wrench setting (see Specifications).
   Do not exceed the figure or the covers will distort and leak oil. Reconnect the ancillary components to the engine in the reverse order to which they were removed.
   It should be noted that in all cases it is best to reassemble the engine as far as possible before refitting it to the car. This means that the inlet and exhaust manifolds, carburettor, dynamo, water thermostat, oil filter, distributor and engine mounting brackets, should all be in position. Ensure that the oil filter is filled with engine oil, as otherwise there will be a delay in the oil reaching the bearings while the oil filter refills.

65 Engine/transmission unit (manual transmission) - replacement

   Although the engine can be replaced with one man and a

suitable winch, it is easier if two are present, one to lower the engine into the engine compartment and the other to guide the engine into position and to ensure it does not foul anything. Generally speaking, engine replacement is a reversal of the procedures used when removing the engine. The sequence is not quite the same however, and the following will be found the easiest and quickest order to follow:

1 Refit the radiator, and radiator hoses. Always use new hoses if the old hoses show any signs of internal or external cracking or general deterioration. The bottom hose is especially susceptible because of the heater take-off portion which tends to crack and leak first.

2 Connect lifting tackle to the lifting hooks or place suitable slings round each end of the transmission casing.

3 Raise the engine and if using a fixed hoist, roll the car under it. Jack-up the front of the car securely so it can be worked on from underneath. Lower the engine/transmission unit into the engine compartment. Stop halfway in and reconnect the speedometer cable to the transmission casing.

4 Keep the sliding joints pushed well back on the drive shafts and ensure that nothing is fouling as the engine is lowered into place. Take particular care to make sure that the radiator matrix is not damaged during this operation.

5 To line up the mounting bracket holes it may be necessary to move the engine about slightly and this will be found much easier to do if the slings are still in position and taking most of the weight. Replace the nuts, bolts, and spring washers to the engine mounting brackets and tighten them finger tight. To avoid vibration it is most important to position the mountings correctly as described below.

6 Refit the exhaust manifold to the exhaust pipe, replace the clamp and secure the joint loosely with the two clamp bolts. It is essential to fit the exhaust properly as otherwise the exhaust downpipe may fracture, or the mounting lug may break away from the pipe due to the rocking motion of the engine on its mountings.

7 Check that the engine tie-bar bush is in good condition and attach the bar to the engine. It may be necessary to move the engine slightly so that the hole in the tie-rod lines up with the engine attachment hole. Under no circumstances should the engine mountings be tightened before the tie-rod holes are aligned. Insert and do up the tie-rod bolt.

8 Remove the sling from the engine and let the full weight of the power unit onto the engine mounting brackets. The nuts and bolts may now be tightened down securely.

9 Check the gap between the exhaust pipe mounting clip and the fixing point on the gearbox extension. Fill the gap with washers and insert and tighten loosely the securing nut and bolt. On early models the hole in the extension was threaded and a set bolt used to secure the pipe. It is best to drill out this hole (use an 8 mm. drill), and replace the set bolt with a 5/16 in. UNF nut, bolt and spring washer.

10 Do up the manifold clamp securing bolts tightly, followed by the gearbox extension to exhaust pipe clip bolt, and the tail pipe support clips.

11 Replace the horn and the starter motor solenoid switch where this is mounted on the flywheel housing.

12 Pull the sliding joints into contact with the flexible coupling, and insert the two 'U' bolts. **Note:** The sides of the 'U' bolts tend to spread apart when removed from the couplings. Nip them gently in a vice, taking care not to damage the threads before refitment. This will ease their replacement considerably. Tighten up the 'U' bolt securing nuts.

13 Refit the clutch slave cylinder to the flywheel housing, and reconnect the earth lead.

14 On models fitted with a tachometer, refit the tachometer drive.

15 Refit the carburettor to the inlet manifold.

16 Reconnect the fuel inlet pipe to the carburettor/s.

17 Refit the distributor cap and reconnect the high tension leads to the appropriate spark plug.

18 Reconnect the high tension lead from the centre of the distributor cap to the coil, and the low tension lead from the terminal 'C' on the coil to the terminal on the side of the distributor.

19 Reconnect the leads to the dynamo or alternator. The different sized terminals on the dynamo ensure that no mistake can be made. Also reconnect the starter motor cable to the starter motor.

20 Reconnect the accelerator and choke cables and replace the air cleaner/s on the carburettor/s.

21 Reconnect the oil pressure sender unit, or the oil pressure gauge pipe line to the threaded take off point at the right-hand near side of the engine.

22 If the small bypass hose between the cylinder head and the water pump was not replaced when the head was refitted then this must be done now. This can sometimes be a difficult operation but should be carried out fairly easily if the small jubilee clips are slipped over each end of the tube which is then squeezed in a vice, and is quickly fitted before the hose has time to expand to its normal length again.

23 Refit the blower motor and heater hose where this is under the bonnet. Always use new hoses if the old hoses show signs of internal or external cracking or flaking.

24 Reconnect the water temperature gauge sender unit where a water temperature gauge is fitted.

25 Reconnect the distributor vacuum advance pipe and refit the front grille if previously removed.

26 Replace the gearlever in the gearbox extension and refit the rubber boot at the base of the gearlever.

27 Replace the windscreen washer bottle and carrier if previously removed.

28 Replace the bonnet (easier with two people).

29 Reconnect the battery.

30 Check that the drain taps are closed or the plugs replaced, and refill the cooling system with water and the engine with the correct grade of oil. Start the engine and carefully check for oil or water leaks. There should be no oil or water leaks if the engine has been reassembled carefully, all nuts and bolts tightened down correctly, and new gaskets and joints used throughout.

---

66 Engine/transmission unit (manual transmission) - replacement with subframe

---

The procedure for replacing the engine and subframe together as a unit is very similar to replacing the engine as described in the previous Section.

Generally, replacement is a reversal of the removal sequence, but as an aid to rapid refitment, the following notes are given:

1 Either wheel the subframe into position under the body, or wheel the body over the subframe as preferred and depending on whether a hoist is available from which to suspend the front of the bodyshell.

2 When replacing the subframe in the body take great care not to get the brake pipes, battery cables, or main electrical leads, nipped between the body and the subframe.

3 Replace the nuts and bolts securing the subframe to the bodyshell but **do not** tighten them right down until they are all in position. This confirms that the subframe is properly aligned with the bodyshell.

4 Reconnect the steering tie-rods to the steering arms and tighten the ball joint nuts to a torque of 25 lb fft (3.4 kg fm).

5 To help ensure lack of engine vibration and to help prevent the exhaust downpipe fracturing or the clip breaking, it is wisest to fit the tie-rod before securing the exhaust system, and to loosen the engine mounting bolts to move the engine slightly if the alignment between the tie bar hole and the engine mounting hole is not perfect. This is described in detail in paras. 6 and 7 of Section 65.

6 After the hydraulic brake pipe to the front brakes is connected up it will be necessary to bleed the braking system.

67 Engine/transmission unit (automatic transmission) - replacement

Refitting the engine and automatic transmission is the reverse sequence to removal and no problems will arise. The two following points should be noted:
a) When lowering the engine/transmission unit into position reconnect the driving flanges and screw the nuts onto the flange studs as soon as possible before the unit is finally positioned.
b) Adjust the selector lever cable and transverse rod, as described in Chapter 6.

68 Engine/transmission unit (automatic transmission) - replacement with subframe

Refitting the engine/automatic transmission unit complete with subframe is the reverse sequence to removal. Refer to Section 67, for two points that should be noted. Information on the subframe and suspension will be found in Section 66.

69 Engine - initial start-up after overhaul or major repair

1 Make sure that the battery is fully charged and that the oil, water and fuel are replenished.

2 If the fuel system has been dismantled it will require several revolutions of the engine on the starter motor to get the petrol up to the carburettor. An initial prime by pouring petrol down the carburettor feed pipe will help the engine to fire quickly thus relieving the load on the battery.

3 As soon as the engine fires and runs, keep it going at a fast tickover only (not faster) and bring it up to normal working temperature.

4 As the engine warms up there will be odd smells and some smoke from parts getting hot and burning off oil deposits. The signs to look for are leaks of oil or water which will be obvious, if serious. Check also the clamp connections of the exhaust pipes to the manifolds as these do not always 'find' their exact gas tight position until the warmth and vibration have acted on them and it is almost certain that they will need tightening further. This should be done, of course, with the engine stopped.

5 When normal running temperature has been reached adjust the idling speed as described in Chapter 3.

6 Stop the engine and wait a few minutes to see if any lubricant or coolant is dripping out when the engine is stationary.

7 Road test the car to check that the timing is correct and giving the necessary smoothness and power. Do not race the engine - when new bearings and/or pistons and rings have been fitted it should be treated as a new engine and run in at reduced revolutions for the first 500 miles (800 km).

70 Fault diagnosis - engine

Symptom	Reason/s	Remedy
Engine will not turn over when starter switch is operated.	Flat battery. Bad battery connections. Bad connections at solenoid switch and/or starter motor.	Check that battery is fully charged and that all connections are clean tight.
	Starter motor jammed.	Turn the square headed end of the starter motor shaft with a spanner to free it.
	Defective solenoid.	Bridge the main terminals of the solenoid switch with a piece of heavy duty cable in order to operate the starter.
	Starter motor defective.	Remove and overhaul starter motor.
Engine turns over normally but fails to fire and run.	No spark at plugs.	Check ignition system according to procedures given in Chapter 4.
	No fuel reaching engine. Too much fuel reaching the engine (flooding).	Check fuel system according to procedures given in Chapter 3.
Engine starts but runs unevenly and misfires.	Ignition and/or fuel system faults.	Check the ignition and fuel systems as though the engine had failed to start.
	Incorrect valve clearances.	Check and reset clearances.
	Burnt out valves. Blown cylinder head gasket.	Remove cylinder heads and examine and overhaul as necessary.
	Worn out piston rings. Worn cylinder bores.	Remove cylinder heads and examine pistons and cylinder bores. Overhaul as necessary.
Lack of power.	Ignition and/or fuel system faults.	Check the ignition and fuel systems for correct ignition timing and carburettor settings.
	Incorrect valve clearances.	Check and reset the clearances.
	Burnt out valves. Blown cylinder head gasket.	Remove cylinder heads and examine and overhaul as necessary.
	Worn out piston rings. Worn cylinder bores.	Remove cylinder heads and examine pistons and cylinder bores. Overhaul as necessary.
Excessive oil comsumption	Oil leaks from crankshaft rear oil seal, timing cover gasket and oil seal, rocker cover gasket, oil filter gasket, transmission unit gasket, drain plug washer.	Identify source of leak and renew seal as appropriate.
	Worn piston rings or cylinder bores resulting in oil being burnt by engine. (Smoky exhaust is an indication).	Fit new rings or rebore cylinders and fit new pistons, depending on degree of wear.
	Worn valve guides and/or defective valve stem seals. (Smoke blowing out from the rocker cover vent is an indication on crankcase breather pipe - early models).	Remove cylinder head, and recondition valve stem bores and valves and seals as necessary.
Excessive mechanical noise from engine	Wrong valve to rocker clearances.	Adjust valve clearances.
	Worn crankshaft bearings. Worn cylinders (piston slap). Worn timing gears.	Inspect and overhaul where necessary.

Note: When investigating starting and uneven running faults do not be tempted into snap diagnosis. Start from the beginning of the check procedure and follow it through. It will take less time in the long run. Poor performance from an engine in terms of power and economy is not normally diagnosed quickly. In any event the ignition and fuel systems must be checked first before assuming any further investigation needs to be made.

Chapter 2 Cooling system

Contents

Specifications

Type ... ... Pump and fan with pressurised radiator and expansion tank

Thermostat settings:
Standard	82° C (180° F)
Cold climates	88° C (190° F)
Hot climates	74° C (165° F)
or	77° C (171° F)

Thermostat type ... ... Wax

Water pump type ... ... Impeller

Fan belt tension ... ... 0.5 in. (12.7 mm) free-movement midway between water pump and generator pulleys

Expansion tank pressure cap setting ... ... 13 lb/in^2 (0.91 kg/cm^2)

Cooling system capacity:
Less heater	5.75 pints (3.27 litres)
With heater	6.75 pints (3.83 litres)

Torque wrench settings:

	lb f ft	kg fm
Water pump retaining bolts	17	2.35
Thermostat housing (water outlet elbow)	8	1.11
Water pump pulley setscrews	18	2.49
Thermal transmitter	16	2.21

1 General description

The engine cooling water is circulated by a thermo-siphon, water pump assisted system, and the coolant is pressurised. This is primarily to prevent premature boiling in adverse conditions. The spill pipe from the radiator is connected to an expansion chamber which makes topping-up unnecessary. The coolant expands when hot, and instead of being forced down the spill pipe and lost, it flows into the expansion chamber. As the engine cools the coolant contracts and because of the pressure differential flows back into the top tank of the radiator.

The expansion tank cap is pressurised to 13 lb./sq.in. (0.91 kg/sq.cm.) which increases the boiling point to 230°F (110° C). If the water temperature exceeds this figure and the water boils the pressure in the system forces the internal part of the cap off its seal, thus exposing the expansion tank overflow pipe down which the steam from the boiling water escapes thus

relieving the pressure. It is, therefore, important to check that the expansion tank cap is in good condition and that the spring behind the sealing washer has not weakened. Most garages have a special machine on which pressure caps can be tested.

The cooling system comprises the raditor, expansion tank, top and bottom water hoses, bypass hose to return water to the block when the thermostat is closed, heater hoses (if heater/ demister fitted), the impeller water pump, (mounted on the front of the engine it carries the fan blades and is driven by the fan belt), the thermostat and the two drain taps or plugs.

The system functions in the following fashion. Cold water in the bottom of the radiator circulates up the lower radiator hose to the water pump where it is pushed round the water passages in the cylinder block, helping to keep the cylinder bores and piston cool.

The water then travels up into the cylinder head and circulates round the combustion spaces and valve seats absorbing more heat. Then, when the engine is at its proper operating temperature, the water travels out of the cylinder head, past the open thermostat into the upper radiator hose, and so into the radiator header tank. The water travels down the radiator where it is rapidly cooled by the rush of cold air through the radiator core. As the radiator is mounted in the wheelarch the fan pushes cold air through the radiator matrix. The water, now cool, reaches the bottom of the radiator, when the cycle is repeated.

When the engine is cold the thermostat (which is a valve which opens and closes according to the temperature of the water) maintains the circulation of the same water in the engine by returning it, via the bypass hose, to the cylinder block. Only when the correct minimum operating temperature has been reached, as shown in the Specifications, does the thermostat begin to open, allowing water to return to the radiator.

2 Cooling system - draining

With the car on level ground drain the system as follows:
1 If the engine is cold remove the pressure cap from the expansion tank by turning the cap anticlockwise. If the engine is hot having just been run, then turn the expansion tank pressure cap very slightly until the pressure in the system has had time to disperse. Use a rag over the cap to protect your hand from escaping steam. If, with the engine very hot, the cap is released suddenly the drop in pressure can result in the water boiling. With the pressure released the cap can be removed (photo).
2 If antifreeze is in the cooling system drain it into a clean bucket or bowl for re-use.
3 Open the two drain taps. When viewed from the side the radiator drain tap is on the bottom right-hand side of the radiator, and the engine drain tap is halfway down the rear right-hand side of the cylinder block. A short length of rubber tubing over the radiator drain tap nozzle will assist draining the coolant into a container without splashing. **Note**: On some later models a drain plug is fitted at the bottom of the radiator, rather than a drain tap (photo).
4 When the water has finished running, probe the drain tap or plug orifices with a short piece of wire to dislodge any particles of rust or sediment which may be blocking the taps and preventing all the water draining out.

3 Cooling system - flushing

1 With time the cooling system will gradually lose its efficiency as the radiator becomes choked with rust scales, deposits from the water, and other sediment. To clean the system out, remove

2.1 The expansion tank cap removed

2.3a The engine drain tap, arrowed and ...

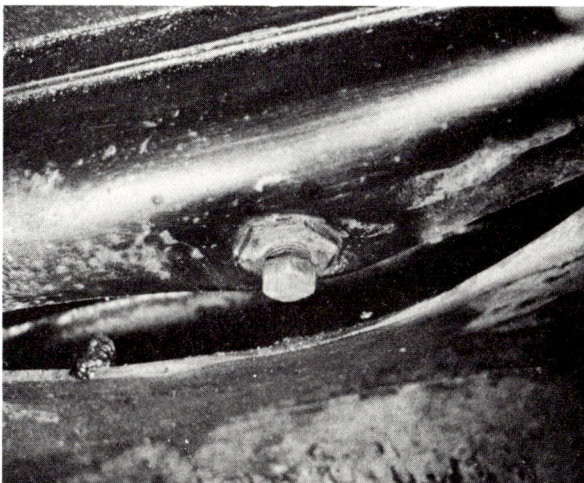
2.3b ... the radiator drain plug used on later models

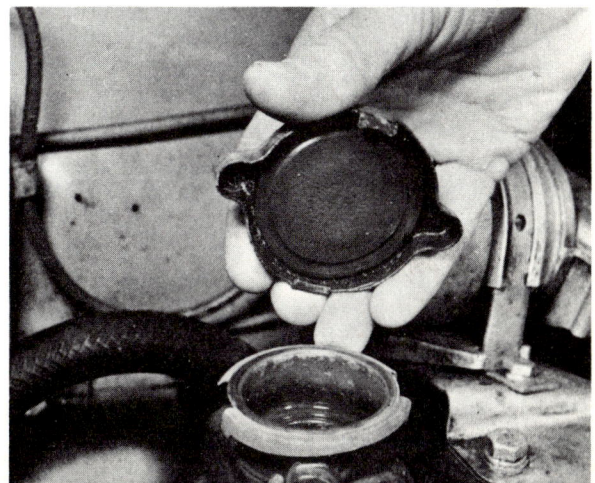
3.1 The radiator cap removed

the radiator cap and drain tap and leave a hose running in the radiator cap orifice for ten to fifteen minutes (photo).

2 In very bad cases the radiator should be reversed flushed. This can be done with the radiator in position. The cylinder block tap is closed and a hose placed over the open radiator drain tap. Water, under pressure, is then forced up through the radiator and out of the header tank filler orifice.

3 The hose is then removed and placed in the filler orifice and the radiator washed out in the usual fashion.

4 Check that the spill pipe to the expansion tank is clear and that there is no sediment in the bottom of the expansion tank.

4 Cooling system - filling

1 Close the two drain taps or refit the plugs as applicable.

2 Fill the system slowly to ensure that no air locks develop. If a heater unit is fitted, check that the valve to the heater unit is open, otherwise an air lock may form in the heater. The best type of water to use in the cooling system is rain water, so use this whenever possible.

3 Completely fill the radiator, replace the cap, remove the expansion chamber cap and check that there is 2.5 in (63.5 mm) of coolant (use a ruler or pencil) in the chamber.

4 Only use antifreeze mixture with a glycerine or ethylene base.

5 Replace the expansion tank cap and turn it firmly clockwise to lock it into position.

5 Radiator - removal and replacement

The radiator on all models is removed in the following manner:

1 Undo and remove the two bolts and spring washers from the bonnet side of each of the two hinges. Carefully lift the bonnet off and place it to one side.

2 Drain the water by removing the drain plug at the base of the radiator, and the similar plug from the side of the block, and remove the radiator cap. **Note:** on some models drain taps may be fitted.

3 Undo the bolts holding the radiator upper support bracket to the top cowl, and the two nuts and spring washers holding the upper support bracket to the thermostat housing. Lift away the radiator upper support bracket (Fig. 2.1).

4 Undo the bolt from the radiator lower support bracket and place the bolt on one side together with its spring washer. The bottom of the radiator is now released from its attachment to the radiator mounting bracket.

5 Unscrew the clip on the upper radiator hose at the thermostat housing outlet pipe, and remove the hose off the pipe.

6 The bottom water hose incorporates a bonded in take-off tube which carries water to the heater, (if no heater is fitted there is no take-off on the bottom hose). Disconnect this tube and then completely remove the bottom hose by unscrewing the clips at each end.

7 Undo the clip which holds the radiator to expansion tank spill pipe in place, pull the pipe away from its attachment to the filler neck and release the pipe from its clip to the cowling.

8 Undo the 8 small bolts which hold the cowlings to the radiator take off the cowl and lift the radiator assembly out of the car.

9 **Note:** On later models fitted with a plastic fan, especially those where the radiator is positioned further from the engine (a longer upper support bracket is used), it is not necessary to separate the radiator from the cowling as it is possible to lift the radiator and cowling assembly from the car.

10 To replace the radiator, first fit the radiator bottom hose to the bottom pipe but do not tighten the clip completely.

11 Fit the top hose in position on the radiator inlet pipe. Do not tighten completely.

12 Replace the drain plug in the base of the radiator and lower

the radiator into the car; refit the top cowl and insert and tighten the 8 small bolts which hold the cowlings to the radiator.

13 Refit the radiator to expansion tank hose to the radiator overflow pipe and the pipe on the expansion tank. Refix the hose to its clip on the cowling.

14 Refit the radiator bottom hose to the input or lower side of the water pump and to the heater return pipe where applicable.

15 Replace and tighten the bolt and spring washer, which holds the radiator lower support bracket to the radiator mounting bracket.

16 Refit the upper radiator hose to the thermostat housing outlet pipe, and tighten the securing clips on the top and bottom hoses.

17 Replace the radiator upper support bracket and do up the nuts and spring washers holding it to the top cowl and the radiator thermostat studs.

18 Carefully refit the bonnet.

19 Replace the drain plug (or close the tap) in the side of the block and refill the system with water.

20 Start the engine to pressurise the system and check for leaks.

21 **Note:**

a) If an engine with the radiator mounted in the original position is being fitted to a modified body with a shortened air box in the inner wing panel, a millboard extension piece should be attached to the air box with rivets or screws.

b) If a new radiator is being fitted, it may be necessary to enlarge the holes in the radiator cowls to accept the securing screws.

6 Radiator - inspection and cleaning

1 With the radiator out of the car any leaks can be soldered up or repaired with a substance such as "Cataloy". Clean out the inside of the radiator by flushing as detailed in Section 3.

2 When the radiator is out of the car it is advantageous to turn it upside down for reverse flushing. Clean the exterior of the radiator by hosing down the radiator matrix with a strong jet of water to clear away road dirt, dead flies, etc.

3 Inspect the radiator hoses for cracks, internal or external perishing, and damage caused by overtightening of the securing clips. Replace the hoses as necessary.

4 Examine the radiator hose securing clips and renew them if they are rusted or distorted. The drain taps should be renewed if leaking, but ensure the leak is not because of a faulty washer behind the tap. If the tap is suspected try a new washer to see if this clears the trouble first.

7 Thermostat - removal, testing and replacement

1 To remove the thermostat partially drain the cooling system (4 pints/2.25 litres is enough), loosen the upper radiator hose at the thermostat elbow end and pull it off the elbow. Unscrew the three set bolts and spring washers from the thermostat housing and the two bolts and spring washers from the radiator cowling. Lift off the radiator support bracket and the advance and retard pipe clip. Lift the housing and paper gasket away. Take out the thermostat.

2 Test the thermostat for correct functioning, by immersing it in a saucepan of cold water together with a thermometer. Heat the water and note when the thermostat begins to open. This should be at 82° C (179.6° F). It is advantageous in winter to fit a thermostat that does not open until 88° C (190.4° F). Discard the thermostat if it opens too early. Continue heating the water until the thermostat is fully open. Then let it cool down naturally. If the thermostat will not open fully in boiling water, or does not close down as the water cools, then it must be exchanged for a new one. If the thermostat is stuck open when cold this will be apparent when removing it from the housing.

3 Replacing the thermostat is a reversal of the removal procedure. Remember to use a new paper gasket between the

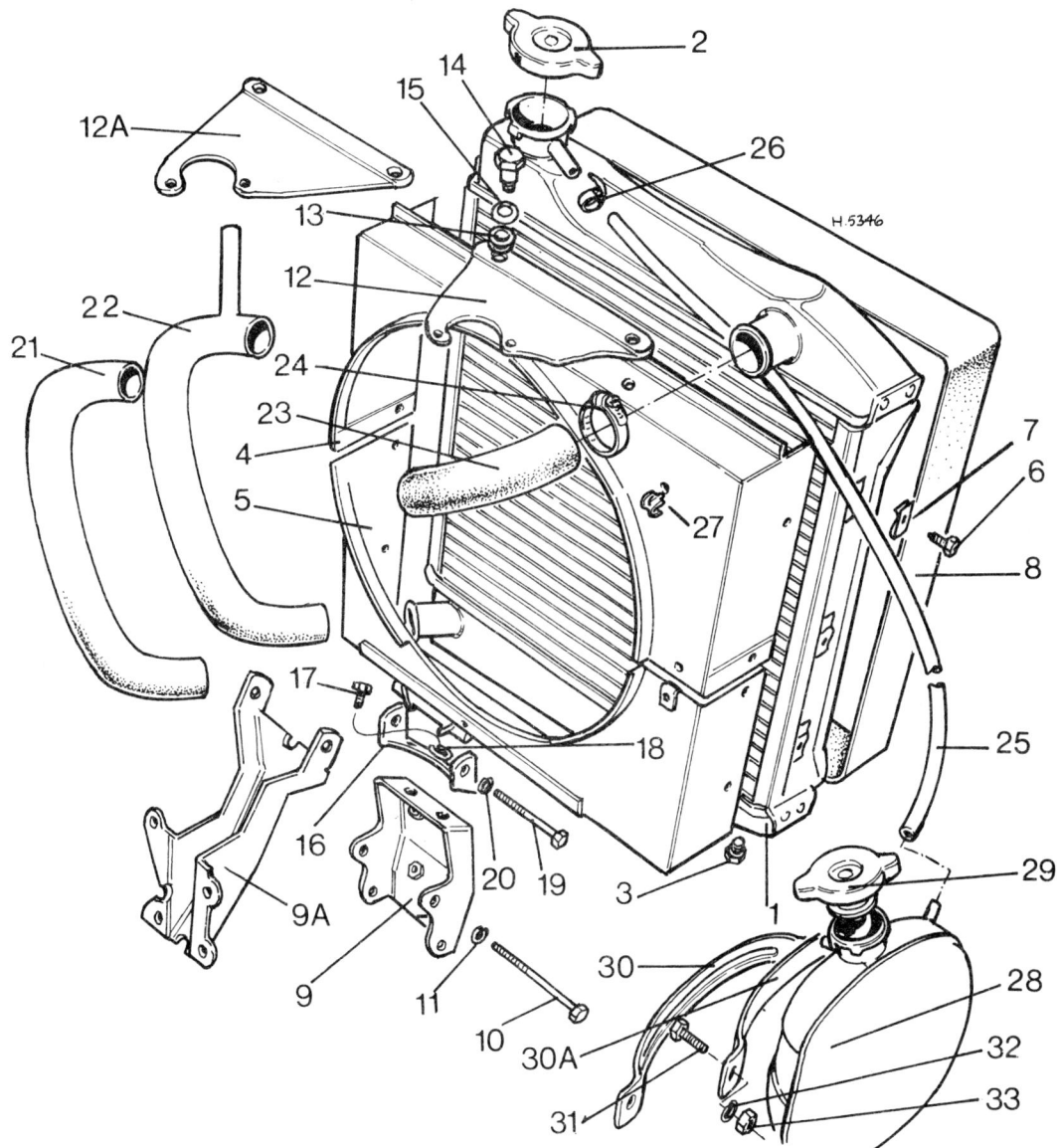

Fig. 2.1. Component parts of radiator and attachments (Sec. 5)

1 Radiator assembly	9a Radiator mounting bracket	17 Screw	26 Hose clip
2 Radiator filler cap	(later type)	18 Shakeproof washer	27 Radiator cowl hose clip
(plain)	10 Bolt	19 Bolt	28 Expansion tank
3 Drain plug (early	11 Spring washer	20 Spring washer	29 Expansion tank cap
assemblies)	12 Radiator upper support	21 Radiator hose to pump	(pressurized)
4 Top cowl	bracket (short)	22 Radiator hose to pump	30 Expansion tank strap
5 Bottom cowl	12a Radiator upper support	(heater)	(metal tank)
6 Screw	bracket (long)	23 Radiator outlet hose	30a Swaged expansion tank strap
7 Spring nut	13 Support bracket grommet	24 Hose clip	(plastic tank)
8 Rubber cowl surround	14 Screw	25 Radiator to expansion tank	31 Screw
(early assemblies)	15 Plain washer	spill hose	32 Spring washer
9 Radiator mounting bracket	16 Radiator lower support		33 Nut
(early type)	bracket (early assemblies)		

thermostat housing elbow and the thermostat. Renew the thermostat elbow if it is badly corroded and eaten away.

4 If a new winter thermostat is fitted, providing the summer unit is functioning correctly, it can be placed on one side and refitted in the spring. Thermostats should last for two or three years at least between renewals.

8 Water pump - removal and replacement

1 Drain the cooling system as described in Section 2.

2 Remove the top radiator support bracket by undoing the bolts securing it to the radiator and thermostat housing. Remove

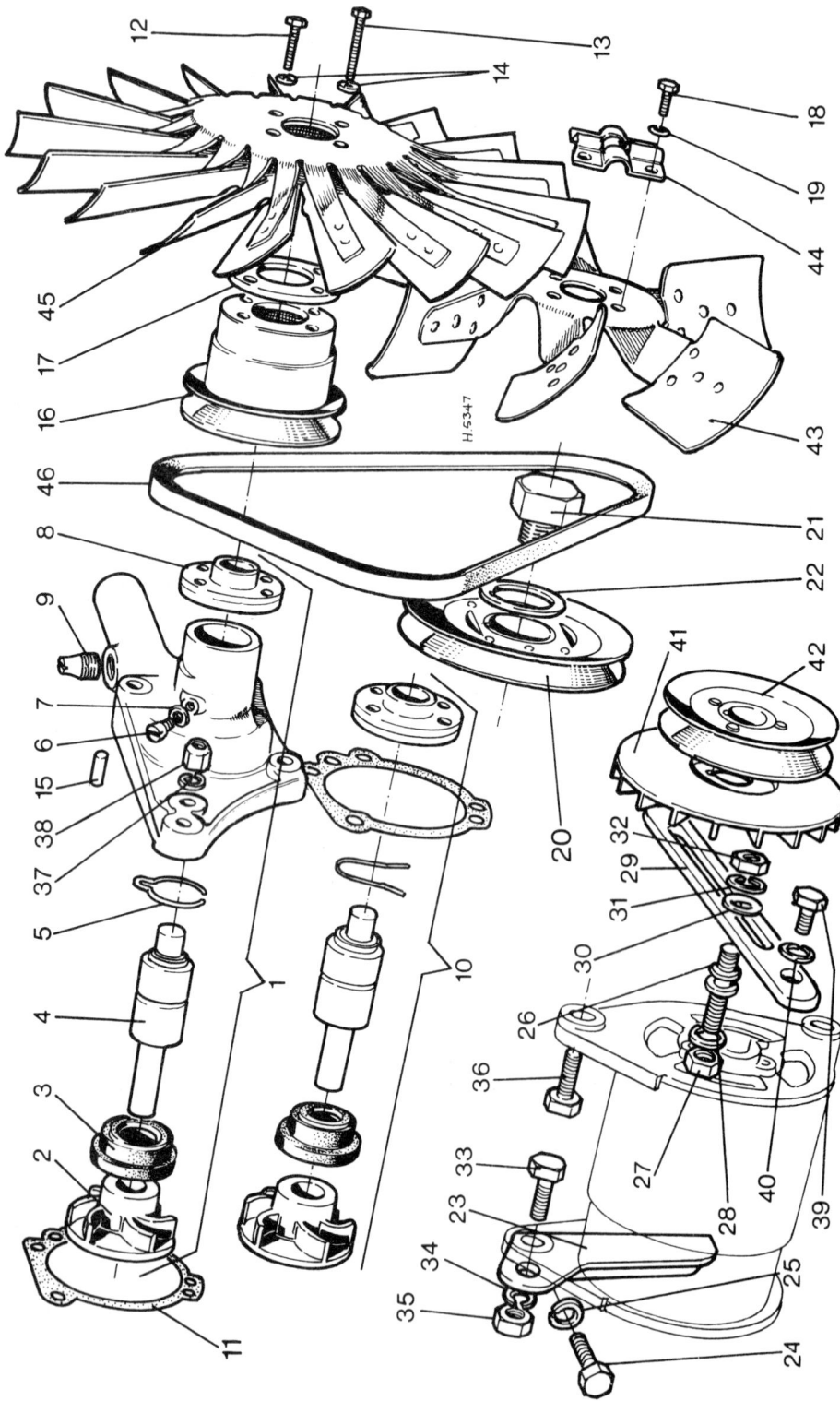

Fig. 2.2. Exploded view of water pump (early type) and ancillary components (Secs. 8 and 9)

1 Water pump assembly
2 Vane
3 Seal
4 Bearing with spindle
5 Bearing locating wire
6 Lubrication point screw
7 Fibre washer
8 Hub pulley
9 By-pass hose adaptor
10 Parts comprising water pump repair kit (BLMC)
11 Gasket
12 Pump screw - long
13 Pump screw - short
14 Spring washer
15 Dowel
16 Fan & water pump pulley
17 Fan & water pump pulley spacer
18 Fan retaining screw
19 Spring washer
20 Crankshaft pulley
21 Retaining bolt
22 Lock washer
23 Rear dynamo bracket
24 Screw
25 Spring washer
26 Pillar
27 Nut
28 Spring washer
29 Dynamo adjusting link
30 Washer
31 Spring washer
32 Nut
33 Bolt
34 Spring washer
35 Nut
36 Bolt
37 Spring washer
38 Nut
39 Screw
40 Spring washer
41 Dynamo fan
42 Dynamo pulley
43 Fan for tropical use
44 Fan blade stiffener
45 16 blade fan
46 Fan belt

H.5347

the top half of the cowling.

3 Either remove the top and bottom radiator hoses and remove the radiator and cowling completely as described in Section 5 or just remove the long bolt which holds the bottom of the radiator and cowling to the support bracket and pull the radiator back against the wing valence to give clearance.

4 Loosen the dynamo securing bolts and remove the fan belt. Undo the four bolts which hold the fan and pulley to the water pump flange and carefully take the fan and pulley off. The easiest way to remove these bolts is to hold the head of a bolt with a spanner, and to then rotate the fan clockwise.

5 Undo and clip on the lower side of the bypass hose and the

clip holding the lower radiator hose to the water pump inlet pipe.

6 Unscrew the four bolts which hold the pump to the front of the cylinder block and lift away the water pump.

7 Refitting is the reverse sequence to removal but note in addition:

a) Clean the mating faces of the water pump body and cylinder block to ensure a good water tight joint.

b) Always use a new gasket.

c) The small bypass hose should be renewed because it is very difficult to replace with the water pump in position.

d) Adjust the fan belt tension as described in Section 11.

9 Water pump - dismantling and overhaul

1 If the water pump starts to leak (make certain it is not the bypass hose) the pump can be dismantled and rebuilt, or an exchange reconditioned pump fitted. It should however be noted that three types of water pump have been fitted to models covered by this manual. Before commencing work ensure that parts are available for the type of pump being dismantled.

2 Remove the four bolts and spring washers which hold the fan blades and fan pulley in place. With these removed, pull or tap off the hub from the end of the spindle, taking great care not to damage it.

3 Then pull out the bearing retaining wire.

4 The spindle and bearing assembly are combined (and are only supplied on exchange as a complete unit), and should now be gently tapped out of the rear of the water pump.

5 The oil seal assembly and the impeller will also come out with the spindle and bearing assembly.

6 The impeller vane is removed from the spindle by judicious tapping and levering, or preferably, to ensure no damage and for ease of operation, with an extractor. The oil seal assembly can then be slipped off.

7 Thoroughly inspect all parts for wear or damage. Replace any faulty parts.

8 Should the interference fit of the fan hub be impaired when the hub was withdrawn from the spindle a new hub must be fitted. The hub must be fitted with its face flush with the end of the spindle.

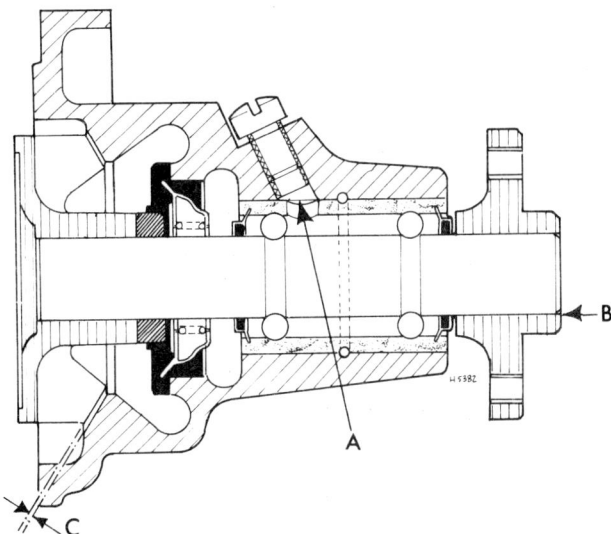

Fig. 2.3. Cross-section through water pump (first type) (Sec. 9)

A Lubricating hole
B Hub face flush with spindle
C 0.020 - 0.030 in (0.51 - 0.76 mm) clearance

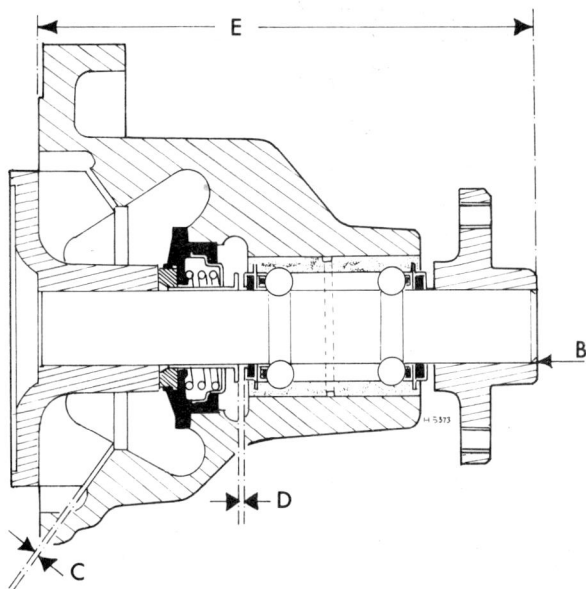

Fig. 2.4. Cross-section through water pump (second type) (Sec. 9)

A 0.534 ± 0.005 in (13.56 ± 0.13 mm)
B Hub face flush with spindle
C 0.020 - 0.030 in (0.51 - 0.76 mm) clearance
D 0.042 - 0.062 in (1.1 - 1.6 mm) clearance
E 3.712 - 3.732 in (94.31 - 94.8 mm)

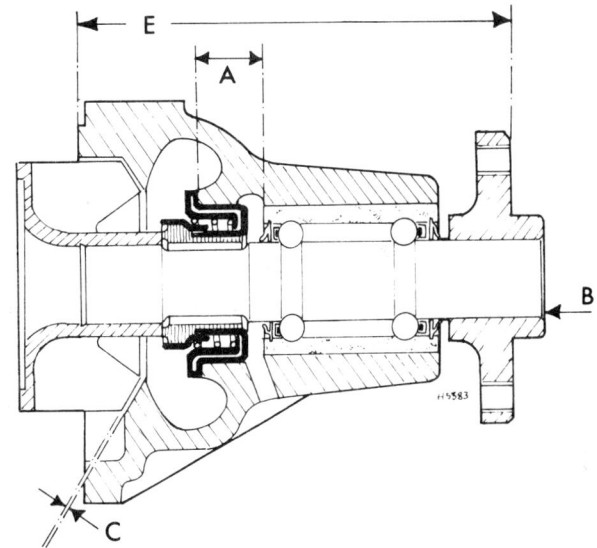

Fig. 2.5. Cross-section through water pump (third type) (Sec. 9)
(See Fig. 2.4 for dimensions)

9 To reassemble press the bearing and spindle assembly into the pump body.

10 On the 3rd type of pump, without the thrower, adjust the position of the spindle to obtain the correct distance from the rear face of the spindle bearing to the seal housing shoulder.

11 On the 2nd type of pump with the thrower, check the bearing to thrower clearance before refitting the spindle.

12 On the 1st type of pump which has a grease plug, ensure that the hole in the bearing is aligned with the bore in the pump body.

13 Fit a new seal. Smear the jointing face of the seal with a mineral based oil to ensure a watertight joint.

14 Carefully press the impeller onto the spindle, ensuring that the correct running clearance is maintained between the impeller vanes and the pump body. This clearance is the same for all three types of pump: 0.020 - 0.030 in. (0.51 - 0.76 mm).

10 Fan belt - removal and replacement

If the fan belt is worn or has stretched unduly, it should be replaced. The most usual reason for replacement is that the belt has broken in service. It is therefore recommended that a spare belt is always carried. Replacement is a reversal of the removal sequence, but as replacement due to breakage is the most usual operation, it is detailed below.

1 Loosen the two dynamo pivots and the nut on the adjusting link and push the dynamo or alternator in towards the engine.

2 Fit the belt by manoeuvring it over each fan blade in turn, through the small gap at the top front side of the radiator.

3 Slip the belt over the crankshaft, dynamo, and water pump pulleys.

4 Adjust the belt as detailed in Section 11 and tighten the dynamo or alternator mounting nuts. **Note:** after fitting a new belt it will require adjustment 250 miles (400 km) later.

11 Fan belt - adjustment

It is important to keep the fan belt correctly adjusted and although not listed by the manufacturer, it is considered that this should be a regular maintenance task performed every 6,000 miles (10,000 km). If the belt is too loose it will slip, wear rapidly and cause the dynamo or alternator and water pump to malfunction. If the belt is too tight the dynamo or alternator and water pump bearings will wear rapidly causing premature failure of these components.

The fan belt tension is correct when there is 0.5 in (12.7 mm) of lateral movement at the midpoint position of the belt between the dynamo pulley wheel and the water pump pulley wheel.

To adjust the fan belt, slacken the dynamo or alternator securing bolts and move the dynamo or alternator either in or out until the correct tension is obtained. It is easier if the dynamo bolts are only slackened a little so it requires some force to move the dynamo. This should not be done with an alternator. In this way the tension of the belt can be arrived at more quickly than by making frequent adjustments. If difficulty is experienced in moving the dynamo or alternator away from the engine a long spanner placed behind the dynamo or alternator and resting against the block serves as a very good lever and can be held in this position while the dynamo or alternator bolts are tightened.

12 Fan and pulley - removal and replacement

1 Remove the fan belt as described in Section 10.

2 On models which have an air box incorporated in the inner wing valance, refer to Section 5 and remove the radiator assembly.

3 On models that do not have an air box it is not necessary to completely remove the radiator. Remove the upper support and detach the lower support bracket by withdrawing the long bolt, and allow the radiator assembly to swing on the hoses. It is not necessary to drain the cooling system.

4 Undo and remove the screws and washers that secure the fan and pulley to the water pump hub.

5 Lift away the fan and pulley and recover the packing disc or spacer which may be fitted between them.

6 Refitting the pulley and fan is the reverse sequence to removal. It should be noted that a special six bladed metal fan with a stiffener is available for models which are to be used in a hot climate. This fan should be fitted as a precaution against overheating in slow moving traffic if temperatures above 35°C (95°F) are likely to occur.

13 Expansion tank - removal and replacement

1 The expansion tank which receives the overflow from the radiator is located under the lower front valance. It is important that care is taken if the pressure cap is to be removed with the cooling system other than cold, see Section 4.

2 To remove the expansion tank first detach the overspill hose from the radiator and its securing clip from the cowling.

3 Undo and remove the two set screws and lift off the expansion tank, spill hose and securing strap (where fitted).

4 Refitting the expansion tank is the reverse sequence to removal. Should the fixing lugs of the later plastic tube expansion tank be broken, it is possible to fit the special swaged securing strap with two 1/16 in (1.6 mm) thick plates between the tanks and brackets on the body.

14 Antifreeze mixture

1 In anticipation of freezing conditions, it is essential that some of the water is drained and an adequate amount of antifreeze is added to the cooling system.

2 Any antifreeze which conforms with the specification 'BS 3151' or 'BS 3152' can be used. Never use an antifreeze with an alcohol base as evaporation is too high.

3 An antifreeze with anti-corrosion additive can be left in the cooling system for up to two years, but after six months it is advisable to have the specific gravity of the coolant checked at your local garage and thereafter, every three months.

4 Listed below are the amounts of antifreeze which should be added to ensure adequate protection down to the temperature given.

Commences freezing at		Solution %	Quantity of antifreeze required
°C	°F		
− 9	16	20	1.75 pints (1.0 litre)
−13	9	25	2 pints (1.1 litres)
−16	3	30	2.25 pints (1.2 litres)

15 Fault diagnosis - cooling system

Symptom	Reason/s	Remedy
Heat generated in cylinder not being successfully disposed of by radiator	Insufficient water in cooling system	Top up radiator, expansion tank.
	Fan belt slipping (accompanied by a shrieking noise on rapid engine acceleration)	Tighten fan belt to recommended tension or replace if worn.
	Radiator core blocked or radiator grille restricted	Reverse flush radiator, remove obstructions.
	Bottom water hose collapsed, impeding flow	Remove and fit new hose.
	Thermostat not opening properly	Remove and fit new thermostat.
	Ignition advance and retard incorrectly set (accompanied by loss of power and perhaps, misfiring)	Check and reset ignition timing.
	Carburettor incorrectly adjusted (mixture too weak)	Tune carburettor.
	Exhaust system partially blocked	Check exhaust pipe for constrictive dents and blockages.
	Oil level in sump too low	Top up sump to full mark on dipstick.
	Blown cylinder head gasket (water/steam being forced down the radiator spill pipe under pressure)	Remove cylinder head, fit new gasket.
	Engine not yet run-in	Run-in slowly and carefully.
	Brakes binding	Check and adjust brakes if necessary.
Too much heat being dispersed by radiator	Thermostat jammed open	Remove and renew thermostat.
	Incorrect grade of thermostat fitted allowing premature opening of valve	Remove and replace with new thermostat which opens at a higher temperature.
	Thermostat missing	Check and fit correct thermostat.
Leaks in system	Loose clips on water hoses	Check and tighten clips if necessary.
	Top or bottom water hoses perished and leaking	Check and replace any faulty hoses.
	Radiator core leaking	Remove radiator and repair.
	Thermostat gasket leaking	Inspect and renew gasket.
	Pressure cap spring worn or seal ineffective	Renew pressure cap.
	Blown cylinder head gasket (pressure in system forcing water/steam down spill pipe)	Remove cylinder head and fit new gasket.
	Cylinder wall or head cracked	Dismantle engine, dispatch to engineering works for repair.

Chapter 3 Fuel system and carburation

Contents

Specifications

Air cleaner:

Type	Disposable paper element type

Fuel pump:

Electric type:

Make and type	SU, SP or AUF 200
Delivery rate	56 pints/hr (32 litres/hr)
Delivery pressure	2.5 - 3 lb/in^2 (0.17 - 0.21 kg/cm^2)

Mechanical type:

Make and type	SU, AUF 700 (AUF 714 model)
Suction (minimum)	6 in. (152 mm) Hg
Pressure (minimum)	3 lb/in^2 (0.21 kg/cm^2)

Carburettor:

Morris 1100 Saloon and Traveller - manual	1962 - 67
Austin 1100 Saloon and Countryman - manual	1963 - 67
Austin and Morris 1100 Mk II - all manual models	1967 - 71
Austin and Morris 1100 Mk III - all manual models	1971
Make and type	SU HS2
Piston spring	Red
Jet size	0.090 in. (2.29 mm)
Needle:	
Standard	AN
Rich	H6
Weak	EB
Idling speed	550 rpm
Fast idle speed	1050 rpm

MG 1100 and 1100 Mk II	**1962 - 67**
Vanden Plas 1100 and 1100 Mk II	**1964 - 67**
Riley Kestrel and Mk II	**1965 - 67**
Wolseley 1100 and 1100 Mk II	**1965 - 67**
Make and type	SU HS2 (Twin)
Piston spring	Blue
Jet size	0.090 in. (2.29 mm)
Needle:	
Standard	D3
Rich	D6
Weak	GV
Idling speed	500 rpm
Fast idle speed	1050 rpm
Austin and Morris 1100 - Automatic	**1966 - 67**
Austin and Morris 1100 Mk II - Automatic	**1967 - 71**
Austin 1100 Mk III - Automatic	**1971**
MG, Riley, Vanden Plas and Wolseley 1100 - Automatic ...	**1967 on**
Make and type	SU HS4
Piston spring	Red
Jet size	0.090 in. (2.29 mm)
Needle:	
Fixed type:	
Standard	DL
Rich	BQ
Weak	ED
Spring loaded type	AAY
Idling speed	650 rpm
Fast idle speed	1050 rpm
1275 cc engines as optional extra for 1100 Mk I	**1967 only**
MG Sports Saloon (USA only)	**1967 only**
Make and type	SU HS4
Piston spring	Red
Jet size	0.090 in. (2.29 mm)
Needle:	
Standard	DZ
Rich	BQ
Weak	CF
Idling speed	650 rpm
Fast idle speed	1050 rpm
Austin and Morris 1100 Mk III (ECE 15)	**1972**
Make and type	SU HS4
Piston spring	Red
Jet size	0.090 in. (2.29 mm)
Needle	AAY
Idling speed	750 rpm
Fast idle speed	1100 to 1200 rpm
Exhaust gas CO content	3.5 to 4.5%
Austin and Morris 1300 - all versions, except GT	**1967 - 1971**
MG, Riley, Vanden Plas and Wolseley 1300 - manual	**1967 - 68**
Wolseley 1300 and 1300 Mk II and Vanden Plas 1300 - Automatic	**1967 on**
MG and Riley Kestrel 1300 - Automatic	**1967 - 69**
Make and type	SU HS4
Piston spring	Red
Jet size	0.090 in. (2.29 mm)
Needle:	
Fixed type:	
Standard	DZ
Rich	BQ
Weak	CF
Spring loaded type	AAR
Idling speed	650 rpm
Fast idle speed	1050 rpm

Wolseley 1300 and 1300 Mk II and Vanden Plas 1300 - manual   **1968 on**
MG and Riley Kestrel 1300 - manual ... ...   **1968 only**

Make and type	SU HS2 (Twin)
Piston spring	Blue
Jet size	0.090 in. (2.29 mm)
Needle:	
Fixed type:	
Standard	EB
Rich	M
Weak	GG
Spring loaded type	AAP
Idle speed	500 rpm
Fast idle speed	1050 rpm

MG 1300 Mk II - manual ... ...   **1968 - 71**
Riley 1300 Mk II - manual ... ...   **1968 - 69**
Austin and Morris 1300 GT ... ...   **1969 - 1971**

Make and type	SU HS2 (Twin)
Piston spring	Blue
Jet size	0.090 in. (2.29 mm)
Needle:	
Fixed type (standard only)	GY
Spring loaded type	AAP
Idling speed	750 rpm
Fast idle speed	1050 rpm

Austin, Morris, Vanden Plas and Wolseley 1300 Mk III
(ECE 15) **1972**

Make and type	SU HS4
Piston spring	Red
Jet size	0.090 in. (2.29 mm)
Needle	ABB
Idling speed	750 rpm
Fast idle speed	1100 to 1200 rpm
Exhaust gas CO content	3.0 to 4.5%

Austin and Morris 1300 GT (ECE 15) **1972**

Make and type	SU HS2 (Twin)
Piston spring	Blue
Jet size	0.090 in (2.29 mm)
Needle	AAP
Idling speed	800 rpm
Fast idle speed	1100 to 1200 rpm
Exhaust gas CO content (maximum)	3%

Austin America
Carburettor and exhaust emission data:

Carburettor:	
Make and type	SU HS4 (Single)
Model:	
Manual transmission:	
Fixed needle	AUD 281
Spring loaded needle	AUD 379
Automatic transmission:	
Fixed needle	AUD 296
Spring loaded needle	AUD 380
Choke diameter	1.5 in. (38.1 mm)
Jet size	0.090 in. (2.28 mm)
Needle:	
Fixed	DZ
Spring loaded	AAG
Piston spring	Red
Idle jet adjustment	13 flats from bridge
Throttle damper setting	0.10 in. (2.54 mm)
Idle speed	850 rpm
Fast idle speed	1050 rpm (maximum)

Exhaust emission:
    Exhaust gas analyser reading:

Engine idle speed	...	...	...	...	...	3.5% CO (maximum)
Air pump test speed	...	...	...	...	...	1200 rpm (engine)

Fuel tank capacity ...   .   8 gallons (36 litres)

Torque wrench settings:

							lb f ft	kg fm
Manifold to cylinder head	...	...	...	...	...	...	12 - 16	1.7 - 2.2

1 General description

The fuel system fitted to models covered by this manual comprises a fuel tank mounted at the rear of the body and under the boot, an electric (early) or mechanical (later) fuel pump, a single or twin SU Carburettor installation, air cleaner and the necessary fuel lines between the tank, pump and carburettors.

All models are fitted with air cleaners which remove dust and dirt from the air before it reaches the carburettors. The air cleaner element is disposable and must be renewed at the recommended mileages.

Operation of the individual components is described elsewhere in this Chapter.

2 Mechanical fuel pump - general description

The mechanically operated fuel pump is located on the bulkhead side of the crankcase and is operated by a separate lobe on the camshaft. As the camshaft rotates the rocker lever is actuated, one end of which is connected to the diaphragm operating rod. When the rocker arm is moved by the cam lobe the diaphragm via the rocker arm moves downwards causing fuel to be drawn in through the filter, past the inlet valve flap and into the diaphragm chamber. As the cam lobe moves round, the diaphragm moves upwards under the action of the spring, and fuel flows via the large outlet valve to the carburettor float chamber.

When the float chamber has the requisite amount of fuel in it, the needle valve in the top of the float chamber shuts off the fuel supply, causing pressure in the fuel delivery line to hold the diaphragm down against the action of the diaphragm spring until the needle valve in the float chamber opens to admit more fuel.

3 Mechanical fuel pump - removal and replacement

1 Remove the fuel inlet and outlet connections from the fuel pump and plug the ends of the pipes to stop loss of fuel or dirt ingress.
2 Unscrew and remove the two pump mounting flange nuts and washers. Carefully slide the pump off the two studs followed by the insulating block assembly and gaskets.
3 Refitting is the reverse sequence to removal. Inspect the gaskets on either side of the insulating block and if damaged obtain and fit new ones.

4 Mechanical fuel pump - dismantling, inspection and reassembly

1 Thoroughly clean the outside of the pump in paraffin and dry. To ensure correct reassembly mark the cover and upper and lower body flanges (Fig. 3.1).
2 Remove the three cover retaining screws, lift away the cover followed by the sealing ring and fuel filter (photos).
3 Remove the three remaining screws holding the upper body to the lower body. Separate the two halves taking care not to damage the diaphragm (photos).
4 As the combined inlet and outlet valve is a press fit into the body, very carefully remove the valve taking care not to damage

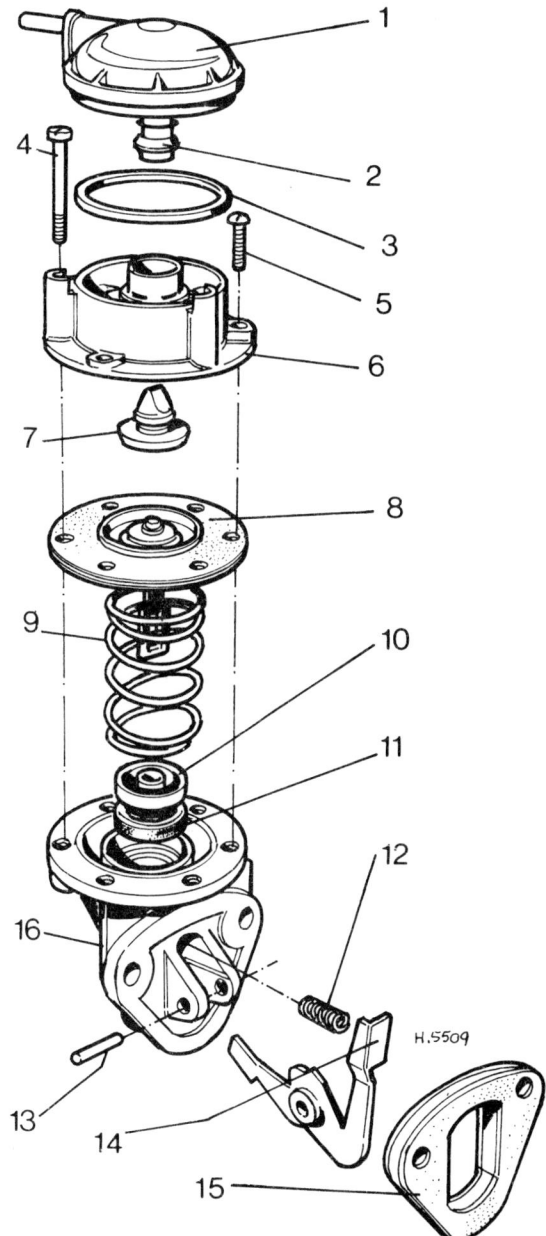

Fig. 3.1. Exploded view of mechanical fuel pump (Sec. 4)

1	Outlet cover	9 Diaphragm spring
2	Insert - outlet cover	10 Retaining cup
3	Sealing washer	11 Crankcase seal
4	Long screws	12 Rocker lever tension spring
5	Short screws	13 Rocker lever pivot pin
6	Upper body	14 Rocker lever
7	Inlet and outlet valve	15 Insulator and gasket
8	Diaphragm assembly	16 Lower body

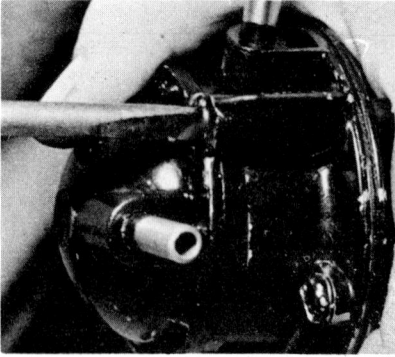
4.2a Removal of cover securing screws ...

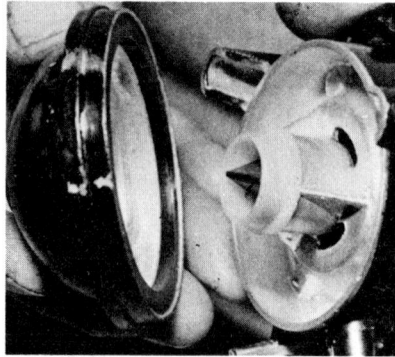
4.2b Lifting away cover from upper body

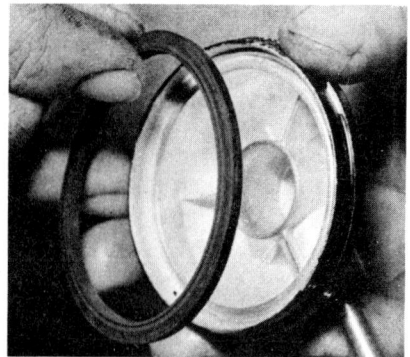
4.2c Removal of sealing washer

4.3a Removal of upper body securing screws

4.3b Lifting away upper body

4.4 Removal of combined inlet and outlet valve from upper body

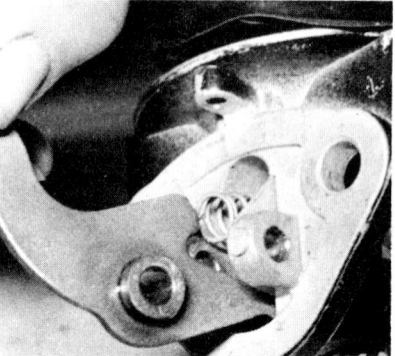
4.6a Withdrawing rocker lever

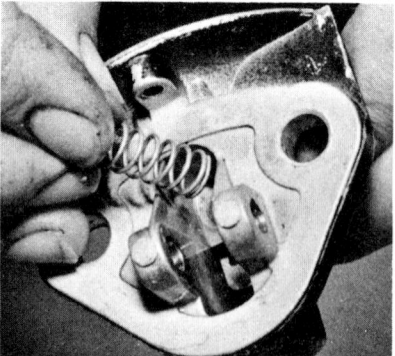
4.6b Renew the tension spring

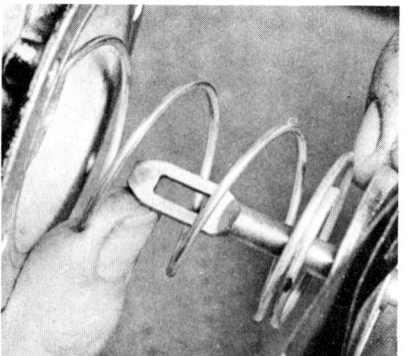
4.7a Removal of diaphragm and spring

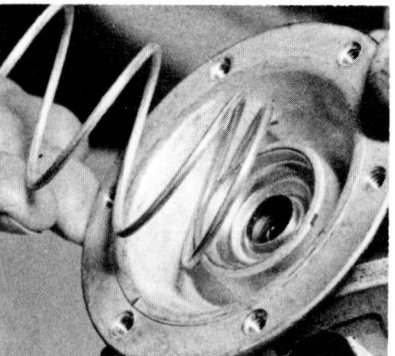
4.7b Note which way round the spring is fitted

4.10 Alignment of diaphram stump ready for refitting the rocker lever

4.12 Upper and lower body alignment marks

the very fine edge of the inlet valve (photo).

5 Lift away the insert from the outlet cover.

6 With the diaphragm and rocker held down against the action of the diaphragm spring tap out the rocker lever pivot pin using a parallel pin punch. Lift out the rocker lever and spring (photos).

7 Lift out the diaphragm and spring having first well lubricated the lower seal to avoid damage as the spindle stirrup is drawn through. Unless the seal is damaged, it is best left in position as a special extractor is required for removal (photos).

8 Carefully wash the filter gauge in petrol and clean all traces of sediment from the upper body. Inspect the diaphragm for signs of distortion, cracking or perishing and fit a new one if suspect.

9 Inspect the fine edge and lips of the combined inlet and outlet valve and check that it is a firm fit in the upper body. Finally inspect the outlet cover for signs of corrosion, pitting or distortion and obtain a new part if necessary.

10 To reassemble first check that there are no sharp edges on the diaphragm spindle and stirrup and well lubricate the oil seals. Insert the stirrup and spindle into the spring and then through the oil seal and position the stirrup ready for rocker lever engagement (photo).

11 Fit the combined inlet/outlet valve ensuring that the groove registers in the housing correctly. Check that the fine edge of the inlet valve contacts its seating correctly and evenly.

12 Match up the screw holes in the lower body and holes in the diaphragm and depress the rocker lever until the diaphragm lies flat, fit the upper body and hold in place by the three short screws, but do not tighten fully yet, (photo).

13 Refit the filter, outlet cover insert, new sealing washer and outlet cover suitably positioned by sligning the previously made marks. Replace the three long screws and then tighten all screws firmly in a diagonal pattern.

14 Insert the rocker lever and spring into the lower body and retain in position using the rocker lever pivot pin.

5 Mechanical fuel pump - testing

If the pump is suspect, or has been overhauled, it may be quickly dry tested holding a finger over the inlet nozzle and operating the rocker lever through three complete strokes. When the finger is released suction noise should be heard. Next hold a finger over the outlet nozzle and press the rocker arm fully. The pressure generated should hold for a minimum of fifteen seconds.

6 Electric fuel pump - general description

The SP and AUF pumps are very similar and it is quite possible to exchange the earlier SP type for the later AUF model. It is as well to know the differences between them and they will be listed in the text as they occur. On early models the fuel pump is situated under the boot on the left-hand side of the car. On later models the pump was moved inside the boot on the right-hand side.

Both of these 12 - volt fuel pumps comprise a long outer body casing housing the diaphragm, armature and solenoid assembly, with at one end the contact breaker assembly protected by a bakelite cover, and at the other end a short casting containing the inlet and outlet ports, filter, valves, and pumping chamber. The joint between the bakelite cover and the body casing is protected with a rubber sheath.

The pump operates in the following manner. When the ignition is switched on current travels from the terminal on the outside of the bakelite cover through the coil located round the solenoid core which becomes energised and acting like a magnet draws the armature towards it. The current then passes through the points to earth.

When the armature is drawn forward it brings the diaphragm with it against the pressure of the diaphragm spring. This creates

sufficient vacuum in the pump chamber to draw in fuel from the tank through the fuel filter and non-return inlet valve.

As the armature nears the end of its travel a 'throw over' mechanism operates which separates the points so breaking the circuit.

The diaphragm return spring then pushes the diaphragm and armature forwards into the pumping chamber so forcing the fuel in the chamber out to the carburettor through the non-return outlet valve. When the armature is nearly fully forward the throw over mechanism again functions, this time closing the points and re-energising the solenoid, so repeating the cycle.

7 Electric fuel pump - removal and replacement

1 Disconnect the earth lead from the battery.

2 Disconnect the earth and the supply wires from their terminals on the pump body.

3 Prepare to seqeeze the rubber portion of the petrol pipe leading from the tank with a mole wrench to ensure the minimum of fuel is lost when the inlet pipe is removed from the pump. Alternatively have a suitable container handy into which the fuel can drain.

4 Remove the fuel inlet and outlet pipes by undoing the union nuts or the clip screws. (Remove the vent pipe connector where fitted, at this stage). On later models with the pump inside the boot undo the inlet and outlet connections under the car so the flexible hoses are still connected to the pump connections.

5 Unscrew the two bolts and spring washers which hold the pump bracket in position and remove the pump. On later models remove the floor from the boot and undo the screws which hold the pump in place. Pull the pump into the boot and disconnect the earth wire.

6 Replacement of the pump is a reversal of the above process. Two particular points to watch are that:

a) The fuel inlet and outlet pipes are connected up the right way round.

b) A good electrical earth connection is made.

8 Electric fuel pump - dismantling, inspection and reassembly

1 The filter and inlet and outlet arrangements differ between the two pumps and for this reason it is necessary to deal with them individually at this stage:

a) Type SP. Remove the inlet nozzle by unscrewing it, and take out the filter from the inlet port. **Note** The fibre washer under the nozzle head. The outlet nozzle is pressed into the end casting and cannot be removed.

b) Type AUF. Release the inlet and outlet nozzles, valves, sealing washers, and filter by unscrewing the two screws from the spring clamp plate which hold them all in place.

2 Mark the flanges adjacent to each other and separate the housing holding the armature and solenoid assembly from the pumping chamber casting, by unscrewing the six screws holding both halves of the pump together. Take great care not to tear or damage the diaphragm as it may stick to either of the flanges as they are separated. On the SP pump, remove the pan-headed screw which holds the valve retainer in place to the floor of the pumping chamber, and remove the retainer and the inlet and outlet valves which have already been removed on the AUF pump.

3 The armature spindle which is attached to the armature head and diaphragm is unscrewed anti-clockwise from the trunnion at the contact breaker end of the pump body. Lift out the armature, spindle and diaphragm, and remove the impact washer from under the head of the armature (this washer quietens the noise of the armature head hitting the solenoid core), and the diaphragm return spring.

4 Slide off the protective rubber sheath and unscrew the terminal nut, connector (where fitted), and washer from the terminal screw, and remove the bakelite contact breaker cover.

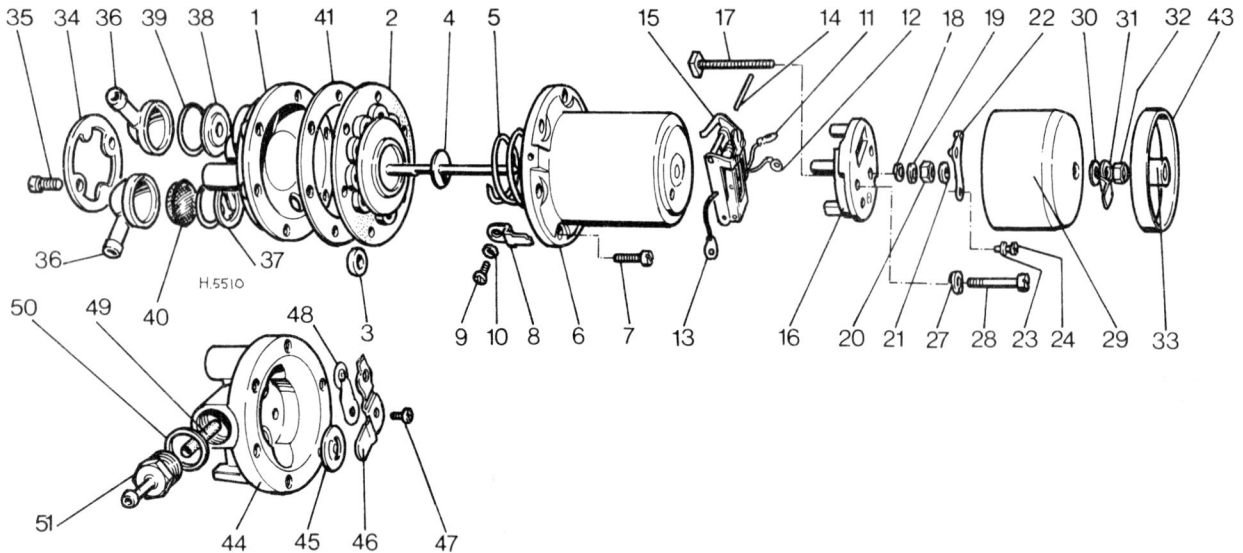

Fig. 3.2. Exploded view of electric fuel pump (Sec. 8)

1 Pump body (AUF 200 only)	12 Terminal tag	28 Screw	41 Gasket
	13 Earth tag	29 End-cover	43 Sealing band
2 Diaphragm and spindle assembly	14 Rocker pivot pin	30 Shakeproof washer	44 Pump body
	15 Rocker mechanism	31 Connector	45 Outlet valve
3 Armature centralizing roller	16 Pedestal	32 Nut	46 Valve retainer
	17 Terminal stud	33 Insulating sleeve	47 Screw
4 Impact washer	18 Spring washer	34 Clamp plate	48 Inlet valve
5 Armature spring	19 Lead washer	35 Set screw	49 Filter
6 Coil housing	20 Terminal nut	36 Inlet and outlet nozzles	50 Washer
7 Set screw	21 End-cover seal washer	37 Inlet valve	51 Inlet nozzle
8 Earth connector	22 Contact blade	38 Outlet valve	
9 Set screw	23 Washer	39 Sealing washer	
10 Spring washer	24 Contact blade screw	40 Filter	
11 Terminal tag	27 Spring washer		

(Items 35–40: AUF 200 only) (Items 41–51: SP only)

5 Unscrew the 5 BA screws which hold the contact spring blade in position and remove it with the blade and screw washer.

6 Remove the cover retaining nut on the terminal screw, and cut through the lead washer under the nut on the terminal screw with a pocket knife.

7 Remove the two bakelite pedestal retaining screws complete with spring washers which hold the pedestal to the solenoid housing, remove the braided copper earth lead, and the coil lead from the terminal screw.

8 Remove the pin on which the rockers pivot by pushing it out sideways and remove the rocker assembly. The pump is now fully dismantled. It is not possible to remove the solenoid core and coil and the rocker assembly must not be broken down, as it is only supplied on exchange as a complete assembly.

9 Remove the filter as has already been detailed and thoroughly clean it in petrol. At the same time clean the points by gently drawing a piece of thin card between them. Do this very carefully so as not to disturb the tension of the spring blade. If the points are burnt or pitted they must be renewed and a new blade and rocker assembly fitted.

10 On either of the pumps fuel starvation combined with rapid operations is indicative of an air leak on the suction side. To check whether this is so, undo the fuel line at the top of the float chamber, and immerse the end of the pipe in a jam jar half filled with petrol. With the ignition on and the pump functioning, should a regular stream of air bubbles emerge from the end of the pipe, air is leaking in on the suction side.

11 If the filter is coated with gum-like substance very like varnish, serious trouble can develop in the future unless all traces of this gum (formed by deposits from the fuel) are removed.

12 To do this boil all steel and brass parts in a 20% solution of caustic soda, then dip them in nitric acid and clean them in boiling water. Alloy parts can be cleaned with a clean rag after they have been left to soak for a few hours in methylated spirits.

13 With the pump stripped right down, wash and clean all the parts thoroughly in paraffin and renew any that are worn, damaged, fractured, or cracked. Pay particular attention to the gaskets and diaphragm.

14 To reassemble first fit the rocker assembly to the bakelite pedestal and insert the rocker pivot pin. The pin is case hardened and wire or any other substitute should never be used if the pin is lost.

15 Place the spring washer, wiring tag from the short lead from the coil, a new lead washer, and the nut on the terminal screws, and tighten the nut down.

16 Attach the copper earth wire from the outer rocker immediately under the head of the nearest pedestal securing screw, and fit the pedestal to the solenoid housing with the two pedestal securing screws and lockwashers. It is unusual to fit an earth-wire immediately under the screw head but in this case the spring washer has been found not to be a particularly good conductor.

17 Fit the lockwasher under the head of the spring blade contact securing screw, then the last lead from the coil, and then the spring blade so that there is nothing between it and the bakelite pedestal. It is important that this order of assembly is adhered to. Tighten the screw lightly.

18 The static position of the pump when it is not in use is with the contact points making firm contact and this forces the spring blade to be bent slightly back. Move the outer rocker arm up and down and position the spring blade so that the contacts on the rocker or blade wipe over the centre line of the other points. When open the blade should rest against the small ledge on the bakelite pedestal just below the points. The points should come into contact with each other when the rocker is halfway forward. To check that this is correct press the middle of the blade gently so that it rests against the ridge with the points just having come into contact. It should now be possible to slide a

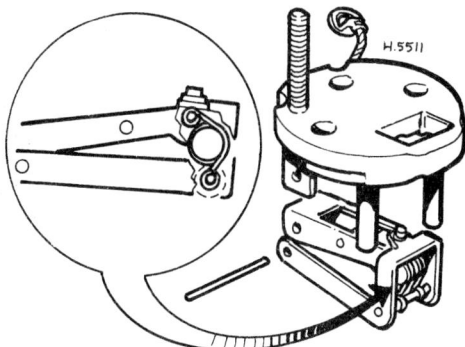

Fig. 3.3. The correct relative positions of the rocker assembly and pedestal. Inset shows correct assembled position of toggle spring (Sec. 8)

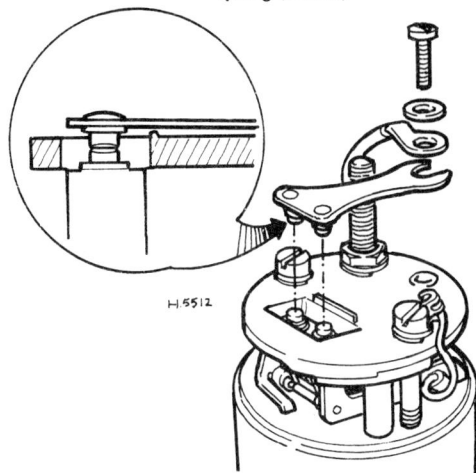

Fig. 3.4. Setting the correct relative position of blade and rocker contact points (Sec. 8)

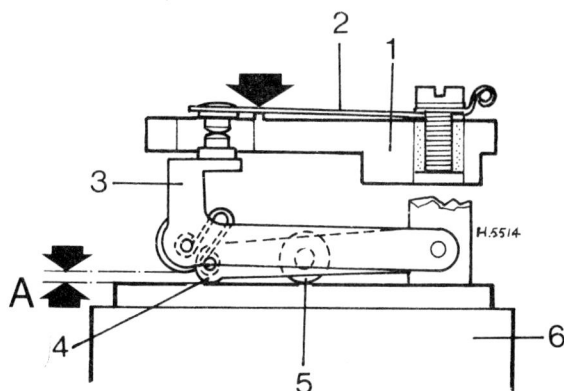

Fig. 3.5. Contact gap setting - earlier type rocker assembly (Sec. 8)

1	Pedestal	4	Inner rocker
2	Contact blade	5	Trunnion
3	Outer rocker	6	Coil housing

A = 0.030 in (0.8 mm)

0.030 in (0.762 mm) feeler gauge between the rocker rollers and the solenoid housing. If the clearance is not correct bend the tip of the blade very carefully until it is.

On the AUF and SP pumps with the outer rocker against the coil housing and the spring blade contact resting against the pedestal, the gap between the points should be 0.030 in (0.762 mm).

19 Tighten down the blade retaining screw, and check that with AUF and SP models a considerable gap exists between the under-side of the spring blade and the pedestal ledge, with the rocker contact bearing against the blade contact and the rocker fully forward in the normal static position. With the rocker arm down, ensure that the underside of the blade rests on the ledge of the pedestal. If not, remove the blade and very slightly bend it until it does.

20 Place the impact washer on the underside of the armature head, fit the diaphragm return spring with the wider portion of the coil against the solenoid body, place the brass rollers in position under the diaphragm and insert the armature spindle through the centre of the solenoid core, and screw the spindle into the rocker trunnion.

21 It will be appreciated that the amount the spindle is screwed into the rocker trunnion will vitally affect the functioning of the pump. To set the diaphragm correctly, turn the steel blade to one side, and screw the armature spindle into the trunnion until, if the spindle was screwed in a further sixth of a turn, the throw-over rocker would not operate the points closed to points open position. Now screw out the armature spindle four holes (2/3 of a turn) to ensure that wear in the points will not cause the pump to stop working. Turn the blade back into its normal position.

22 Reassembly of the valves, filters, and nozzles into the pumping chamber is a reversal of the dismantling process. Use new washers and gaskets throughout.

23 With the pumping chamber reassembled, replace it carefully on the solenoid housing, ensuring that the previously made mating marks on the flanges line up with each other. Screw the six screws in firmly.

24 Fit the bakelite cover and replace the shakeproof washer, lucar conductor, cover nut, and terminal knob to the terminal screw. Then, replace the terminal lead and cover nut, so locking the lead between the cover nut and the terminal nut. Assembly of both types is now complete.

9 Electric fuel pump - testing

If the pump is suspect, or has been overhauled, it may be quickly tested by connecting up to a 12 volt battery and listening to hear it operate. Next hold a finger over the inlet union and slight suction should be felt. Now hold a finger over the outlet union and the pump should stop, and only recommence pumping action when the finger has been removed.

10 SU carburettor - general description

1 The variable choke SU carburettor, shown in component form, is a relatively simple instrument. It differs from most other carburettors in that instead of having a number of various sized fixed jets for different conditions, only one variable jet is fitted to deal with all possible conditions.

2 Air passing rapidly through the carburettor draws petrol from the jet so forming the petrol/air mixture. The amount of petrol drawn from the jet depends on the position of the tapered carburettor needle, which moves up and down the jet orifice according to the engine load and throttle opening, thus effectively altering the size of jet so that exactly the right amount of fuel is metered for the prevailing road conditions.

3 The position of the tapered needle in the jet is determined by engine vacuum. The shank of the needle is held at its top end in a piston which slides up and down the dashpot in response to the degree of manifold vacuum.

4 With the throttle fully open, the full effect of inlet manifold vacuum is felt by the piston which has an air bleed into the choke tube on the outside of the throttle. This causes the piston to rise fully, bringing the needle with it. With the accelerator partially closed, only slight inlet manifold vacuum is felt by the piston (although, of course, on the engine side of the throttle the vacuum is greater), and the piston only rises a little, blocking most of the jet orifice with the metering needle.

5 To prevent the piston fluttering and giving a richer mixture

when the accelerator pedal is suddenly depressed, an oil damper and light spring are fitted inside the dashpot.

6 The only portion of the piston assembly to come into contact with the piston chamber or dashpot is the actual piston rod. All the other parts of the piston assembly, including the lower choke portion, have sufficient clearance to prevent any direct metal to metal contact which is essential if the carburettor is to function correctly.

7 The correct level of the petrol in the carburettor is determined by the level of the float chamber. When the level is correct the float rises and, by means of a lever resting on top of it, closes the needle valve in the cover of the float chamber. This closes off the supply of fuel from the pump. When the level in the float chamber drops as fuel is used in the carburettor, the float drops. As it does, the float needle is unseated so allowing more fuel to enter the float chamber and restore the correct level.

11 SU carburettor - removal and replacement

1 Release the clip which secures the breather hose to the rocker cover, and pull the hose from the rocker cover pipe.
2 Unscrew the union which holds the vacuum advance pipe to the carburettor body.
3 Remove the air cleaner.
4 Unscrew the union or clip securing the fuel inlet pipe to the float chamber and pull away the pipe.
5 Remove the choke and accelerator cables from the carburettor linkages.
6 Remove the two nuts and lock washers which hold the SU carburettor to the inlet manifold. The bottom nut is sometimes difficult to unscrew, but merely requires patience.
7 Lift the carburettor away from the inlet manifold together with the inlet manifold gasket.
8 If twin carburettors are being removed then the procedure is exactly the same as above but both carburettors will have to be lifted off together as they are joined by a common spindle.
9 To replace the carburettor/s reverse the above procedure using new gaskets where required. Do not omit to fit the spring washers.

12 SU carburettor - dismantling and reassembly

1 The SU carburettor with only two normally moving parts - the throttle valve and the piston assembly - makes it a straightforward instrument to service, but at the same time it is a delicate unit and clumsy handling can cause much damage. In particular it is easy to knock the finely tapering needle out of true, and the greatest care should be taken to keep all the parts associated with the dashpot scrupulously clean.
2 Remove the oil dashpot plunger nut from the top of the dashpot.
3 Unscrew the two set screws holding the dashpot to the carburettor body, and lift away the dashpot, light spring, and piston and needle assembly.
4 To remove the metering needle from the choke portion of the piston unscrew the sunken retaining screw from the side of the piston choke and pull out the needle. When replacing the needle ensure that the shoulder is flush with the underside of the piston.
5 Release the float chamber from the carburettor by releasing the clamping bolt and sealing washers from the carburettor base. (The bolt is removed from the side in the case of the H2 type).
6 Normally it is not necessary to dismantle the carburettor further, but if because of wear or for some other reason it is wished to remove the jet, this is easily accomplished by removing the clevis pin holding the jet operating lever to the jet head, and then removing the jet by extracting it from the base of the carburettor. The jet adjusting screw can then be unscrewed together with its locking spring.

7 If the larger jet locking screw above the jet adjusting screw is removed, then the jet will have to be recentred when the carburettor is reassembled. With the jet screws removed on HS.2 carburettors, it is a simple matter to release the jet bearing. On the H2 type of carburettor, dismantling is more complex. With the jet locking screw removed, take out the sealing washer, jet gland spring, brass gland washer, glandwasher, and the top half of the jet bearing in this order.
8 To remove the throttle and actuating spindle release the two screws holding the throttle in the position in the slot in the spindle, slide the throttle out of the spindle and then remove the spindle.
9 Reassembly is a straight reversal of the dismantling sequence.

13 SU carburettor - examination and repair

The SU carburettor is most reliable but even so it may develop one of several faults which may not be readily apparent unless a careful inspection is carried out. The common faults to which the carburettor is prone are:

1 Piston sticking
2 Float needle sticking
3 Float chamber flooding
4 Water and dirt in the carburettor

In addition the following parts are susceptible to wear after high mileages and as they vitally affect the economy of the engine they should be checked and renewed where necessary, every 24,000 miles (38,600 km):

a) The carburettor needle: If this has been incorrectly fitted at some time so that it is not centrally located in the jet orifice, then the metering needle will have a tiny ridge worn on it. If a ridge can be seen than the needle must be renewed. SU carburettor needles are made to very fine tolerances and, should a ridge be apparent, no attempt should be made to rub the needle down with fine emery paper. If it is wished to clean the needle it can be polished lightly with metal polish.
b) The carburettor jet: If the needle is worn it is likely that the rim of the jet will be damaged where the needle has been striking it. It should be renewed, otherwise fuel consumption will suffer. The jet can also be badly worn or ridged on the outside from where it has been sliding up and down between the jet bearing every time the choke has been pulled out. Removal and renewal is the only answer.
c) Check the edges of the throttle and choke tube for wear. Renew if worn.
d) The washers fitted to the base of the jet and under the float chamber lid may leak after a time and can cause a great deal of fuel wastage. It is wisest to renew them automatically when the carburettor is stripped down.
e) After high mileages the float chamber needle and seat are bound to be ridged. They are not an expensive item to replace and must be renewed as a set. They should never be renewed separately.

14 SU carburettor - piston sticking

1 The hardened piston rod which slides in the centre guide tube in the middle of the dashpot is the only part of the piston assembly (which comprises the jet needle, suction disc, and piston choke) which should make contact with the dashpot. The piston rim and the choke periphery are machined to very fine tolerances so that they will not touch the dashpot or the choke tube walls.
2 After high mileages wear in the centre guide tube may allow the piston to touch the dashpot wall. This condition is known as sticking.

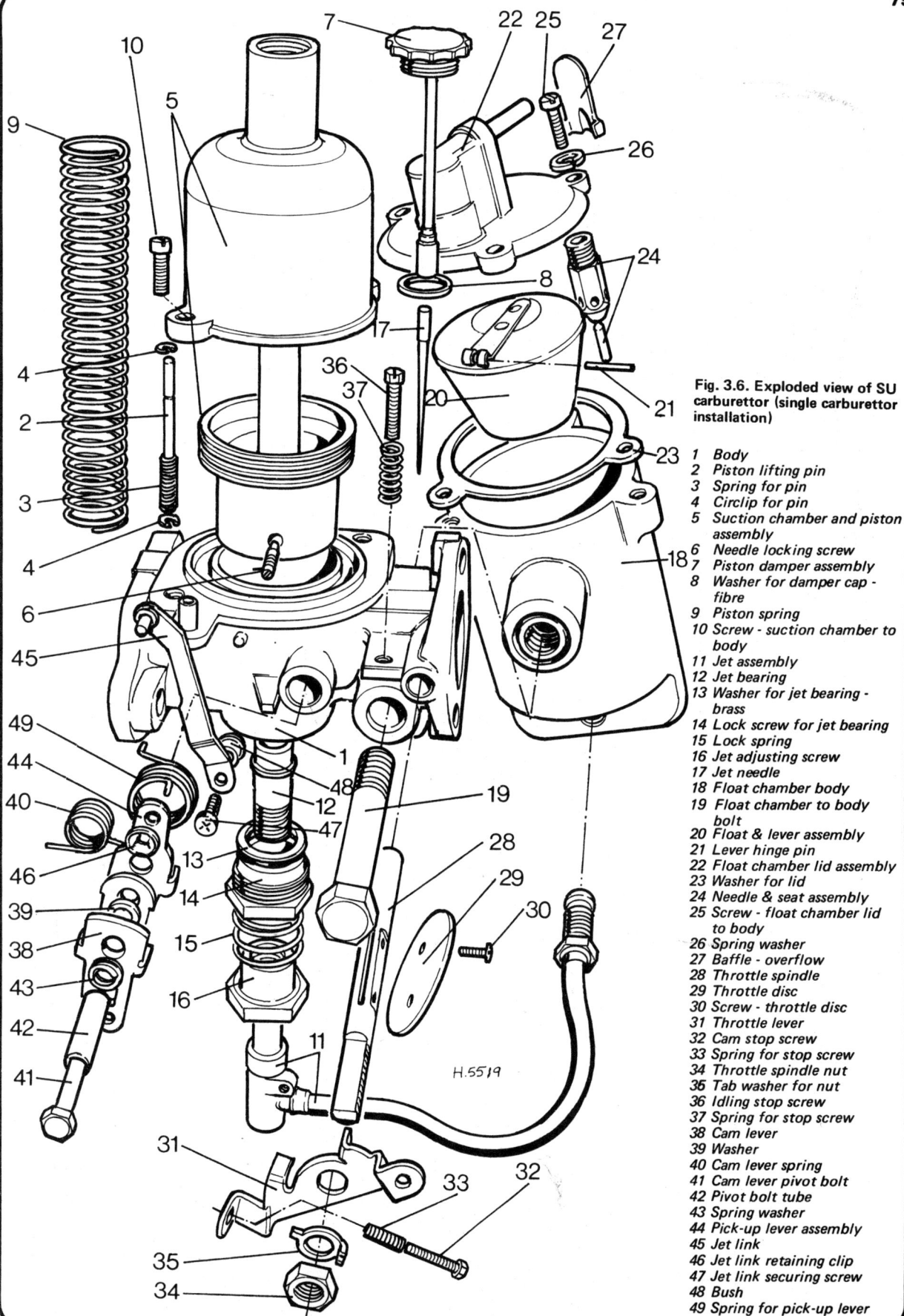

Fig. 3.6. Exploded view of SU carburettor (single carburettor installation)

1 Body
2 Piston lifting pin
3 Spring for pin
4 Circlip for pin
5 Suction chamber and piston assembly
6 Needle locking screw
7 Piston damper assembly
8 Washer for damper cap - fibre
9 Piston spring
10 Screw - suction chamber to body
11 Jet assembly
12 Jet bearing
13 Washer for jet bearing - brass
14 Lock screw for jet bearing
15 Lock spring
16 Jet adjusting screw
17 Jet needle
18 Float chamber body
19 Float chamber to body bolt
20 Float & lever assembly
21 Lever hinge pin
22 Float chamber lid assembly
23 Washer for lid
24 Needle & seat assembly
25 Screw - float chamber lid to body
26 Spring washer
27 Baffle - overflow
28 Throttle spindle
29 Throttle disc
30 Screw - throttle disc
31 Throttle lever
32 Cam stop screw
33 Spring for stop screw
34 Throttle spindle nut
35 Tab washer for nut
36 Idling stop screw
37 Spring for stop screw
38 Cam lever
39 Washer
40 Cam lever spring
41 Cam lever pivot bolt
42 Pivot bolt tube
43 Spring washer
44 Pick-up lever assembly
45 Jet link
46 Jet link retaining clip
47 Jet link securing screw
48 Bush
49 Spring for pick-up lever

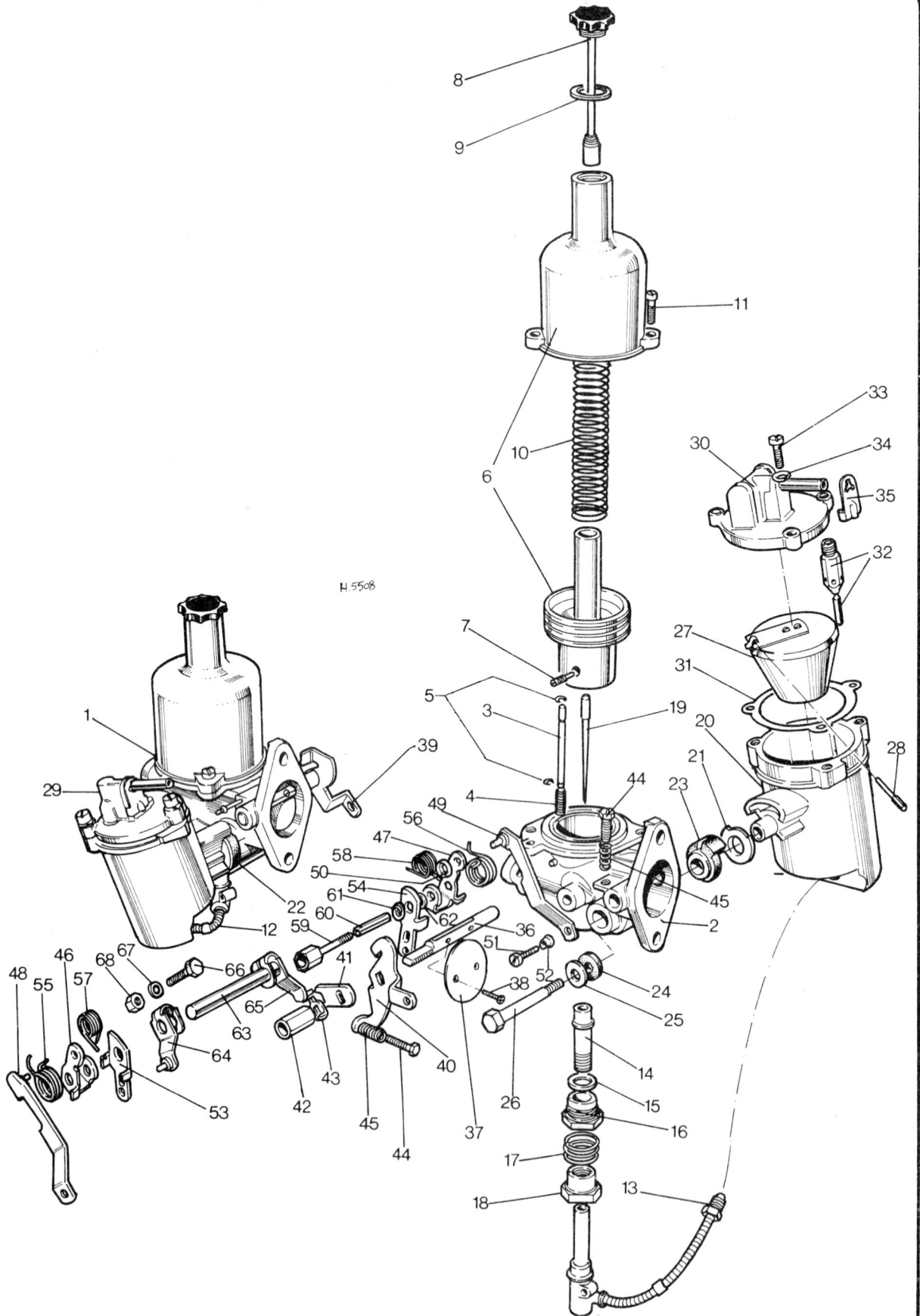

H.5508

Fig. 3.7. Exploded view of SU carburettor (twin carburettor installation)

1   Carburettor body (left)
2   Carburettor body (right)
3   Piston lifting pin
4   Spring
5   Circlip
6   Piston chamber assembly
7   Screw
8   Cap and damper assembly
9   Fibre washer
10 Piston spring
11 Screw
12 Jet assembly (left carburettor)
13 Jet assembly (right carburettor)
14 Bearing
15 Washer
16 Screw
17 Spring
18 Screw
19 Needle
20 Float chamber
21 Support washer
22 Rubber grommet (left carburettor)
23 Rubber grommet (right carburettor)
24 Washer (rubber)
25 Washer (steel)
26 Bolt
27 Float assembly
28 Lever pin
29 Float chamber lid (left carburettor)
30 Float chamber lid (right carburettor)
31 Washer
32 Needle and seat assembly
33 Screw
34 Spring washer
35 Baffle plate
36 Throttle spindle
37 Throttle disc
38 Screw
39 Throttle return lever (left carburettor)
40 Throttle return lever (right carburettor)
41 Lost motion lever
42 Nut
43 Tab washer
44 Throttle screw stop
45 Spring
46 Pick-up lever (left carburettor)
47 Pick-up lever (right carburettor)
48 Link (left carburettor)
49 Link (right carburettor)
50 Washer
51 Screw
52 Bush
53 Cam lever (left carburettor)
54 Cam lever (right carburettor)
55 Pick-up lever spring (left carburettor)
56 Pick-up lever spring (right carburettor)
57 Cam lever spring (left carburettor)
58 Cam lever spring (right carburettor)
59 Bolt
60 Tube
61 Spring washer
62 Distance washer
63 Jet rod
64 Lever and pin assembly (left carburettor)
65 Lever and pin assembly (right carburettor)
66 Bolt
67 Washer
68 Nut

3   If piston sticking is suspected and it is wished to test for this condition, rotate the piston about the centre guide tube at the same time as sliding it up and down inside the dashpot. If any portion of the piston makes contact with the dashpot wall then that portion of the wall must be polished with a metal polish until clearance exists. In extreme cases, fine emery cloth can be used.

The greatest care should be taken to remove only the minimum amount of metal to provide the clearance, as too large a gap will cause air leakage and upset the function of the carburettor. Clean down the walls of the dashpot and the piston rim and ensure that there is no oil on them. A trace of oil may be judiciously applied to the piston rod.

4   If the piston is sticking, under no circumstances try to clear it by trying to alter the tension of the light return spring.

15 SU carburettor - float needle sticking

1   If the float needle sticks, the carburettor will soon run dry and the engine will stop, despite there being fuel in the tank.

The easiest way to check a suspected sticking float needle is to remove the inlet pipe at the carburettor and turn the engine over on the starter motor by pressing on the solenoid rubber button (manual gearbox) or operating the ignition/starter switch (automatic transmission). In the latter case remove the white lead on the ignition coil so that the engine does not start. If fuel spurts from the end of the pipe (direct it towards the ground, into a wad of cloth or into a jar) then the fault is almost certain to be a sticking float needle.

2   Remove the float chamber, dismantle the valve and clean the housing and float chamber out thoroughly.

16 SU carburettor - float chamber flooding

If fuel emerges from the small breather hole in the cover of the float chamber this is known as flooding. It is caused by the float chamber needle not seating properly in its housing: normally this is because a piece of foreign matter is jammed between the needle and needle housing. Alternatively the float may have developed a leak or be maladjusted so that it is holding open the float chamber needle valve even though the chamber is full of petrol. Remove the float chamber cover, clean the needle assembly, check the setting of the float as described later in this chapter and shake the float to verify if any petrol has leaked into it.

17 SU carburettor - water or dirt in carburettor

1   Because of the size of the jet orifice, water or dirt in the carburettor is normally easily cleared. If dirt in the carburettor is suspected, lift the piston assembly and flood the float chamber. The normal level of the fuel should be about 1/16 inch (1.6 mm) below the top of the jet, so that on flooding the carburettor the fuel should flow out of the jet hole.

2   If little or no petrol appears, start the engine (the jet is never completely blocked) and with the throttle butterfly fully open blank off the air intake. This will cause a partial vacuum in the choke tube and help suck out any foreign matter from the jet tube. Release the throttle as soon as the engine speed alters considerably. Repeat this procedure several times, stop the engine and then check the carburettor as described in the first paragraph of this section.

3   If this failed to do the trick then there is no alternative but to remove and blow out the jet.

18 SU carburettor - jet centering

1   This operation is always necessary if the carburettor has been

dismantled: but to check if this is necessary on a carburettor in service, first screw up the jet adjusting nut as far as it will go without forcing it, and lift the piston and then let it fall under its own weight. It should fall onto the bridge making a soft metallic click. Now repeat the above procedure but this time with the adjusting nut screwed right down. If the soft metallic click is not audible in either of the two tests proceed as follows:

2   Disconnect the jet link from the bottom of the jet, and the nylon flexible tube from the underside of the float chamber. Gently slide the jet and the nylon tube from the underside of the carburettor body. Next unscrew the jet adjusting nut and lift away the nut and the locking spring. Refit the adjusting nut without the locking spring and screw it up as far as possible without forcing. Replace the jet and tube but there is no need to reconnect the tube.

3   Slacken the jet locking nut so that it may be rotated with the fingers only. Unscrew the piston damper and lift away the damper. Gently press the piston down onto the bridge and tighten the locknut. Lift the piston using the lifting pin and check that it is able to fall freely under its own weight. Now lower the adjusting nut and check once again. If this time there is a difference in the two metallic clicks, repeat the centering procedure until the sound is the same for both tests.

4   Gently remove the jet and unscrew the adjusting nut. Refit the locking spring and jet adjusting nut. Top up the damper with oil, if necessary, and replace the damper. Connect the nylon flexible tube to the underside of the float chamber and finally reconnect the jet link.

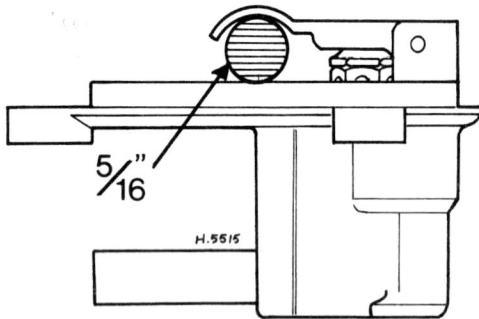

19 SU carburettor - float chamber fuel level adjustment

1   It is essential that the fuel level in the float chamber is always correct as otherwise excessive fuel consumption may occur. Carburettors fitted to the later models have non-adjustable floats.

2   *(Early models only)*. With the carburettor fitted to the engine and the float chamber full of petrol remove the piston dashpot assembly

3   Check that the level of fuel in the jet is about 1/16 inch (1.6 mm) below the top of the jet. If it is above or below this level it may be adjusted by bending the float lever and resetting as shown in Figs. 3.8 or 3.9.

20 SU carburettor - needle replacement

1   Should it be necessary to fit a new needle, first remove the piston and suction chamber assembly, marking the chamber for correct reassembly in its original position.

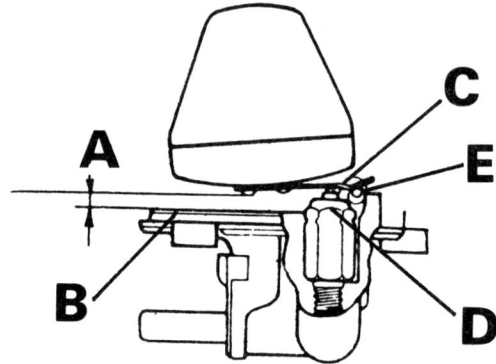

Fig. 3.9. Method of checking correct adjustment of float lever - later carburettors (Sec. 19)

A   *0.125 to 0.1875 in (3.18 to 4.76 mm)*
B   *Machined lip*
C   *Angle of float lever*
D   *Float needle and seat assembly*
E   *Lever hinge pin*

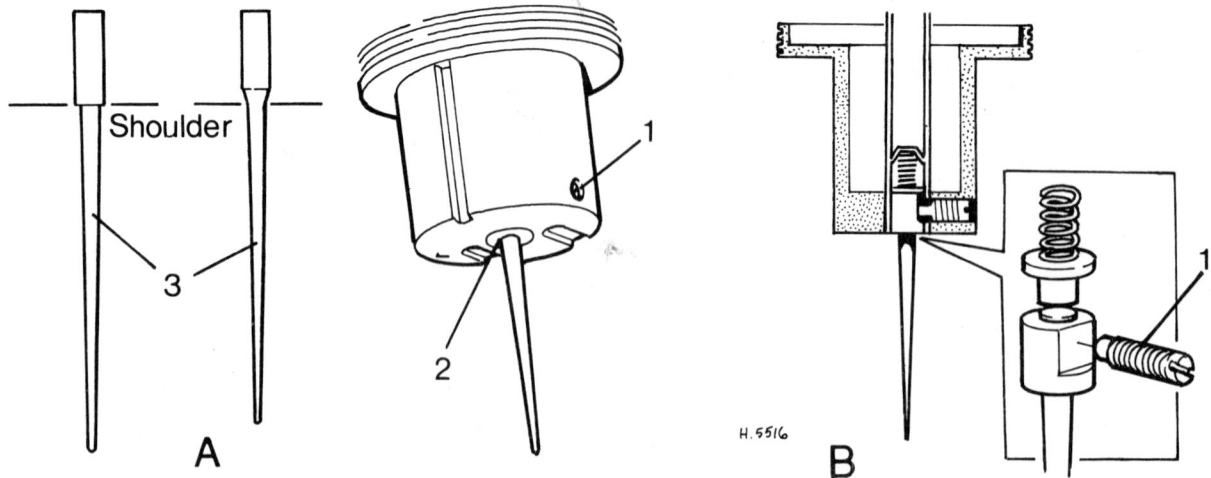

Fig. 3.8. Method of setting correct clearance of the float lever - early carburettors (Sec. 19)

Fig. 3.10. Needle location in piston (Sec. 20)

A   *Fixed needle*   B   *Spring loaded needle*

1   *Needle securing screw*
2   *Needle shoulder flush with bottom of piston*
3   *Needle (two types of shoulder are in use)*

2 *Fixed needle type.* Slacken the needle clamping screw and withdraw the needle from the underside of the piston.

3 *Swing needle type.* Slacken the needle clamping screw and withdraw the needle, guide and spring from the underside of the piston.

4 Refitting the needle (or needle assembly) is the reverse sequence to removal. Ensure that the shoulder or guide is fitted flush with the face of the piston. With the swing needle ensure the flat on the guide is positioned adjacent to the needle guide locking screw.

21 SU carburettor - adjustment and tuning

1 To adjust and tune the SU carburettor proceed as follows: Check the colour of the exhaust at idling speed with the choke fully in. If the exhaust tends to be black and the tail pipe interior is also black, it is a fair indication that the mixture is too rich. If the exhaust is colourless and the deposit in the exhaust pipe is very light grey it is likely that the mixture is too weak. This condition may also be accompanied by intermittent misfiring, while too rich a mixture will be associated with 'hunting'. Ideally the exhaust should be colourless with a medium grey pipe deposit.

2 The exhaust pipe deposit should only be checked after a good run of at least 20 miles. Idling in city traffic and stop/start motoring is bound to produce excessive dark exhaust pipe deposits.

3 Once the engine has reached its normal operating temperature, detach the carburettor air cleaner.

4 Only two adjustments are provided on the SU carburettor. Idling speed is governed by the throttle adjusting screw and the mixture strength by the jet adjusting nut. The SU carburettor is correctly adjusted for the whole of its engine revolution range when the idling mixture strength is correct.

5 To adjust the mixture set the engine to run at about 1000 rpm by screwing in the throttle adjusting screw.

6 Check the mixture strength by lifting the piston of the carburettor approximately 1/32 inch (0.79 mm) with the piston lifting pin so as to disturb the air flow as little as possible. If

a) The speed of the engine increases appreciably the mixture is too rich.

b) The engine speed immediately decreases, the mixture is too weak.

c) The engine speed increases very slightly, the mixture is correct.

To weaken the mixture, rotate the adjusting nut which is at the bottom of the underside of the carburettor, in an anti-clockwise direction, ie. upwards. Only turn the adjusting nut a flat at a time and check the mixture strength between each turn. It is likely that there will be a slight increase or decrease in rpm after the mixture adjustment has been made so the throttle idling screw should be turned so that the engine idles at the recommended speed (see Specifications).

22 SU carburettor - synchronisation of twin carburettors

First ensure that the mixture is correct in each instrument. With twin SU carburettors, in addition to the mixture strength being correct for each instrument, the idling suction must be equal on both. It is best to use a vacuum synchronising device such as the 'Motor Meter synchro tester'. If this is not available it is possible to obtain fairly accurate synchronisation by listening to the hiss made by the air flow into the intake throats of each carburettor using a piece of rubber or plastic hose.

The aim is to adjust the throttle butterfly disc so that an equal amount of air enters each carburettor. Loosen the throttle shaft levers on the throttle shaft which connects the two throttle disc splines. Listen to the hiss from each carburettor and if a

difference in intensity is noticed between them, then unscrew the throttle adjusting screw on the other carburettor until the hiss from both the carburettors is the same.

With a vacuum synchronisation device all that it is necessary to do is to place the instrument over the mouth of each carburettor in turn and adjust the adjusting screws until the reading on the gauge is identical for both carburettors.

Tighten the levers on the interconnecting linkage to connect the throttle disc of the two carburettors together, at the same time holding down the throttle adjusting screws against their idling stops. Synchronisation of the two carburettors is now complete.

23 SU carburettor - twin carburettor linkage adjustment

On models fitted with twin carburetters there must be a gap between the lost motion lever on the throttle spindle and the lever and pin assembly so that when there is no pressure on the accelerator the throttle butterfly valve will be in the fully closed position.

To make sure this clearance exists, first disconnect the choke control. Then loosen the nuts on the bolts which clamp the throttle shaft levers to the throttle shaft. Insert a 0.012 in (.305 mm) feeler gauge blade between the choke control connecting rod, and the accelerator shaft stop. Press down each throttle shaft lever in turn until the pin in the lever lies lightly on the lower arm of the fork in the carburettor throttle lever. Tighten

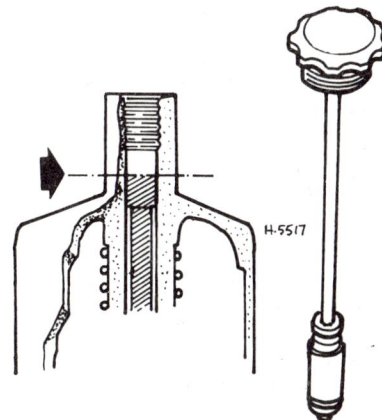

Fig. 3.11. Correct damper oil level

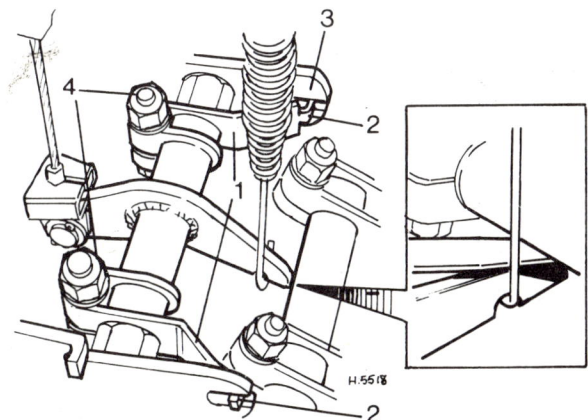

Fig. 3.12. Setting a clearance between the throttle shaft operating lever and the choke interconnecting spindle (twin carburettor installation) (Sec. 23)

1 Throttle shaft levers   3 Throttle spindle lever fork
2 Lever pins   4 Throttle shaft lever clamps

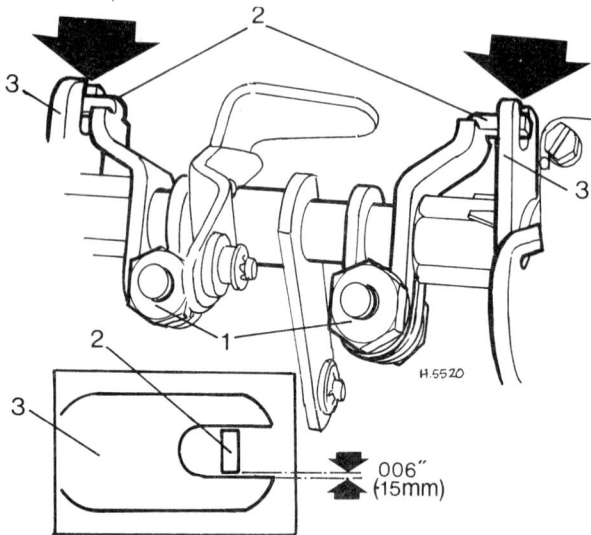

Fig. 3.13. Setting a clearance between the throttle shaft operating levers and spindle forks (9.71 : 1 CR engines) (Sec. 23)

1 Throttle shaft lever clamps
2 Lever and pins
3 Throttle spindle forks

the nuts and bolts (Figs. 3.12 and 3.13).

There should now be a working clearance between the throttle shaft lever pins and the slots when the feeler gauge blade is removed. Reconnect the choke control.

24 SU carburettor - automatic transmission models

The HS4 carburettor (see Specifications) is fitted to models equipped with automatic transmission. The sequence for dismantling and reassembly is identical to that described in previous Sections. The only differences are in the removal and replacement and adjustment sequences. These are described in the following two Sections.

25 SU carburettor (automatic transmission) - removal and replacement

1 Remove the air cleaner as described in Section 29.
2 Disconnect the choke and throttle control cables, the distributor vacuum advance pipe and the fuel inlet hose from the carburettor.
3 Detach the governor control rod fork end from the throttle lever.
4 Undo and remove the securing nuts and spring washers and lift the carburettor and cable abutment plate from the inlet manifold.
5 Refitting the carburettor is the reverse sequence to removal. Always fit new joint washers between the manifold face and the abutment plate and carburettor flange.

26 SU carburettor (automatic transmission) - adjustment

1 Refer to Section 21, and follow the instructions given but with the following exceptions:
2 Move the selector lever to the 'N' position and firmly apply the handbrake.
3 Start and run the engine until it reaches its normal operating

Fig. 3.14. Throttle damper setting (Sec. 27)
Depress the damper with a feeler gauge between the lever pad and damper plunger

temperature.
4 Adjust the jet position, as described in Section 21.
5 With the carburettor correctly tuned now adjust the throttle adjusting screw until a maximum idling speed of 650 rpm is reached (An electric tachometer will be of benefit here).
6 Slowly pull out the choke control to the maximum fast idle position. Check and adjust if necessary the fast idle adjustment screw to obtain a maximum fast idle speed of 1050 rpm.
7 Push in the choke control knob and recheck the idling speed.
8 Refer to Chapter 6 and check the adjustment of the governor control rod.

27 SU carburettor throttle damper (1275 cc engine) - adjustment

1 Slacken off the clamp nut on the damper operating lever and insert a 0.020 in (0.508 mm) feeler gauge between the damper plunger and the damper operating lever.
2 Ensure that the carburettor butterfly is fully closed then depress the operating lever until the plunger is fully depressed.
3 Tighten up the clamp bolt on the operating lever and remove the feeler gauge. If it is found that damping is excessive, increase the feeler gauge by 0.010 in (0.254 mm) at a time until satisfactory damping is obtained. Similarly, if damping is insufficient, reduce the setting by 0.010 in (0.254 mm) and reset the operating lever.

28 In-line fuel filter - removal and replacement

1 The line fuel filter must be replaced every 12,000 miles (20,000 km).
2 To remove the filter, check that the ignition is switched off, unscrew the clips at either end of the filter and pull off the fuel pipes.
3 Discard the old filter and fit a new one in the reverse manner.
4 Having fitted the new filter, switch on the ignition to activate the fuel pump and carefully check for leaks. Start the engine and check for leaks again.

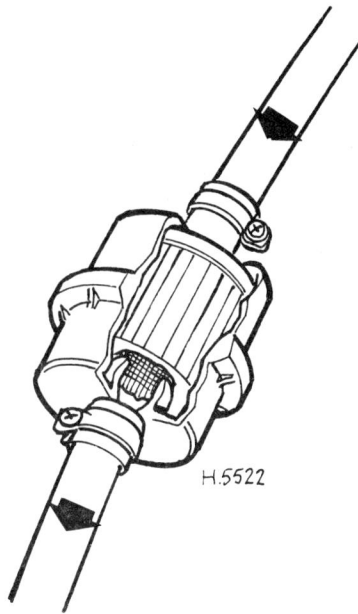

Fig. 3.15. Fuel line filter - arrow shows flow of fuel (Sec. 28)

29 Air cleaner - removal and replacement

1 Unscrew the wing nut(s) from the top of the air cleaner and lift off the cover. (photo).

2 The element(s) may now be lifted away. (photo).

3 Disconnect the rocker cover to air cleaner breather pipe on cars without closed circuit breathing.

4 Detach the throttle return spring when fitted.

5 Lift away the air cleaner assembly body (photo).

6 If it is necessary to remove the air cleaner manifold to the carburettor bodies (other than on 1098 cc single carburettor applications) undo and remove the securing screws.

7 Refitting the air cleaner is the reverse sequence to removal.

8 To avoid carburettor icing in winter the air cleaner intakes should be positioned close to the exhaust manifold. The position of the air cleaner intake is altered by slackening the securing clip on the pipe adjacent to the air cleaner body.

9 For the best performance in summer the intake should be moved as far away from the manifold as possible.

30 Fuel tank - removal and replacement

1 Jack-up the rear of the car by about 18 inches (457 mm) and

support on axle stands located under the subframe. Remove the jack.

2 Remove the tank filter cap and from underneath the car unscrew the drain plug from the tank, draining the contents into a suitable container **Note: Ensure that suitable safety precautions are taken.** When empty, replace the plug and washer securely.

3 Working in the luggage compartment release the hose securing clips and detach the hose from the fuel tank inlet.

4 On models fitted with evaporative loss control equipment remove the two expansion pipe connections from the top of the tank.

5 Standard models. Disconnect the vent pipe.

6 Disconnect and remove the exhaust tail pipe and silencer assembly.

7 Disconnect the fuel outlet pipe at its union with the tank, the clips securing the fuel delivery pipe and the vapour pipe (evaporative loss control equipment models) from either side of the fuel tank.

8 Support the fuel tank and remove the set screws securing the tank to the underside of the body.

9 Lower the tank sufficiently to allow access to the fuel tank sender unit. Detach the Lucar connector.

10 The tank can now be fully lowered and removed from under the car.

11 Refitting the fuel tank is the reverse sequence to removal. Ensure all clips are fully tightened.

31 Fuel tank - cleaning

With time it is likely that sediment will collect in the bottom of the fuel tank. Condensation, resulting in rust and other impurities, is sometimes found in the fuel tank of a car more than three or four years old.

When the tank is removed, it should be vigorously flushed out and turned upside down, and if facilities are available, steam cleaned.

32 Fuel tank sender unit - removal and replacement

1 Disconnect the earth lead from the battery (positive terminal) and remove the petrol tank as described in the previous section.

2 Undo the locking ring which holds the gauge unit to the tank (BLMC have a special gauge locking ring tool, Part No. '18G 1001' for this operation) and carefully lift the complete unit away, ensuring that the float lever is not bent or damaged in the process.

3 If the tool is not available it is possible to remove the lock ring using two crossed screwdrivers.

4 Replacement of the unit is a reversal of the above process. To ensure a fuel tight joint, scrape both the tank and sender gauge mating flanges clean, and always use a new joint washer.

29.1 Removal of wing nuts

29.2 Lifting away element

29.5 Removal of air cleaner assembly body

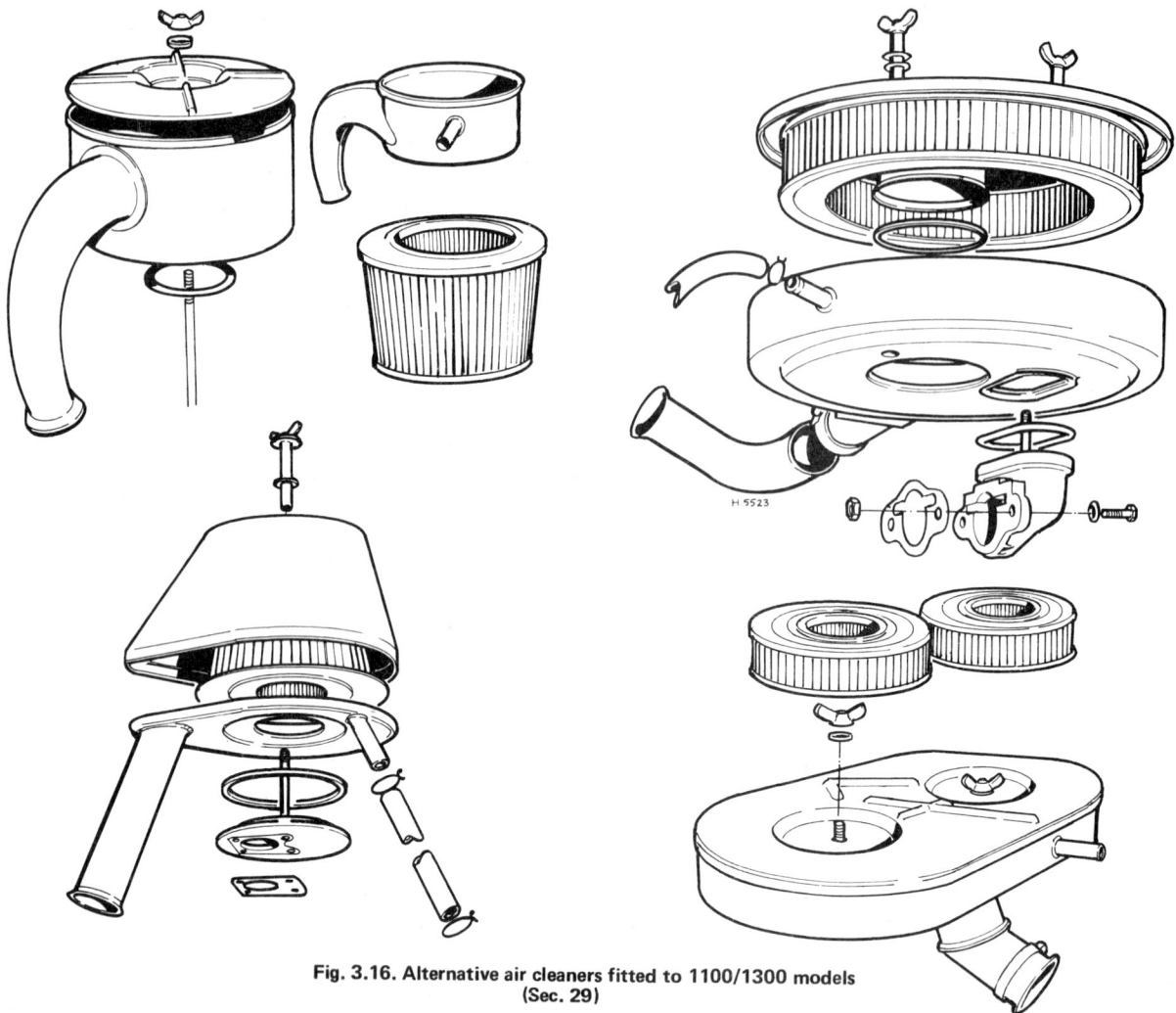

Fig. 3.16. Alternative air cleaners fitted to 1100/1300 models
(Sec. 29)

33 Fuel tank filler extension - removal and replacement

1 The filler extension may be removed independently of the fuel tank.
2 Slacken the securing hose clip and pull the filler outwards from the wings sufficiently to allow the grommet to be pushed back into the luggage compartment.
3 On models fitted with evaporative loss control equipment remove the expansion tank and the expansion pipe from the top of the filler.
4 Remove the filler cap and withdraw the filler extension from inside the luggage compartment.
5 Refitting the filler extension is the reverse sequence to removal. Ensure all clips are fully tightened.

34 Exhaust emission control system - general description

Due to the increasing concern of atmospheric pollution in various countries and the appearance of new regulations apertaining to motor cars, certain modifications have to be made to either the engines, the exhaust system or the fuel tank breathing system. In some cases a combination of two or three modifications has to be incorporated, depending entirely on the local regulations relative to the country in which the car is being operated.

The modifications are not at present enforced - in countries where the regulations exists - for visitors cars.

The three systems are:
1 Crankcase emission control.
2 Exhaust emission control.
3 Fuel evaporative loss control.

It is important for the reader to appreciate that electronic engine tune equipment is very necessary when finally setting the various engine adjustments ie. carburettor settings or ignition timing, otherwise the engine and exhaust emission control modifications will not operate efficiently and could affect the overall engine performance.

At the end of this section are full details for diagnosing faults and these should be used as a guide to tracing the fault, but the rectification may have to be left to the local agents who will have the necessary servicing equipment.

The Austin America and certain other models are fitted with an exhaust emission control system that conforms to the various laws governing the amount of carbon monoxide and hydro-carbons emitting from the exhaust outlets of cars in the USA.

The system fitted to the Austin America allows a maximum of 3.5% of carbon monoxide to be emitted.

35 Exhaust emission control - crankcase emission

1 The valve control portion of the crankcase emission control comprises a diaphragm control valve which is connected by rubber hoses to the inlet manifold and the crankcase. The outlet

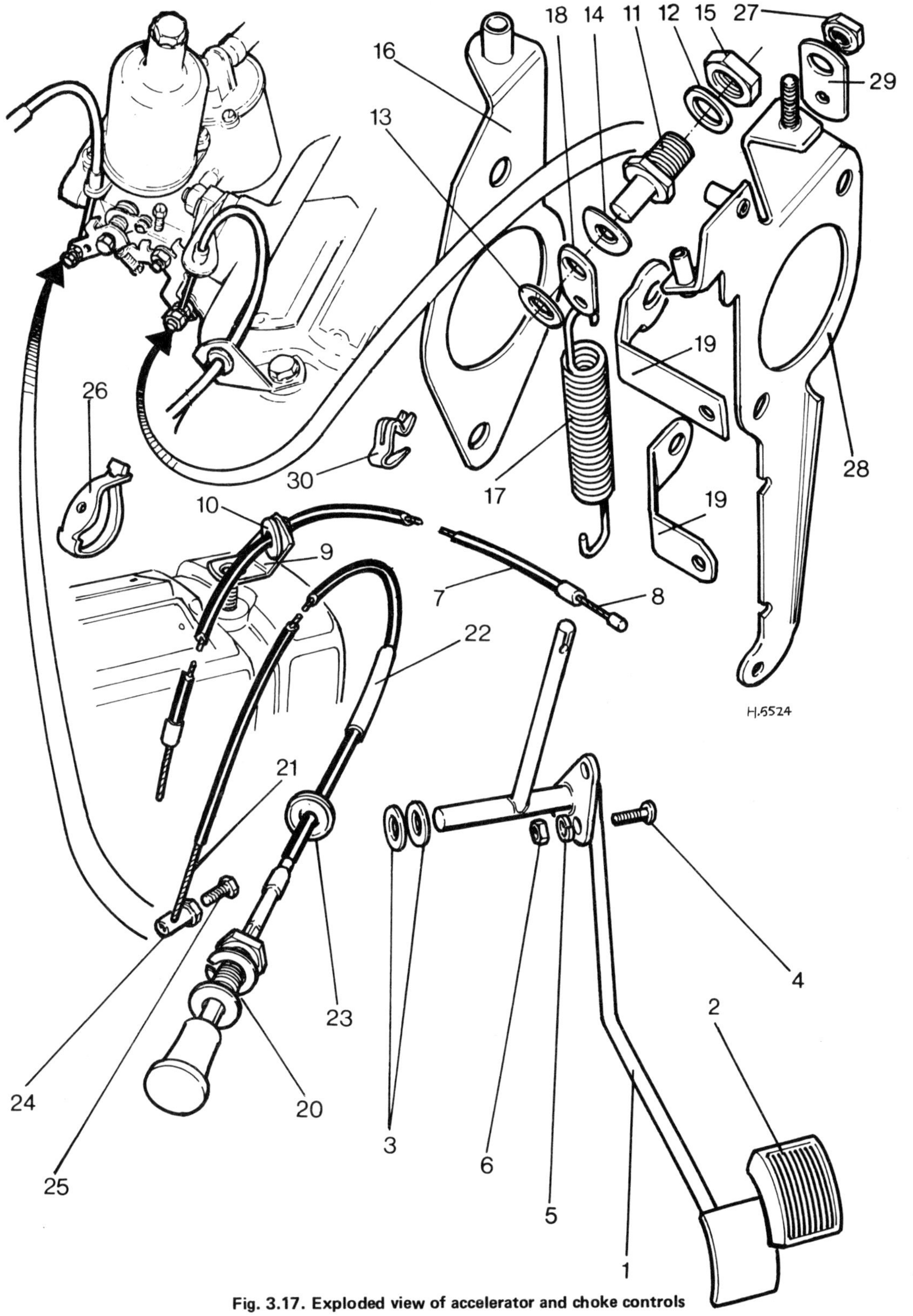

Fig. 3.17. Exploded view of accelerator and choke controls

1	Accelerator pedal	9	Cable bracket	17	Throttle return spring	24	Pin
2	Rubber pedal pad	10	Grommet	18	Tag	25	Screw pin
3	Plain washers	11	Pin	19	Manifold end tag	26	Cable strap
4	Screw	12	Large plain washer	19a	Alternative end tag	27	Pin nut
5	Spring washer	13	Small plain washer	20	Choke cable assembly	28	Abutment bracket
6	Nut	14	Anti-rattle washer	21	Choke cable assembly		
7	Accelerator cable assembly	15	Nut	22	Rubber sleeve	29	End tag
8	Inner cable	16	Throttle abutment bracket	23	Cable grommet	30	Clip

automatic models (27, 28, 29)

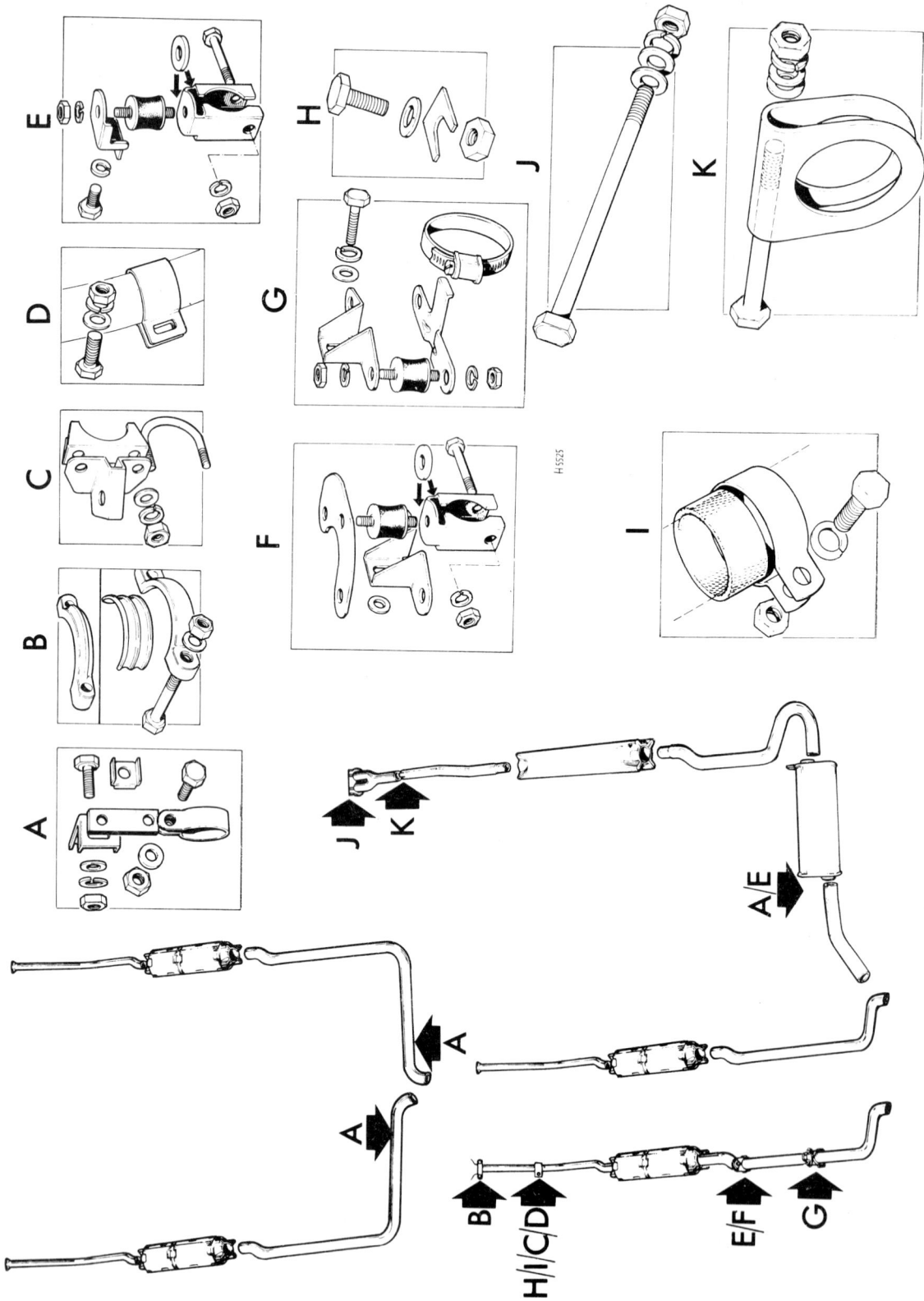

Fig. 3.18. Selection of exhaust systems that have been fitted to 1100/1300 models

H 5525

connection from the crankcase incorporates an oil separator which prevents oil being drawn up to the emission control valve with the oil vapour. A restricted orifice 9/64 inch (3.6 mm) diameter in the oil filler cap on the rocker cover acts as a source of fresh air into the crankcase, as the oil vapour or piston blow-by gas is drawn up into the inlet manifold by normal manifold depression.

2 The emission control valve diaphragm is spring loaded to vary the opening to the inlet manifold depending on the depression within the manifold. When the inlet manifold depression decreases, or alternatively the crankcase pressure increases, the diaphragm opens and allows the oil vapour or piston blow-by gases to be drawn into the inlet manifold.

3 When the engine speed is low or labouring under load the diaphragm automatically closes the valve and therefore restricts the flow of oil vapour or piston blow-by gases into the inlet manifold which will therefore prevent the weakening of the petrol/air charge to the cylinders.

4 The carburettor control portion of the system comprises the engine breather outlet which is connected by rubber hoses to the controlled depression chamber, the part between the piston and the throttle disc butterfly valve of the carburettor installation.

5 The oil vapour or piston blow-by gas is drawn from the crankcase by the depression in the controlled depression chamber, through a special oil separator fitted into the engine crankcase connection and thereafter to the inlet manifold. Fresh air is supplied to the crankcase through a special oil filler cap with a small filter incorporated in it.

6 The carburettor control system - incorporating evaporative loss control equipment uses all the parts from the carburettor control system, with the exception of the special oil filler cap. The system is shown in Fig. 3.19. The fresh air requirement for the crankcase is drawn through a filtered absorption canister of the evaporative loss control system fitted to the rocker cover. A special restrictor valve in the rocker cover connection acts to reduce the air flow to ensure that there is a depression in the crankcase at all times.

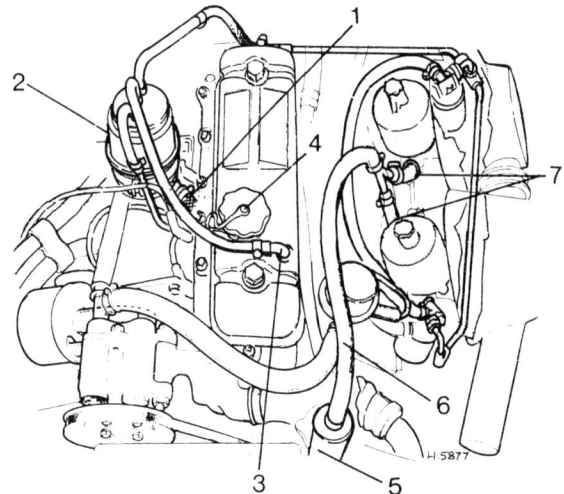

36 Control valve - testing and servicing

1 With the engine at normal operating temperature and running at an even idle speed, remove the oil filler cap. If the engine speed rises slightly this indicates that the valve is functioning correctly. On the other hand if the speed does not rise it is an indication that the control valve requires servicing.

2 The oil filler cap must be renewed every 12,000 miles (20,000 km) or 12 months whichever is sooner.

3 The control valve may be removed for servicing or renewal by disconnecting the two rubber hoses. To dismantle, ease off the spring clip and lift away the cover plate, diaphragm, metering valve and spring.

4 The parts may be cleaned in petrol or paraffin and if deposits are difficult to remove allow to soak overnight. The diaphragm should be cleaned in methylated spirits.

5 All parts should be examined for signs of wear and new parts fitted as necessary.

6 During reassembly ensure that the metering valve fits correctly into its guide and also that the diaphragm is correctly seated. Finally test the valve as previously described.

7 If operation of the system is suspect check the rubber hoses and connections for leaks or blockage.

37 Exhaust emission control - exhaust port air injection

Air under pressure from a pump driven by a 'V' belt is passed to each exhaust valve port via a special air injection manifold. The system is shown in Fig. 3.20. Blow back from high pressure exhaust gases into the air injection system is prevented by a check valve in the air delivery pipe.

The air pump also supplies air through a valve called a 'Gulp

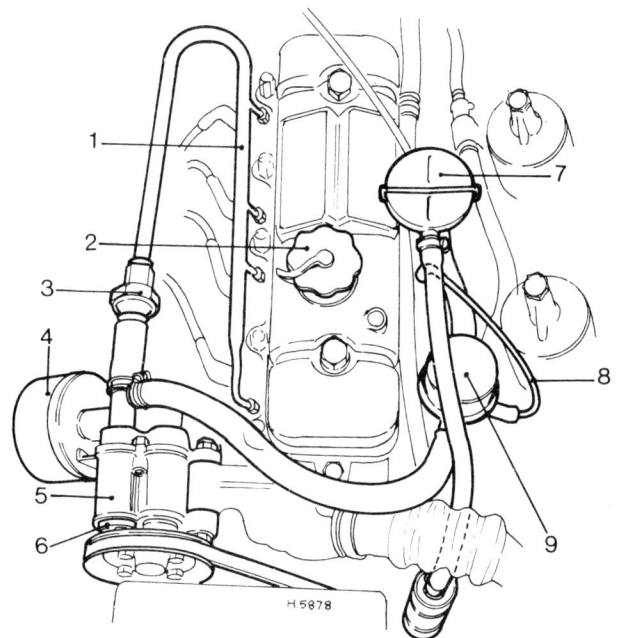

Fig. 3.19. Carburettor control system - incorporating evaporative loss control (Sec. 35)

1 Ventilation air intake
2 Absorption canister
3 Restricted connection to rocker cover
4 Sealed oil filler cap
5 Oil separator
6 Breather hose
7 Carburettor chamber connections

Fig. 3.20. View of the engine emission control layout (Sec. 37)

1 Air manifold
2 Filtered oil filler cap
3 Non-return check valve
4 Air pump air cleaner
5 Air pump
6 Relief valve
7 Crankcase emission control valve
8 Vacuum sensing tube
9 Gulp valve

valve' to the inlet manifold to provide air during deceleration and overrun conditions, thus overriding the carburettor.

The air pump of the rotary vane type is mounted on the front of the cylinder head and is driven from the water pump double pulley. An adjustable lower mounting is fitted to provide adequate belt tension adjustment. Clean air via a dry type renewable element filter is drawn into the pump and is discharged through the pump discharge port. A relief valve is fitted to the discharge port to prevent excessive pressure build up. A check valve is fitted between the air pump and injection manifold which is designed to prevent any exhaust gases passing to the air pump, causing it to be damaged. It closes if the air pressure drops whilst the engine is running, as for instance if the drive belt breaks.

As previously mentioned there is a gulp valve fitted to the inlet manifold and this is connected to the pump discharge line and controls the flow of air for weakening the air/petrol charge present in the inlet manifold immediately after the throttle is closed after full throttle operation. There is a little pipe called a 'Sensing pipe' which connects the inlet manifold depression direct to the underside of the diaphragm and through a small bleed hole to the upper side. Any sudden increases in inlet manifold depression occurring immediately after complete throttle closure acts on the underside of the diaphragm and the valve is open and air is admitted to the inlet manifold. The little bleed hole will allow for any differences in inlet manifold depression acting on the diaphragm to equalise, causing the valve to close. It may be found that on some engines there is a restrictor fitted between the air pump discharge connection and the gulp valve to check any engine surging whilst the gulp valve is in operation.

The carburettors are specially modified incorporating a limit valve in the carburettor throttle disc which will control the inlet manifold depression, so that under conditions of a high inlet manifold depression the petrol/air charge entering the combustion chambers is in the correct proportions for complete burning. It is important that the carburettors are set exactly right and for this electronic engine tune equipment is necessary.

38 Air pump - servicing

1 The air pump is pivot mounted so allowing adjustment to the drive belt to be made. A total deflection of ½ inch should be evident under normal hand pressure at the mid-way point of the longest run of the belt between the two pulleys.
2 To adjust the tension of the belt first slacken the air pump mounting bolt (1) Fig. 3.21 and also the two adjusting link bolts (2). Lift up the air pump, using the hand only, until the correct tension is achieved and tighten the adjusting bolts and mounting bolt using a torque wrench set at 10 lb fft (1.382 kg fm).

3 As special equipment is necessary to test and service the air pump it is recommended that this item be left to the local agents.

39 Check valve - removal, testing and replacement

1 To remove the check valve, first disconnect the air supply hose at the check valve union and holding the air manifold connection firmly in the hand to prevent it twisting, unscrew the check valve. Refitting is the reverse sequence to removal.
2 To test the check valve, using the mouth only, blow through each end of the valve in turn when it should be found that air will only pass through the valve when blown from the air supply hose end. If any air passes through when blown from the air manifold connection it is an indication that there is an internal fault and the valve must be renewed. It is important that a compressed air jet is *not* used for this test.

40 Air manifold and injectors - testing and servicing

1 To test the air manifold and injectors first disconnect the air manifold from the cylinder head connections. Then slacken the air supply hose clip located at the check valve connection. Very carefully rotate the air manifold about its connection axis until the injector connections are easily accessible. Tighten the air supply hose clip again. Start the engine and allow to run at normal idle speed. It should be observed that there is a steady flow of air from each of the air manifold connection tubes. If however the flow is either non-existent or equal from any of the air manifold connection tubes, the manifold should be completely removed and the obstruction cleared using a compressed air jet. With the engine running again at normal idle speed check that there is exhaust gas passing from each cylinder head injector. It is important however that the injectors are free in their cylinder head locations and that they are not displaced during testing.
2 Should an injector be blocked with carbon it may be cleaned by using a 1/8 inch drill in a hand drill and carefully drilling down the injector bore ensuring that the tip of the drill does not touch the valve stem when passing through the end of the injector. Any dust remaining may be cleared using a compressed air jet.

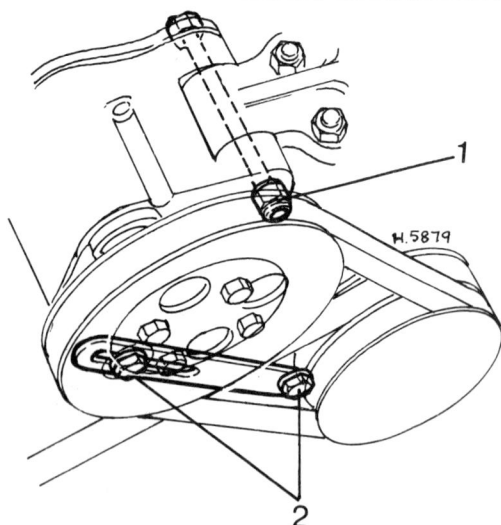

Fig. 3.21. Air pump drive belt adjustment (Sec. 38)

1 Pump mounting bolt   2 Adjusting link bolts

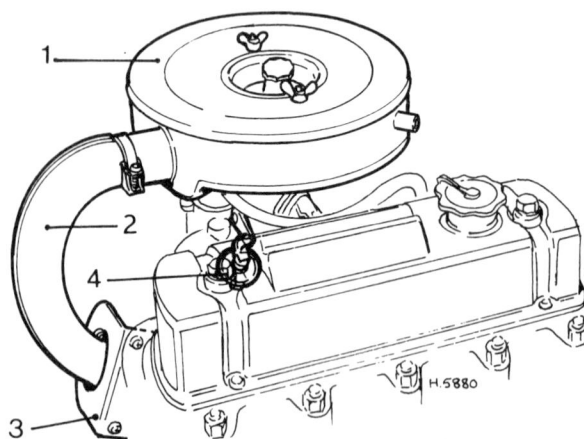

Fig. 3.22. Engine modification exhaust emission control system (Sec. 42)
Note position of air intake for low temperature conditions

1 Air cleaner   3 Manifold shroud
2 Air intake tube   4 Throttle damper

41 Gulp valve and limit valve (inlet manifold depression) - testing

If the operation of the gulp valve or limit valve is suspect the car should be taken to the local agents as accurate gauges are required for testing.

42 Exhaust emission control - engine modification system

This system as shown in Fig. 3.22 is used with a high compression ratio engine fitted with a specially modified carburettor installation.

The carburettor must be specially and accurately tuned to give maximum and most efficient engine performance and this can be done only by using electronic engine tune equipment. A limit valve is built into the carburettor throttle disc so that the inlet manifold depression is limited when under high inlet manifold depression conditions and the petrol/air charge into the combustion chamber is at the correct proportion for complete burning. Also a throttle damper is fitted to act on the throttle lever as it returns to the closed position when the accelerator pedal is released. This ensures a gradual closing of the throttle valve which will give a smooth and progressive deceleration of the car. This is adjustable but should be left to the local agent if the operation of the damper is suspect.

With cars operating in very low temperature conditions the air cleaner intake is positioned in a metal shroud formed over part of the exhaust manifold so that air drawn through by the air cleaner to the carburettor installation is warmed. The air intake may be repositioned away from the exhaust manifold for cars operating in warmer conditions by first slackening the intake tube retaining clip followed by removing the two air cleaner wing nuts. The intake tube can now be extracted from the exhaust manifold shroud and from the air cleaner. Refit the intake tube with its entry positioned adjacent to the rocker cover. Finally replace the wing nuts and tighten the securing clip.

The carburettors that are fitted to cars which have had the engines modified for exhaust emission control regulation purposes are accurately set and it is very important that they are not interchanged or substitute parts fitted. Furthermore resetting and tuning can only be done when the engine is connected up to electronic engine tune equipment, so that any work to be done in the way of testing or adjusting or overhauling the carburettors must be left to the local agents.

43 Exhaust emission control - evaporative loss control

The objective of this system is to collect any petrol vapour that could have evaporated from the petrol in the tank. Also as an ultimate, on the twin carburettor installations even the petrol in the carburettor float chambers is vented to the absorption unit (8) Fig. 3.23. The idea is that the petrol vapour is stored in an absorption canister (Fig. 3.24), whilst the engine is stationary but when the engine is restarted the vapour is passed through the crankcase emission control system to the combustion chambers. With the car in motion any vapours are automatically drawn to the crankcase emission control system. A special ventilation system comprises tubes on the fuel tank and ensures that petrol vapour is vented through the control system when the car is parked on the slope. An expansion tank (4) Fig. 3.23 is of suitable capacity to prevent any spillage of fuel caused by a full tank of petrol becoming heated due to rises in ambient temperatures. The expansion tank connections are so positioned that it is not possible for liquid petrol to find its way to the storage canister (8). Both the petrol filler cap and the oil filler cap seal the complete system and to ensure correct and reliable operation they must always be correctly fitted.

The absorption canister, Fig. 3.24 is located in the engine compartment and contains a special carbon grain with filter pad at each end so that ventilating air is filtered and the carbon grain

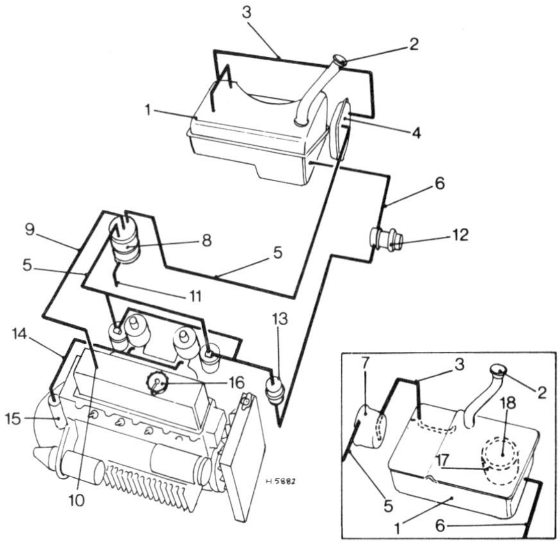

Fig. 3.23. Evaporative loss control system (Sec. 43)

1	Fuel tank	10	Restricted connection
2	Sealed fuel/filler cap	11	Air vent
3	Expansion/vapour line	12	Fuel pump
4	Expansion tank	13	Fuel line filter
5	Vapour pipe	14	Breather pipe
6	Fuel pipe	15	Oil separator
7	Separation tank	16	Sealed oil filler cap
8	Absorption canister	17	Capacity limiting tank
9	Purge line	18	Air lock bleed

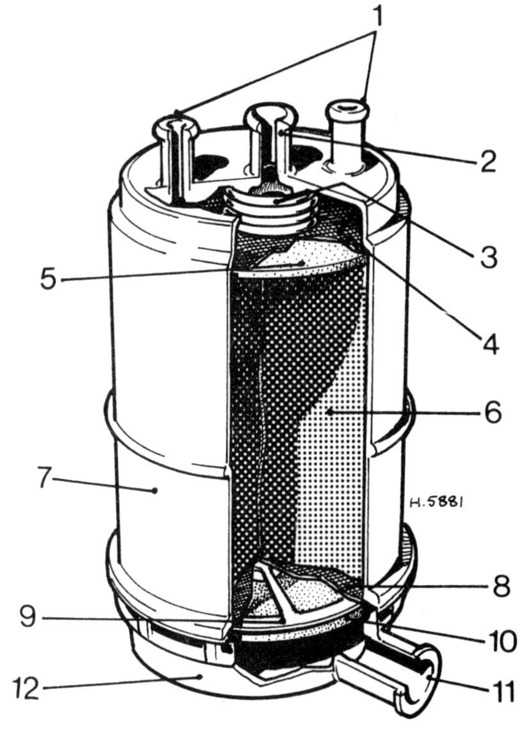

Fig. 3.24. Component parts of absorption canister (Sec. 43)

1	Vapour pipe connections	7	Canister
2	Purge pipe connection	8	Gauze
3	Spring	9	Retainer
4	Gauze	10	Filter pad
5	Filter pad	11	Air vent connection
6	Charcoal granules	12	End cap

keeps in position. The ventilation air filter pad (10) is renewable by unscrewing the end cap (12). The vapour tubes from the petrol tank, the carburettor float chambers and also the surge line from the engine crankcase breather system are connected to the three unions located at the top of the canister. The single union at the bottom of the canister is the connection for the ventilating air tube.

Any petrol vapour enters the canister through the vapour tubes and is absorbed and held by the charcoal. Once the engine is started air is drawn by the crankcase emission control system through the ventilation tube and into the canister. With the air passing between the carbon granules the petrol vapours are given up and are carried with the air through the crankcase emission system to the combustion chambers.

Two methods are used to ensure adequate capacity to accommodate petrol displaced by expansion due to high ambient temperature. Either a separate expansion tank of suitable capacity is fitted, and it is into this that any excess petrol flows, or as an alternate system an air lock chamber is designed into the petrol tank which will stop the tank being filled to maximum fluid capacity so providing additional space for expansion as it occurs. See inset Fig. 3.23.

To act as a safeguard to stop dirt finding its way into the carburettor float chamber and unseating the little needle valve, a small fuel line filter is fitted into the system, this being shown in Fig. 3.15.

A small temperature sensitive valve is sometimes fitted next to the carburettor and the valve is connected between the air cleaner and the controlled depression chamber of the carburettor. If the under bonnet temperatures are abnormally high, causing the petrol to be excessively warm, the valve opens and allows a small quantity of air to pass into the carburettor by passing the jet assembly in the carburettor bridge. This air jet will weaken the charge which would otherwise gradually richen by the vapours from the evaporative loss control system and also by the increase in petrol flow through the carburettor due to the high fuel temperature.

---

44 Evaporative loss control system - servicing

1 *Leak testing.* Should the correct operation of either one part of the system or the system as a whole, other than the absorption canister or fuel liner filter, be suspect the car should be taken to the local agents as specialist equipment is necessary to trace the fault. It is recommended that the filter be renewed every 12,000 miles (20,000 km). It is easily removed from either end. Do not forget to check that the ignition switch is off otherwise the electric fuel pump (if fitted as an alternative to the mechanical pump) will operate. With the new filter fitted run the engine for a few minutes and check the two hose connections for leaks.

3 *Absorption canister.* It is recommended that the air filter located in the bottom section of the canister is renewed every 12,000 miles (20,000 km) for average motoring conditions or

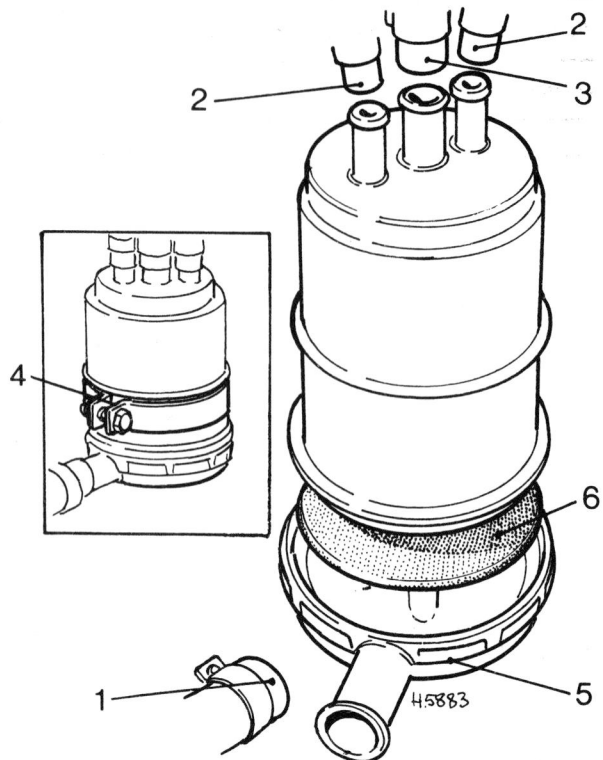

Fig. 3.25. Absorption canister air filter pad (Sec. 44)
Note the correct hose connections

1 Air vent tube	4 Canister securing clip
2 Vapour pipes	5 End cap
3 Surge pipe	6 Air filter pad

more often if the conditions are dusty. The complete absorption canister must be renewed every 50,000 miles (83,600 km) or at any time should the carbon grains be saturated in liquid petrol.

4 To remove the canister first disconnect the air vent tube (1), see Fig. 3.25 from the base of the canister. Then disconnect the vapour (2) and surge pipe (3) from the top of the canister and finally unscrew the mounting clip tightening nut and bolt (4) and lift away the canister.

5 The air filter may be removed by unscrewing the bottom end cap (5) of the canister which will then expose the filter (6). Lift it out and discard, wipe the inside of the cap with a non-fluffy rag and fit a new filter pad followed by the cap.

6 Refit the canister to the mounting clip and reconnect the pipes. The surge pipe from the engine valve rocker cover must be fitted to the centre connection on the top of the canister.

45 Fault diagnosis - Fuel system and carburation

Symptom	Reason/s	Remedy
Fuel consumption excessive	Air cleaner choked and dirty giving rich mixture	Remove, clean and replace air cleaner.
	Fuel leaking from carburettor, fuel pumps, or fuel lines	Check for and eliminate all fuel leaks. Tighten fuel line union nuts.
	Float chamber flooding	Check and adjust float level.
	Generally worn carburettor	Remove, overhaul and replace.
	Distributor condenser faulty	Remove, and fit new unit.
	Balance weights or vacuum advance mechanism in distributor faulty	Remove, and overhaul distributor.
	Carburettor incorrectly adjusted, mixture too rich	Tune and adjust carburettor.
	Idling speed too high	Adjust idling speed.
	Contact breaker gap incorrect	Check and reset gap.
	Valve clearances incorrect	Check clearances and adjust as necessary.
	Incorrectly set spark plugs	Remove, clean, and regap.
	Tyres under-inflated	Check tyre pressures and inflate if necessary.
	Wrong spark plugs fitted	Remove and replace with correct units.
	Brakes dragging	Check and adjust brakes.
Insufficient fuel delivery or weak mixture due to air leaks	Petrol tank air vent restricted	Remove petrol cap and clean out air vent.
	Partially clogged filters in pump and carburettor.	Remove and clean filters.
	Dirt lodged in float chamber needle housing	Remove and clean out float chamber and needle valve assembly.
	Incorrectly seating valves in fuel pump	Remove, dismantle, and clean out fuel pump.
	Fuel pump diaphragm leaking or damaged	Remove, and overhaul fuel pump.
	Gasket in fuel pump damaged	Remove, and overhaul fuel pump.
	Fuel pump valves sticking due to petrol gumming	Remove, and thoroughly clean fuel pump.
	Too little fuel in fuel tank (prevalent when climbing steep hills)	Refill fuel tank.
	Union joints on pipe connections loose	Tighten joints and check for air leaks.
	Split in fuel pipe on suction side of fuel pump.	Examine, locate, and repair.
	Inlet manifold to block or inlet manifold to carburettor gasket leaking	Test by pouring oil along joints - bubbles indicate leak. Renew gasket as appropriate.

Chapter 4 Ignition system

Contents

Specifications

Morris 1100 Saloon and Traveller - manual ... ... *1962 - 67*
Austin 1100 Saloon and Countryman - manual ... *1963 - 71*
Austin and Morris 1100 Mk II - manual ... ... *1967 - 71*
Austin and Morris 1100 Mk III - manual *1971*

Ignition timing:
    Static ... ... 3⁰ btdc
    Stroke at 600 rpm ... ... 5⁰ btdc

General distributor data:
    Make ... ... Lucas
    Type 25 D4
    Rotation ... ... Anticlockwise
    Dwell angle ... ... 60 $\pm$ 3⁰
    Points gap ... ... 0.014 - 0.016 in (0.36 - 0.40 mm)
    Condenser capacity ... ... 0.18 - 0.24 m F

Distributor number: **41142, 41147, 41260**
    Compression ratio ... ... 8.5 : 1
    Deceleration check (vacuum pipe disconnected) ... ... 30⁰ - 34⁰ at 5400 rpm
    17⁰ - 21⁰ at 2500 rpm
    2⁰ - 6⁰ at 1200 rpm
    No advance below ... ... 600 rpm
    Vacuum advance:
        Starts ... ... 6 in (15 cm) Hg
        Finishes ... ... 14⁰ at 13 in (33 cm) Hg

Distributor number: **40849**
    Compression ratio ... ... 8.5 : 1
    Deceleration check (vacuum pipe disconnected) ... ... 24⁰ - 28⁰ at 3700 rpm
    12⁰ - 16⁰ at 2000 rpm
    1⁰ - 5⁰ at 900 rpm
    No advance below ... ... 500 rpm

Vacuum advance:
    Starts ... ...   6 in (15 cm) Hg
    Finishes ... ...   14° at 13 in (33 cm) Hg

Distributor number: **40899, 41025, 41262**
    Compression ratio ... ...   7.5 : 1
    Deceleration check (vacuum pipe disconnected): ... ...   32° - 36° at 5600 rpm
        14° - 18° at 2500 rpm
        1° - 5° at 1200 rpm
    No advance below ... ...   700 rpm
    Vacuum advance:
        Starts ... ...   5 in. (13 cm) Hg
        Finisher ... ...   20° at 17 in. (43 cm) Hg

Spark plugs:
    Make ... ...   Champion
    Type ... ...   N9Y or N5
    Size ... ...   14 mm
    Gap ... ...   0.025 in. (0.64 mm)

Ignition Coil:

	Temperate climates	Cold climates
Make	Lucas	Lucas
Type	LA 12	16 C6
Primary resistance at 20° C (68° F)	3.0 - 3.4 ohms (cold)	1.43 - 1.58 ohm (cold)
Ballast resistance	—	1.3 - 1.4 ohm
Consumption (CB Points closed, ignition on)	3.5 amps	4.5 - 5 amps

Firing order: 1 3 4 2

MG 1100 and 1100 Mk II ... ...   *1962 - 67*
Vanden Plas 1100 and 1100 Mk II ... ...   *1964 - 67*
Riley Kestrel and Mk II ... ...   *1965 - 67*
Wolseley 1100 and 1100 Mk II ... ...   *1965 - 67*

Ignition Timing:
    Static ... ...   5° btdc
    Strobe at 600 rpm ... ...   7° btdc

General distributor data:
    Make ... ...   Lucas
    Type 25 D4
    Rotation ... ...   Anticlockwise
    Dwell angle ... ...   60 $\pm$ 3°
    Points gap ... ...   0.014 - 0.016 in. (0.36 - 0.40 mm)
    Condenser capacity ... ...   0.18 - 0.24 m F

Distributor number: **40853, 41028**
    Compression ratio ... ...   8.9 : 1 (8.1 : 1 available)
    Deceleration check (vacuum pipe disconnected): ... ...   28° - 32° at 5000 rpm
        19° - 23° at 2800 rpm
        1° - 3° at 1000 rpm
    No advance below ... ...   600 rpm
    Vacuum advance:
        Starts ... ...   4 in (10 cm) Hg
        Finishes ... ...   14° at 7 in. (18 cm) Hg

Spark plugs:
    Make ... ...   Champion
    Type N5
    Size ... ...   14 mm
    Gap ... ...   0.025 in. (0.64 mm)

Ignition Coil:
    Make ... ...   Lucas
    Type ... ...   LA 12
    Primary resistance at 20° C (68° F) ... ...   3.0 - 3.4 ohms (cold)
    Consumption (CB Points closed, ignition on) ... ...   3.5 amps

Firing order: 1 3 4 2

Austin and Morris 1100 Automatic ... ...   *1966 - 67*
Austin and Morris 1100 Mk II Automatic ... ...   *1967 - 71*
Austin 1100 Mk III Automatic *1971*
MG, Riley, Vanden Plas and Wolseley 1100
Automatic ... ...   *1967 on*

Ignition Timing:

Static:

High Compression (8.9 : 1)

Distributor number:

41181, 41261	5° btdc
41134	7° btdc

Low Compression (8 : 1)

All 1098 cc automatic transmission models Distributor
number 41181, 41261 ... ... 3° btdc

Strobe:

High Compression (8.9 : 1) at 600 rpm - vacuum pipe disconnected

Distributor number:

41181, 41261	8° btdc
41134	10° btdc

All 1098 cc automatic transmission models Distributor number
41181, 41261 ... ... 8° btdc

General distributor data:

Make	Lucas
Type	25 D4
Rotation	Anticlockwise
Dwell angle	$60^{\circ} \pm 3^{\circ}$
Points gap	0.014 - 0.016 in. (0.36 - 0.40 mm)
Condenser capacity	0.18 - 0.24 m F

Distributor number **41181, 41261**

Deceleration check (vacuum pipe disconnected): ... ... 26° - 30° at 5,500 rpm
                                         18° - 22° at 2,800 rpm
                                         3° –5° at 800 rpm

No advance below ... ...   600 rpm

Vacuum advancer:

Starts	3 in. (8 cm) Hg
Finishes	24° at 13 in. (33 cm) Hg

Distributor number: **41134**

Deceleration check (vacuum pipe disconnected): ... ... 26° - 30° at 5,500 rpm
                                         16° - 20° at 2000 rpm
                                         0° - 4° at 800 rpm

No advance below ... ...   600 rpm

Vacuum advance:

Starts	3 in. (8 cm) Hg
Finishes	18° at 15 in. (38 cm) Hg

Spark plugs:

Make	Champion
Type	N 9Y or N5
Size	14 mm
Gap	0.025 in. (0.64 mm)

Ignition coil:

	Temperate climates	Cold climates
Make	Lucas	Lucas
Type	HA12	16 C6
Primary resistance at 20° C (68° F)	3.0 - 3.4 ohms (cold)	1.43 - 1.58 ohms (cold)
Ballast resistance	—	1.3 - 1.4 ohms
Consumption (CB Points closed, ignition on)	3.5 amps	4.5 - 5 amps

Firing order: 1 3 4 2

1275 cc engine as optional extra for 1100 Mk I ...   *1967 only*
MG Sports Sedan (USA only)

Ignition Timing:

Static	8° btdc
Strobe	10° btdc

Measuring plug gap. A feeler gauge of the correct size (see ignition system specifications) should have a slight 'drag' when slid between the electrodes. Adjust gap if necessary

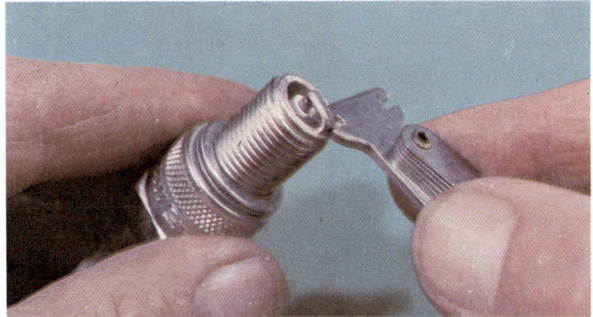

Adjusting plug gap. The plug gap is adjusted by bending the earth electrode inwards, or outwards, as necessary until the correct clearance is obtained. Note the use of the correct tool

Normal. Grey-brown deposits lightly coated core nose. Gap increasing by around 0.001 in (0.025 mm) per 1000 miles (1600 km). Plugs ideally suited to engine and engine in good condition

Carbon fouling. Dry, black, sooty deposits. Will cause weak spark and eventually misfire. Fault: over-rich fuel mixture. Check: carburettor mixture settings, float level and jet sizes; choke operation and cleanliness of air filter. Plugs can be re-used after cleaning

Oil fouling. Wet, oily deposits. Will cause weak spark and eventually misfire. Fault: worn bores/piston rings or valve guides; sometimes occurs (temporarily) during running-in period. Plugs can be re-used after thorough cleaning

Overheating. Electrodes have glazed appearance, core nose very white - few deposits. Fault: plug overheating. Check: plug value, ignition timing, fuel octane rating (too low) and fuel mixture (too weak). Discard plugs and cure fault immediately

Electrode damage. Electrodes burned away; core nose has burned, glazed appearance. Fault: initial pre-ignition. Check: as for 'Overheating' but may be more severe. Discard plugs and remedy fault before piston or valve damage occurs

Split core nose (may appear initially as a crack). Damage is self-evident, but cracks will only show after cleaning. Fault: pre-ignition or wrong gap-setting technique. Check: ignition timing, cooling system, fuel octane rating (too low) and fuel mixture (too weak). Discard plugs, rectify fault immediately

General distributor data:

Make	Lucas
Type	25 D4
Rotation	Anticlockwise
Dwell angle	$60^O \pm 3^O$
Points gap	0.014 - 0.016 in. (0.36 - 0.40 mm)
Condenser capacity	0.18 - 0.24 m F

Distributor number: **41214**

Deceleration check (vacuum pipe disconnected):	18° - 22° at 5000 rpm
	11° - 15° at 2800 rpm
	4° - 8° at 1600 rpm
No advance below	300 rpm
Vacuum advance:	
Starts	3 in. (8 cm) Hg
Finishes	20° at 10 in. (25 cm) Hg

Distributor number: **40819**

Deceleration check:	22° - 26° at 5200 rpm
	10° - 14° at 1600 rpm
	6° - 12° at 1000 rpm
No advance below	450 rpm
Vacuum advance	No vacuum unit fitted

Spark plugs:

Make	Champion
Type	N9Y - originally UN 12Y
Size	14 mm
Gap	0.025 in. (0.64 mm)

Ignition Coil:

Make	Lucas
Type	LA 12
Primary resistance at 20° C (68° F)	3.0 - 3.4 ohms (cold)
Consumption (CB Points closed, ignition on)	3.5 amps

Firing order: 1 3 4 2

Austin and Morris 1100 Mk III (ECE 15) *1972*

Ignition timing:

Static	7° btdc
Strobe at 1000 rpm (vacuum pipe disconnected)	14° btdc

General distributor data:

Make	Lucas
Type	25 D4
Rotation	Anti-clockwise
Dwell angle	$60^O \pm 3^O$
Points gap	0.014 to 0.016 in (0.36 to 0.40 mm)
Condenser capacity	0.18 to 0.24 mfd

Distributor number **41261**

Deceleration check (vacuum pipe disconnected)	24° - 28° at 5500 rpm
	17° - 21° at 2800 rpm
	1^O - 6° at 800 rpm
No advance	300 rpm
Vacuum advance:	
Starts	3 in. (8 cm) Hg
Finishes	24° at 13 in. (33 cm) Hg

Spark plugs:

Make	N9Y or N5
Type	14 mm
Gap	0.025 in (0.64 mm)

Ignition coil:

Make	Lucas
Type	HA 12
Primary resistance at 20^OC (68^OF)	3.0 - 3.4 ohms (cold)
Consumption (CB Points closed, ignition on)	3.5 amps

Austin and Morris 1300 - all models except GT   ...   *1967 - 1971*
MG, Riley, Vanden Plas, and Wolseley 1300 - manual *1967 - 68*
Wolseley 1300 and 1300 Mk II, and Vanden Plas
1300 - automatic ...   .   *1967 on*
MG and Riley Kestrel 1300 - Automatic   ...   ...   *1967 - 69*

Ignition Timing:
  Static:

High compression (8.8 : 1)	8° btdc
Low compression (8.1 : 1)	3° btdc

  Strobe (at 600 rpm)

High compression (8.8 : 1)	10° btdc
Low compression (8.1 : 1)	6° btdc

General distributor data:

Make	Lucas
Type	25 D4
Rotation	Anticlockwise
Dwell angle	$60^o \pm 3^o$
Points gap	0.014 - 0.016 in. (0.36 - 0.40 mm)
Condenser capacity	0.18 - 0.24 m F

Distributor number: **41257, 41214**

Compression ratio	8.8 : 1
Deceleration check (vacuum pipe disconnected):	18° - 22° at 5,000 rpm
	11° - 15° at 2800 rpm
	4° - 8° at 1600 rpm
No advance below	300 rpm

  Vacuum advance:

Starts	3 in. (8 cm) Hg
Finishes	20° at 10 in. (25 cm) Hg

Distributor number: **41233, 41259**

Compression ratio	8.1 : 1
Deceleration check (vacuum pipe disconnected):	28° - 32° at 5600 rpm
	18°- 22° at 3000 rpm
	9° - 13° at 1600 rpm
No advance below	300 rpm

  Vacuum advance:

Starts	6 in. (15 cm) Hg
Finishes	24° at 16 in. (40 cm) Hg

Spark plugs:

Make	Champion
Type	N9Y
Size	14 mm
Gap	0.025 in. (0.64 mm)

Ignition coil:

	Temperate climates	Cold climates
Make	Lucas	Lucas
Type	L A 12	16 C6
Primary resistance at 20° C (68° F)	3.0 - 3.4 ohms (cold)	1.43 - 1.58 ohms (cold)
Ballast resistance	—	1.3 - 1.4 ohms
Consumption (CB Points closed, ignition on)	3.5 amps	4.5 - 5 amps

Firing order: 1 3 4 2

Wolseley 1300 and 1300 Mk II and Vanden Plas
1300 - manual   ...   .   *1968 on*
MG and Riley Kestrel 1300 - manual   ...   .   *1968 only*

Ignition Timing:
  Static:

High compression (8.8 : 1)	5° btdc
Low compression (8.1 : 1)	7° btdc

  Strobe: (at 600 rpm)

High compression (8.8 : 1)	8° btdc
Low compression (8.1 : 1)	10° btdc

General distributor data:

Make ...	Lucas
Type ...	25 D4
Rotation	Anticlockwise
Dwell angle ...	$60^\circ \pm 3^\circ$
Points gap ...	0.014 - 0.016 in. (0.36 - 0.40 mm)
Condenser capacity ...	0.18 - 0.24 m F

Distributor number: ...   **41242, 41134, 41251**

Compression ratio ...	8.8 : 1
Deceleration check (vacuum pipe disconnected):	26° - 30° at 5500 rpm
	16° - 20° at 2000 rpm
	12° - 16° at 1600 rpm
	0° - 4° at 800 rpm
No advance below ...	600 rpm
Vacuum advance:	
Starts ...	3 in. (8 cm) Hg
Finishes ...	18° at 15 in. (38 cm) Hg

Distributor number: ...   **41259**

Compression ratio ...	8.1 : 1
Deceleration check (vacuum pipe disconnected):	28° - 32° at 5600 rpm
	18° - 22° at 3000 rpm
	9° - 13° at 1600 rpm
No advance below ...	300 rpm
Vacuum advance:	
Starts ...	6 in. (15 cm) Hg
Finishes ...	24° at 16 in. (40 cm) Hg

Spark plugs:

Make ...	Champion
Type ...	N9Y
Size ...	14 mm
Gap ...	0.025 in. (0.64 mm)

Ignition coil:

Make ...	Lucas
Type ...	LA 12
Primary resistance at 20° C (68° F) ...	3.0 - 3.4 ohms (cold)
Consumption (CB Points closed, ignition on) ...	3.5 amps

Firing order: ...   1 3 4 2

MG 1300 Mk II - manual ...   *1968 - 71*
Riley 1300 Mk II - manual ...   *1968 - 69*
Austin and Morris 1300 GT ...   *1969 - 1971*

Ignition Timing:

Static ...	2° btdc
Strobe (at 100.0 rpm) ...	9° btdc

General distributor data:

Make ...	Lucas
Type ...	25 D4
Rotation	Anticlockwise
Dwell angle ...	$60^\circ \pm 3^\circ$
Points gap ...	0.014 - 0.016 in. (0.36 - 0.40 mm)
Condenser capacity ...	0.18 - 0.24 m F

Distributor number: ...   **41238**

Compression ratio ...	9.75 : 1
Deceleration check (vacuum pipe disconnected):	22° - 26° at 6,000 rpm
	20° - 24° at 4800 rpm
	14° - 18° at 2800 rpm
	10° - 14° at 1500 rpm
No advance below ...	600 rpm
Vacuum advance:	
Starts ...	2 in. (5 cm) Hg
Finishes ...	14° at 18 in. (46 cm) Hg

Spark plugs:

Make	Champion
Type	N9Y
Size	14 mm
Gap	0.025 in. (0.64 mm)

Ignition coil:

	Temperate climates	Cold climates
Make	Lucas	Lucas
Type	HA 12	16 C6
Primary resistance at 20° C (68° F)	3.0 - 3.4 ohms (cold)	1.43 - 1.58 ohms (cold)
Ballast resistance	—	1.3 - 1.4 ohms
Consumption (CB Points closed, ignition on)	3.5 amps	4.5 - 5 amps

Firing order: 1 3 4 2

Austin, Morris, Vanden Plas and Wolseley 1300 Mk III (ECE 15) *1972*

Ignition timing:

Static	8° btdc
Strobe at 1000 rpm (vacuum pipe disconnected)	13° btdc

General distributor data:

Make	Lucas
Type	25 D4
Rotation	Anti-clockwise
Dwell angle	60° ± 3°
Points gap	0.014 to 0.016 in. (0.36 to 0.40 mm)
Condenser capacity	0.18 to 0.24 mfd

Distributor number **41257, 41214**

Deceleration check (vacuum pipe disconnected)	18° to 22° at 5000 rpm
	11° to 15° at 2800 rpm
	4° to 8° at 1600 rpm
No advance below	300 rpm
Vacuum advance:	
Starts	3 in (8 cm) Hg
Finishes	20° at 10 in. (25 cm) Hg

Spark plugs:

Make	Champion
Type	N9Y
Size	14 mm
Gap	0.025 in. (0.64 mm)

Ignition coil:

Make	Lucas
Type	LA 12
Primary resistance at 20°C (68°F)	3.0 to 3.4 ohms (cold)
Consumption (CB Points closed, ignition on)	3.5 amps

Austin and Morris 1300 GT (ECE 15) *1972*

Ignition timing:

Static	2° btdc
Strobe at 1000 rpm (vacuum pipe disconnected)	9° btdc

General distributor data:

Make	Lucas
Type	25 D4
Rotation	Anti-clockwise
Dwell angle	60° ± 3°
Points gap	0.014 to 0.016 in. (0.36 to 0.40 mm)
Condenser capacity	0.18 to 0.24 mfd

Distributor number **41238**

Deceleration check (vacuum pipe disconnected)	22° to 26° at 6000 rpm
	20° to 24° at 4800 rpm
	14° to 18° at 2800 rpm
	9° to 12½° at 1100 rpm

No advance	600 rpm
Vacuum advance:	
Starts	4 in. (10 cm) Hg
Finishes	14° at 11 in. (28 cm) Hg

Spark plugs:

Make	Champion
Type	N9Y
Size	14 mm
Gap	0.025 in (0.64 mm)

Ignition coil:

Make	Lucas
Type	HA 12
Primary resistance at 20^OC (68^OF)	3.0 to 3.4 ohms (cold)
Consumption (CB Points closed, ignition on)	3.5 arnp

Torque wrench settings:

	lb f ft	kg f m
Spark plugs	30	4.14
Distributor flange retaining screws	8 - 10	1.1 - 1.4

1 General description

In order that the engine can run correctly it is necessary for an electrical spark to ignite the fuel/air mixture in the combustion chamber at exactly the right moment in relation to engine speed and load. The ignition system is based on feeding low tension voltage from the battery to the coil where it is converted to high tension voltage. The high tension voltage is powerful enough to jump the spark plug gap in the cylinders many times a second under high compression pressures, providing that the system is in good condition and that all adjustments are correct.

The ignition system is divided into two circuits. The low tension circuit and the high tension circuit.

The low tension (sometimes known as the primary) circuit consists of the battery, lead to the control box, lead to the ignition switch, lead from the ignition switch to the low tension or primary coil windings (terminal SW), and the lead from the low tension coil windings (coil terminal CB) to the contact breaker points and condenser in the distributor.

The high tension circuit consists of the high tension or secondary coil windings, the heavy igniiton lead from the centre of the coil to the centre of the distributor cap, the rotor arm, and the spark plug leads and spark plugs.

The system functions in the following manner. Low tension voltage is changed in the coil into high tension voltage by the opening and closing of the contact breaker points in the low tension circuit. High tension voltage is then fed via the carbon brush in the centre of the distributor cap to the rotor arm of the distributor. The rotor arm revolves inside the distributor cap and, each time it comes in line with one of the four metal segments in the cap, which are connected to the spark plug leads, the opening and closing of the contact breaker points causes the high tension voltage to build up, jump the gap from the rotor arm to the appropriate metal segment. The voltage then passes via the spark plug lead to the spark plug, where it finally jumps the spark plug gap before going to earth.

The ignition is advanced and retarded automatically, to ensure the spark occurs at just the right instant for the particular load at the prevailing engine speed.

The ignition advance is controlled both mechanically and by a vacuum operated system. Some 1275cc models do not have a vacuum unit fitted - see Specifications.

The mechanical governor mechanism comprises two lead weights, which move out from the distributor shaft, due to centrifugal force, as the engine speed rises. As they move outwards they rotate the cam relative to the distributor shaft, and so advance the spark. The weights are held in position by two light springs and it is the tension of the springs which is largely responsible for correct spark advancement.

The vacuum control consists of a diaphragm, one side of

which is connected via a small bore tube to the carburettor, and the other side to the contact breaker plate. Depression in the inlet manifold and carburettor, which varies with engine speed and throttle opening, causes the diaphragm to move, so moving the contact breaker plate, and advancing or retarding the spark. A fine degree of control is achieved by a spring in the vacuum assembly.

2 Contact breaker points - adjustment

1 To adjust the contact breaker points to the correct gap, first pull off the two clips securing the distributor cap to the distributor body, and lift away the cap. Clean the cap inside and out with a dry cloth. It is unlikely that the four segments will be badly burned or scored, but if they are the cap will have to be renewed.

2 Push in the carbon brush located in the top of the cap once or twice, to make sure that it moves freely. The brush should protrude by at least 0.25 in (6.35 mm).

3 Gently prise the contact breaker points open to examine the condition of their faces. If they are rough, pitted, or dirty, it will be necessary to remove them for resurfacing, or for replacement points to be fitted.

4 Presuming the points are satisfactory, or that they have been cleaned and replaced, measure the gap between the points by turning the engine over until the contact breaker arm is on the peak of one of the four cam lobes. A 0.15 in (0.381 mm) feeler gauge should now just fit between the points.

5 If the gap varies from this amount, slacken the contact plate securing screw, and adjust the contact gap by inserting a screwdriver in the notched hole at the end of the plate, turning clockwise to decrease and anticlockwise to increase the gap. Tighten the securing screw and check the gap again (photo).

6 Replace the rotor arm and distributor cap and clip the spring blade retainers into position.

3 Contact breaker points - removal and replacement

1 If the contact breaker points are burned, pitted or badly worn, they must be removed and either replaced, or their faces must be filed smooth.

2 To remove the points unscrew the terminal nut and remove it together with the steel washer under its head. Remove the flanged nylon bush and then the condenser lead and the low tension lead from the terminal pin. Lift off the contact breaker arm and then remove the large fibre washer from the terminal pin.

3 The adjustable contact breaker plate is removed by unscrewing the one holding down screw and removing it, complete

2.5 The contact plate securing screw and notched hole (arrowed)

with spring and flat washer.

4 To reface the points, rub their faces on a fine carborundum stone, or on fine emery paper. It is important that the faces are rubbed flat and parallel to each other so that there will be complete face to face contact when the points are closed. One of the points will be pitted and the other will have deposits on it.

5 It is necessary to completely remove the built-up deposits, but not necessary to rub the pitted point right down to the stage where all the pitting has disappeared, though obviously if this is done it will prolong the time before the operation of refacing the points has to be repeated.

6 To replace the points, first position the adjustable contact breaker plate, and secure it with its screw spring and flat washer. Fit the fibre washer to the terminal pin, and fit the contact breaker arm over it. Insert the flanged nylon bush with the condenser lead immediately under its head, and the low tension lead under that, over the terminal pin.

7 Fit the steel washer and screw on the securing nut.

8 The points are now reassembled and the gap should be set as detailed in Section 2.

4 Condenser - removal and replacement

1 The purpose of the condenser, (sometimes known as a capacitor) is to ensure that when the contact breaker points open there is no sparking across them which would waste voltage and cause wear.

2 The condenser is fitted in parallel with the contact breaker points. If it develops a short circuit, it will cause ignition failure as the points will be prevented from interrupting the low tension circuit.

3 If the engine becomes very difficult to start or begins to miss after several miles running and the breaker points show signs of excessive burning, then the condition of the condenser must be suspect. A further test can be made by separating the points by hand with the ignition switch on. If this is accompanied by a flash it is indicative that the condenser has failed.

4 Without special test equipment the only sure way to diagnose condenser trouble is to replace a suspected unit with a new one and note if there is any improvement.

5 To remove the condenser from the distributor, remove the distributor cap and the rotor arm. Unscrew the contact breaker arm terminal nut, and remove the nut, washer, and flanged nylon bush and release the condenser lead from the bush. Unscrew the condenser retaining screw from the breaker plate and remove the condenser.

6 Replacement of the condenser is simply a reversal of the removal process. Take particular care that the condenser lead does not short circuit against any portion of the breaker plate.

5 Distributor - lubrication

1 It is important that the distributor cam is lubricated with petroleum jelly at the specified mileages, and that the breaker arm, governor weights, and cam spindle, are lubricated with engine oil once every 6,000 miles (10,000 km).

2 Great care should be taken not to use too much lubricant, as any excess that might find its way onto the contact breaker points could cause burning and misfiring.

3 To gain access to the cam spindle, lift away the rotor arm. Drop no more than two drops of engine oil onto the screw head. This will run down the spindle when the engine is hot and lubricate the bearing.. No more than *one* drop of oil should be applied to the pivot post.

6 Distributor - removal and replacement

1 For safety reasons, disconnect the battery.

2 Release the clips securing the distributor cap to the body and lift away the distributor cap.

3 Remove the inspection plate on the clutch cover, (manual transmission) and slowly turn the crankshaft until the relevant timing marks are in alignment (see Specification). The rotor arm should be pointing to the distributor cap segment which is connected to No 1 spark plug.

4 Disconnect the low tension lead from the terminal on the side of the distributor.

5 Detach the vacuum pipe from the distributor vacuum advance unit - when fitted - see Specifications.

6 Undo and remove the two screws, spring and plain washers securing the distributor clamp plate to the cylinder block. The distributor may now be lifted up together with the clamp plate still attached.

7 If it is not wished to disturb the ignition timing, then under no circumstances should the clamp pinch bolt, which secures the distributor in its relative position in the clamp, be loosened. Providing the distributor is removed without the clamp being loosened from the distributor and the engine is not turned, the ignition timing will not be lost.

8 Replacement is a reversal of the above sequence. If the engine has been turned, it will be necessary to retime the ignition. This will also be necessary if the clamp pinch bolt has been loosened. Tighten the flange retaining screws to a torque wrench setting of 8 - 10 lb f ft (1.1 - 1.4 kg fm).

7 Distributor - dismantling

1 With the distributor removed from the car and on the bench, remove the distributor cap and lift off the rotor arm. If very tight, !ever it off gently with a screwdriver.

2 Remove the points from the distributor as detailed in Section

3 Remove the condenser from the contact breaker plate by releasing its securing screw.

4 Unhook the vacuum unit spring from its mounting pin on the moving contact breaker plate. **Note:** on some 1275cc models no vacuum is fitted to the distributor. This does not affect the dismantling procedure. Ignore reference to the vacuum unit as applicable.

5 Remove the contact breaker plate.

6 Unscrew the two screws and lockwashers which hold the contact breaker base plate in position and remove the earth lead from the relevant screw. Remember to replace this lead on reassembly.

7 Lift out the contact breaker base plate.

8 **Note** the position of the slot in the rotor arm drive in relation to the offset drive dog at the opposite end of the distributor. It is essential that this is reassembled correctly as otherwise the timing may be 180° out.

9 Unscrew the cam spindle retaining screw, which is located in

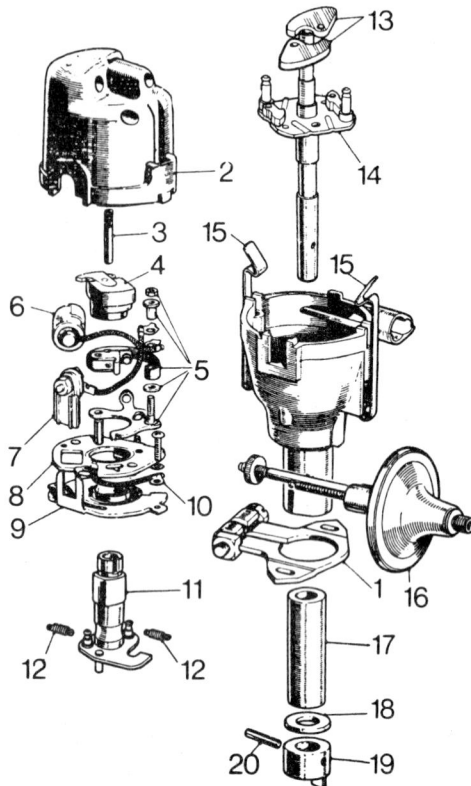

Fig. 4.1. Component parts of distributor (Sec. 7)

1 Clamping plate	10 Earth lead
2 Moulded cap	11 Cam
3 Brush and spring	12 Automatic advance
4 Rotor arm	springs
5 Contacts (set)	13 Weight assembly
6 Capacitor	14 Shaft and action plate
7 Terminal and lead	15 Cap retaining clips
(low tension)	16 Vacuum unit
8 Moving contact breaker	17 Bush
plate	18 Thrust washer
9 Contact breaker base	19 Driving dog
plate	20 Parallel pin

the centre of the rotor arm drive, and remove the cam spindle.
10 Lift out the centrifugal weights together with their springs.
11 To remove the vacuum unit, spring off the small circlip which secures the advance adjustment nut which should be unscrewed. With the micrometer adjusting nut removed, release the spring and the micrometer adjusting nut lock spring clip. This is the clip that is responsible for the 'clicks' when the micrometer adjuster is turned, and it is small and easily lost, as is the circlip so put them in a safe place. Do not forget to replace the lock spring clip on reassembly.
12 It is only necessary to remove the distributor drive shaft or spindle if it is thought to be excessively worn. With a thin punch drive out the retaining pin from the driving tongue collar on the bottom end of the distributor drive shaft. The shaft can then be removed. The distributor is now completely dismantled.

8 Distributor - inspection and repair

1 Thoroughly wash all mechanical parts in petrol and wipe dry using a clean non-fluffy rag.
2 Check the contact breaker points as described in Section 3.
3 Check the distributor cap for signs of tracking indicated by a thin black line between the segments. Replace the cap if any

signs of tracking are found.
4 If the metal portion of the rotor arm is badly burned or loose, renew the arm. If slightly burnt clean the arm with a fine file.
5 Check that the carbon brush moves freely in the centre of the distributor cover.
6 Examine the fit of the breaker plate on the bearing plate and also check the breaker arm pivot for looseness or wear and renew as necessary.
7 Examine the balance weights or cam assembly if a degree of wear is found.
8 Examine the shaft and the fit of the cam assembly on the shaft. If the clearance is excessive compare the items with new units, and renew either, or both, if they show excessive wear.
9 If the shaft is a loose fit in the distributor bushes and can be seen to be worn, it will be necessary to fit a new shaft and bushes. The old bushes in the early distributor, or the single bush in the later ones, are simply pressed out. **Note:** before inserting new bushes they should be stood in engine oil for 24 hours.
10 Examine the length of the balance weight springs and compare them with new springs. If they have stretched they should be renewed.

9 Distributor - reassembly

1 Reassembly is a straight reversal of the dismantling process, but there are several points which should be noted in addition to those already given in the Section on dismantling.
2 Lubricate the balance weights and other parts of the mechanical advance mechanism, the distributor shaft, and the portion of the shaft on which the cam bears, with engine oil, during assembly. Do not oil excessively but ensure these parts are adequately lubricated.
3 On reassembling the cam driving pins with the centrifugal weights, check that they are in the correct position so that when viewed from above, the rotor arm should be at the six o'clock position, and the small offset on the driving dog must be on the right.
4 Check the action of the weights in the fully advanced and fully retarded positions and ensure they are not binding.
5 Tighten the micrometer adjusting nut to the middle position on the timing scale.
6 Finally, set the contact breaker gap to the correct clearance as described in Section 2.

10 Ignition timing

If the clamp plate pinch bolt has been loosened on the distributor and the static timing lost, or if for any other reason it is wished to set the ignition timing, proceed as follows:
1 Undo the two bolts from the inspection plate on the top of the clutch cover and remove the plate. The timing marks can now be checked with the help of a small mirror. The static advance is checked at the exact moment of opening of the points relative to the position of the timing marks on the flywheel, in relation to the pointer in the flywheel housing inspection hole. The ¼ mark on the flywheel indicates tdc and the marks 5, 10 and 15 indicate 5⁰, 10⁰ and 15⁰ advance before tdc respectively (Fig. 4.2).
2 The timing marks are on the torque coverter for models fitted with automatic transmission. On early models the tdc position is indicated by the ¼ mark supplemented with 5⁰ and 10⁰ marks. On later models each degree from 20⁰ btdc to 10⁰ atdc is marked (Fig. 4.3).
3 Check the 'Ignition specification' for the correct position of the flywheel when the points should be just beginning to open. This is shown as the 'static setting'.
4 Having determined whether your engine possesses a high or low compression ratio (by checking the engine number) turn the

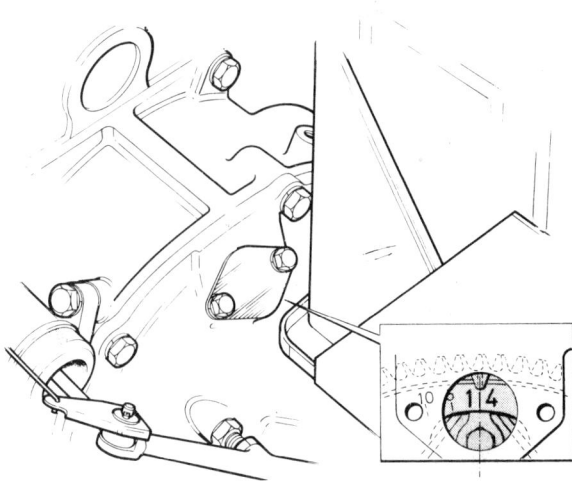

Fig. 4.2. The timing marks 1/4 (TDC), 5°, 10° and 15° BTDC are on the flywheel. They may be seen together with the indicator with the aid of a mirror after removing the plate (arrowed) Manual Transmission (Sec. 10)

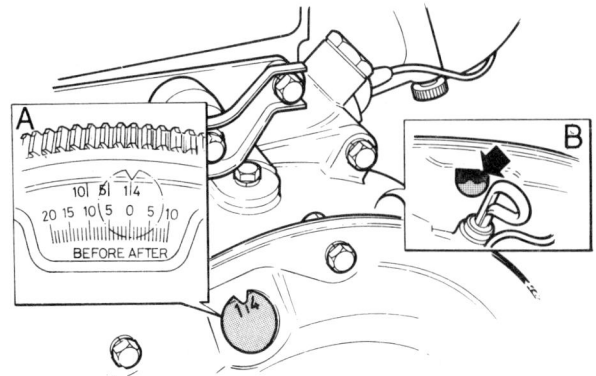

Fig. 4.3. The timing marks on converter (Automatic Transmission) (Sec. 10)

a) *On early models the TDC position is indicated by the 1/4 mark (Inset A) with 5° and 10° marks also provided.*
b) *On later models each degree from 20° BTDC to 10° ATDC is marked.*
c) *The hole in converter housing (Inset B) is used for inserting screwdriver to turn the converter.*

engine over so that No. 1 piston is coming up to tdc on the compression stroke. (This can be checked by removing No. 1 spark plug and feeling the pressure being developed in the cylinder, or by removing the rocker cover and noting when the valves in No. 4 cylinder are rocking ie., the inlet valve just opening and exhaust valve just closing. If this check is not made it is all too easy to set the timing 180° out, as both No. 1 and 4 cylinders come up to tdc at the same time but only one is on the firing stroke.

5 Continue turning the engine until the pointer in the flywheel inspection hole is in line with the correct timing mark on the flywheel periphery.

6 Remove the distributor cover, slacken off the distributor body clamp bolt, and with the rotor arm pointing towards the No. 1 terminal (check this position with the distributor cap and lead to No. 1 spark plug), insert the distributor into the distributor housing. The dog on the drive shaft should match up with the slot in the distributor driving spindle.

7 Insert the two bolts holding the distributor in position.

8 With the engine set in the correct position and the rotor arm opposite the correct segment for No. 1 cylinder, turn the advance/retard knob on the distributor until the contact points are just beginning to open. Eleven clicks of the knurled micrometer adjuster nut represent 1° of timing movement.

9 If the range of adjustment provided by this adjuster is not sufficient, then, if the clamp bolt is not already slackened, it will be necessary to slacken it and turn the distributor body half a graduation as marked on the adjusting spindle barrel. (Each graduation represents 5° timing movement or 55 clicks of the micrometer adjuster). Sufficient adjustment will normally be found available using the distributor micrometer adjuster. When this has been achieved the engine is statically timed.

10 Difficulty is sometimes experienced in determining exactly when the contact breaker points open. This can be ascertained most accurately by connecting a 12-volt bulb in parallel with the contact breaker points (one lead to earth and the other from the distributor low tension terminal). Switch on the ignition, and turn the advance and retard adjuster until the bulb lights up indicating that the points have just opened.

11 If a stroboscopic timing light is being used, attach one lead to No. 1 spark plug, and attach the other lead into the free end of No. 1 plug ignition cable leading from the distributor. Start the engine and shine the light on the flywheel periphery and timing indicators. If the engine idles at more than 600 rpm then the correct static timing will not be obtained as the centrifugal

10.13 The clamp bolt and micrometer adjuster (arrowed)

weights will have started to advance.

12 If the light shows the pointer in the flywheel inspection hole to be to the right of the timing marks, then the ignition is too far retarded. If the pointer appears to the left of the timing marks, then the ignition is too far advanced. Turn the distributor body or micrometer adjuster until the timing pointer appears in just the right position in relation to the timing marks.

13 Tighten the clamp bolt and recheck that the timing is still correct, making any small correction necessary with the micrometer adjuster (photo).

11 Spark plugs and HT leads

1 The correct functioning of the spark plugs is vital for the proper running and efficient operation of the engine.

2 At intervals of 6000 miles (10,000 Km) the plugs should be removed, examined, cleaned, and if worn excessively, renewed. The condition of the spark plug will also tell much about the general condition of the engine.

3 If the insulator nose of the spark plug is clean and white, with no deposits, this is indicative of a weak mixture, or too hot a plug (a hot plug transfers heat away from the electrode slowly - a cold plug transfer heat away quickly).

4 If the insulator nose is covered with hard black looking deposits, then this is indicative that the mixture is too rich. Should the plug be black and oily, then it is likely that the engine is fairly worn, as well as the mixture being too rich.

5 If the insulator nose is covered with light tan or greyish brown deposits, then the mixture is correct, and it is likely that the engine is in good condition.

6 If there are any traces of long brown tapering stains on the outside of the white portion of the plug, then the plug will have to be renewed as this shows that there is a faulty joint between the plug and body and the insulator, and compression is being allowed to leak away.

7 Plugs should be cleaned by a sand blasting machine, which will free them from carbon more than by cleaning by hand. The machine will test the condition of the plugs under compression. Any plug that fails to spark at the recommended pressure should be renewed.

8 The spark plug gap is of considerable importance, as, if it is too large or too small the size of the spark and its efficiency will be seriously impaired. The spark plug gap should be set to 0.25 inch (0.6425 mm).

9 To set it, measure the gap with a feeler gauge, and then bend open, or close, the outer plug electrode until the correct gap is achieved. The centre electrode should never be bent as this may crack the insulation and cause plug failure, if nothing worse.

10 When replacing the plugs, remember to use new washers and replace the leads from the distributor cap in the correct firing order which is 1 3 4 2, No. 1 cylinder being the one nearest the fan.

11 The plug leads require no maintenance other than being kept clean and wiped over regularly. At intervals of 6000 miles (10,000 Km), however, pull each lead off the plug in turn and remove it from the distributor cap. Water can seep down these joints giving rise to a white corrosive deposit which must be carefully removed from the end of each cable (photo).

12 Ignition system - fault diagnosis

There are two general symptoms of ignition fault. Either the engine will not fire, or the engine is difficult to start and misfires. If it is a regular misfire, ie. the engine is only running on two or three cylinders, the fault is almost sure to be in the high tension circuit. If the misfiring is intermittent, the fault could be in either the high or low tension circuits. If the engine stops suddenly, or will not start at all, it is likely that the fault is in the low tension circuit. Loss of power and overheating, apart from faulty carburettor settings, are normally due to faults in the distributor, or incorrect ignition timing.

Engine fails to start

1 If the engine fails to start it is likely that the fault is in the low tension circuit. The way the starter motor spins over will indicate whether there is a good charge in the battery. If the battery is evidently in good condition, then check the distributor.

2 Remove the distributor cap and rotor arm, and check that the contact points are not burnt, pitted or dirty. If the points are badly pitted, or burnt or dirty, clean and reset them as described in Section 3.

3 If the engine still refuses to fire check the low tension circuit further. Check the condition of the condenser as described in Section 4. Switch on the ignition and turn the crankshaft until the contact breaker points have fully opened. With either a voltmeter or bulb, and length of wire, connect the contact breaker plate terminal to earth on the engine. If the bulb lights, the low tension circuit is in order, and the fault is in the points. If the points have been cleaned and reset, and the bulb still lights, then the fault is in the high tension circuit.

11.11 Removing a lead securing screw (early type distributor)

4 If the bulb fails to light, connect it to the ignition coil terminal 'CB' and earth. If it lights, it points to a damaged wire or loose connection in the cable from the 'CB' terminal to the terminal on the contact breaker plate.

5 If the bulb fails to light, connect it between the ignition coil terminal SW and earth. If the bulb lights it indicates a fault in the primary winding of the coil, and it will be necessary to fit a replacement unit.

6 Should the bulb not light at this stage, then check the cable to 'SW' for faults or a loose connection. Connect the bulb from the negative terminal of the battery to the 'SW' terminal of the coil. If the bulb lights, then the fault is somewhere in the switch, or wiring and control box. Check further as follows:

    a) Check the white cable leading from the control box 'A3' terminal to the ignition switch. If the bulb fails to light, then this indicates that the cable is damaged, or one of the connections loose, or that there is a fault in the switch.

    b) Connect the bulb between the ignition switch white terminal cable and earth. If the bulb fails to light, this indicates a fault in the switch or in the wiring leading from the control box.

    c) Connect the bulb to the other ignition switch terminal and then to earth. If the bulb fails to light, this indicates a fault or loose connection in the wiring leading from the control box.

    d) Connect the bulb between the lighting and ignition terminal in the control box, and then to earth. If the bulb fails to light this indicates a faulty control box.

    e) Connect the bulb from the fuse unit terminal to earth. If the bulb fails to light this indicates a fault or loose connection in the wire leading from the starter solenoid to the control box.

    f) Connect the bulb from the input terminal of the solenoid switch to earth. If the bulb fails to light then there is a fault in the cable from the battery to the solenoid switch, or the earth lead of the battery is not properly earthed and the whole circuit is dead.

7 If the fault is not in the low tension circuit check the high tension circuit. Disconnect each plug lead in turn at the spark plug end, and hold the end of the cable about 3/16 in (4.76 mm) away from the cylinder block. Spin the engine on the starter motor solenoid switch (under the bonnet). Sparking between the end of the cable and the block should be fairly strong with a regular blue spark. (Hold the lead with rubber to avoid electric shocks).

8 Should there be no spark at the end of the plug leads, disconnect the lead at the distributor cap, and hold the end of the

lead about ¼ inch (6.35 mm) from the block. Spin the engine as before, when a rapid succession of blue sparks between the end of the lead and the block, indicate that the coil is in order, and that either the distributor cap is cracked, or the carbon brush is stuck or worn, or the rotor arm is faulty.

9   Check the cap for cracks and tracking, and the rotor arm for cracks or looseness of the metal portion and renew as necessary.

10 If there are no sparks from the end of the lead from the coil, then check the connections of the lead to the coil and distributor head, and if they are in order, and the low tension side is without fault, then it will be necessary to fit a replacement coil.

Engine misfires

If the engine misfires regularly, run it at a fast idling speed, and short out each of the plugs in turn by placing a short screwdriver across from the plug terminal to the cylinder. Ensure that the screwdriver has a **wooden** or **plastic, insulated handle.**

No difference in engine running will be noticed when the plug in the defective cylinder is short circuited. Short circuiting the working plugs will accentuate the misfire.

Remove the plug lead from the end of the defective plug and hold it about 3/16 inch (4.76 mm) away from the block. Restart the engine. If the sparking is fairly strong and regular the fault must lie in the spark plug.

The plug may be loose, the insulation may be cracked, or the points may have burnt away giving too wide a gap for the spark to jump. Worse still, one of the points may have broken off.

Either renew the plug, or clean it, reset the gap, and then test it.

If there is no spark at the end of the plug lead, or if it is weak and intermittent, check the ignition lead from the distributor to the plug. If the insulation is cracked or perished, renew the lead. Check the connections at the distributor cap.

If there is still no spark, examine the distributor cap carefully for tracking. This can be recognised by a very thin black line running between two or more electrodes, or between an electrode and some other part of the distributor. These are paths which now conduct electricity across the cap thus letting it run to earth. The only answer is a new distributor cap.

Apart from the ignition timing being incorrect, other causes of misfiring have already been dealt with under the section dealing with the failure of the engine to start. To recap - these are that:

a)   The coil may be faulty giving an intermittent misfire.
b)   There may be a damaged wire or loose connection in the low tension circuit.
c)   The condenser may be short circuiting.
d)   There may be a mechanical fault in the distributor (broken driving spindle or contact breaker spring).

If the igniition timing is too far retarded, it should be noted that the engine will tend to overheat, and there will be a quite noticeable drop in power. If the engine is overheating and the power is down, and the ignition timing is correct, then the carburettor should be checked, as it is likely that this is where the fault lies. See Chapter 3 for further details on this.

Chapter 5 Clutch

Contents

Specifications

Early cars:

Type	Single dry plate (coil springs)
Diameter	7.125 in. (181 mm)
Facing material	Wound yarn. DSW8 or Mintex H26
Facing area	18.25 in^2 (117 cm^2)
Coil springs	6
Colour	Black/white spot

Later cars:

Type	Single dry plate (diaphragm spring)
Colour	Green or blue

Torque wrench settings:

	lb f ft	kg fm
Pressure plate bolts	16	2.21
Driving strap bolts	16	2.21
Flywheel retaining bolt	115	15.87

1 General description

Initially a BLMC coil spring single dry plate 7.125 in (181 mm) clutch was fitted. In 1964 an improved diaphragm clutch of the same diameter was introduced. Both types of clutch are very unusual because there are major parts of the clutch assembly on *both* the *inside* and the *outside* of the flywheel.

The main parts of the clutch assembly on the outside of the flywheel comprise the spring housing, the thrust plate, the release bearing, the 6 pressure springs, or the diaphragm spring in later models and the three driving straps.

The main parts of the clutch assembly on the inside of the flywheel are the clutch disc, and the pressure plate.

The spring housing is firmly bolted to the pressure plate by 3 bolts and spring washers. The spring housing is held to the flywheel by driving straps which are held a little way away from the outer clutch face by spacing washers.

The clutch disc is free to slide along the splines of the primary gear which is fitted to the end of the crankshaft.

Friction lining material is riveted to the clutch disc which has a segmented hub to help absorb transmission shocks and to ensure take-off.

The clutch is actuated hydraulically. The pendant clutch pedal is connected to the clutch master cylinder and hydraulic fluid reservoir by a short pushrod. The master cylinder and

hydraulic reservoir are mounted on the engine side of the bulkhead in front of the driver.

Depressing the clutch pedal moves the piston in the master cylinder forwards, so forcing hydraulic fluid through the clutch hydraulic pipe to the slave cylinder.

The piston in the slave cylinder moves forward on the entry of the fluid and actuates the clutch operating lever by means of a short pushrod. The opposite end of the operating lever, slots, by means of a balljoint, into a throw-out plunger.

As the pivoted operating lever moves backwards it bears against the release bearing pushing it forwards. This in turn bears against the clutch thrust plate, the spring housing and the pressure plate which all move forward slightly so disengaging the pressure plate face from the clutch disc.

When the clutch pedal is released, the pressure plate springs force the pressure plate spring housing outwards, which, because it is attached to the pressure plate brings the pressure plate into contact with the high friction linings on the clutch disc. At the same time the disc is forced firmly against the inner face of the flywheel and so the drive is taken up.

As the friction linings of the clutch disc wear, the clearance between the clutch thrust race and the clutch ring will decrease. The pressure plate will move in closer to the clutch disc to compensate for wear, and unless the wear is taken up by adjustment at the adjustable stop located between the clutch housing and the operating lever, clutch slip will result.

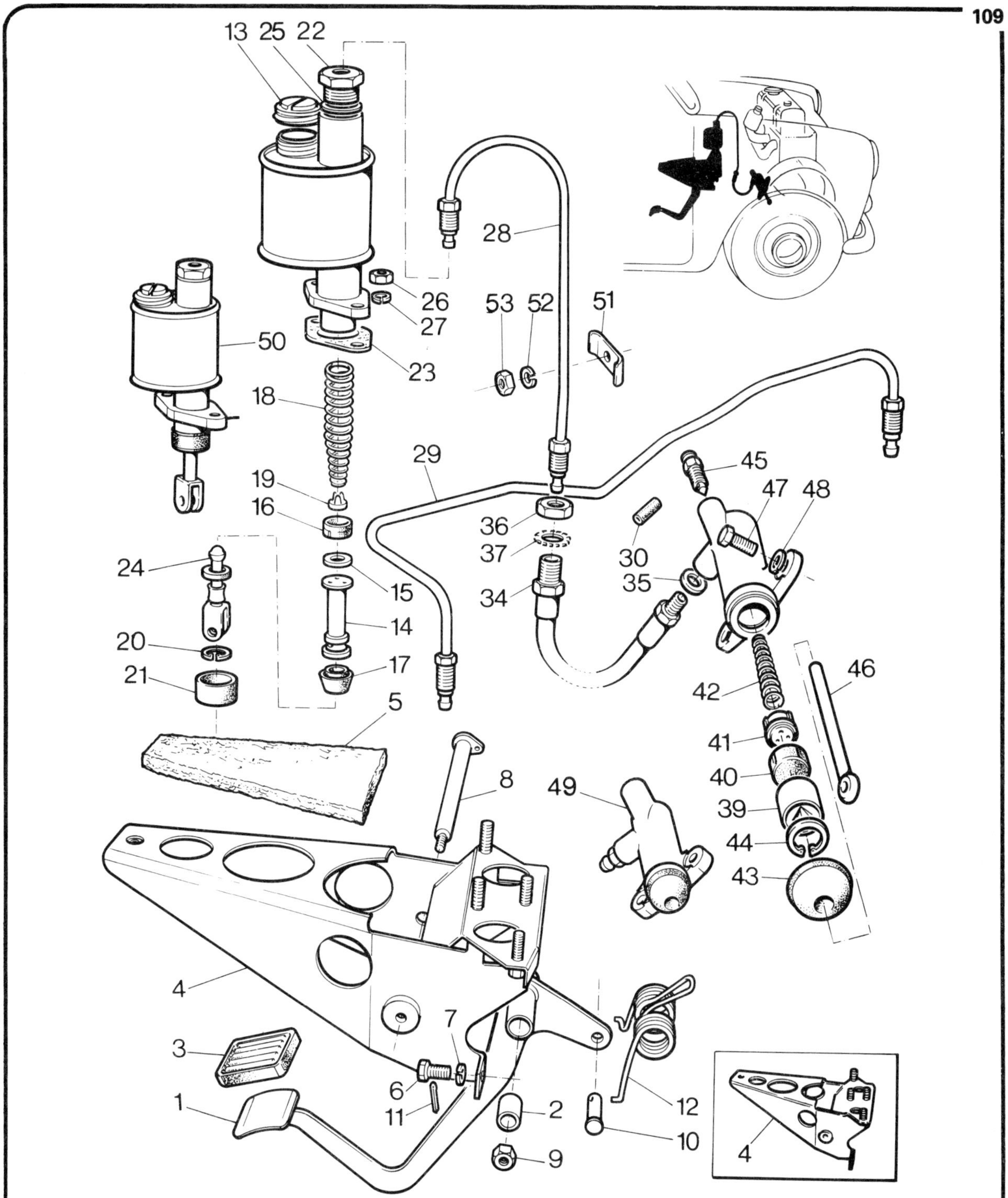

Fig. 5.1. Exploded view of clutch operating system

1	Clutch pedal	10	Clutch pedal to	20	Circlip	29	29 in (736.6 mm)	43	Rubber boot
2	Pedal bush		pushrod clevis pin	21	Rubber boot		pipe (lhd)	44	Circlip
3	Pedal pad	11	Split pin	22	End plug	30	Rubber pipe (lhd)	45	Bleed screw
4	Clutch & brake pedal	12	Return spring	23	Gasket	34	Clutch hose	46	Pushrod
	bracket	13	Filler cap	24	Pushrod	35	Gasket	47	Screw
5	Felt	14	Piston	25	Sealing washer	36	Locknut	48	Spring washer
6	Screw	15	Washer	26	Nut	37	Lock washer	49	Slave cylinder
7	Spring washer	16	Main cup	27	Spring washer	39	Piston	50	Master cylinder
8	Clutch & brake pedal	17	Secondary cup	28	12 in (304.8 mm)	40	Piston cup	51	Bracket
	shaft	18	Return spring		pipe	41	Piston cup filler	52	Washer
9	Nut	19	Retainer spring			42	Filler cup spring	53	Nut

2 Clutch hydraulic system - bleeding

1 Gather together a clean jam jar, a length of plastic or rubber tubing which fits tightly over the bleed nipple in the slave cylinder, a tin of hydraulic brake fluid, and an assistant.

2 Check that the master cylinder is full and if not fill it, and cover the bottom inch of the jar with hydraulic fluid.

3 Remove the rubber dust cap from the bleed nipple on the slave cylinder and with a suitable spanner open the bleed nipple one turn.

4 Place one end of the tube securely over the nipple and insert the other end in the jam jar so that the tube orifice is below the level of the fluid.

5 The assistant should now pump the clutch pedal up and down slowly until air bubbles cease to emerge from the end of the tubing. He should also check the reservoir frequently to ensure that the hdyraulic fluid does not disappear so letting air into the system.

6 When no more air bubbles appear, tighten the bleed nipple on the downstroke.

7 Replace the rubber dust cap over the bleed nipple. Discard the fluid bled from the system.

3 Clutch pedal - removal and replacement

1 From underneath the fascia take off the circlip which retains the fulcrum pin or pedal crossshaft in position. Slip off the hooked ends of the arms of the springs bearing against the pedal levers and push the crossshaft out.

2 Remove the small circlip from the end of the clevis pin fitted to the end of the pushrod and slide out the clevis pin.

3 The pedal is now free and can be lifted out.

4 Replacement is a straight reversal of the above procedure.

4 Clutch - removal and replacement

The clutch can be removed with the engine in the car or with the engine on the bench. If the engine is in the car proceed as follows:

1 Place a jack under the offside end of the transmission casing and take the weight of the engine. Disconnect the battery and remove it together with the battery carrier.

2 Undo the nut securing the starter motor cable to the starter motor, and pull the cable away. Undo the two bolts securing the starter motor in place and lift the motor out. Remove the cover over the timing marks on the flywheel and with the help of a winch turn the engine to tdc (top-dead-centre). If this is not done there is a chance of the flywheel 'C' washer falling and jamming the flywheel.

3 Either the coil or the solenoid switch may be fitted to the top of the flywheel housing. Undo the bolts which hold either in place and disconnect the wires.

4 Undo and remove the two bolts and spring washers which hold the offside engine mounting to the subframe sidemember.

5 Undo the bolt from the engine tie-rod and pull the tie-rod back against the bulkhead. Note: Engine tie-rods are not fitted to all models.

6 Loosen the two nuts and bolts on the exhaust pipe to exhaust manifold clamp. Undo and remove the bolt which holds the clip on the exhaust pipe to the gearlever casing extension.

7 Undo and remove the bolts which hold the top radiator steady bracket in place and remove the bracket.

8 Remove the slave cylinder return spring, undo and remove the two bolts which hold the slave cylinder to the top of the flywheel housing, and pull the cylinder off the short pushrod which is attached to the top of the clutch operating lever.

9 Undo and remove the nine bolts and spring washers which hold the clutch cover to the flywheel housing.

10 Jack up the engine just enough to be able to remove the clutch cover (which comes away with the engine mounting attached to it). While operating the jack frequently check that the fan blades are not damaging or fouling the radiator core.

11 Because the clutch is spread out on both sides of the flywheel, it is necessary to remove the flywheel before access can be gained to the pressure plate and the clutch disc.

12 Knock back the tabs which secure the three nuts to the three thrust plate screws. Note: The clutch thrust plate is only held by a retaining spring on models with diaphragm clutches. Pull off the clutch thrust plate.

13 Knock back the tab on the lockwasher which securely holds the flywheel bolt and undo the bolt three turns.

14 The flywheel is held firmly in place on the end of the crankshaft by means of a taper. A special puller will have to be borrowed to break this seal. See Chapter 1 for details. Note: If the engine is on the bench it is only necessary to carry out the operations described in paragraphs 9, and 11 to 14.

15 To refit the flywheel/clutch assembly on the rear of the crankshaft refer to Chapter 1, for full details.

16 Refit the clutch cover to the flywheel housing and insert and tighten up the nine bolts and washers which hold it in place.

17 Lower the engine and secure the offside engine mounting to the side of the subframe. Do not yet tighten the two bolts fully.

18 Replace and reconnect the slave cylinder. Adjust the clutch as described later in the Chapter.

19 Line up the hole in the tie-rod with the hole in the block so that the minimum strain will be placed on the rod and the engine mountings. It may be necessary to move the engine about 0.25 in (6.35 mm) before the holes line up.

20 Tighten the engine mounting and tie-rod bolts. Tighten the exhaust pipe to manifold clamp. Insert sufficient washers between the exhaust pipe clip and the mounting lug on the gearlever extension to take up any gap. Refit the clip to mounting lug nut and bolt.

21 Refit the coil or solenoid switch, the starter motor and the front grille.

22 Release the jack from under the car.

5 Clutch - dismantling and inspection

1 With the flywheel and clutch removed take great care to keep the assembly upright until any oil in the flywheel annulus has been mopped away.

2 To ensure that the clutch will still be evenly balanced on reassembly mark all the component parts of the clutch/flywheel unit so they can be replaced in their same relative positions. On most units the letter 'A' has been stamped on the edge of the pressure plate, and on the corner of the thrust plate and spring housing. Ensure the laminated driving straps are also marked.

3 Screw in to the flywheel through the holes in the spring housing, three 2½ in. 3/8 in. UNF bolts, or the three studs of Service tool '18G 304'. Tighten down the bolts (or nuts on the studs) finger tight. Then tighten them a further turn at a time until the load is completely taken from the three pressure plate bolts. Undo and remove the pressure plate bolts and their washers. Note: When dismantling the diaphragm spring clutch there is no need to use the bolts or the special studs of the service tool referred to above.

4 Undo and remove the clutch strap bolts and unscrew the bolts or nuts on the special screws a turn at a time until the clutch springs are fully released. The clutch is now fully dismantled.

5 Examine the clutch disc friction linings for wear and loose rivets and the disc for rim distortion, cracks and worn splines.

6 It is always best to renew the clutch disc as an assembly to preclude further trouble, but, if it is wished to merely renew the linings, the rivets should be drilled out and not knocked out with a punch. The manufacturers do not advise that only the linings are renewed and personal experience dictates that it is far more satisfactory to renew the disc complete than to try and economise by only fitting new friction linings.

7 Check the machined faces of the flywheel and the pressure plate. If either are badly grooved they should be machined until

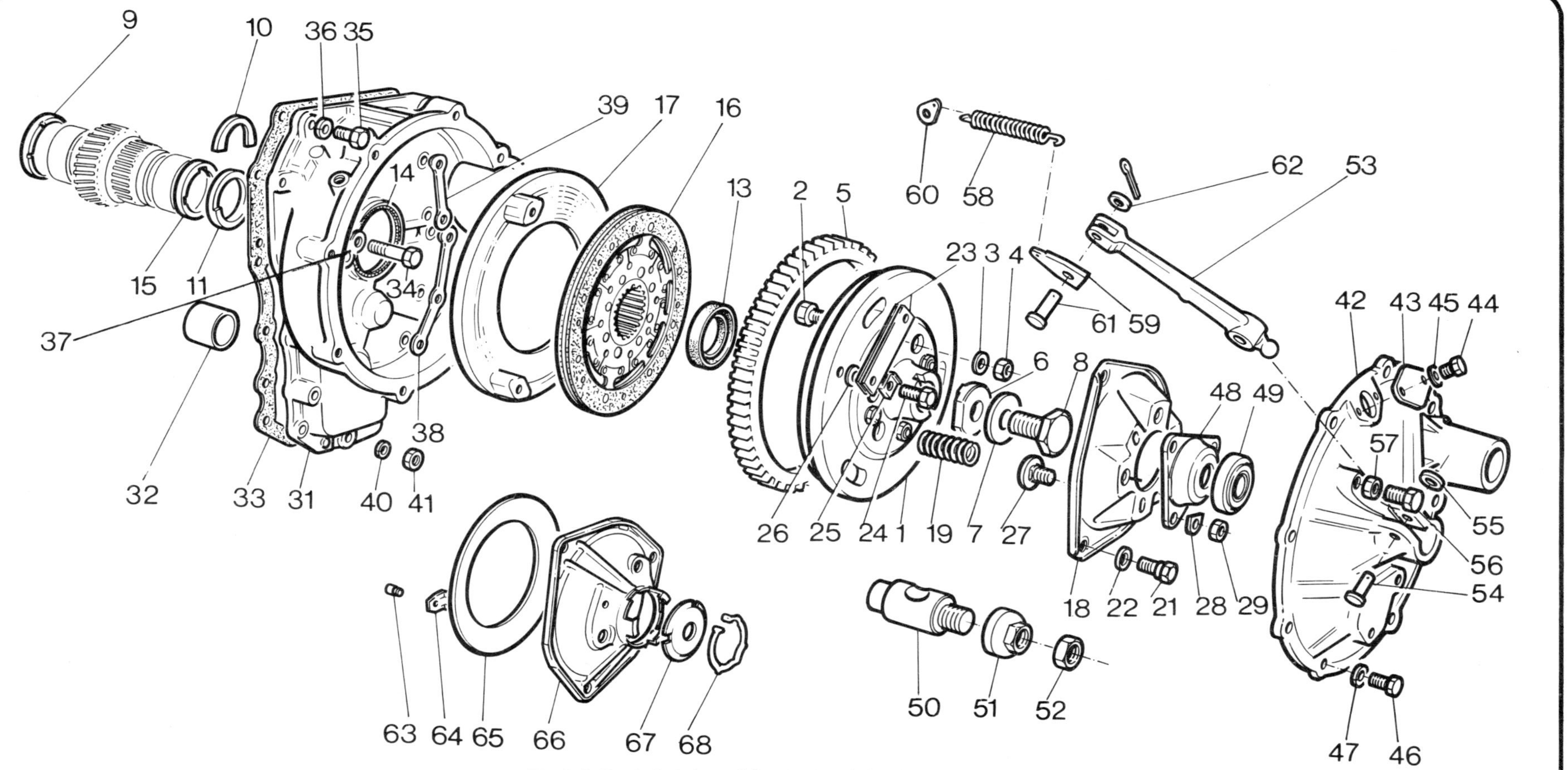

Fig. 5.2. Exploded view of flywheel and clutch components

1 Flywheel assembly
2 Hub screw
3 Lockwasher
4 Nut
5 Starter ring
6 Key
7 Lockwasher
8 Flywheel screw
9 Gear thrust washer (front)
10 Gear thrust washer (rear)
11 Backing ring
13 Flywheel oil seal
14 Housing oil seal
15 Primary gear retaining washer
16 Clutch driven plate
17 Pressure plate
18 Pressure spring housing (coil spring clutch)
19 Pressure spring
21 Pressure plate screw
22 Washer
23 Driving strap
24 Strap screw
25 Lockwasher
26 Washer
27 Thrust plate screw
28 Lockwasher (coil spring clutch)
29 Nut (coil spring clutch)
31 Flywheel housing
32 Idler gear bearing
33 Housing joint
34 Housing screw (long)
35 Housing screw
36 Washer
37 Housing lockwasher
38 Housing lock washer
39 Housing lockwasher
40 Washer
41 Nut
42 Clutch cover
43 Cover plate
44 Screw
45 Washer
46 Cover screw
47 Washer
48 Clutch thrust plate (coil spring clutch)
49 Release bearing
50 Throw-out plunger
51 Throw-out stop
52 Stop locknut
53 Clutch operating lever
54 Lever pin
55 Washer
56 Screw
57 Locknut
58 Lever pull-off spring
59 Spring anchor (lever)
60 Spring anchor (cylinder)
61 Pushrod pin
62 Washer
63 Rivet dowel
64 Retaining clip
65 Diaphragm spring
66 Spring housing
67 Thrust plate
68 Plate retaining spring

Diaphragm spring clutch

smooth. If the pressure plate is cracked or split it must be renewed.

8 Check the thrust plate for cracks and renew it if any are found.

9 Renew any clutch pressure springs that are broken or shorter than standard.

10 Examine the holes in the spring housing through which the pressure plate bolts pass, and if any of the holes are elongated the housing should be renewed.

11 Also examine the shoulders of the pressure plate bolts for ridges or signs of wear, and the driving straps for distortion or hole elongation. **Note**: If any of the bolts or straps require renewal they should be renewed as a set. Failure to do this will result in the clutch being thrown out of balance.

12 All 1100 Mk II, 1300 Mk I and II and 1300GT models are fitted with a 'Borg and Beck' diaphragm spring clutch. The clutch driven plate can be replaced in the normal way but it is not possible to service the pressure plate and diaphragm spring and these must be renewed as a unit if faulty in any way.

6 Clutch - reassembly

1 During clutch reassembly ensure that all the components are placed in their correct relative positions.

2 It is most important that no oil or grease gets on the clutch disc friction linings, or the pressure plate and flywheel faces. It is advisable to rebuild the clutch with clean hands and to wipe down the pressure plate and flywheel faces with a clean dry rag before assembly begins.

3 Renew the oil seal in the flywheel where one is fitted (coil spring type clutch). Reassemble the driving straps to the flywheel and ensure the spacing washers are in position.

4 Place the pressure plate, lugs facing upwards, on two blocks of wood on the assembly bench so there is about 1.5 in (38.1 mm) clearance between the centre of the pressure plate and the bench.

5 Place the clutch disc in the exact centre of the pressure plate using the polished working area on the pressure plate face as an accurate guide if the special centralising tool BLMC part No.'18G 571' is not available. Ensure that the longer end of the splined hub faces the bench away from the flywheel.

6 Carefully place the flywheel on the clutch disc so as not to disturb the position of the disc on the pressure plate. Also ensure the flywheel is in its correct relative position.

7 Stand the clutch pressure springs in their recessed holes in the flywheel.

8 Hold the spring housing in its correct relative position about 1 foot above the flywheel and note which springs lie underneath the elongated holes in the spring housing.

9 Place the three thrust plate bolts on top of the springs which will lie under the elongated holes and lower the spring housing over them. Ensure the flat flanks of the bolts register properly in the holes in the housing.

10 Compress the springs with the aid of the three 5/16 in. UNF bolts or the special tool. (Not necessary with diaphragm clutches).

11 Replace and do up the three pressure plate bolts using new washers under their heads and tighten them down to a torque of 16 lb f ft (2.21 kg f m).

12 Ensure the bolts which hold the driving straps to the flywheel are also tightened down to a torque of 16 lb f ft (2.21 kg f m) and that the tabs of the locking washer are turned up.

7 Clutch master cylinder - removal and replacement

1 Individual master cylinders and reservoirs are fitted for the brake system and the clutch system. Spring off the circlip from the end of the clevis pin which holds the clutch pushrod to the clutch pedal. Slide out the clevis pin.

2 Unscrew the union nut from the end of the hydraulic pipe where it enters the clutch master cylinder and gently pull the pipe clear.

3 Unscrew the two nuts and spring washers holding the clutch master cylinder mounting flange to the mounting bracket.

4 Remove the master cylinder and reservoir.

5 Refitting the master cylinder is the reverse sequence to removal. It will be necessary to bleed the clutch hydraulic system as described in Section 2.

8 Clutch master cylinder - dismantling, examination and assembly

1 Unscrew the filler cap, and drain the hydraulic fluid into a clean container.

2 Remove the rubber boot or dust cover, and extract the circlip from the end of the body with a pair of long-nosed pliers.

3 Pull out the pushrod and stop washer and shake out the piston, secondary cup, copper piston and spring washer.

4 Clean all the components thoroughly with hydraulic fluid or methylated spirits and then dry them off.

5 Carefully examine the parts, especially the rubber primary and secondary cups for signs of swelling, distortion, or splitting, and check the piston and cylinder wall for wear and score marks. Replace any parts that are faulty.

6 Reassembly is a straight reversal of the dismantling procedure, but **note** the following points:

a) As the components are returned to the cylinder barrel, lubricate them with the correct grade of hydraulic fluid.

b) Insert the return spring into the barrel with its broader base first.

9 Clutch slave cylinder - removal and replacement

The clutch slave cylinder is located at the top of the flywheel housing on the offside of the car.

1 Unscrew the union nut retaining the pipe to the slave cylinder and remove the pipe. Catch the hydraulic fluid in a suitable clean container and plug the end of the pipe to ensure no dirt enters.

2 Free the clutch slave cylinder pushrod from the clutch release arm by pulling out the split pin from the end of the clevis pin, and removing the clevis pin.

3 Unscrew the two bolts and spring holding the clutch slave cylinder to the clutch housing and lift the slave cylinder away.

4 Refitting the slave cylinder is the reverse sequence to removal. It will be necessary to bleed the clutch hydraulic system as described in Section 2. Also check the clutch adjustment as described in Section 11.

10 Clutch slave cylinder - dismantling, examination and re-assembly

1 Pull off the rubber boot or dust cap, remove the pushrod, and release the circlip with a pair of long-nosed pliers. Tap or shake out the piston, piston cup, cup filler and the small spring.

2 Clean all the components thoroughly with hydraulic fluid or methylated spirits and then dry them off.

3 Carefully examine the rubber components for signs of swelling, distortion, splitting or other wear, and check the piston and cylinder wall for wear and score marks. Replace any parts that are found faulty.

4 Reassembly is a straight reversal of dismantling procedure. As the component parts are refitted to the slave cylinder barrel smear them with hydraulic fluid.

11 Clutch - adjustment

As the friction linings of the clutch disc wear, the distance

Fig. 5.4. Cross-sectional view of clutch slave cylinder (Sec. 10)

1	Spring	5	Body
2	Cup filler	6	Circlip
3	Cup	7	Rubber boot
4	Piston	8	Pushrod

between the clutch release bearing and the clutch thrust plate will decrease. The pressure plate moves in closer to the clutch disc to compensate for wear. Unless the wear is taken up by adjustment of the stop located between the clutch housing and the operating lever, the clutch will start to slip.

1 Unhook the release spring from the clutch operating lever.

2 Pull the lever back until all the free movement is taken up. Hold the operating lever in this position and check the gap between the lever and the adjustable stop with a feeler gauge.

3 The gap should be 0.020 in. (0.508 mm). If this is not so, slacken the adjusting stop lock bolt and screw the bolt in or out till the clearance is correct. Tighten the lock bolt, and replace the release spring. After a clutch overhaul the throw out stop fitted in the centre of the flywheel cover boss must be reset:-

a) Slacken fully the locknut and the throw-out stop in the middle of the clutch cover.

b) Press down the clutch pedal, and holding the pedal in this position, screw the throw-out stop up to the cover boss.

c) Release the clutch pedal and screw in the stop a further 0.002 to 0.005 in. (0.05 to 0.12 mm) (about 1 flat of the lock-nut). Tighten the locknut and check the clearance between the operating lever and the stop screw which should be reset to 0.020 in (0.508 mm) if not already correct.

12 Clutch - overthrow

The purpose of adjusting the clutch is to prevent clutch slip, and to ensure that clutch overthrow does not overload the crankshaft thrust bearings. Even with the stop adjustment correct, clutch overthrow can occur if the clutch operating lever spring or the clutch pressure springs have weakened or the operating mechanism is stiff. Test for overthrow as follows:

1 Start the engine and allow it to warm up to its usual running temperature.

2 With the engine idling at no more than 500 rpm press the clutch pedal three or four times rapidly.

3 If the engine slows down much or stalls overthrow is occurring.

4 Increase the distance between the operating lever and the stop bolt to 0.075 in (1.91 mm).

5 If there is no improvement check the lever for stiffness.

6 If overthrow is still present replace the operating lever pull off spring with a stronger one.

7 Should no improvement be noticed then the clutch must be dismantled and new pressure plate springs fitted.

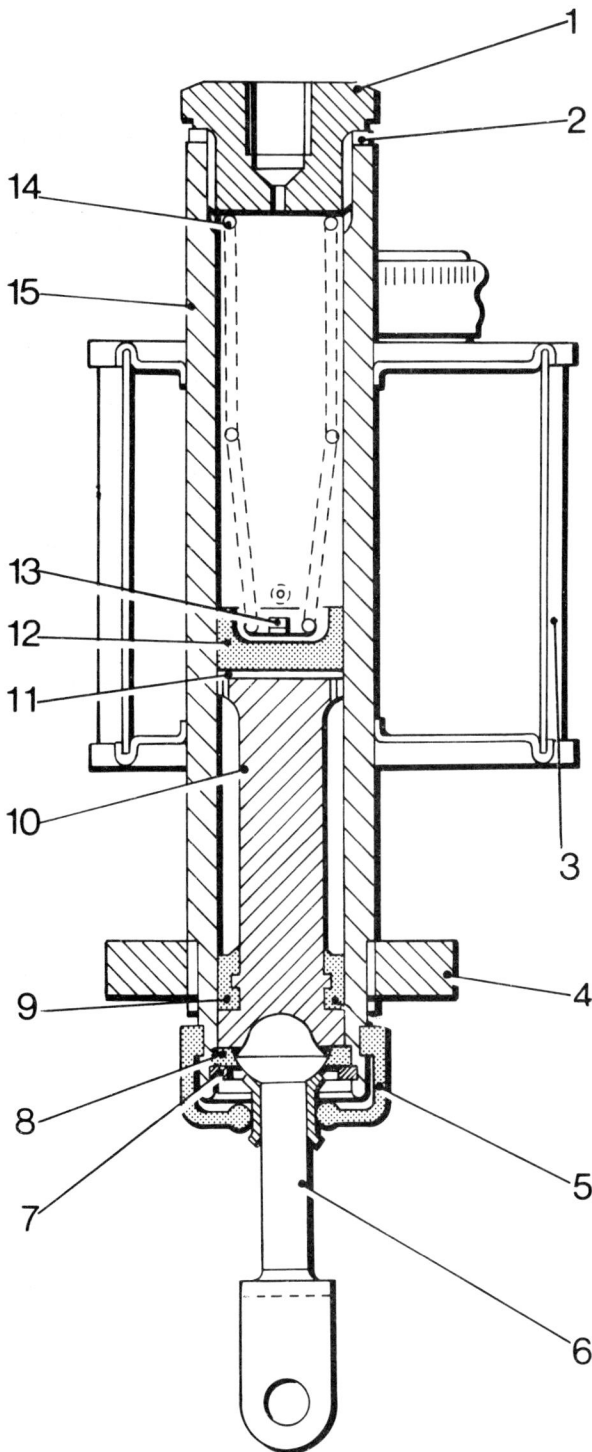

Fig. 5.3. Cross-sectional view of clutch master cylinder (Sec. 8)

1	End plug	9	Secondary cup
2	Washer	10	Piston
3	Supply tank	11	Piston washer
4	Mounting flange	12	Main cup
5	Rubber boot	13	Spring retainer
6	Pushrod	14	Return spring
7	Circlip	15	Body
8	Stop washer		

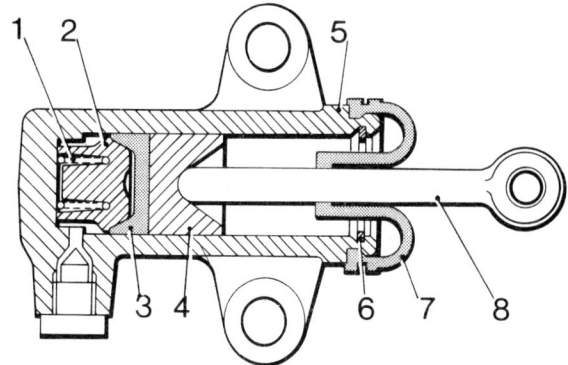

Clutch - removal and replacement (Early type shown. Many photos also applicable to later type diaphragm spring clutch)

1 Undo the bolts holding the clutch cover in place and remove the cover. The clutch is unusual in that it is spread out on both sides of the flywheel

2 The next step is to undo the three nuts which hold the thrust plate in position and lift away the plate

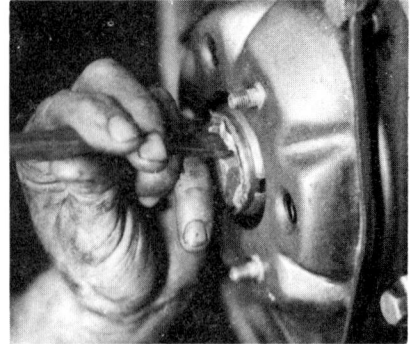

3 Part of the clutch is on the inside of the flywheel, this must be removed. Knock back the tab washer from flywheel retaining bolt and undo 3 turns

4 Screw down finger tight three 3/8 in UNF bolts, or three studs from BLMC tool 18G 304 into the flywheel through three holes in the spring housing

5 If bolts are used this plate must be placed under their heads. If studs are being used tighten the nuts down evenly

6 Prevent the engine rotating by a screwdriver jammed against flywheel tooth and casing. Tighten the large centre bolt to break the flywheel crankshaft seal

7 With the seal broken and the flywheel now loose on the crankshaft taper remove the special plate, undo the retaining bolt completely, and lift the flywheel away

8 Generally, dismantling the flywheel is a reversal of assembly shown in the following photographs. Ensure parts marked 'A' line up with the ¼ mark on the flywheel

9 Support the pressure plate so it is raised at least 2 in (50.8 mm) off the ground and fit the clutch driven plate with the long splined centre portion facing down

10 Gently replace flywheel making sure the '¼' mark on the rim is adjacent to the 'A' mark on the pressure plate

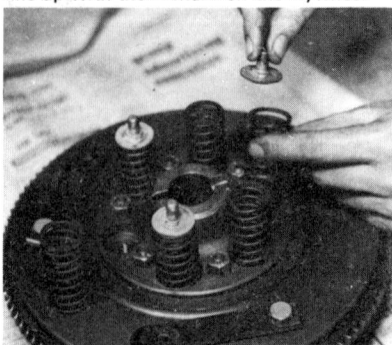

11 Replace clutch pressure springs and thrust plate screws (shown). Then carefully lower the spring housing into place

12 If a clutch compressing tool is not to hand standing on the housing compresses springs enough for the bolts to be fitted

13 With the flywheel back on the crankshaft replace the flywheel retaining bolt. Stop the flywheel from turning by inserting a cold chisel in the position shown

14 Tighten the flywheel retaining bolt to a torque of 115 lb f ft (15.87 kg f m)

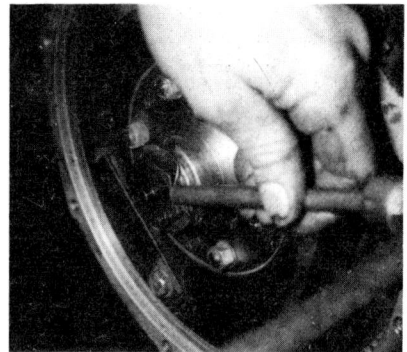

15 Knock back the tab of the lockwasher with the aid of a drift. The clutch housing can also be fitted with the flywheel in place as shown in the next 4 photos

16 Either a diaphragm or a coil spring housing may be fitted. In either case ensure the mark 'A' lines up with the ¼ mark on the flywheel

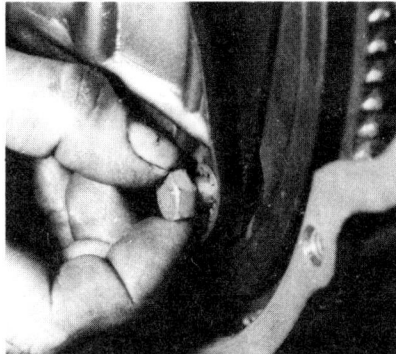

17 Then replace the three bolts and washers which hold the spring housing to the pressure plate

18 The next step is to replace the thrust plate which is simply held in place with a retaining spring on diaphragm clutches

19 In this photograph the retaining spring and thrust plate have been replaced and the method of attachment can be clearly seen

20 The next step is to fit the starter motor which is held in place with two bolts

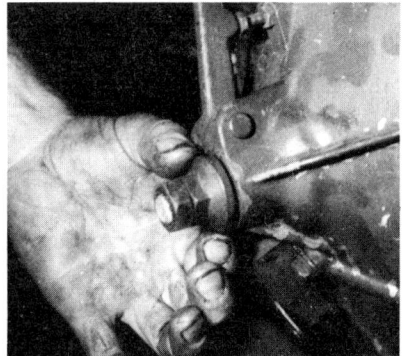

21 Then refit the clutch cover and adjust the clutch throw-out stop as follows: Screw the locknut and stop as far out from the cover as possible

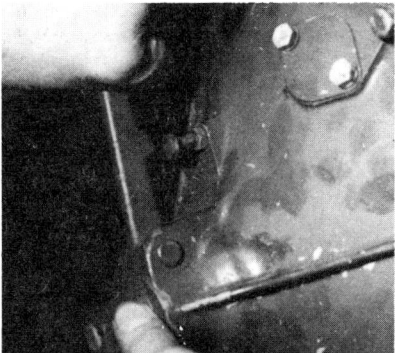

22 Pull and hold out the clutch lever as far as it will go and then do up the throw-out stop until it touches the cover boss

23 Release clutch lever and turn throw-out stop a further flat of hexagon (0.002 - 0.005 in/0.0508 - 0.127 mm). Tighten locknut

24 Check clearance of clutch lever against adjustable bolt on casing and screw bolt in or out to a gap of 0.020 in (0.508 mm)

13 Flexible hose - inspection, removal and replacement

Inspect the condition of the flexible hydraulic hose leading from the clutch metal pipe. If swollen, damaged, cut or chafed, it must be renewed.

1 Unscrew the metal pipe union nut from its connection to the flexible hose, and then, holding the hexagon on the hose with a spanner, unscrew the attachment nut and washer.

2 The end of the flexible hose can now be withdrawn from the mounting bracket and will be quite free.

3 Disconnect the flexible hose from the slave cylinder by unscrewing it, using a spanner.

4 Refitting is the reverse sequence to removal.

5 It will be necessary to bleed the hydraulic system as described in Section 2.

14 Fault diagnosis and remedy - clutch

There are four main faults to which the clutch and release mechanism are prone. They may occur by themselves or in conjunction with any of the other faults. They are clutch squeal, slip, spin, and judder.

Clutch squeal

1 If on taking up the drive or when changing gear, the clutch squeals, this is a sure indication of a badly worn clutch release bearing.

2 As well as regular wear due to normal use, wear of the clutch release bearing is much accentuated if the clutch is ridden, or held down for long periods in gear, with the engine running. To minimise wear of this component the car should always be taken out of gear at traffic lights and for similar hold-ups.

3 The clutch release bearing is not an expensive item.

Clutch slip

1 Clutch slip is a self-evident condition which occurs when the clutch friction plate is badly worn, the release arm free travel is insufficient, oil or grease have got onto the flywheel or pressure plate faces, or the pressure plate itself is faulty.

2 The reason for clutch slip is that, due to one of the faults listed above, there is either insufficient pressure from the pressure plate, or insufficient friction from the friction plate to ensure solid drive.

3 If small amounts of oil get onto the clutch, they will be burnt off under the heat of clutch engagement, in the process gradually darkening the linings. Excessive oil on the clutch will burn off leaving a carbon deposit which can cause quite bad slip, or fierceness, spin and judder.

4 If clutch slip is suspected, and confirmation of this condition is required, there are several tests which can be made.

5 With the engine in second or third gear and pulling lightly up a moderate incline, sudden depression of the accelerator pedal may cause the engine to increase its speed without any increase in road speed. Easing off the accelerator will then give a definite drop in the speed without the car slowing.

6 Drive the car at a steady speed in top gear and braking with the left leg, try and maintain the same speed by pressing down on the accelerator. Providing the same speed is maintained a change in the speed of the engine confirms that slip is taking place.

7 In extreme cases of clutch slip the engine will race under normal acceleration conditions.

8 If slip is due to oil or grease on the linings a temporary cure can sometimes be effected by squirting carbon tetrochloride into the clutch. The permanent cure, of course, is to renew the clutch driven plate and trace and rectify the oil leak.

Clutch spin

1 Clutch spin is a condition which occurs when there is a leak in the clutch hydraulic actuating mechanism where this system of actuation is used; the release arm free travel is excessive; there is an obstruction in the clutch either on the primary gear splines, or in the operating lever itself; or the oil may have partially burnt off the clutch linings and have left a resinous deposit which is causing the clutch disc to stick to the pressure plate or flywheel.

2 The reason for clutch spin is that due to any, or a combination of, the faults just listed, the clutch pressure plate is not completely freeing from the centre plate even with the clutch pedal fully depressed.

3 If clutch spin is suspected, the condition can be confirmed by extreme difficulty in engaging first gear from rest, difficulty in changing gear, and very sudden take-up of the clutch drive at the fully depressed end of the clutch pedal travel as the clutch is released.

4 Check the operating lever free travel. If this is correct examine the clutch master and slave cylinders and the connecting hydraulic pipe for leaks. Fluid in one of the rubber boots fitted over the end of either the master or slave cylinders, where fitted, is a sure sign of a leaking piston seal.

5 If these points are checked and found to be in order than the fault lies internally in the clutch, and it will be necessary to remove the clutch for examination.

Clutch judder

1 Clutch judder is a self-evident condition which occurs when the gearbox or engine mountings are loose or too flexible; when there is oil on the faces of the clutch friction plate; or when the clutch pressure plate has been incorrectly adjusted.

2 The reason for clutch judder is that due to one of the faults just listed, the clutch pressure plate is not freeing smoothly from the friction disc, and is snatching.

3 Clutch judder normally occurs when the clutch pedal is released in first or reverse gears, and the whole car shudders as it moves backwards or forwards.

Chapter 6
Manual Gearbox and automatic transmission

Contents

Specifications

Manual gearbox

1098 cc power units

Number of forward speeds 4

Synchromesh action:

Early models	Second, third and top gears
Later models	All forward gears

Ratios:

Gearbox		3 speed synchromesh	4 speed synchromesh
Top		1.0 : 1	1.0 : 1
Third		1.412 : 1	1.43 : 1
Second		2.172 : 1	2.22 : 1
First		3.627 : 1	3.53 : 1
Reverse		3.627 : 1	3.54 : 1

Overall:			
Top		4.13 : 1	4.13 : 1
Third		5.83 : 1	5.90 : 1
Second		8.98 : 1	9.17 : 1
First		14.99 : 1	14.57 : 1
Reverse		14.99 : 1	14.65 : 1

Speedometer gear ratio 17/6

Road speed in top gear at 1000 rpm ... ... 15 mph (24 kph) approx.

1275 cc and 1300 cc power units

Number of forward speeds 4

Synchromesh action:

1300 models	All forward gears
1275 cc engines	Second, third and fourth

Ratios:

Gearbox	Early 1275 cc engines	Later 1275 cc engines	1300 models 8.8 : 1 C.R.	1300 models 9.75 : 1 C.R.
Top	1.0 : 1	1.0 : 1	1.0 : 1	1.0 : 1
Third	1.426 : 1	1.412 : 1	1.43 : 1	1.35 : 1
Second	2.420 : 1	2.172 : 1	2.22 : 1	2.07 : 1
First	3.829 : 1	3.627 : 1	3.52 : 1	3.33 : 1
Reverse	3.829 : 1	3.627 : 1	3.54 : 1	3.35 : 1

Overall:

	Early 1275 cc	Later 1275 cc	1300 8.8	1300 9.75
Top	3.44 : 1	3.65 : 1	3.65 : 1	3.65 : 1
Third	4.91 : 1	5.16 : 1	5.22 : 1	4.93 : 1
Second	8.3 : 1	7.92 : 1	8.09 : 1	7.57 : 1
First	13.16 : 1	13.21 : 1	12.85 : 1	12.04 : 1
Reverse	13.16 : 1	13.21 : 1	12.92 : 1	12.22 : 1

Speedometer gear ratio	17/6

Road speed in top gear at 1000 rpm:

3.65 : 1 ratio *	17 mph (27.5 kph)
3.44 : 1 ratio *	18 mph (29 kph)
3.9 : 1 ratio *	16 mph (25 kph)

* See Specifications Chapter 8.

Automatic transmission:

Ratio

Gearbox:

Top	1.0 : 1
Third	1.46 : 1
Second	1.845 : 1
First	2.69 : 1
Reverse	2.69 : 1

Overall:

	Early 1100 models	Later 1100 and 1300 models
Top	4 : 1	3.76 : 1
Third	5.84 : 1	5.49 : 1
Second	7.38 : 1	6.94 : 1
First	10.76 : 1	10.11 : 1
Reverse	10.76 : 1	10.11 : 1

Speedometer gear ratio	7/17

Capacities:

Manual transmission casing	8.5 Imp pints, 4.83 litres
Automatic transmission:	
Dry	13 Imp pints, 7.38 litres
Refill	9 Imp pints, 5 litres

Torque wrench settings:

	lb f ft	kg f m
Manual		
Transmission case to crankcase	6	0.8
Transmission case studs 3/8 in. UNC	8	1.1
5/16 in. UNC	6	0.8
Transmission case stud nuts 3/8 in. UNF	25	3.5
5/16 in. UNF	18	2.5
Bottom cover setscrew 1/4 in. dia. UNC (change speed tower)	6	0.8
First motion shaft nut:		
Early	90	12.4
Later	150	20.74
Third motion shaft nut	150	20.74
Automatic		
Converter centre bolt	110 - 115	15.2 - 15.9
Converter (6 centre bolts)	22 - 24	3.04 - 3.32
Converter drain plugs	18 - 20	2.5 - 2.77

							lb f ft	kg f m
Converter housing bolts	...	...	...	...	...	...	18	2.5
Input shaft nut	...	...	...	...	...	...	70	9.6
Oil filter bowl (centre bolt)	...	...	...	...	...		12 - 16	1.7 - 2.2
Transmission to engine securing nut:	...	...	...	...			12	1.7
5/16 in. UNF bolt	...	...	...	...	...		18 - 20	2.5 - 2.77
3/8 in. UNF bolt	...	...	...	...	...		30	4.15
'Kickdown' control assembly bolts	...	...	...	...			5	0.7

1 General description

The manual gearbox fitted to all models contains four forward gears and reverse. On earlier models synchromesh was fitted between second and third gears and between the third and fourth. With the introduction of the 1300 models in 1968 a four speed all synchromesh gearbox was fitted to all models.

The early gearboxes made use of bush bearings in the second and third gear clusters whilst needle roller bearings were fitted to post October 1964 models. The two forward gear selector forks were also modified.

With the introduction of all synchromesh gearbox major changes in design were necessary to the casing and all shafts. The laygear was lengthered by 1.0 inch (25.4 mm) and supported on the needle roller bearings. For these reasons the components of this gearbox are not interchangeable with earlier types.

Automatic transmission was offered as an optional fitment to many models. Information on this unit will be found later on in this Chapter.

2 Gearbox - removal and replacement

The gearbox is removed from the car together with the engine and differential assembly. Full information on removal, and separation from the engine, will be found in Chapter 1. Replacement of the gearbox is the reverse sequence to removal.

3 Gearbox (earlier type) - dismantling

Before the gearbox can be dismantled it is necessary to separate the engine and the differential unit from the gearbox casing. Refer to Chapters 1 and 8, respectively, for full information.

Place the gearbox on a strong bench so it is at a comfortable working height and quite accessible. If a bench is not available then lay the gearbox on the floor, but make sure the latter is clean and dirt free and preferably covered with paper.

To make the dismantling and rebuilding sequence as easy as possible, the task has been keyed to Fig. 6.2, except where otherwise stated. Throughout the text the numbers in brackets, ie., (15), refer to the parts shown in this illustration. Strip the gearbox in the following sequence:

1 Remove the remote control extension housing after undoing the bolts which hold it to the transmission casing.

2 To dismantle the extension prise off the dust cover at the change speed lever end, and undo and remove the bolt and spring washer from the primary shaft lever. Remove the cap nut, spring and plunger and pull the primary shaft out of the extension.

3 Unscrew the clamping bolt (131) which secures the lever (130) to the remote control shaft (129) in the rear of the transmission casing, and slide the shaft out. On early models a nylon cup and spring were fitted to the bottom of the shaft. On later models the cup and spring were omitted. If found during overhaul discard the nylon cup and also the spring. This helps to give a positive and easier gearchange.

4 Remove the spring plug (135), the plug washer (136), the spring (134) and the reverse check plunger (133) which serves to locate the gearchange shaft (120).

5 Take off the intermediate gear (43) together with its thrust washers (44) from the rear of the transmission casing. Make sure that the washers are kept in their correct relative positions either side of the gear.

6 Undo the bolt (97) on the speedometer pinion housing and take off the pinion housing cover (95). Pull out the speedometer pinion (93). Undo the two bolts and washers (103, 104), from the front cover (137), and remove the end plate, joint gasket, and speedometer gear (101, 102, 100).

7 Unscrew the clamp bolt and washer (124, 125) from the selector lever (122) and remove the gear change shaft (120), the selector lever (122), and the oil seal (121), from the transmission casing (1). **Note:** There is a Woodruff key (123) fitted to the lower end of the gearchange shaft (120). Ensure this key is extracted before removing the shaft.

8 Undo and remove the bolts, nuts and spring washers (139, 143, 142, 140) which hold the front cover (137) in position. Pull the cover (137), and gasket (138) from the transmission casing.

9 Knock back the tab of the lock washer (32) from the bolt (31) which holds the oil suction pipe support bracket to the lug on the gearbox casing. Undo the two bolts (37) which hold the oil pipe flange (33) to the casing, and remove the suction pipe (33) and joint gasket (34). The oil strainer (26) cannot yet be removed.

10 Knock back the tabs of the locking washers (87) and undo the bolts (88) which hold the mainshaft bearing retainer (86) to the web in the centre of the casing. Take off the retainer (86) and remove the bearing shim (89).

11 Lock together two gears by pressing the shifter fork rods in. This will prevent the mainshaft from turning.

12 Undo and remove the nut and washer (91, 92) which holds the final drive pinion (90) to the mainshaft (65). Pull the pinion off the mainshaft.

13 Remove the circlip and the roller bearing from the end of the first motion shaft, unlock the lock washer (47), undo the nut (46), and take off the driving gear (45). The locked gears may now be freed.

14 Measure the endfloat of the laygear (54) with a feeler gauge. If the endfloat exceeds 0.006 in (0.152 mm) or is less than 0.002 in (0.0508 mm) then new thrust washers must be fitted on re-assembly. A single locating plate (55) holds both the layshaft (53), and the reverse shaft (50) in place by means of slots in the ends of the shafts into which the plate fits. Remove the plate from the centre web so freeing the shafts.

15 Tap the layshaft out of the transmission casing and lift the laygear (54) together with the thrust washers (59, 60) out of the gearbox.

16 Unscrew the 2 plugs (117) from the transmission housing (1) and remove the plungers (115) and plunger springs which locate in the 1st and 2nd, and 3rd and 4th gear shifter rods.

17 Remove the circlip (64) from the transmission housing, and carefully tap out the first motion shaft ball bearing (63).

18 Release the locknut (114) from the 1st and 2nd gear shifter fork (108), unscrew the shifter fork bolt (112) and remove the 1st and 2nd gear shifter rod (109). Lift the shifter fork out of the transmission casing.

19 With a suitable drift drive the mainshaft (65), about 1 in. to the rear of the transmission casing. Because the mainshaft bearing is held with a circlip against the forward edge of the centre web it will be prevented from emerging on the other side of the web with the mainshaft. Insert the BLMC special tool '18G 613' in the gap now created between the 1st speed gear (68) and the mainshaft bearing (66).

20 Drive the mainshaft forward towards the front of the casing, taking care not to damage the shifter forks, until the bearing is nearly clear of the centre housing. Carefully lever the bearing off. If the special tool '18G 613' is not used the splines or

shoulder of the lst gear may damage the centre web. **Note:** Two thick metal packing pieces may be used instead of the tool if if it is not available.

21 Remove the bearing, the mainshaft, and the associated parts from the transmission casing.

22 Knock back the other tab on the lockwasher (32), unscrew the remaining bolt (31) from the strainer bracket (28) and lift the strainer (6) and bracket out of the gearbox casing.

23 Loosen the locknut (114) from the 3rd and 4th gear shifter fork (110), unscrew the shifter fork bolt (112) and remove the gear shifter rod (111). Lift the shifter fork (110) out of the transmission casing. Repeat this operation with the reverse gear shifter rod (106) and shifter fork (107).

24 Remove the reverse gear shaft (50), the reverse gear (48), and the reverse gear shifter fork (105). Remove the plunger (115), and the plunger spring (116).

25 Remove the circlip (52) from the top of the reverse gear shifter lever (51) and extract the lever from the casing, together with the lever pin (22).

26 The gearbox is now completely stripped. The component parts should now be examined for wear as detailed later, and the layshaft, first motion shaft, and mainshaft broken down further as shown in Section 4.

4 Gearbox (early type) - examination and renovation

Carefully examine all the component parts starting with the synchronising baulk rings. If badly worn or if the rings are loose on their gears, they must be renewed. It is normal practice to purchase new gears and synchronising rings complete.

Examine the gearwheels for excessive wear and chipping of the teeth and renew them as necessary.

If the laygear endfloat is above the permitted tolerance (see para. 14 in Section 3), the thrust washers must be renewed.

Measure the distance between the larger gearwheel and the side of the casing, immediately below the layshaft.

When gap is	Fit shim
0.125 to 0.127 in (3.18 to 3.22mm)	88G325
0.128 to 0.130 in (3.25 to 3.30mm)	88G326
0.131 to 0.133 in (3.32 to 3.37mm)	88G327
0.134 in (3.41mm)	88G328

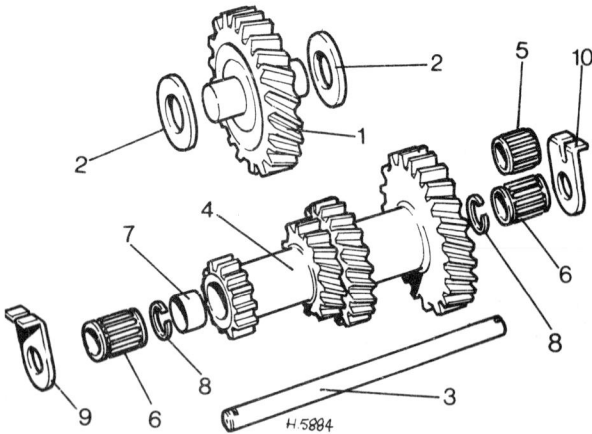

Fig. 6.1. Exploded view of layshaft and idler gear (earlier models)

1 Idler gear
2 Thrust washers - various sizes available
3 Layshaft
4 Laygear
5 Needle roller bearing
6 Alternative needle roller bearing
7 Distance piece
8 Spring clip
9 Thrust washer
10 Thrust washer

H·5884

Fig. 6.2. Exploded view of early type gearbox (Sec. 3)

1 Transmission case
2 Control shaft bush
3 Differential cover stud
4 Differential cover stud
5 Differential cover dowel
6 Differential cover joint washer (upper)
7 Differential cover joint washer (lower)
8 Differential cover stud nut
9 Washer
10 Washer
12 Differential cover stud nut
13 Washer
14 Flywheel housing stud
15 Front cover stud (long)
16 Front cover stud (long)
17 Front cover stud (short)
18 Front cover dowel
19 Flywheel housing dowel
20 Idler gear bearing
21 Bearing circlip
22 Operating lever pin
23 Exhaust pipe bracket
24 Drain plug
25 Plug washer
26 Oil strainer
27 Sealing ring
28 Strainer bracket
29 Screw to strainer
30 Washer
31 Screw to casing
32 Washer
33 Oil suction pipe
34 Joint washer
35 Pipe flange
36 Joint washer
37 Pipe screw
38 Washer
39 Sealing ring
40 Primary gear
41 Gear bush (front)
42 Gear bush (rear)
43 Idler gear
44 Idler gear thrust washer
45 First motion shaft gear
46 Nut
47 Lockwasher
48 Reverse gear
49 Bush
50 Reverse shaft
51 Reverse operating lever
52 Pivot pin circlip
53 Layshaft
54 Laygear
55 Locating plate
56 Bearing
57 Distance piece
58 Retaining ring
59 Thrust washer (rear)
60 Thrust washer (front)
61 First motion shaft
62 First motion shaft roller bearing
63 First motion ball bearing
64 Circlip
65 Third motion shaft
66 Third motion shaft bearing
67 Circlip
68 First speed gear
69 Synchronizer ball
70 Spring
71 Second speed synchronizer plunger
72 Baulk ring
73 Second speed gear
74 Second speed gear thrust washer
75 Bush
76 Interlocking ring
77 Third speed gear
78 Bush
79 Third motion shaft thrust washer
80 Thrust washer peg
81 Spring
82 Third/top synchronizer
83 Ball
84 Spring
85 Baulk ring
86 Bearing retainer
87 Lockwasher
88 Screw
89 Bearing shim
90 Final drive pinion
91 Nut
92 Washer
93 Speedometer pinion
94 Bush
95 Bush assembly
96 Joint washer
97 Bush screw
98 Washer
99 Washer
100 Speedometer spindle and gear
101 End plate
102 Plate joint
103 Screw
104 Washer
105 Reverse fork
106 Reverse fork rod
107 Fork rod selector
108 First and second speed fork
109 First and second speed fork rod
110 Third and fourth speed fork
111 Third and fourth speed fork rod
112 Selector screw
113 Washer
114 Locknut
115 Plunger fork end
116 Plunger spring
117 Plug
118 Plug washer
119 Change speed gate
120 Gear change shaft
121 Oil seal
122 Operating lever
123 Key
124 Lever screw
125 Washer
126 Change shaft lever
127 Lever screw
128 Washer
129 Remote control shaft
130 Shaft lever
131 Lever screw
132 Washer
133 Reverse check plunger
134 Plunger spring
135 Spring plug
136 Plug washer
137 Front cover
138 Cover joint
139 Cover screw
140 Washer
141 Mounting adaptor stud
142 Washer
143 Nut
144 Crankcase joint washer rh
145 Crankcase joint washer lh
146 Bearing cap oil seal
147 Transmission to crankcase screw
148 Transmission to crankcase screw (long)
149 Transmission to crankcase stud
150 Nut
151 Washer
152 Gear change remote control shaft lubricator
153 Lubricator washer

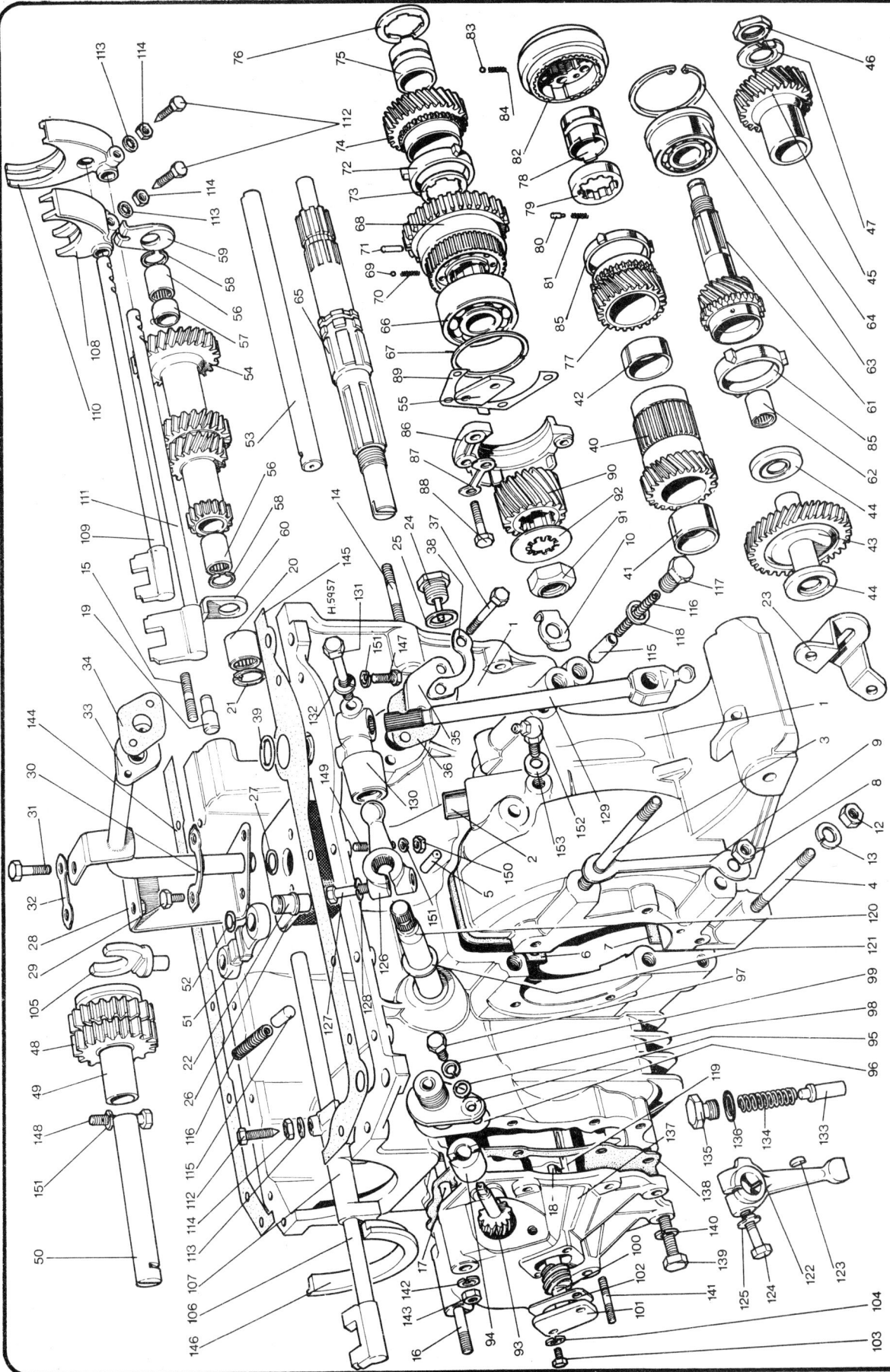

A needle roller bearing is fitted internally to each end of the laygear. To examine them, prise out the retaining clips from each end, and with a finger pull out the outer race, needle rollers, and inner race. At the end of the laygear with the smaller gear, also extract the distance piece and the inner spring rings from both ends. Renew the roller bearings and races, if worn.

Dealing first with the smaller end of the laygear, place it upright with the smaller end at the top and fit the inner spring ring, the distance piece, and slide the new roller bearing into position. Slip the spring retaining ring into the groove. Repeat this procedure for the larger end of the laygear, turning the laygear round, and omitting, of course, the distance piece.

Examine the condition of the main ball bearings, one on the first motion shaft, and the other on the mainshaft. If there is looseness between the inner and outer races the bearings must be renewed.

If it is wished to renew the synchronisers, or to examine the second and third gear bushes or needle roller bearings the third motion shaft must be dismantled in the following sequence which will ensure the job is done rapidly, correctly, and easily.

If new bushes are being fitted they must be first heated to about 190° C (374° F). Expansion will allow them to slide on the mainshaft easily and as they cool the subsequent contraction will ensure they fit securely in position.

5 Mainshaft (early type) - dismantling

1 Slide the synchroniser hub (82) for third/top gears from off the rear of the mainshaft. **Note:** the plain part of the hub faces towards the rear of the transmission casing.
2 With an electrical screwdriver or piece of thin rod, press down the spring loaded plunger (80, 81), and turn the splined thrust washer (79) so that a spline holds the plunger down, and the thrust washer is so positioned that it can slide forwards off the rear of the mainshaft. Now slide the baulk ring synchroniser (85) and the third gear (77) off the mainshaft in the same manner.
3 Remove the now exposed plunger and spring (80, 81) and take off the third gear bush (78), (or needle roller bearings) and the interlocking ring (76).
4 Remove the second gear (74) together with the baulk ring synchroniser (72) and the second gear bush (75). **Note:** in post 1965 models a needle roller bearing replaces the bush. Take off the thrust washer (73).
5 Slide the first gear and hub (68) off the front of the mainshaft.
6 If it is wished to remove the hubs from the centre of the gearwheels, ensure a rag is placed round the assembly to catch the three spring loaded balls (69, 70) contained in each hub.

6 Mainshaft (early type) - reassembly

On reassembly of the gearwheel to the hub ensure that the cut-away on the spline in the gearwheel lines up with the hole for the plunger. Also ensure that the teeth on the first gear are on the cone side of the first gear hub.
1 Replace the second gear thrust washer (73) and slide the second gear bush (75), or needle roller bearing, onto the rear of the mainshaft so the smooth end of the bush abuts the thrust washer. Oil the bearings.
2 Fit the second gear and synchroniser (72, 74) over the second gear thrust washer and slide on the interlocking ring (76) so that two of the cut-outs mate with the two protrusions on the end of the second gear bush (75).
3 Replace the first gear and hub assembly (68) on the front of the mainshaft (65), pushing it firmly up to the second gear (74). Ensure that the flat end of the hub assembly (68) will abut the roller bearing (66) when the latter is replaced.
4 Moving to the rear of the mainshaft, fit the third gear bush (78) ensuring that the two protrusions slide into the two remain-

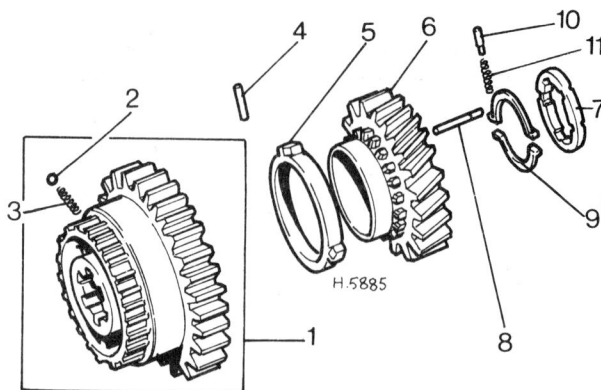

Fig. 6.3. Exploded view of first and second gears

1	First gear with second gear synchroniser	6	Second gear
2	Ball	7	Locking collar
3	Spring	8	Needle roller
4	Second gear plunger	9	Locking washer
5	Baulk ring synchroniser	10	Peg
		11	Spring

ing slots in the interlocking ring (76).
5 Slide the third gear (77) onto the rear of the mainshaft, flat side first, and drop the spring (81) and locking plunger (80) into the mainshaft drilling.
6 Press down the plunger (80), slide the thrust washer (79) up the splines of the mainshaft over the depressed plunger, and rotate the washer in the circular mainshaft groove one spline width. Turning the thrust washer in this way allows the plunger to slide up into one of the internal spline grooves, so locking the washer in place.
7 Measure the endfloat of the second and third speed gears which should be between o.0035 and 0.0055 in. (0.09 and 0.13 mm.).
8 Replace the synchroniser hub (82) for third/top gears with the plain side facing the rear of the transmission casing. Mainshaft assembly is now complete.

7 Gearbox (early type) - reassembly

Thoroughly clean the gearbox casing, and scrape all traces of old gaskets off the gearbox flanges. Clean in paraffin, and, if possible, blow dry with an airline, the internal components of the gearbox. Reassembly should proceed as follows:
1 Press the reverse lever operating pin (22) into its bore in the bottom of the casing with the groove in the pin uppermost.
2 Press the reverse operating lever (51) into place on the operating pin (22), and fit operating lever retaining circlip (52) to the operating pin (22).
3 Replace the reverse fork (105) in the hole in the reverse operating lever (51). Ensure the cut-out on the fork faces the front of the gearbox.
4 Place the reverse gear and bush (48. 49) in position so the flange on the end of the gear slides over the prongs of the reverse fork (105).
5 Oil the reverse gear shaft (50) and pass it through the centre web of the transmission case, into the reverse gear (49), with the slotted end of the shaft (50) facing towards the front of the casing.
6 Fit and hold the reverse gear shifter rod spring (116A) and plunger (115A) in place, and then slide in the reverse fork rod (106) from the front of the casing so the fork rod selector (107) picks up the reverse fork.
7 Place the third and fourth gear shifter fork (110) in the casing and push the third and fourth gear shifter rod (111) in from the front of the casing so the rod enters the lower hole in

the fork (110).

8 Place the first and second gear shifter fork (108) in the casing and push the first and second gear shifter rod (109) in from the front of the casing so the rod enters the locating hole in the first and second gear selector fork (108) and also passes through the clearance hole in the third and fourth gear shifter fork (110).

9 Line up the indentations in the rods (106, 111, 109) with the holes in the forks (107, 110, 108) and insert and tighten down the selector screws (112), lockwashers (113), and locknuts (114). Make certain the locknuts (114) are properly tightened down, and on no account omit the lockwashers (113). As the selectors lie in the bottom of the transmission casing if one works loose the whole gearbox must be stripped to tighten it.

10 Place the oil strainer sealing ring (27) in the recess in the oil strainer (26), and lightly grease the ring to help the oil pipe pass through easily when it is fitted later. Attach the oil strainer bracket (28) to the oil strainer (26), fit the lockwasher (30), and insert and tighten the two bolts (29) securely. Turn up the tabs on the lockwasher. Place the strainer in position in the bottom of the casing. Do not yet insert the bolts (31) which hold the bracket to the lugs on the casing.

11 Replace the mainshaft assembly with the forked end of the shaft (65) facing the front of the gearbox casing and with the synchroniser hubs in place over the shifter forks.

12 Press the first motion shaft ball bearing (63) onto the end of the first motion shaft (61) and insert the assembly into the casing.

13 Place the circlip (67) in the retaining groove of the mainshaft bearing (66); ensure that both the mainshaft and the first motion shaft are correctly aligned and then carefully drift both bearings into position in the casing. **Note:** When drifting in the bearings ensure the load is spread over both the inner and outer ball race cases. Oil both bearings.

14 With a pair of circlip pliers replace the circlip (64) retaining the first motion shaft ball bearing (63) in its housing.

15 Replace the first and second and third and fourth gear selector rod plungers (115) into their drillings on the outside of the casing, and follow them up with their locating springs (116), plugs and plug washers (117, 118). If possible use new plug washers, and on no account omit them or oil leaks will develop.

16 Fit the final drive pinion (90), a new locking washer (92), and screw on the pinion retaining nut. Tighten the nut down to a torque of 150 lb f ft (20.74 kg fm). Turn up the edge of the lockwasher.

17 Place the first motion shaft gearwheel (45) on the locating splines at the front of the first motion shaft (61); fit a new lockwasher (47), making sure that the two protrusions on the washer locate in the two holes in the gearwheel; and tighten down the securing nut (46) to a torque of 90 lb f ft (12.4 kg fm); later models 150 lb f ft (20.74 kg fm). Turn up the edge of the lockwasher.

18 Place a thrust washer (60) in position (hold it with a dab of grease), and carefully fit the laygear (54) taking care not to disturb the washer. Oil the layshaft (53) and by judicious manipulation insert it through the hole in the centre web, through the thrust washer (60) to the far end of the laygear (54). Then fit the second thrust washer (59) and push the layshaft right home in the housing. **Note:** The slot in the side of the layshaft must be towards the front of the gearbox casing.

19 Measure the end clearance which should be between 0.002 in. and 0.006 in. (0.0508 and 0.1524 mm) as already described. Thrust washers sized from 0.121 to 0.132 in. (3.048 to 3.353 mm) compensate for wear.

20 Do not yet fit the mainshaft bearing retainer shim (89) in position, but fit the bearing retainer (86). Turn the slots in the sides of the layshaft (53), and the reverse gear shaft (50), until they are at approximately 90° to each other and then refit the locating plate (55), which fits *between* the shim (89) (not yet fitted) and the retainer (86).

21 Replace the two tab lockwashers (87), tighten down the four bolts (88), and then with a feeler gauge measure the gap between the mainshaft bearing retainer, and the wall of the housing as

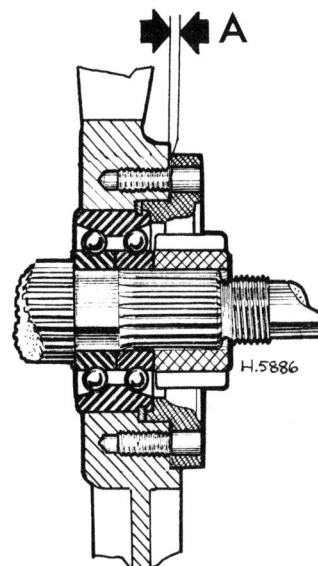

Fig. 6.4. Cross-section through third motion shaft bearing retainer (Sec. 7)
Gap 'A' to be measured with feeler gauges to determine shim thickness

indicated in Fig. 6.4. Use the table below to determine the correct thickness of shim to use.

Measured Gap	Fit shims totalling
0.005 to 0.006in (0.127 to 0.152mm)	0.005in (0.127mm)
0.006 to 0.008in (0.152 to 0.203mm)	0.007in (0.178mm)
0.008 to 0.010in (0.203 to 0.254mm)	0.009in (0.229mm)
0.010 to 0.012in (0.254 to 0.304mm)	0.011in (0.279mm)
0.012 to 0.014in (0.304 to 0.356mm)	0.013in (0.330mm)
0.014 to 0.015in (0.356 to 0.381mm)	0.015in (0.381mm)

22 Remove the retainer (86), fit the appropriate shims under the locating plate (55), and replace and tighten down the bolts holding the retainer and locating plate in position. Knock up the tabs of the locking washers (87).

23 Lightly grease the end of the oil suction pipe (33) and insert it into the hole in the centre of the oil strainer (26) taking care not to dislodge the rubber sealing ring (27).

24 The top flange on the bracket (28) lies under the lug on the side of the gearbox casing. The oil pipe bracket lies on the top of the lug. Position the lockwasher (32), and insert the two bolts (31) through the two holes in the lug into the fixed nuts under the bracket flange (28). Place a new joint gasket (36) between the pipe blanking plate (35) and the flange on the outside of the casing, and a new gasket (34) between the oil pipe flange (33) and inside of the casing. Fit a new lockwasher (38) and tighten up the two pairs of bolts (37, 31). Turn up the tabs on both lockwashers (32, 38).

25 Refit the change speed gate (119); fit a new front cover gasket (138) to the flange on the front of the casing; fit the front cover (137), and insert and tighten up the bolts (139), nuts (143) and springwasher (140, 142), as appropriate.

26 Replace the oil seal (121), and partially insert the gear change shaft (120) into the transmission casing. Refit the Woodruff key (123) to the shaft, position the selector lever in the casing, making sure its lower end engages with the change speed gate (119) and push the gear change shaft (120) through the hole in the lever (122) so the Woodruff key (123) mates with the slot in the selector lever (122). Push the shaft (120) right into its housing in the transmission case, and line up the cut-out in the shaft (120) with the hole for the clamp bolt in the lever (122). Insert and tighten the clamp bolt (124), and turn up the tab on the lockwasher (125).

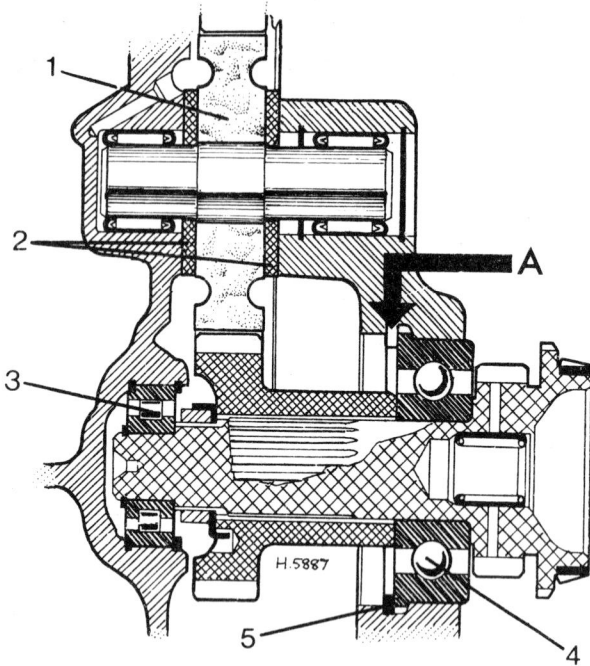

Fig. 6.5. Cross-section through the idler gear and first motion shaft (Sec. 7)
Ideally the gap 'A' should be measured with service tool '18G 569' to enable selection of appropriate circlip

1 Idler gear	4 First motion shaft ball
2 Idler gear thrust washers	bearing
3 First motion shaft roller	5 First motion shaft
bearing	circlip

27 Replace the reverse check plunger (133), and the plunger spring (134) in the hole in the casing; make sure the washer (136) is under the head of the spring plug (135) and tighten the plug securely.
28 Insert the speedometer spindle and gear (100), through the front cover (137) so the spindle engages the slot in the end of the mainshaft (65). Replace the joint gasket (102), end plate (101), and tighten down the two securing bolts and lockwashers (103, 104).
29 Replace the speedometer pinion (93) in the side of the front cover (137), and carefully fit the brush (94), the joint gasket (96), and the pinion housing cover (95). Insert and tighten down the speedometer pinion housing bolt, flat and spring washers (98, 99).
30 Refit the differential assembly to the gearbox casing as described in Chapter 8.
31 Refit the remote control shaft (129) and the lever (130) in place. **Note:** Leave off the nylon cup and spring if previously fitted. Replace the bottom cover plate on the underside of the gear change extension and refit anti-rattle spring, plunger and hexagon cap. The gearbox is now completely assembled with the exception of the intermediate gear which is dealt with in Section 9.

8 Transfer gears - general description

Drive is transmitted from the clutch to the gearbox by means of three transfer gears. On the end of the crankshaft is the primary gear. When the clutch pedal is depressed the primary gear remains stationary while the crankshaft revolves inside it.

On releasing the clutch pedal the drive is taken up and the primary gear revolves with the crankshaft at crankshaft speed.
Drive is taken from the primary gear, through an intermediate gear, to the first motion shaft drive gear which is a splined fit on the nose of the first motion shaft.

9 Transfer gears - removal and replacement

Removal and replacement of the primary gear (40) has already been covered in Chapter 1. Please see pages 32 and 48 for details. To remove the first motion shaft gear knock back the locking tab on the lockwasher (47), undo the retaining nut (46), and pull off from the end of the first motion shaft, the first motion shaft gearwheel (45). Replacement is a straight reversal of this procedure.
The intermediate gear (43) is removed by pulling it out of its housing on the rear end of the gearbox casing. Make sure the thrust washers (one on either side) are kept in their correct relative positions. Replacement is a straight reversal of this process. **Note:** It is important to check the endfloat as described below, and to ensure the thrust washers are replaced with the chamfered bores against the gear face.
Make sure the mating flanges of the flywheel housing and gearbox casing are thoroughly clean and fit a new flywheel housing gasket in place.
Fit the bearing rollers on the end of the first motion shaft with a trace of grease to hold them in place, replace the circlip, and carefully refit the flywheel housing to the transmission casing. The usual reason for the housing not mating properly first time, is that one of the roller bearings has tilted, so causing an obstruction. Never use force to fit the flywheel housing.
Tighten down the flywheel housing nuts to the correct torque and measure the endfloat of the intermediate gear between the side of the gear and the casing. Endfloat should be between 0.003 in. and 0.008 in. (0.076 and 0.203 mm.). Thrust washers from 0.132 to 0.139 in (3.34 to 3.54 mm.) are available to correct any deficiency.
Undo the flywheel housing nuts, and pull the housing away from the transmission casing. The engine and gearbox may now be fitted together and the flywheel housing replaced. **Note:** Always use a new uncompressed flywheel housing gasket, and never use the one used to take the intermediate gear endfloat measurement. The flywheel housing gasket contains a small cut-out on its outer edge. When assembled the gasket should be compressed to 0.030 in (0.762 mm) which can be measured at the cut-out with a feeler gauge.

10 Flywheel housing bearing (early type) - removal and replacement

If the intermediate gear bearing in the flywheel housing is worn and requires replacement it can be removed and refitted as follows:
1 Heat the flywheel housing in boiling water. On no account apply a direct flame to the housing. If a receptacle large enough to hold the flywheel housing is not available slowly pour boiling water over the area round the bearing.
2 Remove the retaining ring (where fitted) and carefully prise the bearing out of the casting taking great care not to damage the bearing housing. If possible use BLMC service tool '18G 582'.
3 When fitting a new bearing carefully drift it into position (having previously heated the housing as described above) until it is clear of the retaining ring recess (where fitted). On no account press the bearing right into the recess in the housing, as this would mask the bearing oil supply hole which is at the rear of the recess.
4 If the outer race of the first motion shaft roller bearing requires renewal use the system described above, but if possible borrow BLMC service tool '18G 617'.

Manual gearbox dismantling and reassembly sequence (earlier type shown). Note: All the numbers in brackets in the captions to the photographs refer to Fig. 6.2.

1 The first step in dismantling the gear-box is to remove the flywheel housing, and lift away the engine. The gears etc. are then exposed as above

2 Then undo the clamp bolt (127) from the operating shaft lever (126). Note: the spring washer (128) under the head of the clamp bolt

3 Remove the differential unit from the gearbox casing as described in detail in Chapter 8

4 Undo the nuts, bolts, and spring washers (142, 143, 139, 140) retaining the front cover (137) and carefully knock the cover off with a length of wood as shown

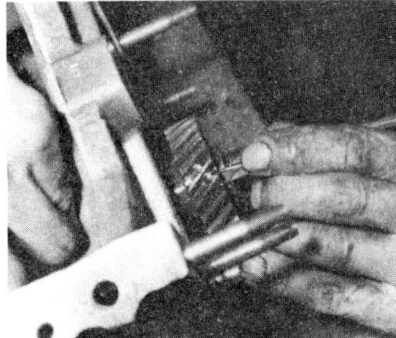

5 Take the intermediate gear (43), together with its thrust washers (44) off the rear of the transmission casing

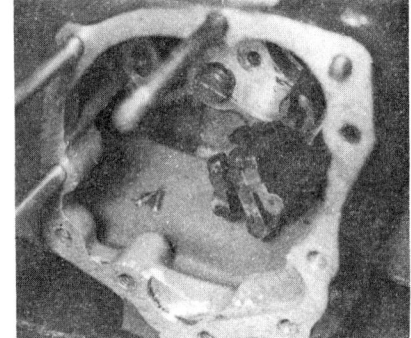

6 Lock the gearbox solid by knocking in two of the three selector rods as shown in the above photograph

7 Then knock back the tab of the lock-washer (47) and undo the nut (46) off the end of the first motion shaft

8 The first motion shaft gear (45) is then removed off the splines on the first mot-ion shaft

9 With a pair of circlip pliers pinch together the enlarged ends of the circlip (64) and remove the clip from the trans-mission casing

10 Then lock up the gearbox again by driving in the two selectors with the aid of a screwdriver

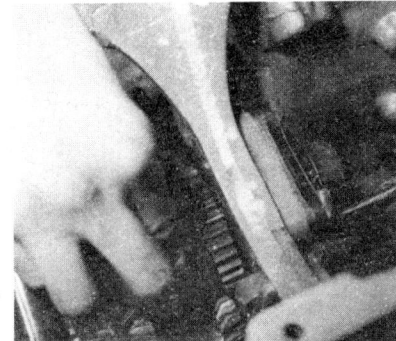

11 Before the nut (91) holding the final drive pinion (90) in place can be undone knock back the lockwasher tab (92)

12 Loosen the final drive pinion nut (90) and then unscrew it as shown above

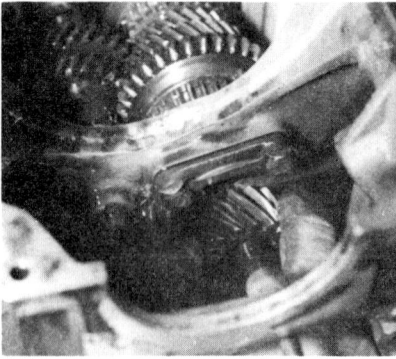
13 Then remove the lockwasher (92) and pull the final drive pinion (90) off the end of the mainshaft

14 Free the gearbox by lining up the selector rod cut-outs

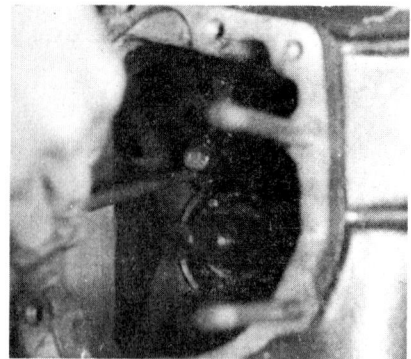
15 The next step is to knock back the tabs of the locking washers (87) which hold the bearing retainer (86) in place

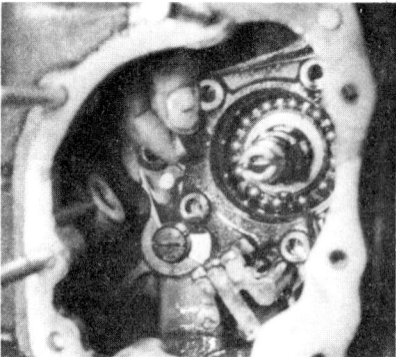
16 Undo the bolts (88) which hold the bearing retainer (86) in position and lift the retainer out

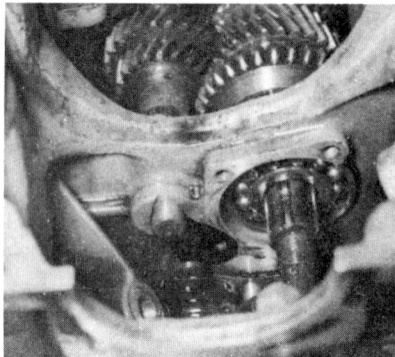
17 With the bearing retainer removed the position of the locating plate (55) which engages in the slots on the layshaft (53) reverse shaft (50) can be seen

18 Carefully remove the plate, noting which way round it is fitted

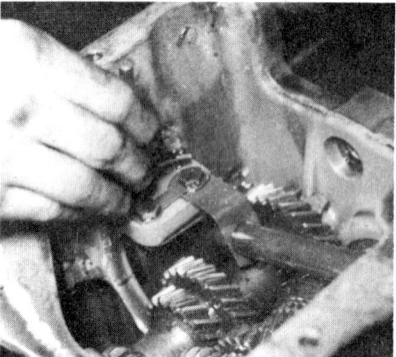
19 The next step is to knock back the tabs on the lockwasher (32) and undo the two bolts (31) holding the oil suction pipe in place

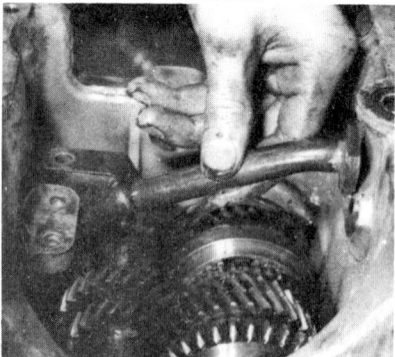
20 Undo the two bolts (37) which hold the oil suction pipe flange to the gearbox casing and then lift the pipe out of the gearbox

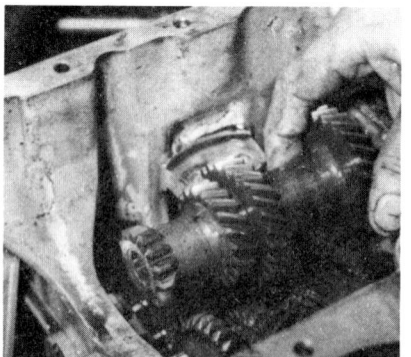
21 Measure and note the laygear endfloat and then tap the layshaft (53) out of the laygear (54). Lift the laygear from the gearbox

22 Tap out first motion shaft, bearing and circlip (67). Loosen shifter forks, drive mainshaft rearwards and drift out bearing (66)

23 The mainshaft bearing can then be removed from the end of the mainshaft. Note which way round it was fitted

24 Now pull back the mainshaft assembly so as to clear the hole in the centre web

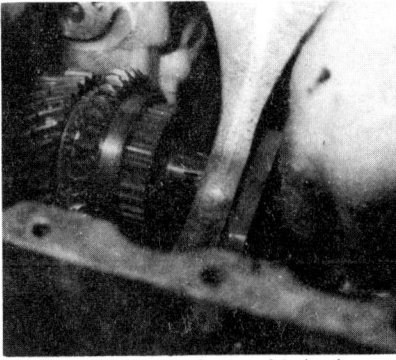

25 Move the mainshaft assembly back as far as possible as shown above

26 The mainshaft assembly can now be lifted out of the transmission casing

27 With the mainshaft removed examine the gearwheel teeth carefully for chipping and wear. First gear (68) in this case is badly worn

28 On removal of the hubs from the gearwheels it is vital that a rag is placed round the assembly to prevent loss of the three spring loaded balls (69, 70)

29 On hub reassembly the three spring loaded balls must enter the cut-outs arrowed

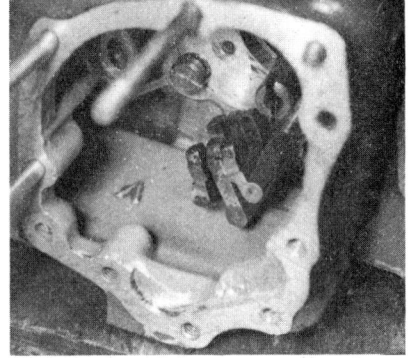

30 Under normal circumstances there is no need to remove the selector rods. If it is wished to extract them undo the selector screws and locknuts (112, 114)

31 It is vital that the selector screws and locknuts are tightened securely on reassembly. If a gear shifter fork comes loose the whole gearbox has to be stripped

32 The selector screw and locknut for the first and second gear shifter fork can be tightened through the hole for the differential unit

33 The reverse shifter fork selector screw and locknut rests in the bottom of the gearbox casing facing upwards

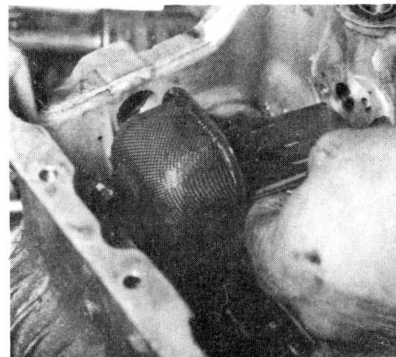

34 Before replacing gears the oil strainer must be positioned as above, and turned through 90⁰ under the lug

35 This shows the strainer in position but not yet secured to the lug. Smear the oil sealing ring (27) with grease

36 Replace mainshaft assembly, forked end of shaft (65) facing front, and synchroniser hubs in the shifter forks

37 Carefully fit the mainshaft bearing (66) drifting it into place and then secure it with the circlips (67)

38 This is how the gearbox should now look. The roller bearing on the right runs inside the first motion shaft (61) which is fitted next

39 With the first motion shaft ball bearing (63) in place on the shaft fit the first motion gear so it engages with the mainshaft

40 It may be necessary to drift the assembly into place especially when the ball bearing (63) meets the gearbox casing

41 With the first motion shaft properly in position replace the circlip (64) which holds the bearing in place

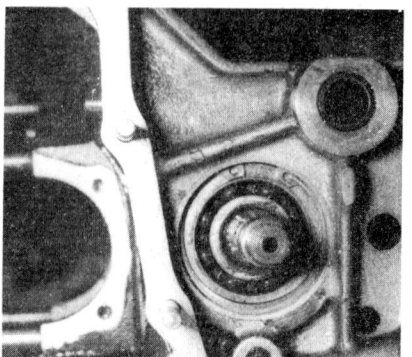
42 Make sure that the circlip fits properly into its recess as shown

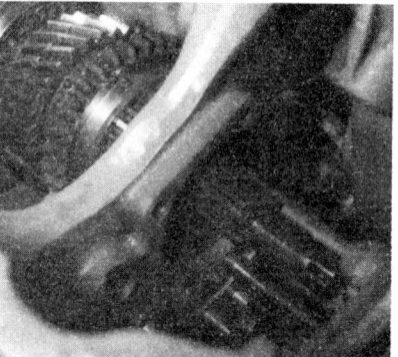
43 If the first motion shaft has been correctly fitted to the mainshaft the assembly will now look like this

44 Replace the distance piece (57) in the end of the laygear (54)

45 Then fit the needle roller bearing (56) into the smaller end of the laygear (54) and secure it with the retaining ring (58)

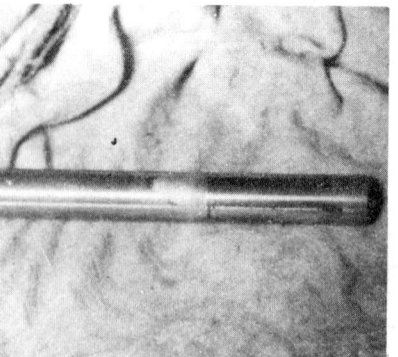
46 New bearings and layshaft were fitted to the laygear in this instance because the old layshaft case hardening had failed

47 Place new thrust washers (47) at each end of the casing so they rest on the lugs between which the laygear fits

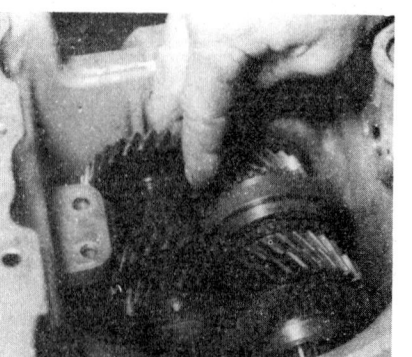
48 Drop the laygear (54) into position with the larger end adjacent to the gearbox end casing as shown above

49 Then fit the layshaft carefully pushing it through the centre of the laygear until the retaining slot emerges through the hole in the centre web

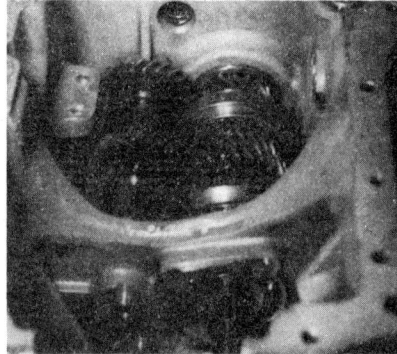

50 With the laygear in place and layshaft fitted the gearbox should now look like this. The laygear endfloat should be 0.002 to 0.006 in (0.0508 to 0.1524 mm)

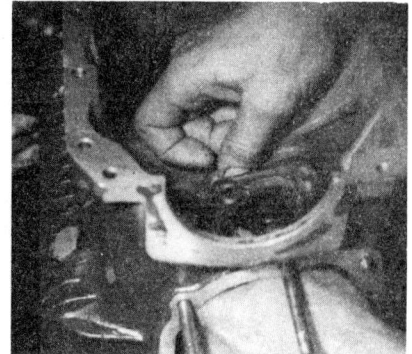

51 Fit appropriate mainshaft bearing shims (89), replace the locating plate (55) so it enters the notches on the shafts (50, 53) and fit the bearing retainer (86)

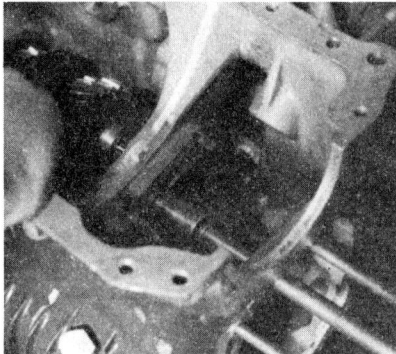

52 Fit new lockwashers (87) and then insert and do up the four retaining bolts (88)

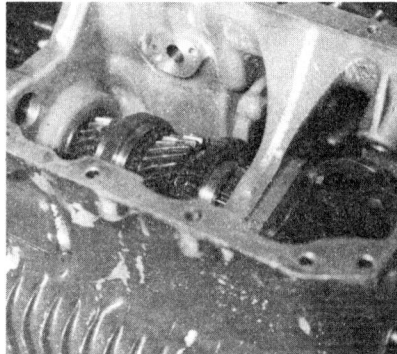

53 Turn up the tabs of the lockwashers to firmly secure the bolts

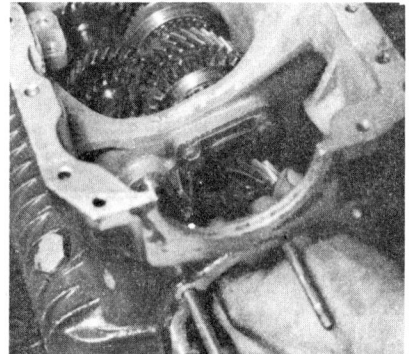

54 Then fit the pinion (90) onto the splines on the end of the mainshaft

55 It may be necessary to drift the pinion into place. To ensure the pinion slides on squarely tap each side of the gear in turn

56 With the pinion firmly in place fit a new lockwasher. This is vital

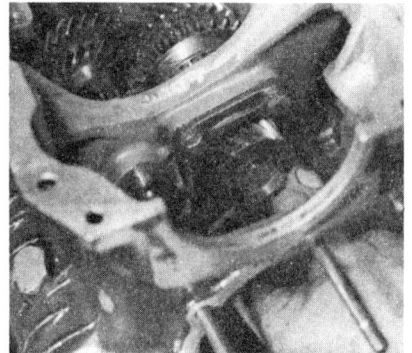

57 The next step is to screw the pinion retaining nut (91) onto the end of the mainshaft

58 This shows the ends of two selector rods in the unlocked position. Lock the gearbox by first punching in the lower rod

59 Punch in top selector rod engaging two gears and preventing gears turning when tightening main or first motion shaft nuts

60 Tighten up the pinion retaining nut (91) on the mainshaft with a torque wrench to 150 lb f ft (20.74 kg f m)

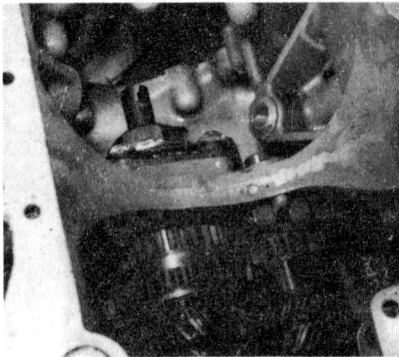

61 Knock over the edge of the lock-washer (92) to securely hold the nut (91) from working loose

62 Moving to the clutch end of the gearbox casing fit the first motion shaft gear (45) over the splines of the first motion shaft (61) as shown above

63 Then fit a new lockwasher (47) so the two lips engage in the two holes in the gearwheel (45)

64 Now fit the nut (46) on the end of the first motion shaft

65 Tighten up the first motion shaft gearwheel nut (46) with a torque spanner

66 The next step is to lock the nut in place by bending over the edge of the lockwasher

67 Now fit the oil suction pipe (33) to the oil strainer (26) and secure the pipe flange to the casing by doing up the two bolts shown

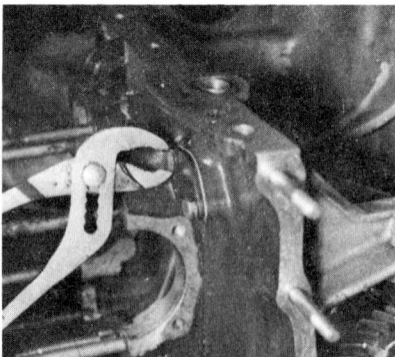

68 Make sure new joint gaskets (34, 36) are fitted and remember to turn up the lips of the one-piece lockwasher

69 The bolts actually register in a thread cut in the flange shown, so holding it to the side of the casing

70 Insert the two bolts holding the oil strainer bracket (28) and through the lug on the casing. Turn up the lockwasher tabs

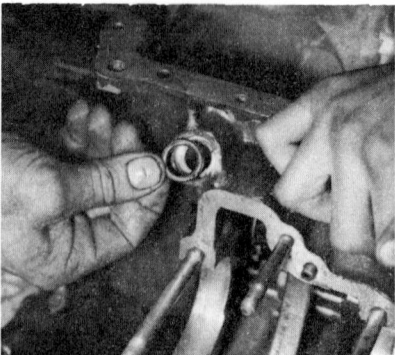

71 Moving to the other end of the gearbox casing fit a new oil seal (121) in the recess after greasing it

72 Very carefully slide in the gear change shaft (120) so as not to damage the oil seal

73 Fit the selector lever (122) over the end of the gear change shaft so the Woodruff key enters the flange and the cut-out lies parallel with the hole for the bolt

74 Position the cut-out in the gear change shaft inside the selector lever so that the clamp bolt (124) can be inserted

75 Remember to fit a lockwasher (125) under the head of the clamp bolt and tighten the latter firmly

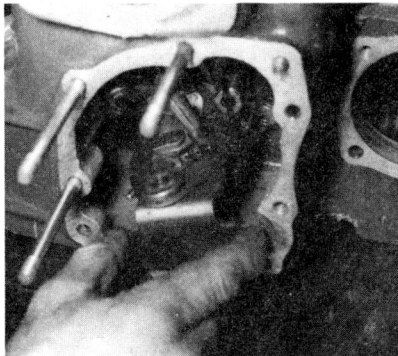

76 The next step is to fit the change speed gate (119) so the jaws lie in the selector rod cut-outs with the selector lever between the two jaw points

77 In this photograph the change speed gate (119) is shown correctly assembled to the gearbox casing

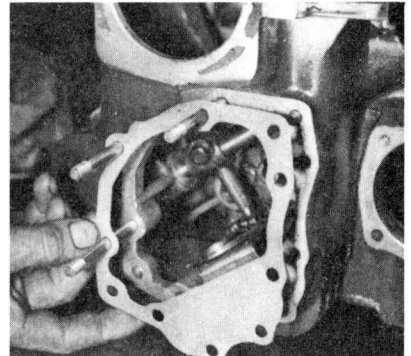

78 Fit a new cover gasket (138) in place after making sure that all traces of the old gasket have been removed

79 The next step is to fit the front cover (137) in position as shown

80 Make sure the end of the speedometer spindle engages the slot in the end of the mainshaft

81 Replace the speedometer pinion (93) and then the joint gasket (96), and the pinion housing cover (95)

82 At the other end of the transmission casing fit a new roller bearing over the nose of the first motion shaft

83 With a pair of circlip pliers fit the circlip which holds the bearing in place

84 Then fit the differential unit in place. For full details see Chapter 8

85 The next step is to fit the intermediate gear (43) with a thrust washer (44) on either side of the gear

86 Make sure the grooves on the thrust washers face outwards from the intermediate gear

87 Fit a new transfer gear case gasket and carefully fit gear case to the gearbox. Ensure the roller bearings on the first motion shaft enters its recess cleanly

88 Tighten down the nuts holding the transfer gear case in place to a torque of 18 lb f ft (2.49 kg f m)

89 Then measure with a feeler gauge the intermediate gear endfloat which should be between .003 to .008 in. If incorrect different size thrust washers are available

90 Fit a new 'O' rubber sealing ring in the circular groove in the gearbox casing flange. On no account use the old ring as it may leak resulting in low oil pressure

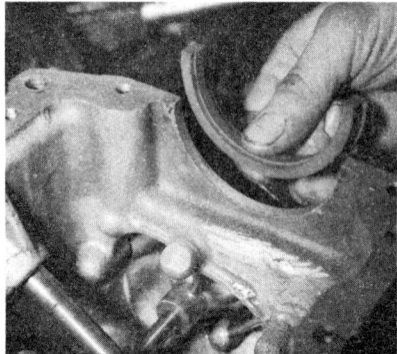

91 Clean the gearbox casing front cut-out in preparation for fitting a new gasket. When fitted it should stand not more than 1/16 in proud

92 The gearbox is now rebuilt and ready to be mated with the engine

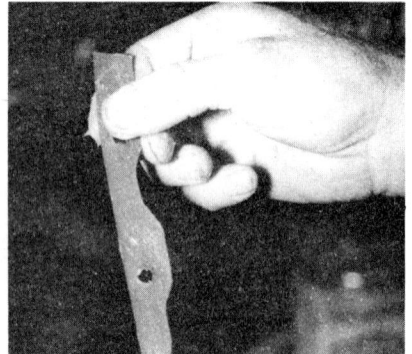

93 Lightly grease the two halves of the crankcase to gearbox casing gasket and place them in position on the crankcase flanges

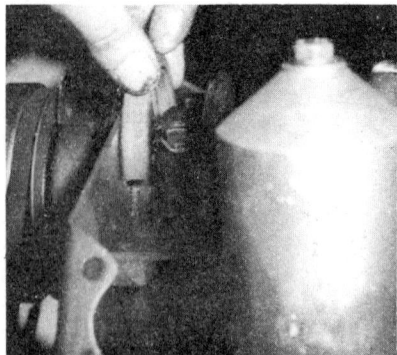

94 Fit a new seal at the front of the engine having previously checked it for correct fitting in the gearbox front cut-out

95 Carefully lower the engine onto the gearbox making sure the locating dowels enter their corresponding holes cleanly

96 Then refit the gearbox casing to crankcase bolts, tightening them to a torque of 6 lb f ft (0.83 kg f m)

97 Next place the primary gear thrust washer, bevelled side away from the gearwheel, on the crankshaft and follow it with the crankshaft primary gear

98 Then fit the outer thrust washer (not fitted on early models) so the raised portion lies at the bottom of the crankshaft

99 Turn the crankshaft so Nos. 1 and 4 pistons are at TDC. Fit the horseshoe or 'C' ring so it engages the two slots cut into the crankshaft

100 Then measure the primary gear endfloat which should be between 0.0035 to 0.0065 in (0.089 to 0.165 mm). Different sized thrust washers are available

101 With the intermediate gear and thrust washers fitted all is now ready to fit the flywheel housing or transfer gear case

102 Fit a new gasket in place. Do not re-use the gasket used to get the intermediate gear endfloat measurement

103 Then offer up the flywheel housing to the cylinder block and gearbox endfaces

104 With the flywheel housing in place next fit a new tab washer

105 Then replace the flywheel housing nuts and bolts and tighten them up to a torque of 18 lb f ft (2.49 kg f m)

106 Turn up the tabs of the lockwashers to secure the nuts and bolts

107 A new oil seal can be fitted with the primary gear on or off the crankshaft. The procedure is identical in both cases

108 Protect the new seal from the primary gear splines by using the special sleeve (shown) or binding splines with tape

109 Push the seal over the sleeve until it abuts the gearwheel and then remove the sleeve

110 If the primary gear was removed for the new seal to be fitted it should now be replaced

111 To press the seal into position either use the special tool shown above or a short length of suitably sized tubing

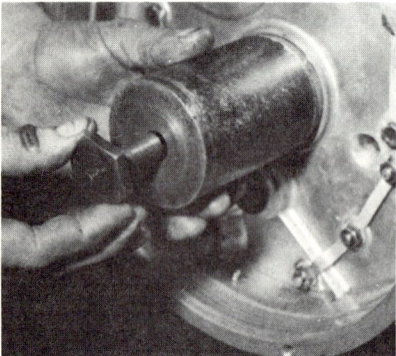
112 If using the special tool, the bolt shown above screws into the end of the crankshaft. As the bolt is tightened the sleeve slides forward, pressing in the seal

113 With the primary gear, thrust washers, and 'C' ring back in place all is now ready for replacement of the flywheel/clutch assembly

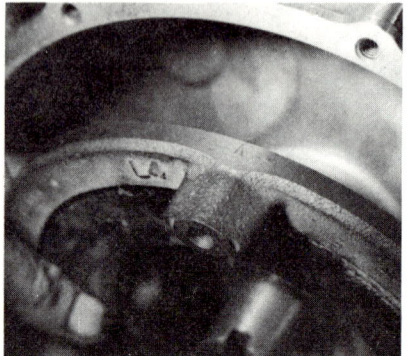
114 With the crankshaft set so pistons Nos. 1 and 4 are at TDC replace the pressure plate with the lugs facing outwards and the mark 'A' at TDC

115 Then fit the clutch disc with the longer side of the boss facing towards the pressure plate

116 Press the clutch disc firmly home against the pressure plate. Always renew the disc if linings are worn or oil saturated

117 Then fit the flywheel after making certain that the area which contacts the clutch lining is perfectly clean

118 Ensure the ¼ mark on the flywheel periphery lines up with the 'A' mark on the pressure plate lug

119 The next step is to replace the locking key followed by the lockwasher shown in the next photograph

120 Then replace the flywheel bolt etc as shown in Chapter 5 which deals with the clutch

11 Gearbox (later type) - dismantling

The sequence for dismantling the later type all synchromesh gearbox is basically identical to that given in Section 3. However, the following two additional points should be noted:
a) The layshaft must be removed from the casing at the clutch end as it is stepped with two diameters.
b) There are three needle roller bearings in the laygear and in these gearboxes they are caged. These caged bearings are interchangeable with the earlier non-caged type.

12 Gearbox (later type) - examination and renovation

Follow the sequence described in Section 4 with the exception of the laygear endfloat check. The new settings will be found in Section 14.

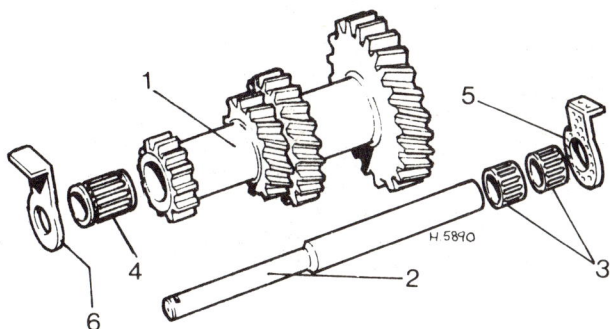

Fig. 6.6. Exploded view of later type gearbox (Sec. 11)

1 *Laygear*
2 *Layshaft (un-stepped on three-speed synchromesh units)*
3 *Needle roller bearings (one only on three-speed synchromesh units)*
4 *Needle roller bearing*
5 *Large thrust washer*
6 *Small thrust washer*

13 Mainshaft (later type) - dismantling and reassembly

1 Refer to Section 5, and follow the instructions given in paragraphs 1 and 2.
2 Slide the first gear from the shaft followed by the baulk ring.
3 Remove the needle roller bearing and the journal.
4 Slide off the reverse mainshaft gear together with the synchro hub for 1st and 2nd gears.
5 Remove the second baulk ring.
6 Depress and twist the thrust-washer so that it lines up with the splines on the shaft and can be drawn off.
7 Finally remove the 2nd gear and roller bearing.
8 Reassembly is the reverse sequence to removal. Follow the instructions given in paragraphs 2 to 6 inclusive in this Section, and then Section 6 from paragraph 5 onwards.

14 Gearbox (later type) - reassembly

1 The thrust washers on the laygear differ from the earlier types with synchromesh on three speeds only. On the three speed synchromesh models the smaller thrust washer is standard and the larger one selective; on the four speed synchromesh the larger thrust is standard and the smaller one selective.
2 The laygear endfloat should be between 0.002 and 0.006 in. (0.0508 and 0.1524 mm).
3 With the standard washer fitted and the gap between the end of the laygear and the casing measured, the selective washer can be decided upon.

When gap is	Fit shim
0.125 to 0.127 in (3.18 to 3.22mm)	22G 856
0.128 to 0.130 in (3.25 to 3.30mm)	22G 857
0.131 to 0.133in (3.32 to 3.37mm)	22G 858
0.134in. (3.41mm)	22G 859

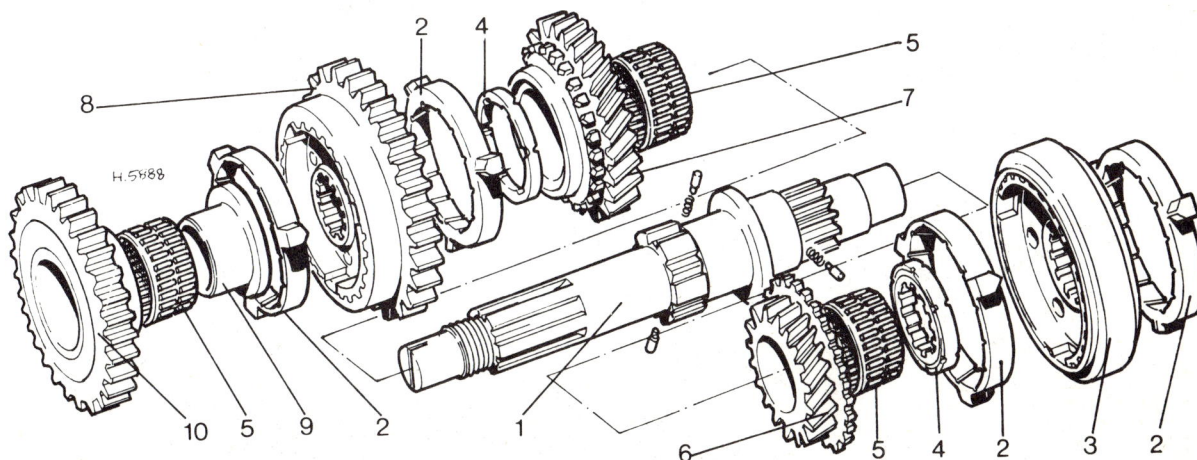

Fig. 6.7. Third motion shaft assembly as fitted to later type gearbox

1 *Third motion shaft*
2 *Baulk rings*
3 *3rd and 4th speed synchroniser*
4 *Thrust washers*
5 *Needle roller bearings*
6 *Third speed gear*
7 *Second speed gear*
8 *Reverse mainshaft gear and 1st and 2nd speed synchroniser*
9 *Needle roller bearing journal*
10 *First speed gear*

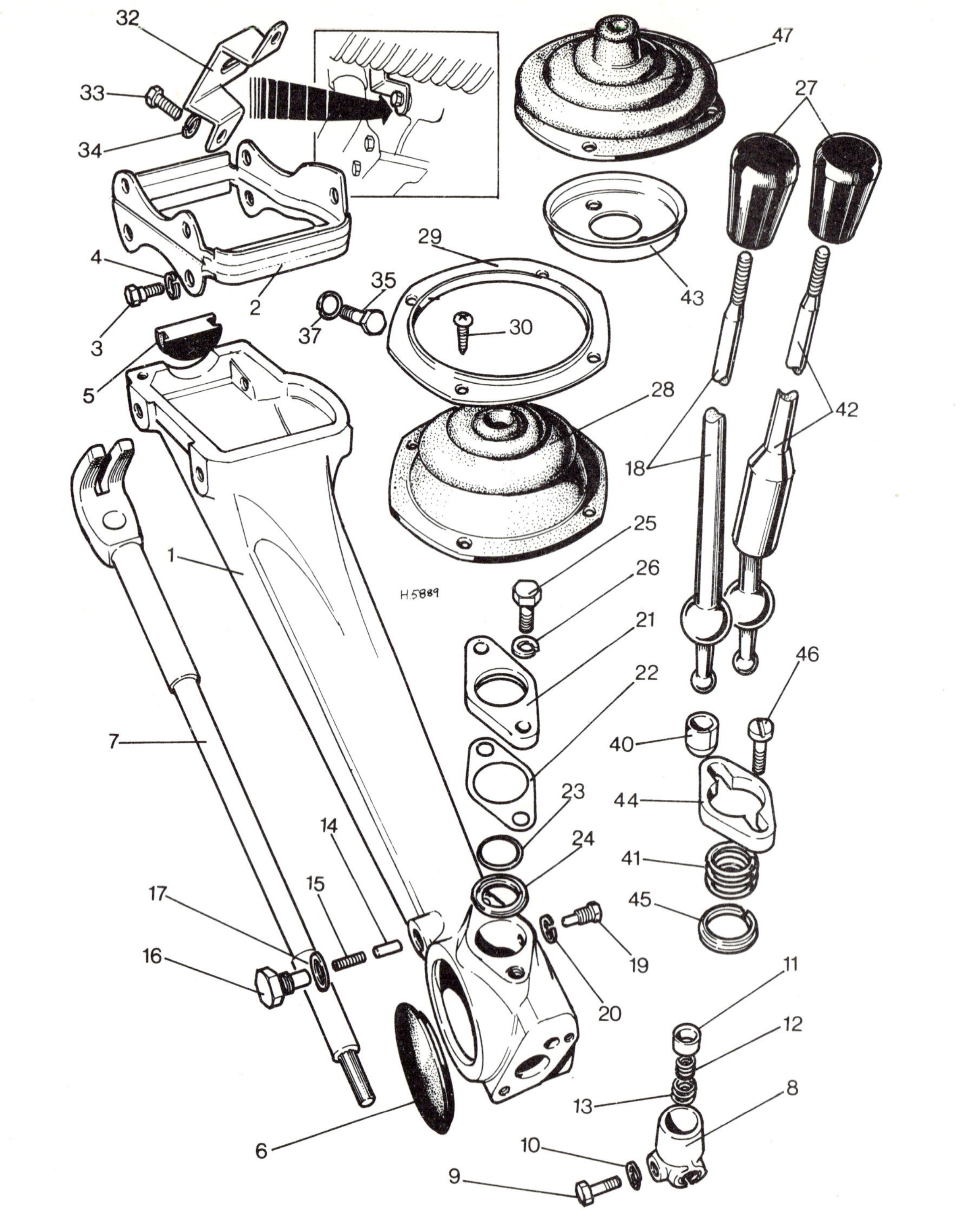

Fig. 6.8. Gearchange lever and remote control assembly (manual gearbox) - earlier type (Sec. 15)

1 **Remote control housing**	12 **Anti-rattle inner spring**	23 **Rubber ring**	35 **Screw**
2 **Housing adaptor**	13 **Anti-rattle outer spring**	24 **Nylon retainer flange**	37 **Spring washer**
3 **Screw**	14 **Plunger**	25 **Screw**	40 **Split bush**
4 **Spring washer**	15 **Plunger spring**	26 **Spring washer**	41 **Gearlever spring**
5 **Rubber plug**	16 **Spring retaining cap**	27 **Gearchange knob**	42 **Alternative gearlever**
6 **Dust cover**	17 **Washer**	28 **Rubber gaiter**	43 **Distance piece**
7 **Remote control primary**	18 **Gearchange lever**	29 **Retaining ring**	44 **Lever retainer**
shaft	19 **Locating gearlever pin**	30 **Phillips screw**	45 **Nylon flange retainer**
8 **Shaft lever**	20 **Spring washer**	32 **Exhaust mounting bracket**	46 **Screw**
9 **Screw**	21 **Lever retaining plate**	33 **Screw**	47 **Gearchange lever gaiter**
10 **Spring washer**	22 **Retainer gasket**	34 **Spring washer**	
11 **Anti-rattle thrust button**			

15 Gearchange remote control assembly (early type) - removal and replacement

1 Working inside the car, remove the floor covering and then unscrew the gearlever knob.
2 Undo and remove the four self-tapping screws securing the rubber gaiter metal plate to the floor. Lift away the plate and rubber gaiter.
3 Undo and remove the two shouldered securing screws from the rear extension support bracket and lift off the flat plate.
4 Working under the car undo and remove the four bolts that secure the extension to the transmission casing adaptor.
5 The extension housing assembly may now be lifted away.
6 Refitting the extension housing assembly is the reverse sequence to removal. Ensure that the rubber plug is correctly located between the extension and transmission casing.

16 Gearchange remote control assembly (early type) - dismantling and reassembly

1 Refer to Section 15, and remove the housing assembly from the car.
2 Slacken the lever locating pin and remove the screws that secure the change speed lever retainer. Withdraw the lever with nylon locating flange, spring and retainer.
3 Lift away the distance piece.
4 Remove the remote control shaft damper assembly, the rubber dust cover and screw that secures the remote control shaft to the primary shaft lever.
5 Carefully withdraw the shaft and lever from the housing.
6 With all parts clean inspect for wear or damage and obtain new parts as necessary.
7 Reassembly is the reverse sequence to dismantling but the following additional points should be noted:
a) Lubricate the operating surfaces of all parts with a little grease.
b) Ensure that the forked end of the primary shaft is correctly aligned with the splined primary shaft lever before refitting the clamping screw.

17 Gearchange remote control assembly (later type) - removal and replacement

1 Working inside the car unscrew and remove the gearchange lever knob (Fig. 6.9).
2 Remove the front floor carpeting.
3 Undo and remove the self-tapping screws that secure the gaiter ring retainer. Slide the gaiter up the lever.
4 Depress and turn the bayonet cap fixing so as to release the lever from the remote control assembly.
5 The gearchange lever may now be lifted away.
6 Working under the car drift out the roll pin that attaches the extension rod to the selector rod at the final drive housing end.
7 Undo and remove the nut and bolt that secures the remote control steady rod to the final drive housing on the gearbox.
8 Undo and remove the one nut and bolt securing the remote control housing to the mounting bracket and lift away the assembly.
9 Refitting the remote control assembly is the reverse sequence to removal.

18 Gearchange remote control assembly (later type) - dismantling and reassembly

1 Refer to Section 17, and remove the remote control assembly.
2 Mount the assembly up-side-down in a vice and undo and remove the bottom cover plate six securing screws. Lift away the cover plate noting which way round it is fitted.

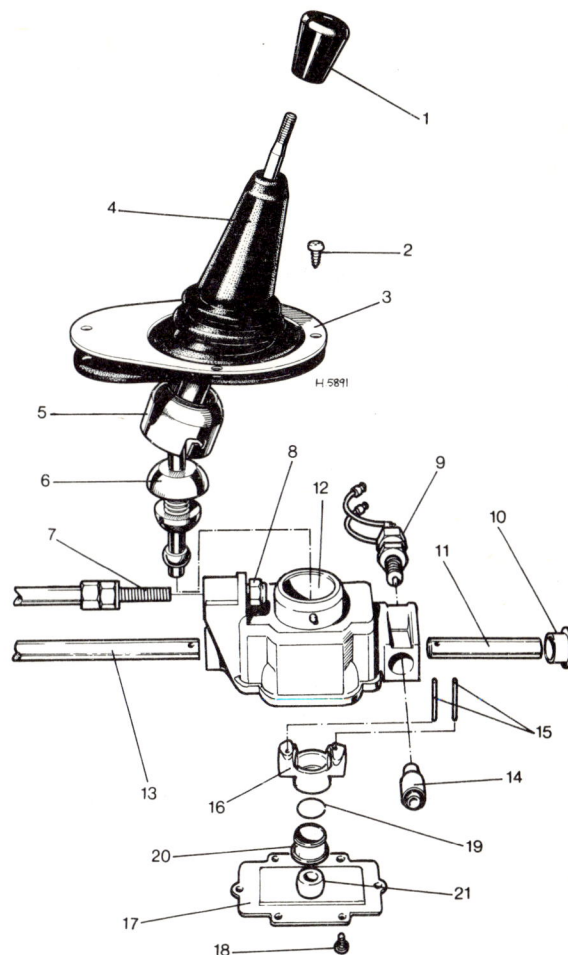

Fig. 6.9. Exploded view of later type remote gearchange assembly (manual gearbox) (Sec. 17)

1 Knob	11 Support rod
2 Screw	12 Casing
3 Plate	13 Extension rod
4 Gaiter	14 Plunger
5 Bayonet cap	15 Roll pin
6 Gearchange lever	16 Extension rod eye
7 Steady rod	17 Bottom cover
8 Nut	18 Screw
9 Reverse light switch (or plug)	19 Circlip
	20 Bearing seat
10 Bush	21 Bearing

3 Undo and remove the large nut and washer securing the steady rod to the housing. Remove the steady rod.
4 Move the extension rod eye rearwards and using a suitable diameter parallel pin punch remove the roll pin attaching the extension rod to the rod eye.
5 The extension rod may now be removed.
6 Move the extension rod eye forward and remove the roll pin retaining the support rod to the extension rod eye.
7 The support rod should now be drifted from the housing.
8 Finally lift away the extension rod eye.
9 Wash all parts, wipe dry and carefully examine all parts for wear. Obtain new parts as necessary.
10 Reassembly is the reverse sequence to dismantling. Well lubricate all moving parts with grease.

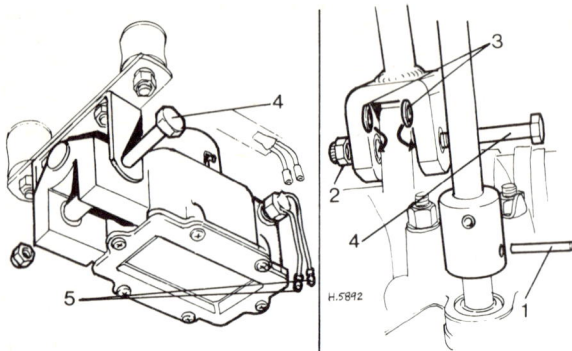

Fig. 6.10. Remote control assembly attachments (later type) (Sec. 17)

1 Roll pin	*4 Bolt*
2 Nut	*5 Reverse light switch*
3 Plain washers	

19 Gearchange remote control assembly mountings (later type) - removal and replacement

1 Working inside the car remove the front floor carpeting.
2 Undo and remove the nuts and spring washers that secure the remote control mountings to the tunnel panel.
3 Lower the remote control assembly by a sufficient amount to gain access to the lower mounting nuts.
4 Undo and remove the nuts and spring washers that secure the mountings to the support bracket.
5 Refitting the mountings is the reverse sequence to removal.

20 Reverse light switch - removal and replacement

Early type
1 The reverse light switch is screwed into the front of the transmission casing in place of the reverse check plunger, spring and plug.
2 To remove the switch, disconnect the electrical connections and unscrew it from the casing. No adjustment is possible when it is refitted.

Later type
1 The reverse light switch is screwed into the side of the remote control unit casing and may be removed by detaching the electrical connections, slackening the locknut and unscrewing the switch.
2 Refitting the switch is the reverse sequence to removal but it is necessary to adjust its setting. First engage reverse gear.
3 Disconnect the electrical connections from the reverse light switch and slacken the locknut (if this has not already been done).
4 Connect a test light and battery across the switch terminals. Slowly screw the switch out from the casing until the test light goes out.
5 Now screw the switch in until the test light comes on. Screw in a further half-turn and secure with the locknut.
6 Remove the test light and battery, reconnect the electrical connections and check correct operation of the switch.

21 Automatic transmission - general description

The automatic transmission offered as optional fitment to most models covered by this manual incorporates a three-element hydraulic torque converter with a maximum torque conversion ratio of 2:1 coupled to a bevel gear train which provides four forward gears and reverse.

Power from the engine is transmitted from the crankshaft converter output gear through an idler gear to the input gear which drives the bevel reduction gears in the gear train assembly.

The final drive is transmitted from a drivegear to a conventional type differential unit which in turn transmits engine power through two flange type coupling driveshafts employing constant velocity joints to the wheels.

The complete gear train assembly, including the reduction gear and differential unit runs below, and parallel to, the crankshaft and is housed in the transmission casing which serves also as the engine sump.

The gear trains are controlled by a selector lever within a gated quadrant marked in seven positions. It is mounted centrally on the floor panel.

The reverse, neutral and drive positions are for normal automatic driving with the first, second, third and fourth positions used for manual operation or over-ride as required by the driver.

This allows the system to be used as a fully automatic four speed transmission, from rest to maximum speed with the gears changing automatically according to throttle position and load. Should a lower ratio be required to obtain greater acceleration, an instant full throttle position (kick-down) on the accelerator immediately produces a ratio change.

Complete manual control of all four forward gears by use of the selector lever provides rapid changes. However it is very important that downward changes are effected at the correct road speeds otherwise serious damage may result to the automatic transmission unit. The second, third and top gears provide engine braking whether in automatic or manual control positions. In first gear a free wheel condition exists when decelerating.

Manual selection to third or second gear gives engine braking and also allows the driver to stay in a particular lower gear to suit road conditions or when descending steep hills.

Due to the complexity of the automatic transmission unit, if performance is not up to standard, or overhaul is necessary, it is imperative that this be undertaken by the local BLMC garage who will have special equipment for accurate fault diagnosis and rectification. It is important that the fault is diagnosed before the unit is removed from the car.

The content of the following Sections is therefore solely general and servicing information.

22 Automatic transmission - removal and replacement

It is necessary to remove the engine and transmission as one unit and then separate the two parts. Full information will be found in Chapter 1.

Although refitting the two units together in a direct reversal of the separation sequence there are many points which have to be considered. Full information will be found in the following Section.

23 Automatic transmission - separation and refitment to engine

For full information on separation of the two units refer to Chapter 1. To refit the two units proceed as follows:
1 **Important:** If a replacement transmission unit is being fitted check the casing to determine whether it is the later type with a cast in oil reservoir (to improve idler gear bearing lubrication). Should it be an earlier casing discuss this with the local BLMC garage as it may be necessary to modify the unit slightly. This is an instance of quoting correct car numbers when ordering spare parts.
2 Immerse the front main bearing cap moulded rubber oil seal in oil and fit with the lip facing the rear of the engine.
3 Refit the rubber sealing ring onto the main oil strainer pipe and fit new gaskets to the transmission case.
4 Lower the engine onto the transmission. Take care that the moulded rubber seal is correctly located.
5 Refit and tighten the set screws and nuts as the engine is being lowered into position.
6 Refit the transmission to engine oil feed pipe.

7　Refit the oil filter assembly. **Note:** The oil filter head to front cover joint washer (with copper inserts) fitted to later units is **not** interchangeable with those fitted to the earlier units. The two 'O' ring oil seals are not used on the later units.

8　Refit the main oil pump to transmission oil pipe.

9　Using a razor blade or sharp knife trim off any excess transmission joint from the rear of the unit. Clean the surfaces and fit a new converter housing gasket.

10　Refit the converter output gear. When refitting make certain that the correct running clearance of 0.0035-0.0065 in (0.089 - 0.165 mm) is maintained between the inner thrust-washer and the converter output gear.

11　If the clearance is outside these limits, select and fit the appropriate washer from the size range, with the chamfered inner edge of the washer to face the crankshaft.

Converter output gear thrust washers.

0.112 - 0.114 in	(2.84 - 2.89 mm)
0.114 - 0.116 in	(2.89 - 2.94 mm)
0.116 - 0.118 in	(2.94 - 3.00 mm)
0.118 - 0.120 in	(3.00 - 3.05 mm)

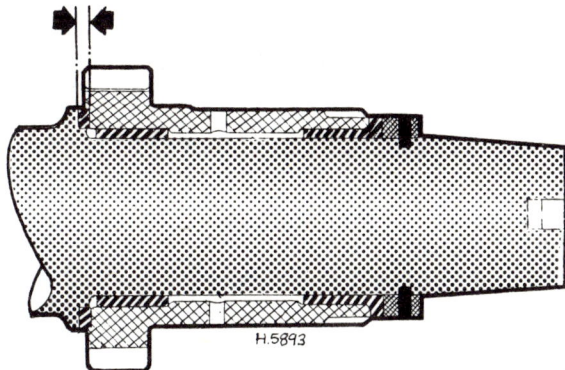

Fig. 6.11. Converter output gear (Sec. 23)
Measure the gap indicated and fit the appropriate thrust washer

12　Idler and input gear adjustment. Two types of input gears have been used, those fitted to earlier units having two thrust-washers. The later gear, of increased hub thickness, has a number of thin shims fitted to the outer hub face of the gear for adjustment.

13　Provided the original idler and input gears are being used the original thrust-washer/shims can be used. However, if new gears or converter housing are being used special tools are necessary. It is better to discuss this adjustment with the local BLMC garage.

Idler gear thrust washer (early models)

0.130 - 0.131 in	(3.30 - 3.32 mm)
0.132 - 0.133 in	(3.35 - 3.37 mm)
0.134 - 0.135 in	(3.40 - 3.42 mm)
0.136 - 0.137 in	(3.45 - 3.47 mm)
0.138 - 0.139 in	(3.50 - 3.53 mm)

Input gear thrust washers (early models)

0.128 - 0.130 in	(3.25 - 3.30 mm)
0.132 - 0.134 in	(3.35 - 3.40 mm)
0.140 - 0.142 in	(3.55 - 3.61 mm)
0.148 - 0.150 in	(3.76 - 3.81 mm)
0.152 - 0.154 in	(3.86 - 3.91 mm)

Input gear
0.003 in (0.076 mm)
0.012 in (0.305 mm)

14　Refit and align the converter outlet pipe.

15　Discard the old converter housing joint washer and fit a new one. Offer up the converter housing and retain with the nuts and set screws.

16　Refit the input gear nut and tighten to a torque wrench setting of 70 lb f ft (9.6 kg fm).

17　Remove each pair of bolts in turn from the converter and fit new locking plates. Tighten the bolts to a torque wrench setting of 22-24 lb f ft (3.04 - 3.32 kg fm). **Do not** remove all six bolts from the converter centre at one time.

18　Lubricate the converter oil seal and refit the converter.

19　Refit the washer (offset pegs) and the centre bolt with its lockwasher. Tighten the bolt to a torque wrench setting of

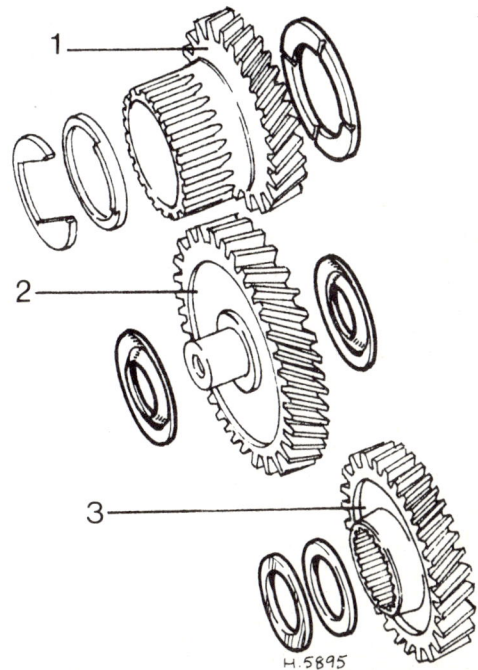

Fig. 6.12. Converter output (1), idler (2) and input gear (3) with their respective thrust washers and shims (Sec. 23)

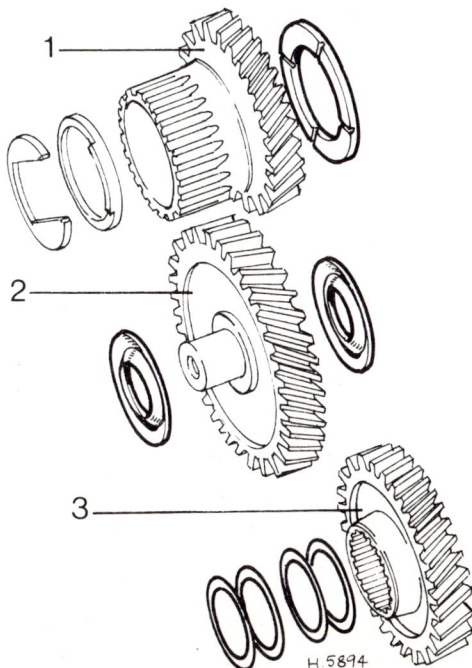

Fig. 6.13. Converter output (1), idler (2) and input gear (3) with their respective thrust washers (Sec. 23)

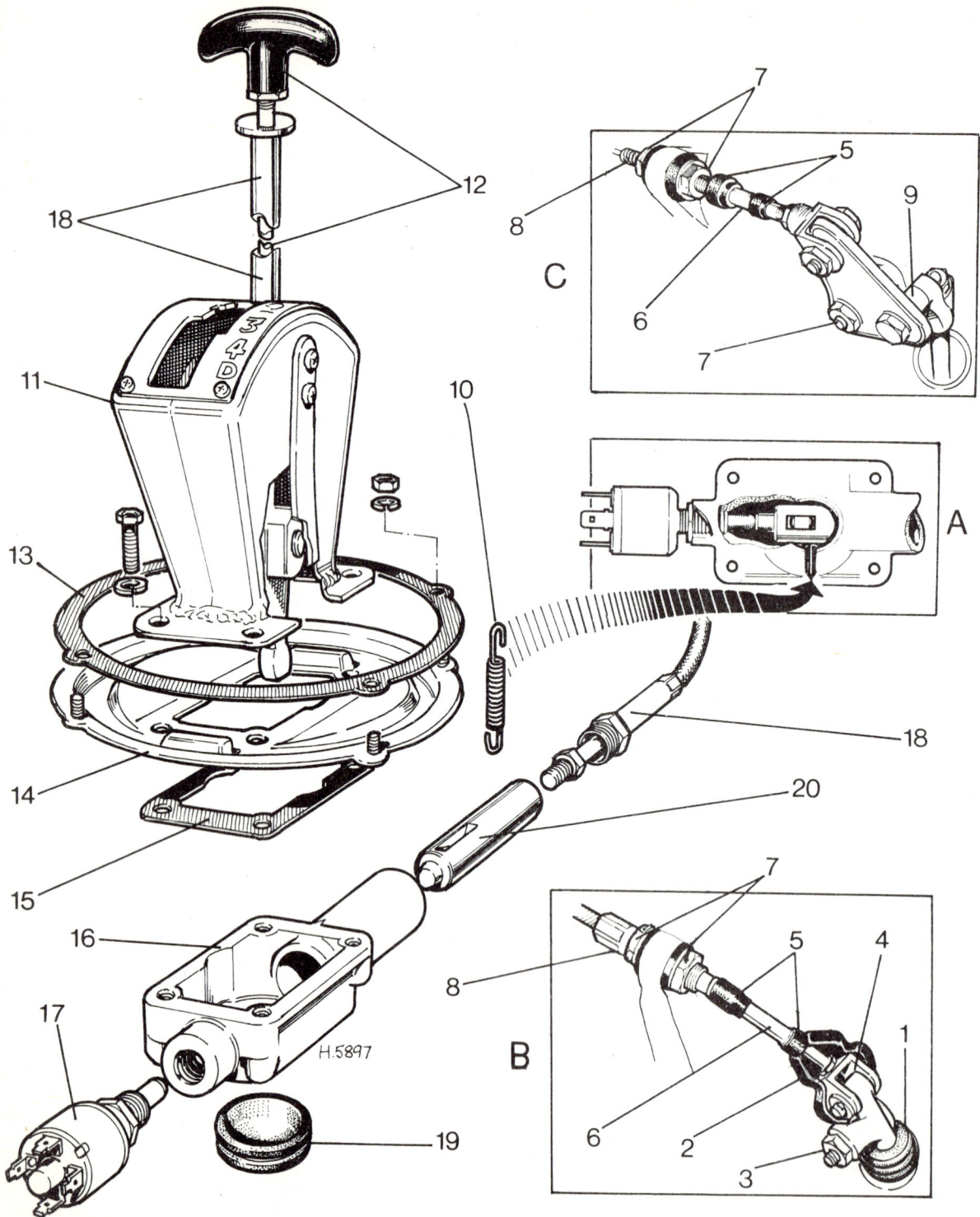

Fig. 6.14. Selector lever housing and cable components (Sec. 24)

Inset A Reverse return spring location
       B Earlier type bellcrank lever connections
       C Later type bellcrank lever connections

1	Rubber bellows early	7	Cable adjusting nuts
2	Rubber sleeve models	8	Cable
3	Pivot pin nut	9	Spacer
4	Yoke	10	Reverse return spring
5	Rubber ferrules	11	Quadrant
6	Cable sleeve	12	Gear selector lever
13	Joint washer - baseplate	17	Inhibitor switch (early type)
14	Baseplate	18	Spring loaded sleeve (later models)
15	Joint washer - housing	19	Rubber grommet - housing
16	Gearchange housing	20	Lever plunger

H.5897

110-115 lb f ft (15.2 - 15.9 kg fm). Lock the bolt with the washer.

20 Refit the low pressure valve and gasket.

21 Refit the gear selector bellcrank lever and its pivot and reconnect it with the transverse rod. Do not forget to refit the rubber boot (early models) or guard (later models).

22 Finally refit the converter cover, starter motor and rear engine mounting, this being a direct reversal of the removal sequence.

24 Automatic transmission selector lever assembly - removal and replacement

1 Earlier type bellcrank lever assembly (see Fig. 6.15). Remove the bellcrank lever guard (later models) from the converter housing or pull back the rubber sleeve (early models). Remove the clevis pin and disconnect the gearchange cable.

2 Later type bellcrank lever assembly (see Fig. 6.16). Remove the modified bellcrank lever guard from the connector housing and then disconnect the gearchange cable by undoing and removing the nut and bolt from the yoke.

3 Slacken the yoke's locknut and remove the yoke, locknut, bolt rubber ferrules and the cable sleeve.

4 Undo and remove the front adjusting nut from the outer cable and pull the cable clear of the transmission unit.

5 Release the cable clip from the floor panel.

6 Remove the front floor carpeting.

7 Disconnect the electrical leads from the inhibitor switch.

8 Undo and remove the four nuts that secure the gear change housing plate to the floor panel and remove the housing and cable assembly.

9 Refitting the selector lever assembly is the reverse sequence to removal but there are several points which must be noted. These are given in the following paragraphs.

10 If necessary fit a new joint washer to the housing base plate.

11 Fill the bellows of early models with a little Duckhams Lamol grease.

12 If seizure of early versions of the first type bellcrank lever has occurred due to overtightening of the pivot pin nut, the pivot pin and distance tube must be renewed. A modified pivot pin with a shoulder should be used.

13 If the backlash of the selector lever mechanism with the original forged type bellcrank lever is excessive, fit the first type minimum backlash bellcrank lever assembly. Remove the forged bellcrank lever and its pivot pin, the front cover and the transverse rod. Renew the oil seal behind the pressed cup in the transmission casing with one of an increased bore size and fit the non-adjustable transverse rod, which has a larger diameter.

Fit the modified type of pivot pin, the pressed type of bellcrank lever, and replace the gearchange clevis pin with a bolt. Refit the front cover and the bellcrank lever guard, which must be reshaped.

14 On transmission units with the minimum backlash ballcrank lever assembly, the reverse position of the selector lever indicator gate should be modified to ensure that the selector valve detent is fully engaged when reverse gear is selected.

a) Unscrew the gear selector handle from its lever.

b) Undo and remove the four screws that secure the indicator gate to the quadrant.

c) File a radius (0.0625 in (1.59 mm) deep in the end of the gate (see Fig. 6.17) and reassemble the quadrant components.

Important: If slip or loss of drive in reverse gear occurs on replacement transmissions which incorporate the minimum backlash bellcrank lever check that the selector gate has been lengthened. If it has not and adjustment of the selector cable does not cure the trouble carry out the previously described modification.

15 Adjust the selector lever cable and the transverse rod (early type only) as described in Section 26. Also adjust the inhibitor switch as described in Section 27.

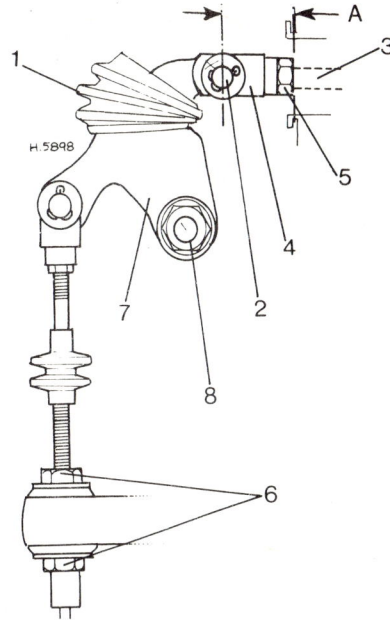

Fig. 6.15. Gearchange cable and transverse rod adjustment (forged type bellcrank) (Secs. 24 and 26)

A = 0.781 in (19.84 mm)
1 Rubber boot
2 Clevis pin
3 Transverse rod
4 Transverse rod yoke (adjustable)
5 Yoke locknut
6 Cable adjusting nuts
7 Bellcrank lever arm
8 Bellcrank lever pivot and securing nut

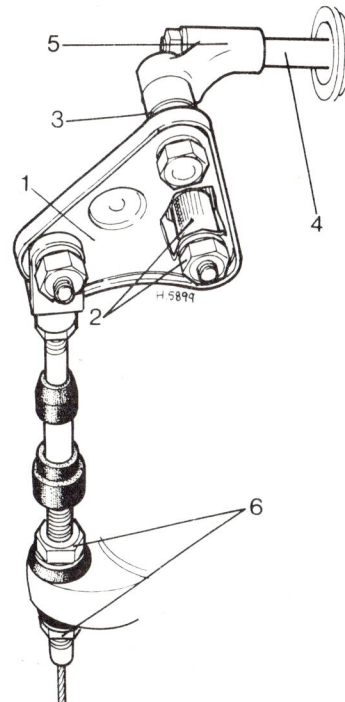

Fig. 6.16. Pressed type minimum backlash bellcrank lever assembly (Secs. 24 and 26)

1 Bellcrank lever arm
2 Bellcrank lever pivot and securing nut
3 Spherical joint
4 Transverse rod
5 Transverse rod bracket (fixed)
6 Cable adjusting nuts

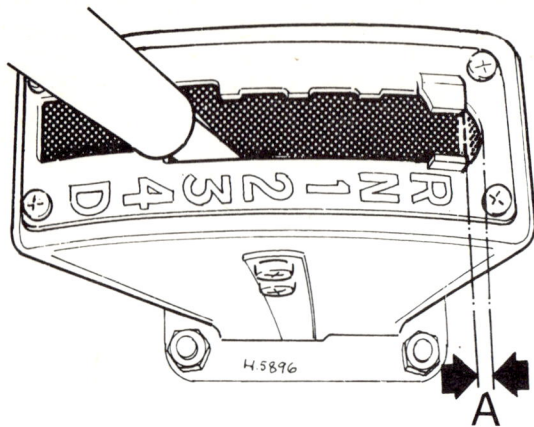

Fig. 6.17. Modification to selector lever indicator gate (Sec. 24)

A = 0.0625 in (1.59 mm)

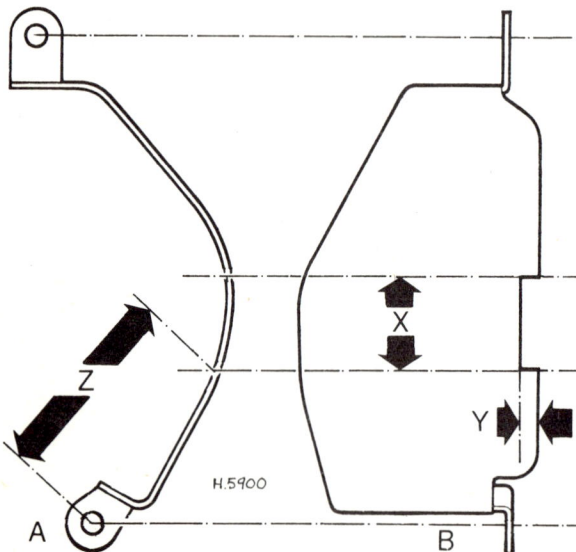

Fig. 6.18. Modified lever guard (Sec. 26)
Reset the earlier type bellcrank lever guard to use with the later type bellcrank by bending it to the revised shape (A) and adding to the cut-out (B)

X = 1.375 in (35.0 mm)
Y = 0.375 in (9.5 mm)
Z = 2.625 in (67 mm)

25 Automatic transmission selector lever assembly - dismantling and reassembly

1 Refer to Section 24, and remove the selector lever assembly.
2 Mount the assembly in a vice and remove the set screws that secure the quadrant to the housing.
3 Detach the reverse return spring from the base of the housing. Lift away the quadrant and lever assembly.
4 Unscrew the cable securing nut from the front of the housing. Pull the cable and plunger from the housing and release it from the gearchange lever plunger.
5 Remove the handle from its lever and the indicator gate and external leaf spring from the quadrant.
6 Separate the cross-shaft into its two component parts once the end circlip has been removed.

7 The lever assembly may now be lifted away.
8 The spring loaded sleeve which is fitted to later assemblies may be removed once the retaining circlip has been removed.
9 Wash all parts, wipe dry and carefully examine all parts for wear. Obtain new parts as necessary.
10 Reassembling the selector lever assembly is the reverse sequence to removal but the following two additional points should be noted.
a) Lubricate all moving parts with a little grease.
b) Ensure that the gear selector lever is refitted into the relieved side of the plunger.

26 Selector lever cable and transverse rod - adjustment

1 Apply the handbrake and chock the front wheels.
2 Move the selector lever to the 'R' position and check that reverse is engaged.
3 Slowly move the lever back towards the 'N' position and check that the gear is disengaged just before or as soon as the lever drops in the 'N' position on the quadrant.
4 Repeat the above sequence in the first gear '1' position.
5 If the conditions in paragraph 3 do not exist then adjustment is necessary.

Selector lever transverse rod (early type)
1 Ease back the rubber boot and remove the clevis pin.
2 Make sure that the transverse selector rod is screwed in tightly and pushed fully into the transmission case.
3 **Never start the engine with the transverse selector rod disconnected.**
4 Swivel the bellcrank lever arm clear of the transverse selector rod yoke and refit the clevis pin.
5 Refer to Fig. 6.15 and measure dimension 'A' which should be 0.781 in (19.85 mm).
6 If adjustment is necessary slacken the locknut and turn the yoke until the correct measurement is obtained.
7 Set the yoke square to the bellcrank and tighten the locknut.

Selector lever transverse rod (later type)
    The transverse rod is not adjustable and is fitted on units having the later type minimum backlash bellcrank lever assembly.

Selector lever cable
1 Select 'N' position in the transmission unit by pulling the transverse selector rod fully out and then pushing it back in one detent on all transmissions which have seven selector positions on the indicator plate, or two detents on those which have only six positions.
2 *Early models:* Engage 'N' with the selector lever and adjust the selector cable until the hole in the cable fork aligns with the bellcrank lever and the clevis pin can easily be inserted. (See Fig. 6.15).
3 *Later models:* On units fitted with the minimum backlash bellcrank lever, the adjustment procedure is as previously described with the exception that the cable fork must align with the bore of the spherical joint in the bellcrank lever so that the bolt can be easily inserted. Make sure that the yoke end on the selector cable is secured square to the bellcrank lever before re-connecting.
4 Now carry out the adjustment check as described in the first part of this Section. It may be found that slight re-adjustment is necessary so that the amount of movement to engage or disengage gears is equalized in both directions.
5 Tighten all adjustment/locknuts and ensure that the clevis pin (when fitted) is secured. When rubber boots are fitted pack with a little 'Duckhams Lamol Grease'. Refit the boots and the bellcrank lever guard.
6 *Important:* The bellcrank lever guard fitted to units having the minimum backlash bellcrank is reshaped, but the earlier type guard can be modified to use with the later type bellcrank. (Fig 6.18).

7   Finally road test the car to ensure correct operation of the automatic transmission unit.

27 Inhibitor switch - adjustment

1   The switch is located on the rear of the gear selector housing and must be adjusted to ensure that the engine can only be started when the selector lever is in the 'N' position on the quadrant. The earlier type switches have four terminals, two of which are connected through the ignition starter circuit. Later type switches have two terminals only.
2   Should adjustment be suspect check that the starter only operates when the selector lever is in the 'N' position and also that the reverse light (when fitted) operates only when 'R' position is selected.
3   Before adjusting the inhibitor switch check the selector lever cable and transverse rod adjustment first.
4   Select 'N' and disconnect the electrical connections from the switch.
5   Slacken the locknut and unscrew the switch until it is almost out of the housing.
6   Connect a test light and battery across the switch terminals numbered 2 and 4.
7   Screw the switch into the housing until the circuit is made, and mark the switch body.
8   Continue screwing in the switch and note the number of turns required until the circuit breaks.
9   Remove the test light and battery and unscrew the switch from the housing half the number of turns counted.
10 Tighten the locknut and refit the electrical leads to the appropriate terminals:

    2 and 4   Ignition/starter circuit
    1 and 3   Reverse light

11 **Note:** If the switch cannot be adjusted to operate correctly it must be renewed.

28 Governor control rod ('kick-down') - adjustment

1   Start the engine and run until normal operating temperature is reached.
2   If possible connect a tachometer to the ignition system and set the carburettor to give an engine idle speed of 650 rpm.
3   Disconnect the governor control rod at the carburettor, insert a 0.25 in (6.4 mm) diameter rod through the hole in the intermediate bellcrank lever and locate in the hole in the transmission case (Fig. 6.20).
4   Check if the control rod can now be re-connected to the carburettor with its fulcrum pin an easy sliding fit through its forked end and the carburettor linkage.
5   If it is not, slacken the control rod locknut and disconnect the forked end at the carburettor linkage. Turn the rod until the correct length is obtained.
6   Reconnect the carburettor end and tighten the locknut. Do not forget to remove the checking rod.
7   Road test the car and check that the change speeds occur at the correct time. If the change speeds are low disconnect the forked end of the rod, slacken the locknut and *shorten* the rod. If the change speeds are too high *lengthen* the rod.

29 Fault diagnosis - automatic transmission

To enable a complete fault diagnosis sequence to be carried out certain special tools and equipment are necessary. These will be found at the local BLMC garage so it is best to leave the checking of any suspected faults to them. Also it is important that the fault be found before the unit is stripped out of the car. There are, however, several checks that the reader can carry out before seeking the advice of a specialist.

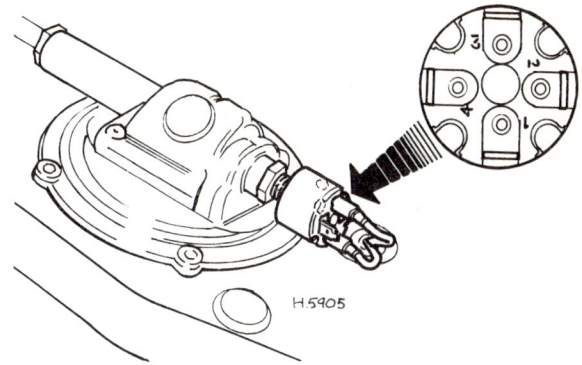

Fig. 6.19. Inhibitor switch on gearchange lever housing (Sec. 27)
Inset shows connections marked on switch

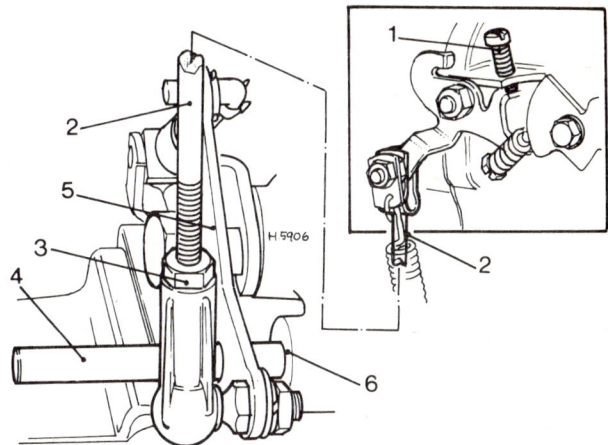

Fig. 6.20. Governor control rod adjustment (Sec. 28)

1 Throttle adjustment
*   screw*
2 Governor control rod
3 Locknut

4 0.25 in (6.4 mm) dia. rod
5 Intermediate bell-crank
*   lever*
6 Transmission case hole

Preliminary check
a) Check oil level
b) Check engine idle speed
c) Check adjustment of selector lever cable, transverse rod, and inhibitor switch.

Road test
Check the operation of the gear selector in all seven positions.

'N'	Check that there is key start in this position only and not in the drive positions.
'I'	Confirm that there is drive and *no* engine braking.
'2', '3' or '4'	(if latter provided) Confirm that there is drive with engine braking.
'D'	See 'Change speed' table at the end of this Section.
'R'	Confirm that there is drive *with* engine braking.
'Kick-down'	Check the 'kick down' up change speeds in the 'D' position. See 'Change speed' table at end of this Section.

Change speed table

Selector position	Throttle position	Gearshift	1100 (Up to 10AG/A/H1207)		1100 (From 10AG/A/H1208) 1300 - All models	
			mph	kph	mph	kph
'D'	Light	1-2	10-14	16-22	11-15	18-24
		2-3	15-19	23-29	16-20	26-32
		3-4	20-24	33-39	22-26	36-42
'D'	'Kick-down'	1-2	25-33	41-53	27-35	44-56
		2-3	37-45	60-72	39-47	64-76
		3-4	49-57	78-91	52-60	85-97
'D'	'Kick-down'	4-3	47-39	76-64	50-42	80-68
		3-2	39-31	62-50	41-33	66-54
		2-1	26-18	41-29	27-19	43-31
'D'	Closed (roll out)	4-3	20-16	32-26	21-17	33-27
		3-2	14-10	22-16	15-11	24-18
		2-1	8-4	12-6	9-5	14-8

30 Fault diagnosis - manual gearbox

Symptom	Reason/s	Remedy
Weak or ineffective synchromesh	Synchronising cones worn, split or damaged	Dismantle and overhaul gearbox. Fit new gear wheels and synchronising cones.
	Baulk ring synchromesh dogs worn, or damaged	Dismantle and overhaul gearbox. Fit new baulk ring synchromesh.
Jumps out of gear	Broken gear change fork rod spring	Dismantle and replace spring.
	Gearbox coupling dogs badly worn	Dismantle gearbox. Fit new coupling dogs.
	Selector fork rod groove badly worn	Fit new selector fork rod.
	Selector fork rod securing screw locknut loose	Remove gearbox and tighten.
Excessive noise	Incorrect grade of oil being used	Drain complete unit and refill with correct grade of oil.
	Brush or needle roller bearings worn or damaged	Dismantle and overhaul gearbox. Renew bearings.
	Gear teeth excessively worn or damaged	Dismantle and overhaul gearbox. Renew gear wheels.
	Laygear thrust washers worn allowing excessive end play	Dismantle and overhaul gearbox. Renew thrust washers.
Excessive difficulty in engaging gear	Clutch pedal adjustment incorrect	Adjust clutch pedal movement (Chapter 5).

Chapter 7 Driveshafts and universal joints

Contents

Specifications

Type: Solid shaft reverse spline with rubber bush, Hardy-Spicer or constant velocity inner joint - depending on model and year of production. Constant velocity outer joint.

Torque wrench settings:	lb f ft	kg f m
Front hub nut (driveshaft)	60	8.3
Balljoint nut	25	3.4

1 General description

Drive is transmitted from the differential to the front wheels by means of two driveshafts. Fitted at each end of each shaft are universal joints which allow for vertical movement of the front wheels. Fore and aft movement is absorbed by a sliding spline on the inner ends of the shafts.

The outer universal joints are of the 'Birfield' constant velocity type and are manufactured by Hardy-Spicer. The driveshaft fits inside the circular outer CV joint which is also the driven-shaft. Drive is transmitted from the driveshaft to the driven-shaft by six steel balls which are located in curved grooves machined in line with the axis of the shaft on the inside of the driven-shaft to hinge freely on the driveshaft, but at the same time keeps them together. Enclosing the CV joint is a rubber boot.

The inner universal joints have been the subject of several changes. The first type used was of the rubber bushed type and made by Dunlop. The second type used on automatic transmission models was that of the Hardy-Spicer design as usually found at the ends of a conventional propeller shaft. The third type uses constant velocity joints which are mounted on the ends of the differential gears.

Note that a small rubber boot covers the joint between the flange and shaft and on early driveshafts a grease nipple was fitted to the flange and covered by the rubber boot.

Before commencing work identify which type is fitted to the car and ensure that spare parts are available if overhaul is necessary.

2 Driveshaft - removal and replacement

1 Remove the wheel trim from the wheel from which the driveshaft is to be removed.
2 Place the car in gear and apply the handbrake firmly. Extract the split pin locking the hub nut, and undo and remove the nut.
3 Loosen the front roadwheel securing nuts and jack-up the car on the same side.

4 As it will be necessary to work underneath the car, supplement the jack with a stand or support blocks. This will minimise the danger should the jack collapse.
5 Remove the roadwheel.
6 Undo the self-locking nut from the balljoint on the end of the steering tie-rod three turns. Free the tapered balljoint pin from the steering arm with either a balljoint separator or by hitting the opposite sides of the steering arm eye at the same time, until the balljoint pin is free. Remove the nut (which was kept in place to protect the balljoint threads from accidental damage) and pull the balljoint pin from the steering arm.
7 Because the inner end of the shaft is a sliding fit on the flange it will now be necessary to partially free the end of the driveshaft from the centre of the hub. With a soft drift and hammer tap the end of the shaft until it is seen to move inwards slightly.
8 Undo the securing nuts which hold the upper and lower suspension arms to the steering swivel, and disconnect the arms.
9 Undo and remove the nut and washer from the lower suspension arm inner hinge pin, and tap the pin clear to release the arm.
10 Having previously started separating the driveshaft from the hub swivel axle and brake assembly it should now be fairly easy to pull the latter off. Rest the hub and disc assembly on a wooden block or similar to ensure no strain is placed on the flexible brake hose. On no account allow the hub assembly to hang freely on the hydraulic hose.
11 The procedure now differs depending on the type of driveshaft fitted.

12 Early type
a) Mark the drive flange and flexible joint so on reassembly they can be placed in the same relative positions.
b) Undo and remove the four outside nuts from the 'U' bolts holding the driveshaft flange to the flexible rubber coupling. The shaft can now be extracted from the car through the wheelarch.

13 Hardy-spicer universal joint type
a) Mark the drive flanges so on reassembly they can be placed in the same relative positions.
b) Undo and remove the four nuts, bolts and washers that

secure the two drive flanges together, part the two flanges and withdraw the driveshaft through the wheelarch.

14 Constant velocity type

a) Refer to Fig. 7.1 and using a metal lever as shown carefully detach the driveshaft from the differential. It is possible to use two large screwdrivers to release the constant velocity joint from the spring clip on the differential gear shaft but extreme care must be taken.

b) Lift away the complete driveshaft assembly.

15 Replacement of the driveshaft assembly is the reverse sequence to removal but the following additional points should be noted.

16 Early type

a) Replace the driveshaft in the car in its correct relative position to the flexible rubber coupling. Before replacing the 'U' bolts, thread their nuts on a few turns and lightly nip the ends of the 'U' bolts in a vice. They tend to 'spread' when removed from the coupling and nipping them in this way will greatly ease their replacement.

b) Replace the 'U' bolts and tighten down the nuts. **Note:** Do not overtighten.

c) Replace the hub, swivel axle and brake assembly on the end of the driveshaft.

d) Refit the lower suspension arm inner hinge pin.

e) Refit the upper and lower suspension arms to the steering swivel, and refit the balljoint to the steering arm. Tighten the balljoint nut to a torque wrench setting of 25 lb f ft (3.4 kg fm).

f) Replace and tighten down the hub nut; replace the split pin.

17 Hardy-Spicer universal joint type

a) A new rubber boot must be fitted and refilled with ¾ oz (21 gms) of Duckhams M-B grease.

18 Constant velocity type

a) Make sure that the chamfers on the end of the shaft and the shaft splines are free from damage or burrs before entering the shaft into the differential unit.

b) Should any difficulty be found in engaging the shaft into the differential circlip try fitting a 3.5 inch (89 mm) diameter jubilee clip round the pot joint housing and apply an even and sustained pressure by and onto the shaft. Use a drift located on the jubilee clip to drive the shaft into its full engagement position.

---

3 Constant velocity joint rubber boot - removal and replacement

---

If a rubber boot on one of the CV joints has split or been damaged it should be replaced with the minimum of delay. Although it is necessary to remove the driveshaft before the boot can be removed, speedy action will ensure that a large bill for a new driveshaft is avoided.

1 Remove the driveshaft as described in the previous Section.

2 Undo the wire securing the smaller rubber boot in place, and pull the flange and boot off the end of the driveshaft.

3 Undo the clips or wires holding the larger boot in place on the CV joint and pull the boot off the inner splined end of the shaft.

4 Carefully clean all traces of rubber from both ends of the shaft and the flange, and wipe all traces of the old grease from the CV joint. **Note:** If grit is present in the grease then it is essential that the CV joint is thoroughly cleaned out.

5 Fit the new boot from the inner splined end and carefully slide it down the driveshaft.

6 Lubricate the CV joint and replace the rubber boot with about 1 oz. of Duckhams Q.5795 grease. It is important not to use any other type.

7 Carefully pull the boot over the joint so that the moulded lips of the boot fit on the shallow machined depression in the outer circumference of the joint, and on the shaft.

8 Secure the rubber boot to the shaft with two turns of soft

1 Latest type driveshaft with inboard constant velocity joint

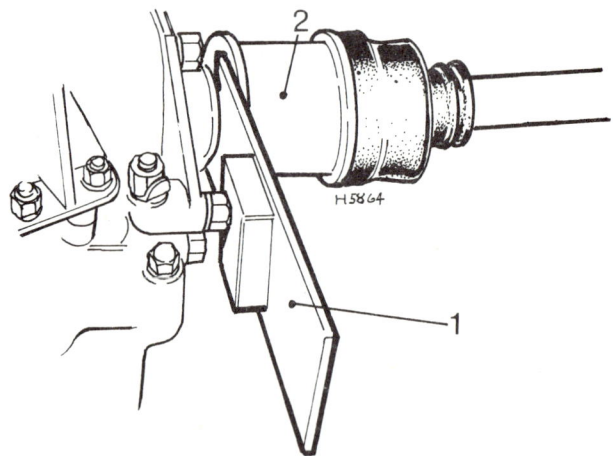

Fig. 7.1. Use of tool to detach latest type of inner constant velocity joint (Sec. 2)

1 Metal lever   2 Constant velocity joint

2 Nylon dust/water shield which must always be in good condition

iron wire. Twist the ends together and turn them to face away from the direction of forward rotation of the shaft. **Note:** Ensure the wires are correctly located on the area of the boot directly over the shallow depressions.

9 Moving to the inner end of the shaft fit the smaller rubber boot, sliding it up the shaft until the moulded lip fits in the shallow machined depression about 2 in (50.8 mm) beyond the end of the splines.

10 Fill the cavity in the joint flange with Duckhams Q.5795 grease up to the old grease nipple hole (now blocked with a bolt).

11 Slide the flange onto the end of the shaft, and pull the larger lip of the rubber boot over the end of the flange.

12 Secure the rubber boot to the flange with two turns of soft iron wire. Twist the ends together and turn them away from the direction of forward rotation.

13 When clips are to be used in securing the rubber gaiter pull the clip tight and clinch in the order shown in Fig. 7.2.

14 Place the driveshaft in a vice and push the flange fully onto the shaft. At the same time, hold the lip of the boot off the shaft with a screwdriver to allow surplus grease to escape.

15 With the flange fully home on the spline, check that the diameter of the rubber boot bellows does not exceed 1¾ in. (44.45 mm). If in excess of this figure, squeeze grease out of the boot until correct. If this is not done the life of the boot will be considerably shortened.

16 Secure the rubber boot to the shaft with two turns of soft iron wire as described in paragraph 12.

4 Outer constant velocity joint - dismantling, overhaul and re-assembly

There is little point in dismantling the outer CV joints if they are known to be badly worn. In this case it is best to remove the joint from the driveshaft and fit a new unit. To remove and then dismantle the CV joints proceed as follows.

1 Remove the driveshaft from the car, and the rubber boot from the CV joint as previously described.

2 Mount the shaft vertically in a vice with the CV joint facing downwards.

3 Before the joint can be dismantled it must be removed from the driveshaft. This is easily done by firmly tapping the outer edge of the CV joint with a hide or plastic headed hammer. The CV joint is held to the shaft by an internal circular section circlip ('B' in Fig. 7.4) and tapping the joint in the manner described forces the circlip to contract into a groove so allowing the joint to slide off.

4 Carefully note which way round the joint was fitted to the shaft. With the joint now free, the inner race can tilt sufficiently for the six balls to be released one at a time. Mark the relative positions of the balls, inner race and cage, and the outer race. This will ensure the same mating surfaces are adjacent on re-assembly. (Fig. 7.5).

5 Remove and separate the inner race and cage. The CV joint is now completely dismantled. (Fig. 7.6).

6 Thoroughly clean all the component parts of the joint by washing in paraffin.

7 Examine each ball in turn for cracks, flat spots, or signs of surface pitting.

8 The cage which fits between the inner and outer races must be examined for wear in the ball cage windows and for cracks which are especially likely to develop across the narrower portions between the outer rims and the holes for the balls.

9 Wear is most likely to be found in the ball tracks on the inner and outer races. If the tracks have widened the balls will no longer be a tight fit and, together with excessive wear in the ball cage windows, will lead to the characteristic 'knocking' on full lock described previously.

10 If wear is excessive then all the parts must be renewed as a matched set.

11 Reassemble the inner race into the cage, and then the cage

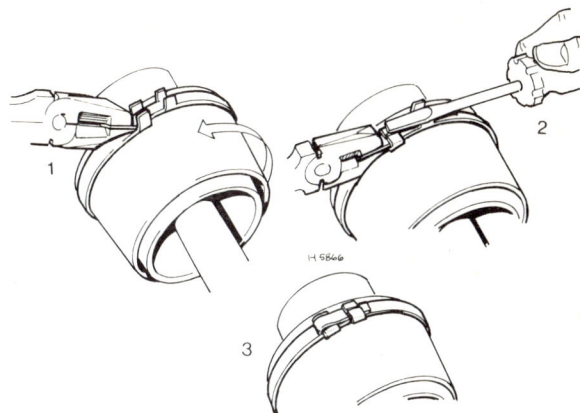

Fig. 7.2. When clips are to be used in securing rubber gaiter pull clip tight and clinch in the order shown. Arrow shows normal direction of rotation (Sec. 3)

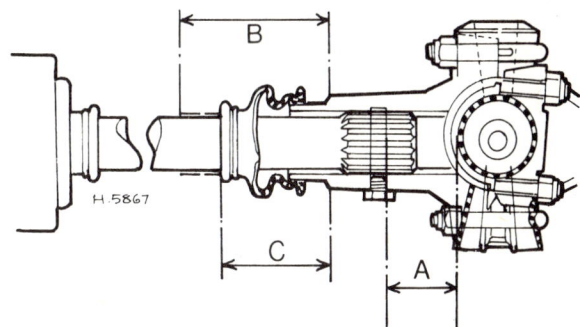

Fig. 7.3. Pack the hollow portion of the flange with the amount of grease shown at 'A'. Adjust the flange and shaft to 2.5 in (63.5 mm) as shown at 'B' before securing the boot to the shaft. 'C' represents the correct measurement of 1.875 in (47.625 mm) from the flange shoulder to the end of the boot when the shaft is adjusted to 'B' (Sec. 3)

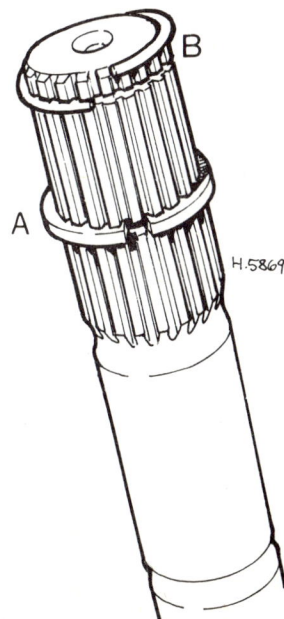

Fig. 7.4. Detail of driveshaft end (Sec. 4)

A Spring ring   *B Round section circlip*

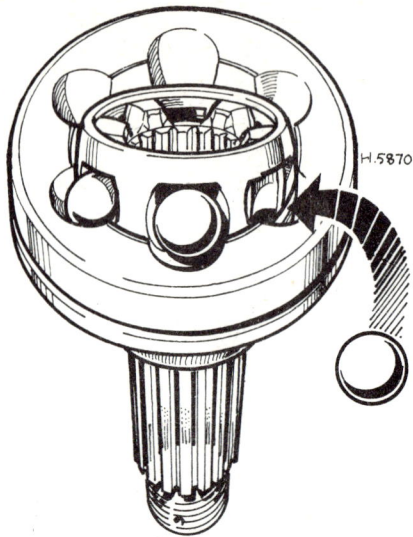

Fig 7.5. Extract each ball in turn by tilting the inner race as illustrated (Sec. 4)

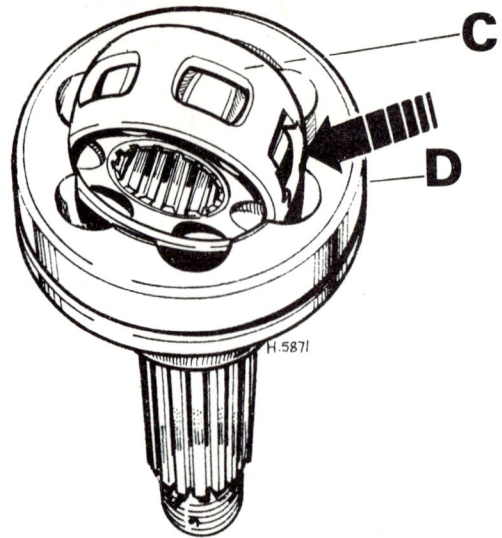

Fig. 7.6. With all the balls removed the cage and inner race can be removed as illustrated. Then remove the inner race 'C' from the cage 'D' (Sec. 4)

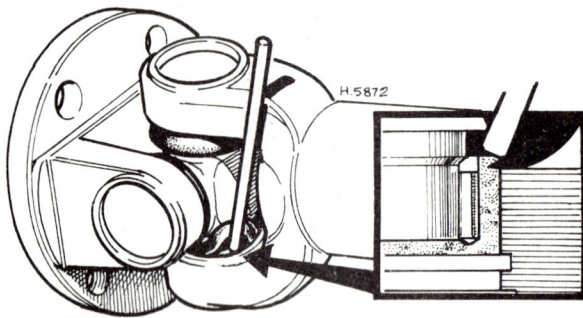

Fig. 7.7. Universal joint bearing removal using a small diameter rod. To be used if bearing cup is really tight (Sec. 7)

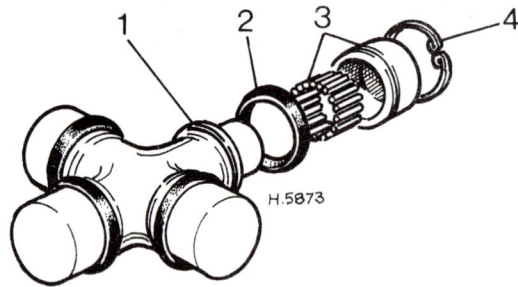

Fig. 7.8. Universal joint component parts (Sec. 7)

1   Journal spider   3   Needle rollers and bearing
2   Rubber seal   cup
                                     4   Circlip

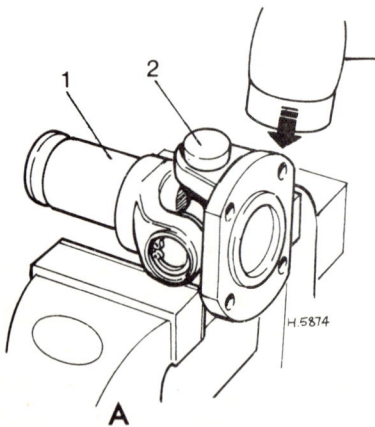

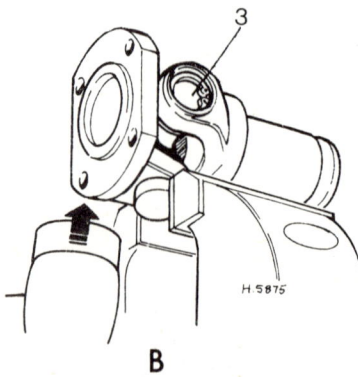

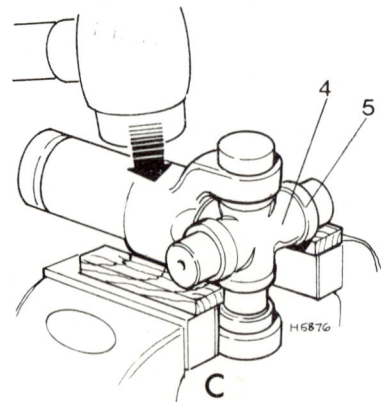

A   B   C

Fig. 7.9. Alternative sequence of operations to be used when removing needle bearings from the universal joint (Sec. 7)

1   Yoke   2   Needle bearing race   4   Journal spider
                                3   Retaining circlip   5   Rubber seal

into the outer race. Tilt the cage and replace the balls one at a time.

12 Pack the joint with the contents of a tube of special Duckhams M–B grease.

13 Fit the CV joint onto the shaft the correct way round and with the joint pressing against the circlip. Contract the circlip right into its groove in the shaft with the aid of two screwdrivers, so the inner race of the CV joint will slide over it. It may be necessary to tap the outside end of the joint smartly with a soft faced hammer in order to close the circlip completely. Tap the joint till it is fully home with the inner race resting against the large retaining clip 'A'. The circlip 'B' should now have expanded inside the joint. (Fig. 7.4).

14 Replace the rubber boot, and refit the driveshaft to the car as described in Section 2.

5 Inner constant velocity joint - dismantling, overhaul and re-assembly

The principle of dismantling, overhaul and reassembly is basically identical to that from the outer constant velocity joint as described in Section 4.

6 Inner Hardy-Spicer type joint - inspection

Wear in the needle roller bearings is characterised by vibration in the transmission, 'clonks' on taking up the drive, and in extreme cases of lack of lubrication, metallic squeaking, and ultimately grating and shrieking sounds as the bearing break up.

It is easy to check if the needle roller bearings are worn with the driveshaft in position, by trying to turn the shaft with one hand, the other hand holding the drive coupling flange.

Any movement between the driveshaft and the half coupling is indicative of considerable wear. If worn, the old bearings and spiders will have to be discarded and a repair kit, comprising new universal joint spiders, bearings, oil seals and retainers purchased.

Check also by trying to lift the shaft and notice any movement in the joints.

Examine the driveshaft splines for wear. If worn it will be necessary to purchase a new half coupling, or if the yokes are badly worn, a new or exchange driveshaft will be required. It is not possible to fit oversize bearings and journals to the trunnion bearing holes.

7 Inner Hardy-Spicer type joint - dismantling, overhaul and reassembly

1 Clean away all traces of dirt and grease from the circlips located on the ends of the spiders, and remove the clips by pressing their open ends together with a pair of pliers and lever them out with a screwdriver. **Note:** If they are difficult to remove tap the bearing face resting on top of the spider with a mallet which will ease the pressure on the circlip.

2 Hold the joint assembly in one hand and remove the bearing cups and needle rollers by tapping the yoke at each bearing with a copper or hide faced hammer. As soon as the bearings start to emerge they can be drawn out with the fingers. If the bearing cup refuses to move then place a thin bar against the inside of the bearing and tap it gently until the cup starts to emerge.

3 With the bearings removed it is relatively easy to extract the spiders from their yokes. If the bearings and spider journals are thought to be badly worn this can easily be ascertained visually with the universal joints dismantled.

4 Thoroughly clean out the yokes and journals.

5 Fit new rubber seals and retainers on the spider journal, place the spider on the shaft yoke, and assemble the needle rollers in the bearing races with the assistance of some thin grease.

6 Pack the bearing cup ends with 0.125 in (3 mm) of grease and refit into the spider. Tap the bearings home so that they lie squarely in position.

7 Replace the circlips and ensure complete freedom of movement. If necessary tap the bearings and yoke to settle the bearing cups.

Chapter 8 Differential unit

Contents

Specifications

Ratio:

1098 cc manual	...	...	...	...	...	...	4.133 : 1
1275 cc manual							
Early models	...	...	...	...	...	...	3.44 : 1
Later models	...	...	...	...	...	...	3.65 : 1
Special export	...	...	...	...	...	...	3.9 : 1
1098 cc Automatic:							
Early models	...	...	...	...	...	...	3.48 : 1
Later models	...	...	...	...	...	...	3.27 : 1
1275 cc Automatic	...	...	...	...	...	...	3.27 : 1

Torque wrench settings:

	lb f ft	kg f m
End-cover bolts	1.8	.25
Driven gear to differential case	60	8.3
Nut, driving flange to differential	70	9.6
Pinion securing nut	150	20.7
Flange bolts (automatic transmission)	40 - 45	5.53 - 6.62

1 General description

The differential is located on the bulkhead side of the engine/transmission unit and is held in place by nuts and studs. The crownwheel or drive-gear, together with the differential gears, is mounted in the differential unit. The drive pinion is mounted on the end of the mainshaft in the gearbox.

All repairs can be carried out to the component parts of the differential unit, only after the engine/transmission unit has been removed from the car. If it is wished to attend to the pinion it will be necessary to separate the transmission casing from the engine.

Although pinion renewal is relatively simple for manual transmission models it is a little more involved for automatic transmission models.

2 Differential unit (manual transmission) - removal and replacement

1 Refer to Chapter 1, and remove the engine/transmission unit.
2 On early models fitted with the earlier type gearchange, remove the remote control housing from its adaptor if this has not already been done.
3 Separate the transmission from the engine, as described in Chapter 6, if it is necessary to fit a new final drive pinion to the transmission unit or if the final drive components have suffered damage with the result that swarf has been created.

4 On early models fitted with the earlier type gearchange, release the control shaft lever from the top of the remote control shaft. Withdraw the remote control shaft.
5 Early models. A split pin locks each of the driveshaft flange securing nuts. Remove the split pins and holding the flange stationary with either special BLMC tool '18G669' or a large wrench, undo and remove each nut in turn and pull the flanges off the gear shafts.
6 Undo and remove the five bolts and spring washers which hold the end-covers in place. Take off the end-covers together with their gaskets.
7 Carefully note the number of shims fitted between the drive-gear bearing and the end-cover housing.
8 Undo and remove the seven nuts and spring washers securing the differential casing to the main transmission casing. On later models lock-washers are used instead of spring-washers.
9 Pull the differential casing up off the transmission casing studs and then lift out the differential assembly.
10 To refit the differential unit first place the differential assembly in the transmission casing with the drive-gear furthest away from, but with a bias towards, the clutch end.
11 Ensure the differential casing flanges are clean and free from all traces of the old gasket, fit a new gasket, and then carefully lower the casing over the studs.
12 Refit the seven nuts and washers and tighten them down lightly so that, although the drive gear bearings are firmly held, they can still be moved slightly together with the differential unit.
13 Clean the end cover flanges, fit a new right-hand end cover

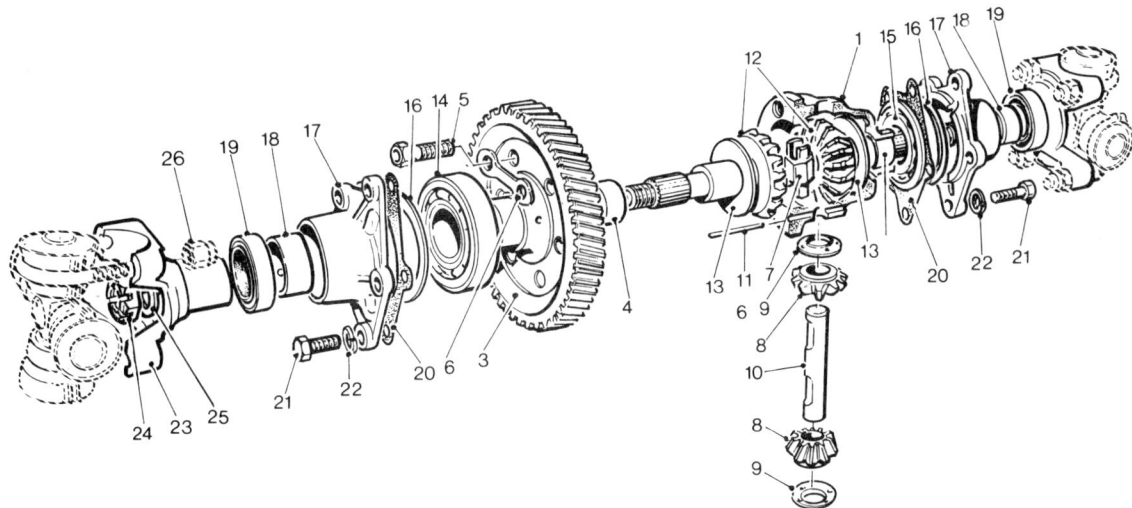

Fig. 8.1. Exploded view of differential assembly (manual transmission)

1	Differential case	8	Differential pinion	15	Case bearing	22	Washer
2	Case bush	9	Pinion thrust washer	16	Bearing shim	23	Driving flange
3	Drive gear	10	Centre pin	17	End cover	24	Flange nut
4	Gear bush	11	Pin peg	18	Cover bush	25	Washer
5	Gear bolt	12	Differential gear	19	Oil seal	26	Locknut
6	Lockwasher	13	Gear thrust washer	20	Cover joint		
7	Thrust block	14	Drive gear bearing	21	End cover screw		

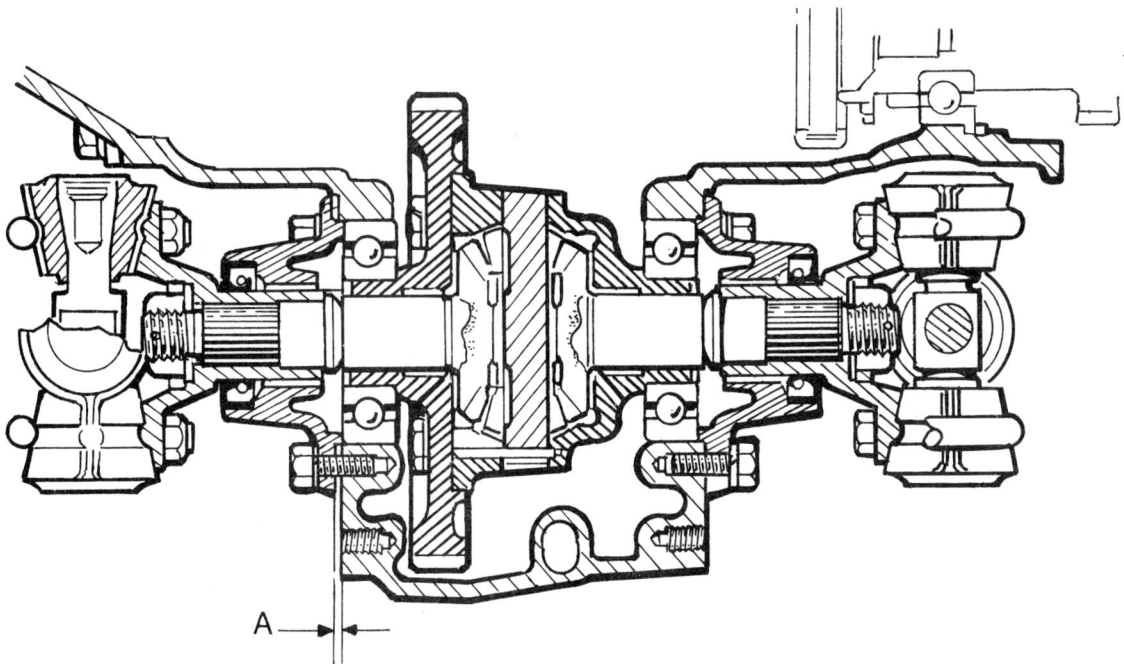

Fig. 8.2. Cross-sectional view of differential unit (manual transmission) (Sec. 2)
Measure the gap 'A' without a gasket to ensure the bearing pre-load is correct

gasket and replace the right-hand end cover. Ensure the holes in the cover flange and the tapped hole in the transmission casing and differential housing are correctly aligned.

14 Screw in the five bolts and spring washers an equal amount so that the inner face of the cover bears evenly on the differential bearing outer race. As the bolts are tightened a little at a time the differential assembly will move away from the flywheel end of the casing, so centralising the assembly in the differential housing.

15 Now fit the left-hand end cover but **omit** the gasket. Tighten

the bolts so that the cover register just seats the bearing outer race. Do not overtighten the bolts or the end cover flange will be distorted.

16 Measure the gap between the end cover and the differential casing in several places to ensure the end cover is seating squarely on the differential assembly. Variations in measurement indicate that the bolts have been tightened unevenly so pulling the differential assembly out of alignment. Alternatively the end cover flange may be distorted. Adjust the tension on the bolts accordingly. (Fig. 8.2).

Differential assembly - removal and replacement (earlier type shown)

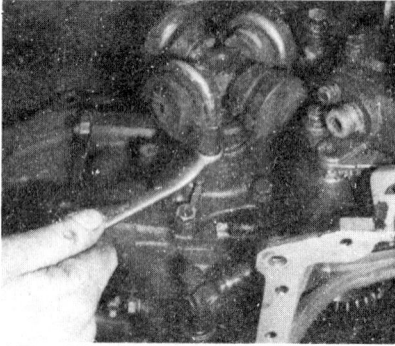

1 The differential assembly can be removed without separating transmission and engine, although it has been done in this instance. Undo remaining 'U' bolt nuts

2 Remove the 'U' bolts and the rubber UJ's. If the UJ's are worn they must be replaced

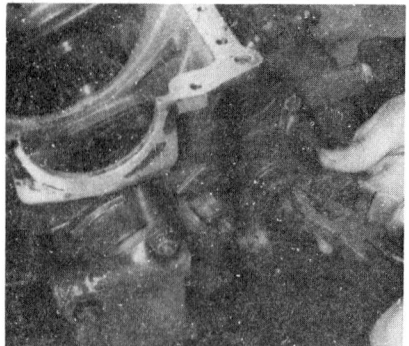

3 With a pair of pliers remove the split pins from the castellated nuts on either side of the differential unit

4 BLMC mechanics use a special spanner which engages the four 'U' bolt holes on the driving flanges and prevents them turning when undoing the flange nuts

5 The driving flange can normally be locked in place with a couple of steel rods jammed against the casing. Remove the nuts and pull the flanges off the shafts

6 Next undo the end cover bolts and remove them from the differential unit together with the split washers

7 Pull the end covers away from the differential unit and place on one side

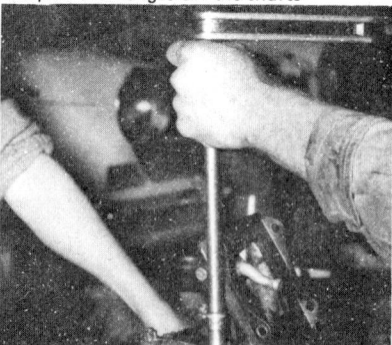

8 The differential cover is removed next from the gearbox casing. Undo the retaining nuts and remove them together with the washers

9 In this photograph the nuts have been removed from the differential cover studs, and it can be seen that the end-covers have also been removed

10 Carefully lift the differential cover away from the casing

11 The differential assembly can be lifted out as shown. To remove the pinion it is necessary to take off the end-cover

12 Thoroughly clean all traces of the old gasket from the casing and differential flanges

13 Refit the differential assembly and drive gear and fit new gaskets as shown

14 Remember to replace differential bearing shims. These might have to be changed if the correct clearance with end-cover flanges cannot be obtained (see text)

15 Prise out the old cover flange oil seals unless they are obviously nearly new

16 Carefully press in new end-cover flange oil seals. This will help ensure no oil leaks develop from the transmission casing

17 Refit the driving flanges to the end-covers on the bench. This is easier than fitting the flanges after the endcovers have been fixed to the differential casing

18 Refit the driving flanges without a gasket, gently tighten the cover bolts (do not overtighten or the flange will distort) and measure the gap (see text)

19 When the gap of 0.008 to 0.009 in (0.2032 to 0.2286 mm) is even all the way round fit a new gasket, and replace the end-cover

20 Fit the end-cover bolts and washers and tighten them down to a torque of 18 lb f ft (2.49 kg f m)

21 Replace the differential cover and do up the retaining nuts. One is actually inside the gearchange extension and difficult to reach as shown

22 Fit the flange washer and the flange nut. Holding the flange securely tighten the nut to 70 lb f ft (9.6 kg f m)

23 Turn the castellated nut on so the next slot lines up with the hole in the gear shaft and fit a new split pin

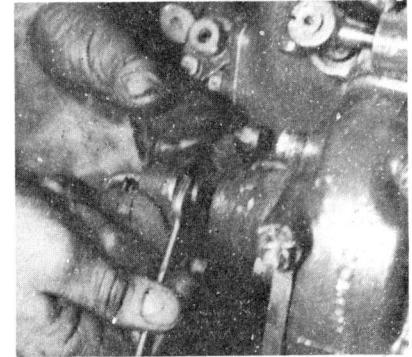

24 Finally refit rubber UJ's. It is helpful to nip the 'U' bolt ends (after replacing the nuts) in a vice prior to refitting

17 The correct gap necessary to give the required preload to the bearings without the gasket fitted is 0.008 to 0.009 in (0.2032 to 0.2286 mm). As the gasket when compressed is 0.007 in (0.1778 mm) thick, the correct gap with the gasket fitted is 0.001 in to 0.002 in (0.0254 to 0.0508 mm) before the bolts are finally tightened down.

18 Any deviation from 0.008 to 0.009 in. (0.2032 to 0.2286 mm) must be rectified by fitting appropriate shims between the register on the inside of the end cover and the bearing outer race.

Measured gap (No gasket)	Shim thickness
0.000 to 0.001 in	0.008 in
0.001 to 0.002 in	0.006 to 0.007 in
0.002 to 0.003 in	0.005 to 0.006 in
0.003 to 0.004 in	0.004 to 0.005 in
0.004 to 0.005 in	0.003 to 0.004 in
0.006 to 0.007 in	0.002 to 0.003 in
0.007 to 0.008 in	0.001 to 0.002 in
0.008 to 0.009 in	None necessary

Note: No metric dimensions given. Shims only available in imperial measurement.

19 Remove the end cover. Fit the necessary shims. Replace the cover complete with gasket, and tighten down the securing bolts evenly to a torque of 18 lb f ft (2.49 kg fm).

20 Tighten the differential housing nuts.

21 **Note:** On later assemblies increased thrust capacity bearings are used and they must be fitted with the identification word 'THRUST' facing the outside , towards the end cover. As the pre-load is increased to 0.003-0.004 in (0.08 - 0.1 mm) adjust the gap A (Fig. 8.2) with shims until it is 0.010 - 0.011 in (0.25 - 0.28 mm) wide before the gasket is fitted.

22 Early models: Refit the driving flanges; replace the driving flange washers and nuts and tighten to 70 lb f ft (9.6 kg fm). (Turn the slotted nut as necessary to align with the next split pin hole). Insert new split pins.

23 Early models: Refit the remote control shaft, the shaft lever, and the extension cover plate. Replace the engine/transmission unit in the car, as described in Chapter 1.

3 Differential unit (manual transmission) - dismantling, examination and reassembly

1 With the aid of a universal puller (or BLMC tool '18G2') pull off the two bearings from the right and left-hand gearshafts.

2 Mark the differential case and the drive-gear so that they can be reassembled in their original positions.

3 Knock back the tabs of the three lockwashers and unscrew the six set bolts which hold the drive-gear to the differential case.

4 Remove the drive-gear complete with the left gearshaft. Pull the drive-gear off the shaft together with the thrust-washer.

5 Gently tap out the tapered peg which holds the centre pin in place.

6 Remove the centre pin and the component parts of the differential case. The differential case can now be removed from the right gearshaft.

Check the bearings for side play and the rollers and races for general wear. Examine the centre pin, the thrust block, and the thrust washers for score marks and pitting, and renew these components as necessary.

7 Examine the teeth of the drive-gear for pitting, score marks, chipping and general wear. If a new drive-gear is required a mated drive-gear and drive pinion must be fitted. It is asking for trouble to renew one without the other. Examine the oil seals in the end flanges and renew them if worn.

8 Reassembly is a straight reversal of the above sequence. **Note:** When replacing the differential gear thrust-washers ensure the slightly chamfered bores rest against the machined faces of the differential gears. The six driven gear bolts should be tightened to a torque of 60 lb f ft (8.3 kg fm) each.

4 Final drive pinion (manual transmission) - removal and replacement

1 Refer to Chapter 1, and remove the engine/transmission unit.

2 Separate the engine from the transmission casing, as described in Chapter 6.

3 Refer to Section 2, and remove the differential unit.

4 Undo the plug on the forward facing side of the transmission casing. This plug holds the change speed reverse detent plunger in place. Remove the plug, washer, spring and plunger.

5 Undo the clamp screw from the selector lever and the Woodruff key from the end of the gear change operating shaft.

6 Pull the gearchange operating shaft up out of the transmission casing.

7 Undo the speedometer pinion housing bolt, remove the housing and extract the pinion. Undo the two bolts which hold the speedometer gear retaining plate to the transmission case front cover, remove the plate and then the speedometer spindle and gear.

8 Knock back the securing tag of the lockwasher which holds the drive pinion securing nut in place, and undo and remove the nut.

9 The final drive pinion can then be pulled off the splines on the mainshaft.

10 Replacement is a straightforward reversal of the removal sequence. Use a new pinion lock-washer and tighten the pinion securing nut to 150 lb f ft (20.7 kg gm).

5 Differential unit (automatic transmission) - removal and replacement

1 Refer to Chapter 1, and remove the engine/transmission unit.

2 Hold the drive flange with either special BLMC tool '18G 1100' or a large wrench and undo and remove each flange centre securing bolt.

3 Remove the flanges from the splined shafts.

4 Carefully knock back the lock-washer and then undo and remove the nuts securing the final drive housing. Lift away the tab washers.

5 Undo and remove the screws securing the "kick-down" linkage to the transmission casing. Pull the linkage from the casing.

6 Undo and remove the two set-screws securing the end cover to the transmission.

7 Lift away the final drive and housing assembly.

8 Undo and remove the remaining securing bolts from the end-cover. Remove the cover and adjustment shims noting the number of shims fitted.

9 The differential unit may now be removed from its casing.

10 To refit the differential unit first place the differential assembly into the transmission casing and push the assembly towards the converter. The slot in the spacer must be in alignment with the dowel in the transmission case.

11 Smear a little Hylomar, or similar jointing compound, onto a new gasket and fit to the transmission casing.

12 Make sure that the oil seal is pressed squarely against the face of the spacer and refit the differential housing.

13 Fit new tabwashers and lightly tighten the securing nuts.

14 Refit the end-cover less the joint washer but with the original shims fitted and tighten the cover bolts evenly but only by a sufficient amount so that the cover register nips the bearing outer race. Overtightening will only distort the flange.

15 Measure the gap between the end-cover and the differential casing in several places to ensure the end-cover is seating squarely on the differential casing. Variations in measurement indicate that the bolts have been tightened unevenly so pulling the differential assembly out of alignment. Alternatively, the end-cover flange may be distorted. Adjust the tension on the bolts as necessary.

16 The compressed thickness of a new cover joint washer is

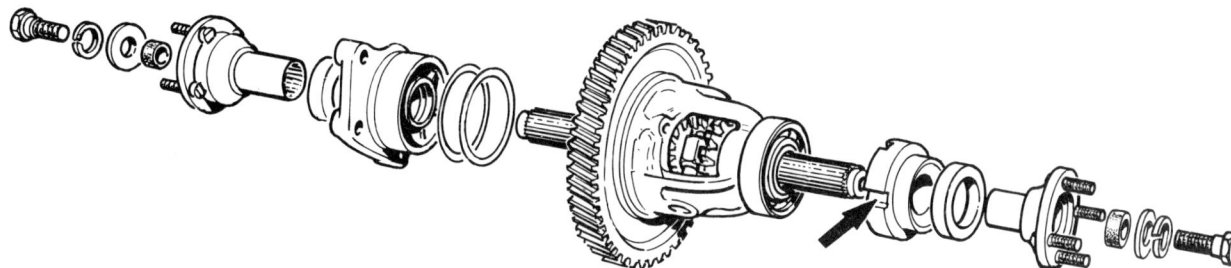

Fig. 8.3. Exploded view of differential assembly (automatic transmission) (Sec. 5)
Arrow shows alignment slot in the spacer

0.007 in (0.178 mm) and the required preload on the bearings is 0.002 in (0.051 mm). The correct gap should therefore be 0.009 in (0.229 mm) and any deviation from this figure must be made up by adding or subtracting shims.

17 **Note:** On later assemblies increased thrust capacity bearings are used and they must be fitted with the identification word 'THRUST' facing the outside, towards the end-cover. As the preload is increased to 0.003 - 0.004 in (0.08 - 0.1 mm) adjust the gap with shims until it is 0.011 in (0.28 mm) before the joint washer is fitted.

18 Remove the end-cover, fit shims as necessary and refit the cover with a new joint washer coated with Hylomar, or similar jointing compound.

19 Tighten the differential housing nuts and the cover bolts to a torque wrench setting of 18 lb f ft (2.5 kg fm).

20 Bend up the locking-washer tabs except on the nut which secures the exhaust pipe bracket.

21 Tighten the end-cover bolts to a torque wrench setting of 18 lb f ft (2.5 kg fm).

22 Lubricate the driving flange oil seals and refit the flanges ensuring the split collets are correctly located inside the flanges.

23 Fit new rubber seals to and refit the central securing bolts to a torque wrench setting of 40 - 45 lb f ft (5.53 - 6.62 kg fm).

24 Refit the governor control linkage to the transmission not forgetting to use a new washer. Make sure the lever is correctly positioned relative to the governor.

25 Replace the engine/transmission unit in the car as described in Chapter 1.

6 Differential unit (automatic transmission) - dismantling, examination and reassembly

1 Remove the oil seal housing.

2 With the aid of a universal puller (or BLMC tool '18G2') pull off the two bearings from the right and left-hand gearshafts.

3 Carefully knock back the locking-plate tabs and remove the bolts securing the driving gear to the cage. Mark the gear and cage so that they may be refitted in their original positions.

4 Separate the driving gear from the cage and remove the differential gear and thrust-washer from the driving gear.

5 Using a suitable diameter parallel pin punch tap out the roll pin and remove bolt pinions and thrust-washers, pinion spacer, and the other differential gear and thrust-washer.

6 Check the bearings for side-play and the rollers and races for general wear. Examine the roll pin, spacer, and the thrust-washer for score marks, and pitting, and renew these components as necessary.

7 Examine the teeth of the drive-gear for pitting, score marks, chipping and general wear. If a new drive-gear is required a mated drive-gear and drive pinion must be fitted. It is asking for trouble to renew one without the other. Examine the oil seals in the end flanges and renew them if worn.

8 Reassembly is a straight reversal of the above sequence. **Note:** When replacing the differential gear thrust-washers ensure the slightly chamfered bores rest against the machined faces of the differential gears. The six drive-gear bolts should be tightened to a torque of 60lb f ft (8.3 kg fm) each.

Chapter 9 Braking system

Contents

Specifications

Make:	... ...	Lockheed
Type:	... ...	Hydraulic. Front disc, rear drum with leading and trailing shoes. Handbrake operating on rear wheels only.

Front brakes (fixed caliper type)

Disc diameter	... ...	8.0 in. (20.3 cm)
Disc thickness	... ...	0.43 - 0.44 in. (10.92 - 11.18 mm)
Pad area (total)	... ...	16.5 sq in. (106.5 cm^2)
Swept area (total)	... ...	133.2 sq in. (859.4 cm^2)
Lining material	... ...	Mintex M78FG (except Sweden and USA) Ferodo 2426F.FG. (Sweden and USA)
Minimum pad thickness	... ...	0.0625 in. (1.59 mm)
Maximum disc run-out	... ...	0.002 in. (0.05 mm)

Front brakes (swinging caliper type)

Disc diameter ...	... ...	8.4 in. (213.36 mm)
Pad area (total)	... ...	18.6 sq in. (120 cm^2)
Swept area (total)	... ...	146 sq in. (955 cm^2)
Lining material	... ...	Mintex M78.FG
Minimum pad thickness...	... ...	0.0625 in. (1.59 mm)
Cylinder diameter	... ...	2.0 in. (50.8 mm)
Maximum disc run-out	... ...	0.002 in. (0.05 mm)

Rear brakes

Drum diameter	... ...	8.00 - 8.005 in. (20.32 - 20.333 cm)
Lining dimensions	... ...	7.68 x 1.25 x 0.094 in. (195.0 x 31.7 x 2.39 mm)
Minimum lining material thickness	... ...	0.06 in. (1.59 mm)
Swept area (total)	... ...	63 sq in. (406 cm^2)
Lining material	... ...	Ferodo AM8.FE or Mintex M79
Wheel cylinder diameter (1300 and 1100 Mk II)	...	0.80 in. (20.32 mm)
Pressure regulating valve closing pressure	... ...	450 lb/sq in. (31.65 Kg cm^2)
Servo unit type	... ...	Lockheed Series 6

Torque wrench settings:

	lb f ft	Kg f m
Disc to hub	38 - 45	5.3 - 6.2
Backplate retaining bolts	25	3.5
Front swivel hub to caliper	50 - 60	7 - 8.3
Brake caliper pivot pin screws (swinging caliper)	65 - 80 lb f in	0.75 - 0.92
Front brake bleed screws	7 - 8	0.95 - 1.15
Rear brake bleed screws	4 - 5	0.55 - 0.7
Servo shell securing bolts	13	1.5
Pressure failure switch assembly		
Nylon switch	12 - 15	1.4 - 1.7
Inertia valve end plug	45	6.2

1 General description

The front brakes on all Mk I models and early 1100 Mk II manual control models are of the rotating disc and rigidly mounted caliper type. Each caliper contains two friction pad assemblies between which the disc rotates.

The friction pads are pressed against the sides of the disc by means of two hydraulically operated pistons and are automatically retracted when the hydraulic pressure is released. Wear on the friction pad linings is automatically compensated for and no adjustment is required.

Hydraulic fluid under pressure enters the mounting half of the caliper and passes through internal drillings to the rim half thus exerting equal pressure on both operating pistons simultaneously and moving the friction pads into contact with the faces of the disc.

The front brakes on 1300, 1100 Mk II automatic transmission, and later 1100 Mk II manual control models are of the single swinging caliper type.

The friction pads are pressed against the disc by means of a single piston operated by hydraulic pressure. Hydraulic fluid under pressure enters the piston, which pushes its friction pad onto the disc. The resultant reaction on the piston cylinder pulls on the swinging caliper to which it is attached, so that the friction pad on the opposite side of the disc is simultaneously drawn onto the disc face with equal force. The rear brakes are of the internal expanding type with one leading and one trailing shoe in each assembly. Pressure on the brake pedal expands the shoes in the drums hydraulically. When the pressure is released return springs retract them onto their stops on the expander units.

A valve is fitted in the hydraulic line to limit the pressure on the rear brakes.

The handbrake operates the rear brakes only through mechanical linkage and does not require separate adjustment except at major overhaul times.

2 Drum brakes - adjustment

1 Jack-up the rear of the car.
2 The brakes on all models are taken up by turning a square-headed adjuster on the rear of each backplate. The edges of the adjuster are easily burred if an ordinary spanner is used. Use a square-headed brake adjusting spanner, if possible (BLMC part no. '18G419'). **Note**: When adjusting the rear brakes make sure the handbrake is off (photos).
3 Turn the adjuster a quarter of a turn at a time until the wheel is locked. Then turn back the adjuster one notch so the wheel will rotate without binding.
4 Spin the wheel and apply the brakes hard to centralise the shoes. Recheck that it is not possible to turn the adjusting screw further without locking the shoe. **Note**: A rubbing noise when the wheel is spun is usually due to dust in the brake drum. If there is no obvious slowing of the wheel due to brake binding there is no need to slacken off the adjusters until the noise disappears. Better to remove the drum and brush out the dust.
5 Repeat this process on the other brake drum. A good tip is to paint the head of the adjusting screws white which will facilitate future adjustment by making the adjuster heads easier to see.

3 Drum brake shoe - inspection, removal and replacement

After high mileages it will be necessary to fit replacement brake shoes with new linings. Refitting new brake linings to old shoes is not always satisfactory, but if the services of a local garage or workshop with brake lining equipment are available, then there is no reason why your own shoes should not be successfully relined.

1 Remove the hub cap, loosen off the wheel nuts, securely jack-up the car, and remove the road wheel.
2 Completely slacken off the brake adjustment and prise off

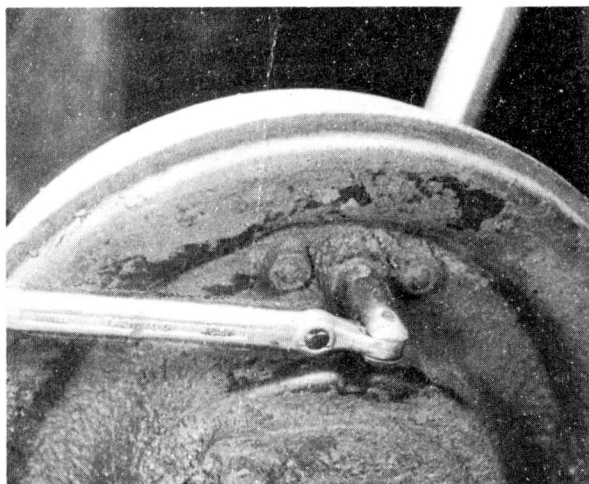

2.2a A brake adjusting spanner ...

2.2b ... and adjuster (rear brakes)

the small grease cap in the centre of the wheel BLMC garages use a special puller to draw off the brake drum. We have found an excellent way to get round this. Take out from the boot the steel cup which holds the spare wheel in place. Remove the split pin, hub nut (left-hand rear- left-hand thread) and flat washer. Place the steel cup in the centre of the brake drum and then replace roadwheel. As the wheel nuts are evenly tightened down the drum is pulled off the hub.

3   The brake linings should be renewed if they are so worn that the rivet heads are flush with the surface of the lining. If bonded linings are fitted they must be removed when the material has worn down to 0.06 in (1.59 mm) at its thinnest point. On early models fitted with a single leading shoe it will be found that the linings do not wear evenly. On no account should the shoes be swapped around in an attempt to get even wear.

4   Detach the shoes and return springs by pulling one end of the shoes away from the slot in the closed end of one of the brake cylinders and in the case of rear wheel brakes pull the ends of both shoes out of the pivot post. Carefully note the holes in the brake shoes into which the return springs fit, and that the springs are fitted so that they are on the inside of the shoes facing the backplate. Allow the return spring to pull the free end of the brake shoe down the side of the brake cylinder. Repeat this process and then lift both brake shoes away.

5   Thoroughly clean all traces of dust from the shoes, back-plates, and brake drums with a dry paint brush and compressed air, if available. Brake dust can cause squeal and judder and it is

therefore important to clean out the brakes thoroughly.

6   Check that the pistons are free in their cylinders and that the rubber dust covers are undamaged and in position and that there are no hydraulic fluid leaks. Secure the pistons with wire or string. On no account press the brake pedal while the brake drum is off, as this would force the pistons out of the brake cylinders resulting in complete loss of hydraulic fluid.

7   Prior to reassembly, smear a trace of white brake grease to all sliding surfaces. The shoes should be quite free to slide on the closed end of the cylinder and the piston anchorage point. It is vital that no grease or oil comes in contact with the brake drums or the brake linings.

8   Replacement is a straight reversal of the removal procedure, but note the following points:
a)   Check that the adjusters are backed right off.
b)   Ensure that the return springs are in their correct holes in the shoes and lie between them and the backplate.

---

4   Drum brake wheel cylinder - inspection and overhaul

If hydraulic fluid is leaking from one of the brake cylinders it will be necessary to dismantle the cylinder and replace the piston rubber and sealing ring. If brake fluid is found running down the side of the wheel, or it is noticed that a pool of liquid forms alongside one wheel and the level in the master cylinder has dropped, proceed as follows:

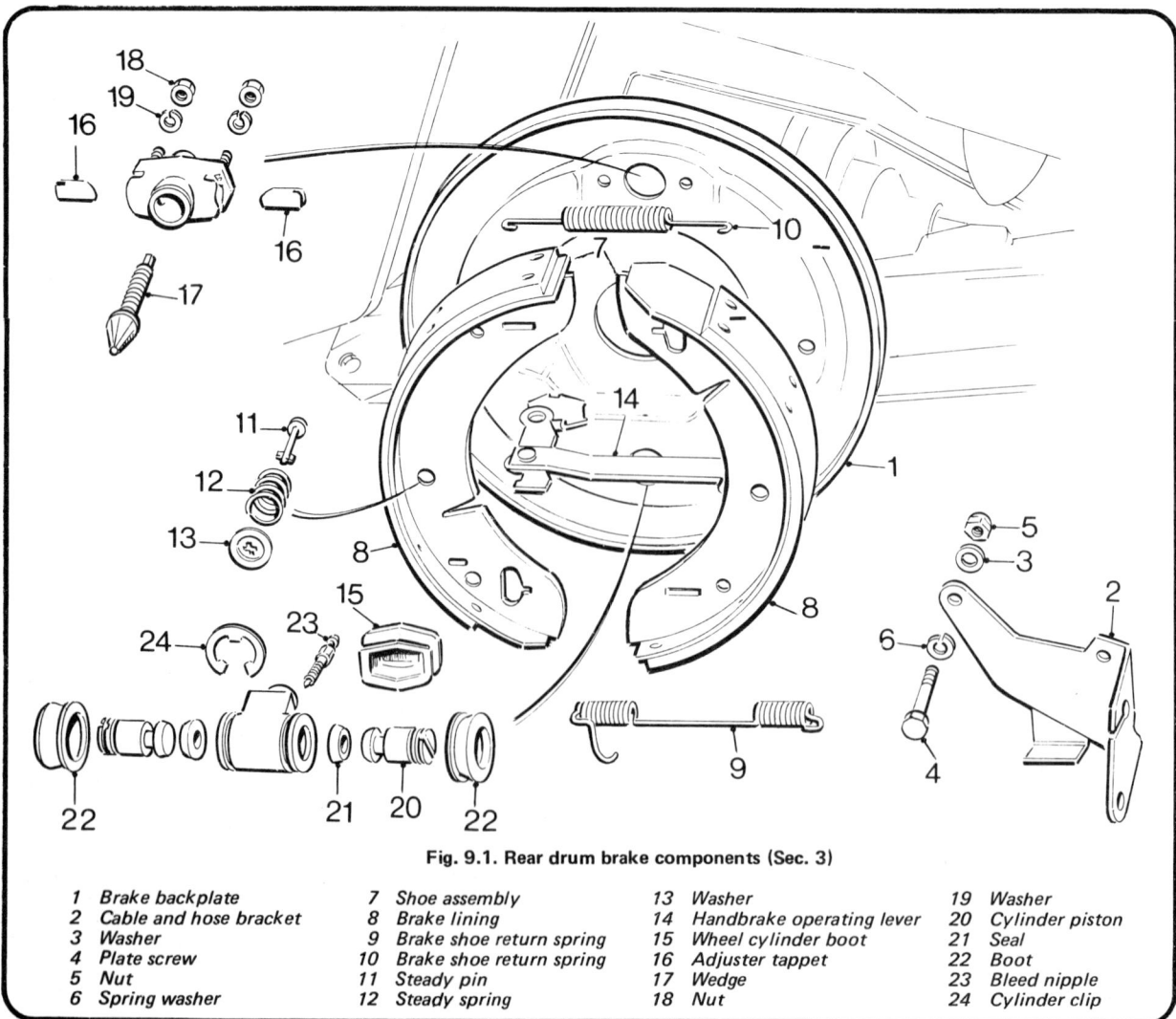

Fig. 9.1. Rear drum brake components (Sec. 3)

1	Brake backplate	7	Shoe assembly	13	Washer	19	Washer
2	Cable and hose bracket	8	Brake lining	14	Handbrake operating lever	20	Cylinder piston
3	Washer	9	Brake shoe return spring	15	Wheel cylinder boot	21	Seal
4	Plate screw	10	Brake shoe return spring	16	Adjuster tappet	22	Boot
5	Nut	11	Steady pin	17	Wedge	23	Bleed nipple
6	Spring washer	12	Steady spring	18	Nut	24	Cylinder clip

Rear brake drum — removal and lining inspection

1 Grease cap removal

2 Withdraw hub nut split pin

3 Removal of hub nut

4 With brake adjustment released, ease the drum and hub assembly from radius arm stub axle

5 Lift away brake drum

6 Brake assembly cleaned ready for inspection

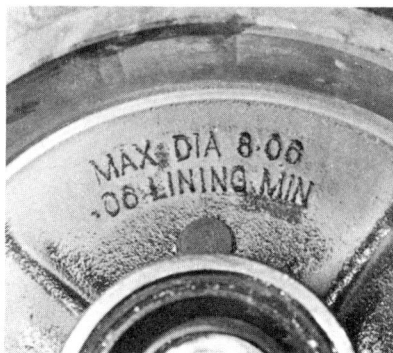

7 Brake drum machining limits

8 Handbrake cable attachment to actuating lever on backplate

1   Remove the brake drum and brake shoes as described in Section 3.

2   Remove the piston, piston rubber and seal from the leaking cylinder by applying gentle pressure to the foot brake. Place a quantity of rag under the backplate or a tray to catch the hydraulic fluid as it pours out of the cylinder.

3   Inspect the inside of the cylinder for score marks caused by impurities in the hydraulic fluid. If any are found the cylinder and piston will require renewal.

4   If the cylinder is sound thoroughly clean it out with fresh hydraulic fluid.

5   The old rubbers will probably be swollen and visibly worn. Smear the new rubbers with hydraulic fluid and reassemble in the cylinder. Fit new seals to the recesses in the piston and replace both pistons in the operating cylinder.

6   Replenish the brake fluid, replace the brake shoes and brake drum, and bleed the hydraulic system as previously detailed.

7   If the cylinder is scored and is to be renewed, remove the flexible hose as detailed in Section 8.

8   Unscrew the bleed screw, remove the circlip and the dished washer from off the wheel cylinder boss which protrudes through the brake backplate. Remove the wheel cylinder. Re-assembly is a direct reversal of this process.

9   In the case of the rear brake assembly, remove the hydraulic pipe, the flexible cable, bleed screw, and circlip from the cylinder boss which protrudes through the backplate. With the brake drum and brake shoes removed the cylinder can now be released. Reassembly is a direct reversal of this process.

5   Drum brake backplate - removal and replacement

1   In the case of the rear brakes the backplate securing bolts can be removed and the backplate lifted away after:

a)   The road wheels, brake drum, handbrake lever rod, and hydraulic pipe have been disconnected.

1 Handbrake lever assembly
2 Lever
3 Release knob
3a Alternative release knob
4 Locking nut
5 Felt washer
6 Spring
7 Plain washer
8 Release rod
8a Alternative release rod
9 Rivet
9a Alternative rivet
10 Pawl
10a Alternative pawl
11 Clevis
11a Alternative clevis pin
12 Plain washer
13 Fulcrum pin
14 Washer
15 Ratchet
16 Trunnion
17 Washer

18 Starlock washer
19 Screw
20 Spring washer
21 Nut
22 Handbrake cable
23 Return spring
24 Adjusting spring
25 Adjusting nut
26 Plain washer
27 Clevis pin
28 Cable fairlead
29 Rubber fairlead seal
30 Seal retaining plate
31 Screw
32 Spring washer
33 Tapped plate
34 Cable swivel assembly
35 Swivel bush
36 Distance tube
37 Nut
38 Plain washer

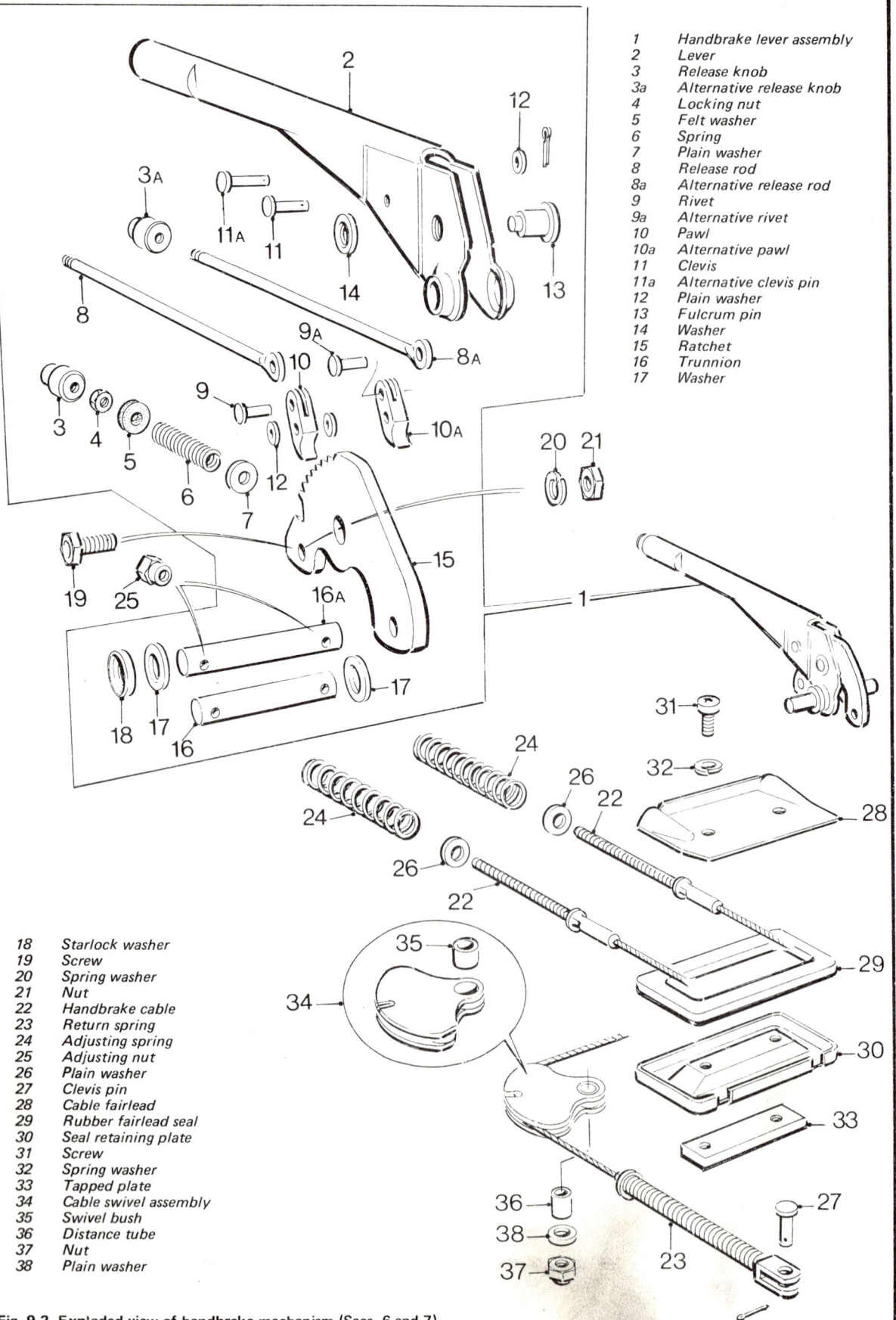

Fig. 9.2. Exploded view of handbrake mechanism (Secs. 6 and 7)

b) The hub assembly has been removed.

2 Replacement in both cases is a straight reversal of the removal sequence.

6 Handbrake - adjustment

If the handbrake requires adjustment it is more than likely that the footbrake will require adjustment also. Excess travel in the footbrake is compensated by adjusting the brake shoes, this automatically compensates for excess travel in the handbrake lever as well.

Never try to adjust the handbrake to compensate for wear on the rear brake linings. It is very seldom that the handbrake will require adjustment, and that only after very high mileages due to slight stretching of the cable. Usually it is badly worn rear brake linings that lead to excessive handbrake travel. If the rear brake linings are in good condition or have been recently renewed and the handbrake tends to reach the end of its ratched travel before the brakes come on, adjust the handbrake as follows:

1 Lock the rear brake shoes by rotating the adjustment screw as far as it will turn clockwise.

2 Apply the handbrake on the fourth notch of its ratchet.

3 Remove the slackness in the cable by adjusting the nuts at the handbrake lever trunnion. **Do not overtighten** the cables or the rear brakes will bind.

4 Release the handbrake and check that neither of the rear wheels is binding.

7 Handbrake cable - removal and replacement

If the handbrake cables have stretched to the extent where adjustment is no longer possible, or if they are badly corroded or worn, they can be replaced as follows:

1 Remove the hub cap and loosen the four securing nuts on the rear road wheel on the side from which the cable is to be removed.

2 Place the car in bottom gear, and with a jack under the rear subframe raise the rear of the car, and remove the roadwheel.

3 Undo the cable adjusting nuts on the handbrake lever trunnion and take off the cable fairlead which is positioned in the middle of the floor towards the rear of the front seats.

4 From underneath the floor of the car pull the cable out from inside the body and free the cable from its guide channel on the rear subframe crossmember.

5 Undo the nut which holds the quarter circular cable swivel to the radius arm. The corners of the cable swivel are squeezed together so gripping the cable firmly.

6 Free the cable from the handbrake actuating lever on the brake backplate, and pull the cable through the subframe and remove complete with the cable swivel.

7 Replacement is a direct reversal of the removal sequence but the following two points should be noted:

a) Always ensure that the cable swivel holds the cable securely.

b) The handbrake should be adjusted as described in Section 6.

8 Flexible hoses - inspection, removal and replacement

Inspect the condition of the flexible hydraulic hoses leading from the chassis mounted metal pipe to the brake backplates. If any are swollen, damaged, cut, or chaffed, they must be renewed.

1 Unscrew the metal pipe union nut from its connection to the hose, and then holding the hexagon on the hose with a spanner, unscrew the attachment nut and washer.

2 The chassis end of the hose can now be pulled from the chassis mounting bracket and will be quite free.

3 Disconnect the flexible hydraulic hose at the backplate by unscrewing it from the brake cylinder. **Note**: When releasing the hose from the backplate, the chassis end must always be freed

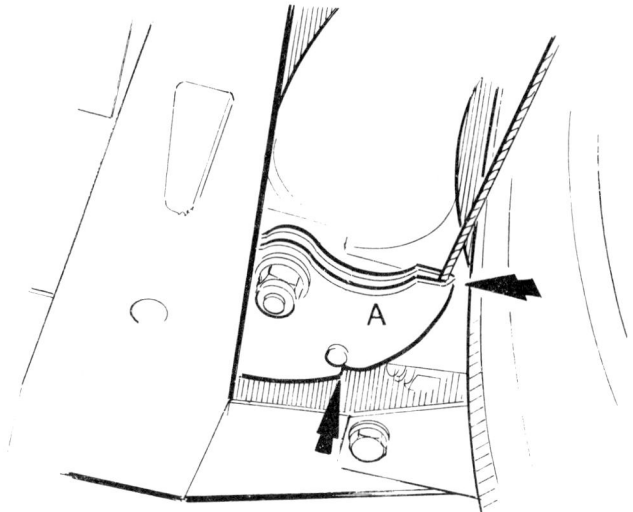

Fig. 9.3. The handbrake cable sector (A) mounted on the underside of the rear radius arm. Ensure the sector is nipped at corner when fitting a new cable (Sec. 7)

first.

4 Replacement is a straight reversal of the above procedure.

9 Brake hydraulic system - bleeding

Single master cylinder

Gather together a clean glass jar, a 9 in (230 mm) length of tubing which fits tightly over the bleed nipples and a tin of the correct brake fluid. Then proceed as follows:

1 Fill the master cylinder and the bottom inch (25.4 mm) of the jar with hydraulic fluid.

2 On the wheel furthest away from the master cylinder, remove the rubber dust cap from the bleed screw and with a suitable spanner unscrew the bleed screw ¾ of a turn.

3 Place one end of the tube over the wheel cylinder bleed screw and insert the other open end in the jar so that it is covered by the fluid.

4 An assistant should now pump the brake pedal up and down, slowly, replenishing the master cylinder as necessary, until all air bubbles cease to emerge with the fluid from the end of the tube.

5 Tighten the bleed screw on the next down stroke, and replace the rubber dust cap.

6 Repeat this process with the other three bleed screws, finishing up at the nipple nearest the brake master cylinder.

Note: Never re-use fluid bled from the hydraulic system. It should always be discarded.

Tandem master cylinder

1 To bleed the hydraulic system when a tandem master cylinder is fitted the sequence is slightly different.

2 Top-up the hydraulic fluid reservoir to the correct level and thereafter do not allow the level to fall by more than 0.5 in (1.25 mm).

3 Attach bleed tubes to the front and rear bleed screws on the right-hand side of the car.

4 Submerge the open end of each tube in a small amount of clean brake fluid in a glass jar.

5 Open both bleed screws half a turn and fully depress the brake pedal. Hold it in this position.

6 Close both bleed screws and allow the pedal to return slowly.

7 Repeat the sequence in paragraphs 5 and 6 until clean, air free, fluid issues from both tubes.

8 Repeat the above sequence four more times and with the brake pedal depressed tighten both bleed screws fully.

9 Transfer the bleed tubes to the left-hand bleed screws and repeat the sequence in paragraphs 6, 7 and 8.

10 Disc brake friction pad (fixed caliper) - inspection, removal and replacement

1 Remove the front wheels and inspect the amount of friction material left on the friction pads. The pads must be renewed when the thickness of the material has worn down to 0.0625 in (1.59 mm).
2 Press down on the pad retaining spring and extract the retaining spring split pins.
3 Take off the spring clip and with a slight rotational movement, remove the friction pads and anti-squeak shims, using a pair of sharp-nosed pliers if necessary.
4 Carefully clean the recesses in the caliper in which the friction pad assemblies lie, and the exposed face of each piston from all traces of dirt and dust.
5 Remove the cap from the hydraulic fluid reservoir and place a large rag underneath the unit. Press the pistons in each half of the caliper right in - this will cause the fluid level in the reservoir

to rise and possibly to spill over the brim onto the protective rag.
6 After checking that the cut away face of each piston is facing upwards, fit the new friction pads into the calipers and position the anti-squeak shims between the friction pad and the piston.
7 Check that the new friction pad assemblies move freely in the caliper recesses and remove any high spots on the edges of the pressure plate by careful filing.
8 Check that the retaining spring clips show no sign of damage or loss of tension and then, if sound, replace them, press them down and insert the split pins.
9 Replace the road wheels and remove the jacks. Press the brake pedal several times to adjust the brake. Top-up the master cylinder as required.

11 Disc brake caliper and disc (fixed caliper) - removal, overhaul and replacement

1 Jack up the car and remove the roadwheel.

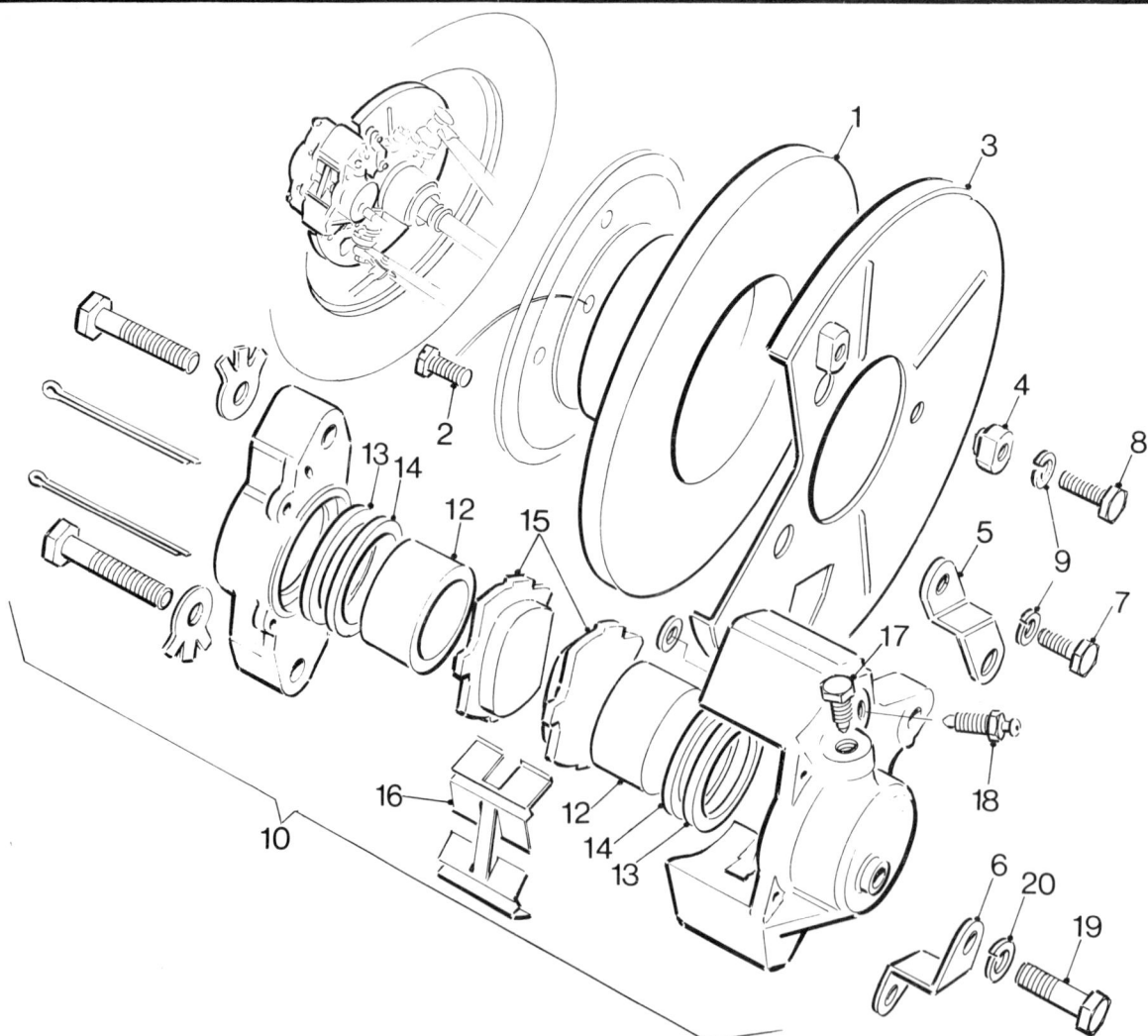

Fig. 9.4. Exploded view of front disc brake components (fixed caliper type) (Secs. 10 and 11)

1 Brake disc	6 Dust protector bracket - bottom	12 Piston	17 Plug
2 Flange bolt	7 Protector bolt	13 Inner seal	18 Bleed nipple
3 Dust protector	8 Protector bolt	14 Seal	19 Caliper bolt
4 Nut	9 Spring washers	15 Pad assembly	20 Spring washer
5 Dust protector bracket - top	10 Caliper assembly	16 Spring	

2 Undo the two nuts and screws which hold the locking plate to the disc brake dust cover.

3 Remove the disc brake friction pads and anti-squeal shims as previously detailed.

4 Unscrew the two caliper mounting bolts and lockwashers and remove the caliper assembly from the disc, together with the dust cover.

5 Meticulously clean the caliper, and place the caliper on a block or similar support, or get an assistant to hold it to avoid it hanging on the hydraulic hose which could damage the latter.

6 Clamp the piston in either the mounting half or the rim half of the caliper with wire or a suitable clamp, depending on which side of the caliper the piston is to be removed from first.

7 Gently apply the footbrake so forcing the unclamped piston out of the caliper until it is in a position where it can be removed by hand.

8 Gently prise the dust seal retainer from the cylinder by carefully inserting a penknife blade between the dust seal retainer and the dust seal, and then extract the seal.

9 Remove the inner hydraulic fluid seal from its groove in the caliper cylinder with a blunt nosed tool. **Note**: Great care should be taken not to damage or scratch the cylinder bore or fluid seal groove.

10 After the piston and rubber seals in one side of the caliper have been checked and replaced as necessary, and the piston reassembled to the caliper as detailed later in this Section, the piston in the other half of the caliper can be removed by clamping the rebuilt piston assembly in place and then repeating the process used to remove the first piston.

11 If it is wished to remove the brake disc, first prise off the hub bearing cover, then extract the split pin, unscrew the hub nut, and pull off the hub flange and disc.

12 To separate the hub from the disc, unscrew the four set screws and lift the disc away from the flange.

13 To reassemble, first replace the disc on the hub flange and tighten down the four set screws.

14 Refit the hub flange and disc to the swivel axle assembly.

15 Check the run out at the outer periphery of the disc. If it exceeds 0.006 in (0.152 mm.) remove the disc and reposition it on the hub casing.

16 Coat a new rubber fluid seal with hydraulic brake fluid and fit the seal to the groove in the cylinder.

17 Slacken the bleed screw in the caliper one turn.

18 Lubricate the piston with hydraulic fluid and press the piston into the cylinder carefully, with the undercut portion facing upwards and out. Press the piston in squarely until approximately 0.25 in (6.35 mm) protrudes from the cylinder.

19 Smear a new dust seal with hydraulic fluid and fit it to its retainer.

20 Place the dust seal assembly with the seal resting on the raised portion of the piston and press the piston and seal home with a suitable clamp. Tighten the bleed screw. Repeat this procedure with the remaining cylinder in the other half of the caliper.

21 Refit the caliper to the disc. Replace the two screws which hold the dust cover in place. Tighten the caliper bolts to a torque of 50 to 60 lb f ft (7.00 to 8.3 kg f m).

22 Fit the anti-squeal plates and disc brake friction pads as previously described and bleed the hydraulic system. Reassembly is now complete.

12 Disc brake friction pad (swinging caliper) - inspection, removal and replacement

1 Jack-up the car, remove the front wheels and inspect the amount of friction material left on the friction pads. The pads must be renewed when the thickness of the material has worn down to 0.0625 in (1.59 mm).

2 Press down on the pad retaining spring and extract the retaining spring split pins.

3 Take off the pad retaining spring and with a slight rotational movement, remove the friction pads, using a pair of sharp nosed

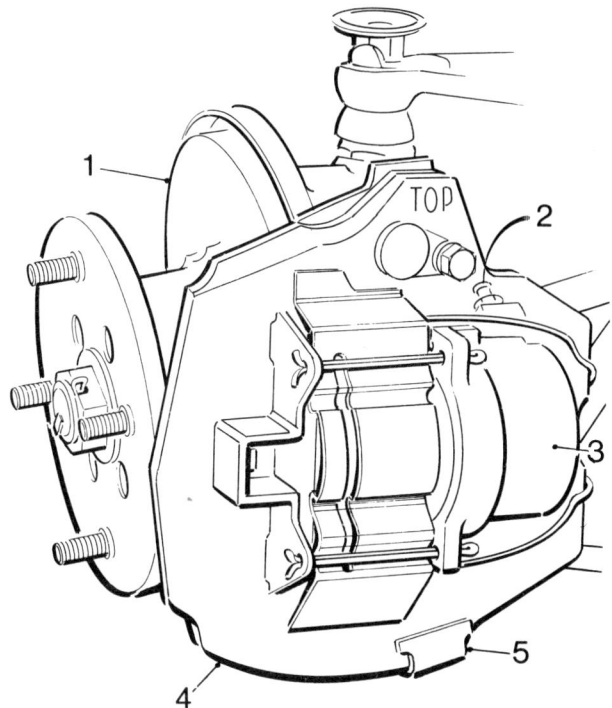

Fig. 9.5. Swinging caliper disc brake assembly (Sec. 12)

1 Brake disc
2 Bleeder screw
3 Piston assembly

4 Swinging caliper
5 Fixed to swinging caliper securing clip

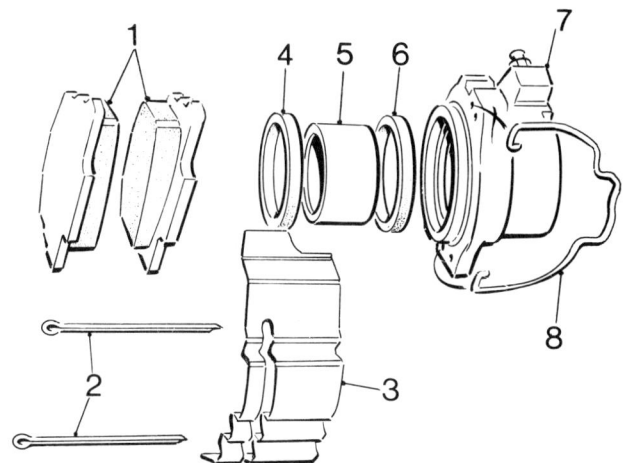

Fig. 9.6. Exploded view of swinging caliper type piston and brake pad assembly (Sec. 12)

1 Friction pads
2 Retaining pins
3 Pad retaining spring
4 Piston dust seal

5 Piston
6 Piston fluid seal
7 Piston cylinder
8 Piston assembly clip

pliers if necessary.

4 Carefully clean the exposed face of the single piston, the recess upon which the moving pad slides, and the face of the caliper against which the fixed pad rests.

5 Remove the cap from the hydraulic fluid reservoir and place a large absorbent rag underneath the unit. Press the piston back into its cylinder - this will cause the fluid level in the reservoir to rise and possibly spill over the brim onto the protective rag.

6 Fit new friction pad assemblies to the caliper, ensuring that

Disc-brake caliper-pad and caliper removal (swinging caliper shown)

1 Remove the roadwheel

2 The two pins must be straightened

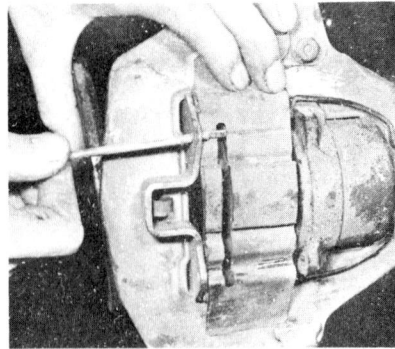
3 Withdraw the pins taking care of the pad retaining spring

4 Lift away the outer pad and then the inner pads

5 Removal of caliper bolts. Note the pads have been removed

6 Lifting away caliper. Do not stretch the flexible hose

the pad operated by a single piston can move easily in its recess in the caliper.

7 Check that the pad retaining springs show no sign of damage or loss of tension; if sound replace them and insert the split pins.

8 Slacken the nut on the top of the caliper adjacent to the pivot pin boss, press the brake pedal several times to centralise the brake pads on the brake disc and retighten the nut to a torque of 65 to 80 lb f in (0.75 - 0.92 kg f m).

9 Check the level in the master cylinder reservoir and top-up if necessary. Replace the roadwheels and remove the jacks.

---

13 Disc brake caliper and disc (swinging caliper) - removal, overhaul and replacement

---

1 Jack-up the car and remove the roadwheel.

2 Remove the disc brake friction pads as described in Section 12.

3 Unscrew the two caliper mounting bolts and lockwashers and remove the caliper assembly from the disc and hub.

4 Meticulously clean the caliper, and place the caliper on a block or similar support so that there is no tension on the hydraulic hose which could easily become damaged during this operation.

5 Remove the piston assembly retaining clip and then gently tap the piston assembly from the caliper with a soft faced hammer. The footbrake can also be used to free the piston from the cylinder.

6 Gently prise the dust seal retainer from the cylinder by carefully inserting a penknife blade between the dust seal retainer and the dust seal, and then extract the seal.

7 Remove the inner hydraulic fluid seal from its groove in the caliper cylinder with a blunt nosed tool. **Note:** Great care should be taken not to damage or scratch the cylinder bore or fluid seal groove.

8 If it is wished to remove the brake disc, first prise off the hub bearing cover, then extract the split pin, unscrew the hub nut and pull off the hub flange and disc.

9 First, scratch a small mating mark on the disc and hub. To separate the hub from the disc, unscrew the four set screws and lift the disc away from the flange.

10 To reassemble, first replace the disc on the hub flange in the same position it was in originally and tighten down the four set screws.

11 Refit the hub flange and disc to the swivel axle assembly.

12 Check the run out at the outer periphery of the disc. If it exceeds 0.002 in (0.05 mm) remove the disc and reposition it on the hub casing.

13 Coat a new rubber fluid seal with hydraulic fluid and fit the seal to the groove in the cylinder.

14 Slacken the bleed screw in the caliper one turn.

15 Lubricate the piston with hydraulic fluid and press the piston into the cylinder carefully until approximately 0.25 in (6.35 mm) protrudes from the cylinder.

16 Smear a new dust seal with hydraulic fluid and fit it to its retainer.

17 Place the dust seal assembly with the seal resting on the raised position of the piston and press the piston and seal home with a suitable clamp.

18 Refit the piston assembly retaining clip and ensure that the pivot pin and the sliding face between the fixed and moving parts of the caliper are completely free from rust and dirt, so that the moving part of the caliper can swing freely.

19 Refit the caliper to the disc and hub noting that the thick steel washer is fitted to the lower of the two bolts attaching the caliper to the hub, and that both bolts have spring washers.

20 Fit the disc friction pads as described in Section 12 and bleed the hydraulic system as described in Section 9. Reassembly is now complete.

14 Brake master cylinder (single) - removal, overhaul and replacement

1   Individual master cylinders and reservoirs are fitted for the brake system and the clutch system and although they look the same they are not interchangeable. Spring off the circlip from the end of the clevis pin which holds the brake pushrod to the brake pedal. Slide out the clevis pin.

2   Unscrew the union nut from the end of the hydraulic pipe where it enters the brake master cylinder and gently pull the pipe clear.

3   Unscrew the two nuts and spring washers holding the brake cylinder mounting flange to the mounting bracket.

4   Remove the master cylinder and reservoir, unscrew the filler cap, and drain the hydraulic fluid into a clean container.

5   Remove the rubber boot or dust cover, and extract the circlip from the end of the body with a pair of long-nosed pliers. (Fig. 9.7).

6   Pull out the pushrod and stop washer and shake out the piston, secondary cup, copper piston washer, the primary or main cup, and the spring and valve assembly.

7   Clean all the components thoroughly with hydraulic fluid or alcohol and then dry them off.

8   Carefully examine the parts, especially the rubber primary and secondary cups for signs of swelling, distortion, or splitting. and check the piston and cylinder wall for wear and score marks. Replace any parts that are faulty.

9   Reassembly is a straight reversal of the dismantling procedure, but note the following points:
a) As the components are returned to the cylinder barrel, lubricate them with clean hydraulic fluid.
b) Insert the return spring into the barrel with its broader base first.
c) On completion of assembly top up the reservoir tank with the correct grade of hydraulic fluid and bleed the system.

15 Brake master cylinder (single) - pushrod to piston clearance

It is unlikely that the master cylinder pushrod to piston clearance will have to be reset, unless the adjusting nuts have been disturbed. If they have, then reset the nuts to give 0.156 in (3.97 mm) clearance at the foot pedal before the piston begins to move. If the pedal is depressed by hand the point when the piston begins to move is quite obvious by the greatly increased pressure required to depress the pedal further.

16 Brake master cylinder (tandem) - removal, overhaul and replacement

1   Spring off the circlip from the end of the clevis pin which holds the brake pushrod to the brake pedal. Slide out the clevis pin.

2   Unscrew the union nuts from the end of the hydraulic pipes where they enter the brake master cylinder and gently pull the pipes clear. Plug the pipe ends to prevent loss of fluid and the entry of dirt.

3   Remove the two nuts and spring washers securing the brake master cylinder to the bulkhead and lift it clear. Drain the fluid from the reservoir and refit the cap to prevent the entry of dirt.

4   Plug the pipe connections on the body and thoroughly clean the exterior of the assembly, then remove the pushrod rubber boot. (Fig. 9.8).

5   Place the master cylinder with the mouth of the bore uppermost in a soft jawed vice.

6   Compress the return spring and remove the Spirolox ring from its groove in the primary piston. Take extreme care not to distort the coils of the spring or damage the bore of the cylinder.

7   Using a pair of long nosed circlip pliers remove the piston retaining circlip.

8   Gently move the piston up and down in the cylinder bore to free the nylon guide bearing and the cap seal. Remove the plain washer.

9   Using a pair of long nosed circlip pliers remove the inner circlip.

10 Withdraw the primary and secondary piston assembly from the bore together with the stop washer. Remove the stop washer.

11 Compress the spring that separates the two pistons and tap out the pin which retains the piston link.

12 Make a careful note of the positions of the rubber cups by

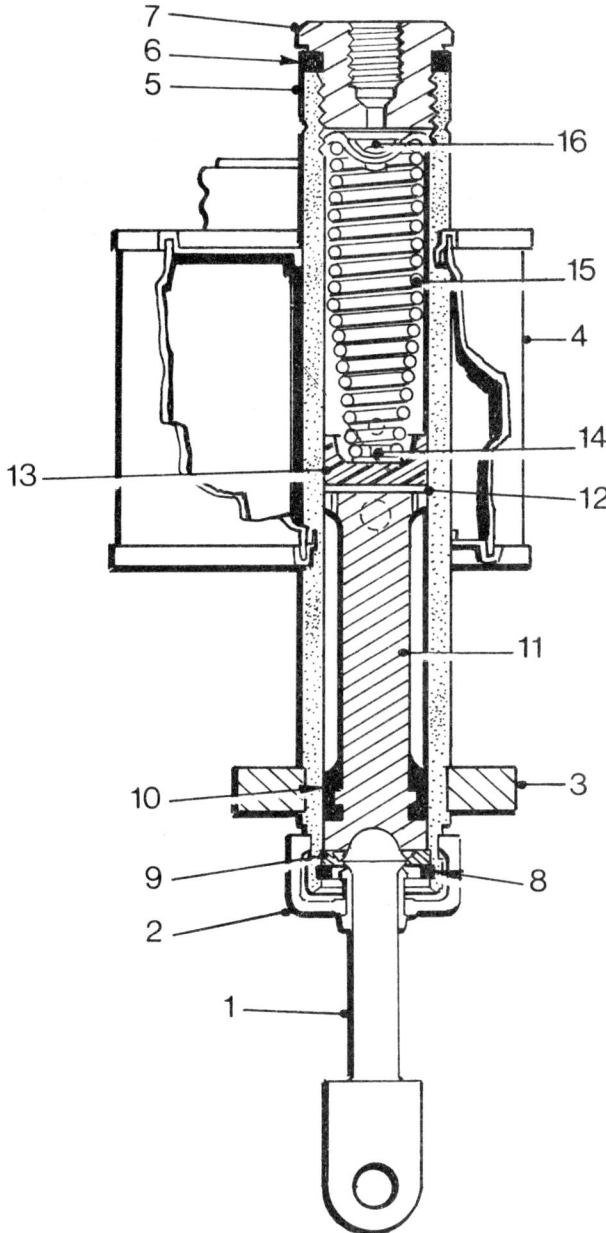

Fig. 9.7. Cross-sectional view of brake master cylinder (single) (Sec. 14)

1	Pushrod	9	Stop washer
2	Rubber boot	10	Secondary cup
3	Mounting flange	11	Piston
4	Supply tank	12	Piston washer
5	Body	13	Main cup
6	Washer	14	Spring retainer
7	End plug	15	Return spring
8	Circlip	16	Non-return valve

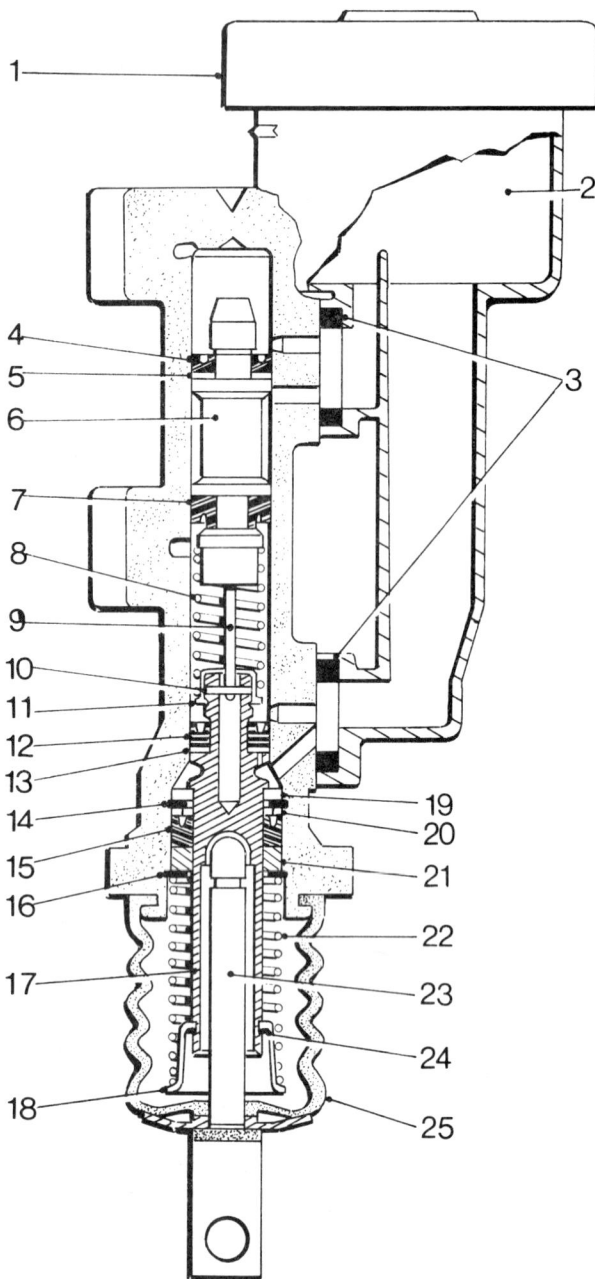

Fig. 9.8. Cross-sectional view of tandem master cylinder (Sec. 16)

1 Filler cap	14 Circlip
2 Plastic reservoir	15 Cup
3 Reservoir seals	16 Circlip
4 Main cup	17 Piston
5 Piston washer	18 Spring retainer
6 Piston	19 Stop washer
7 Main cup	20 Washer
8 Spring	21 Bearing
9 Piston link	22 Spring
10 Pin	23 Pushrod
11 Pin retainer	24 Spirolox ring
12 Main cup	25 Rubber boot
13 Piston washer	

their moulded shape and then remove the cups and washers from the pistons.

13 Remove the four bolts which secure the plastic reservoir to the cylinder body and lift off the reservoir. Remove the two reservoir sealing rings.

14 Clean all the components thoroughly with hydraulic fluid or methylated spirits and dry them with a clean absorbant rag.

15 Carefully examine the parts, especially the rubber cups for signs of swelling, distortion, or splitting, and check the pistons and cylinder bore for wear and score marks. Replace any parts that are faulty.

16 Prior to reassembly dip all the internal components in the recommended hydraulic fluid as they must not be assembled dry.

17 Reassembly is a straightforward reversal of the dismantling proceedure but NOTE the following points.

a) Locate the piston washers on the head of the pistons prior to fitting the main cups.

b) When repairing the main cups carefully ease them lip last, over the end of the pistons, using the fingers and seat them in the grooves adjacent to the washers.

18 After reassembling and refitting the master cylinder fill the reservoir with fresh hydraulic fluid and bleed the system as described in Section 9.

17 Pressure regulating valve - removal, overhaul and replacement

1 Thoroughly clean all dirt away from the body of the valve (located under the floor on the rear subframe front cross-member) and from the brake line unions to ensure no dirt enters the system on removal of the unit. (photo).

2 Undo the three nuts which hold the brake pressure pipes to the valves and pull the pipes clear of the unit. Loosen the large end plug.

3 Undo and remove the nut and washer which secures the valve to the crossmember and lift away the valve assembly.

4 Remove the end plug together with its sealing washer and extract the valve piston, and the return spring. (Fig. 9.9).

5 Examine the rubber seals on the piston. If they are worn or perished new seals will have to be fitted.

6 Carefully clean the interior of the valve body and lubricate the bore with hydraulic fluid prior to reassembly of the piston.

7 Fit new taper and piston seals and make certain that the taper seal is fitted so that the smaller diameter enters the valve bore first.

8 Insert the return spring first, followed by the piston assembly, followed by the sealing washer and end plug.

9 Replace the valve assembly to the subframe, tighten the end plug, reconnect the three brake pressure pipes and finally bleed the system as described in Section 9.

18 Inertia valve - removal, overhaul and replacement

On all Austin America models an Inertia Valve replaces the pressure regulating valve described in Chapter Nine. It is fitted in the fluid line to the rear brakes and its purpose is to reduce the possibility of the rear wheels skidding due to weight transfer during heavy braking.

Referring to Fig. 9.10 the angle at which the assembly is mounted allows the steel ball inside the body to hold the valve in the open position so that fluid may pass to the rear brakes. Under heavy braking, the weight transfer to the front of the car causes the ball to move away from the valve, which is then closed by a light spring. In this way further pressure is prevented from reaching the rear brakes and all additional pressure is transferred to the front brakes.

1 To dismantle, remove the hydraulic pipes and plug the ends to prevent loss of fluid or dirt entering.

2 The inertia valve is located beneath the rear subframe cross-member on the right-hand side and is fixed by two bolts. Remove these bolts and lift the assembly from the car.

Fig. 9.9. Exploded view of brake pressure regulating valve (Sec. 17)

17.1 Location of pressure regulating valve

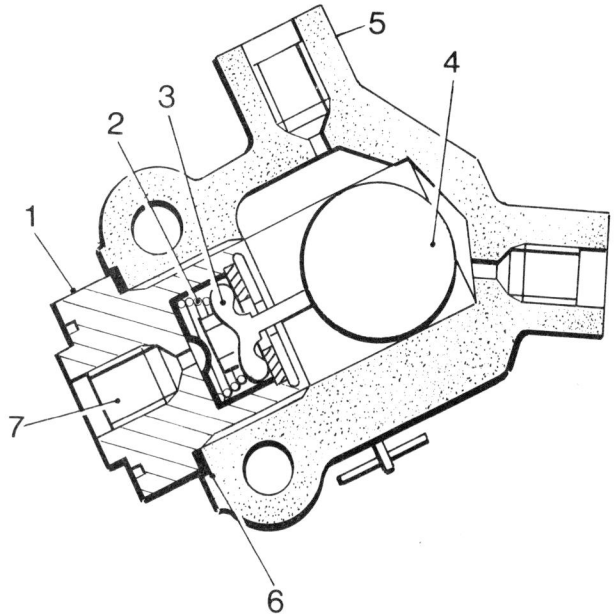

Fig. 9.10. Cross-sectional view of inertia valve assembly

1 End plug sub-assembly	5 Inertia valve body
2 Light spring	6 End plug washer
3 Valve	7 Fluid supply from the
4 Steel ball	master cylinder

sub-assembly fitting a new copper washer.

7   Make sure that the seating faces of both the body and end plug are clean and undamaged and then tighten the end plug down to a torque of 50 lb f ft (6.91 kg f m).

8   Refit the inertia valve to the car noting the marking 'FRONT' on the inertia valve body.

9   Bleed the brakes starting with the rear wheels then inspect the inertia valve for fluid leaks both with the brake pedal fully depressed and also with the system at rest.

19 Pressure failure switch - removal, overhaul and replacement

On all Austin America models and some home market models a pressure failure switch is incorporated in the hydraulic braking system with a warning light on the fascia panel.

1   Disconnect the wiring from the switch and thoroughly clean the assembly and its surroundings, paying particular attention to the area round the hydraulic pipe connections.

2   Disconnect the hydraulic pipes and plug the ends to prevent fluid loss or dirt entering.

3   Unscrew the retaining bolt and remove the assembly from the car.

4   Referring to Fig. 9.11 remove the end plug and discard the copper washer, as it is not advisable to refit an old one.

5   Unscrew the nylon switch and then remove the shuttle valve piston assembly from the bore using a low pressure air line to free the piston if necessary.

6   Remove the two piston seals from the assembly and discard them.

7   Thoroughly clean all the parts and inspect the bore of the casing for scoring or other damage. If the bore is not in perfect

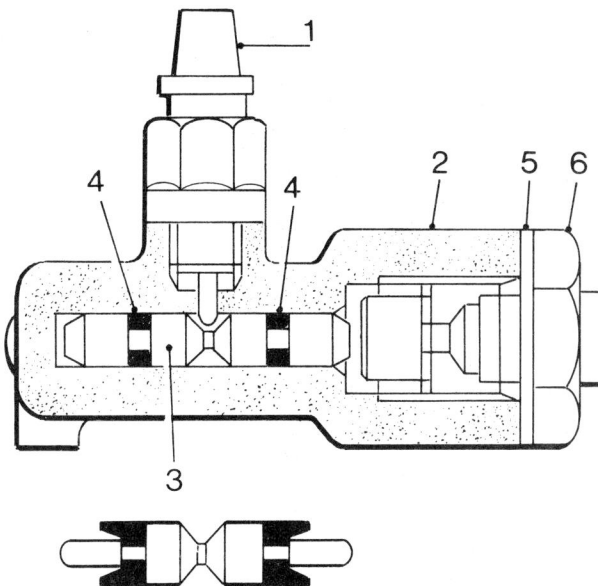

Fig. 9.11. Cross-sectional view of pressure failure switch assembly
Inset - early type piston and seals

1 Nylon switch	4 Piston seal
2 Switch body	5 Copper washer
3 Shuttle valve piston	6 End plug

3   Remove the end plug sub-assembly and washer from the inertia valve body and extract the steel ball.

4   Thoroughly clean and dry the body and steel ball.

5   Carefully examine all the component parts as they must be in perfect condition if they are to be reused. A new end plug washer must always be used.

6   Insert the steel ball into the body and screw in the end plug

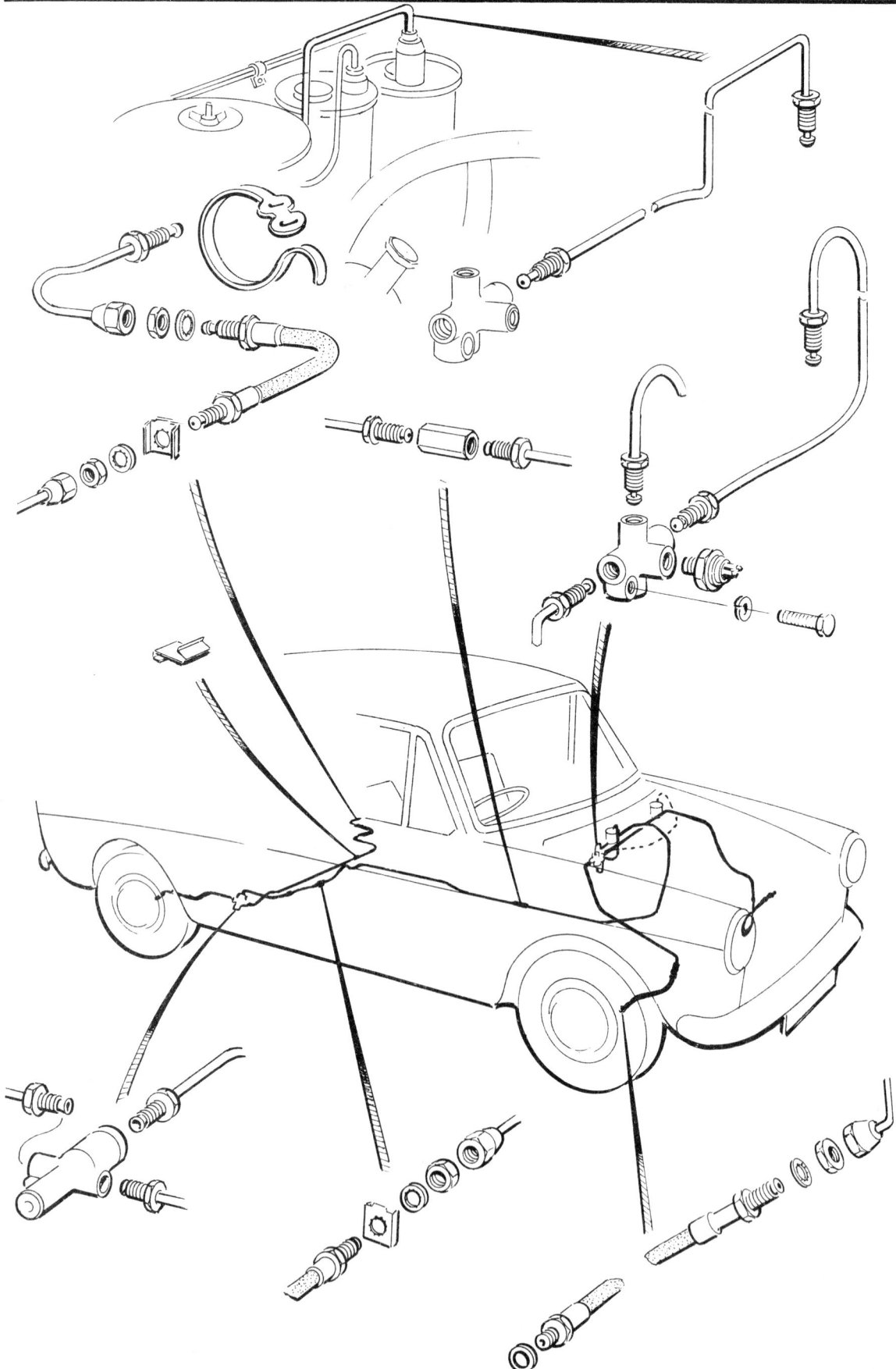

Fig. 9.12. Exploded view of the layout of the hydraulic brake circuit (single master cylinder application shown) (Sec. 21)

condition the complete assembly must be replaced.

8 Connect up the wiring to the switch and actuate the switch plunger to check the switch operation, and check that the warning light inside the car is functioning correctly.

9 Fit the two new piston seals to the piston with the lips facing outwards.

10 Thoroughly lubricate the piston assembly with fresh hydraulic fluid and fit the piston into the bore. Care must be taken to ensure that the lip of the leading seal does turn under.

11 Fit a new copper washer to the end plug. Replace the plug and tighten it down to a torque of 200 lb f in. (2.3 kg f m).

12 Screw in the switch and tighten it down to a torque of 15 lb f in (0.17 kg f m).

13 Replace the assembly on the car by reversing the removal procedure and finally bleed the brakes as described in Section 9.

20 Brake pedal - removal and replacement

1 From underneath the fascia take off the circlip which retains the fulcrum pin or pedal cross-shaft in position. Slip off the hooked ends of the arms of the springs bearing against the pedal levers and push the cross-shaft out.

2 Remove the small circlip from the end of the clevis pin fitted to the end of the pushrod and slide out the clevis pin.

3 The pedal is now free and can be lifted out.

4 Replacement is a straight reversal of the above procedure.

21 Hydraulic pipes and hoses - general

1 Carefully examine all brake pipes, pipe connections and unions periodically.

2 First examine for signs of leakage where the pipe unions occur. Then examine the flexible hoses for signs of chafing and fraying and, of course, leakage. This is only a preliminary part of the flexible hose inspection, as exterior condition does not necessarily indicate the interior condition, which will be considered later.

3 The steel pipes must be examined carefully and methodically. They must be cleaned off and inspected for any signs of dents, corrosion, or other damage. Corrosion should be scraped off and, if the depth of pitting in the pipes is significant, they will need renewing. This is particularly likely in those areas underneath the car body where the pipes are exposed to road and weather conditions.

4 If any section of pipe is to be taken off, first wipe and then remove the fluid reservoir cap and place a piece of polythene over the reservoir. Refit the cap. This will stop syphoning during subsequent operations.

5 Rigid pipe removal is usually quite straightforward. The unions at each end are undone, the pipe and union pulled out and the centre sections of the pipe removed from the body clips. Where the pipe unions are exposed to full force of road and weather they can sometimes be very tight. As one can only use an open-ended spanner and the unions are not large, burring of the flats is not uncommon when attempting to undo them. For this reason a self-locking grip wrench (Mole) is often the only way to remove a stubborn union.

6 Removal of flexible hoses is described in Section 8.

7 With the flexible hose removed, examine the internal bore. If it is blown through first, it should be possible to see through it. Any specks of rubber which come out, or signs of restriction in the bore means that the rubber lining is breaking up and the pipe must be renewed.

8 Rigid pipes which need renewing can usually be purchased at any garage where they have the pipe, unions and special tools to make them up. All they need to know is the total length of the pipe, the type of flare used at each end with the union, and the length and thread of the union.

9 Replacement of the pipe is a straightforward reversal of the removal procedure. If rigid pipes have to be made up it is best to get all the sets (bends) in them before trying to install them.

Also if there are any acute bends, ask your supplier to put these in for you on a special tube bender, otherwise you may kink the pipe and thereby decrease the bore area and fluid flow.

10 With the pipes replaced, remove the polythene from the reservoir cap and bleed the system as described in Section 9.

22 Stop light switch - removal and replacement

Type 1: Cars fitted with hydraulic pressure failure switch.

1 The switch which operates the rear stop lights is mounted behind and controlled by the brake pedal.

2 To remove the switch, pull off the two Lucar connectors and the locknut, and remove the switch assembly from the pedal stop.

3 Refitting the switch is the reverse sequence to removal but it must be adjusted.

4 Depress the brake pedal to take up any free-movement and slacken the brass locknut.

5 Screw the switch inwards or outwards as necessary until the plunger just makes contact with the brake pedal arm.

6 Tighten the locknut, reconnect the two electrical leads and check the switch for correct operation.

Type 2: Cars not fitted with hydraulic pressure failure switch

The switch is of the hydraulic type and is screwed into a four way pipe connector on the bulkhead. If faulty the switch must be renewed as a complete unit. Renewal is a straightforward operation after which the hydraulic system must be bled as described in Section 9.

23 Servo unit - general description

The vacuum unit offered as an optional extra on some models is fitted into the brake hydraulic circuit in series with the master cylinder to provide 'power' assistance to the driver when the brake pedal is depressed.

The unit is operated by vacuum obtained from the inlet manifold and comprises basically a booster diaphragm, and vacuum cylinder, an air valve assembly, and the slave cylinder which is connected in the hydraulic circuit between the main master cylinder and the wheel cylinders.

Under light braking hydraulic fluid is allowed to pass directly to the wheel cylinders via the hollow centre of the slave piston and no braking assistance is obtained. Hydraulic pressure acting on the air valve piston closes the diaphragm thus separating the chamber behind the main servo diaphragm from the one in front.

Under heavy braking further movement of the air valve piston opens the air valve and allows air to enter the chamber behind the main diaphragm, so destroying the vacuum. The central rod is pushed to the left, sealing the hollow centre of the slave piston and pushing it down its bore, so increasing the fluid pressure at the wheel cylinders.

When the brake pedal is released, the pressure beneath the air valve piston is released, the diaphragm re-opens and the air valve closes. A suspended vacuum is re-created around the main diaphragm via the non-return valve.

Under the action of the spring and diaphragm, the pushrod and thus the slave piston are returned to there original positions and the pressure in the wheel cylinders is lost.

24 Servo unit - removal and replacement

1 Wipe the top of the brake master cylinder and remove the cap. Place a piece of polythene over the reservoir and refit the cap. This will prevent syphoning during subsequent operations.

2 Unscrew both the brake pipe unions from the slave cylinder and detach the vacuum pipe from the non-return valve in the servo unit shell.

3 Unscrew and remove both nuts from the two mounting studs on the servo unit end-cover. Note the third stud is not used.

4 Slacken the clamp around the neck of the slave cylinder and carefully lift out the complete servo unit. Note that the mounting bracket holes are slotted to facilitate removal.

5 Refitting the servo unit is the reverse sequence to removal. It will be necessary to bleed the brake hydraulic system as described in Section 9.

25 Servo unit - dismantling, examination and reassembly

There would normally be two reasons for dismantling part or all of the servo unit:

a) Maintenance - cleaning the air filter (see paragraphs 3 and 34, of this Section)

b) Non-operation.

In the case of the latter the most likely reason would be due to faults in the hydraulic seals in either the slave cylinder or air valve piston. It would be wise therefore to buy a repair kit for all these before starting work, as once the servo is taken out of the system there are no hydraulic brakes of any sort unless provision has already been made for a servo by-pass.

Proceed with dismantling as follows under scrupulously clean conditions.

1 Grip the servo unit on a well padded vice by the slave cylinder body (1) (Fig. 9.13) with the air valve (23) uppermost.

2 Remove the rubber pipe (29) from the end-cover connection.

3 Undo the screws securing the plastic air valve cover and lift off the cover assembly complete, which comprises the filter and

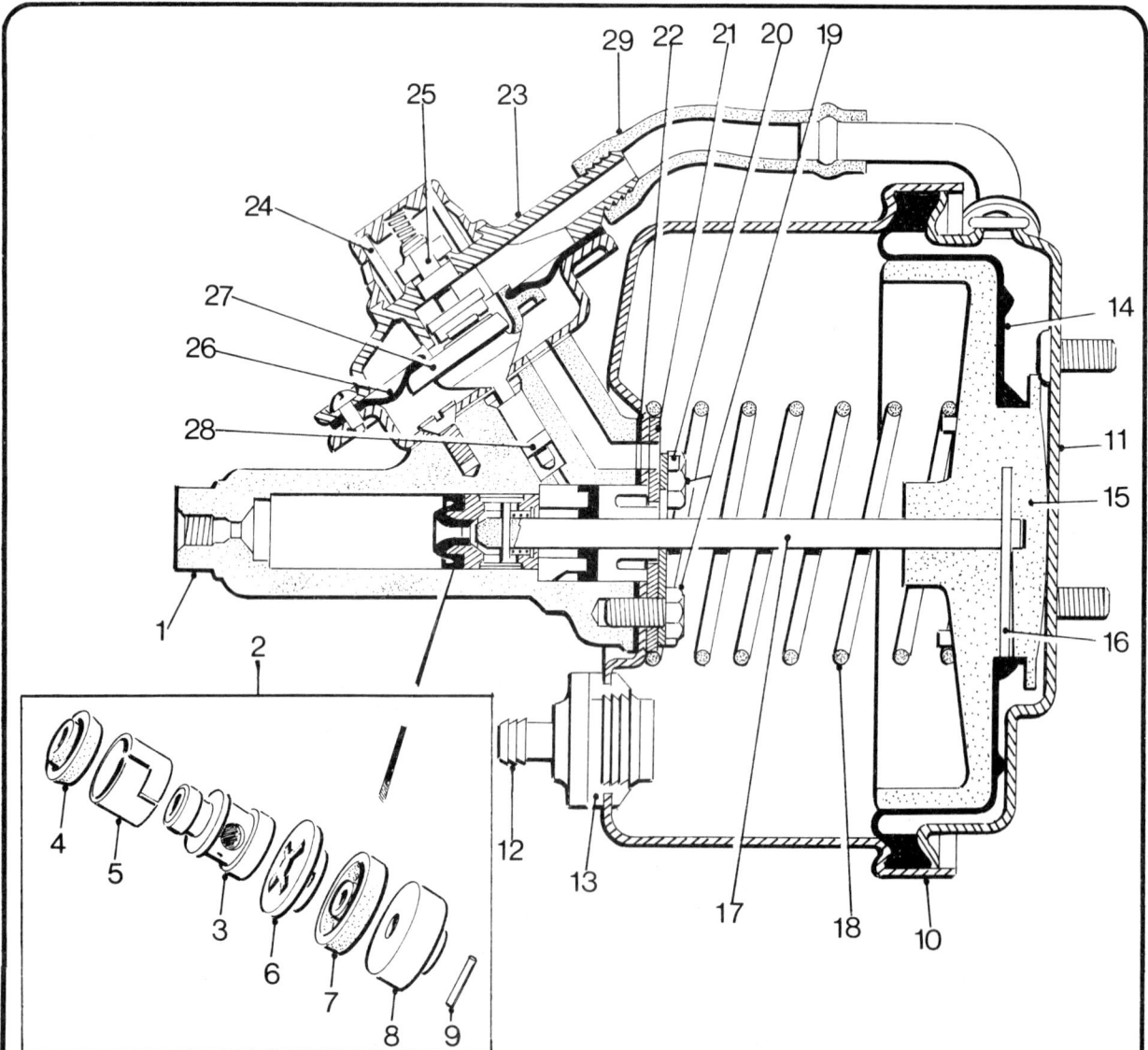

Fig. 9.13. Cross-sectional view of servo unit (Sec. 25)

1	Slave cylinder	8	Bearing	15	Diaphragm support
2	Slave piston assembly	9	Pin	16	Retaining key
3	Slave piston	10	Servo shell	17	Pushrod
4	Seal	11	End cover	18	Main return spring
5	Retaining clip	12	Non-return valve	19	Servo shell retaining bolts
6	Spacer	13	Rubber mounting	20	Locking plate
7	Cup	14	Main servo diaphragm	21	Abutment plate

22	Gasket
23	Air valve cover
24	Filter
25	Air valve
26	Air valve diaphragm
27	Diaphragm support
28	Air valve piston
29	Rubber pipe

valve. If the air valve is suspect a new assembly which is part of the complete repair kit will have to be obtained. (ie. these individual parts cannot be obtained separately).

3a The dome containing these items is a snap fit into the air valve cover.

4 Remove the rubber diaphragm and its plastic support, and the three valve housing securing screws will then be revealed. Undo these and take off the housing and joint washer.

5 To get the air control valve piston (28) out of its cylinder will require a low pressure inside the slave cylinder. This can be done by blocking one of the two hydraulic fluid unions on the slave cylinder with a finger and applying air pressure from a foot pump to the other. When it is out remove the rubber cup from the piston (for replacement).

6 The non-return valve (12) which is mounted in a rubber grommet (13) can be pushed out by thumb pressure. Remove the grommet also.

7 It is now necessary to remove the end cover (11) from the main servo shell (10). This is a twist fit bayonet type of connection and to remove it calls for an anti-clockwise twist as far as the stops in the cover will permit, when it will come off. Although there is a special tool for this (C2030) one can achieve the same result by remounting the servo on the car mounting bracket by the three end cover studs and gripping the shell and twisting it anti-clockwise. The end cover can be left on the mounting bracket.

8 Put the unit back into the vice as before. To remove the diaphragm it is not necessary to free the retaining key (16) from the pushrod (17).

Turn the diaphragm support (15) so that the retaining key (16) points downwards. Then supply light fluctuating pressure to the backplate against the main return spring (18) and the retaining key will drop out.

9 Hold on to the diaphragm support and take it and the diaphragm and the return spring from the servo shell.

10 The bolts (19) holding the servo shell to the slave cylinder are now exposed. Bend back the locking plate tabs (20) from the bolt heads and remove the bolts, locking plate (20) and abutment plate (21).

11 The shell can now be taken from the slave cylinder. Retrieve the washer between the two.

12 The pushrod (17) can now be drawn from the slave cylinder together with piston assembly.

13 Slide the bearing (8), cup (7) and spacer (6) off the pushrod noting the order and position in which they came off.

14 Prise the rubber seal (4) off the slave piston (3).

15 If the rod is to be detached from the piston the following action will be required but a new retaining clip (9) will be needed. It should not normally be necessary to separate them. Open up the retaining clip (5) by twisting a small screwdriver in the join and this will expose the connecting pin (9) which can be pushed out. This disconnects the slave piston from the connecting rod. This unit is now completely dismantled.

16 Examine all rubber cups and seals for wear and replace as necessary. If the air valve unit is in good condition and it is only necessary to clean the filter, blow it through with a tyre foot pump. Do not use any cleaning fluids or lubricants on the filter.

17 Wash all slave cylinder components in clean hydraulic fluid, and remove any deposits from the slave cylinder walls in the same way. If the slave cylinder is scored then it must be replaced.

18 Reassembly must be done in very clean conditions as a single speck of grit in the wrong place can cause total malfuntion. It is best to wash your hands, get new clean cloths and lay out all the components on a sheet of clean white paper. 5 minutes extra attention now could save you another complete dismantling operation later.

19 Use clean hydraulic fluid as a lubricant when reassembling the hydraulic components.

20 If the piston and pushrod were separated push the rod into the rear of the piston against the spring until the connecting pin hole is open. Fit the pin followed by the retaining clip. It is important to ensure that the clip fits snugly in its groove. Any

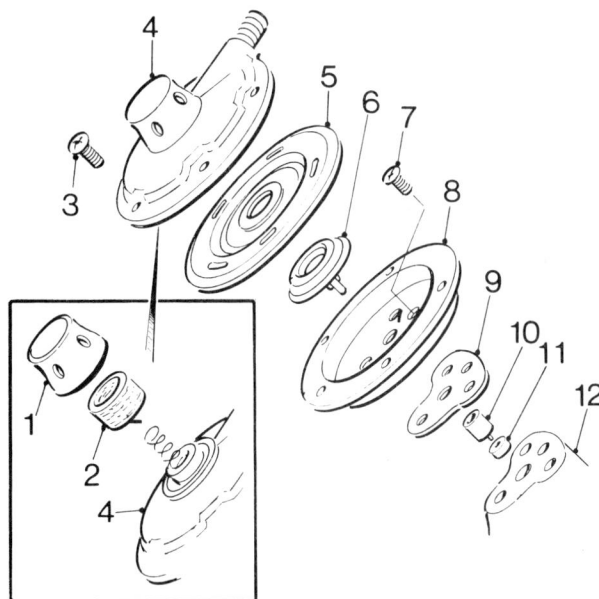

Fig. 9.14. Components of servo unit air valve assembly and controlling piston (Sec. 25)

1	Domed cover for filter	7	Valve housing securing
2	Air filter		screw
3	Air valve cover securing	8	Valve housing
	screw	9	Joint washer
4	Air valve cover	10	Piston
5	Diaphragm	11	Piston cup
6	Diaphragm support	12	Slave cylinder

protrusions will score the cylinder wall.

21 Refit the rubber seal (4) to the slave piston (3) using only the fingers ensuring that the lips of the seal face away from the pushrod.

22 Lubricate (with hydraulic fluid only) the cylinder bore and insert the piston. Then replace in correct order, over the pushrod the spacer (6) cup (7) and bearing (8) into the mouth of the slave cylinder. Ensure that each item placed into the cylinder has its sealing lips neither bent nor turned back and that each is bedded individually in turn.

23 The servo shell is now refitted in the reverse order to that given in paragraph 10. If the locking plate (20) has been used more than once before (ie. if the servo has already been twice dismantled) a new one should be fitted. Tighten the bolts evenly to a torque figure of 17 lb f ft (2.35 kg f m) and tap up the locking plate tabs.

24 To replace the diaphragm, support and spring pull out the pushrod as far as possible. Fit the spring and diaphragm support ensuring that the spring ends are correctly located over the abutment plate (21) and the diaphragm support boss.

25 Press the diaphragm support over the pushrod with the key slot facing upwards and when the groove in the pushrod and the slot in the diaphragm are lined up insert the key.

26 Ensuring that the support and diaphragm are quite clean and dry fit the diaphragm to the support, gently stretching the inner edge to ensure that it seats properly in the groove of the support.

27 Smear the outer edge of the diaphragm with disc brake lubricant (not grease or hydraulic oil). This prevents it from binding when the lid cover is refitted to the servo shell.

28 If no service tool is available fix the end cover onto the vehicle mounting bracket (if you did not leave it there when taking it off) using the normal mounting units. Offer up the servo unit to the end cover so that when twisted clockwise the pipe will line up with the elbow on the end cover when the turn is completely up to the stops.

29 With the unit back on the bench replace the non-return valve and its mounting grommet.

30 To replace the air valve assembly first fit the rubber piston

cup (11) to the spigot of the piston (10) ensuring that the lips face away from the spigot shoulder. Lubricate the cup with a little hydraulic fluid and insert it into the slave cylinder taking care that the lips do not get bent back.

31 Fit the joint washer (9 in Fig. 9.14) and valve housing (8) to the slave cylinder (12) using the three securing screws (7).

32 Fit the diaphragm support (6) into the diaphragm (5) and make sure that the inner ring fits snugly into the groove in the support. Then place the spigot of the support into the hole in the air valve piston. Use no lubricants.

33 Line up the screw holes in the diaphragm (5) and the valve housing (8).

34 If the air filter, and dome have been removed (1&2) now is the time to snap the complete assembly back into the air valve cover (4).

35 Place the valve cover over the diaphragm so that the projections in the cover engage the slots in the diaphragm. Replace all five securing screws (3) finger tight. Tighten them down firmly, but not over-tight, in a progressive pattern roughly North South, East, West. This tightening sequence is important as the air valve must seat evenly and precisely. Any leak renders the whole servo inoperative.

36 Refit the rubber pipe from the valve cover port to the end-cover elbow.

26 Fault diagnosis - Braking system

Symptom	Reason/s	Remedy
Pedal travels almost to floor before brakes operate	Brake fluid level too low	Top up master cylinder reservoir. Check for leaks.
	Wheel cylinder or caliper leaking	Dismantle wheel cylinder or caliper, clean, fit new rubbers and bleed brakes.
	Master cylinder leaking (bubbles in master cylinder fluid)	Dismantle master cylinder, clean, and fit new rubbers. Bleed brakes.
	Brake flexible hose leaking	Examine and fit new hose if old hose leaking. Bleed brakes.
	Brake line fractured	Replace with new brake pipe. Bleed brakes.
	Brake system unions loose	Check all unions in brake system and tighten as necessary. Bleed brakes.
Normal wear	Linings over 75% worn	Fit replacement shoes and brake linings.
Brake pedal has "springy" feel	New linings not yet bedded-in	Use brakes gently until springy pedal feeling leaves.
	Brake drums or discs badly worn and weak or cracked	Fit new brake drums or discs.
	Master cylinder securing nuts loose	Tighten master cylinder securing nuts. Ensure spring washers are fitted.
Brake pedal has "spongy" feel	Wheel cylinder or caliper leaking	Dismantle wheel cylinder or caliper, clean, fit new rubbers, and bleed brakes.
	Master cylinder leaking (bubbles in master cylinder reservoir)	Dismantle master cylinder, clean, and fit new rubbers and bleed brakes. Replace cylinder if internal walls scored.
	Brake pipe line or flexible hose leaking	Fit new pipe line or hose.
	Unions in brake system loose	Examine for leaks, tighten as necessary.
Brake operation uneven - car pulls to one side during braking	Linings and brake drums or discs contaminated with oil, grease, or hydraulic fluid	Ascertain and rectify source of leak, clean brake drums, fit new linings.
	Tyre pressures unequal	Check and inflate as necessary.
	Brake backplate caliper or disc loose	Tighten backplate caliper or disc securing nuts and bolts.
	Brake shoes or pads fitted incorrectly	Remove and fit shoes or pads correct way round.
	Different type of linings fitted at each wheel	Fit the linings specified all round.
	Anchorages for front or rear suspension loose	Tighten front and rear suspension pick-up points including spring locations.
	Brake drums or discs badly worn, cracked or distorted.	Fit new brake drums or discs.
Brakes bind or tend to lock on	Brake shoes adjusted too tightly	Slacken off rear brake shoe adjusters two clicks.
	Handbrake cable over-tightened	Slacken off handbrake cable adjustment.
	Master cylinder pushrod out of adjustment giving too little brake pedal free movement	Reset to specifications.
	Reservoir vent hole in cap blocked with dirt	Clean and blow through hole.
	Master cylinder by-pass port restricted - brakes seize in 'on' position	Dismantle, clean, and overhaul master cylinder. Bleed brakes.
	Wheel cylinder seizes in 'on' position	Dismantle, clean and overhaul wheel cylinder. Bleed brakes.
	Drum brake shoe pull-off springs broken, stretched or loose	Examine springs and replace if worn or loose.
	Drum brake shoe pull-off springs fitted wrong way round, omitted, or wrong type used	Examine, and rectify as appropriate.

Chapter 10 Electrical system

Contents

Specifications

System type:

1100 Mk I and Mk II	12 volt positive earth return
1100 Mk III	12 volt negative earth return
Austin and Morris 1300; Riley and MG 1300 and 1300 Mk II; Princess 1300 and Wolseley 1300 and 1300 Mk II (up to 1971); Austin America (dynamo equipped)	12 volt positive earth return
Austin and Morris 1300 Mk III; Princess 1300 and Wolseley 1300 Mk II (1971 on); Austin America (alternator equipped)	12 volt negative earth return

Battery:

Type	Lucas D9/DZ9
	Lucas A9/AZ9
	Lucas A11/AZ11
Capacity at 20 hr rate:	
D9 and A9	40 amp/hr
A11	50 amp/hr
Charging rate:	
D9 and A9	3.5 amp
A11	5 amp

Electrolyte to fill one cell:

D9 and DZ9	0.667 pint (380 cc, 0.8 US pint)
A9 and AZ9	0.75 pint (410 cc, 0.875 US pint)
A11 and AZ11	0.875 pint (520 cc, 1.125 US pint)

Starter motor:

Type	Lucas, M35G or M35J
Lucas M35G:	
Brush spring tension	15 - 25 oz (425 - 709 gms)
Minimum brush length	0.3125 in. (7.9 mm)
Light running:	
Speed	9,500 - 11,000 rpm
Current	45 amps
Voltage	8.8 - 9.2 volts
Lock torque	11 lb f ft (1.38 Kg f m)
Current	420 - 440 amps
Voltage	7.8 - 7.4 volts
Lucas M35J:	
Brush spring tension	28 oz (0.8 kg)
Minimum brush length	0.375 in. (9.5 mm)
Minimum commutator thickness	0.08 in. (2.05 mm)
Lock torque	7 lb f ft (0.97 Kg f m)
Current	350 - 375 amps
Torque at 1000 rpm	4.4 lb f ft (0.61 Kg f m)
Current	260 - 275 amps
Light running current	65 amps at 8,000 - 10,000 rpm

Dynamo:

Type:	Lucas C40
Cutting in speed	1200 - 1400 rpm
Maximum output	13.5 volts, 22 amps
Field resistance	6.0 ohms

Control box:

Type:	
MkI, Mk II and LHD Mk III models	Lucas RB 340
Mk III (UK only)	Lucas RB 106
RB340:	
Cut in voltage	12.6 - 13.4 volts
Drop off voltage	9.3 - 11.2 volts
Open circuit setting at 20° C (68° F)	14.2 - 14.8 volts at 1500 dynamo rpm
RB340 - Flat armature type:	
Cut in voltage	12.7 - 13.3 volts
Drop off voltage	9.5 - 11.5 volts
Open circuit setting at 20° C (68° F)	14.5 - 15.5 volts at 3000 dynamo rpm
RB106:	
Cut in voltage	12.7 - 13.3 volts
Drop off voltage	8.5 - 11.0 volts
Open circuit setting at 20° C (68° F)	16.0 - 16.6 volts at 3000 dynamo rpm

Alternator:

Type:	Lucas 11AC, 16ACR or 17ACR
11AC:	
Nominal output	43 amps
Brush spring tension	8 - 16 oz (227 - 454 gms)
Minimum brush length	0.3125 in. (7.938 mm)
Control unit type	4TR
Relay type	6RA
Warning light control type	3AW
16ACR:	
Nominal output	34 amps at 6000 alternator rpm
Nominal system voltage	14.2 volts at 20% nominal output
Brush spring tension	7 - 10 oz (193 - 283 gms)
Minimum brush length	0.2 in. (5 mm)
17ACR:	
Nominal output	36 amps at 6000 alternator rpm
Nominal system voltage	14.2 volts at 20% nominal output
Brush spring tension	7 - 10 oz (193 - 283 gms)
Minimum brush length	0.2 in (5 mm)

Windscreen wiper:

Type:	Lucas 3WA - 14W
Wiper arm spring pressure	11 - 13 oz (312 - 369 gms)

3WA:

Normal running current	2.7 - 3.4 amps
Stall current	14 amps (cold) 8 amps (hot)
Resistance between adjacent commutator segments ...	0.3 - 0.41 ohms
Field coil resistance	12.8 - 14 ohms
Armature endfloat	0.008 - 0.012 in. (0.20 - 0.30 mm)

14W:

Light running speed (rack disconnected):

Normal speed	1.5 amps
Fast speed	2 amps
Brush spring pressure	5 - 7 oz (140 - 200 gms)
Minimum brush length	0.1875 in. (4.8 mm)
Armature endfloat	0.002 - 0.008 in. (0.05 - 0.2 mm)
Maximum pull to move rack in tube	6 lb (2.7 kg)

Horns:

Type:	Lucas 9H, 9H modified, 6N or Clear Hooters F725/N
Maximum current consumption:	3.5 amps
9H modified	4 amps (connectors set wide apart)
6H (when fitted)	3 amps

Fuse unit:

Type:	Lucas 4FJ (2 live, 2 spare)
Fuse rating	35 amps

Bulbs:

Mk I models　　Watts

Headlights (LHD except USA and Europe)	50/40
Headlights (LHD Europe except France)	45/40
Headlights (France only)	45/40
Headlights (RHD Left dip)	50/40
Sidelights:	
Austin Morris, Wolseley, Riley, MG	6
Princess	5
Direction indicator lights (front and rear)	21
Tail and stop lights	6/21
Number plate illumination light:	
Morris, MG	6
Austin, Wolseley, Princess, Riley	6
Panel and warning lights (screw in type)	2.2
Panel and warning lights (bayonet type)	2
Interior light	6
Direction indicator arm	1.5
Radiator badge (Wolseley)	6
Fog light (Princess)	48
Reverse light (Princess)	21

Mk II and III models

As for Mk I with following exceptions:-
Direction indicator repeater lights.

Capless bulb	5
Bayonet bulb	6
Direction indicator warning light	2.2
Number plate light	
Austin, Morris, Princess, Riley 1300, Wolseley 1300 ...	6
MG, Riley 1300 Mk II, Wolseley 1300 Mk II	6
Brake test warning light (Austin America)	1.5
Reverse light (Austin America and GT)	21

Torque wrench settings:	lb f ft	Kg f m
Alternator shaft nut	25 - 30	3.46 - 4.5
Alternator brush box screws	10 (lb f in.)	0.12 (Kg f m)

1 General description

The electrical system is of the 12 volt type and the major components comprise a battery, dynamo or alternator, and control unit, starter motor, lights and auxiliary equipment.

The system incorporates compensated voltage control for the charging circuit. The electrical system may be either positive or negative earth return and the correct polarity must be maintained at all times otherwise serious damage will result. The correct polarity for an individual model will be found by referring to the relevant wiring diagram.

The battery is mounted on a platform located on the right-hand wing valance under the bonnet.

The dynamo or alternator (depending on model) is mounted on the right-hand side of the cylinder block and is driven by the fan belt tension.

The starter motor is mounted on the flywheel housing on the right-hand side of the engine and operates in the flywheel or torque converter adaptor plate (automatic transmission models) through a sliding pinion assembly.

The instruments are voltage controlled by means of a bi-metal resistance in order to maintain accuracy. Electrical circuits are protected by fuses which are carried in external holders mounted under the bonnet on the right-hand inner wing panel.

When fitting electrical accessories to cars with a negative earth system it is important, if they contain silicone diodes or transistors, that they are connected correctly, otherwise serious damage may result to the components concerned. Items such as radios, tape players, electronic ignition systems, automatic headlight dipping etc should all be checked for correct polarity.

When an alternator is fitted it is very important that the battery positive lead is always disconnected if the battery is to be boost charged. Also if body repairs are to be carried out using electric arc welding equipment, the alternator must be disconnected otherwise serious damage can be caused to the more delicate instruments.

2 Battery - removal and replacement

1 The battery is carried in a special carrier fitted to the right-hand wing valance of the engine compartment. It should be removed once every three months for cleaning and testing. Disconnect the positive and then the negative leads from the battery terminals by slackening the retaining nuts and bolts, or by unscrewing the retaining screws if these are fitted.
2 Remove the battery clamp and carefully lift the battery out of its compartment. Hold the battery vertical to ensure that none of the electrolyte is spilled.
3 Replacement is a direct reversal of this procedure. **Note:** Replace the negative lead before the earth (positive) lead and smear the terminals with petroleum jelly (vaseline) to prevent corrosion. **Never** use an ordinary grease as applied to other parts of the car.

3 Battery - maintenance and inspection

1 Normal weekly battery maintenance consists of checking the electrolyte level of each cell to ensure that the separators are covered by ¼ in. of electrolyte. If the level has fallen, top up the battery using distilled water only. Do not overfill. If the battery is overfilled or any electrolyte spilled, immediately wipe away the excess as electrolyte attacks with very rapidly. (photo)
2 As well as keeping the terminals clean and covered with petroleum jelly, the top of the battery, and especially the top of the cells, should be kept clean and dry. This helps prevent corrosion and ensures that the battery does not become partially discharged by leakage through dampness and dirt.
3 Once every three months remove the battery and inspect the battery securing bolts, the battery clamp plate, tray, and the battery leads for corrosion (white fluffy deposits on the metal which are brittle to touch). If any corrosion is found, clean off the deposits with ammonia and paint over the clean metal with an anti-rust/anti-acid paint.
4 At the same time inspect the battery case for cracks. If a crack is found, clean and plug it with one of the proprietary compounds marketed by firms such as 'Holts' for this purpose. If leakage through the crack has been excessive then it will be necessary to refill the appropriate cell with fresh electrolyte as detailed later. Cracks are frequently caused to the top of battery cases by pouring in distilled water in the middle of winter *after* instead of *before* a run. This gives the water no chance to mix with the electrolyte and so the former freezes and splits the battery case.
5 If topping up the battery becomes excessive and the case has been inspected for cracks that could cause leakage, but none are found, the battery is being overcharged and the voltage regulator will have to be checked and reset.
6 With the battery on the bench at the three monthly interval check, measure its specific gravity with a hydrometer to determine its state of charge and condition of the electrolyte. There should be very little variation between the different cells and if a variation in excess of 0.025 is present it will be due to either:
a) Loss of electrolyte from the battery at some time caused by

3.1 Lucas Pacemaker with filler/vent top raised

spillage or a leak resulting in a drop in the specific gravity of the electrolyte, when the deficiency was replaced with distilled water instead of fresh electrolyte.
b) An internal short circuit caused by buckling of the plates or a similar malady pointing to the likelihood of total battery failure in the near future.
7 The specific gravity of the electrolyte for fully charged conditions at the electrolyte temperature indicated, is listed in Table A. The specific gravity of a fully discharged battery at different temperatures of the electrolyte is given at Table B.

TABLE A

Specific Gravity - Battery fully charged

1.268 at 100°F or 38°C electrolyte temperature
1.272 at 90°F or 32°C   "   "
1.276 at 80°F or 27°C   "   "
1.280 at 70°F or 21°C   "   "
1.284 at 60°F or 16°C   "   "
1.288 at 50°F or 10°C   "   "
1.292 at 40°F or 4°C   "   "
1.296 at 30°F or −1.5°C "   "

TABLE B

Specific Gravity - Battery fully discharged

1.098 at 100°F or 38°C electrolyte temperature
1.102 at 90°F or 32°C   "   "
1.106 at 80°F or 27°C   "   "
1.110 at 70°F or 21°C   "   "
1.114 at 60°F or 16°C   "   "
1.118 at 50°F or 10°C   "   "
1.122 at 40°F or 4°C   "   "
1.126 at 30°F or −1.5°C "   "

4 Electrolyte replenishment

1 If the battery is in a fully charged state and one of the cells maintains a specific gravity reading which is 0.025 or more lower than the others, and a check of each cell has been made with a voltage meter to check for short circuits (a four to seven second test should give a steady reading of between 1.2 to 1.8 volts), then it is likely that electrolyte has been lost from the cell with the low reading at some time.

2 Top the cell up with a solution of 1 part sulphuric acid to 2.5 parts of water. If the cell is already fully topped up draw some electrolyte out of it with a pipette.

3 When mixing the sulphuric acid and water **never add water to sulphuric acid** - always pour the acid slowly onto the water in a glass container. **If water is added to sulphuric acid it will explode.** Continue to top up the cell with the freshly made electrolyte and then recharge the battery and check the hydrometer readings.

5 Battery charging

1 In winter time when heavy demand is placed upon the battery, such as when starting from cold, and much electrical equipment is continually in use, it is a good idea to occasionally have the battery fully charged from an external source at the rate of 3.5 to 4 amps.

2 Continue to charge the battery at this rate until no further rise in specific gravity is noted over a four hour period.

3 Alternatively a trickle charger, charging at the rate of 1.5 amps, can be safely used overnight.

4 Special rapid 'boost' charges which are claimed to restore the power of the battery in 1 to 2 hours are damaging unless they are thermostatically controlled as they can cause plate buckling resulting in the shredding of active material from the plates and the possibility of internal shorts.

6 Dynamo - maintenance

1 Maintenance of the dynamo consists of checking the tension of the fan belt, and lubricating the dynamo rear bearing at the recommended interval (see Routine Maintenance).

2 To check the fan belt tension see Chapter 2.

3 Lubrication of the dynamo consists of inserting three drops of engine oil in the small hole in the centre of the commutator end bracket, to lubricate the rear bearing. The front bearing is preloaded with grease and requires no attention.

7 Dynamo - testing in position

1 If, with the engine running no charge comes from the dynamo, or the charge is very low, first check that the fan belt is in place and is not slipping. Then check that the leads from the control box to the dynamo are firmly attached and that one has not come loose from its terminal.

2 The lead from the 'D' terminal on the dynamo should be connected to the 'D' terminal on the control box, and should also be connected together.

3 Disconnect the leads from terminals 'D' and 'F' on the dynamo and then join the terminals together with a short length of wire. Attach to the centre of this length of wire the negative clip of a 0-20 volts voltmeter and run the other clip to earth. Start the engine and allow it to idle at approximately 750 rpm.

4 At this speed the dynamo should give a reading of about 15 volts on the voltmeter. There is no point in raising the engine speed above a fast idle as the reading will then be inaccurate.

5 If no reading is recorded then check the brushes and brush connections. If a very low reading of approximately 1 volt is observed then the field winding may be suspect.

6 On early dynamos it was possible to remove the dynamo cover band and check the dynamo and brushes in position. With the Lucas C40 windowless yoke dynamo, fitted to all models, the dynamo has to be removed and dismantled before the brushes and commutator can be attended to.

7 If the voltmeter shows a good reading then with the temporary link still in position connect both leads from the control box to 'D' and 'F' on the dynamo ('D' to 'D' and 'F' to 'F'). Release the lead from the 'D' terminal at the control box end and clip one lead from the voltmeter to the end of the cable, and

the other lead to a good earth. With the engine running at the same speed as previously, an identical voltage to that recorded at the dynamo should be noted on the voltmeter.

8 If no voltage is recorded then there is a break in the wire.

9 If the voltage is the same as recorded at the dynamo then check the 'F' lead in similar fashion. If both readings are the same as at the dynamo then it will be necessary to test the control box.

8 Dynamo - removal and replacement

1 Slacken the two dynamo retaining bolts, and the nut on the sliding link, and move the dynamo in towards the engine so that the fan belt can be removed.

2 Disconnect the two leads from the dynamo terminals. **Note:** If the ignition coil is mounted on top of the dynamo, remove the high tension wire from the centre of the coil by unscrewing the knurled nut, and unscrew the nuts holding the two low tension wires in place.

3 Remove the nut from the sliding link bolt, and remove the two upper bolts. The dynamo is then free to be lifted away from the engine.

4 Replacement is a reversal of the above procedure. Do not finally tighten the retaining bolts and the nut on the sliding link until the fan belt has been tensioned correctly.

5 If it is wished to fit a replacement dynamo, check the identification marks which will be found on the yoke, and quote these to your local BLMC or Lucas agent prior to handing the dynamo in to ensure a replacement is available.

9 Dynamo - dismantling and reassembly

1 Remove the dynamo pulley after unscrewing the nut and lockwasher which retains it to the armature shaft. (It is not necessary to do this if only the brushes and commutator are to be examined). Fig. 10.1.

2 From the commutator end bracket remove the nuts, spring, and flat washers from the field terminal post. (Not necessary where LUCAR connectors are fitted).

3 Unscrew the two through bolts and remove them together with their spring washers.

4 Take off the commutator end bracket, and remove the driving end bracket complete with the armature.

5 Lift the brush springs and draw the brushes out of the brush holders. Unscrew the screws and lockwashers holding the brush leads to the commutator end bracket.

6 The bearings need not be removed, or the armature shaft separated from the drive end bracket unless the bearings or the armature are to be renewed. If it is wished to remove the armature shaft from the drive end bracket and bearing (and this is necessary for bearing renewal) then the bearing retaining plate must be supported securely, and with the Woodruff key removed the shaft pressed out of the end bracket.

7 When a new armature is fitted or the old one replaced, it is most important that the inner journal of the ball bearing is supported by a steel tube of suitable diameter so that no undue strain is placed on the bearing as the armature shaft is pressed home.

8 Reassembly is a straight reversal of the above process. A point worth noting is that when fitting the commutator end plate with brushes attached, it is far easier to slip the brushes over the commutator if the brushes are raised in their holders and held in this position by the pressure of the springs resting against their flanks rather than on their heads.

10 Dynamo - inspection and repair

1 First check the brushes for wear. Any brush less than 0.25 in (6.35 mm) long on the C40 unit, must be replaced. Check that the brushes move freely and easily in their holders by removing

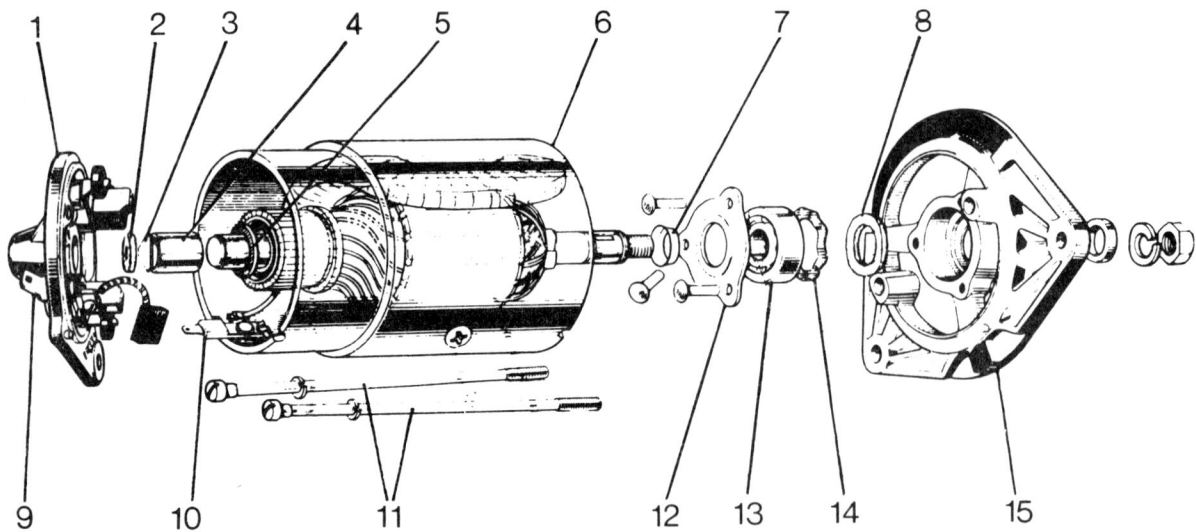

Fig. 10.1. Exploded view of dynamo

1	Commutator end bracket	5	Fibre washer	9	Output terminal 'D'	13	Drive end bearing
2	Felt ring	6	Yoke	10	Field terminal 'F'	14	Corrugated washer
3	Felt ring retainer	7	Shaft collar retaining cup	11	Through bolts	15	Driving end bracket
4	Bronze bush	8	Felt ring	12	Bearing retaining plate		

the retaining springs and then pulling gently on the wire brush leads. If either of the brushes tend to stick in their holders clean the brushes wih a petrol moistened rag and if still stiff, lightly polish the sides of the brush with a fine file until the brush moves quite freely and easily in its holder.

2 If the brushes are but little worn and are to be used again then ensure that they are placed in the same holders from which they were removed. Check the tension of the brush springs with a spring balance. The tension of the springs when new was 26 oz. falling to 18 oz. when the brush was sufficiently worn to warrant replacement.

3 Check the condition of the commutator. If the surface is dirty or blackened, clean it with a petrol dampened rag. If the commutator is in good condition the surface will be smooth and quite free from pits or burnt areas, and the insulated segments clearly defined.

4 If, after the commutator has been cleaned, pits and burnt spots are still present, then wrap a strip of glass paper round the commutator and rotate the armature.

5 In extreme cases of wear the commutator can be mounted in a lathe and with the lathe turning at high speed, a very fine cut may be taken off the commutator. Then polish the commutator with glass paper. If the commutator has worn so that the insulators between the segments are level with the top of the segments, then undercut the insulators to a depth of 0.031 in (0.8 mm). The best tool to use for this purpose is half a hacksaw blade ground to the thickness of the insulator, with the handle end of the blade covered in insulating tape to make it comfortable to hold. On later models using generators of the moulded type, the commutator should not be undercut more than 0.020 in. (0.508 mm) deep, or 0.040 in. (1.016 mm) wide.

6 Check the armature for open or short circuited windings. It is a good indication of an open circuited armature when the commutator segments are burnt. If the armature has short circuited the commutator segments will be very badly burnt, and the overheated armature windings badly discoloured. If open or short circuits are suspected then test by substituting the suspect armature for a new one.

7 Check the resistance of the field coils. To do this, connect an ohmmeter between the field terminal and the yoke and note the reading on the ohmmeter which should be about 6 ohms. If the ohmmeter reading is infinity this indicates an open circuit in the field winding. If the ohmmeter reading is below 5 ohms this

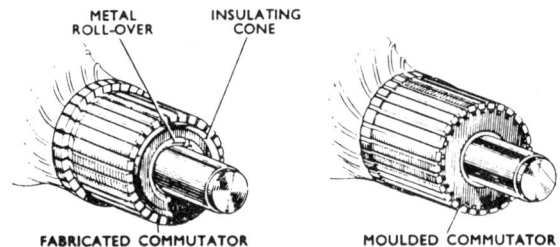

Fig. 10.2. The dynamo commutator (Sec. 10)

indicates that one of the field coils is faulty and must be replaced.

8 Field coil replacement involves the use of a wheel operated screwdriver, a soldering iron, caulking and riveting and this operation is considered to be beyond the scope of most owners. Therefore, if the field coils are at fault either purchase a rebuilt dynamo, or take the casing to a reputable electrical engineering works for new field coils to be fitted.

11 Dynamo bearings - inspection, removal and replacement

With the dynamo stripped down, check the condition of the bearings. They must be renewed when wear has reached such a state that they allow visible side movement of the armature shaft. A bush bearing is fitted to the commutator end bracket and a ball bearing to the drive end bracket. To renew the bush bearing proceed as follows:

1 With a suitable extractor pull out the old bush from the commutator end bracket. Alternatively screw a 5/8 in. tap into the C40 bush and pull out the bush together with the tap.

2 **Note:** when fitting the new bush bearing that it is of the porous bronze type, and it is essential that it is allowed to stand in engine oil for at least 24 hours before fitment.

3 Carefully fit the new bush into the end plate, pressing it in until the end of the bearing is flush with the inner side of the end plate. If available press the bush in with a smooth shouldered mandrel the same diameter as the armature shaft.

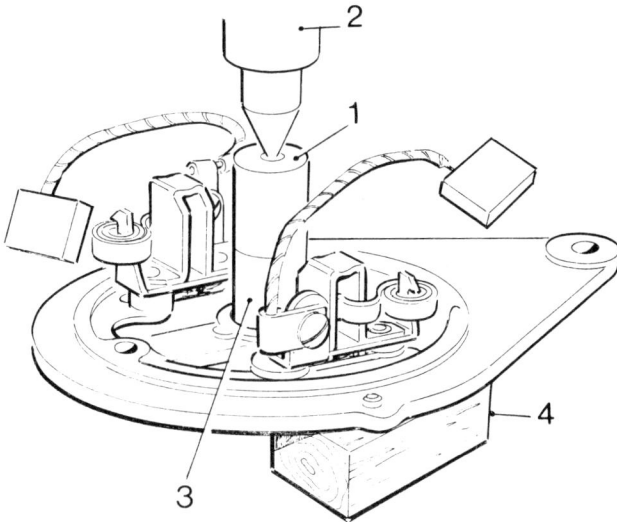

Fig. 10.3. Pressing in commutator end bracket bush (Sec. 11)

1 *Shouldered mandrel*   3 *Bearing bush*
2 *Hand press*   4 *Support block*

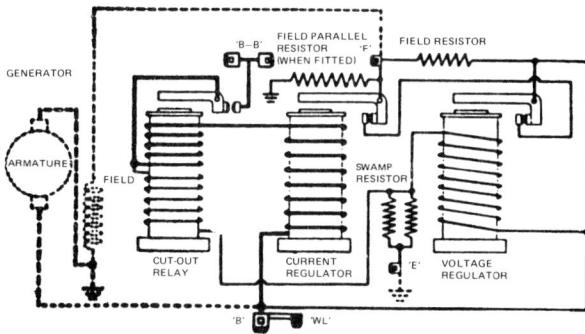

Fig. 10.4. Dynamo charging circuit (Sec. 12)

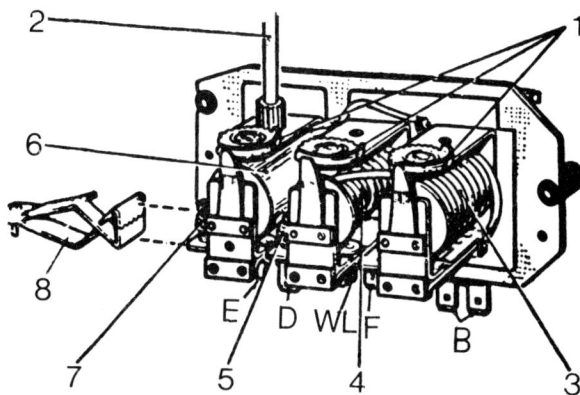

Fig. 10.5. Lucas RB 340 control box with cover removed (Sec. 13)

1 *Adjustment cams*   5 *Current regulator contacts*
2 *Tool for setting adjustment*   6 *Voltage regulator*
3 *Cut-out relay*   7 *Voltage regulator contacts*
4 *Current regulator*   8 *Clip to close points manually*

To renew the ball bearing fitted to the drive end bracket remove the armature from the end bracket, as detailed in Section 9, and then proceed as follows:
1 Drill out the rivets which hold the bearing retainer plate to the end bracket and lift off the plate.
2 Press out the bearing from the end bracket and remove the corrugated washer and felt washer from the bearing housing.
3 Thoroughly clean the bearing housing, and the new bearing and pack with high melting-point grease.
4 Place the felt washer and corrugated washer in that order in the end bracket bearing housing, and then press in the new bearing.
5 Replace the plate and fit new rivets opening out the rivet ends to hold the plate securely in position. (**Note** that on the C40 dynamo the rivets are fitted from the outer face of the end bracket).

12 Control box - general description

The control box comprises the voltage and current regulators and the cut-out. The voltage regulator controls the output from the dynamo depending on the state of the battery and the demands of the electrical equipment, and ensures that the battery is not over-charged. The cut-out is really an automatic switch and connects the dynamo to the battery when the dynamo is turning fast enough to produce a charge. Similarly it disconnects the battery from the dynamo when the engine is idling or stationary so that the battery does not discharge through the dynamo.

13 Control box cut-out and regulator contacts - maintenance

Every 12,000 miles (20,000 km) check the cut-out current and regulator contacts. If they are dirty or rough or burnt, place a piece of fine glass paper (**do not use emery paper or carborundum paper**) between the cut-out contacts, close them manually and draw the glass paper through several times.
Clean the regulator and current contacts in exactly the same way, but use emery or carborundum paper and not glass paper. Carefully clean both sets of contacts of all traces of dust with a rag moistened in methylated spirits.

14 Voltage regulator - adjustment

If the battery is in sound condition, but is not holding its charge, or is being continually over-charged, and the dynamo is in sound condition, then the voltage regulator in the control box must be adjusted.
Connect a wire from the negative battery terminal to the SW connector on the coil. Pull off the connectors from the control box terminals 'B' under the cut-out. Then connect the negative lead of a 20 volt voltmeter to the 'D' terminal on the dynamo and the positive lead to a good earth. Start the engine and increase its speed until the voltmeter needle flicks and then steadies. This should occur at about 3,000 rpm. If the needle flickers it is likely that the contact points are dirty. If the voltage at which the needle steadies is outside the limits listed below, then remove the control box cover and turn the adjusting cam on top of the voltage regulator with the special Lucas tool, clockwise, to raise the setting, and anticlockwise to lower it.

Air Temperature	Type RB 340 Open circuit voltage
10°C or 50°F	14.9 to 15.5
20°C or 68°F	14.7 to 15.3
30°C or 86°F	14.5 to 15.1
40°C or 104°F	14.3 to 14.9

It is vital that the adjustments be completed within 30 seconds of starting the engine as otherwise the heat from the shunt coil will affect the readings.

15 Current regulator - adjustment

The dynamo should be able to provide 22 amps. at 4,500 rpm irrespective of the state of the battery.

To test the dynamo output take off the control box cover, and short out the voltage regulator contacts by holding them together with a bulldog clip.

Pull off the Lucar connectors from the control box terminals 'B' and connect an ammeter reading to 40 volts to the two cables just disconnected and to **one** of the 'B' Lucar connectors.

Turn on all the lights and other electrical equipment and start the engine. At about 4,500 rpm the dynamo should be giving between 21 and 23 amps as recorded on the ammeter. If the ammeter needle flickers it is likely that the contact points are dirty.

To increase the current turn the cam on top of the current regulator clockwise, and to lower, anticlockwise.

16 Cut-out - adjustment

Check the voltage required to operate the cut-out by connecting a voltmeter between the control box terminals 'D' and 'WL'. Remove the control box cover, start the engine and gradually increase its speed until the cut-outs close. This should occur when the reading is between 12.7 to 13.3 volts. If the reading is outside these limits turn the adjusting cam on the cut-out relay a fraction at a time clockwise to raise the voltage cut-in point and anti-clockwise to lower it. To adjust the drop off voltage bend the fixed contact blade carefully. The adjustment to the cut-out should be completed within 30 seconds of starting the engine as otherwise heat build-up from the shunt coil will affect the readings.

If the cut-out fails to work, clean the contacts, and, if there is still no response, renew the cut-out and regulator unit.

17 Alternator - general description

On later produced models an alternator was fitted instead of a dynamo. Initially a Lucas 11AC alternator with control unit type 4TR was fitted but was soon replaced with the 16ACR and 17ACR types, with integral control systems.

When an alternator is fitted the positive earth system is replaced with a negative earth system.

Alternators are a sophisticated means for electrical generation, incorporating the fruits of modern technical research into the fields of semi conductors and micro circuitry technique. With the exception of one or two items there is little that the average owner can hope to achieve in the case of difficulties or failure. Some components are hermetically sealed and the test equipment alone to check the circuitry would be rarely found in the most enthusiastic owners workshop. The present high cost of alternators (about 4-5 times that of the dynamo) also discourages non-specialist repair.

The main advantage of the alternator lies in its ability to provide a high charge at low revolutions. This is especially welcome to city dwellers as driving slowly in heavy traffic with a dynamo invariably means no charge is reaching the battery. In similar conditions even with the wiper, lights, heater and perhaps radio switched on, the alternator will ensure a charge reaches the battery.

An important feature of the alternator is its built-in output control regulator, based on 'thick film' hybrid integrated microcircuit techniques, which results in Models 16ACR and 17ACR being self-contained generating and control units.

The system provides for direct connection of a charge

17.A The alternator

indicator light, and eliminates the need for a field switching relay or warning light control unit, necessary with former systems.

The alternator is of rotating field, ventilated design. It comprises principally: a laminated stator on which is wound a star-connected 3-phase output winding; and a 12-pole rotor carrying the field windings. Each end of the rotor shaft runs in ball race bearings which are lubricated for life; natural finish aluminium die cast end brackets, incorporating the mounting lugs; a rectifier pack for converting the a.c. output of the machine to d.c. for battery charging; and an output control regulator.

The rotor is belt driven from the engine through a pulley keyed to the rotor shaft. A pressed steel fan adjacent to the pulley draws cooling air through the machine. This fan forms an integral part of the alternator specification: it has been designed to provide adequate air flow with a minimum of noise, and to withstand the high stresses associated with maximum speed. Rotation is clockwise viewed on the drive end. Maximum continuous rotor speed is 12,500 rev./min.

Rectification of alternator output is achieved by six silicone diodes housed in a rectifier pack and connected as a 3-phase full-wave bridge. The rectifier pack is attached to the outer face of the slip ring end bracket and contains also three 'field' diodes; at normal operating speeds, rectified current from the stator output windings flows through these diodes to provide self-excitation of the rotor field, via brushes bearing on face type slip rings.

The slip rings are carried on a small diameter moulded drum attached to the rotor shaft, outboard of the slip ring end bearing. The inner ring is centred on the rotor shaft axis, while the outer ring has a mean diameter of 0.75 in (19.05 mm) approximately. By keeping the mean diameter of the slip rings to a minimum, relative speeds between brushes and rings, and hence wear, are also minimal. The slip rings are connected to the rotor field winding by wires carried in grooves in the rotor shaft.

The brushgear is housed in a moulding screwed to the outside of the slip ring end bracket. This moulding thus encloses the slip ring and brushgear assembly, and, together with the shielded bearing, protects the assembly against the entry of dust and moisture.

The regulator is set during manufacture and requires no further attention. Briefly, the 'thick film' regulator comprises resistors and conductors screen printed on to a 1in (25.4 mm) square alumina substrate. Mounted on the substrate are Lucas semiconductor dice consisting of three transistors, a voltage reference diode and a field recirculation diode, and also two capacitors. The internal connections between these components and the substrate are made by special Lucas-patented connectors. The whole assembly is 0.0625 in (1.5875 mm) thick and is housed in a recess in an aluminium heat sink, which is attached to the slip ring end bracket. Complete hermetic sealing is achieved by a silicone rubber encapsulant to provide environmental protection.

Electrical connections to external circuits are brought out to Lucar connector blades, these being grouped to accept a moulded connector socket which ensures correct connections.

18 Alternator - maintenance

1 The equipment has been designed for the minimum amount of maintenance in service, the only items subject to wear being the brushes and bearings.

2 Brushes should be examined after about 75,000 miles (120,000 km), and renewed if necessary. The bearings are pre-packed with grease for life, and should not require any further attention.

19 Alternators - special procedures

1 A replacement alternator must always be checked to ensure that polarity connections are correct. They are clearly marked and wrong connection can damage the equipment.

2 Never reverse battery connections. The rectifiers could be damaged.

3 Always connect up the battery earth terminal first.

4 Disconnect the alternator/control unit whenever the battery is being charged in position, as a safety precaution.

5 Never disconnect the battery with the engine running, nor run the alternator with the output cable disconnected anywhere

or any other alternator circuits disconnected.

6 The cable between battery and alternator is always "live". Take care not to short it to earth.

20 Alternator - removal and replacement

1 Withdraw the connector terminal block from the alternator terminal output in the end cover, (16ACR and 17ACR) or remove the output terminal nut and detach the cable (11AC).

2 Remove the bolt holding the fan belt tensioning link to the alternator.

3 Slacken the alternator mounting bolts and slip the fan belt over the pulley.

4 Remove the mounting bolts completely and lift away the alternator.

5 Refitting the alternator is the reverse sequence to removal. Ensure that the fan belt is correctly tensioned as described in Chapter 2.

21 Alternator - fault diagnosis and repair

Due to the specialist knowledge and equipment required to test or service an alternator it is recommended that if the performance is suspect, the car be taken to an automobile electrician who will have the facilities for such work. Because of this recommendation no further detailed service information is given other than that for brush renewal.

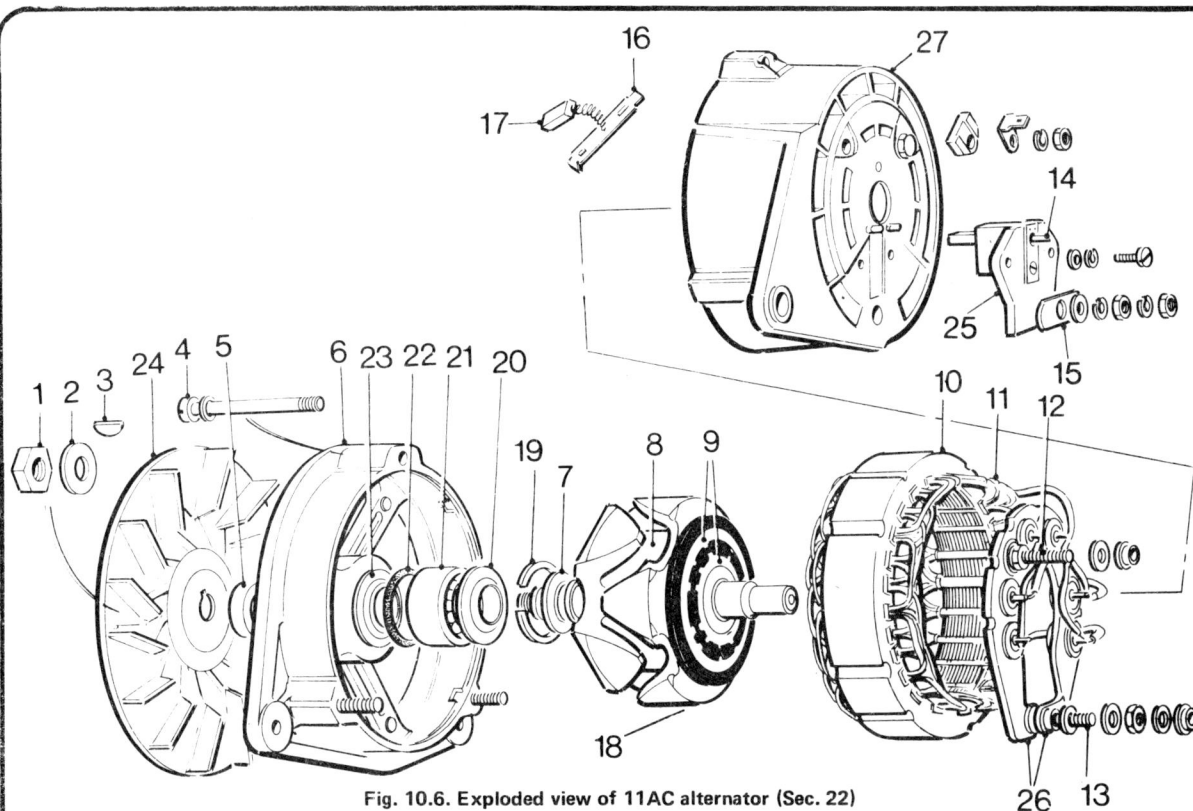

Fig. 10.6. Exploded view of 11AC alternator (Sec. 22)

1	Shaft nut	8	Rotor (field) winding	15 Output terminal plastic strip	21 Ball bearing
2	Spring washer	9	Slip rings	16 Terminal blade retaining	22 'O' ring oil seal
3	Key	10	Stator laminations	tongue	23 'O' ring retaining washer
4	Through bolt	11	Stator windings	17 Brush	24 Fan
5	Distance collar	12	Warning light terminal	18 Rotor	25 Brush box
6	Drive end bracket	13	Output terminal	19 Bearing circlip	26 Heat sink assemblies
7	Jump ring shroud	14	Field terminal blade	20 Bearing retaining plate	27 Slip ring end cover

Fig. 10.7. Exploded view of 16ACR and 17ACR alternator (Sec. 23)

1 Regulator
2 Slip ring end bracket
3 Stator
4 Rotor
5 Fan
6 Pulley
7 Drive end bracket
8 Bearing
9 Bearing
10 Slip rings
11 Rectifier
12 Brush gear
13 Cover

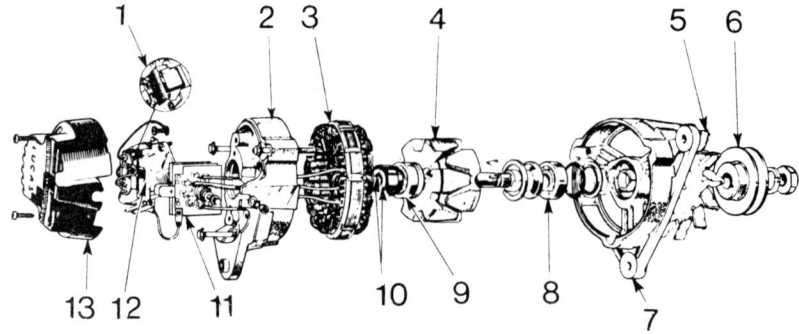

22 Alternator (11AC) - brush renewal

1 The brush gear can be removed from the alternator with the latter still in position.
2 Undo and remove the output terminal nut and detach the output cable.
3 Undo and remove the retaining screws and withdraw the brush box.
4 Close the retaining tongues on the brush terminal blades and withdraw the terminals from the brush box.
5 Brushes worn below 0.3125 in (7.938 mm) must be renewed.
6 The new brush complete with spring and Lucar terminal blade should be pushed into the brush holder until the tongue registers.
7 To retain the terminal, carefully lever up the retaining tongue with a thin blade.
8 Check that the brush moves freely in its holder. If sluggish, clean the brush sides with a petrol moistened cloth or polish with a very fine file.
9 Refit the brush box assembly to the alternator, this being the reverse sequence to removal.

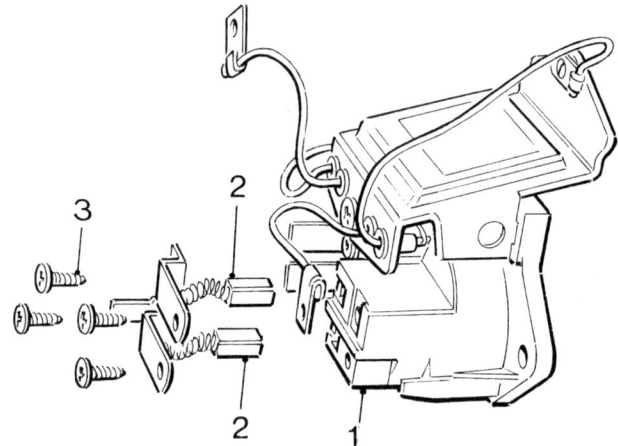

23 Alternator (16ACR and 17ACR) - brush renewal

1 Referring to Fig. 10.7 remove the end cover by undoing the screws.
2 To inspect the brushes correctly the brush holder moulding should be removed complete by undoing the two bolts and disconnecting the 'Lucar' connection to the diode plates.
3 With the brush holder moulding removed and the brush assemblies still in position check that they protrude from the face of the moulding by at least 0.2 in (5 mm). Also check that when depressed, the spring pressure is 7-10 oz. (193-283 gms) when the end of the brush is flush with the face of the brush moulding. To be done with any accuracy this requires a push type spring gauge.
4 Should either of the foregoing requirements not be fulfilled the spring assemblies should be replaced.
5 This can be done simply by renewing the holding screws of each assembly and replacing them.
6 With the brush holder moulding removed the slip rings on the face end of the rotor are exposed. These can be cleaned with a petrol soaked cloth and any signs of burning may be removed very carefully with fine glass paper. On no account should any other abrasive be used or any attempt at machining be made.
7 When the brushes are refitted they should slide smoothly in their holders. Any sticking tendency may first be rectified by wiping with a petrol soaked cloth or, if this fails, by carefully polishing with a very fine file where any binding marks may appear.
8 Reassemble in the reverse order of dismantling. Ensure that leads which may have been connected to any of the screws are reconnected correctly.

Fig. 10.8. Exploded view of alternator brush and spring assembly (16ACR and 17ACR) (Sec. 23)

1 Brush box moulding
2 Brush and spring assembly
3 Four retaining screws

Fig. 10.9. Warning light simulator terminals (Sec. 24)

1 Alternator 'AL'
2 Positive '+'
3 Warning light 'WL'

24 Warning light control - general description

With an alternator, a warning light is fitted and its function is similar to the ignition warning light system fitted with dynamo charging systems. The warning light is illuminated when the alternator is stationary or is being driven slowly. The light is extinguished when the output voltage beings to rise.

The light control unit is a thermally operated relay for controlling the switching on, and off, of the facia panel warning light. It is connected through the alternator terminal 'AL' to the centre point of the six alternator control diodes and to earth.

Should the warning light indicate lack of charge check this unit before the alternator. If it is suspect if must be replaced with a similar new unit. Although similar in design to the direction indicator flasher unit it is not interchangeable.

25 Starter motor - general description

Two types of starter motor have been fitted to models covered by this manual depending on date of manufacture and specification.

The starter motor is mounted on the right-hand lower side of the engine backplate and is held in position by two bolts which also clamp the flywheel housing.

The relay for the starter motor is located on the right-hand side of the engine compartment.

The principle of operation of the interior type starter motor is as follows: When the ignition switch is turned, current flows from the battery to the starter motor solenoid switch which causes it to become energised. Its internal plunger moves inwards and closes an internal switch so allowing full starting current to flow from the battery to the starter motor. This creates a powerful magnetic field to be induced into the field coils which causes the armature to rotate.

Mounted on helicoil splines is the drive pinion which, because of the sudden rotation of the armature, is thrown forwards along the armature shaft and so into engagement with the flywheel ring gear. The engine crankshaft will then be rotated until the engine starts to operate on its own and, at this point, the drive pinion is thrown out of mesh with the flywheel ring gear.

26 Starter motor - testing on engine

1 If the starter motor fails to operate then check the condition of the battery by turning on the headlamps. If they glow brightly for several seconds and then gradually dim, the battery is in an uncharged condition.
2 If the headlamps glow brightly and it is obvious that the battery is in good condition, then check the tightness of the battery wiring connections (and in particular the earth lead from the battery terminal to its connection to the bodyframe). Check the tightness of the connections at the relay switch and at the starter motor. Check the wiring with a voltmeter for breaks or shorts.
3 If the wiring is in order then check that the starter motor switch is operating. To do this, press the rubber covered button in the centre of the relay switch under the bonnet. If it is working the starter motor will be heard to 'click' as it tries to rotate. Alternatively check it with a voltmeter. **Note:** It is not possible to operate the solenoid from under the bonnet on models fitted with automatic transmission.
4 If the battery is fully charged, the wiring in order, and the switch working and the starter motor fails to operate then it will have to be removed from the car for examination. Before this is done, however, ensure that the starter pinion has not jammed in mesh with the flywheel. Check by turning the square end of the armature shaft with a spanner. This will free the pinion if it is stuck in engagement with the flywheel teeth.

27 Starter motor - removal and replacement

1 Disconnect the earth lead from the battery, for safety reasons.
2 Disconnect the starter motor cable from the terminal on the starter motor end plate.
3 Unscrew the two starter motor bolts.
4 Lift the starter motor out of engagement with the teeth on the flywheel ring and pull it forward until it can be lifted clear.
5 Replacement is a straight reversal of the removal procedure.

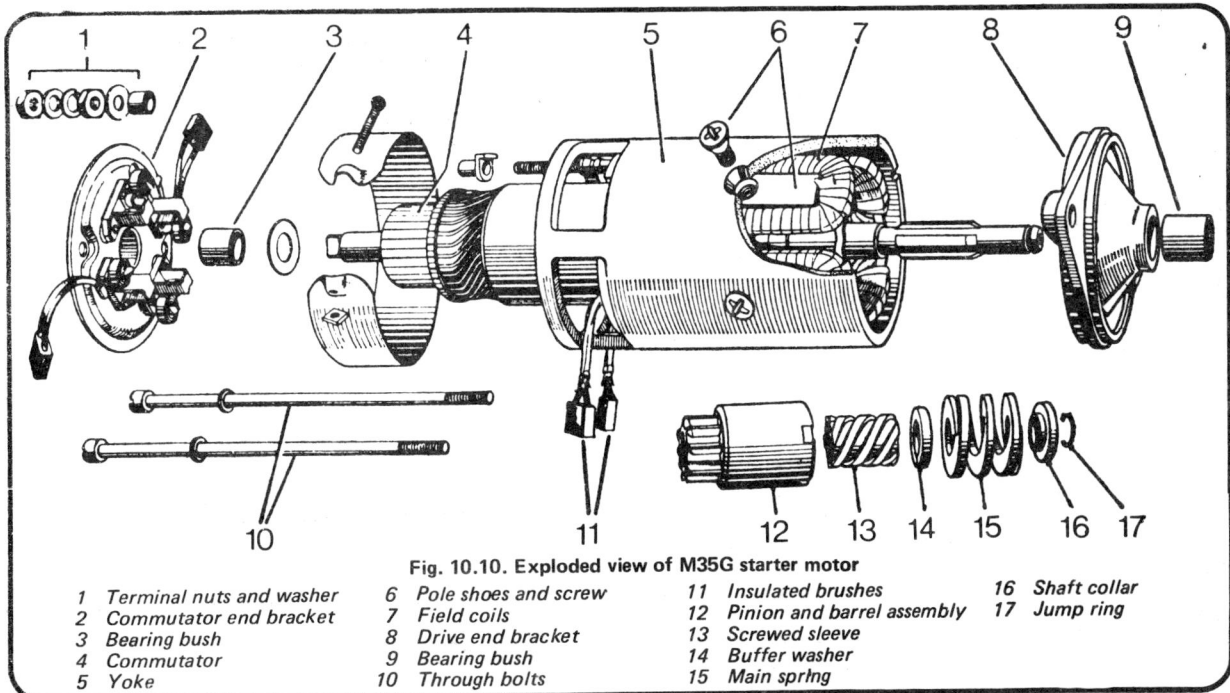

Fig. 10.10. Exploded view of M35G starter motor

1	Terminal nuts and washer	6	Pole shoes and screw
2	Commutator end bracket	7	Field coils
3	Bearing bush	8	Drive end bracket
4	Commutator	9	Bearing bush
5	Yoke	10	Through bolts
11	Insulated brushes	16	Shaft collar
12	Pinion and barrel assembly	17	Jump ring
13	Screwed sleeve		
14	Buffer washer		
15	Main spring		

28 Starter motor (M35G) - dismantling and reassembly

1 With the starter motor on the bench, loosen the screw on the cover band and slip the cover band off. With a piece of wire bent into the shape of a hook, lift back each of the brush springs in turn and check the movement of the brushes in their holders by pulling on the flexible connectors. If the brushes are so worn that their faces do not rest against the commutator, or if the ends of the brush leads are exposed on their working face, they must be renewed.

2 If any of the brushes tend to stick in their holders then wash them with a petrol moistened cloth and, if necessary, lightly polish the sides of the brush with a very fine file, until the brushes move quite freely in their holders.

3 If the surface of the commutator is dirty or blackened, clean it with a petrol dampened rag. Secure the starter motor in a vice and check it by connecting a heavy gauge cable between the starter motor terminal and a 12-volt battery.

4 Connect the cable from the other battery terminal to earth in the starter motor body. If the motor turns at high speed it is in good order.

5 If the starter motor still fails to function or if it is wished to renew the brushes, then it is necessary to further dismantle the motor.

6 Lift the brush springs with the wire hook and lift all four brushes out of their holders one at a time.

7 Remove the terminal nuts and washers from the terminal post on the commutator end bracket.

8 Unscrew the two through bolts which hold the end plates together and pull off the commutator end bracket. Also remove the driving end bracket which will come away complete with the armature.

9 At this stage if the brushes are to be renewed, their flexible connectors must be unsoldered and the connectors of new brushes soldered in their place. Check that the new brushes move freely in their holders as detailed above. If cleaning the commutator with petrol fails to remove all the burnt areas and spots, then wrap a piece of glass paper round the commutator and rotate the armature. If the commutator is badly worn, remove the drive gear as detailed in the following Section. Then mount the armature in a lathe and with the lathe turning at high speed, take a very fine cut out of the commutator and finish the surface by polishing with glass paper. **Do not undercut the mica insulators between the commutator segments.**

10 With the starter motor dismantled, test the four field coils for an open circuit. Connect a 12-volt battery with a 12-volt bulb in one of the leads between the field terminal post and the tapping point of the field coils to which the brushes are connected. An open circuit is proved by the bulb not lighting.

11 If the bulb lights, it does not necessarily mean that the field coils are in order, as there is a possibility that one of the coils will be earthing to the starter yoke or pole shoes. To check this, remove the lead from the brush connector and place it against a clean portion of the starter yoke. If the bulb lights the field coils are earthing. Replacement of the field coils calls for the use of a wheel operated screwdriver, a soldering iron, caulking and riveting operations and is beyond the scope of the majority of owners. The starter yoke should be taken to a reputable electrical engineering works for new field coils to be fitted. Alternatively, purchase an exchange Lucas starter motor.

12 If the armature is damaged this will be evident after visual inspection. Look for signs of burning, discolouration, and for conductors that have lifted away from the commutator. Reassembly is a straight reversal of the dismantling procedure.

29 Starter motor drive (M35G) - removal and replacement

1 Extract the split pin from the shaft nut on the end of the starter drive.

2 Holding the squared end of the armature shaft at the commutator end bracket with a suitable spanner, unscrew the

shaft nut which has a right-hand thread, and pull off the mainspring.

3 Slide the remaining parts with a rotary action off the armature shaft.

4 Reassembly is a straight reversal of the above procedure. Ensure that the split pin is refitted.

Note: It is most important that the drive gear is completely free from oil, grease and dirt. With the drive gear removed, clean all the parts thoroughly in paraffin. **Under no circumstances oil the drive components.** Lubrication of the drive components could easily cause the pinion to stick.

30 Starter motor bushes (M35G) - inspection, removal and replacement

With the starter motor stripped down check the condition of the bushes. They should be renewed when they are sufficiently worn to allow visible side movement of the armature shaft.

The old bushes are simply driven out with a suitable drift and the new bushes inserted by the same method. As the bearings are of the phospher bronze type it is essential that they are allowed to stand in engine oil for at least 24 hours before fitment.

31 Starter motor (M35J) - dismantling and reassembly

1 With the starter motor on the bench, first mark the relative positions of the starter motor body to the two end brackets.

2 Undo and remove the two screws and spring washers securing the drive end bracket to the body. The drive end bracket, complete with armature and drive, may now be drawn forwards from the starter motor body.

3 Lift away the thrust washer from the commutator end of the armature shaft.

4 Undo and remove the two screws securing the commutator end bracket to the starter motor body. The commutator end bracket may now be drawn back about an inch allowing sufficient access so as to disengage the field brushes from the bracket. Once these are free, the end bracket may now be completely removed.

5 With the motor stripped, the brushes and brush gear may be inspected. To check the brush spring tension, fit a new brush into each holder in turn, and, using an accurate spring balance, push the brush on the balance tray until the brush protrudes approximately 0.0625 in (1.588 mm) from the holder. Make a note of the reading which should be approximately 28 ounces. If the spring pressures vary considerably the commutator end bracket must be renewed as a complete assembly.

6 Inspect the brushes for wear and renew a brush which is nearing the minimum length of 0.375 in (9.525 mm). To renew the end bracket brushes, cut the brush cables from the terminal posts and, with a small file or hacksaw, slot the head of the terminal posts to a sufficient depth to accommodate the new leads. Solder the new brush leads to the posts.

7 To renew the field winding brushes, cut the brush leads approximately 0.25 in (6.35 mm) from the field winding junction and carefully solder the new brush leads to the remaining stumps, making sure that the insulation sleeves provide adequate cover.

8 If the commutator surface is dirty or blackened, clean it with a petrol dampened rag. Carefully examine the commutator for signs of excessive wear, burning or pitting. If evident it may be reconditioned by having it skimmed at the local engineering works or BLMC dealer who possesses a centre lathe. The thickness of the commutator must not be less than 0.08 inch. For minor reconditioning, the commutator may be polished with glass paper. **Do not under cut the mica insulator between the commutator segments.**

9 With the starter motor dismantled, test the field coils for open circuit. Connect a 12 volt battery with a 12 volt bulb in one of the leads between each of the field brushes and a clean part of the body. The lamp will light if continuity is satisfactory

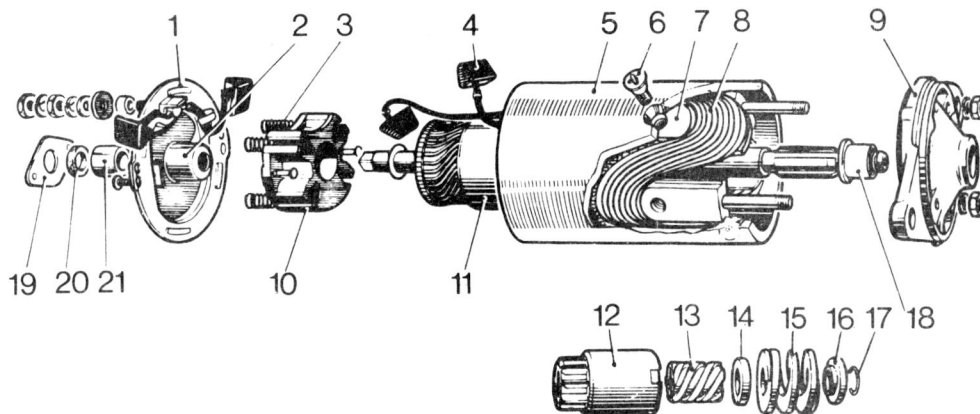

Fig. 10.11. Exploded view of M35J starter motor (Sec. 31)

1	Commutator end bracket	7	Pole shoe	13	Screwed sleeve	19	Bush cover
2	Bush housing	8	Field coils	14	Buffer washer	20	Felt washer
3	Brush spring	9	Drive end brackets	15	Main spring	21	Bearing bush
4	Brushe	10	Brush box moulding	16	Cup spring		
5	Yoke	11	Armature	17	Jump ring		
6	Pole screw	12	Pinion and barrel	18	Bearing bush		

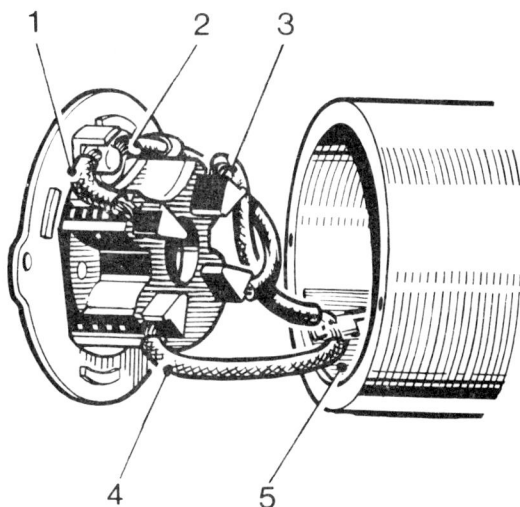

Fig. 10.12. View of commutator end bracket assembly (M35J)

1 Short brush - flexible, commutator end bracket
2 Long brush - flexible, commutator end bracket
3 Long brush - flexible, field winding
4 Short brush - flexible, field winding
5 Yoke insulator - field connection joint

between the brushes, windings and body connection.

10 Replacement of the field coils calls for the use of a wheel operated screwdriver, a soldering iron, caulking and riveting operations and is beyond the scope of the majority of owners. The starter motor body should be taken to an automobile electrical engineering works for new field coils to be fitted. Alternatively purchase an exchange Lucas starter motor.

11 Check the condition of the bushes and they should be renewed when they are sufficiently worn to allow visible side movement of the armature shaft.

12 To renew the commutator end bracket bush, drill out the rivets securing the brush box moulding and remove the moulding, bearing seal retaining plate and felt washer seal.

13 Screw in a ½ inch tap and withdraw the bush with the tap.

14 As the bush is of the phosphor bronze type it is essential that

it is allowed to stand in engine oil for at least 24 hours before fitment. Alternatively soak in oil at 100° C (212° F) for 2 hours.

15 Using a suitable diameter drift, drive the new bush into position. Do not ream the bush as its self lubricating properties will be impaired.

16 To remove the drive end bracket bush it will be necessary to remove the drive gear as described in paragraphs 18 and 19.

17 Using a suitable diameter drift remove the old bush and fit a new one as described in paragraphs 14 and 15.

18 To dismantle the starter motor drive, first use a press to push the retainer clear of the circlip which can then be removed. Lift away the retainer and main spring.

19 Slide off the remaining parts with a rotary action of the armature shaft.

20 It is most important that the drive gear is completely free from oil, grease and dirt. With the drive gear removed, clean all parts thoroughly in paraffin. Under no circumstances oil the drive components. Lubrication of the drive components could easily cause the pinion to stick.

21 Reassembly of the starter motor drive is the reverse sequence to dismantling. Use a press to compress the spring and retainer sufficiently to allow a new circlip to be fitted to its groove on the shaft. Remove the drive from the press.

32 Fuses - general

1 Two fuses are fitted to a separate fuse holder positioned adjacent to the control box. (photo) The fuse marked A1 - A2 protects the electrical items such as the horn and lights, which function irrespective of whether the ignition is on or not.

2 The fuse marked A3 - A4 protects the ignition system and items which only operate when the ignition system is switched on, ie., the stop lights, fuel gauge, flasher unit, and windscreen wiper motor.

3 If either of these fuses blows due to a short circuit or similar trouble, trace and rectify the cause before renewing the fuse.

4 A further fuse for the rear and pilot lights can be found in a small tube adjacent to the wiring loom under the fascia or battery. Access to this fuse is achieved by holding the small tube at each end and then pushing in, twisting, and pulling off the serrated portion.

32.1 Fuse unit

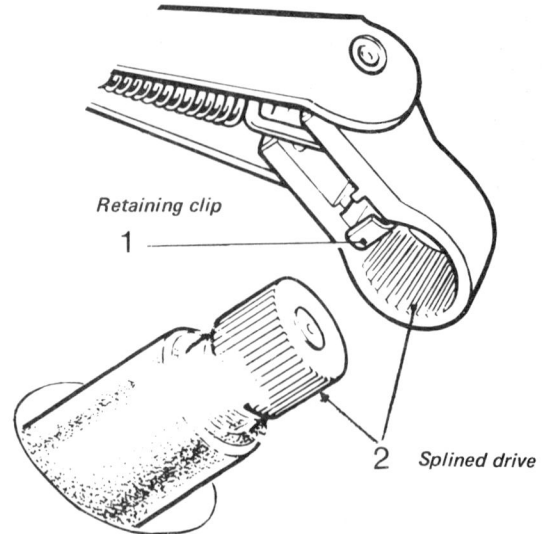

Fig. 10.13. Method of attaching wiper arm to spindle

33 Flasher circuit - fault diagnosis and rectification

The flasher unit fitted to Mk I 1100 models is enclosed in a small cylindrical metal container located on the right-hand side of the engine compartment. On Mk II 1100 and 1300 models the unit is located in a small rectangular container situated in the wiring loom behind the fascia.

In both cases the unit is actuated by the direction indicator switch.

If the flasher unit fails to operate, or works very slowly or very rapidly, check out the flasher indicator circuit as detailed below. before assuming there is a fault in the unit itself.

1 Examine the direction indicator bulbs front and rear for broken filaments.

2 If the external flashers are working but the internal flasher warning light has ceased to function check the filament of the warning bulb and replace as necessary.

3 With the aid of the wiring diagram check all the flasher circuit connections if a flasher bulb is sound but does not work.

4 In the event of total direction indicator failure, check the 'A3' - 'A4' fuse.

5 With the ignition turned on check that current is reaching the flasher unit by connecting a voltmeter between the 'plus' or 'B' terminal and earth. If this test is positive connect the 'plus' or 'B' terminal and the 'L' terminal and operate the flasher switch. If the flasher bulb lights up the flasher unit itself is defective and must be replaced as it is not possible to dismantle and repair it.

6 Renewal of the earlier cylindrical type is straightforward and will present no problems. Access to the later type is from inside the car, via the parcel tray. It is detached by gently pulling it from the Lucar connector terminals.

34 Windscreen wiper mechanism - fault diagnosis and rectification

1 Should the windscreen wipers fail, or work very slowly, then check the terminals for loose connections, and make sure the insulation of the external wiring is not cracked or broken. If this is in order then check the current the motor is taking by connecting up a 1-20 volt voltmeter in the circuit and turning on the wiper switch. Consumption should be between 2.3 to 3.1 amps.

2 If no current is passing through check the A3 - A4 fuse. If the fuse has blown replace it after having checked the wiring of the motor and other electrical circuits serviced by this fuse for short

circuits. If the fuse is in good condition check the wiper switch.

3 If the wiper motor takes a very high current check the wiper blades for freedom of movement. If this is satisfactory check the gearbox cover and gear assembly for damage and measure the armature endfloat which should be between 0.009 to 0.012 in (0.20 to 0.30 mm) early type or 0.002 to 0.008 in (0.05 to 0.2 mm) - later models. The endfloat is set by the adjusting screw. Check that excessive friction in the cable connecting tubes caused by too small a curvature is not the cause of the high current consumption.

4 If the motor takes a very low current ensure that the battery is fully charged. Check the brush gear after removing the commutator end bracket and ensure that the brushes are bearing on the commutator. If not, check the brushes for freedom of movement and if necessary, renew the tension spring. If the brushes are very worn they should be replaced with new ones. The brush levers should be quite free on their pivots. If stiff, loosen them by moving them backwards and forwards by hand and by applying a little thin machine oil. Check the armature by substitution if this unit is suspect.

5 If the windscreen wipers fail to park or only park intermittently, then the fault is almost certain to be that the limit switch is incorrectly set. (Early models).

6 To reset the limit switch remove the four screws which hold the gearbox cover in position and turn the circular cover until the setting pip on top of the cover lines up, and is nearest to, the slightly offset groove in the gearbox cover.

7 If it is wished to change the area through which the wiper blades move this is simply done by removing each blades in turn from each splined drive, and then replacing it on the drive in slightly different position.

8 Should the wheelboxes or rack drive be worn it is possible to further their life by following the instructions in the following paragraphs.

9 Park the wipers and remove the arms from their spindles. Slacken the pipe union nut at the gearbox and then undo and remove the four screws securing the gearbox cover. Lift away the cover.

10 Withdraw the circlip holding the limit switch and connecting link in place. Remove the limit switch and connecting link.

11 The cable rack may now be drawn out of the tube.

12 Rotate the splined drive spindles through 180°.

13 Turn the cable rack over and slide it back into place.

14 Reassembly is the reverse sequence to removal. The wipers will now operate on an unworn segment of the gearwheel and cable rack.

35 Windscreen wiper motor, gearbox and wheelboxes (early type) - removal and replacement

1   Remove the windscreen wiper arms by lifting the blades, carefully raising the retaining clip and then pulling the arms off the splined drive shafts.

2   The windscreen wiper motor and gearbox is attached to a bracket on the radiator valance by three nuts and studs. The bracket is held in position by three bolts. Disconnect the electrical cables from the wiper motor and release the outer cable from the gearbox housing. Undo the wiper securing nuts.

3   Take out the fascia panel as described in Chapter 12.

4   Remove the cable rack from the motor and gearbox. First undo the pipe union nut. Then remove the gearbox cover, and the retaining washer from the crankpin and final gearwheel. The connecting link can now be lifted out and the wiper motor removed.

5   The windscreen wiper arm wheelboxes are located immediately underneath the splined drive shafts over which the wiper arms fit. To remove these wheelboxes release the cable rack outer casings by slackening the wheelbox cover screws. Remove the external nut, bush, and washer from the base of the splines and pull out the wheelboxes from under the fascia.

6   Replacement is a straight reversal of the removal sequence but take care that the cable rack emerges properly and that the wheelboxes are correctly lined up.

36 Windscreen wiper motor (early type) - dismantling, inspection and reassembly

If the motor is not functioning check first that current is reaching it. If this test is positive then the motor can be dismantled, inspected, and reassembled in the following sequence:

1   Undo the four bolts holding the motor gearbox cover in place and remove the cover.

2   Unscrew and remove the two through bolts at the commutator bracket end and pull off the connectors.

3   Pull the commutator end bracket away from the yoke so exposing the brushes.

4   Note which way round the brushes fit so that they can be replaced in their original positions. Remove the brushes in their assembly as one piece.

5   If it is wished to remove the field coil, first mark the two screws which hold the pole piece to the yoke so the screws can be replaced in their original positions. Undo them.

6   Press out the pole piece and field coil, mark the pole piece so

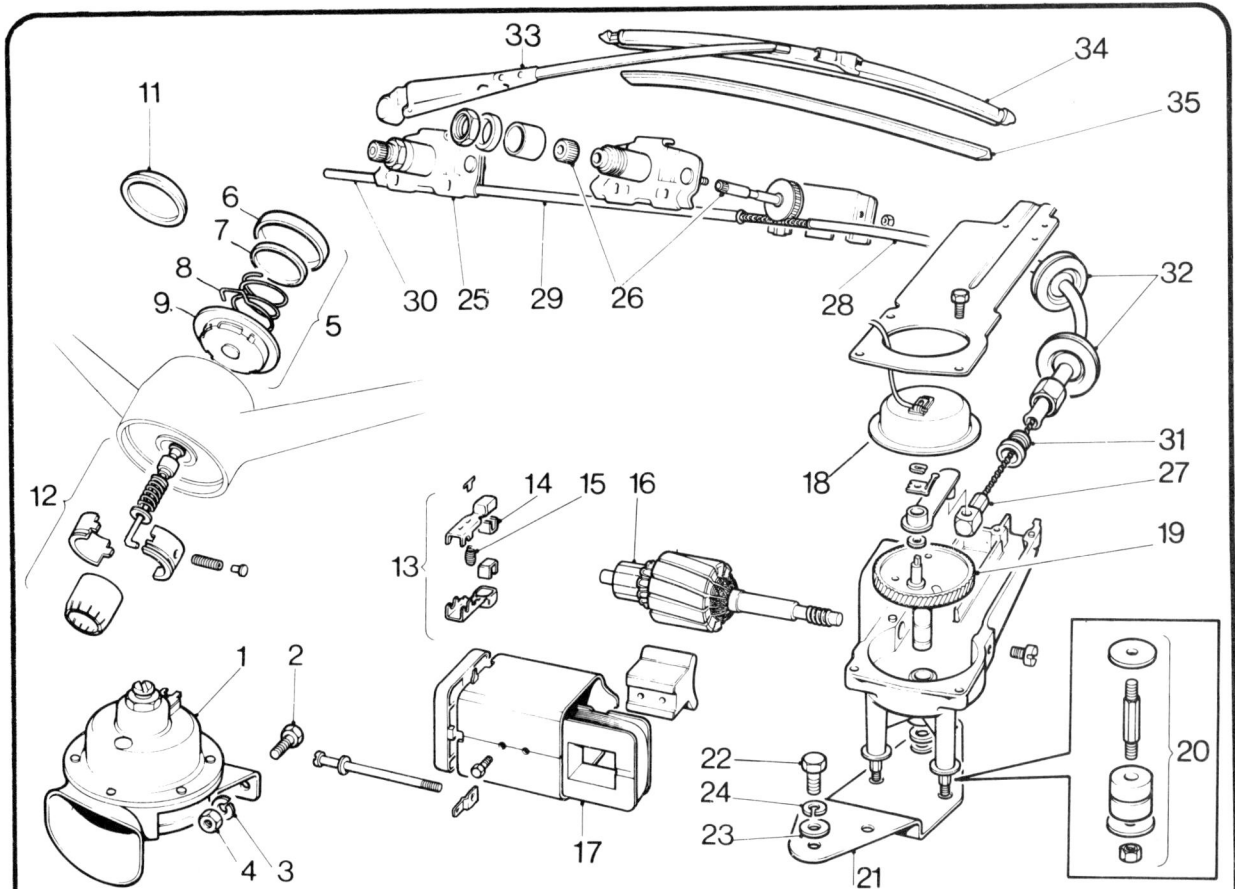

Fig. 10.14. Exploded view of horn and windscreen wiper (3WA) components

1 Horn	11 Motif	20 Stud	28 Drive casing - motor to box
2 Screw	12 Slip ring and rotor	21 Mounting bracket	29 Drive casing - wheelbox
3 Washer	13 Brush gear	22 Bracket screw	30 Drive casing - end
4 Nut	14 Brush	23 Plain washer	31 Ferrule
5 Horn - push	15 Brush spring	24 Spring washer	32 Grommet
6 Retaining ring	16 Armature	25 Wheelbox	33 Wiper arm
7 Contact (upper)	17 Field coil	26 Spindle and gear	34 Wiper blade
8 Motif spring	18 Switch	27 Cross-head and rack	35 Rubber
9 Cover and contact	19 Shaft and gear		

it can be replaced in its original position inside the yoke, and then press the pole piece out of the field coil.

7   Inspect the internal wiring in the motor for signs of burning indicating a short circuit. Insulate any chaffed or burnt wire. Examine the internal wiring for breaks and repair as necessary.

8   Small pieces of carbon can short circuit adjacent commutator segments. The pressure of carbon will also cause high current consumption. Clean both the commutator and the brushes and replace the latter if badly worn.

9   Check the resistance between adjacent segments of the commutator. The correct reading is between 0.34 and 0.41 ohms. Check the resistance of the field coil. It should be between 12.8 and 14 ohms. If it is lower than 12.8 ohms it is likely that there is a short circuit in the winding, which means that a new field coil must be fitted.

10   Reassembly is a straightforward reversal of the dismantling instructions. **Note:** The armature bearings, the commutator end of the armature shaft, and the felt lubricator in the gearbox must be lubricated with engine oil during re-assembly. The self-aligning bearing should be immersed in the same grade of oil for 24 hours before it is refitted. The cable

rack and wheelhouses, the worm wheel bearings, cross head, guide channel, connecting rod, crankpin, worm and final gear shaft should all be packed generously with grease.

37 Windscreen wiper motor, gearbox and wheelboxes (later type) - removal and replacement

1   For safety reasons, disconnect the battery.

2   Remove the windscreen wiper arms by lifting the blades, carefully raising the retaining clip and then pulling the arms off the splined driveshafts.

3   Withdraw the terminal connector from the motor and detach the earth wire from the valance.

4   Unscrew the union on the Bundy tube at the gearbox and release the strap from the mounting bracket.

5   Withdraw the assembly, pulling the cable rack from the Bundy tube.

6   The windscreen wiper arm wheelboxes are located immediately underneath the splined driveshafts over which the wiper arms fit. To remove these wheelboxes release the cable rack

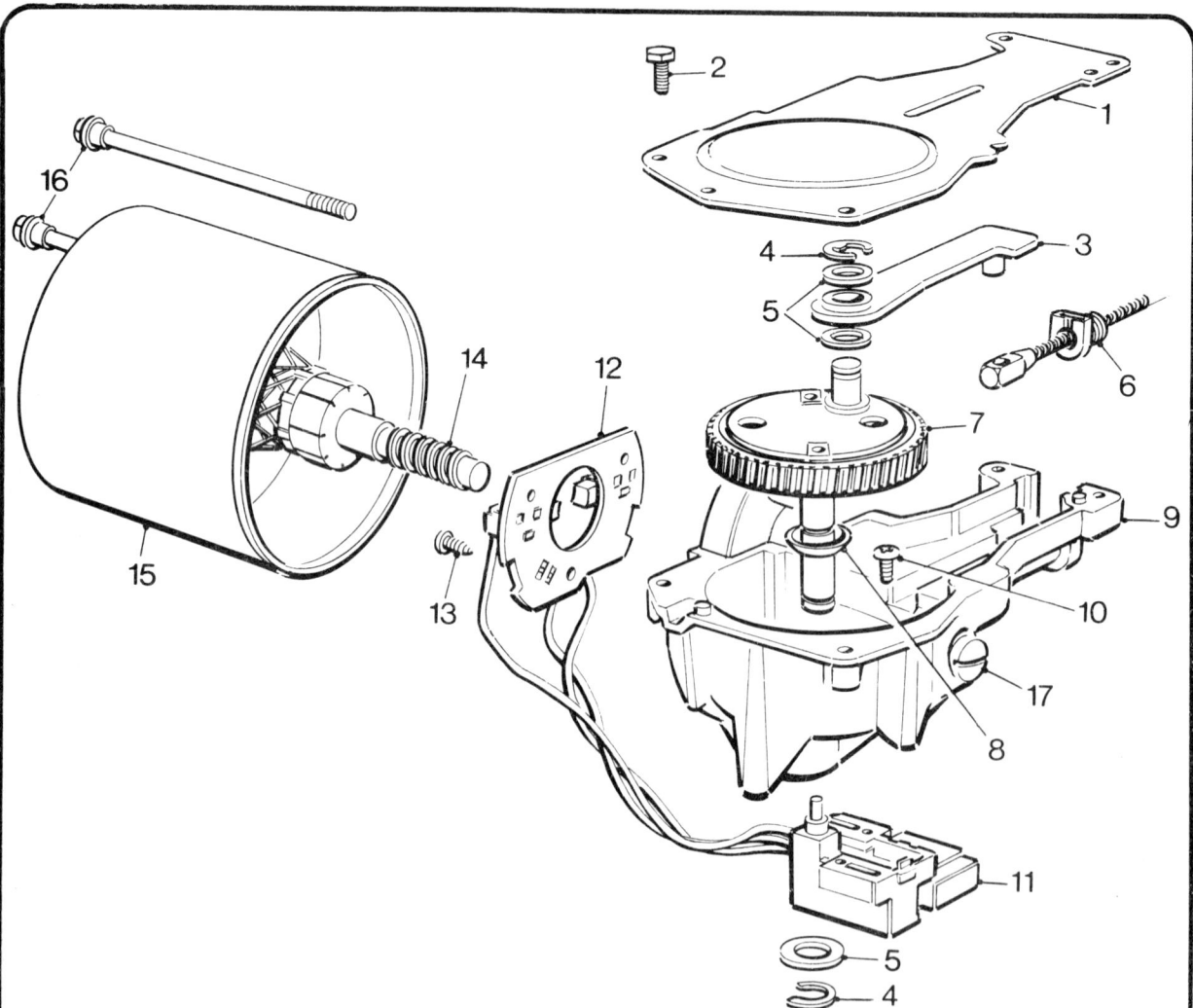

Fig. 10.15. Exploded view of 14W windscreen wiper motor and gearbox (Sec. 38)

1 Gearbox cover	5 Plain washers	9 Gearbox	13 Screw for brush gear
2 Screw for cover	6 Cross-head and rack	10 Screw for limit switch	14 Armature
3 Connecting rod	7 Shaft and gear	11 Limit switch assembly	15 Yoke assembly
4 Circlip	8 Dished washer	12 Brush gear	16 Yoke bolts
			17 Armature thrust screw

outer casings by slackening the wheelbox cover screws. Remove the external nut, bush, and washer from the base of the splines and pull out the wheelboxes from under the fascia.

7   Replacement is a straight reversal of the removal sequence. Leave the wheelbox covers slack until after the cable rack has been inserted and the motor secured.

38 Windscreen wiper motor (later type) - dismantling, inspection and reassembly

1   Refer to Fig. 10.15 and remove the four gearbox cover retaining screws and lift away the cover. Release the circlip and flat washer securing the connecting rod to the crankpin on the shaft and gear. Lift away the connecting rod followed by the second flat washer.
2   Release the circlip and washer securing the shaft and gear to the gearbox body.
3   De-burr the gear shaft and lift away the gear making a careful note of the location of the dished washer.
4   Scribe a mark on the yoke assembly and gearbox to ensure correct reassembly and unscrew the two yoke bolts from the motor yoke assembly. Part the yoke assembly including armature from the gearbox body. As the yoke assembly has residual magnetism ensure that the yoke is kept well away from metallic dust.
5   Unscrew the two screws securing the brush gear and the terminal and switch assembly and remove both the assemblies.
6   Inspect the brushes for signs of excessive wear. If the main brushes are worn to a limit of 0.188 in (4.763 mm) or the narrow section of the third brush is worn to the full width of the brush fit a new brush gear assembly. Ensure that the three brushes move freely in their boxes. If a push type spring gauge is available, check the spring rate which should be between 5 to 7 ounces when the bottom of the brush is level with the bottom of the slot in the brush box. Again, if the spring rate is incorrect, fit a new brush gear assembly.
7   If the armature is suspect take it to an automobile electrician to test for open or short circuiting.
8   Inspect the gear wheel for signs of excessive wear or damage and fit a new one if necessary.
9   Reassembly is the reverse procedure to dismantling but there are several points that require special attention.
10 Use only Ragosine Listate grease to lubricate the gearwheel teeth and cam, the armature shaft worm gear, connecting rod and its connecting pin, the cross head slide and cable rack and the wheelbox gear wheels.
11 Use only Shell Turbo 41 oil to lubricate the bearing bushes, the armature shaft bearing journals (sparingly), the gear wheel shaft and crankpin, the felt washer in the yoke bearing (thoroughly soak) and the wheelbox spindles.
12 The yoke assembly fixing the bolts should be tightened using a torque wrench set to 14 lb f ft (1.94 kg fm).
13 When a replacement armature is to be fitted, slacken the thrust screw so as to provide end float for fitting the yoke.
14 The thrust disc inside the yoke bearing should be fitted with the concave side towards the end face if the bearing. The dished washer fitted beneath the gear wheel should have its concave side towards the gear wheel as shown in Fig. 10.15.
15 The larger of the two flat washers is fitted underneath the connecting rod and the smaller one on top, under the retaining circlip.
16 To adjust the armature endfloat, tighten the thrust screw and then turn back one quarter of a turn so giving an endfloat of between 0.004 and 0.008 inch (0.102 and 0.204 mm). The gap should be measured under the head of the thrust screw. Fit a shim of suitable size beneath the head, and tighten the screw.

39 Horns - fault diagnosis and rectification

1   If a horn works badly or fails completely, first check the wiring leading to it for short circuits and loose connections. Also

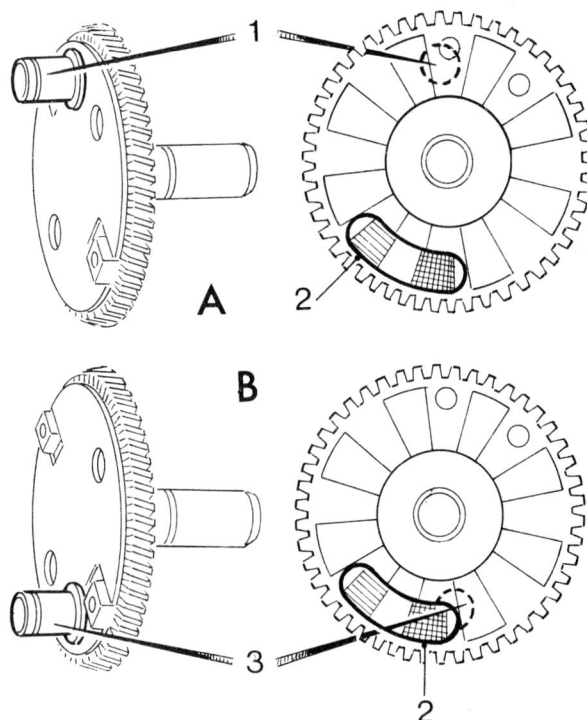

Fig. 10.16. Gear wheel showing alternative positions of crankpin (14W) (Sec. 38)

A   *RHD cars: cable rack retracted with the crankpin (1) opposite the ramp (2)*
B   *LHD cars: cable rack extended with the crankpin (3) adjacent to the ramp (2)*

check that the horn is firmly secured and that there is nothing lying on the horn body.

If the fault is not an external one remove the horn cover and check the leads inside the horn. If these are sound, check the contact breaker contacts. If these are burnt or dirty, clean them with a fine file and wipe all traces of dirt and rust away with a petrol moistened rag. Test the current consumption of the horn which should be between 3 and 3½ amps.

To adjust the contact breaker to compensate for wear turn the small serrated adjustment screw anticlockwise, at the same time pushing the horn push to sound the horn. As soon as the horn stops turn the screw clockwise about a quarter of a turn. This will start the horn again and represents the correct adjustment.

On models fitted with twin horns adjust each horn singly by disconnecting the other instrument. Wrap a piece of insulating tape round the disconnected wires to prevent the live one touching an earth and blowing the '1' to '2' fuse.

40 Headlight unit - removal and replacement

The headlight units fitted to models destined for the North American or UK markets are of the sealed beam type. Pre-focus bulbs are normally fitted for other markets.

UK models
1   Release the retaining screw at the bottom of the rim, ease the rim up whilst lifting the bottom of the rim forwards.
2   Carefully remove the rubber dust excluder.
3   Undo and remove the inner rim securing screws and draw the light unit forwards. Detach the three pin socket and remove the light unit.
4   Refitting the light unit is the reverse sequence to removal.

Headlight unit removal (UK models)

1 Removal of outer rim securing screw

2 Removal of inner rim securing screws

3 Lifting out headlight unit

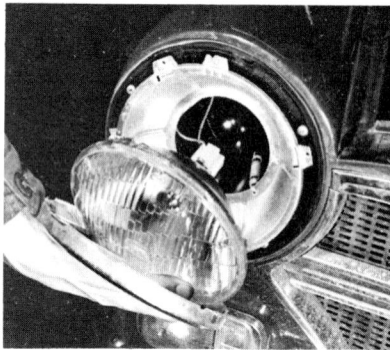

4 Headlight rim, light unit and body

5 Detaching multi pin connector from rear of light

Ensure the registers moulded on the rear edge of the unit engages in the slots in the rear shell.

North American models

1 Release the retaining screw at the bottom of the rim, ease the rim up whilst lifting the bottom of the rim forwards.
2 Carefully remove the rubber dust excluder.
3 Slacken the three crosshead screws securing the light unit retaining rim and turn the rim anticlockwise to remove. Do not forget to support the light unit lens. Detach the three pin plug from the rear of the light unit.
4 Refitting the light unit is the reverse sequence to removal.

LHD and European models

Except Europe and North America

1 The headlight units fitted to these models are of the double filament bulb type.
2 To remove the light unit for bulb replacement unscrew the rim retaining screw, ease the rim up whilst lifting the bottom of the rim forwards.
3 Carefully remove the rubber dust excluder.
4 Press the light unit inwards against the tension of the springs and turn it in an anti-clockwise direction until the heads of the screws can pass through the enlarged ends of the keyhole slots in the light rim.
5 The light unit may now be drawn forwards to expose the wiring and bulb.

European type

The headlights fitted to LHD models for use in European countries are fitted with special front lenses giving an asymmetrical light beam to the right-hand side.

The bulb is released from the reflector by withdrawing the three pin socket and pinching the two ends of the wire retaining clip to clear the bulb flange.

When replacing the bulb ensure the rectangular pip on the

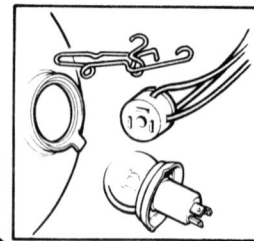

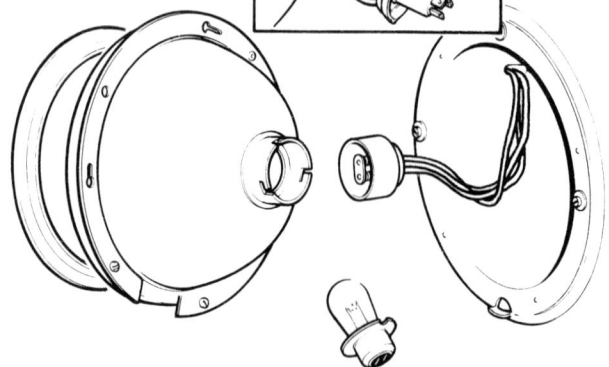

Fig. 10.17. Headlight unit - LHD except Europe and North America. Inset shows European type bulb and socket (Sec. 40)

bulb flange engages in the reflector seating.

Replace the spring clip with its coils resting in the base of the bulb flange and engaging the two retaining lugs on the reflector seating.

LHD (except Europe and North America)

Access to the bulb is obtained in the same manner as that

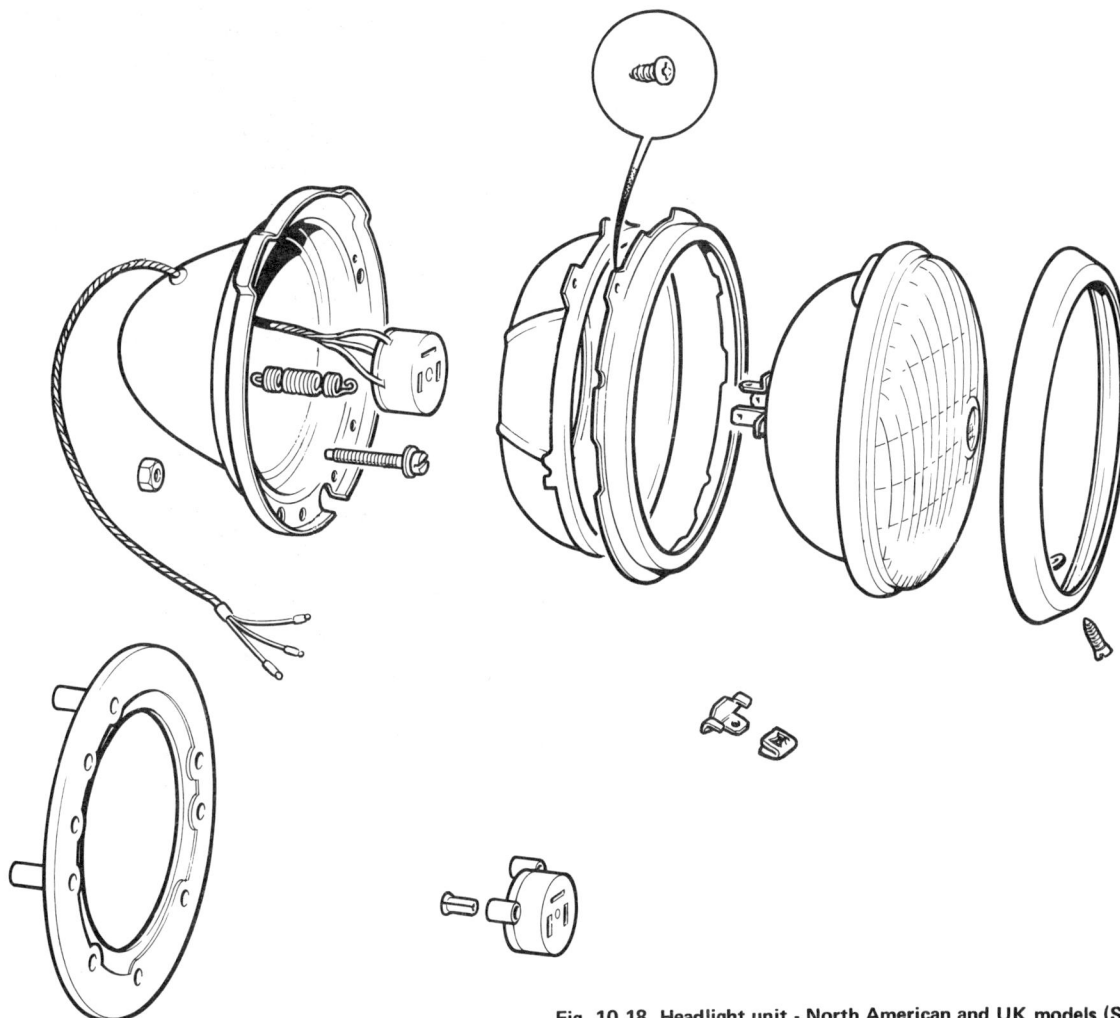

Fig. 10.18. Headlight unit - North American and UK models (Sec. 40)

described for the 'European type' headlights.

Twist the back shell anticlockwise and pull it off. The bulb can then be withdrawn from its holder.

Refitting the bulb is the reverse sequence to removal.

41 Headlight beam - adjustment

The headlights may be adjusted for both vertical and horizontal beam positions by two screws, one at the top, and one at the side, of each light unit.

They should be set so that on full or high beam, the beams are set slightly below parallel with a level road surface. Do not forget that the beam position is affected by how the car is normally loaded for night driving and set the beams with the car loaded to this position.

Although this adjustment can be approximately set at home it is recommended that this be left to a local garage who will have the necessary equipment to do the job more accurately.

42 Side and front flasher bulbs - removal and replacement

Austin, Morris, Wolseley, Riley

1 To gain access to the side and front flashing direction indicator bulbs undo and remove the screws that secure the light lens to the light body and lift away the lens.

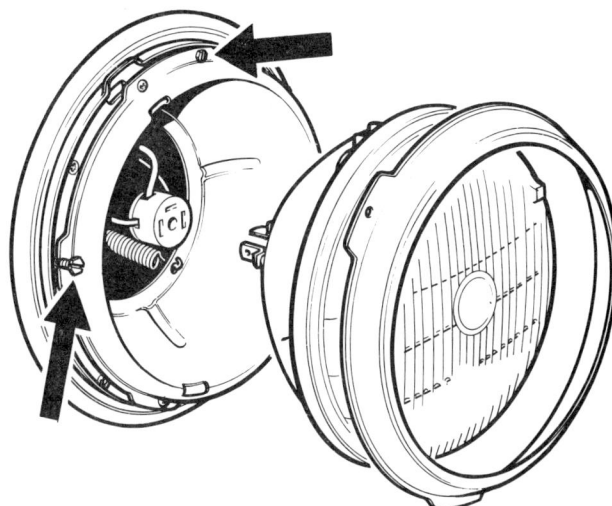

Fig. 10.19. Headlight unit adjustment screws (arrowed) (Sec. 41)

2 Each bulb is retained by a bayonet fixing so to remove a bulb push in slightly and rotate in an anticlockwise direction.

3 Refitting is the reverse sequence to removal. Take care not to overtighten the two lens retaining screws as the lenses can be easily cracked.

MG

1 To gain access to the side and front flashing direction indicator bulbs, press the cover inwards and turn anticlockwise to release the cover locating tongues from the retaining catches.
2 The bulbs are the same as for the other models. Refer to paragraph 2, of the previous sub-Section for information.

Princess

1 To gain access to the side and front flashing direction indication bulbs, undo and remove the screw retaining the plated rim and lens. Lift away the rim and lens.
2 The sidelight bulb is of the capless type whilst the direction indicator bulb is of the bayonet fixing type.
3 To remove a capless bulb simply pull from the contacts, and for a bayonet fixing type, push in slightly and rotate in an anticlockwise direction.
4 Refitting is the reverse sequence to removal.

43 Stop, tail and rear flasher bulbs - removal and replacement

1100 Mk 1 and all Countryman/Traveller models

1 The tail light bulbs are of the double filament type.
2 Access to the bulbs is gained from inside the luggage compartment. On MG and Wolseley models the floor panel and side trim must first be removed.
3 Pull the bulb holder from its socket in the rear of the light body.
4 Each bulb is retained by a bayonet fixing (offset pins are used for the stop/tail light bulb) so to remove a bulb push in slightly and rotate in an anticlockwise direction.
5 Should it be necessary to remove the light body unscrew and remove the three retaining nuts from their studs. Lift away the light body.
6 To renew the lenses remove the three screws securing the upper lens and the two screws securing the lower lens and lift away the lens.
7 Refitting in all cases is the reverse sequence to removal.

1100 Mk II and 1300 Saloon models

1 To gain access to the bulbs undo and remove the two external screws securing the lens to the light body. Lift away the lens. (photo).
2 For bulb removal refer to paragraph 4, of the previous sub-Section.
3 Should it be necessary to remove the light body remove the interior side trim, then undo and remove the two securing nuts from their studs. Lift away the light body.
4 Refitting in all cases is the reverse sequence to removal. Take care not to overtighten the lens securing screws as it is easy to crack the lens.

Repeater wing light

Undo and remove the two screws that secure the lens to the wing. Lift away the lens and unclip the festoon bulb.

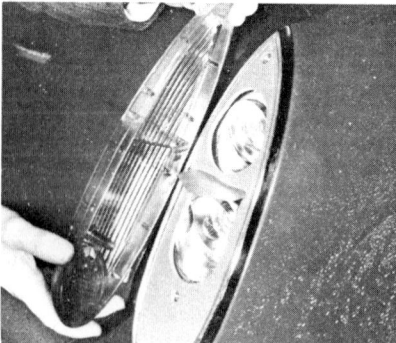

44 Rear number plate light bulb - removal and replacement

Austin, Riley and Princess models

1 The number plate is illuminated by a separate light with twin bulbs. (photo).
2 To remove the cover, undo and remove the two securing screws and lift away the cover which will give access to the bulbs.
3 The bulb is simply rotated in an anticlockwise direction to release the bayonet fitting.
4 Refitting is the reverse sequence to removal.

Morris and MG models

1 The number plate is illuminated by a separate light with one bulb.
2 To remove the cover unscrew the two retaining screws and lift off the cover.
3 The bulb is simply rotated in an anticlockwise direction to release the bayonet fitting.
4 Refitting is the reverse sequence to removal.

Wolseley models

1 The rear number plate is illuminated by two separate lights with twin bulbs.
2 Access to the bulbs is obtained by unscrewing the one slotted screw and lifting away the dowel cover and glass.
3 The bulb is simply rotated in an anticlockwise direction to release the bayonet fitting.
4 Refitting is the reverse sequence to removal.

45 Interior light bulb - renewal

Austin, Morris, Wolseley, Riley and MG

1 The interior light is located at the top of the centre door pillar. The light has a switch incorporated in it and an automatic switch is fitted to each front foor pillar and also to each rear door pillar on Riley and Wolseley 1300 Mk II models. The Countryman/Traveller models have an additional interior light which is controlled manually by a switch in the light body.(photo).
2 To gain access to the festoon type bulb gently squeeze the plastic cover to release the four small tongues and lift away the cover.
3 To remove the bulb simply detach from the spring contacts.
4 Refitting the bulb and cover is the reverse sequence to removal.

Princess

1 To gain access to the bulb undo and remove the two screws that secure the cover to the light body. Lift away the cover.
2 To remove the bulb simply detach from the spring contacts.
3 Refitting the bulb and cover is the reverse sequence to removal.

43.1 1100 Mk II and 1300 Saloon. Removal of rear light assembly lens

44.1 Morris and MG rear number plate light

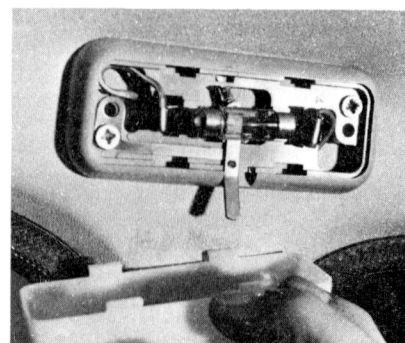

45.1 Interior light with cover removed

46 Fog light bulb - removal and replacement

1 This Section is applicable to Princess models only.
2 Access to the light bulb is obtained by slackening the clamp screw at the bottom of the unit and withdrawing the light unit.
3 Carefully lift the bulb retaining clip and remove the bulb from its holder.
4 Refitting the bulb is the reverse sequence to removal but the following two additional points should be noted:
a) Ensure the slot in the bulb disc engages with the projection in the holder.
b) When refitting the light unit make sure that the lugs are correctly positioned in the light shell before attempting to tighten the light unit clamp screw.

47 Panel and warning light bulbs - removal and replacement

All Mk I models - (In all cases disconnect the battery).
Morris
1 Undo and remove the four crosshead screws securing the instrument cowling and lift away the cowling.
2 Undo and remove the three crosshead screws that secure the instrument panel to the fascia and carefully ease the instrument panel forwards.
3 The relevant bulb holder may now be pulled out from the rear of the instrument panel.
4 Refitting the bulb, instrument panel and cowling is the reverse sequence to removal.

Austin and MG
Access to the panel and warning lights is gained from under the fascia by withdrawing the push-in type holders from the rear of the instrument panel.

Wolseley, Riley, MG and GT (positive earth)
1 Carefully remove the access hole cover from within the glovebox and then working through the aperture pull the bulb holders that are within reach from the rear of the instrument or panel.
2 To gain access to the remaining holders it is necessary to remove the instrument panel. First remove the ashtray and ashtray illumination light (when fitted).
3 Release the ashtray holder clamp wing nut and lift away the clamp and ashtray holder.
4 Remove the ignition switch escutcheon or chrome screw.
5 Carefully pull the instrument panel rearwards as far as the steering column will allow. Access may now be gained to the remaining bulb holders.
6 Reassembly in all cases is the reverse sequence to removal.

Princess
1 To gain access to the panel and warning lights it is necessary to remove the fascia panel. First detach the choke control cable and then remove the choke control bracket.
2 Unscrew the ignition/starter and wiper/washer switch bezels and push out the switches.
3 Undo and remove the wing nut located directly below and behind the ball mounted air duct on the driver's side.
4 Remove the glovebox lid and self-tapping screws securing the glovebox to the fascia board.
5 Undo and remove the wing nut located directly below and behind the ball mounted duct on the passenger's side. Also remove the centre wing nuts which are on either side of the ashtray.
6 Remove the steering inner column clamp bolt and disconnect the wiring from behind the fascia. Note that on earlier models it is necessary to release the outer column to body cross-member bracket. On later models fitted with a steering lock extract the horizontal shear bolt which clamps the outer column and completley remove the steering column assembly.
7 Carefully pull the fascia board forwards at the bottom and lift it away from the fascia surround.

8 The bulb holders can then be pulled out from the rear of the instrument panel.
9 Refitting and reassembly is the reverse sequence to removal. Refer to Chapter 11, for additional information on refitting the steering column.

Mk II and Mk III models
This sub-Section is applicable to 1100 Mk II and Mk III and all 1300 models. (In all cases disconnect the battery).

Austin and Morris Super De-luxe and GT (negative earth)
Access to the relevant bulb is gained by pulling the appropriate bulb holder from the rear of the instrument or instrument panel. Unscrew the bulb from its holder.

Austin and Morris GT (positive earth)
Refer to the instructions for Mk I models.

Wolseley, Riley, MG and Princess
Refer to the instructions for the Mk I models.

Austin and Morris De-Luxe
Undo and remove the four screws securing the fascia panel and pull forwards to allow the speedometer head to be withdrawn sufficiently to enable the necessary holder to be pulled from the rear of the speedometer head. To remove the bulb twist and pull from its holder.
Refitting and reassembly is the reverse sequence to removal.

48 Switches - removal and replacement

All Mk I models (In all cases disconnect the battery).
Lighting, panel and windscreen wiper (toggle type)
1 Disconnect the Lucar connectors, unscrew the fixing nut and remove the switch assembly complete with its 'D' shaped locking washer.
2 On MG, Wolseley and Riley models it is necessary to remove the instrument panel assembly and on Morris 1100 Mk 1 models the instrument cowl and panel to gain access to the switches. Refer to Chapter 12, for full information.
3 Refitting a switch is the reverse sequence to removal.

Ignition/Starter
1 To gain access to the switch assembly it is necessary to remove the instrument panel assembly on all MG, Riley and Wolseley models, on Austin models the top fascia panel and Morris models the instrument cowl and panel. Full information will be found in Chapter 12.
2 On Vanden Plas models the switch can be reached from beneath the fascia panel.
3 Disconnect the Lucar connectors, unscrew the fixing nut, and remove the switch assembly complete with its 'D' shaped washer.
4 To remove the locking barrel from the switch body insert the key and turn to the 'ignition on' position. This will align the barrel retaining plunger with the small hole in the switch body.
5 Using a small screwdriver or carpenters awl depress the plunger and withdraw the barrel complete with key.
6 Refitting and reassembly in all cases is the reverse sequence to removal.

Headlight dip switch
1 Undo and remove the screws securing the switch to the floor and withdraw the switch assembly.
2 Note the cable connections and disconnect from the switch.
3 Refitting the switch is the reverse sequence to removal.

Steering column switch
1 Undo and remove the switch cover securing screws and lift away the cover.
2 Make a note of the cable connections and disconnect the

switch wiring from the snap connectors located behind the fascia panel.

3   Undo and remove the switch securing screws and remove the switch.

4   Refitment of the switch is the reverse sequence to removal but the following additional points should be noted:

a) Make sure the locating peg on the switch fits into the hole/slot in the outer column.

b) Ensure the trip stud is parallel to the axis of the inner column and that it makes full width contact with the cancelling tongue of the switch.

c) On early models, if re-alignment is necessary, slacken the column bracket screws and slide the outer column upwards or downwards as necessary.

d) On later models, if re-alignment is necessary, slacken the outer column horizontal clamp screw and adjust the position of the outer column to obtain a gap of 0.125 in (3 mm) between the nacelle and lower boss of the steering wheel.

1100 mk II and 1300 models - (In all cases disconnect the battery for safety reasons)
Lighting and windscreen wiper Austin and Morris

1   These models are fitted with wide rocker type switches and to remove these a special tool part number '18G1145' is required.

2   To gain access to the switches remove the top fascia panel on Super De-luxe and USA models and the fascia panel from the parcel tray trim on De-luxe models. Full information will be found in Chapter 12.

3   Working behind the instrument panel slide Service tool '18G1145/1' over the tongues of each bezel so as to release the bezel and switch assembly.

4   If necessary separate the bezel from the switch using Service tool '18G1145/2'.

5   Refitting the switch is the reverse sequence to removal.

Wolseley, Riley and MG 1300 mk II

1   These models are fitted with narrow rocker type switches.

2   To gain access to the switches remove the instrument panel as described in Chapter 12.

3   Note the electrical cable connections and detach from the switch.

4   Carefully depress the spring clips, remove the steel retaining plates and withdraw each switch from the front of the fascia.

5   Refitting the switch is the reverse sequence to removal.

Vanden Plas, Wolseley, Riley and MG 1100 mk II and 1300 models

For full information refer to the first sub-Section that deals with Mk I models.

Ignition/Starter

1   To gain access to the switch assembly on Austin and Morris Super De-luxe models first remove the top fascia panel. On De-luxe models remove the fascia panel and pull the speedometer forwards. On all Wolseley, Riley and MG models remove the instrument panel. Full information will be found in Chapter 12.

2   On Vanden Plas models the switch is accessible from beneath the fascia panel.

3   Note their relative positions and then detach the leads from the switch assembly and then unscrew the switch assembly securing nuts.

4   The switch assembly and 'D' shaped washer may now be removed.

5   To dismantle the switch refer to the information given for the Mk I models.

6   Reassembly and refitting is the reverse sequence to removal.

Steering column switch

For full information, refer to the first sub-Section that deals with Mk I models.

49 Impulse type tachometer - fault diagnosis and rectification

The impulse type tachometer works from the ignition pulses given off by the coil. The impulse lead is connected in series between the coil and the ignition switch. (Fig. 10.20).

Incorrect readings, or no reading at all may be due to poor or broken wiring connections in the circuit or to the indicator head. It is also important to ensure that the impulse lead forms a symmetrical loop on the rear of the instrument as shown at 'A' in Fig. 10.20 and not tight against the plastic former.

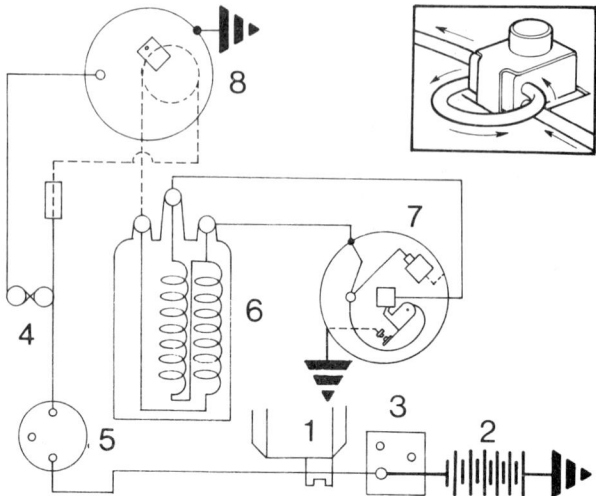

Fig. 10.20. Tachometer circuit (Sec. 49)

1 Control box	5 Ignition switch
2 Battery	6 Ignition coil
3 Starter solenoid	7 Distributor
4 A3-A4 fuse	8 Tachometer

Inset: The pulse lead assembly showing gentle radius loop

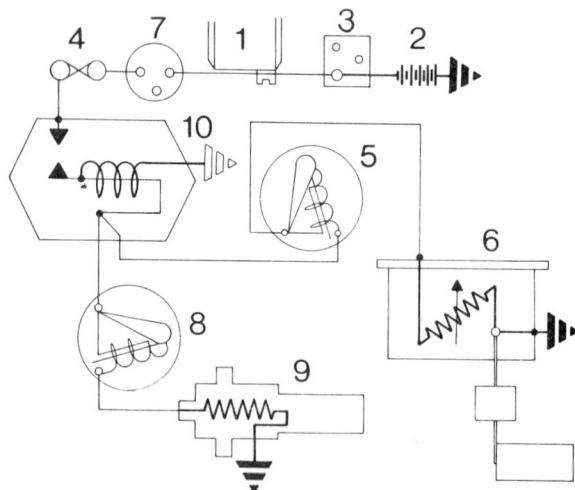

Fig. 10.21. Bi-metal resistance instrumentation circuit

1 Control box	6 Fuel tank unit
2 Battery (12 volt)	7 Ignition switch
3 Starter solenoid	8 Coolant temperature gauge
4 Fuse - A3-A4	9 Coolant temperature
5 Fuel gauge	transmitter
	10 Voltage stabiliser

50 Fuel and temperature gauges - fault diagnosis

1 The bi-metal resistance equipment for the fuel and temperature gauges comprises an indicator head and transmitter unit which are connected to a common voltage stabilizer.

2 The system by which the equipment functions is voltage sensitive and a voltage stabilizer is necessary to ensure a constant supply of a pre-determined voltage to the equipment.

3 If the system operation is suspect the units can be quickly tested using a test light and battery and also an accurate voltmeter.

4 Connect the voltmeter to the control box terminal 'B' and earth. With the engine stationary the reading should be 12 volts, and with it running at 1000 rpm 12-13 volts.

5 Systematically, check all connections for good contact and all wiring for continuity. Refer to the relevant wiring diagram at the end of this Chapter for guidance.

6 Check that the voltage stabilizer and transmitters are correctly earthed.

7 Disconnect the lead from the stabilizer to the gauge at the gauge and connect it to the voltmeter. The other meter terminal should be earthed. Switch on the ignition and after two minutes a reading of 10 volts should be obtained.

8 If the stabilizer is at fault is should be renewed. Ensure that the terminals 'B' and 'E' are uppermost and not exceeding an angle of 20° from the vertical.

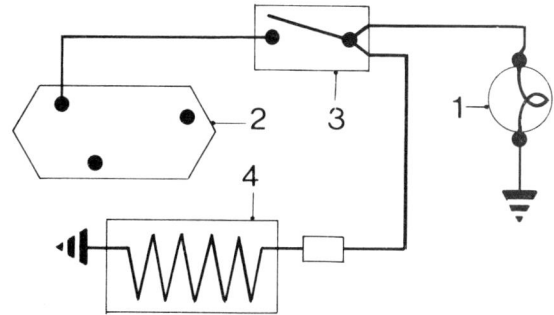

Fig. 10.22. Heated backlight circuit

1 *Warning light (when fitted)*
2 *Voltage stabiliser*
3 *Heated backlight switch*
4 *Heated backlight*

9 Test the gauges for continuity between terminals with the wiring disconnected. **Do not** short circuit a gauge to earth.

10 Check the transmitter(s) for continuity between the case and terminal with the lead disconnected. If the unit is faulty it must be renewed.

See next page for 'Fault diagnosis - electrical system'.

51 Fault diagnosis - electrical system

Symptom	Reason/s	Remedy
Starter motor fails to turn engine	Battery discharged	Charge battery
	Battery defective internally	Fit new battery
	Battery terminal leads loose or earth lead not securely attached to body	Check and tighten leads
	Loose or broken connections in starter motor circuit	Check all connections and tighten any that are loose. Renew all broken connections. Test and renew faulty components.
	Starter motor switch or solenoid faulty	
	Starter motor pinion jammed in mesh with flywheel gear ring	Disengage pinion by turning squared end of armature shaft
	Starter brushes badly worn, sticking, or brush wires loose	Examine brushes, replace as necessary, tighten down brush wires
	Commutator dirty, worn or burnt	Clean commutator, recut if badly burnt
	Starter motor armature faulty	Overhaul starter motor, fit new armature
	Field coils earthed	Overhaul starter motor
Starter motor turns engine very slowly	Battery in discharged condition	Charge battery
	Starter brushes badly worn, sticking, or brush wires loose	Examine brushes, replace as necessary, tighten down brush wires
	Loose wires in starter motor circuit	Check wiring and tighten as necessary
Starter motor operates without turning engine	Starter motor pinion sticking on the screwed sleeve	Remove starter motor, clean starter motor drive
	Pinion or flywheel gear teeth broken or worn	Fit new gear ring to flywheel, and new pinion to starter motor drive
Starter motor noisy or excessively rough engagement	Pinion or flywheel gear teeth broken or worn	Fit new gear teeth to flywheel, or new pinion to starter motor drive
	Starter drive main spring broken	Dismantle and fit new main spring
	Starter motor retaining bolts loose	Tighten starter motor securing bolts. Fit new spring washer if necessary.
Battery will not hold charge for more than a few days	Battery defective internally	Removal and fit new battery
	Electrolyte level too low or electrolyte too weak due to leakage	Top up electrolyte level to just above plates
	Plate separators no longer fully effective	Remove and fit new battery
	Battery plates severely sulphated	Remove and fit new battery
	Fan belt slipping	Check belt for wear, replace if necessary, and tighten
	Battery terminal connections loose or corroded	Check terminals for tightness, and remove all corrosion
	Dynamo or alternator not charging properly	Trace and rectify. Check terminals and wires. Take car to specialist.
	Short in lighting circuit causing continual battery drain	
	Regulator unit not working correctly	Take car to specialist
Ignition light fails to go out, battery runs flat in a few days	Fan belt loose and slipping or broken	Check, replace and tighten as necessary
	Dynamo or alternator faulty	Repair dynamo or seek specialist advice (alternator)

Failure of individual electrical equipment to function correctly is dealt with alphabetically, item-by-item, under the headings listed below.

Symptom	Reason/s	Remedy
Fuel gauge gives no reading	Fuel tank empty!	Fill fuel tank
	Electric cable between tank sender unit and gauge earthed or loose	Check cable for earthing and joints for tightness
	Fuel gauge case not earthed	Ensure case is well earthed
	Fuel gauge supply cable interrupted	Check and replace cable if necessary
	Fuel gauge unit broken	Replace fuel gauge
Fuel gauge registers full all the time	Electric cable between tank unit and gauge broken or disconnected	Check over cable and repair as necessary
Horn operates all the time	Horn push either earthed or stuck down	Disconnect battery earth. Check and rectify source of trouble
	Horn cable to horn push earthed	Disconnect battery earth. Check and rectify source of trouble
Horn fails to operate	Blown fuse	Check and renew if broken. Ascertain cause
	Cable or cable connection loose, broken or disconnected	Check all connections for tightness and cables for breaks
	Horn has an internal fault	Remove and fit new horn

Key to wiring diagrams on pages 198 to 208

1	Dynamo or alternator	49	Reverse lamp switch **
2	Control box (except with 16ACR alternator)	50	Reverse lamp **
3	Battery (12 volt)	53	Foglamp(s) switch
4	Starter solenoid	54	RH foglamp
5	Starter motor	55	LH foglamp (Princess)
6	Lighting switch	56	Clock
7	Headlamp dip switch	57	Cigar lighter
8	RH headlamp	60	Radio *
9	LH headlamp	64	Bi-metal instrument voltage stabiliser
10	Main beam warning lamp	65	Luggage compartment lamp switch (Countryman/Traveller)
11	RH sidelamp		
12	LH sidelamp	66	Luggage compartment lamp (Countryman/Traveller)
13	Panel lamps switch (when fitted)		
14	Panel lamps	67	Line fuse (35 amp)
15	Number plate lamp(s)	75	Automatic transmission safety switch (when fitted)
16	RH stop and tail lamp	77	Electric windscreen washer (Princess)
17	LH stop and tail lamp	78	Windscreen washer switch (Export)
18	Stop lamp switch	81	Ashtray illumination lamp
19	Fuse unit (35 amp 1-2; 35 amp 3-4)	82	Panel lamp heater switch illumination **
20	Interior light(s)	83	Induction heater and thermostat **
21	RH door switch(es) (Combined with ignition	84	Suction chamber heater **
22	LH door switch(es) key buzzer - 1970 America)	94	Oil filter switch (early synchromesh models)
23	Horn(s)	95	Tachometer (Riley, MG 1300 Mk II and GT)
24	Horn push	99	Radiator badge lamp (Wolseley)
25	Flasher unit	105	Oil filter warning lamp (early synchromesh models)
26	Direction indicator, headlamp flasher, and dip switch	106	Rear interior lamp (Mk III Countryman/Traveller)
27	Direction indicator warning lamp(s)	110	RH repeater flasher (except America)
28	RH front flasher lamp	111	LH repeater flasher (except America)
29	LH front flasher lamp	115	Rear window demister switch *
30	RH rear flasher lamp	116	Rear window demister unit *
31	LH rear flasher lamp	118	Combined windscreen washer and wiper switch (Princess)
32	Heater or fresh-air motor switch **		
33	Heater or fresh air motor **	131	Combined reverse switch and automatic safety switch (when fitted)
34	Fuel gauge		
35	Fuel gauge tank unit	139	Alternative number plate lamp connections for Germany
36	Windscreen wiper switch (except Princess)		
37	Windscreen wiper motor	150	Rear window demist warning lamp *
38	Ignition/starter switch (combined with steering lock - certain models)	153	Hazard warning switch
		154	Hazard warning flasher unit
39	Ignition coil	159	Brake pressure warning lamp and lamp push (All Austin America)
40	Distributor		
41	Fuel pump	160	Brake pressure failure switch
42	Oil pressure switch (when fitted)	164	Ballast resistance or cable (except very early models)
43	Oil pressure gauge or warning lamp		
44	Ignition warning lamp	168	Ignition key warning buzzer
45	Speedometer	170	RH front marker lamp
46	Water temperature gauge (Except Austin/	171	LH front marker lamp (1970 Austin
47	Water temperature transmitter Morris De Luxe)	172	RH rear marker lamp America)
		173	LH rear marker lamp
48	Ammeter (Princess)		

Optional extra   ** Optional extra but standard on some models*

Cable colour code

N	Brown	P	Purple	W	White
U	Blue	G	Green	Y	Yellow
R	Red	LG	Light Green	B	Black

When a cable has two colour code letters the first denotes the main colour and the second denotes the tracer colour.

Wiring Diagrams — special note

For reasons of space, it has not been possible to include individual wiring diagrams for every model covered by this manual. We have provided eleven diagrams which cover a wide range of different models. Even if a diagram for your specific model is not included here you should find that one of the diagrams given is for a model of similar specification.

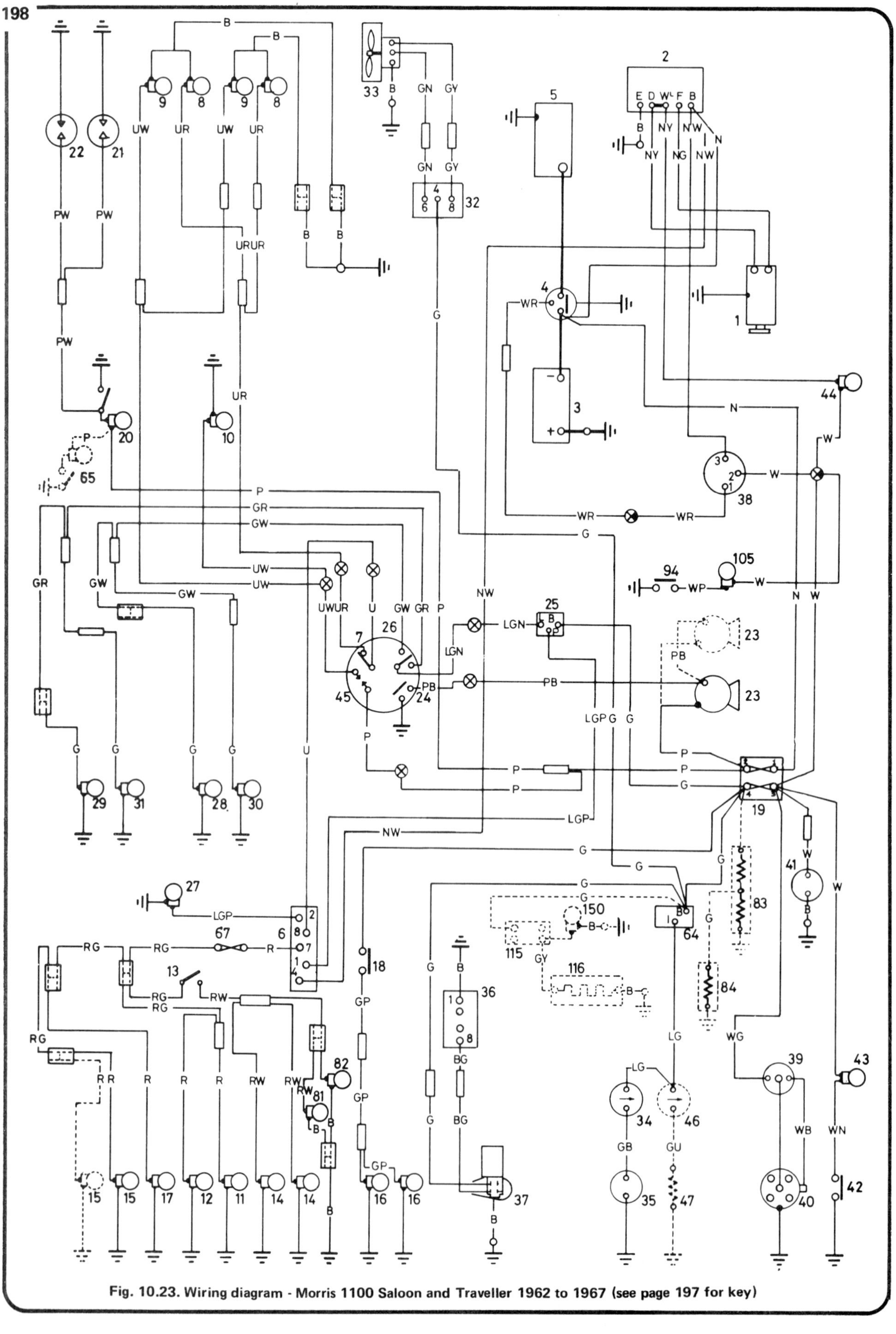

Fig. 10.23. Wiring diagram - Morris 1100 Saloon and Traveller 1962 to 1967 (see page 197 for key)

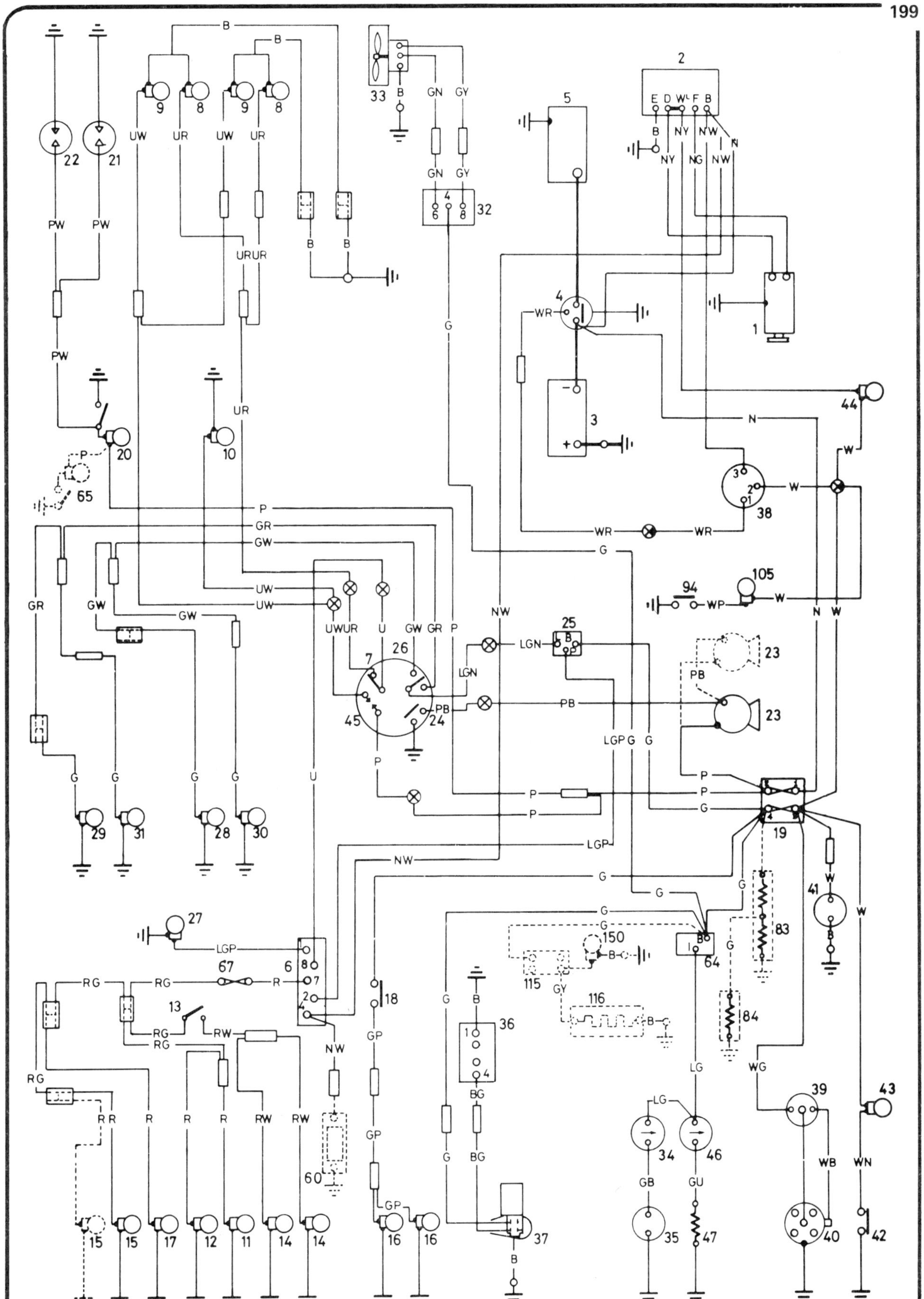

Fig. 10.24. Wiring diagram - Austin 1100 Saloon and Countryman 1963 to 1967 (see page 197 for key)

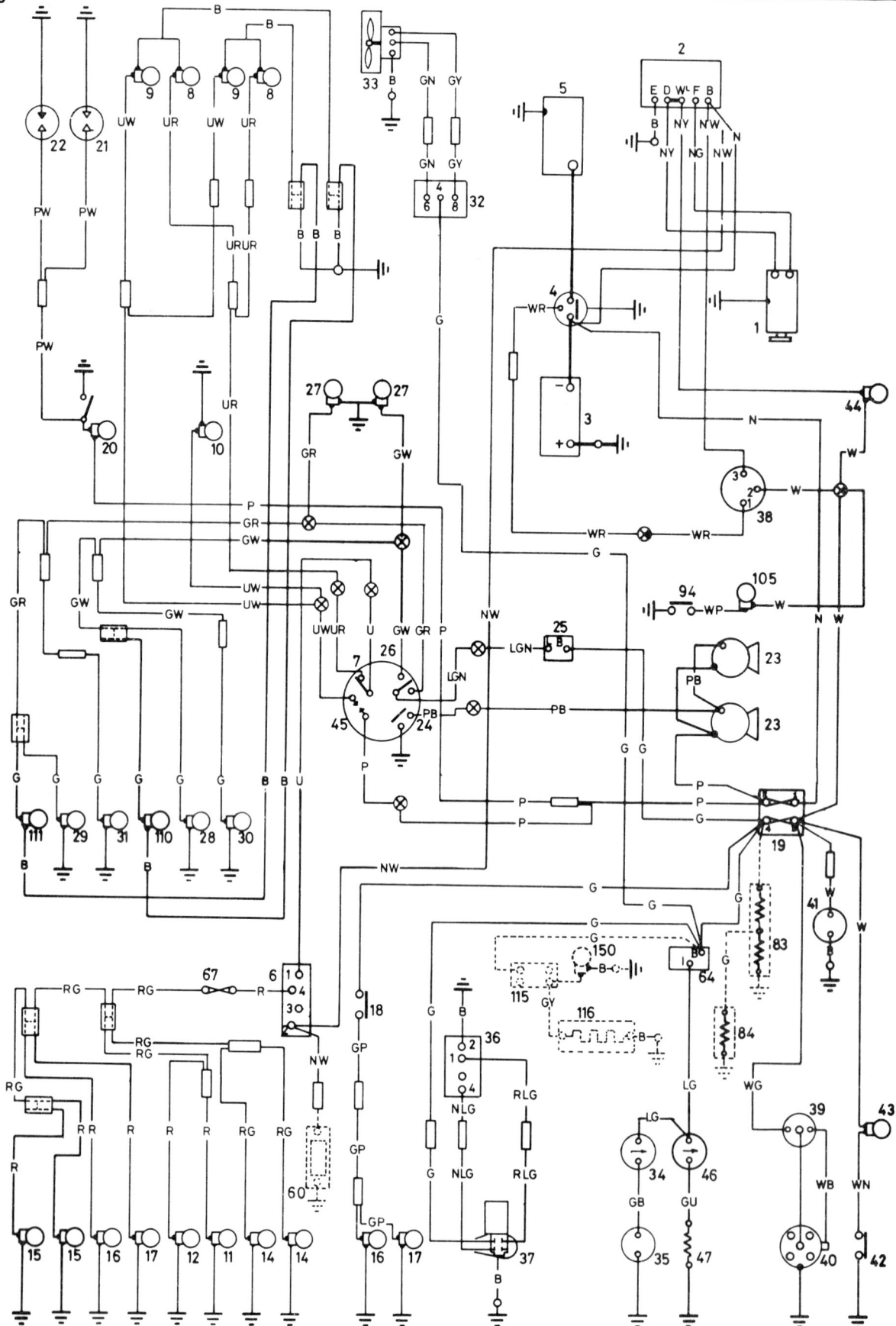

Fig. 10.25. Wiring diagram - Austin and Morris 1100 Mk II and 1300 Super De Luxe 1967 to 1971 (see page 197 for key)

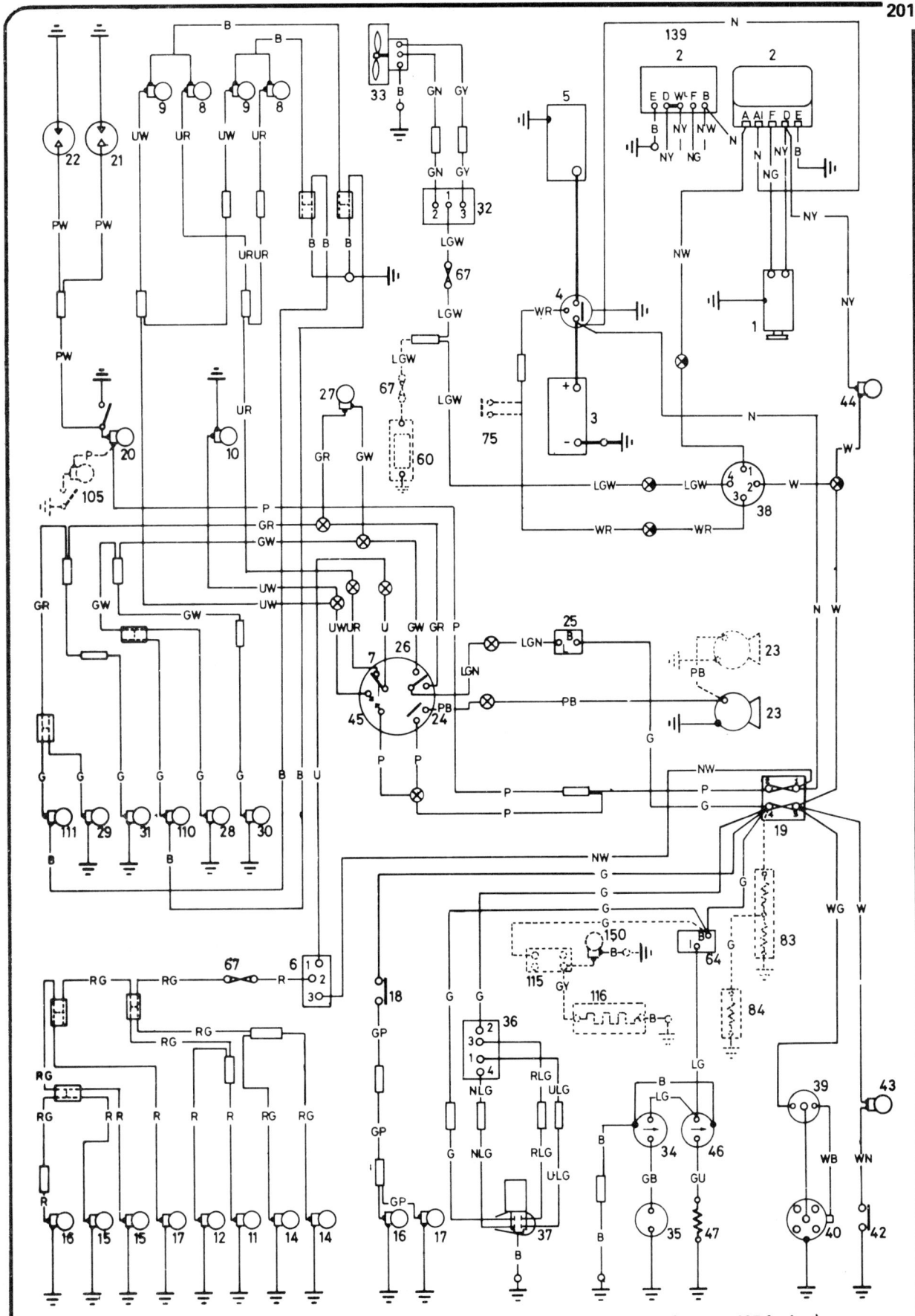

Fig. 10.26. Wiring diagram - Austin and Morris 1100 and 1300 Mk III 1971 onwards (see page 197 for key)

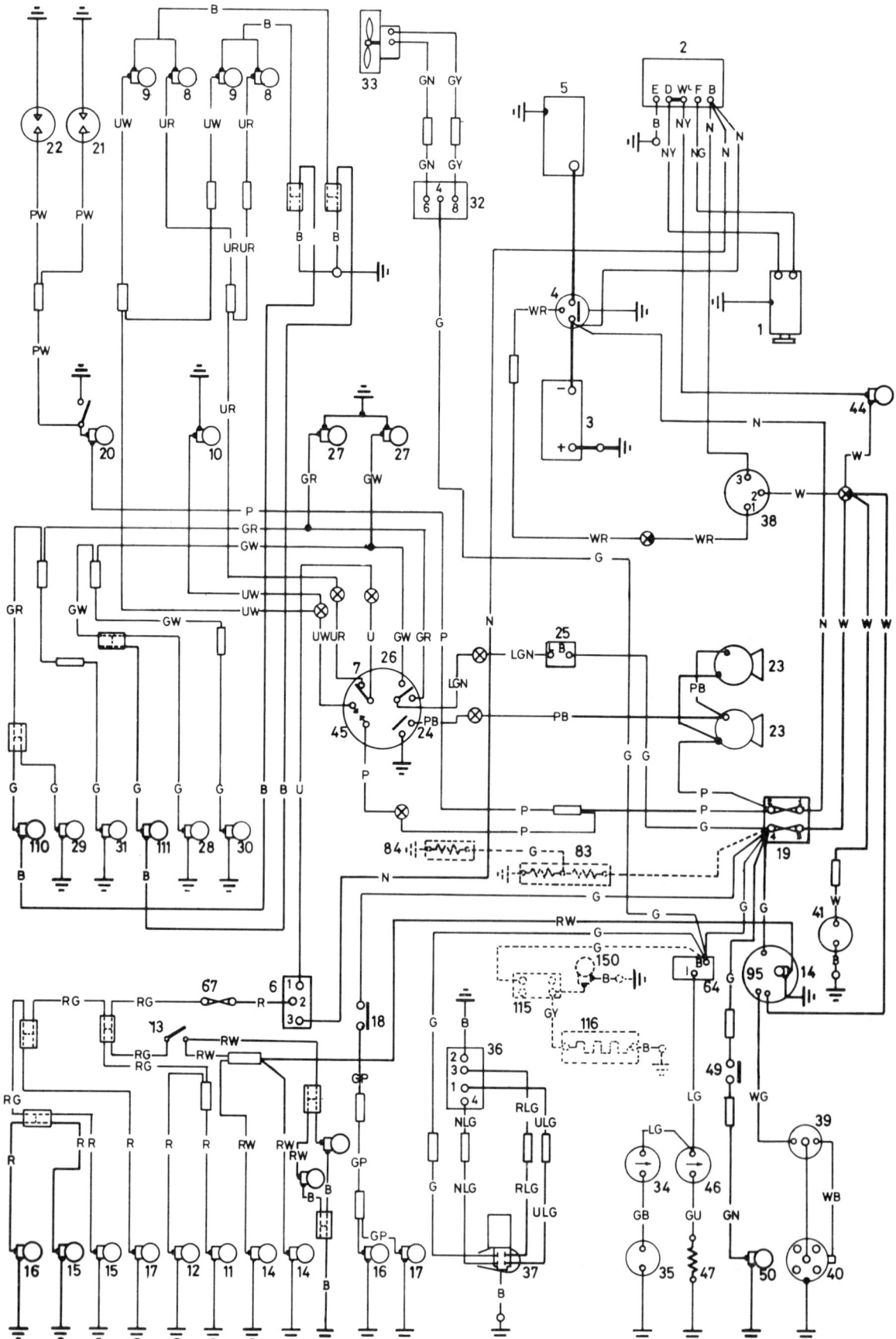

Fig. 10.27. Wiring diagram - Austin and Morris 1300GT 1969 to 1971 (see page 197 for key)

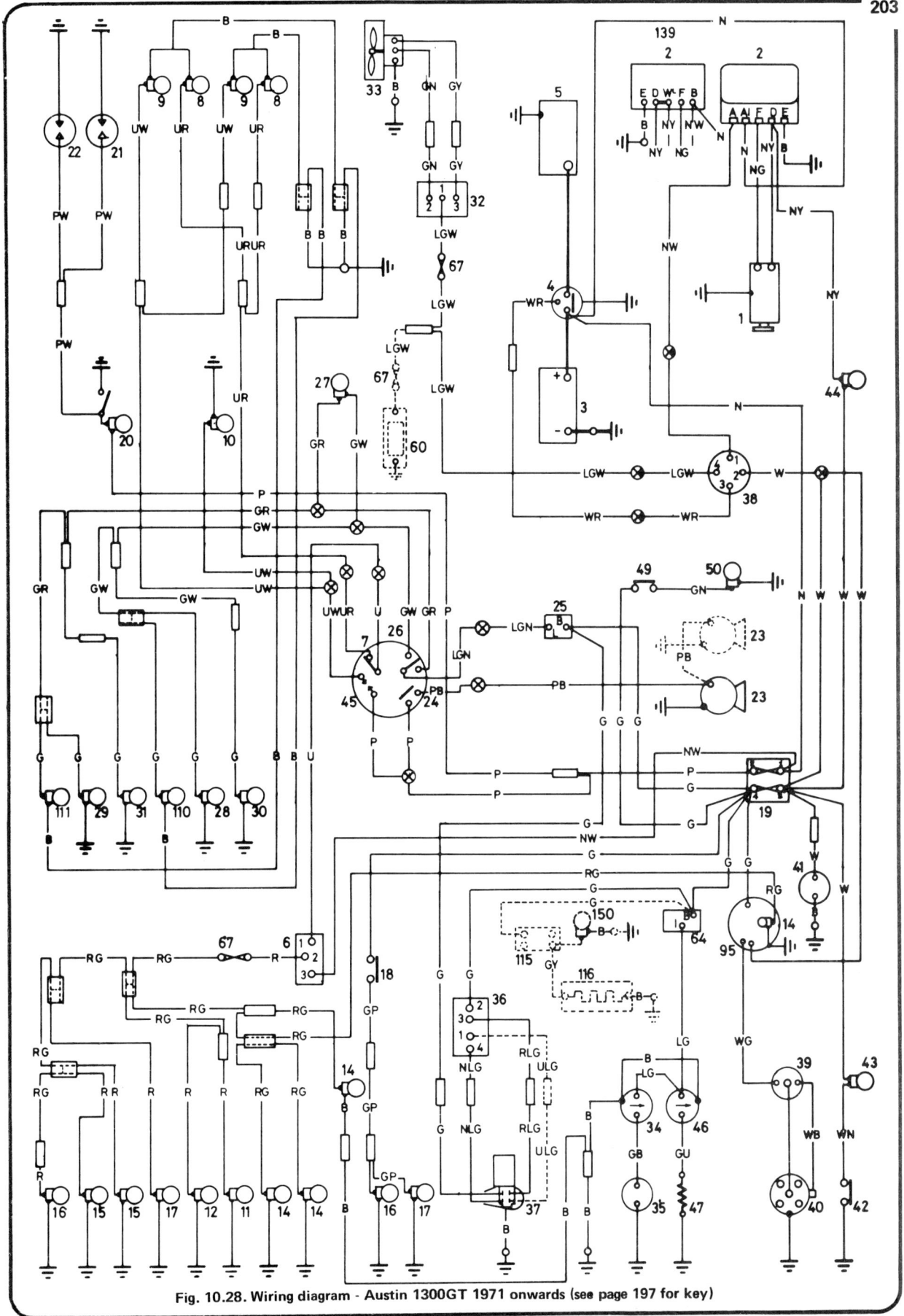

Fig. 10.28. Wiring diagram - Austin 1300GT 1971 onwards (see page 197 for key)

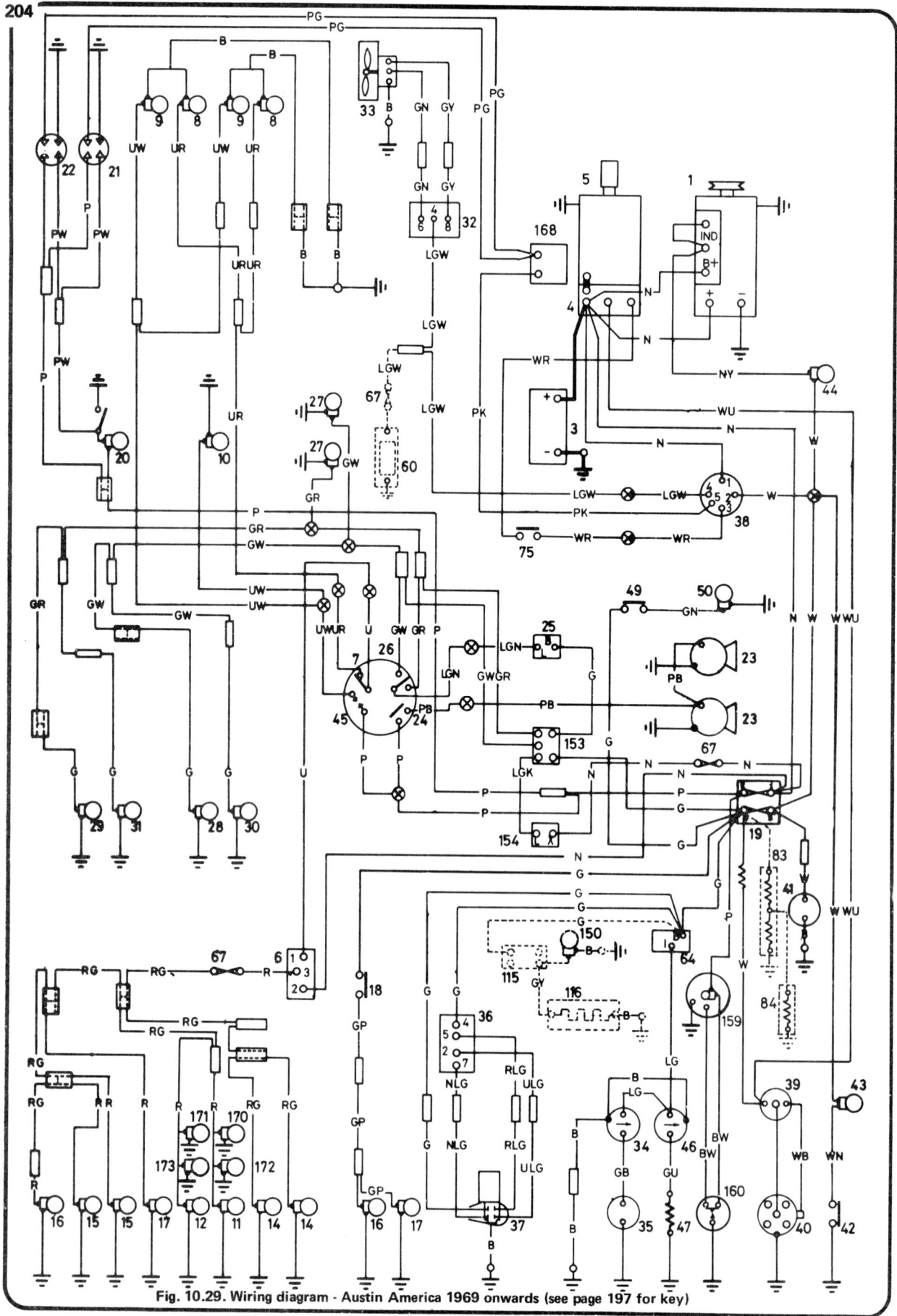

Fig. 10.29. Wiring diagram - Austin America 1969 onwards (see page 197 for key)

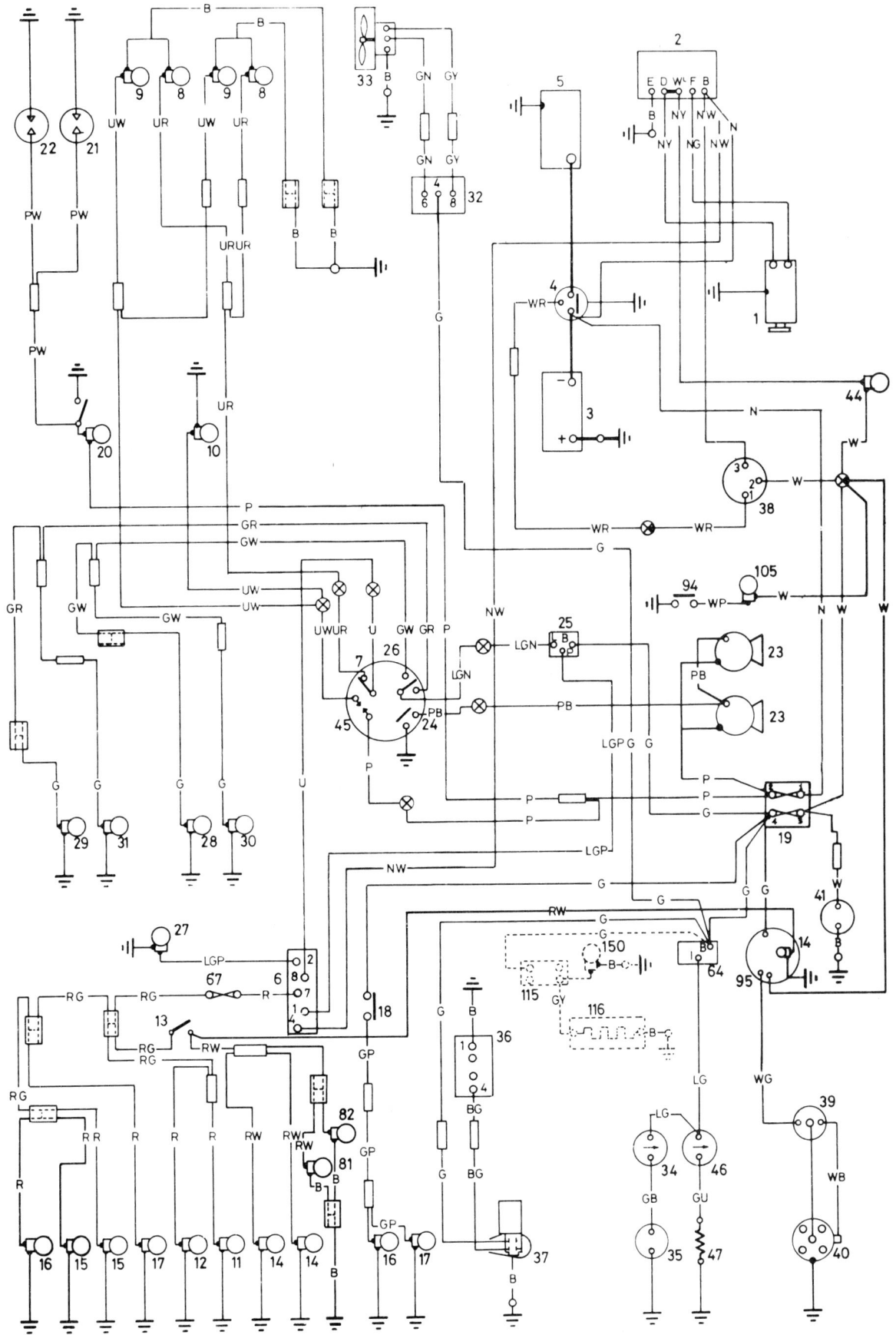

Fig. 10.30. Wiring diagram - Riley Kestrel 1965 to 1967 (see page 197 for key)

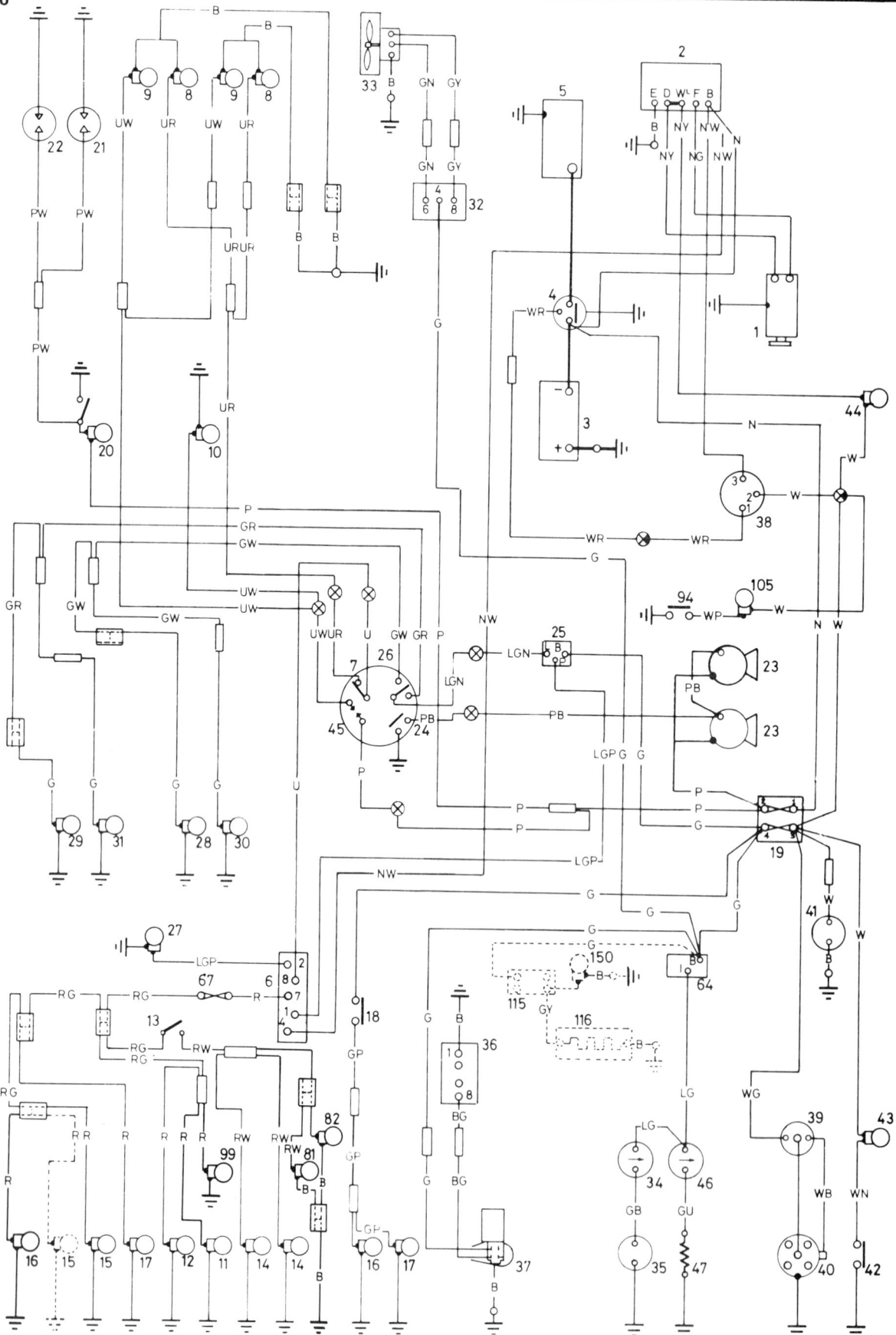

Fig. 10.31. Wiring diagram - Wolseley and MG 1100 1962 to 1965 and 1967 (see page 197 for key)

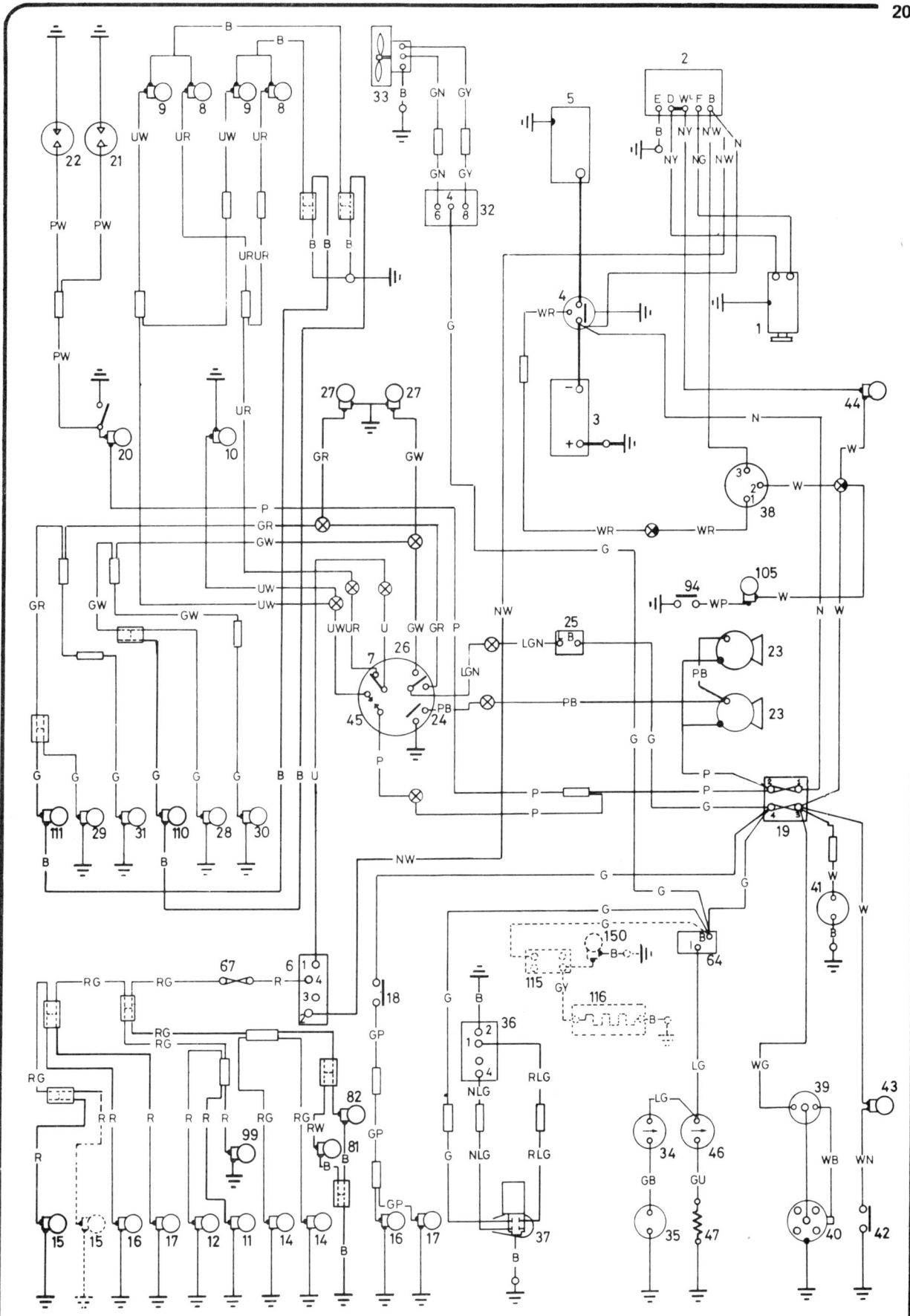

Fig. 10.32. Wiring diagram - Wolseley and MG 1100 Mk II and 1300 1967 to 1968 (see page 197 for key)

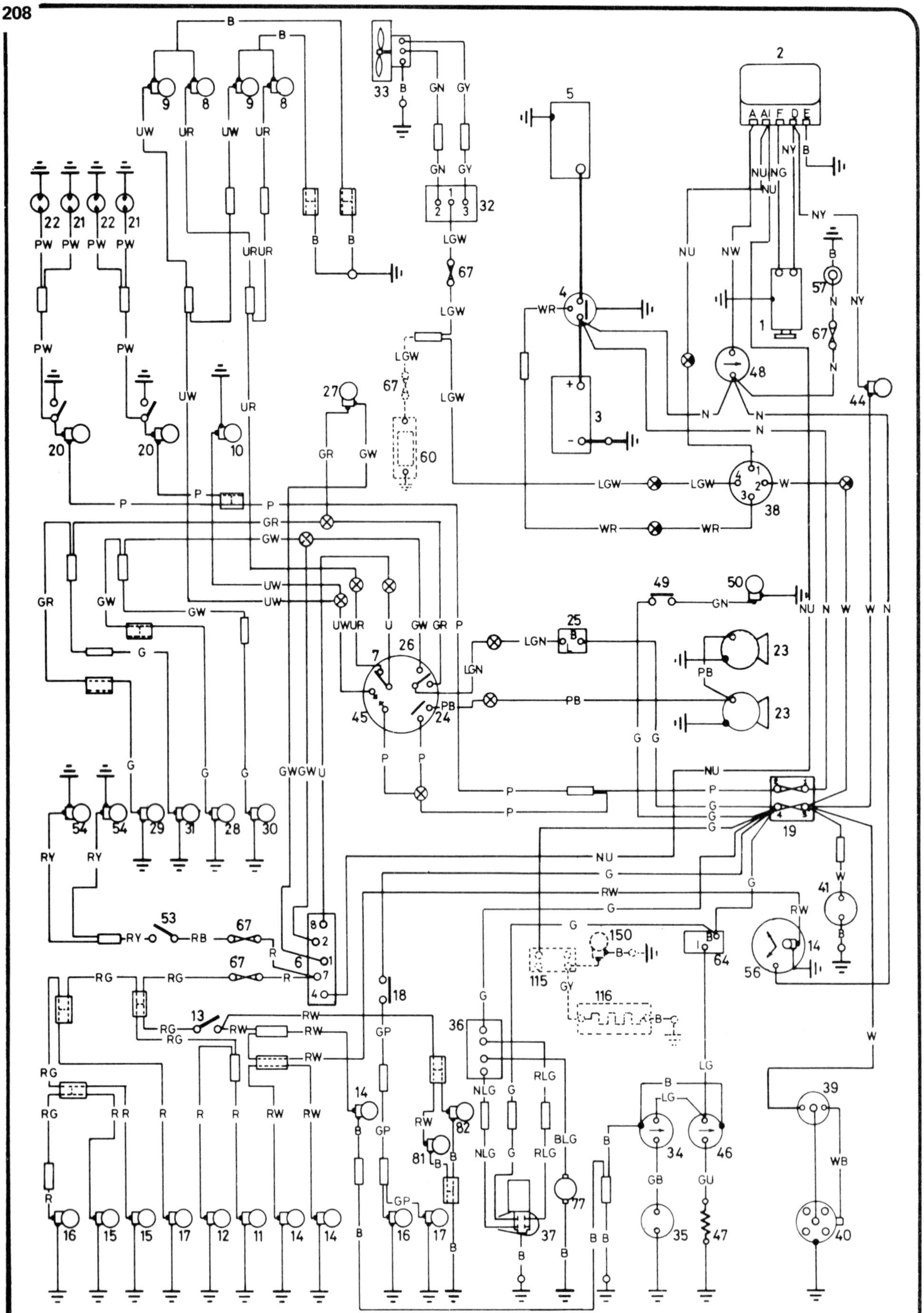

Fig. 10.33. Wiring diagram - Vanden Plas Princess 1300 1971 onwards (see page 197 for key)

Chapter 11 Suspension and steering

Contents

Specifications

Front suspension:

Type:	Independent by interconnected hydrolastic displacers and unequal length arms
Dampers	None - Suspension self-damping
Castor angle	5½° positive - Static unladen condition
Camber angle...	¾° positive - Static unladen condition
King pin inclination	10° - Static unladen condition
Toe-out	1/16 in. (1.59 mm) - Static unladen condition
Track	4 ft 3½ in. (1.297 m) - Static unladen condition

Rear suspension:

Type:	Independent by interconnected hydrolastic displacers, radius arms, and anti-roll bar
Dampers	None - Suspension self-damping
Camber angle	1° positive - Static unladen condition
Toe-out	1/8 in. (3.18 mm)
Track	4 ft 2 7/8 in. - Static unladen condition

Steering:

Type:	Rack and pinion
Steering wheel turns - lock to lock	3 1/8 in.
Steering wheel diameter	16¼ in. (41.2 cm)
Steering lock angles of wheels	Outer wheel: 19° Inner wheel: 20°
Turning circle	34 ft 9 in. (10.59 m)

Wheels:

Type:	4J x 12—Ventilated disc

Tyres:

Size	5.50 by 12
Pressures (Normal):	
Front	28 lb/sq in. (1.97 Kg/cm^2)
Rear	24 lb/sq in. (1.7 Kg/cm^2)

Wing heights and fluid pressures:

	front wing height*	approximate fluid pressure
Austin, Morris, Wolseley, Riley, and MG 1100 Mk I	13 5/8 $\pm$ 3/8 in. 346 $\pm$ 9 mm	205 lb/sq in. 14.41 kg/cm^2
MG (Normalair)	13 5/8 $\pm$ 3/8 in. 346 $\pm$ 9 mm	220 lb/sq in. 15.46 kg/cm^2

	front wing height*	approximate fluid pressure
Princess 1100	13 5/8 ± 3/8 in. 346 ± 9 mm	230 lb/sq in. 16.17 kg/cm^2
Austin and Morris 1100 Mk II and 1300 with arch rear spring ...	14 ± 3/8 in. 355 ± 9 mm	195 lb/sq in. 13.71 kg/cm^2
Austin and Morris 1100 Mk II and 1300 ... . (Manual and Automatic) and Wolseley, Riley ... ... and MG 1300 Manual	13 5/8 ± 3/8 in. 346 ± 9 mm	225 lb/sq in. 15.82 kg/cm^2
Austin and Morris 1300 GT	13 ± 3/8 in. 330 ± 9 mm	205 lb/sq in. 14.41 kg/cm^2
Austin America Manual and Automatic	13 5/8 ± 3/8 in. 346 ± 9 mm	220 lb/sq in. 15.46 kg/cm^2
Wolseley, Riley, and MG 1300 Automatic	13 5/8 ± 3/8 in. 346 ± 9 mm	212 lb/sq in. 14.9 kg/cm^2
Princess 1300	13 5/8 ± 3/8 in. 346 ± 9 mm	245 lb/sq in. 17.22 kg/cm^2

Hub centre to underside of wing

Torque wrench settings:

	lb f ft	Kg f m
Steering lever to hub bolts	30 to 35	4.15 to 4.8
Steering lever ball joint nut	25	3.5
Steering knuckle ball pin bottom nut	35 to 40	4.8 to 5.5
Steering knuckle ball pin top nut	35 to 40	4.8 to 5.5
Steering knuckle ball pin housing	70	9.6
Front hub nut (driveshaft)	150 min. (align to next split pin hole)	20.75 min.
Rear suspension anti-roll bar fixing bolts	70	9.6
Rear suspension stub axle nut	60 (align to next split pin hole)	8.3
Rear suspension radius arm shaft pivot nuts	28 to 30	3.9 to 4.15
Front suspension upper arm pivot pin nut	35 to 40	4.8 to 5.5
Front suspension lower arm pivot pin nuts	35 to 40	4.8 to 5.5
Road wheel nuts	42	5.8
Steering-wheel nut	32 to 37	4.4 to 5.1
Steering-column clamp bolt	8 to 9	1.1 to 1.25
Steering pinion bearing cover bolt	12 to 18	1.7 to 2.5
Steering pinion damper cover bolt	12 to 18	1.7 to 2.5
Subframe mounting bracket bolts—5/16 in. UNF	15	2.1
Tie-rod nut: Welded disc type	35 to 40	4.8 to 5.5
Shouldered end type	30 to 35	4.15 to 4.8
Disc to hub	38 - 45	5.3 - 6.2
Backplate retaining bolts	25	3.5
Front swivel hub to caliper	45 - 50	6.2 - 6.9

1 General description

The hydrolastic suspension makes use of a special displacer unit at each wheel. The front and rear displacer units are connected together by tubes and piping.

Made from sheet steel and rubber, each displacer unit comprises a lower and upper chamber housing, and a nylon re-inforced rubber diaphragm which is connected to the top suspension arm by way of a strut and tapered piston. Damper valves in the top of the fluid separating chamber perform the function done by separate telescopic dampers on other cars.

The displacer units are fitted with a mixture of water, alcohol, and anti-corrosive additives and work in the following manner.

When either of the front wheels hits a bump the strut attached to the top suspension link forces the piston up, which displaces the diaphragm. This increases the pressure in the unit and so forces some of the fluid from the lower to the upper chamber.

This causes the rubber spring to deflect and to transfer some of the liquid via the interconnecting pipe, to the rear displacer unit on the same side. As the fluid enters the rear top chamber it pushes down on the piston which results in the rear of the car being raised. This all occurs far more quickly than it takes to describe.

The same process happens when a rear wheel meets a bump,

but in reverse, as the fluid is now forced into one of the front displacer units. In this way it is possible to obtain a very comfortable ride with the minimum of roll and pitching.

Rack and pinion steering is fitted with $3^{1/8}$ turns of the wheel from lock to lock, giving a 34ft. 9in. turning circle.

The rack and pinion steering gear is held in place against the engine bulkhead by a 'U' bolt at each end of the rack housing. Tie-rods from each end of the steering gear housing operate the steering arms via both exposed, and rubber gaitered enclosed, ball joints. The upper splined end of the helically toothed pinion protrudes from the rack housing and engages with the splined end of the steering column. The pinion spline is grooved and the steering column is held to the pinion by a clamp bolt which partially rests in the pinion groove.

It is necessary to depressurise the system of all hydrolastic models if it is wished to overhaul the upper suspension arm, strut, or displacer unit, or to remove the front or rear subframes. On reassembly it will be necessary to repressurise the system. This involves the use of special servicing equipment which most BLMC garages of any size possess.

A hydrolastic car can be driven for short distances with the system depressurised, providing it is driven slowly (ie. 30 mph/48 kph). It is, therefore, quite feasible for the private owner to carry out repairs himself, providing his local BLMC garage is willing to depressurise and pressurise his hydrolastic system for him.

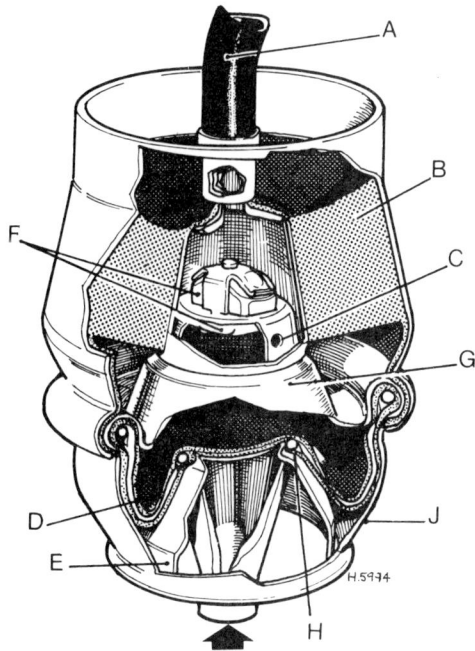

Fig. 11.1. Hydrolastic unit (Sec. 1)

A Interconnecting pipe
B Rubber spring
C Damper bleed
D Butyl liner
E Tapered piston

F Damper valves
G Fluid separating member
H Rubber diaphragm (nylon reinforced)
J Tapered cylinder

2 Suspension and steering - inspection for wear

1 To check for wear in the outer ball joints of the tie-rods place the car over a pit, or lie on the ground looking at the ball joints, and get someone to rock the steering wheel from side to side. Wear is present if there is play in the joints.

2 To check for wear in the rubber and metal bushes jack-up the front of the car until the wheels are clear of the ground. Hold each wheel in turn, at the top and bottom and try to rock it. If the wheel rocks continue the movement at the same time inspecting the upper link bushes, and the rubber bushes at the inner ends of the wishbone, for play.

3 If the wheel rocks and there is no side movement in the rubber bushes, then the swivel hub ball pins will be worn. Alternatively, if the movement occurs between the wheel and the brake backplate, then the hub bearings require replacement.

4 Sideplay or vertical or horizontal movement of the upper link relative to the body is best checked with the outer end of the link freed from the swivel hub. If play is present the bearings are worn and a replacement should be purchased.

5 Excessive play in the steering gear will lead to wheel wobble, and can be confirmed by checking if there is any lost movement between the end of the steering column and rack. Rack and pinion steering is normally very accurate and lost motion in the steering gear indicates a considerable mileage or lack of lubrication.

6 The outer ball joints at either end of the tie-rods are the most likely items to wear first, followed by the rack balljoints at the inner end of the tie-rods.

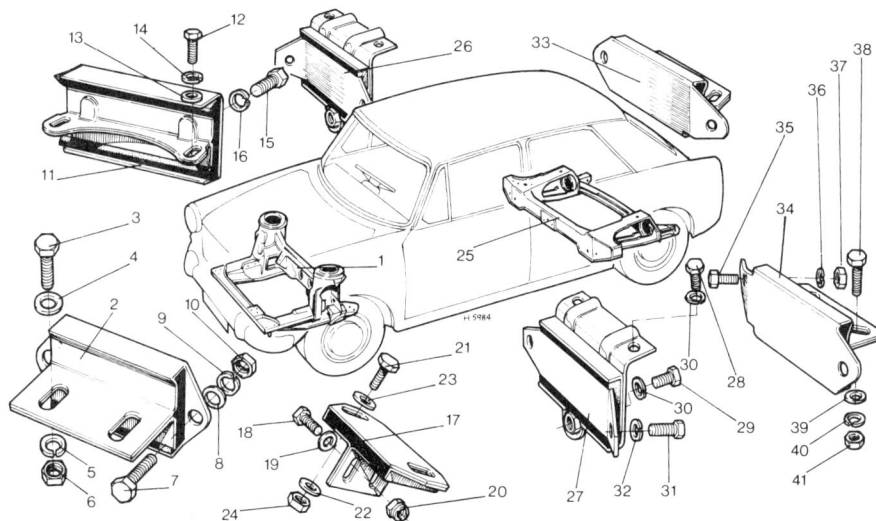

Fig. 11.2. Front and rear subframes and mounting components (Sec. 1)

1 Front subframe assembly
2 Front subframe front mounting
3 Screw
4 Plain washer
5 Spring washer
6 Nut
7 Screw
8 Plain washer
9 Spring washer
10 Nut
11 Rear upper subframe mounting

12 Screw
13 Plain washer
14 Spring washer
15 Screw
16 Spring washer
17 Rear lower front subframe mounting
18 Screw
19 Plain washer
20 Nut
21 Screw
22 Plain washer

23 Washer
24 Nut
25 Rear subframe assembly
26 Front RH rear subframe mounting
27 Front LH rear subframe mounting
28 Screw - long
29 Screw - short
30 Spring washer
31 Screw
32 Spring washer

33 Rear RH rear subframe mounting
34 Rear LH rear subframe mounting
35 Screw
36 Spring washer
37 Nut
38 Screw
39 Washer
40 Spring washer
41 Nut

3   Front displacer unit and upper suspension arm - removal and replacement

Removal of one of the displacer units means that first the system must be depressurised. Then, when the component concerned has been replaced, repressurise to the correct pressure. It is essential that this work is done at a BLMC garage as special service equipment is called for.

After the system has been depressurised, the car can be driven home slowly.

1   Remove the hubcap and loosen the roadwheel nuts.

2   Jack-up the front of the car from underneath the sump. Interpose a piece of wood between the sump and the jack to spread the load and prevent damage to the sump cooling ribs.

3   Chock-up each end of the piece of wood, so there is no danger involved if the jack collapses.

4   Undo the roadwheel nuts and take off the wheel.

5   Undo the hose to the displacer unit at its union on the bulk-head, and plug the open ends to keep out dirt.

6   Undo and remove the nut from the top of the steering swivel and lift the upper suspension arm off the ball pin shank.

7   Undo the pivot pin nut and then remove the upper arm pivot pin together with the washers.

8   Pull away the upper suspension arm together with the displacer strut foot.

9   The displacer unit can now be lifted out from inside the wheelarch.

10   Replacement is mainly a straightforward reversal of the removal sequence. The following additional points should be noted.

11   Pack the bearings in the upper suspension arm with a molybdenum disulphide grease before refitting the pivot pin.

12   Use the same spacer originally fitted. If this has been lost or it is wished to compensate for wear then use one of the nine spacers of different thicknesses that are available from BLMC garages. When fitting a new spacer only lightly tighten the nut and washer. If the spacer is too wide the bearings will be crushed as the nut is tightened.

13   The spacer is the correct thickness when the torque required to turn the shaft is between 5-10 lb f in. It is essential that the inner race of the bearings is turning with the shaft, rather than the inner race turning on the shaft.

4   Swivel hub ball joints - removal and replacement

The normal function of the king pin is undertaken by two ball joints, one at the top, and one at the bottom of each of the swivel hub units. To remove and replace the ball joints proceed as follows:

1   Have the suspension depressurised at your local BLMC garage. Although this is desirable it is not essential provided that care is taken.

2   Loosen the wheel nuts, jack-up the car, and remove the roadwheel. Place a support stand under the front subframe.

3   Remove the caliper assembly as described in Chapter 9 and support it on a block so as not to strain the hydraulic hose. Pull out the split pin from the drive shaft nut and undo it. Then pull off the hub casing and disc assembly.

4   Undo the nut from the bolt which holds the front tie-rod to the lower suspension arm.

5   Undo the nuts and washers from the ball pin shanks on the end of the upper and lower suspension arms. Use an extractor to free the arms from the ball pin taper. Alternatively strike in unison with two hammers the opposite sides of the suspension arm ball joint eyes to "jar" the pin free.

6   Pull the arms away from the ball joints, remove the ball joint housing dust seal, take off the lubricator, knock up the tab of the lockwasher and unscrew the housing to release the ball and ball seat. **Note** the spring fitted underneath the lower ball seat joint.

7   Carefully clean all the component parts and examine them

Fig. 11.3. Exploded view of front suspension

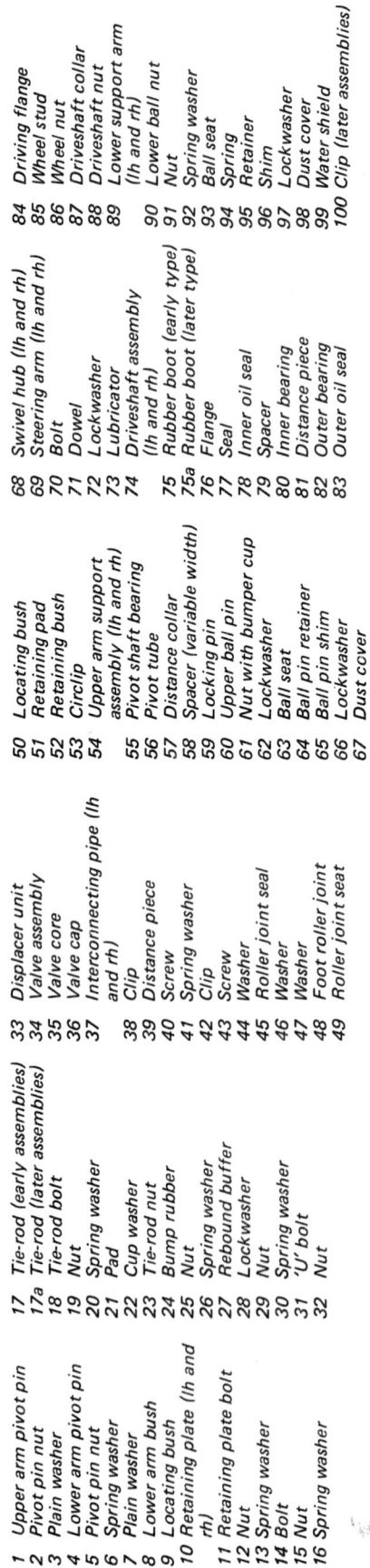

1   Upper arm pivot pin
2   Pivot pin nut
3   Plain washer
4   Lower arm pivot pin
5   Pivot pin nut
6   Spring washer
7   Plain washer
8   Lower arm bush
9   Locating bush
10   Retaining plate (lh and rh)
11   Retaining plate bolt
12   Nut
13   Spring washer
14   Bolt
15   Nut
16   Spring washer
17   Tie-rod (early assemblies)
17a   Tie-rod (later assemblies)
18   Tie-rod bolt
19   Nut
20   Spring washer
21   Pad
22   Cup washer
23   Distance piece
24   Bump rubber
25   Nut
26   Spring washer
27   Rebound buffer
28   Lockwasher
29   Nut
30   Spring washer
31   'U' bolt
32   Nut
33   Displacer unit
34   Valve assembly
35   Valve core
36   Valve cap
37   Interconnecting pipe (lh and rh)
38   Clip
39   Distance piece
40   Screw
41   Spring washer
42   Clip
43   Screw
44   Washer
45   Roller joint seal
46   Washer
47   Washer
48   Foot roller joint
49   Roller joint seat
50   Locating bush
51   Retaining pad
52   Retaining bush
53   Circlip
54   Upper arm support assembly (lh and rh)
55   Pivot shaft bearing
56   Pivot tube
57   Distance collar
58   Spacer (variable width)
59   Locking pin
60   Upper ball pin
61   Nut with bumper cup
62   Lockwasher
63   Ball seat
64   Ball pin retainer
65   Ball pin shim
66   Lockwasher
67   Dust cover
68   Swivel hub (lh and rh)
69   Steering arm (lh and rh)
70   Bolt
71   Dowel
72   Lockwasher
73   Lubricator
74   Driveshaft assembly (lh and rh)
75   Rubber boot (early type)
75a   Rubber boot (later type)
76   Flange
77   Seal
78   Inner oil seal
79   Spacer
80   Inner bearing
81   Distance piece
82   Outer bearing
83   Outer oil seal
84   Driving flange
85   Wheel stud
86   Wheel nut
87   Driveshaft collar
88   Driveshaft nut
89   Lower support arm (lh and rh)
90   Lower ball nut
91   Nut
92   Spring washer
93   Ball seat
94   Spring
95   Retainer
96   Shim
97   Lockwasher
98   Dust cover
99   Water shield
100   Clip (later assemblies)

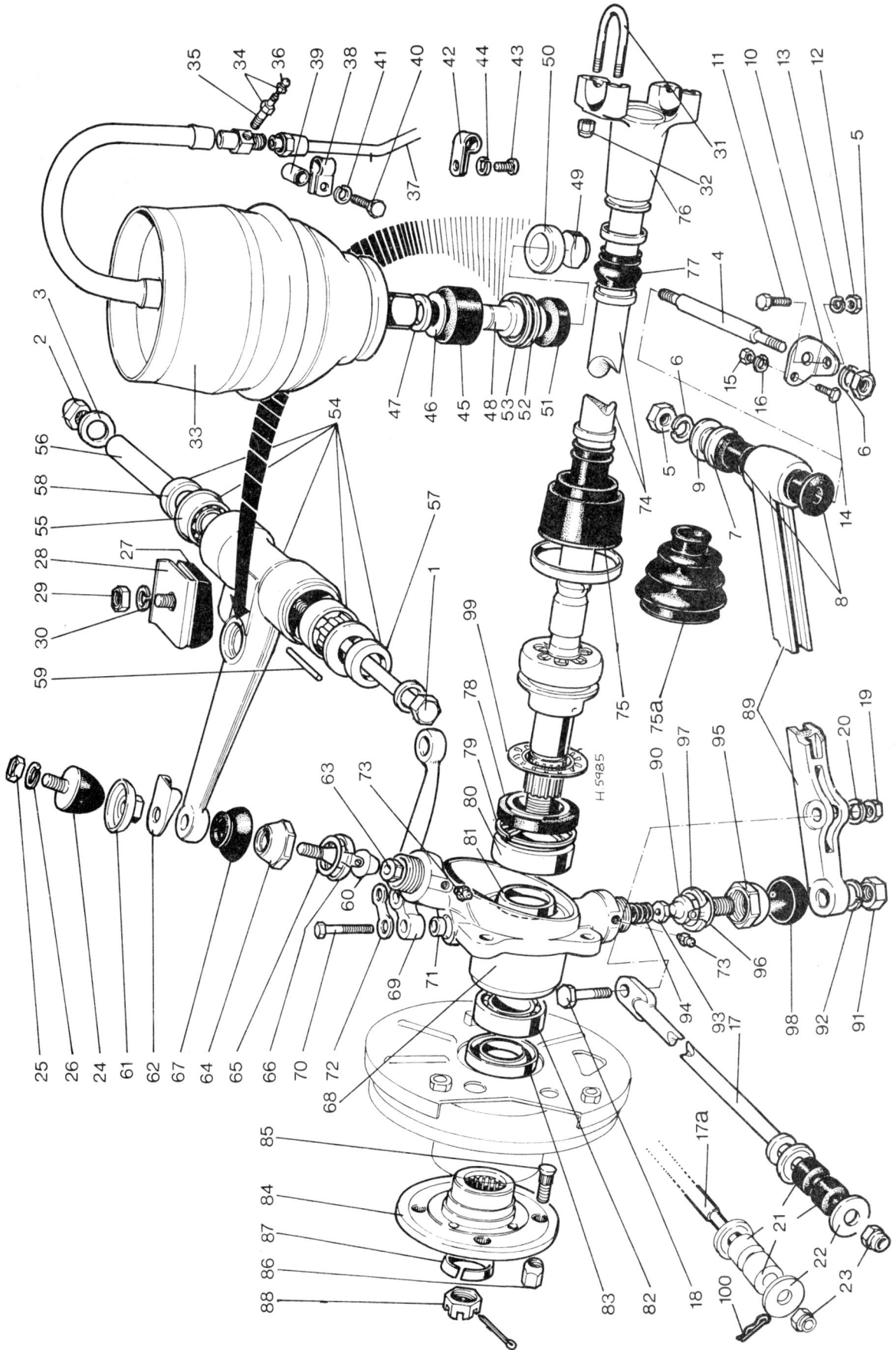

H 5985

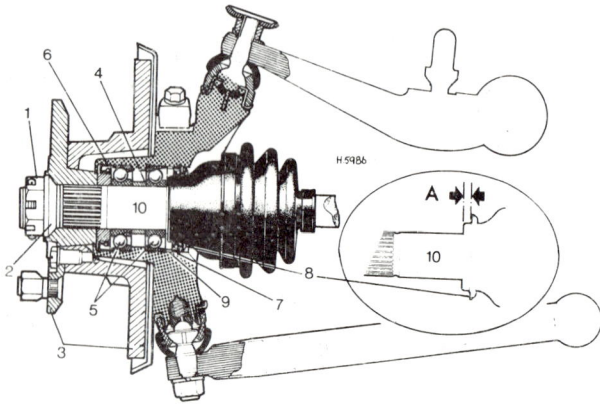

Fig. 11.4. Front hub assembly (Sec. 4)
Inset - initial fitted position of the water shield

1	Driveshaft nut	6	Outer oil seal
2	Tapered collar	7	Inner oil seal
3	Hub and disc assembly	8	Water shield (later assemblies)
4	Bearing distance piece		
5	Bearings	9	Oil seal spacer
		10	Driveshaft

Distance 'A' = 1/4 ± 1/16 in (6.3 ± 1.5 mm)

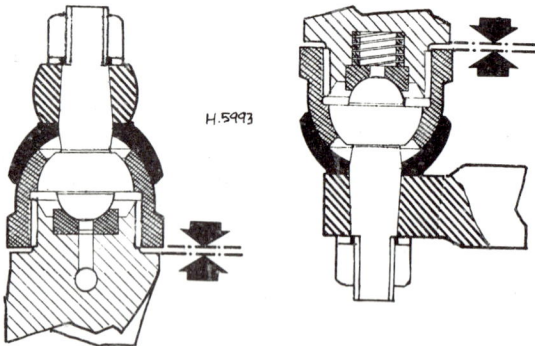

**Fig. 1.5. Cross-sectioned view through swivel hub balljoints.
Take feeler gauge measurements at the positions shown (Sec. 4)**

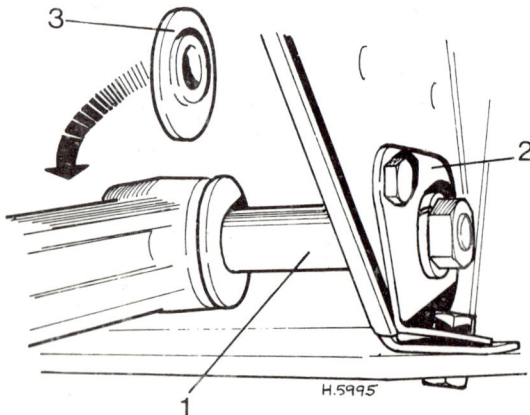

Fig. 1.6. Lower support arm mounting (Sec. 7)

1	Pivot pin	3	Body locating bush
2	Returning plate		

for excessive wear. Renew them as necessary. Normal wear can be taken up by shims.

8 Reassemble the ball seats, pins, and ball housings to the swivel hub without the lockwashers, or lower seat spring in position. Screw down the ball housings till there is no free movement between the ball seating and the ball, and then take a measurement with a feeler gauge in the gap between the housings and the swivel hubs.

9 Dismantle the ball joints, pack with Castrol LM Grease or similar, and then reassemble with the lockwashers, and lower seat spring. Add shims to the thickness of the feeler gauge measurement less 0.036 in (0.91mm) which is the thickness of the washer.

10 Fully tighten the ball housing and ensure the joint is not too tight, or that play is present. If the initial gap was measured accurately the joint will be perfect fit.

11 Knock up the housing washer to lock the housing in position.

12 Refit the dust seals, suspension arm, washers, and ball pin nuts and tighten the latter to a torque of 35 to 40 lb f ft (4.8 to 5.5 kg fm).

13 Refit the tie-rod to the lower suspension arm, replace the wheel, and lower the car to the ground.

5 Swivel hub assembly - removal and replacement

1 Jack-up the front of the car and support on firmly based axle stands. Remove the roadwheel.

2 If the hub assembly is to be dismantled, extract the split pin and slacken the hub flange nut before jacking up the front of the car.

3 Remove the tie-rod ball joint to steering lever securing nut and using a universal ball joint separator detach the ball joint from the steering lever.

4 Release the driveshaft inner coupling. For full information refer to Chapter 7.

5 Refer to Chapter 9, and remove the brake caliper assembly. It is not necessary to detach the hose but support it on string or wire.

6 Disconnect the tie-rod from the lower support arm.

7 Remove the upper and lower support arm retaining nuts and lockwashers and using a universal ball joint separator release the arms from the ball pins.

8 The complete hub assembly and driveshaft may now be lifted away.

9 Replacement is the reverse sequence to removal. Tighten all attachments to the recommended torque wrench settings.

6 Front hubs - removal and replacement

1 Remove the hub cap from the appropriate front wheel, loosen the wheelnuts and lift the front of the car by a jack placed under the transmission casing. Ensure a length of wood is interposed between the casing and the jack to spread the load.

2 Remove the wheelnuts and take off the roadwheel.

3 Undo and remove the two bolts which hold the disc brake caliper to the front hub. **Note:** The caliper is still connected to the hydraulic hose, on no account allow the caliper to hang. Support it on a suitable block to avoid straining the hose.

4 With a pair of pliers pull out the split pin from the hub retaining nut. Undo and remove the nut.

5 With the aid of a puller (BLMC tool '18G304' used with adaptor '18G304B') pull off the hub casing and disc assembly.

6 To separate the disc from the hub assembly undo the securing set screws.

7 Replacement is a straightforward reversal of the removal process but the following points should be noted.

a) Repack the bearing with a high melting point grease.

b) When the bearings are pushed into the hub make sure they are fitted so the sides marked 'THRUST' lie against the bearing spacer.

7 Lower support aim and tie-rod - removal and replacement

1 Jack-up the front of the car and support on firmly based axle stands. Remove the roadwheel.
2 Steady the suspension by placing a jack beneath the hub and release the tie-rod from the lower support arm.
3 Remove the lower ball pin to support arm securing nut and using a universal ball joint separator detach the ball pin from the support arm.
4 Undo and remove both pivot pin nuts and the bolts that secure the retaining plate.
5 Withdraw the pivot pin and the body locating bush.
6 The support arm may now be lifted away.
7 To remove the tie-rod, pull out the securing clip (later assemblies), undo the self-locking nut, lift off the outer cupped washer and bush and pull out the tie-rod.
8 Refitting the tie-rod and lower support arm is the reverse sequence to removal but the following additional points should be noted:
a) Support the lower arm in the normal fitted position when the pivot shaft nuts are being tightened. This will avoid pre-loading the rubber bushes.
b) Later tie-rods have a shouldered end, instead of a welded locating disc. Ensure that the inner cupped washer is fitted against this shoulder and the securing clip is replaced.
c) Tighten all securing nuts to the recommended torque wrench settings.

8 Tie-rod outer ball joint - removal and replacement

1 If the tie-rod outer ball joints are worn it will be necessary to renew the whole ball joint assembly as they cannot be dismantled and repaired. To remove a ball joint, free the ball joint shank from the steering arm and mark the position of the lock nut on the tie-rod accurately to ensure near accurate 'toe-out' on reassembly.
2 Slacken off the ball joint locknut, and holding the tie-rod by its flat with a spanner, to prevent it from turning, unscrew the complete ball assembly from the rod. Replacement is a straight reversal of this process. Visit your local BLMC garage to ensure that toe-in is correct.

9 Rear displacer unit - removal and replacement

1 First have the system depressurised at your local BLMC agent

and then remove the rear subframe as described in Chapter 12.
2 Next separate the brake hose from the brake pipe on the side of the subframe from which the displacer unit and radius arm is to be removed. Plug the open ends of the pipe and hose to prevent the entrance of dirt.
3 Remove the handbrake cable from the lever protruding through the backplate, after pulling out the split pin and then taking out the clevis pin.
4 Undo the nut and washer from the swivelling segment which holds the handbrake cable in place under the radius arm. Pull off the swivelling segment.
5 To remove the handbrake cable from the bracket unscrew the ferrule and slide the cable through the slot in the bracket.
6 Take off the rear anti-roll bar and auxiliary springs as described in Section 11.
7 Undo and remove the nut and washer at each end of the radius arm pivot shaft. Then undo and remove the four bolts which hold the pivot shaft retaining plate to the subframe.
8 The radius arm, complete with displacer unit can now be pulled away from the subframe.
9 Replacement is a straightforward reversal of the removal sequence. Make certain that the displacer unit strut foot is correctly positioned in the radius arm. Also ensure that the thrust washer is fitted with the relieved portion facing the bearing.

10 Rear radius arm - dismantling, overhaul and reassembly

1 The roller foot joint is removed from the radius arm extension after the retaining circlip has been taken out.
2 Pull out the pivot shaft and the bearing assemblies from the radius arm. It may be necessary to use BLMC tool '18G704' to remove the outer races.
3 Examine the bearings for wear and for any signs of free play between the inner and outer races. Replace them if worn.
4 Reassembly proceeds in the following manner: First press the outer spacer onto the retaining plate end of the pivot shaft until the side face of the spacer is flush with the step in the shaft.
5 Then fit the retaining plate to the pivot shaft with the nut and spring washer. Do not tighten the nut so much that it moves the outer spacer.
6 Press the coil seals into the radius arm and ensure they are located squarely in the bore. Thoroughly grease the bearings with a molybdenum disulphide grease and then fit them to the radius arm. The larger bearing lies at the retaining plate end of the radius arm.
7 Next fit the dust shield in place flush with the outer end of the radius arm.

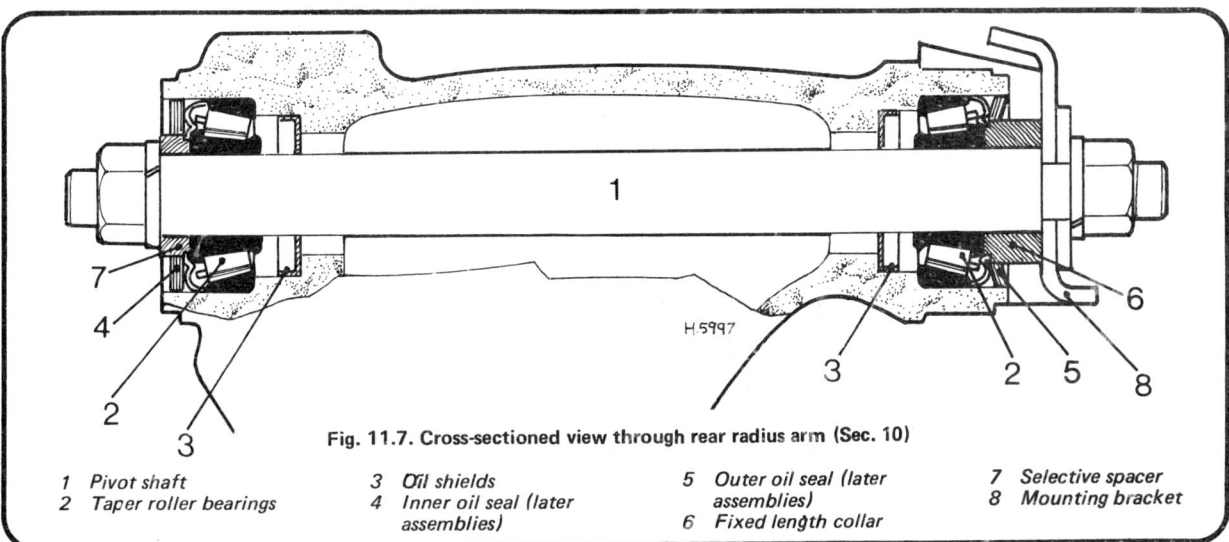

H.5997

Fig. 11.7. Cross-sectioned view through rear radius arm (Sec. 10)

1 Pivot shaft	3 Oil shields	5 Outer oil seal (later assemblies)	7 Selective spacer
2 Taper roller bearings	4 Inner oil seal (later assemblies)	6 Fixed length collar	8 Mounting bracket

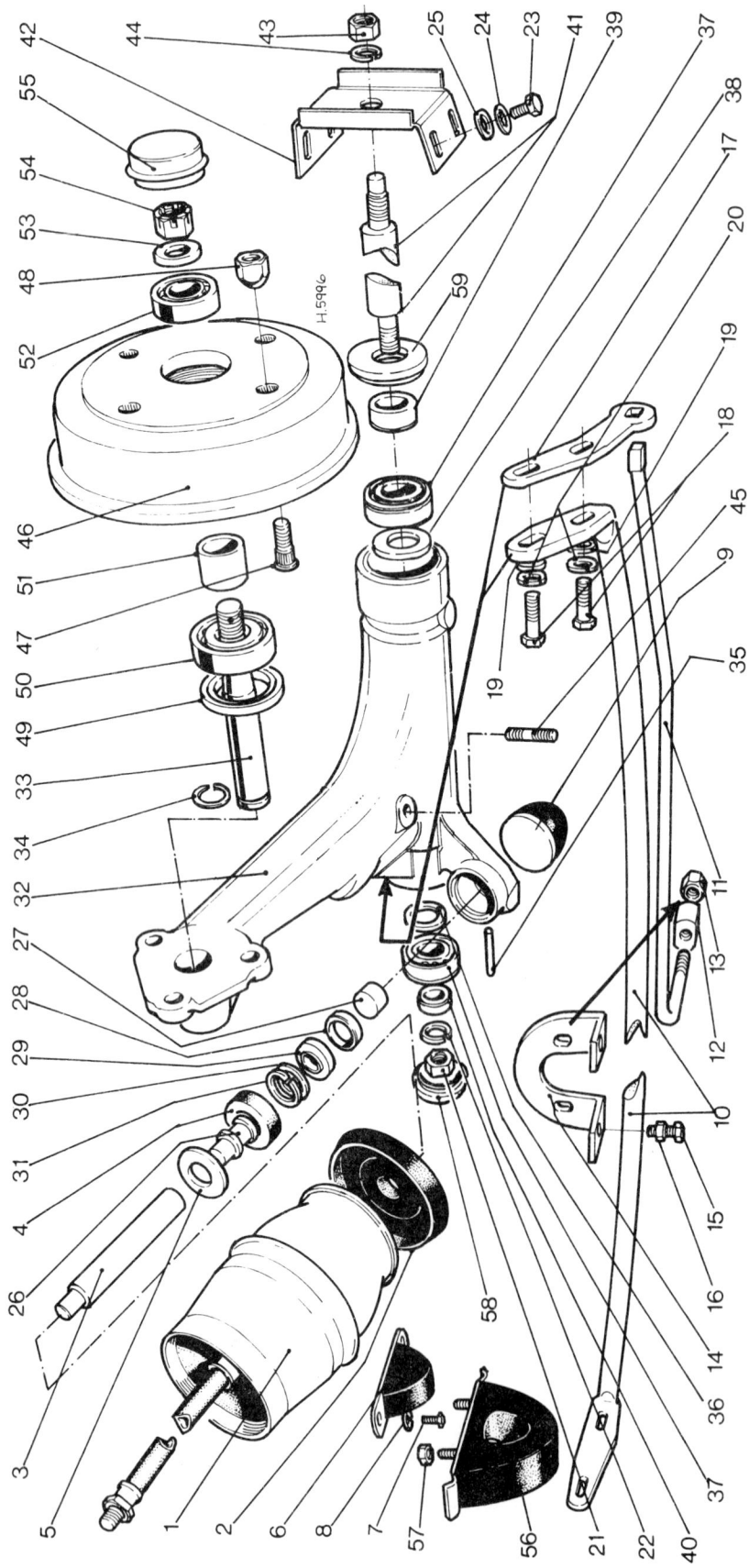

H.5996

Fig. 11.8. Exploded view of rear suspension

1 Displacer unit
2 Piston sleeve
3 Displacer strut
4 Seal
5 Washer
6 Bump rubber
7 Screw
8 Spring washer
9 Rebound buffer
10 Anti-roll bar
11 Auxiliary spring (lh and rh) (where fitted)
12 Bearing
13 Nut
14 Bracket
15 Screw
16 Nut
17 Bracket (lh and rh)
18 Bolt
19 Plain washer
20 Spring washer
21 Nut
22 Spring washer
23 Screw
24 Shakeproof washer
25 Plain washer
26 Roller joint foot
27 Roller joint seat
28 Locating brush
29 Retaining pad
30 Retainer
31 Circlip
32 Radius arm (lh and rh)
33 Stub shaft (lh and rh)
34 Circlip
35 Locking pin
36 Oil shield (inner)
37 Pivot shaft bearing
38 Oil shield (outer)
39 Outer spacer
40 Inner spacer (selective)
41 Pivot shaft
42 Retaining plate (lh and rh)
43 Nut
44 Spring washer
45 Stud
46 Brake drum hub assembly
47 Wheel stud
48 Wheel nut
49 Oil seal
50 Inner bearing
51 Spacer
52 Outer bearing
53 Washer
54 Nut (lh and rh)
55 Grease-retaining cap
56 Arch spring (some two-door models)
57 Nut
58 Oil seal (inner)
59 Oil seal (outer)

8 Slide the pivot shaft inner end first, into the retaining plate end of the radius arm.

9 Use the same spacer originally fitted. If this has been lost or it is wished to compensate for wear then use one of the nine spacers of different thickness available from BLMC garages, starting with one 0.301 in. (7.6 mm.) thick. When fitting a new spacer only lightly tighten the nut. If the spacer is too wide the bearings will be crushed as the nut is tightened. The spacer is of the correct thickness when with the nut fully tightened the torque required to turn the shaft is between 5 to 10 lb f ft (0.7 - 1.38 kg fm). It is essential that the inner race of the bearings turns with the shaft, as opposed to the inner race turning on the shaft.

11 Anti-roll bar and auxiliary springs - removal and replacement

An anti-roll bar and auxiliary springs are fitted on the rear subframe. The springs can be adjusted to raise or lower the rear of the car as necessary. Before the anti-roll bar and the auxiliary springs can be removed, the system must be depressurised and the rear subframe taken off as described in Chapter 12. Then proceed as follows:

1 Load the subframe so the radius arms are in the full bump position.

2 Undo the four bolts which hold the ends of the anti-roll bar and the spring brackets to the inside face of the radius arms.

3 Undo and remove the nuts which secure the auxiliary springs to the subframe. The anti-roll bar and springs are now free,

4 Replacement is a straightforward reversal of the removal procedure.

5 The nominal gap between the underside of the rear subframe and the inside faces of the bracket lugs is 0.125 in. (3.2 mm). The minimum gap is 0.000 in., and the maximum permitted 0.250 in. (6.4 mm). (Fig. 11.9).

6 To raise the riding height of the rear end loosen the two auxiliary spring bar nuts undo the locknuts on the adjusting screws and undo the screws, each by the same amount to decrease the gap (Fig. 11.10). To lower the riding height, first take up the tension on the springs by weighting the subframe down so the radius arms are in full bump position. The screws must then be done up to increase the gap between the underside of the subframe, and the inside faces of the bracket lugs.

12 Rear hub - removal and replacement

1 Remove the hub cap from the appropriate rear wheel; loosen the wheelnuts and jack up the rear of the car under the subframe crossmember.

2 Remove the wheelnuts and take off the roadwheel.

3 Remove the hub as detailed in Chapter 9.

4 Replacement is a straightforward reversal of this sequence. If the bearings have been extracted from the hub ensure they are refitted with the sides marked 'THRUST' against the bearing spacer.

13 Arch springs - removal and replacement

On later 1100 and 1300 models rubber arch springs replace the anti-roll bar and auxiliary springs. The arch springs are in permanent contact with the radius arms.

1 To remove an arch spring, jack-up the rear of the car and remove the roadwheel on the appropriate side thus removing as much weight as possible from the radius arm and thereby removing tension on the spring.

2 Remove the boot floor and undo the two nuts securing the arch spring in position and lift the spring clear.

3 Refitting is a direct reversal of the above procedure, but note that 'FRONT' is marked on the arch spring.

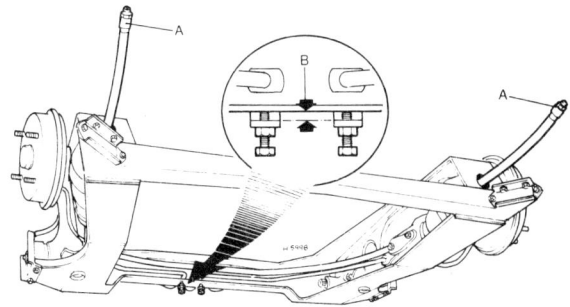

Fig. 11.9. Rear subframe and suspension assembly (Sec. 11)

A   *Displacer unit hoses*
B   *Auxiliary spring bracket clearance*

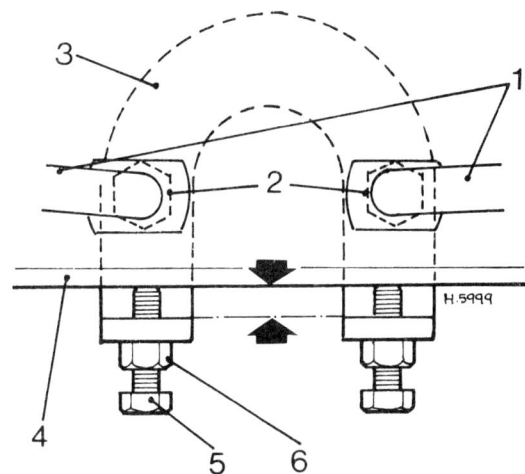

Fig. 11.10. Auxiliary springs attachment bracket (Sec. 11)
Arrowed: nominal gap between the bracket and subframe

| 1 | *Auxiliary springs* | 3 | *Spring bracket* | 5 | *Adjuster screws* |
| 2 | *Centre securing nuts* | 4 | *Subframe* | 6 | *Locknuts* |

14 Rear radius arm - removal and replacement

On all models fitted with rubber arch springs in place of the anti-roll bar and auxiliary springs it is possible to remove and replace a radius arm without removing the complete rear subframe.

1 To remove a radius arm under these conditions, jack-up the car, remove the required roadwheel and depressurise the hydrolastic system on that side of the car (this depressurisation must be done by the local BLMC garage).

2 Release the handbrake and fully slacken off the adjuster mechanism.

3 Remove the clevis pin from the lever on the brake backplate and then remove the handbrake cable swivel sector from its pivot on the under side of the radius arm.

4 Disconnect the brake hydraulic pipe at the union on the sub-frame.

5 Undo the radius arm shaft inner pivot nut, remove the outer support bracket and the hydrolastic displacer strut and then carefully manoeuvre the radius arm assembly from the car.

6 Replacement is a direct reversal of the above procedure but remember to bleed the brakes and re-adjust the handbrake mechanism. Take the car to your local BLMC garage to have the hydrolastic system repressurised.

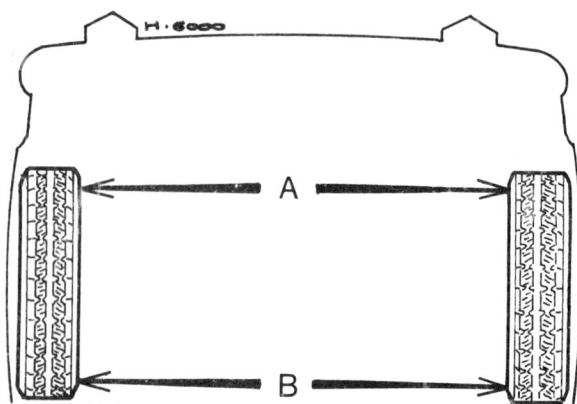

Fig. 11.11. Front wheel alignment (Sec. 15)
To be taken with front wheels in straight ahead position

A = 1/16 ± 1/32 in (1.6 ± 0.8 mm) greater than B

15 Front wheel alignment

1 The front wheels are correctly aligned when they turn out at the front 0.0625 in. (1.59 mm.). It is important that this measurement is taken on a 14.5 in. (368.3 mm.) diameter on the side wall of the tyre at a distance of 9.4 in. (239 mm.) above the surface of the floor. Adjustment is effected by loosening the lock nut on each tie-rod ball joint, and the clips on the gaiters, and turning both tie-rods equally until the adjustment is correct. (Fig. 11.11).

2 This is a job that your local BLMC garage must do, as accurate alignment requires the use of expensive base bar or optical alignment equipment.

3 If the wheels are not in alignment, tyre wear will be heavy and uneven, and the steering will be stiff and unresponsive.

16 Steering wheel - removal and replacement

All models except Austin America and GT
1 For safety reasons, disconnect the battery.

2 Mk I models: Lever out the horn push control from the steering wheel hub with a small screwdriver.

3 Mk II and Mk III (except Super de luxe) models: Lever out the motif from the steering wheel hub with a small screwdriver.

4 Mk III Super de luxe models: Carefully pull off the safety pad.

5 With a suitable socket unscrew the nut which retains the steering wheel to the steering inner column.

6 Mark the steering wheel hub and inner column to assist re-assembly and pull the steering wheel off the splines on the column.

7 Refitting the steering wheel is the reverse sequence to removal but the following additional points should be noted:
a) Tighten the nut to a torque wrench setting of 50 lb f ft (6.9 kg fm).
b) If on Mk I models the horn push control continually pops out a special three pronged clip may be fitted. To do this remove the horn push and steering wheel and drill a 0.219 in (5.60 mm) hole 0.25 in (6.4 mm) deep in the steering wheel hub at a point 0.75 in (19.00 mm) above the centre of the hub. Refit the steering wheel and fit the retaining clip in place of the lock washer with its tag in the drilled hole. Secure both with a new special nut.
Remove the two spring clips from the horn push and replace it after aligning the earthing contact.

Austin America and GT models
1 Carefully lever out the safety boss and if the hub is to be removed unscrew the steering wheel nut.

2 Turn back the lock ring tabs and remove the bolts, lock ring and steering wheel.

3 To remove the hub either carefully tap it off with a soft faced hammer or draw it off using a universal puller. Mark the position of the hub and inner column to assist refitting.

4 Refitting the hub and steering wheel is the reverse sequence to removal.

17 Steering column bush - removal and replacement

1 If there is any play in the top of the steering column, it will be necessary to replace the felt, or nylon, bush which is fitted between the top of the inner and outer steering columns.

2 The bush is replaced after removing the steering wheel and prising the old bush out. The new bush should be soaked in engine grade oil and slid into place.

18 Steering column - removal and replacement

1 For safety reasons, disconnect the battery.

2 Disconnect the direction indicator and horn control cable connectors located beneath the parcel shelf.

3 Undo and remove the nut, bolt and spring washer that clamps the inner column to the steering pinion shaft. To gain access it will be necessary to pull back the rubber shroud.

4 Remove the column support bracket from the body cross-member with the distance pieces (Princess cars), or remove the horizontal shear screw which clamps the outer column on later models.

5 On models with a steering column lock, extract the shear screw(s) as described in Section 21.

6 Carefully pull the column assembly upwards so as to dis-engage it from the pinion shaft splines.

7 Visually check the condition of the splines and if worn new parts must be obtained.

8 If heavy steering is experienced the inner column should be inspected for distortion. To check refit the inner column only onto the steering pinion shaft and with the car jacked-up at the front turn the wheels between both locks. The total run-out at the top bearing face must not exceed 0.25 in (3.1 mm). Straighten the original inner column or obtain new.

9 Refitting the steering column assembly is the reverse sequence to removal but the following additional points should be noted.
a) Ensure that the slot in the column clamp is correctly located with the roadwheels in straight ahead position.
b) On rhd models the clamp must be underneath the column and horizontal in order to bring the direction indicator can-celling lug into the correct position.
c) On lhd models or where the switch is moved to the left-hand side of the column the clamp must be positioned with the slot uppermost.
d) Tighten the steering column clamp pinch bolt to a torque wrench setting of 8-9 lb f ft (1.1 - 1.25 kg fm).
e) On models fitted with a steering column lock check all com-ponents for correct operation before shearing the column support screws.

19 Steering rack - lubrication

1 No provision is made for regular lubrication of the steering rack as replenishment is only necessary when there is evidence of oil loss from the rack housing or rubber gaiters.

2 To top-up the oil level after the source of leakage has been traced and rectified remove the retaining clip from the right-hand end of the rack housing. On lhd models remove the left-hand clip.

3 Move the rack to the straight ahead position.

4 Inject not more than 0.3 pint (0.44 US pints, 0.19 litres) into

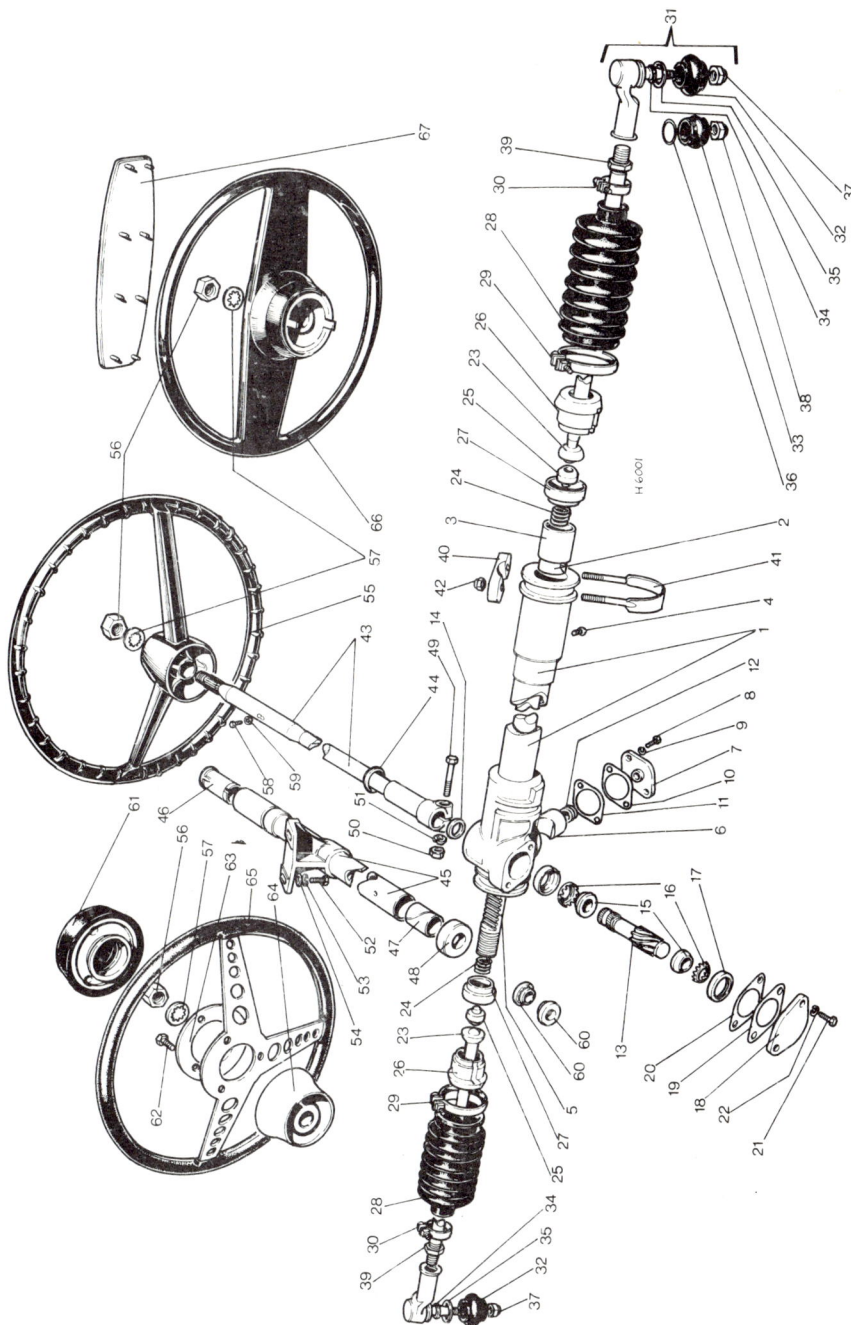

Fig. 11.12. Exploded view of steering assembly

1 Rack housing
2 Rack housing bush
3 Bush housing (early felt bushes only)
4 Housing screw
5 Rack
6 Damper yoke
7 Damper cover
8 Cover bolt
9 Spring washer
10 Yoke shim
11 Cover gasket
12 Disc spring
13 Pinion
14 Oil seal
15 Ball cone
16 Ball cage
17 Ball cup
18 End cover
19 Cover shim
20 End cover gasket
21 Spring washer
22 Boot washer
23 Tie-rod
24 Thrust spring
25 Ball seat
26 Ball housing
27 Locking ring
28 Rubber gaiter
29 Seal clip (inner)
30 Seal clip (outer)
31 Ball socket assembly
32 Rubber boot
33 Rubber boot
34 Boot washer
35 Circlip
36 Circlip
37 Nut
38 Nut
39 Locknut
40 Clamp base
41 'U' bolt
42 Nut
43 Column assembly
44 Washer
45 Column tube
46 Column bearing (upper)
47 Column bearing (lower)
48 Sealing washer
49 Pinion clamp bolt
50 Nut
51 Washer
52 Column screw
53 Spring washer
54 Washer
55 Steering wheel
56 Steering wheel nut
57 Washer
58 Stud
59 Locknut
60 One-piece pinion bearing assemblies (later models)
61 Safety boss
62 Bolt
63 Lock ring
64 Steering wheel hub
65 Steering wheel
66 Steering wheel
67 Safety pad

the end of the rack housing. Always use an Extreme Pressure SAE 90 oil.

5   Reconnect the rubber gaiter, refit the clip and move the rack from side-to-side to distribute oil throughout the housing.

20 Nylon tie-rod ball ends

1   Ball joints have nylon seats which are sealed for life and protected by rubber boots.

2   The rubber boots must be kept in good condition and if it is found that a boot has become damaged both boot and joint must be renewed.

3   If the rubber boot was accidentally damaged in the garage or workshop it may be renewed only if there was no possibility of dirt entry.

21 Steering lock and ignition switch - removal and replacement

1   For safety reasons, disconnect the battery.

2   Disconnect the electrical connections from the underside of the fascia. On the first type fitted the electrical connections are on the rear of the switch.

First type only

3   The first type is identified by the markings 'lock', 'acc', 'garage', 'ignition', 'start'. If it develops a fault it is only renewable as a complete assembly.

4   Remove the lock securing shear screws with a stud extractor or by cutting slots in their heads and using a screwdriver or by punching them round with a centre punch.

5   Withdraw the lock and switch assembly from the steering column.

Second type only

6   The second type is identified by the markings 'halt', 'garage', 'fahrt', 'start' or 'O', '1', '11', '111'.

7   Where fitted remove the nacelle that covers the steering column lock. The lower half can be left in position unless the complete lock assembly is being removed.

8   With the exception of Austin America models it is possible to renew the switch unit with the lock assembly in situ.

9   Remove the grub screw with a magnetic screwdriver through the access hole in the lock body and pull the switch from the barrel.

10   On Austin America models there is an additional wire which is connected to the warning buzzer. This entails removal of the lock and barrel assembly to which the wire is attached, before the switch unit can be removed.

11   To remove the lock and barrel assembly, first extract the three shear screws that secure the two halves of the lock body together by one of the methods described in paragraph 4.

12   The part of the lock body which is secured to the outer steering column need not be removed.

13   On Austin America models if the switch unit is to be removed, release the moulded terminal of the additional wire from the lock barrel. Remove the grub screw and withdraw the switch.

14   To remove the complete lock assembly, extract the two shear screws securing the cap to the lock body and lift away the lock from the steering column.

Third type only

15   The third type is identified by the markings 'O', 'I', 'II', 'III', and incorporates either a press button or a push-in release key.

16   Remove the self-tapping screws securing the nacelle covering the steering column lock. If only the switch is being replaced, the lower half need not be removed.

17   It is possible to remove the switch unit in-situ. Extract the grub screw, which is recessed on the press button type and withdraw the switch.

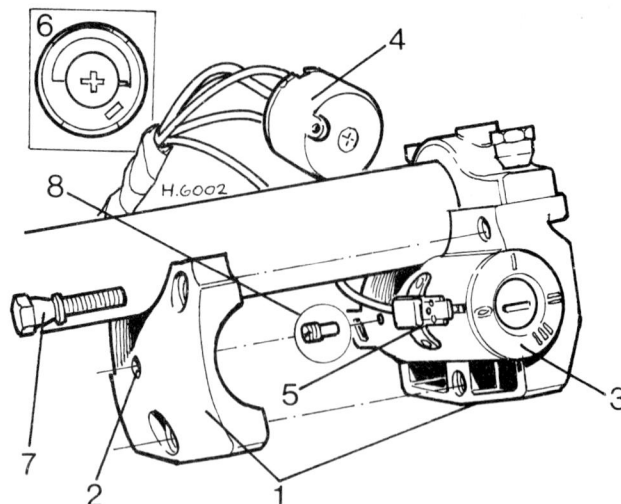

Fig. 11.13. Components of 2nd type steering lock and ignition switch assembly (Sec. 21)

1   *Lock body*
2   *Access hole*
3   *Lock and barrel assembly*
4   *Switch unit (showing cut back spline aligned with pip)*
5   *Moulded terminal for warning buzzer (Austin America only)*
6   *(Inset) The fitted position of the spring loaded device*
7   *Shear screws (five off)*
8   *Grub screw*

18   When an audible buzzer warning buzzer is fitted, also detach the additional wire from its connection on the side of the lock body.

19   If it is necessary to remove the complete lock assembly, extract the two shear screws; the method used is described in paragraph 4.

20   Withdraw the lock from the steering column.

Refitting and reassembly - all types

21   Refitting and reassembly is the reverse sequence to removal but the following additional points should be noted:

a)   When refitting the switch to the barrel on the second type of lock ensure that the cut back spline is aligned with the pip in the switch body and that the key has been turned to the 'O' or 'halt' position and withdrawn. Should the spring loaded device become displaced, it must be refitted to the splines of the centre shaft so that the end of the spring contacts the stop nearest the retaining lug when the key has been withdrawn.

b)   On both of the third types of lock the switch cannot be refitted out of synchronization with the lock mechanism. It may be necessary to turn the key whilst fitting the switch to the barrel to assist engaging the drive.

c)   When a multiple plug is not fitted to the wiring harness ensure that the colours of the individual cables are matched.

d)   Always use new shear screws and before fully tightening ensure that the switch and lock operates correctly.

22 Rack and pinion assembly - removal and replacement

The rack and pinion steering gear is held to the bottom of the turned up portion of the bodyshell floor by two 'U' bolts. It is sandwiched tightly between the floor and the front subframe. Before the steering gear can be removed it is necessary to lower the front subframe four or five inches to make enough room for removal of the 'U' bolts securing the rack. A good centre lift jack, several supports and a few load spreaders made from odd pieces of wooden plank are essential. Removing and replacing the steering gear will take about three hours.

Note: The hydraulic hoses, displacer hoses, control etc., have not been disconnected for this task. Therefore, to avoid damaging them, the subframe must not be lowered more than is absolutely necessary.

1   Jack-up the rear of the car, and place wooden blocks under the rear wheels. Remove the jack.

2   Loosen the front wheel securing nuts, and with the jack resting under the centre of the subframe jack the front of the car about 15 in. off the ground. Support the front subframe at each side with suitable chocks.

3   Take off the front wheels.

4   Remove the track rod ends from the steering arms, after undoing the securing nuts, by impact hammering.

5   From inside the car free the upper end of the steering column from the fascia by undoing the two screws which hold the mounting bracket in place. At the bottom of the steering column unscrew the pinch bolt which secures it to the serrated pinion shaft. Carefully pull the column off the pinion shaft so it just clears it.

6   Lift back the front carpet and undo the two nuts from each of the two 'U' bolts.

7   From underneath the car undo the bolts and nuts which hold the subframe to the bodyshell. Then free the exhaust pipe support from the lug on the gear lever extension.

8   Lowering the subframe is achieved by removing the chocks at each side of the subframe and replacing them under the body just behind the front wheelarches. Carefully lower the jack together with the subframe, and watch the pipe from the multi-way union on the nearside of the car. It may be necessary to disconnect the displacer hoses.

9   Remove the 'U' bolts from under the car. It may be necessary to prise the subframe down further by using a lever between the wing valance and the subframe to get sufficient clearance. Remove the rack and pinion from the driver's side of the car.

10   Replacement is a straightforward reversal of the removal operation but note the following points:

a)   Make sure the pinion shaft is in the centre of the hole in the toeboard, before fully tightening the 'U' bolts.

b)   Reconnect the track rod ends to the steering arms and make sure the wheels are facing straight ahead and the rack in the centre of its travel before fitting the column.

c)   Slacken the bolts holding the steering column bracket to the parcel shelf so the column can be easily centralised if necessary.

d)   Make sure the lower end of the steering column is pushed onto the pinion shaft sufficiently for the clamp bolt to enter the recess in the shaft fully. Also ensure the split portion of the clamp lines up with the marked pinion spline. The clamp

bolt should be tightened to 9 lb f ft (1.2 kg fm) torque.

23 Rack and pinion assembly - dismantling, overhaul and reassembly

It is not possible to make any adjustments to the rack and pinion steering gear unless it is removed from the car. With it removed it is as well to dismantle and examine the whole unit before making any adjustments. This will save having to remove the unit again later because of initial non-detection of wear. If wear is very bad it is best to fit an exchange reconditioned unit.

1   Mark the position of the lock nuts on the tie rods so that the 'toe-out' is approximately correct on reassembly.

2   Slacken the locknuts and gripping the tie-rods firmly with a mole wrench screw off the track rod ends.

3   The rack and pinion steering gear assembly is filled with oil. Ensure a 1 pint container is available before proceeding further.

4   Unscrew the clips holding the rubber gaiters to the rack housing and tie-rods. Drain the oil from the housing and carefully remove the gaiters.

5   Unscrew the two damper cover bolts and spring washers and remove the damper cover gasket shims, springs and yoke. **Note:** Early models make use of a coil spring and plunger in place of the disc springs fitted to later models as shown in Fig. 11.12.

6   Undo the two end cover bolts and remove the end plate, shim and gasket.

7   Carefully extract the lower ball bearing and then pull out the pinion. Access can now be gained to the upper ball bearing nearest the rack housing which can now be removed. If difficulty is experienced wait until the rack is removed from the housing. Extract the pinion shaft oil seal.

8   Each inner tie-rod ball joint is locked to a slot in the end of the rack by means of tabs on a locknut and also to the ball housing. Punch or prise up these tabs and then loosen the locknut. The ball housing can then be undone so freeing the tie-rod, ball seat and the thrust spring.

9   Pull the rack out from the pinion end of the housing so as not to damage the felt (plastic on later models) bush fitted at the other end.

10   Undo the bush securing screws from the housing and carefully remove the bush and metal housing with the aid of a pair of long nosed pliers.

11   Thoroughly clean all the parts with paraffin. Carefully inspect the teeth on the rack and also the pinion for chipping, roughness, uneven wear, hollows, or fractures. Replace both components if either is badly worn.

12   Carefully inspect the component parts of the inner ball joints

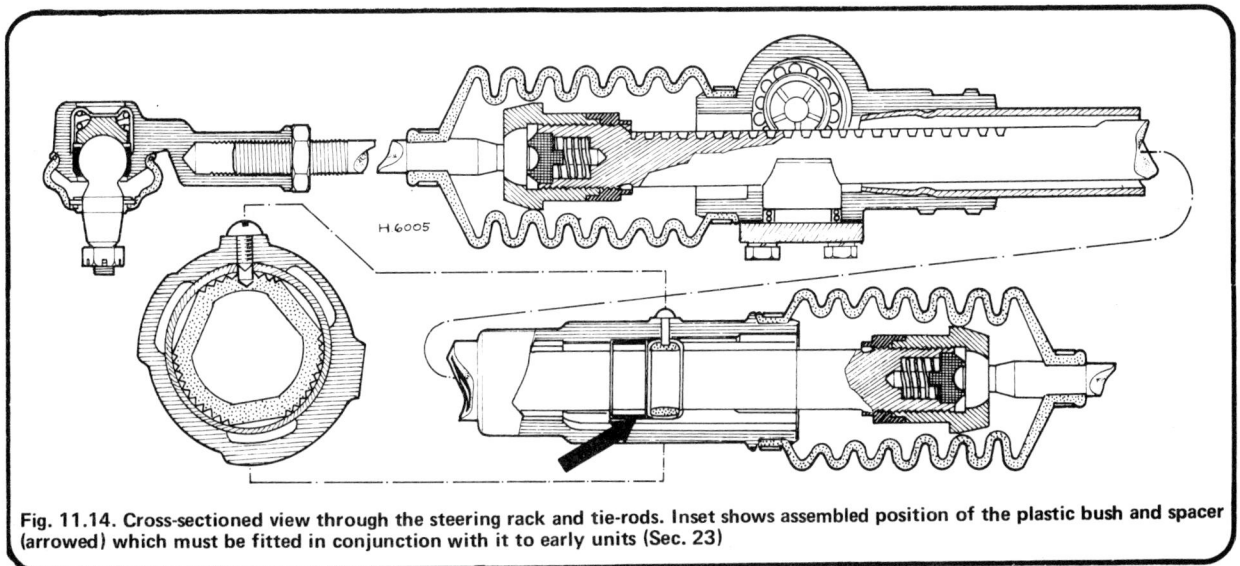

Fig. 11.14. Cross-sectioned view through the steering rack and tie-rods. Inset shows assembled position of the plastic bush and spacer (arrowed) which must be fitted in conjunction with it to early units (Sec. 23)

for wear or ridging and renew as necessary.

13 The outer track rod joints cannot be dismantled and if worn must be renewed as a complete assembly. Examine the component parts of the damper and renew any that show signs of wear. Pay particular attention to the oil seals, and as a precautionary measure it is always best to renew them.

14 As it is very difficult to refill the rack and pinion assembly with oil once it is fitted to the car, make sure the rubber gaiters are sound before refitting them. If they are in the least torn or perished complete oil loss could occur later and they must be renewed.

15 If the steering gear is of the early type the felt bush in the end of the rack furthest from the pinion housing, must be replaced with a plastic bush and a new steel sleeve bush and spacer.

16 Push the spacer, plain end first (not shown in Fig. 11.12 into the end of the rack housing. Insert the plastic bush inside the steel sleeve and slide the sleeve into the housing plain end first.

17 **Note:** The flats on the plastic bush must be so positioned as to be offset to the retaining screw hole in the bottom of the rack housing.

18 Very carefully drill the bush through the retaining screw hole with a 0.11 in (2.7 mm) drill. Carefully clean all traces of swarf away, liberally coat the threads of the retaining screw with jointing compound and screw it into the retaining screw hole. Make sure that the screw does not break right through the bush into the bore. (Fig. 11.14).

19 Lubricate the upper ball bearing nearest the rack housing and fit it into place.

20 Push the rack into the housing from the pinion end and then fit the pinion splined end first.

21 Lubricate the lower ball bearing and fit it in place on the lower end of the pinion shaft.

22 Fit the end cover without any shims and gently tighten down the two end cover bolts till all endfloat is taken up. Measure with a feeler gauge the gap between the end cover and the housing. (See Fig. 11.15). Remove the end cover.

23 Gather together packing shims to the measurement of the feeler gauge less 0.002 in (0.051 mm), treat the mating faces with shellac to make an oil tight joint, and refit the gasket, shims and end cover. Ensure the spring washers are refitted and tighten down the bolts.

24 Screw the ball housing locknuts tightly into the ends of the rack (always use a new locknut). Refit the thrust spring, ball seat, the tie-rod and the ball housing.

25 Tighten up the ball housing till the tie-rod is firmly nipped and rotate the locking nut to meet the ball housing.

26 Undo the ball housing an eighth of a turn and then tighten the locking nut to a torque of 35 lb f ft (4.8 kg fm).

27 Test the ball joints by measuring the pull required to move them by means of a spring balance connected to the track rod ends of the tie-rods. Between 2 to 4 lb. (0.90 to 1.8 Kg.) should be all that is necessary to move the rods. If a heavier pull is required the ball housing has been overtightened and must be slackened off.

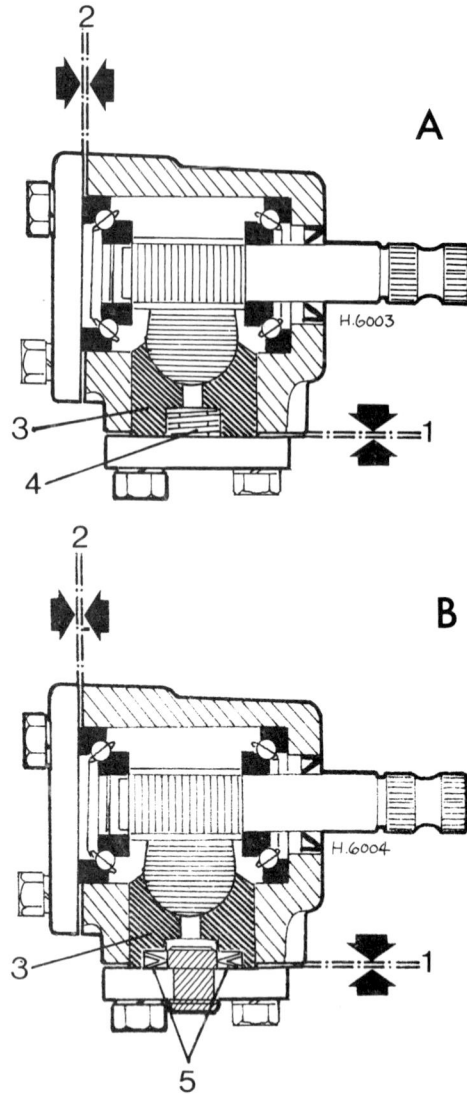

Fig. 11.15. Cross-sectioned view of steering pinion and rack damper (Sec. 23)

A   Later type   B   Early type
1   Clearance between pinion cover and housing
2   Clearance between damper cover and housing
3   Damper yoke
4   Damper spring (later type)
5   Damper spring halves (early type)

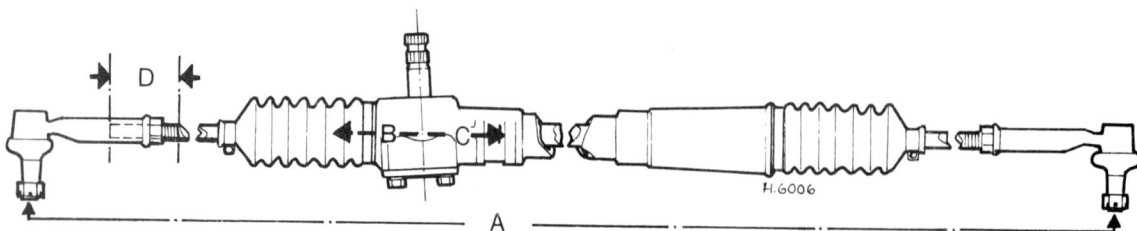

Fig. 11.16. Steering rack assembly dimensions (Sec. 23)

A   The assembled length between the ball pins 45.34 in (115.16 cm)
B   Rack travels from the central position 2.5 in (6.35 cm)
C   Rack travel from the central position 2.5 in (6.35 cm)
D   The threaded length of the tie-rod

28 Punch the lips of the locking nut into the slots in the rack and ball housing so the ball joint is held securely in place.

29 On early models fitted with a coil spring in the damper, assemble the damper plunger and then replace the damper cover leaving out the spring and shims. On later models replace the damper cover after fitting the yoke *and* disc springs, also leaving out the shims.

30 With the damper cover in place refit the two bolts, and ensure the rack is centralised (so both front wheels would face straight ahead if connected).

31 Tighten down the bolts till all backlash is taken up and it is just possible to turn the pinion by the splined end by rotating it between finger and thumb. Do not overtighten the bolts.

32 Measure, with a feeler gauge, the gap between the underside of the damper cover and the rack housing. (See Fig. 11.15). On early models add to the measured figure 0.002 in. (0.05 mm)

and on later models subtract 0.001 to 0.003 in. (0.025 to 0.076 mm). The total figure represents the thickness of shims which must be fitted under the cover.

33 Remove the damper cover; in the case of early models refit the coil spring; fit the necessary gasket, shims, and cover and tighten the bolts and spring washer securely. **Note:** It is sound practice to paint the cover joint to rack housing faces with shellac to ensure an oil tight joint.

34 Fit a new pinion shaft oil seal and replace the rubber gaiters.

35 Tighten down the gaiter clips at one end of the assembly, turn the unit upright and pour in 0.3 pint (0.44 US pint, 0.19 litre) of Extreme Pressure S.A.E. 90 oil through the free end of the upper gaiter. Tighten down all the gaiter clips securely.

36 Replace the locknuts and the trackrod ends. Reassembly is now complete.

24 Fault diagnosis - suspension and steering

Symptom	Reason/s	Remedy
Steering feels vague; car wanders and floats at speed	Tyre pressure uneven	Check pressures and adjust as necessary.
	Steering gear balljoints badly worn	Fit new balljoints.
	Suspension geometry incorrect	Check and rectify.
	Steering gear free play excessive	Adjust or overhaul steering gear.
	Front suspension and rear suspension pick-up points out of alignment	Normally caused by poor repair work after a serious accident. Extensive rebuilding necessary.
Steering stiff and heavy	Tyre pressure too low	Check pressures and inflate tyres.
	No oil in steering gear	Top-up steering gear.
	No grease in suspension balljoints	Dismantle, clean and re-lubricate.
	Front wheel toe-out incorrect	Check and reset toe-out.
	Suspension geometry incorrect	Check and rectify.
	Steering gear incorrectly adjusted too tightly	Check and readjust steering gear.
	Steering column badly misaligned	Determine cause and rectify (usually due to bad repair after severe accident damage and difficult to correct).
Wheel wobble and vibration	Wheel nuts loose	Check and tighten as necessary.
	Front wheels and tyres out of balance	Balance wheels and tyres and add weights as necessary.
	Steering or suspension balljoints badly worn	Replace balljoints.
	Hub bearings badly worn	Remove and fit new hub bearings.
	Steering gear free play excessive	Adjust or overhaul steering gear.
Car settles too low on suspension (one or both sides)	Loss of pressure in Hydrolastic system	Arrange for your Leyland dealer to check and rectify.
Car leans excessively when cornering	Rear anti-roll bar defective or mountings loose	Check and rectify.
	Rear auxiliary springs defective or mountings loose	Check and rectify.

Chapter 12 Bodywork and subframes

Contents

1 General description

The models covered by this manual have a combined body and main underframe of all welded steel construction. This makes a very strong and torsionally rigid shell.

In addition there are two subframes which are attached to the front and rear of the underside of the body. It is onto these that the power unit, front suspension assemblies and rear suspension assemblies are mounted.

Depending on the marque, two door, four door or Countryman (Traveller) versions are available.

Since the introduction of the 1100 in September 1963 there have been various minor modifications and body style changes; but in the main, the basic body shell has changed little.

Due to the simplicity of the body and its attachments, maintenance and repair work is very simple and well within the capabilities of the average Do-it-Yourself motorist.

2 Maintenance - body and subframes

1 The condition of your car's bodywork is of considerable importance as it is on this that the second hand value of the car will mainly depend. It is much more difficult to repair neglected bodywork than to renew mechanical assemblies. The hidden portions of the body, such as the wheel arches and the underframe and the engine compartment are equally important, although obviously not requiring such frequent attention as the immediately visible paintwork.

2 Once a year or every 12,000 miles, (20,000 Km) it is a sound scheme to visit your local main agent and have the underside of the body steam cleaned. This will take about 1½ hours. All traces of dirt and oil will be removed and the underside can then be inspected carefully for rust, damaged hydraulic pipes, frayed electrical wiring and similar maladies. The car should be greased on completion of this job.

3 At the same time the engine compartment should be cleaned in the same manner. If steam cleaning facilities are not available then brush 'Gunk' or a similar cleanser over the whole engine and engine compartment with a stiff paint brush, working it well in where there is an accumulation of oil and dirt. Do not paint the ignition system and protect it with oily rags when the Gunk is washed off. As the Gunk is washed away it will take with it all traces of oil and dirt, leaving the engine looking clean and bright.

4 The wheel arches should be given particular attention as undersealing can easily come away here and stones and dirt thrown up from the road wheels can soon cause the paint to chip and flake, and so allow rust to get in. If rust is found, clean down to the bare metal with wet and dry paper, paint on an anti-corrosive coating such as Kurust, or if preferred, red lead, and renew the paintwork and under-coating.

5 The bodywork should be washed once a week or when dirty. Thoroughly wet the car to soften the dirt and then wash the car down with a soft sponge and plenty of clean water. If the surplus dirt is not washed off very gently, in time it will wear the paint down as surely as wet and dry paper. It is best to use a hose if this is available. Give the car a final washdown and then dry with a soft chamois leather to prevent the formation of spots.

6 Spots of tar and grease thrown up from the road can be removed with a rag dampened with petrol.

7 One every six months, or every three months is wished, give the bodywork and chromium trim a thoroughly good wax polish. If a chromium cleaner is used to remove rust on any of the car's plated parts remember that the cleaner also removes part of the chromium, so use sparingly.

3 Maintenance - upholstery and carpets

1 Remove the carpets and thoroughly vacuum clean the interior of the car every three months, or more frequently if necessary.
2 Beat out carpets and shampoo them if they are very dirty. If the headlining or upholstery is soiled apply an upholstery cleaner with a damp sponge and wipe off with a clean dry cloth.

4 Minor body damage - repair

See photo sequences on pages 230 and 231.

Repair of minor scratches in the car's bodywork

If the scratch is very superficial, and does not penetrate to the metal of the bodywork - repair is very simple. Lightly rub the area of the scratch with a paintwork renovator (eg. "T-Cut"), or a very fine cutting paste, to remove loose paint from the scratch and to clear the surrounding bodywork of wax polish. Rinse the area with clean water.

Apply touch-up paint to the scratch using a thin paint brush; continue to apply thin layers of paint until the surface of the paint in the scratch is level with the surrounding paintwork. Allow the new paint at least two weeks to harden, then, blend it into the surrounding paintwork by rubbing the paintwork in the scratch area with a paintwork renovator (eg. "T-Cut"), or a very fine cutting paste. Finally apply a wax polish.

An alternative to painting over the scratch is to use Holts "Scratch-Patch". Use the same preparation for the affected area; then simply, pick a patch of a suitable size to cover the scratch completely. Hold the patch against the scratch and burnish its backing paper; the patch will adhere to the paintwork, freeing itself from the backing paper at the same time. Polish the affected area to blend the patch into the surrounding paintwork.

Where a scratch has penetrated right through to the metal of the bodywork, causing the metal to rust, a different repair technique is required. Remove any loose rust from the bottom of the scratch with a penknife, then apply rust inhibiting paint (eg. "Kurust") to prevent the formation of rust in the future. Using a rubber or nylon applicator fill the scratch with body-stopper paste. If required, this paste can be mixed with cellulose thinners to provide a very thin paste which is ideal for filling narrow scratches. Before the stopper paste in the scratch hardens, wrap a piece of smooth cotton rag around the top of a finger. Dip the finger in cellulose thinners and then quickly sweep it across the surface of the stopper-paste in the scratch; this will ensure that the surface of the stopper-paste is slightly hollowed. The scratch can now be painted over as described earlier in this Section.

Repair of dents in the car's bodywork

When deep denting of the car's bodywork has taken place, the first task is to pull the dent out, until the affected bodywork almost attains its original shape. There is little point in trying to restore the original shape completely, as the metal in the damaged area will have stretched on impact and cannot be re-shaped fully to its original contour. It is better to bring the level of the dent up to a point which is about 1/8 inch (3 mm) below the level of the surrounding bodywork. In cases where the dent is very shallow anyway, it is not worth trying to pull it out at all.

If the underside of the dent is accessible, it can be hammered out gently from behind, using a mallet with a wooden or plastic head. Whilst doing this, hold a suitable block of wood firmly against the outside of the dent. This block will absorb the impact from the hammer blows and thus prevent a large area of body-work from being 'belled-out'.

Should the dent be in a section of the bodywork which has double skin or some other factor making it inaccessible from behind, a different technique is called for. Drill several small holes through the metal inside the dent area - particularly in the deeper sections. Then screw long self-tapping screws into the

holes just sufficiently for them to gain a good purchase in the metal. Now the dent can be pulled out by pulling on the pro-truding heads of the screws with a pair of pliers.

The next stage of the repair is the removal of the paint from the damaged area, and from an inch or so of the surrounding 'sound' bodywork. This is accomplished most easily by using a wire brush or abrasive pad on a power drill, although it can be done just as effectively by hand using sheets of abrasive paper. To complete the preparations for filling, score the surface of the bare metal with a screwdriver or the tang of a file, or alter-natively, drill small holes in the affected area. This will provide a really good 'key' for the filler paste.

To complete the repair see the Section on filling and re-spraying.

Repair of rust holes or gashes in the car's bodywork

Remove all paint from the affected area and from an inch or so of the surrounding 'sound bodywork', using an abrasive pad or a wire brush on a power drill. If these are not available a few sheets of abrasive paper will do the job just as effectively. With the paint removed you will be able to gauge the severity of the corrosion and therefore decide whether to replace the whole panel (if this is possible) or to repair the affected area. Replace-ment body panels are not as expensive as most people think and it is often quicker and more satisfactory to fit a new panel than to attempt to repair large areas of corrosion.

Remove all fittings from the affected area except those which will act as a guide to the original shape of the damaged body-work (eg. headlamp shell etc). Then, using tin snips or a hacksaw blade, remove all loose metal and any other metal badly affected by corrosion. Hammer the edges of the hole inwards in order to create a slight depression for the filler paste.

Wire brush the affected area to remove the powdery rust from the surface of the remaining metal. Paint the affected area with rust inhibiting paint (eg. "Kurust"); if the back of the rusted area is accessible treat this also.

Before filling can take place it will be necessary to block the hole in some way. This can be achieved by the use of one of the following materials: Zinc gauze, Aluminium tape or Poly-urethane foam.

Zinc gauze is probably the best material to use for a large hole. Cut a piece to the approximate size and shape of the hole to be filled, then position it in the hole so that its edges are below the level of the surrounding bodywork. It can be retained in position by several blobs of filler paste around its periphery.

Aluminium tape should be used for small or very narrow holes. Pull a piece off the roll and trim it to the approximate size and shape required, then pull off the backing paper (if used) and stick the tape over the hole; it can be overlapped if the thickness of one piece is insufficient. Burnish down the edges of the tape with the handle of a screwdriver or similar, to ensure that the tape is securely attached to the metal underneath.

Polyurethane foam is best used where the hole is situated in a section of bodywork of complex shape, backed by a small box section (eg. where the sill panel meets the rear wheel arch - most cars). The usual mixing procedure for this foam is as follows: Put equal amounts of fluid from each of the two cans provided in the kit, into one container. Stir until the mixture begins to thicken, then quickly pour this mixture into the hole, and hold a piece of cardboard over the larger apertures. Almost immediately the polyurethane will begin to expand, gushing frantically out of any small holes left unblocked. When the foam hardens it can be cut back to just below the level of the surrounding bodywork with a hacksaw blade.

Having blocked off the hole the affected area must now be filled and sprayed - see Section on bodywork filling and re-spraying.

Bodywork repairs - filling and re-spraying

Before using this Section, see the Sections on dent, deep scratch, rust hole, and gash repairs.

Many types of bodyfiller are available, but generally speaking those proprietary kits which contain a tin of filler paste and a

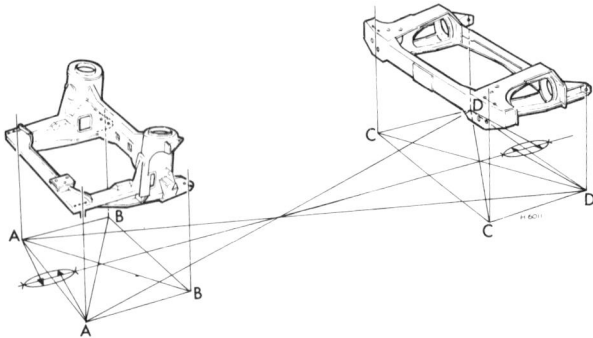

Fig. 12.1. Horizontal alignment check (Sec. 5)

A—A   *Width between centres of the front subframe front*
       mounting set screws 30 7/16 in (773.11 mm)
B—B   *Width between centres of the front subframe rear*
       mounting rear mounting set screws 28¼ in
       (717.35 mm)
C—C   *Width between centres of the rear subframe front*
       mounting setscrews 42¼ in (1073.15 mm)
D—D   *Width between centres of the rear subframe rear*
       mounting setscrews 43 7/16 in (1103.31 mm)

tube of resin hardener (eg. "Holts Cataloy") are best for this type of repair. A wide, flexible plastic or nylon applicator will be found invaluable for imparting a smooth and well contoured finish to the surface of the filler.

Mix up a little filler on a clean piece of card or board - use the hardener sparingly (follow the maker's instructions on the pack), otherwise the filler will set very rapidly.

Using an applicator, apply the filler paste to the prepared area; draw the applicator across the surface of the filler to achieve the correct contour and to level the filler surface. As soon as a contour that approximates the correct one is achieved, stop working the paste - if you carry on too long the paste will become sticky and begin to 'pick-up' on the applicator.

Continue to add thin layers of filler paste at twenty-minute intervals until the level of the filler is just 'proud' of the surrounding bodywork.

Once the filler has hardened, excess can be removed using a Surform plane or Dreadnought file. From then on, progressively finer grades of abrasive paper should be used, starting with a 40 grade 'wet-and-dry' paper. Always wrap the abrasive paper around a flat rubber, cork, or wooden block - otherwise the surface of the filler will not be completely flat. During the smoothing of the filler surface the 'wet-and-dry' paper should be periodically rinsed in water - this will ensure that a very smooth finish is imparted to the filler at the final stage.

At this stage the 'dent' should be surrounded by a ring of bare metal, which in turn should be encircled by the finely 'feathered' edge of the good paintwork. Rinse the repair area with clean water, until all the dust produced by the rubbing-down operation is gone.

Spray the whole repair area with a light coat of grey primer - this will show up any imperfections in the surface of the filler. Repair these imperfections with fresh filler paste or body-stopper and once more smooth the surface with abrasive paper. If bodystopper is used, it can be mixed with cellulose thinners to form a really thin paste which is ideal for filling small holes. Repeat this spray and repair procedure until you are satisfied that the surface of the filler, and the feathered edge of the paintwork are perfect. Clean the repair area with clean water and

allow to dry fully.

The repair area is now ready for spraying. Paint spraying must be carried out in a warm, dry, windless and dust free atmosphere. This condition can be created artificially if you have access to a large indoor working area, but if you are forced to work in the open, you will have to pick your day very carefully. If you are working indoors, dousing the floor in the work area with water will 'lay' the dust which would otherwise be in the atmosphere. If the repair area is confined to one body panel, mask off the surround panels, this will help to minimise the effects of a slight mis-match in paint colours. Bodywork fittings (eg. chrome strips, door handles etc) will also need to be masked off. Use genuine masking tape and several thicknesses of news-paper for the masking operation.

Before commencing to spray, agitate the aerosol can thoroughly, then spray a test area (an old tin, or similar) until the technique is mastered. Cover the repair area with a thick coat of primer, the thickness should be built up using several thin layers of paint rather than one thick one. Using 400 grade 'wet-and-dry' paper, rub down the surface of the primer until it is really smooth. While doing this, the work area should be thoroughly doused with water, and the wet-and-dry paper periodically rinsed in water. Allow to dry before spraying on more paint.

Spray on the top coat, again building up the thickness by using several thin layers of paint. Start spraying in the centre of the repair area and then using a circular motion, work outwards until the whole repair area and about 2 inches of the surrounding original paintwork is covered. Remove all masking material 10 to 15 minutes after spraying on the final coat of paint. Allow the new paint at least 2 weeks to harden fully; then, using a paint-work renovator (eg. "T-Cut") or a very fine cutting paste, blend the edges of the new paint into the existing paintwork. Finally, apply wax polish.

---

5   Major body and underframe damage - repair

Because the body is built on the monocoque principle and is integral with the underframe, major damage must be repaired by competent mechanics with the necessary welding and hydraulic straightening equipment.

If the damage is serious it is vital that the bodyshell is in correct alignment, as otherwise the handling of the car will suffer and many other faults such as excessive tyre wear, and wear in the transmission and steering, may occur. The BLMC recommend a special alignment jig is used to ensure that all is correct; also a repaired car should be checked on this jig.

Alternatively, with the bodyshell jacked-up off a level floor a series of measurement checks can be carried out to determine whether misalignment is present or not. Start by ensuring that the body is quite parallel with the floor and make certain that one side is not higher than the other. This is best done by measuring with a steel tape the distance from the floor at each side and at the front and rear.

Refer to Fig. 12.1 and spread a little chalk on the ground directly under the subframe check points. Drop a bob line from each of the check points and mark the point where it touches the ground with a pencilled 'X'.

When all the datum points have been plotted generously dust a piece of string with chalk powder and secure each end under weights between two opposite 'X' marks. Moving to the centre of the string, lift it vertically a few inches and then allow it to spring back against the floor. A clear line will be made by chalk from the string. Repeat this from different diagonally opposite 'X' marks as shown in Fig. 12.1. All the lines should intersect at the same point. If the lines do not intersect at the same point or there are considerable differences in length between the lines 'A' - 'D', 'D' - 'C', etc., (ie., by several inches) then the body will be known to be badly distorted.

A further check can be made by determining a centre line through drawing intersecting arcs with the aid of a large pair of compasses opposite check points.

6 Door - removal and replacement

Each door is held in place by two hinges and a check link. Free the check link by taking out the split pin, washer, and clevis pin. With a pencil mark the position of the hinges on the door pillar so they can be put back in exactly the same place.

Open the door and place suitable chocks underneath it for support. Then unscrew the three bolts holding each hinge to the door pillar and lift the door off.

Replacement is straightforward reversal of the removal sequence. It is possible to alter the position of the hinge slightly so that the door can be made to fit differently if required.

7 Door trim pad - removal and replacement

Austin, Morris, M.G, Wolseley and Riley models

1 *Mk I and 4 door models:* Remove the centre screw and spring washer that retains each handle and finisher. (Fig. 12.2.) Note which way the handle is fitted and lift away. (photo)

2 Undo and remove the two screws that secure the door pull or arm rest to the door assembly. Lift off the door pull or arm rest. (photo)

3 *2 door Mk II and 1300 models:* Remove the anti-burst door lock remote control retainer halves by easing the top half upwards and the bottom half downwards. (photo)

4 Undo and remove the screws that secure the door map pocket.

5 Using a wide bladed screwdriver carefully lever the trim pad from the door inner panel. (photos)

6 Refitting the door pad is the reverse sequence to removal.

Princess

1 Remove the door lock handle, window regulator handle and the drive screws that secure the chrome plated door pull to the arm rest.

2 Undo and remove the wood screws that secure the arm rest to the map pocket and lift away the map pocket.

3 Undo and remove the drive screws that secure the door trim pad to the door inner panel.

4 Using a wide bladed screwdriver carefully lever the trim pad from the door inner panel.

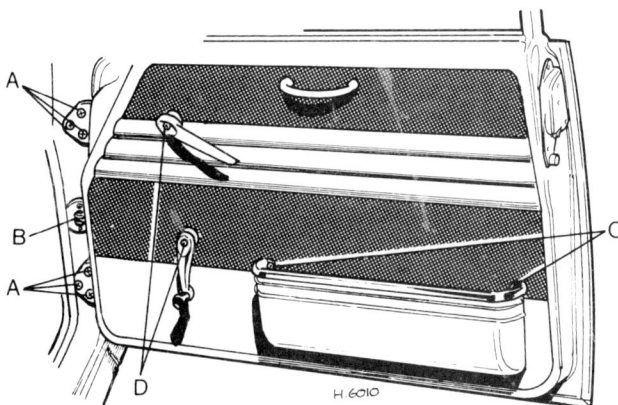

Fig. 12.2. Door trim pad and attachments (earlier models)

A Hinge screws
B Check link
C Door map pocket screws
D Door handle and window regulator screws

5 Undo and remove the drivescrews that secure the wooden door finisher to the door and lift away the door finishers.

6 Refitting the door finishers and trim pad is the reverse sequence to removal.

8 Door glass - removal and replacement

1 This Section is applicable to four door models only.

2 Refer to Section 7, and remove the door trim pad.

3 Carefully lever off the waist finisher strips.

4 Release the glass channel which is attached to the regulator assembly.

5 Remove the glass stop and lower the glass to the bottom of the door.

6 Remove the regulator arm from the glass regulator channel and the vertical and door top glass felt channel.

7 Remove the regulator securing screws and carefully remove the regulator assembly.

8 The door glass assembly may now be lifted up and away through the top of the door panel.

9 Refitting the door glass is the reverse sequence to removal. Lubricate all moving parts with a little grease.

9 Door glass regulator - removal and replacement

1 This Section is applicable to four door models only.

2 Refer to Section 7, and remove the door trim pad.

3 Remove the regulator securing screws and the regulator bracket securing screws.

4 Remove the regulator arm from the bottom of the window glass.

5 Raise the window glass to the top of the aperture and support with a tapered wedge.

7 The regulator and bracket assembly may now be lifted away.

8 Refitting the regulator and bracket assembly is now the reverse sequence to removal.

10 Door glass and regulator (2 door models) - removal and replacement

1 Refer to Section 7, and remove the door trim pad.

2 Remove the door glass stop and lower the door glass to the bottom of the door.

3 Lever off the outer weatherstrip and the inner door waist rail.

4 Remove the ventilator screw and the screw on the top edge of the door.

5 Lift out the fixed quarterlight assembly.

6 Centralise the bottom control channel and twist the glass forwards and upwards to remove it.

7 Undo and remove the ten screws that secure the window winder mechanism and remove it from inside the door.

8 Refitting the regulator and door glass is the reverse sequence to removal.

11 Door lock - removal and replacement

1 This Section is applicable to two door Mk I and 4 door models only.

2 Before attempting to remove any part of the door lock mechanism because of faulty operation, always check that the apparant condition is not caused by bad or incorrect installation.

3 Refer to Section 7, and remove the door trim pad.

4 Release the remote control bar from the door lock by removing the spring clip and wavy washer.

5 Undo and remove the set screws that secure the door lock to the door panel.

6 The door lock assembly may now be lifted away.

7 Refitting the door lock assembly is the reverse sequence to

7.1 Removal of window regulator handle securing screw

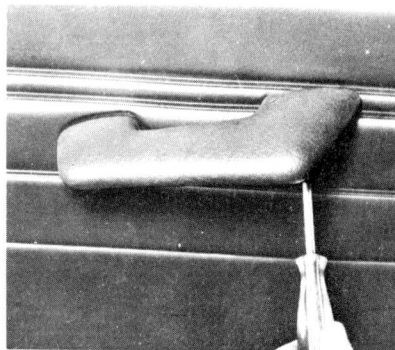

7.2 Removal of arm rest securing screw

7.3 Remote control retainer removal

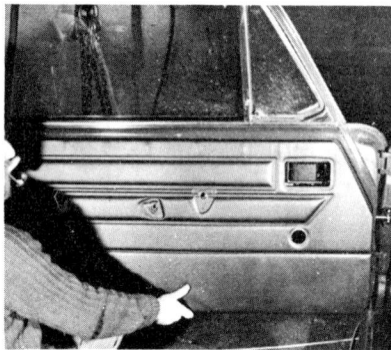

7.5A Lifting away trim pad

7.5B All apertures are sealed with tape

removal. Lubricate all moving points with a little engine grade oil.

12 Door lock (anti-burst type) - removal and replacement

1   This Section is applicable to 2 door 1300 and 1100 Mk II models.
2   Undo the single screw holding the window winder handle and take it off together with the door pull which is held in place by two screws. (Fig. 12.8.)
3   Remove the anti-burst door lock remote control retainer and if fitted remove the door map pocket by unscrewing the two retaining screws.
4   Lever the trim panel away from the door panel and remove the grey door liners.
5   Release the metal clips securing the remote control rods to the door lock and pull the anti-rattle clips from the door.
6   Undo the four screws that secure the remote control assembly to the door panel and lift it clear.
7   Remove both the small and large push button retaining clips and withdraw the push button assembly from the outside.
8   Remove the screws holding the lock mechanism to the door panel and pull the assembly outwards.
9   Refitting of the anti-burst door lock mechanism is a straight-forward reversal of the removal procedure.

13 Door lock striker - removal and replacement

If the striker plate becomes worn and it is wished to replace it, first mark its position on the door pillar so that the new plate can be fixed in the correct position. Unscrew the set screws holding the plate to the door pillar and lift the plate away. Replacement is a direct reversal of the removal process.

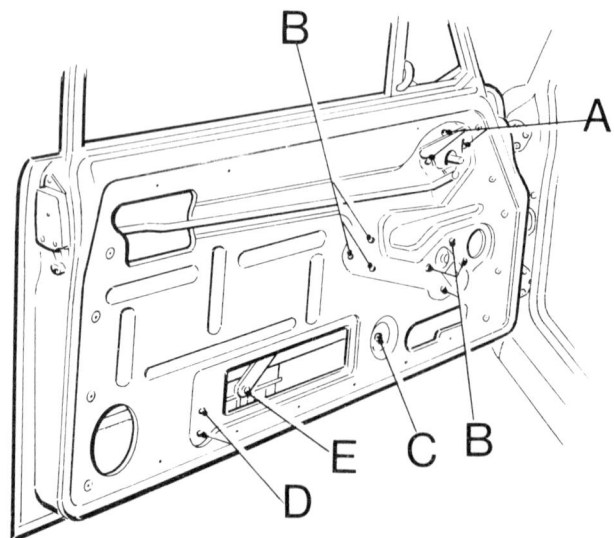

Fig. 12.3. Front door with trim pad removed (4 door models)

A   Door lock
    remote control

B   Window regulator
    and bracket
    screws

C   Ventilator screw
D   Door stop screws
E   Door glass
    regulator arm

14 Exterior door handle - removal and replacement

1   Refer to Section 7, and remove the door trim pad.
2   Undo and remove the door handle to door panel securing set

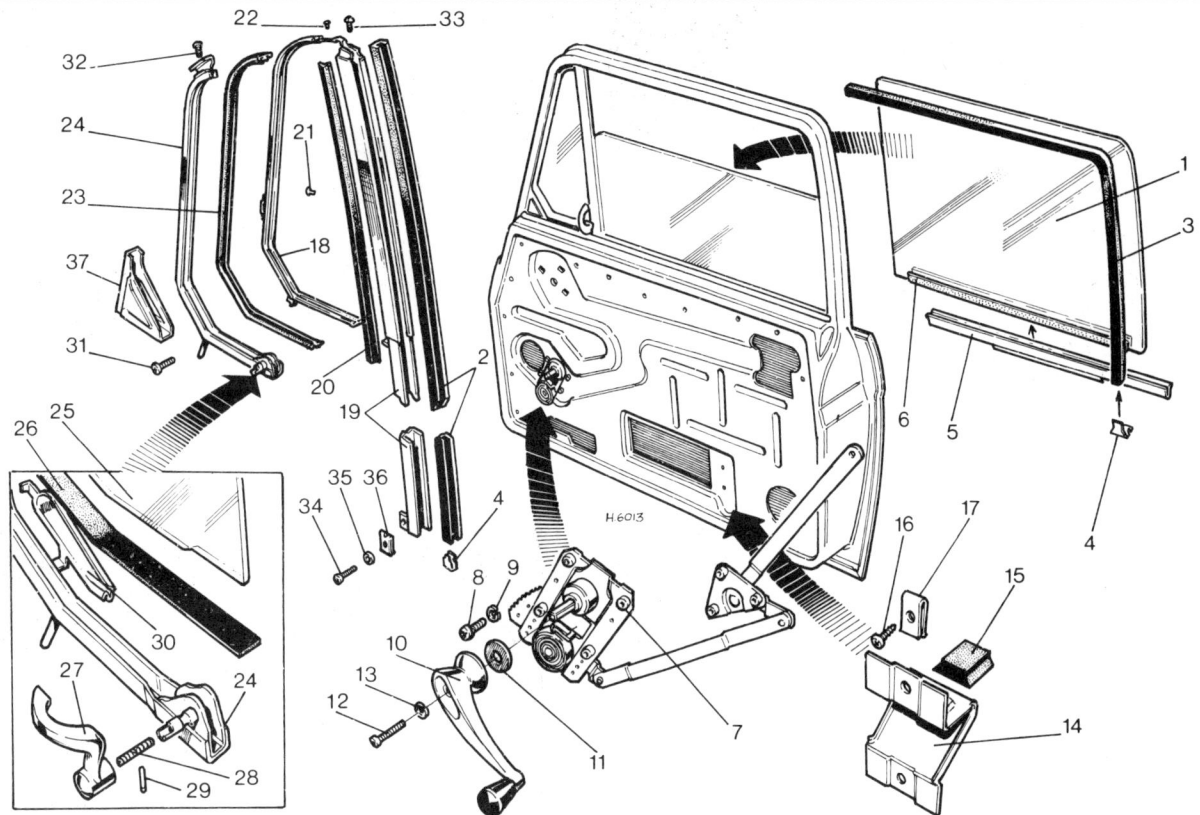

Fig. 12.4. Front door and glass assemblies

1	Window glass	11	Fibre washer	20	Rubber sealing channel
2	Glass channel - front	12	Screw		vertical
3	Glass channel - top and rear	13	Spring washer	21	Rivet
4	Clip	14	Glass stop bracket	22	Rivet
5	Channel assembly	15	Glass stop rubber buffer	23	Sealing rubber
6	Rubber glazing	16	Screw	24	Inner frame assembly
7	Window regulator - rh	17	Plate nut	25	Glass
8	Screw	18	Ventilator frame assembly	26	Rubber glazing
9	Spring washer	19	Channel assembly - vertical	27	Handle catch
10	Window regulator handle				

28	Spring
29	Pin
30	Drain channel
31	Screw
32	Screw
33	Screw - short
34	Screw - long
35	Plain washer
36	Plate nut
37	Corner capping

screws and lift away the outer handle.

3   On Mk I and all 4 door models the push button assembly is contained within the outer handle.

4   Refitting the exterior door handle is the reverse sequence to removal.

15 Door ventilator - removal and replacement

1   Refer to Section 7, and remove the door trim pad.

2   Refer to Section 8, and release but do not remove the window assembly.

3   The ventilator may now be lifted away from the door.

4   Refitting the door ventilator is the reverse sequence to removal.

16 Bonnet - removal and replacement

1   Mark the position of the hinges relative to the bonnet bracket to assist with refitting.

2   Undo and remove the screws that secure the telescopic bonnet stay to the bonnet.

3   Suitably support the bonnet. Undo and remove the securing nuts, spring and plain washers and bolts which secure the bonnet to the bonnet hinges.

4   The bonnet assembly may now be lifted away. (photo)

5   Refitting the bonnet is the reverse sequence to removal. If necessary adjust the bonnet to hinge position to ensure even seating between the two wings and vent panel.

17 Luggage compartment lid - removal and replacement

1   When the number plate light is fitted to the lid disconnect the cable at the terminal connector.

2   Suitably support the lid. Undo and remove the bolts and washers that secure the lid to the hinge bars.

3   The luggage compartment lid may now be lifted away.

4   Refitting the luggage compartment lid is the reverse sequence to removal. Note that the mounting holes are oversize to permit adjustment of the lid in the aperture.

18 Luggage compartment lock - removal and replacement

1   **Warning:** Do not, under any circumstances, close the luggage compartment lid when the lock mechanism is in the process of being removed or refitted.

2   Carefully remove the notched locking ring and withdraw the push button assembly.

3   Unhook the connecting link and then undo and remove the crosshead screws that secure the lock catch mechanism to the lid.

4   The catch assembly may now be lifted away.

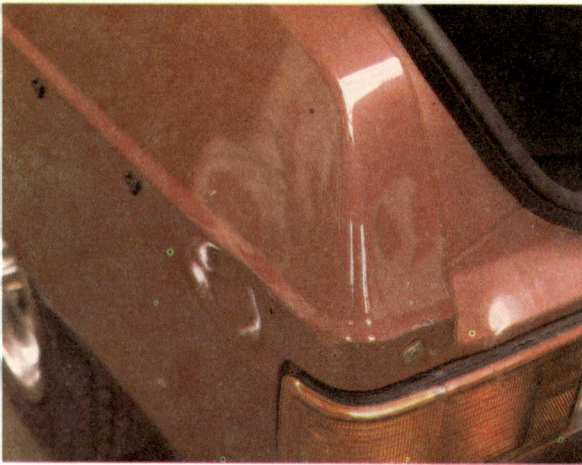

This sequence of photographs deals with the repair of the dent and scratch (above rear lamp) shown in this photo. The procedure will be similar for the repair of a hole. It should be noted that the procedures given here are simplified - more explicit instructions will be found in the text

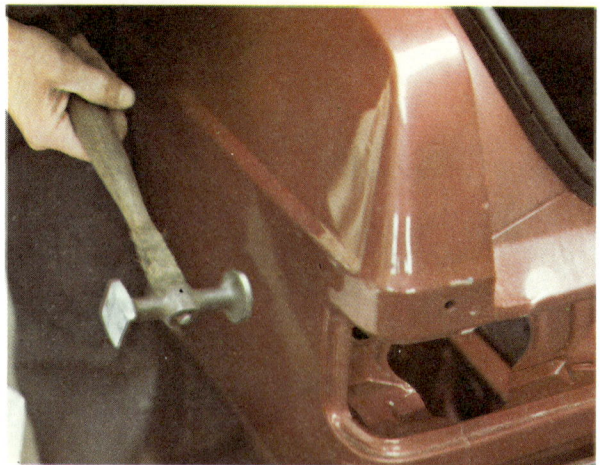

In the case of a dent the first job - after removing surrounding trim - is to hammer out the dent where access is possible. This will minimise filling. Here, the large dent having been hammered out, the damaged area is being made slightly concave

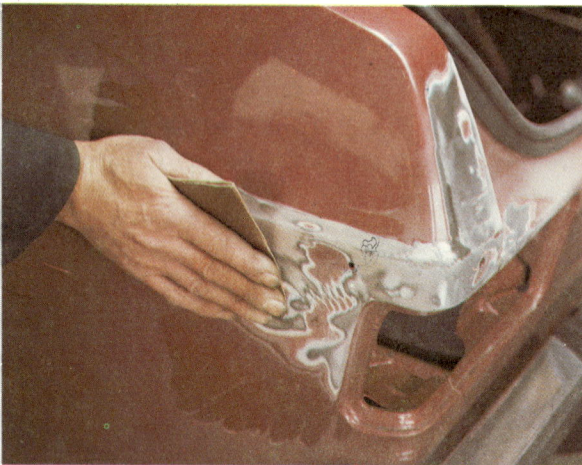

Now all paint must be removed from the damaged area, by rubbing with coarse abrasive paper. Alternatively, a wire brush or abrasive pad can be used in a power drill. Where the repair area meets good paintwork, the edge of the paintwork should be 'feathered', using a finer grade of abrasive paper

In the case of a hole caused by rusting, all damaged sheet-metal should be cut away before proceeding to this stage. Here, the damaged area is being treated with rust remover and inhibitor before being filled

Mix the body filler according to its manufacturer's instructions. In the case of corrosion damage, it will be necessary to block off any large holes before filling - this can be done with zinc gauze or aluminium tape. Make sure the area is absolutely clean before ...

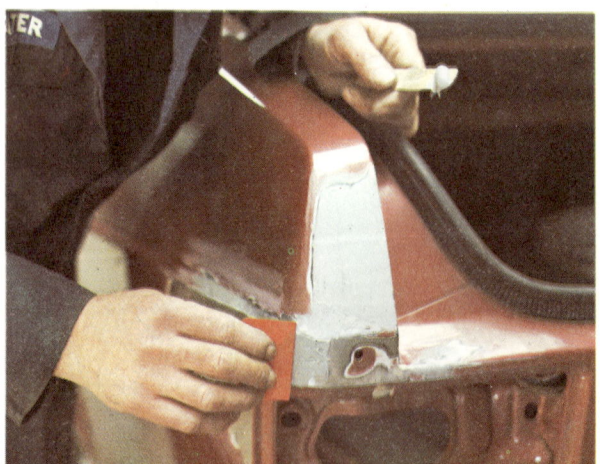

... applying the filler. Filler should be applied with a flexible applicator, as shown, for best results: the wooden spatula being used for confined areas. Apply thin layers of filler at 20-minute intervals, until the surface of the filler is slightly proud of the surrounding bodywork

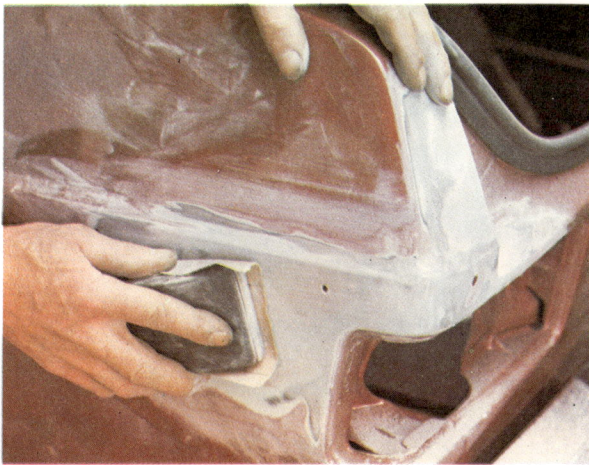

Initial shaping can be done with a Surform plane or Dreadnought file. Then, using progressively finer grades of wet-and-dry paper, wrapped around a sanding block, and copious amounts of clean water, rub-down the filler until really smooth and flat. Again, feather the edges of adjoining paintwork

The whole repair area can now be sprayed or brush-painted with primer. If spraying, ensure adjoining areas are protected from over-spray. Note that at least one-inch of the surrounding sound paintwork should be coated with primer. Primer has a 'thick' consistency, so will fill small imperfections

Again, using plenty of water, rub down the primer with a fine grade of wet-and-dry paper (400 grade is probably best) until it is really smooth and well blended into the surrounding paint-work. Any remaining imperfections can now be filled by carefully applied knifing stopper paste

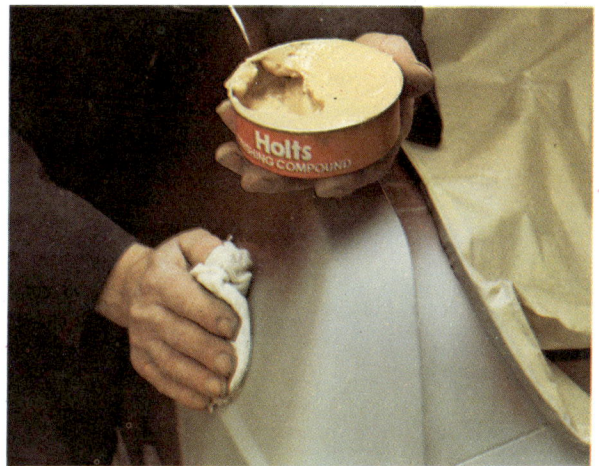

When the stopper has hardened, rub-down the repair area again before applying the final coat of primer. Before rubbing-down this last coat of primer, ensure the repair area is blemish-free - use more stopper if necessary. To ensure that the surface of the primer is really smooth use some finishing compound

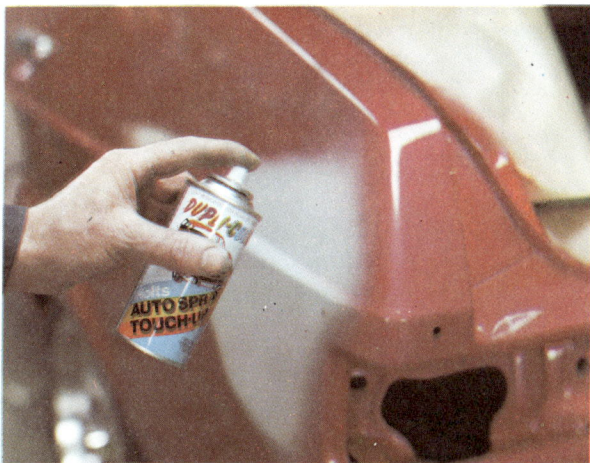

The top coat can now be applied. When working out of doors, pick a dry, warm and wind-free day. Ensure surrounding areas are protected from over-spray. Agitate the aerosol thoroughly, then spray the centre of the repair area, working outwards with a circular motion. Apply the paint as several thin coats.

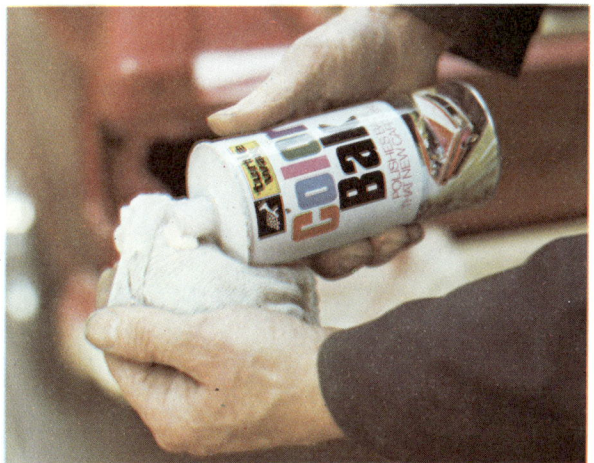

After a period of about two-weeks, which the paint needs to harden fully, the surface of the repaired area can be 'cut' with a mild cutting compound prior to wax polishing. When carrying out bodywork repairs, remember that the quality of the finished job is proportional to the time and effort expended

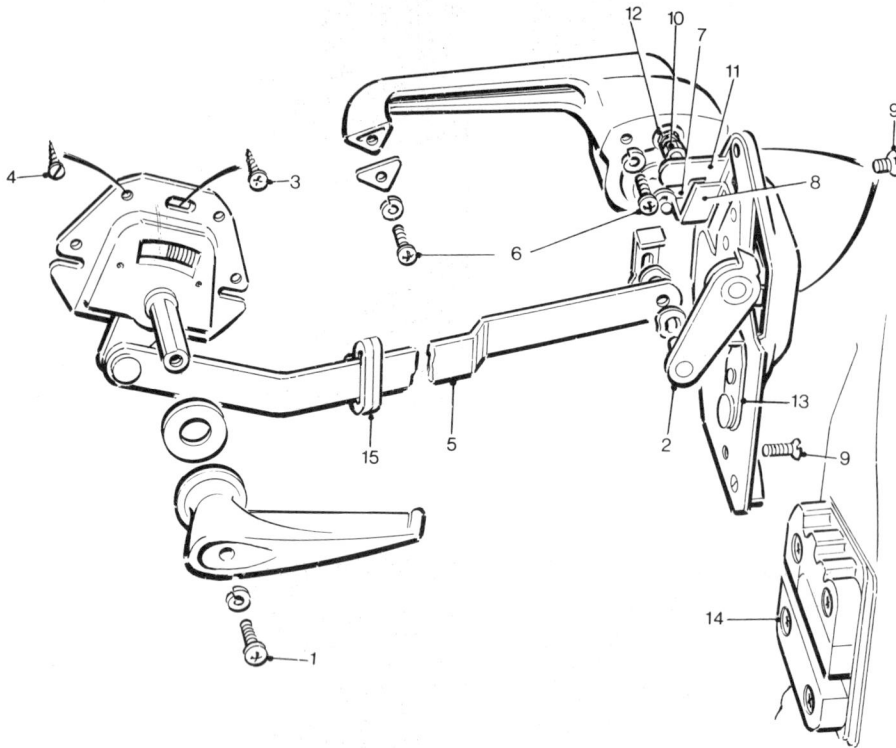

Fig. 12.5. Door lock and striker mechanism (Mk I and 4 door models)

1 Inner door handle
   retaining screw
2 Lock operating lever
3 Remote control to door
   retaining screws

4 Self-tapping screw
5 Connecting link
6 Outer door handle
   retaining screws
7 Key operating arm

8 Lock frame
9 Lock to door retaining
   screws
10 Push button plunger
   bolt

11 Lock contactor
12 Locknut
13 Children's safety catch
14 Striker to door pillar
   retaining screws
15 Anti-rattle clip

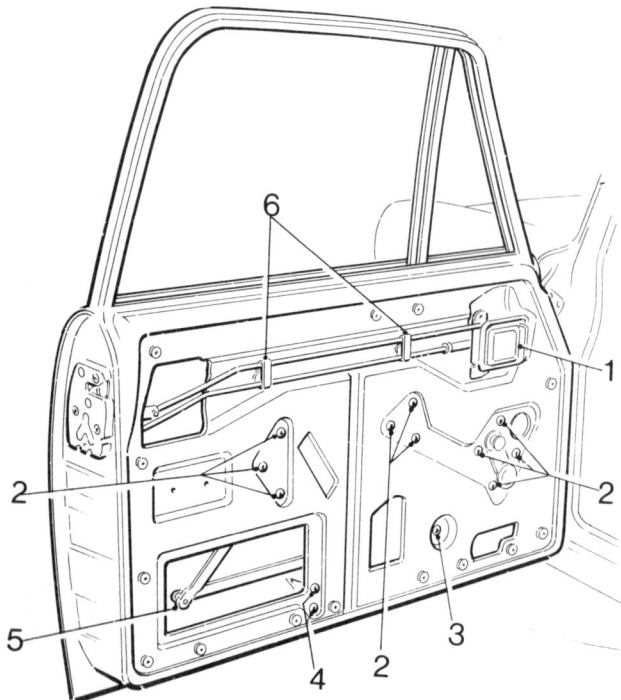

Fig. 12.6. Front door with trim pad removed (1300 and 1100 Mk II)

1 Door lock remote control
2 Window regulator and bracket screws
3 Ventilator screw
4 Door stop screws
5 Door glass regulator arm
6 Anti-rattle clips

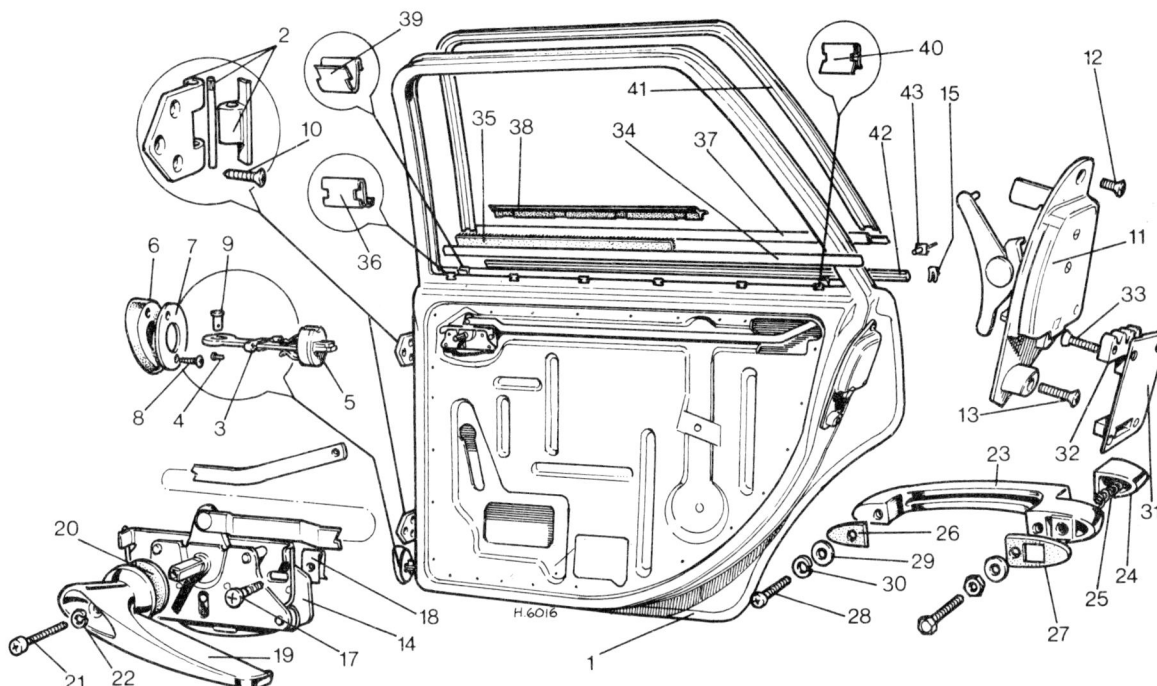

Fig. 12.7. Rear door components

1 Door shell	11 Lock assembly	23 Door handle - rh	34 Waist rail - inner
2 Door hinge	12 Screw - short	24 Push button	35 Weatherstrip - inner
3 Check arm guide spring	13 Screw - long	25 Button return spring	36 Clip
4 Rivet	14 Remote control assembly	26 Washer - front	37 Waist rail - outer
5 Door check arm	15 Clip	27 Washer - rear	38 Waist rail seal - outer
6 Check arm seal	17 Screw	28 Screw	39 Clip - outer
7 Retaining plate seal	18 Plate nut	29 Plain washer	40 Clip - inner
8 Screw	19 Remote control handle	30 Spring washer	41 Finisher
9 Clevis pin	20 Fibre washer	31 Dovetail assembly - rh	42 Door moulding
10 Screw	21 Screw	32 Striker - rh	43 Clip and rivet
	22 Spring washer	33 Screw	assembly

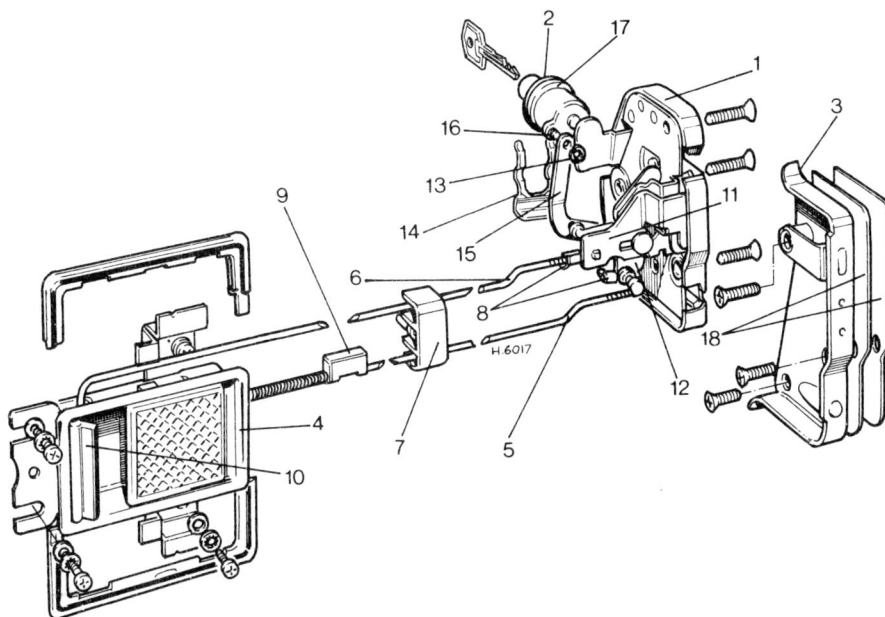

Fig. 12.8. Door lock components as fitted to 1300 and 1100 Mk II 2 door models

1 Lock assembly
2 Push button unit
3 Striker assembly
4 Remote control unit
5 Latch release rod
6 Lock control rod
7 Anti-rattle guides
8 Spring retaining clip (two)
9 Plastic connector
10 Safety locking lever
11 Locking slide
12 Latch release lever
13 Small circlip
14 Large spring slip
15 Key-operated lock link
16 Push-button operating arm
17 Fibre washer
18 Striker shims

16.4 Lifting away bonnet

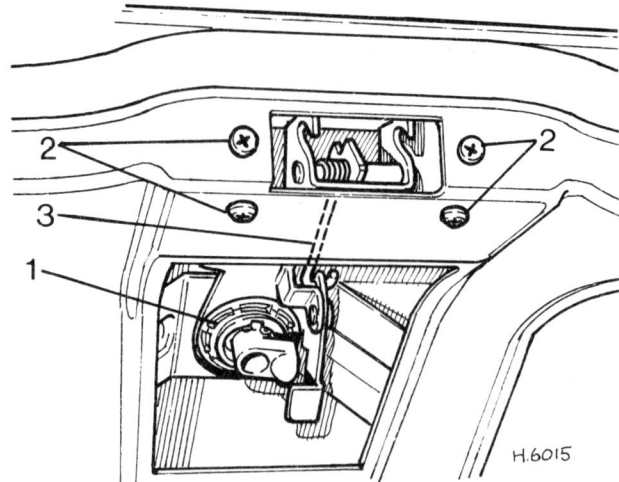

Fig. 12.9. Luggage compartment lock (Sec. 18)

1 *Notched locking ring*   3 *Connecting link*
2 *Cross-head screws*

5 Refitting the luggage compartment lock is the reverse sequence to removal.

19 Luggage compartment hinges and torsion bars - removal and replacement

Hinge

1 Refer to Section 17, and remove the luggage compartment lid.
2 Remove the rear seat as described in Section 29.
3 Remove the rear shelf by pulling it upwards to release the spring clips.
4 Remove the rear upper quarter liner from the side of the car from which the hinge is being removed.
5 *Two door models:* Open the rear quarterlight and pull the seal away from the bottom corner by a sufficient amount to allow the side trim to be pulled back to expose the hinge pivot bolt.
6 *Four door models:* Pull the door seal away by a similar amount just above the waist rail.
7 Support the free end of the torsion bar with a wooden block to release its tension from the hinge.
8 Unscrew the pivot bolt from inside the car and remove the hinge from the body.
9 Refitting the hinge is the reverse sequence to removal.

Torsion bar

1 Remove the hinges as described earlier in this Section.
2 Undo and remove all six retaining bolts from the mounting brackets at both ends.
3 Remove the central support bracket and withdraw both torsion bars with their mounting brackets as a complete assembly.
4 Refitting the torsion bar is the reverse sequence to removal.

20 Rear door (Countryman and Traveller) - removal and replacement

1 Suitably support the rear door and then remove the locknut and bolt from each of the two door brackets.
2 Undo and remove the three captive screws from each of the two hinge plates in the drain channel.
3 The rear door assembly may now be lifted away.
4 Refitting the rear door is the reverse sequence to removal.

21 Rear door lock, remote control and link bar (Countryman and Traveller) - removal and replacement

1 Undo and remove the six self-tapping screws, spring and plain washers from the lock, remote control and link bar.
2 Carefully lift the lock and remote control from the panel.
3 Refitting the rear door lock assembly is the reverse sequence to removal. Lubricate all moving parts with engine oil.

22 Rear door exterior handle (Countryman and Traveller) - removal and replacement

1 Remove the trim pad by carefully levering the fixing clips away from the interior panel.
2 Undo and remove the two small nuts, spring and plain washers from the exterior handle studs and lift the handle from the door.
3 Remove the connecting pin and separate the lock from the remote control bar.
4 Should it be necessary to adjust the handle check that the bolt action is 0.8125 in (20.638 mm) and reset if necessary.
5 Later type lock and striker adjustment: Slacken the lock securing bolts until the lock is just nipped. Open and close the tailgate several times with the bolt retracted to centralise the lock around the pin on the striker plate. If this cannot be done pack the striker with spacers to the required height.
6 Refitting the exterior handle assembly is the reverse sequence to removal. If a later type lock and striker is being fitted to replace the earlier type it will be necessary to drill a hole in the door panel so as to align with the striker pin.

23 Rear door lock, remote control and link bar (Countryman and Traveller) - removal and replacement

1 Undo and remove the six self-tapping screws, spring and plain washers from the lock, remote control and link bar.
2 The lock and remote control may now be lifted from the panel.
3 Refitting the rear door lock assembly is the reverse sequence to removal. Lubricate all moving parts with a little engine oil.

24 Windscreen and backlight glasses - removal and replacement.

1 Removal and replacement of a windscreen or backlight is no

light task. Leave this to the specialist if possible; for the ambitious instructions are given below.

2 Windscreen removal: Refer to Chapter 10 and remove the windscreen wiper arms.

3 Cover the surrounding paintwork with a blanket to protect the paintwork.

4 Prise out the end of the rubber locking filler strip and pull it away from its channel in the sealing rubber.

5 Press hard on one corner of the glass from inside the car until the glass forces the rubber away from the metal edge of the windscreen aperture. Ease the rubber out carefully.

6 Now is the time to remove all pieces of glass if the screen has shattered. Use a vacuum cleaner to extract as much as possible. Switch on the heater boost motor and adjust the controls to 'Screen defrost' but watch out for flying pieces of glass which might be blown out of the ducting.

7 Carefully inspect the rubber moulding for signs of splitting or deterioration. Clean all traces of sealing compound from the rubber moulding and windscreen aperture flange. Position the sealing rubber over the metal edge of the windscreen aperture. Lubricate the rubber channel into which the glass fits with soap

and water and fit the glass to the bottom portion of the channelling. With a small screwdriver, the end of which should be bent over 180°, insert the end of the screwdriver under the lip of the rubber channel starting from one of the bottom corners and working all round the windscreen glass. Generously lubricate the strip of rubber locking filler with soap and water and force it into the outside channel of the surround rubber. When the rubber filler has been fitted all round cut it off, leaving an overlap of 0.25 in (6.35 mm) so that the ends of the rubber are against each other under pressure.

25 Rear quarterlight glass - removal and replacement

1 Undo the three crosshead screws which hold the side window retaining catch to the body and open the side window to give access to the hinge. (Fig. 12.10.)

2 To remove the window frame from the glass carefully press out the glass.

3 Replacement is a straight reversal of removal sequence.

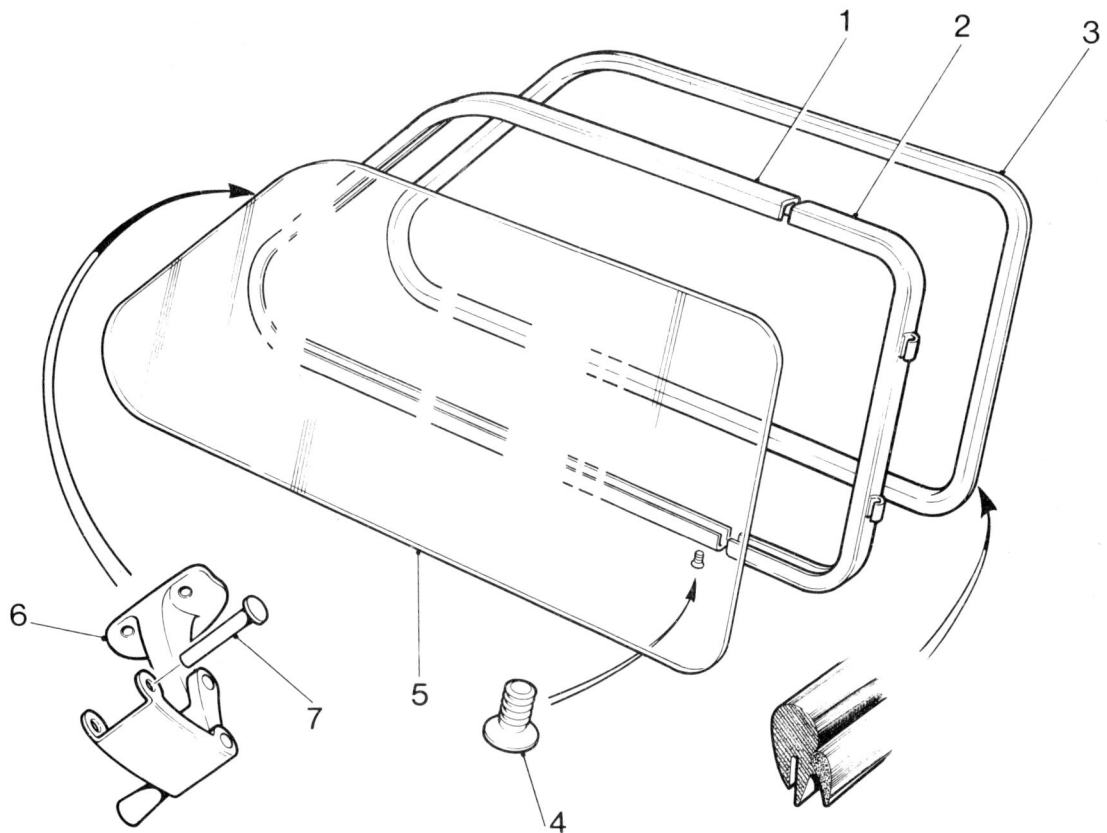

Fig. 12.10. Rear quarterlight (Sec. 25)

1 Frame assembly (rear rh)
2 Frame assembly (front rh)
3 Glazing rubber
4 Screw
5 Glass
6 Catch assembly
7 Rivet

26 Rear side windows (Countryman and Traveller) - removal and replacement

1 Unscrew and remove the two window catches.
2 Release and remove the two closing clips and detach the outer and inner finishers.
3 Remove the eight inner finisher retaining clips.
4 Drill out the five rivets that hold the glass channel retainer to the body.
5 The assembly may be removed by levering the glass channel retainer up and out from the bottom.
6 To remove the glasses from the assembly carefully flex the spring steel channel retainer and lift them out.
7 To reassemble first fit the window glasses into the channel retainer.
8 Fit the assembly into the body aperature, sealing it with a little 'Dum-Dum' putty.
9 Refit the eight inner finisher retaining clips.
10 Rivet the glass channel and retainer into position.
11 Reseal between the glass channel retainer and the body with a little 'Dum-Dum' putty. Take care not to seal over the water outlets.
12 Refit the inner and outer finishers with their appropriate clips and replace the two window catches.

27 Bumpers - removal and replacement

Austin, Morris, Wolseley, Riley, M.G.
Front
1 Undo and remove the bolts that secure the bumper to the lower front valance and lift off the assembly.
2 Refitting the front bumper is the reverse sequence to removal.

Rear
1 Undo and remove the bolts that secure the bumper to the rear valance and lift off the assembly.
2 Refitting the rear bumper is the reverse sequence to removal.

Princess
Front
The sequence for removal and replacement of the front bumper is identical to that for all 1100/1300 models.

Rear
1 Undo and remove the bumper to rear valance securing set screws and nuts.
2 Working in the luggage compartment remove the side cover and side panel to bumper set screws.
3 Disconnect the electrical connector on the rear number plate light and lift away the bumper assembly.
4 Refitting the rear bumper assembly is the reverse sequence to removal.

28 Front grille - removal and replacement

1 Open the bonnet to give access to the rear of the front grille.
2 Undo and remove the front grille securing screws and lift away the front grille assembly.
3 Refitting the front grille is the reverse sequence to removal.

29 Front and rear seats - removal and replacement

Front
1 Undo and remove the set screws that secure the seat to the floor panel centre section and lift away the seat assembly.
2 Refitting the front seat is the reverse sequence to removal.

Rear - Saloon
1 On Mk I models undo and remove the seat to floor tunnel securing nut.
2 Pull the seat forwards and lift away from inside the car.
3 On Mk II and 1300 models unscrew the self-tapping screw from the floor tunnel bracket and pull the front of the seat upwards.
4 To remove the squab remove the lower body securing screws and lift it up and over the locating tags on the rear body section.
5 Refitting the rear seat and squab is the reverse sequence to removal.

Rear - Countryman and Traveller
1 Undo and remove the four hexagon head metal thread screws which secure the rear seat cushion assembly to the pivot bracket.
2 Lift away the rear seat cushion.
3 To remove the squab lift the rear mat and unscrew the nine self-tapping screws which secure the squab to the hinges on the floor.
4 Lift away the rear seat squab.
5 Refitting the rear seat and squab is the reverse sequence to removal.

30 Electrically heated backlight - removal and replacement

1 Carefully remove both rear quarter trim liners.
2 Note their relative positions and then disconnect the wires at the snap connectors inside the body right-hand quarters and from the earth connection in the body left-hand quarter.
3 Remove the backlight glass as described in Section 24. Withdraw the wires through the holes in the body and surrounding rubber.
4 Refitting the electrically heated backlight is the reverse sequence to removal.

31 Parcel shelf - removal and replacement

Earlier models
1 Refer to Chapter 11, and remove the steering column assembly.
2 Detach the heater control panel from the parcel shelf rail.
3 Wolseley, Riley, M.G., Princess: Disconnect and remove the bonnet pull cable.
4 Undo and remove the screws that secure the parcel shelf to the body and lift away the assembly.
5 Refitting the parcel shelf is the reverse sequence to removal.

Austin and Morris de Luxe 1300 and 1100 Mk II models
1 Undo and remove the seven screws that secure the lower edge of the parcel tray to the body.
2 Using a suitable tool such as a bent screwdriver, bend the top edges of the parcel tray down to clear the padded top rail. Take care not to split the material.
3 Lift away the parcel tray assembly.
4 Refitting the parcel tray is the reverse sequence to removal. Carefully push its top edges beneath the padded top rail, starting at the inside first and working outwards.

Austin and Morris Super de Luxe 1300 and 1100 Mk II models
The sequence is basically identical to that for earlier Mk I models. There are however two additional screws in the centre and behind the fascia panel.

32 Fascia assembly - removal and replacement

Different fascia panels are fitted to Austin, Morris, Wolseley, Riley, M.G., and Princess models. In each case the battery must be disconnected before work commences.

Fig. 12.11. Fascia panel components (Morris 1100 Mk I) (Sec. 32)

1 Fascia panel assembly
2 Screw
3 Plate nut
4 Screw
5 Ashtray case
6 Ashtray
7 Screw
8 Instrument cowl
9 Screw
10 Screw
11 Plate nut
12 Front speaker grille
13 Screw
14 Screw
15 Spring washer
16 Nut
17 Cap-screw
18 Fascia pocket
19 Fascia pocket finisher
20 Finisher strip - long
21 Finisher strip - short
22 Glovebox
23 Glovebox - finisher
24 Finisher strip - long
25 Finisher strip - short
26 Clip
27 Rivet
28 Fascia tray
29 Screw
30 Cup washer
31 Plate nut
32 Support bracket
33 Rivet
34 Bulb holder bracket
35 Rivet
36 Heater control blanking escutcheon
37 Push-on fix
38 Windscreen washer pump hole plug
39 Plain washer
40 Push-on fix
41 Fascia support rail
42 Rivet
43 Stay
44 Screw
45 Plain washer
46 Nut
47 Screw
48 Stay
49 Screw
50 Screw
51 Spring washer
52 Nut

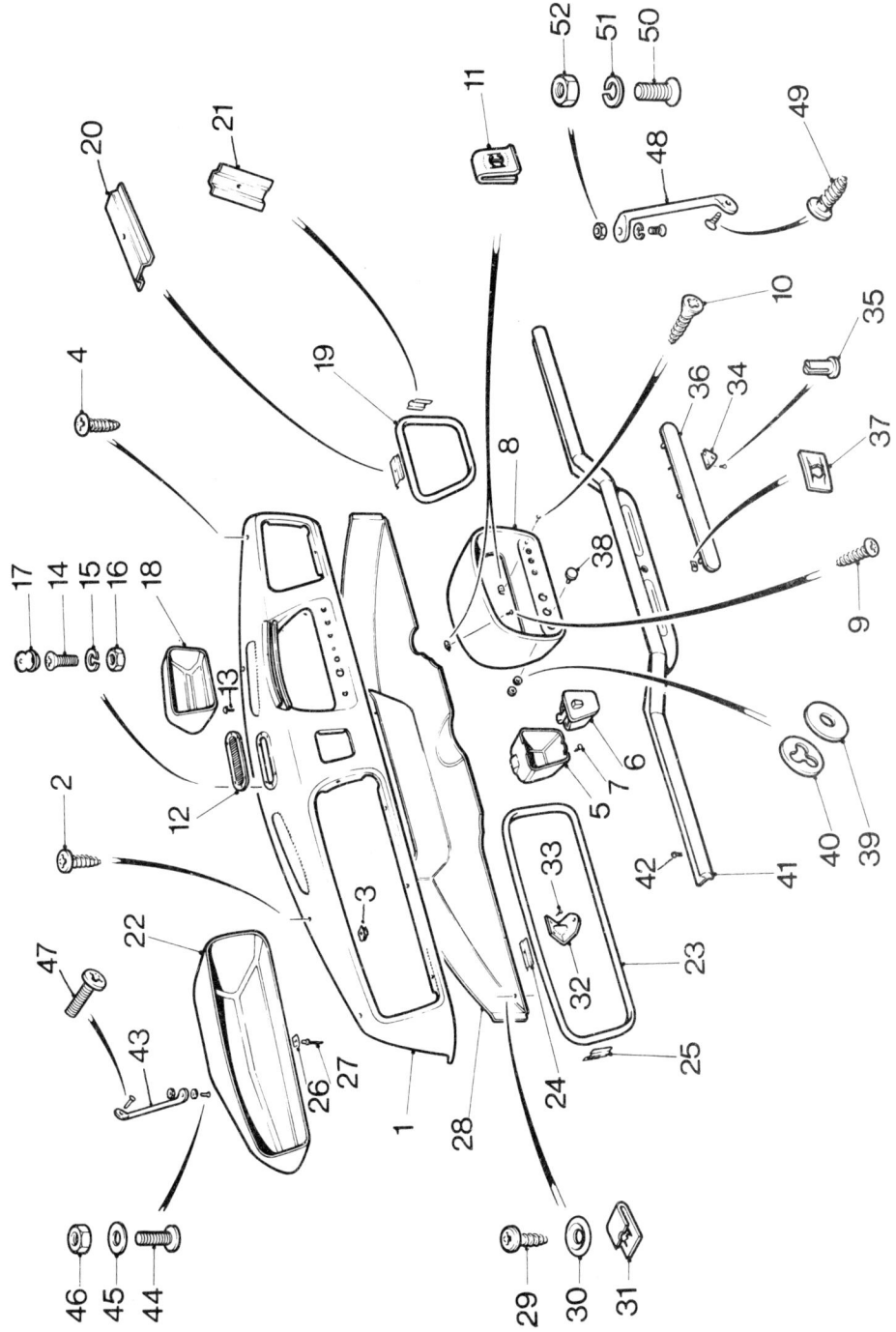

Fig. 12.12. Fascia panel components (Wolseley, Riley, MG and 1300GT) (Sec. 32)

1 Fascia panel assembly - rh
2 Fascia panel assembly - lh
3 Fascia panel assembly - centre
4 Screw, washer, nylon nut
5 Bracket
6 Bracket
7 Screw
8 Screw
9 Instrument panel assembly (all Wolseley and MG 1100 and 1300 models)
9a Instrument panel assembly (all Riley and MG 1300 Mk II and 1300GT)
10 Instrument panel finisher (all Wolseley and MG 1100 and 1300)
11 Instrument bezel
12 Screw
14 Glovebox lid assembly
15 Outer hinge
16 Inner hinge
17 Screw
18 Glovebox lid support
19 Screw
20 Handle
21 Screw
22 Magnetic lock
23 Magnetic lock keeper
24 Plug
25 Ashtray assembly
26 Ashtray case assembly
26a Wing nut
27 Ashtray retaining strip
28 Demister slot finisher
29 Push on fix
30 Fascia tray
31 Screw
32 Washer
33 Nut
34 Bracket
35 Rivet
36 Bracket
37 Rivet
38 Rivet
39 Washer
40 Support rail
41 Rivet
42 Stay
43 Screw
44 Plain washer
45 Nut
46 Screw
47 Stay
48 Screw
49 Screw
50 Nylon nut

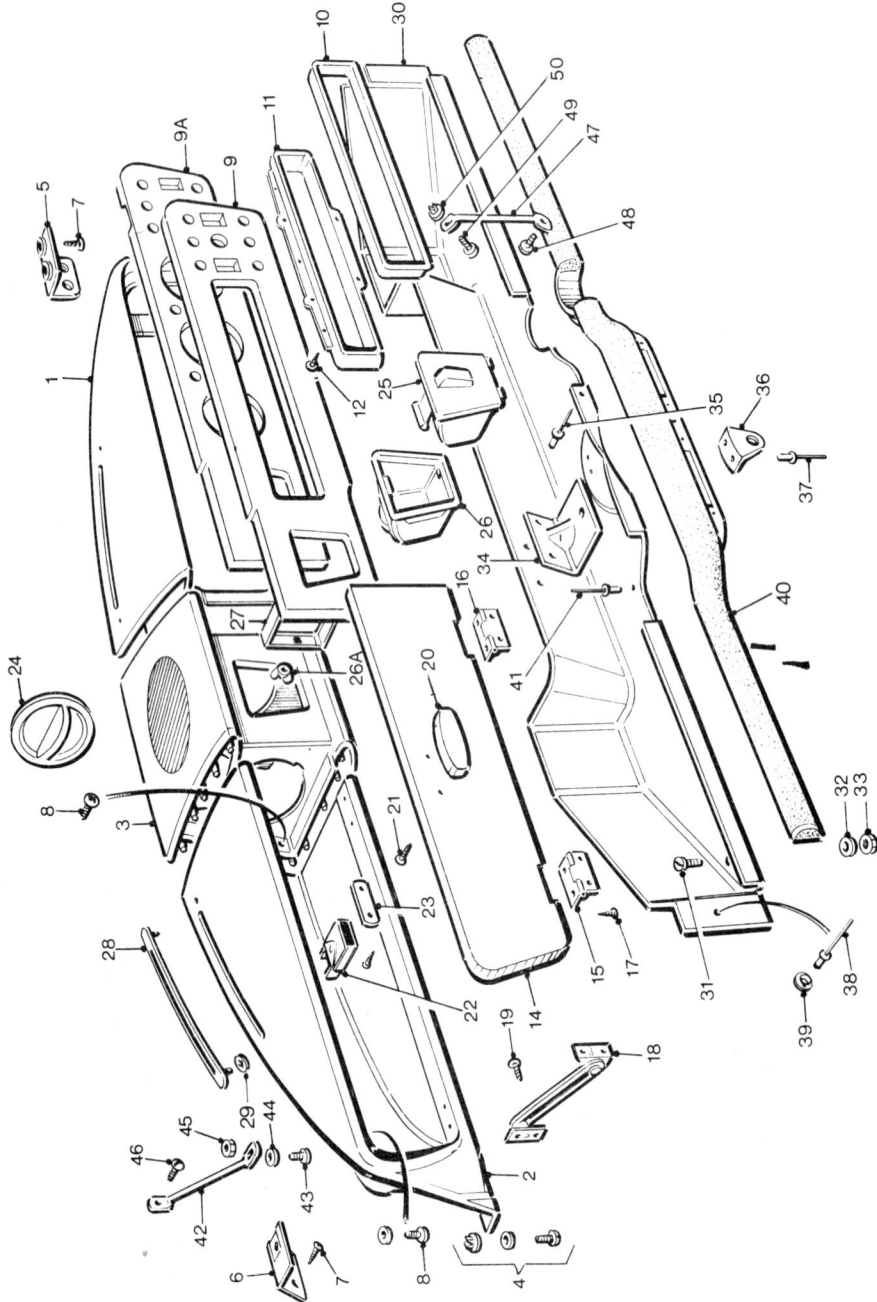

Fig. 12.13. Fascia panel components (Austin [except De Luxe], Morris 1300/1100 Mk II Super De Luxe and MG Sedan) (Sec. 32)

1 Top fascia panel
2 Panel retaining channel
3 Rivet
4 Lower fascia panel (Austin Mk I and MG Sedan)
4a Lower fascia panel (Austin and Morris 1300/1100 Mk II Super De Luxe)
5 Screw
6 Plate nut
7 Nut
8 Spring washer
9 Plain washer
10 Screw
11 Screw
12 Plain washer
13 Spring washer
14 Nut
15 Finisher
16 Rivet
17 Crash rail (lower fascia panel)
18 Rivet
19 Radio aperture mask
20 Plain washer
21 Spring washer
22 Nut
23 Steering column bracket
24 Screw
25 Plain washer
26 Spring washer
27 Parcel shelf
28 Crash pad (parcel shelf)
29 Rivet
30 Ashtray frame shield
31 Rivet
32 Screw
33 Plain washer
34 Spring washer
35 Screw
36 Ashtray
37 Ashtray case
38 Spring clip
39 Distance piece
40 Screw
41 Plain washer
42 Curved washer

H 6014

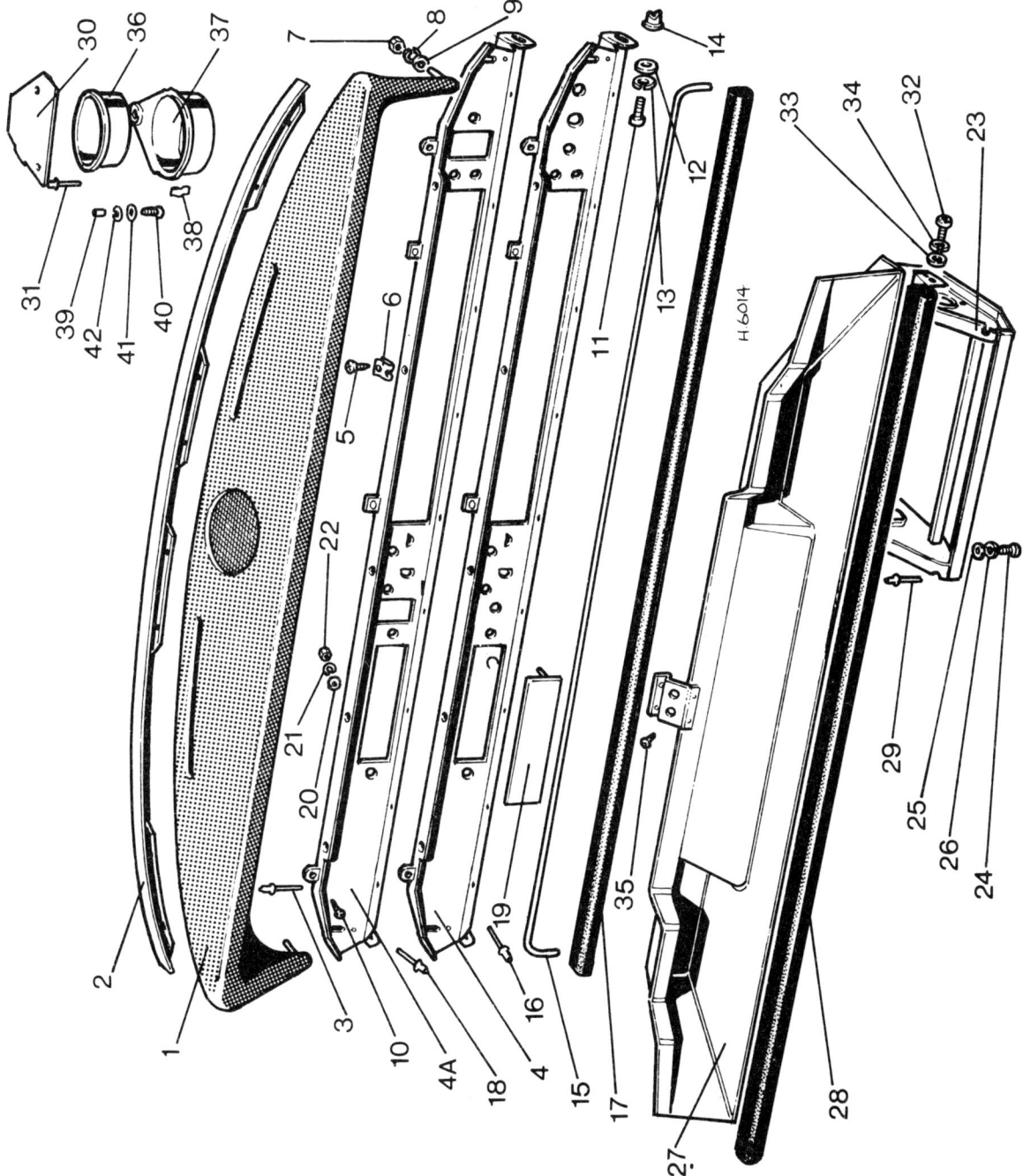

Fig. 12.14. Fascia panel components (Princess) (Sec. 32)

1 Fascia surround
2 Screw
3 Plain washer
4 Shakeproof washer
5 Screw
6 Plain washer
7 Shakeproof washer
8 Screw
9 Nut
10 Plain washer
11 Fascia board
12 Hinge
13 Stud and plate
14 Stud and plate
15 Wing nut
16 Plain washer
17 Spring washer
18 Lock
19 Lock striker plate
20 Magnetic catch
21 Quadrant
22 Box
23 Switch panel
24 Knob
25 Blanking plug
26 Panel illumination light casing
27 Instrument surround
28 Fresh air louvre
29 Fresh air hose
30 Mixture control bracket
31 Screw
32 Plain washer
33 Plate nut
34 Ashtray
35 Ashtray case
36 Ashtray retaining clip
37 Demister finisher slot
38 Push-on fix
39 Fascia support stay
40 Screw
41 Plain washer
42 Nut
43 Screw
44 Finisher 'A' post rh
45 Finisher 'A' post lh

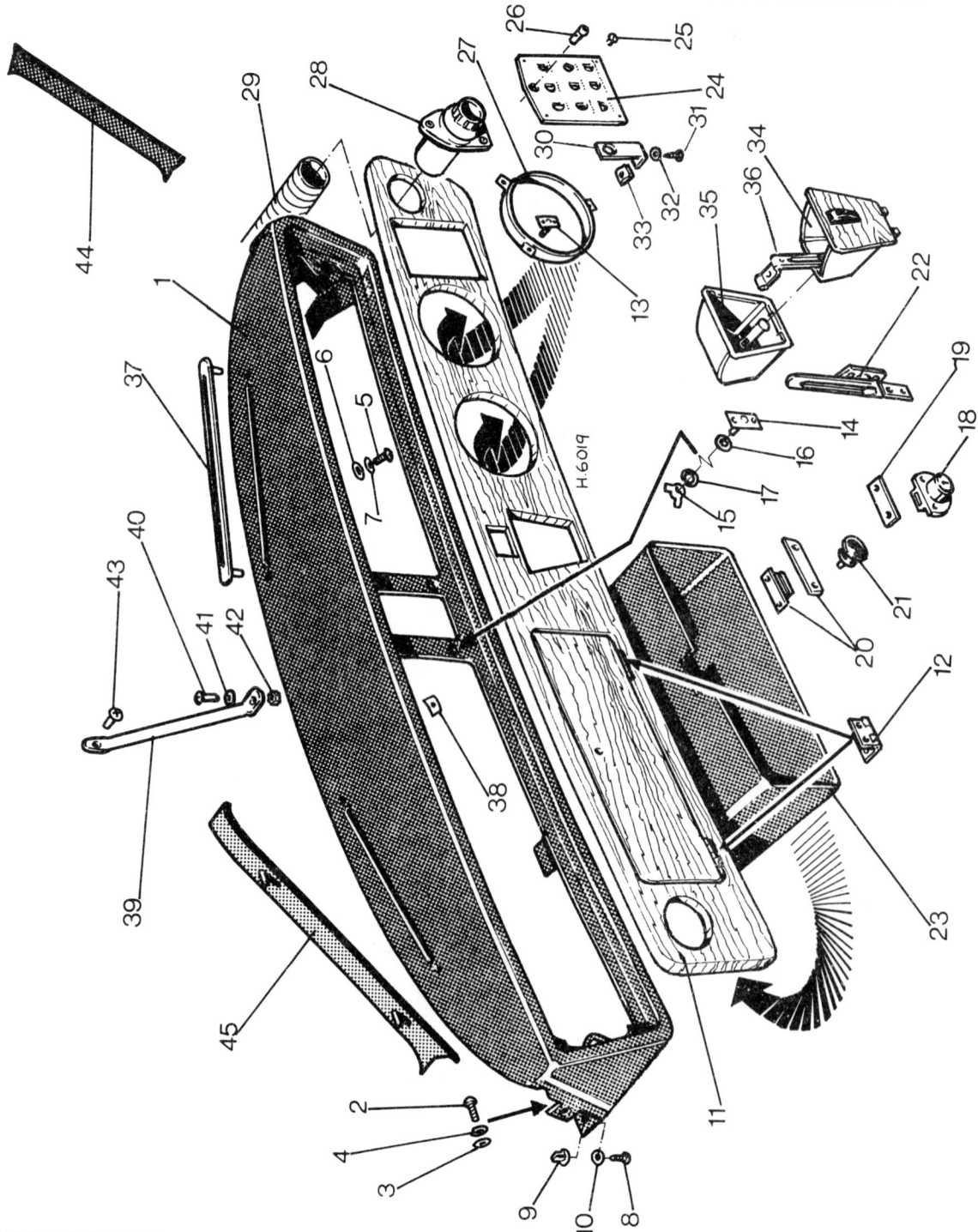

H.6019

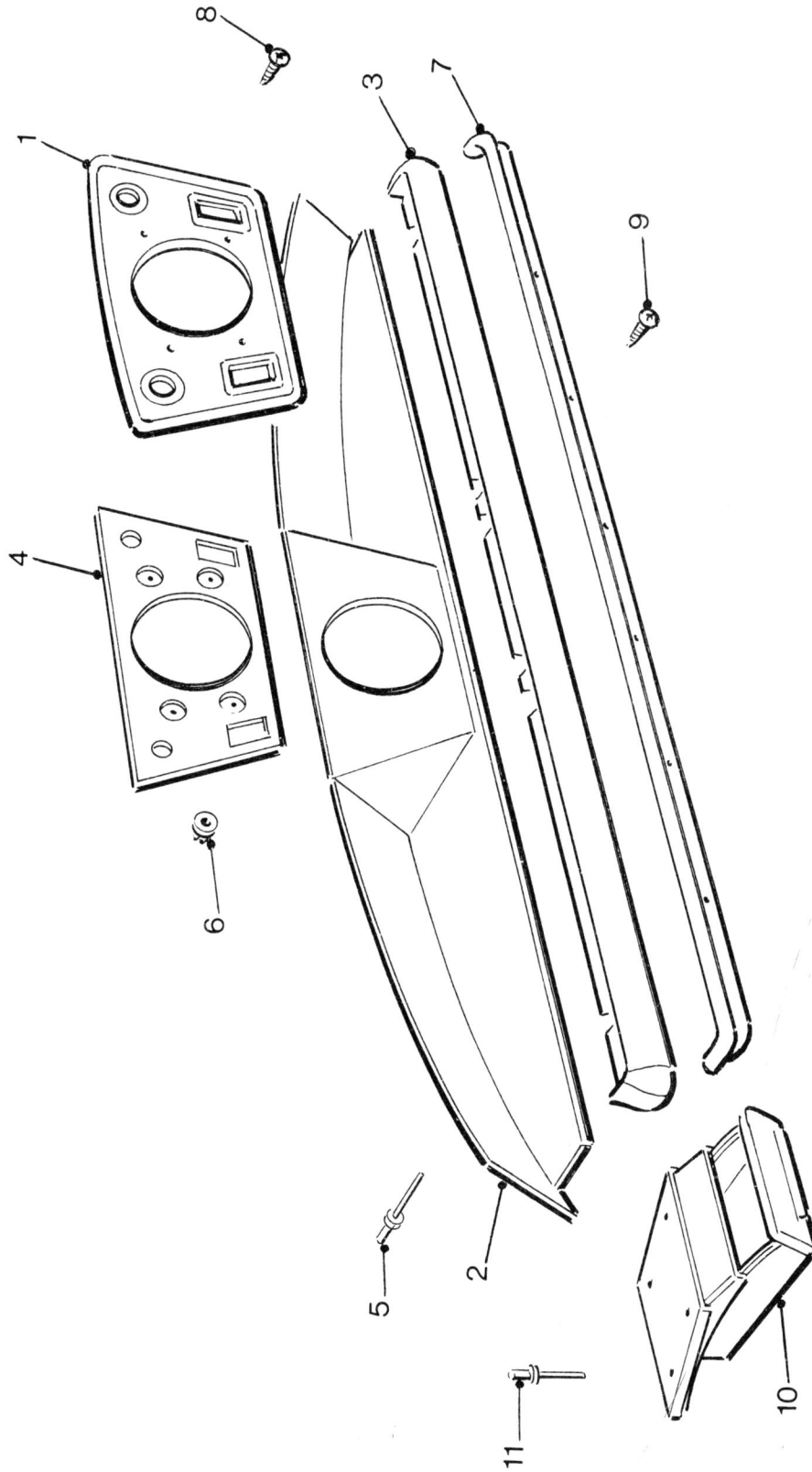

Fig. 12.15. Fascia panel components (Austin and Morris 1300/1100 Mk II De Luxe) (Sec. 32)

1 Finisher - instrument panel
2 Shelf panel
3 Crash pad
4 Plate backing - instrument panel
5 Rivet
6 Nut - speedometer (nylon)
7 Finisher - crash pad
8 Screw - instrument panel
9 Screw - crash-pad finisher
10 Ashtray
11 Rivet and washer

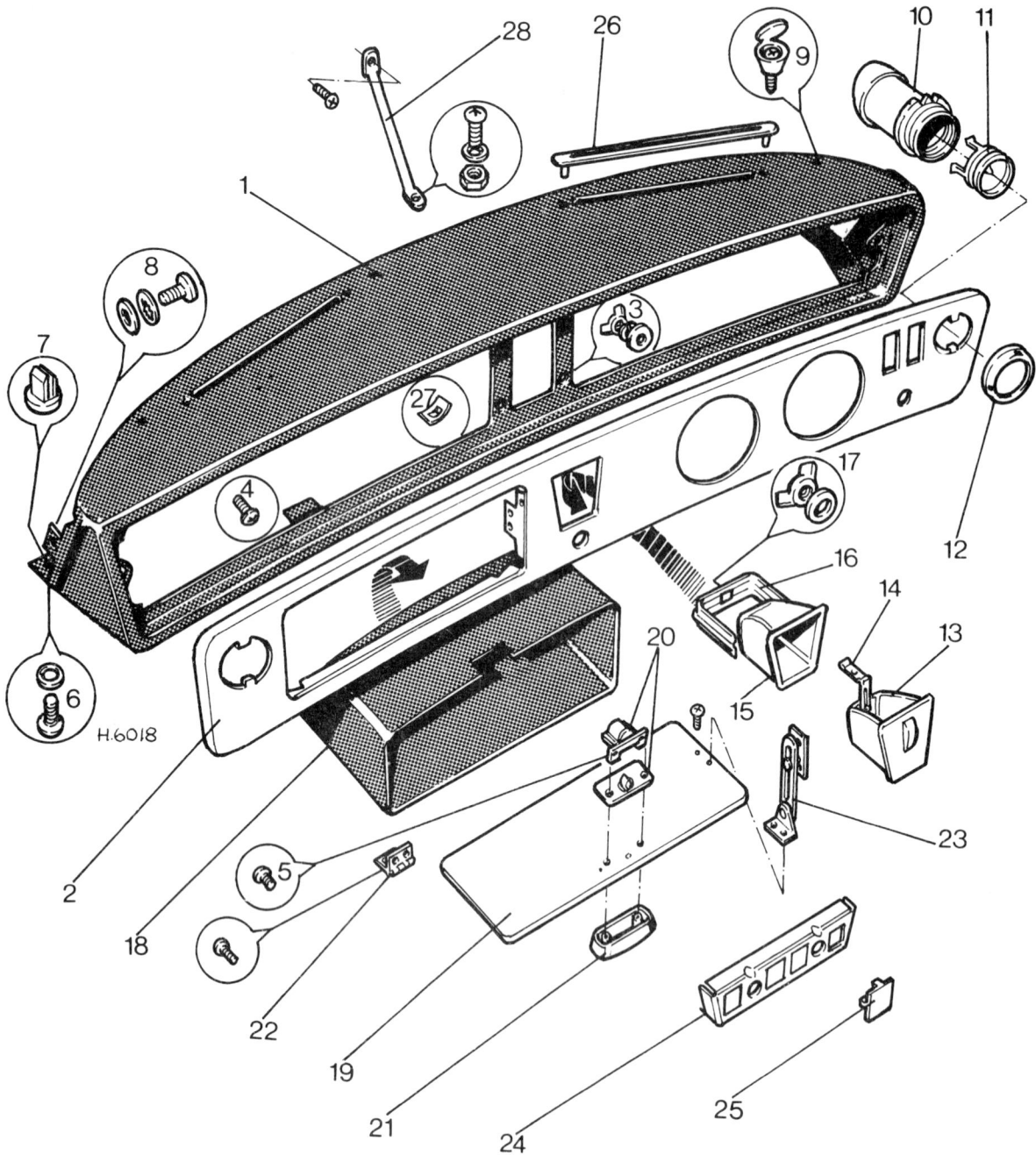

H.6018

Fig. 12.16. Fascia panel components (Austin and Morris Super De Luxe Mk III and later GT models) (Sec. 32)

1 Fascia panel surround
2 Fascia panel (Mk III type shown)
3 Fascia securing washer, spring washer, and wing nut (4 off)
4 Fascia securing lower screws (2 off)
5 Glovebox catch (fascia securing upper screws)
6 Fascia surround lower securing screw and washer
7 Anti-rattle bush
8 Surround side securing screw and washers

9 Surround upper securing screws with domed caps
10 Fascia vent
11 Fascia vent butterfly
12 Fascia vent securing ring
13 Ashtray
14 Ashtray securing clip
15 Ashtray case
16 Ashtray clamp
17 Wing nut and washer

18 Glovebox
19 Glovebox lid
20 Glovebox lid catch
21 Glovebox lid handle
22 Glovebox lid hinge
23 Quadrant
24 Supplementary panel (when fitted)
25 Blank
26 Demister finisher slot
27 Push-on fastener
28 Fascia support stay

Wolseley, Riley and M.G. Mk I models

1   From inside the glovebox take out the cover from the hole that gives access to the wing nut and bracket on the rear of the ashtray.

2   Undo the nut and remove the bracket, free the ashtray bulb holder and pull the assembly clear.

3   Take off the direction indicator switch and its cowling from the steering column surround and place them in the parcel shelf under the fascia.

4   Undo the ignition key locking ring or chromed screw and from under the bonnet free the choke cable from the carburettor.

5   Undo the bracket on the steering column supporting the fascia and pull the instrument panel sufficiently forward to gain access to the rear of the instruments.

6   Undo the knurled nut holding the speedometer cable to the speedometer head, remove the windscreen washer pipes; the trip mileage reset control (on early models only); all the electrical connections, and the oil pressure gauge pipe from its union on the rear of the oil pressure gauge when an oil gauge is fitted. The instrument panel assembly is now free and can be removed.

7   Undo the screws under the glovebox, and the panel securing screw inside the glovebox. Take off the glovebox.

8   With the glovebox removed next move on to the screws on the top and bottom of the instrument panel section. Undo them and lift the section out. Undo the screws retaining the centre section in place and remove it.

9   Replacement is a straightforward reversal of removal sequence.

Austin and MG Saloon Mk I models

The fascia consists of two separate parts which must be taken off and refitted separately. The top part comprises a padded rail, while the bottom part holds the instruments and controls. The fascias on early models were fixed differently to those on later cars.

1   On early models undo the single nut at each end of the top panel and remove together with the washers. Undo the countersunk screws which hold the top and bottom panels together.

2   On later models undo the screws which hold the top and bottom panels together.

3   On both models the top panel can now be lifted off.

4   Undo the locking rings securing the ignition switch and windscreen washer control in place.

5   Undo the hexagon nuts securing the headlight, panel light, and windscreen wiper switches to the instrument panel.

6   Open the bonnet and undo the choke cable from its connection to the carburettor.

7   Undo the speedometer cable from the rear of the speedometer and pull out the bulb holders. Disconnect the wires from the rear of the instruments. To facilitate replacement tag the wires and connections with masking tape and identify with numbers, ie. wire No. 1 fits on connection No. 1.

8   On early models undo the six screws which hold the lower panel in place and then remove it from the passenger's side of the car.

9   On later models undo the screws under the fascia and the two screws on the windscreen scuttle. Undo the screws holding the steering column bracket in place and remove the lower panel.

10 Replacement is a straightforward reversal of the dismantling sequence.

Morris Mk I models

1   On Morris models it is necessary to remove the steering column, as described in Chapter 11.

2   Undo the screws holding the cowling in place and pull the cowling away.

3   Free the switches and controls from the fascia panel assembly. Do not disconnect the choke cable or the wiring from the combined instrument.

4   Undo the screws holding the fascia panel in place and lift the panel away after easing off the windscreen demisting ducts.

5   Replacement is a straightforward reversal of the removal sequence.

Princess Mk I models

1   Disconnect the choke control cable from the carburettor.

2   Working within the car remove the mixture control bracket and bezels and push out the ignition/starter and wiper/washer switches.

3   Remove the wing-nut positioned directly below and behind the ball mounted air duct on the driver's side.

4   Remove the glove box lid and also the self-tapping screws that secure the glove box to the fascia board.

5   Remove the wing-nut that is positioned directly below and behind the ball mounted air duct on the passenger's side and both the centre wing nuts, which are on either side of the ashtray.

6   Refer to Chapter 11, and remove the steering column.

7   Pull the fascia board forwards at the bottom and lift it away from the fascia surround.

8   Disconnect all instruments and switches and remove the fascia board complete with instruments and switches.

9   Remove the self-tapping screws that secure the fascia surround to the body crossmember.

10 Remove the self-tapping screws that secure the surround to the 'A' post and the surround to the top crossmember.

11 Remove the 'A' post finishers and lift away the surround.

12 Refitting the fascia is the reverse sequence to removal.

The fascia board must be fitted with the board securing clips located in the fascia surround.

Austin and Morris De Luxe 1300 and Mk II models

1   Disconnect the battery, for safety reasons.

2   Undo and remove the four screws that hold the fascia to the parcel tray trim and pull it forwards complete with the lighting and windscreen wiper switches.

3   Disconnect the electrical connections and lift away the fascia panel.

4   Refitting the fascia panel is the reverse sequence to removal.

Austin and Morris Super de Luxe 1300 and 1100 Mk II models

1   Disconnect the battery, for safety reasons.

2   Undo and remove the four screws that hold the top rail in position after bending back the hinged metal caps from the outer two screws. Lift off the rail.

3   Undo and remove the six screws that secure the fascia panel, ease back the door trim adjacent to the fascia and pull it forwards.

4   Disconnect the choke cable at the carburettor, pull all Lucar connectors from the rear of the switches making a careful note of their locations.

5   Unscrew the drive from the speedometer and remove the earth lead.

6   The fascia panel complete with switches may now be lifted away.

7   Refitting the fascia panel assembly is the reverse sequence to removal.

Riley, M.G., Wolseley, Princess 1300 and 1100 Mk II models

For full information, refer to the instructions given for the Mk I models.

Austin and Morris Super de Luxe Mk II and later GT models

1   Disconnect the battery, for safety reasons.

2   Refer to Chapter 11, and remove the steering column.

3   Disconnect the choke inner cable at the carburettor.

4   Note the electric cable connections at the rear of the instruments and switches and disconnect.

5   Remove the two capped screws from each end of the top face

Fig. 12.17. Heater components (Sec. 33)

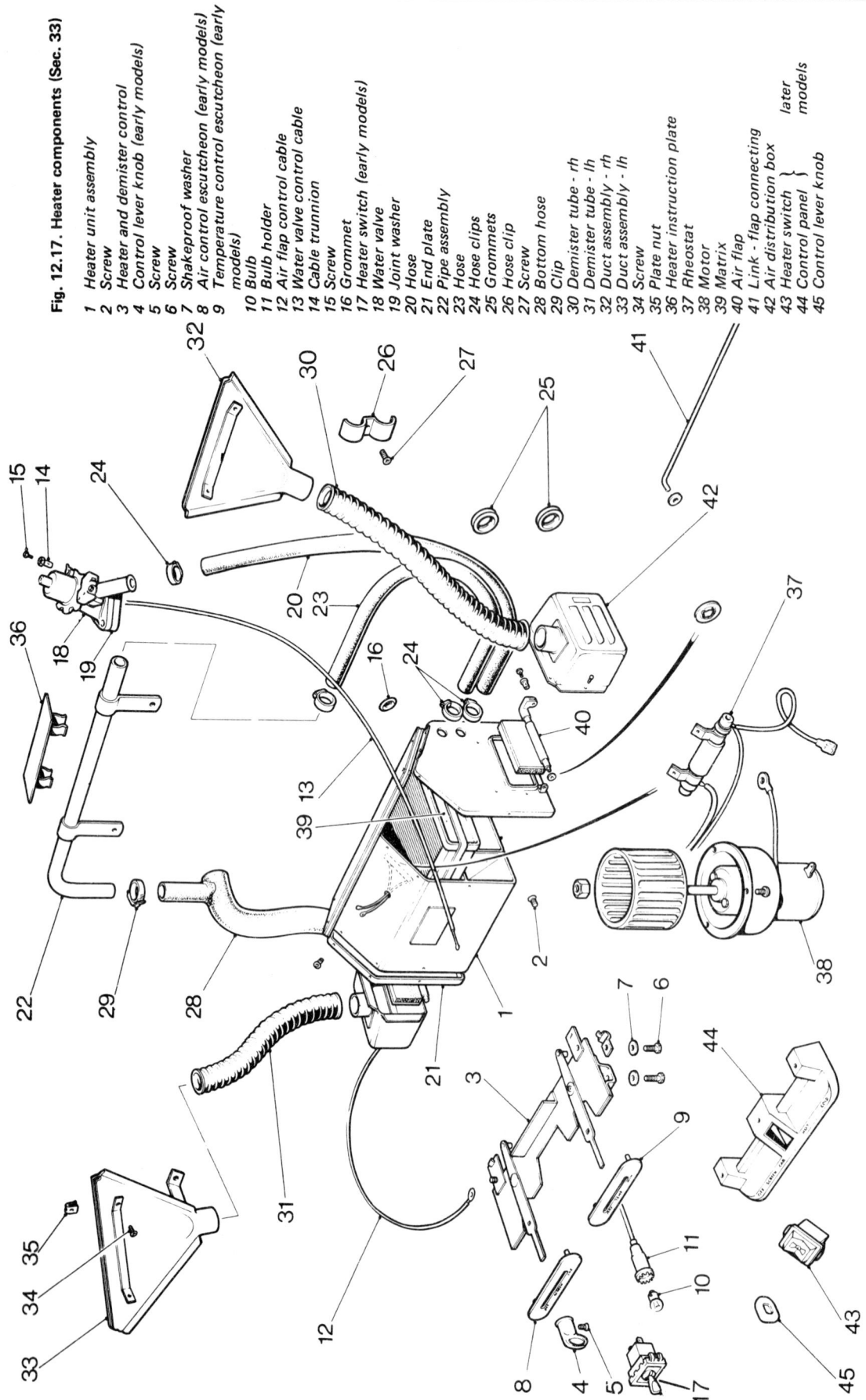

1 Heater unit assembly
2 Screw
3 Heater and demister control
4 Control lever knob (early models)
5 Screw
6 Screw
7 Shakeproof washer
8 Air control escutcheon (early models)
9 Temperature control escutcheon (early models)
10 Bulb
11 Bulb holder
12 Air flap control cable
13 Water valve control cable
14 Cable trunnion
15 Screw
16 Grommet
17 Heater switch (early models)
18 Water valve
19 Joint washer
20 Hose
21 End plate
22 Pipe assembly
23 Hose
24 Hose clips
25 Grommets
26 Hose clip
27 Screw
28 Bottom hose
29 Clip
30 Demister tube - rh
31 Demister tube - lh
32 Duct assembly - rh
33 Duct assembly - lh
34 Screw
35 Plate nut
36 Heater instruction plate
37 Rheostat
38 Motor
39 Matrix
40 Air flap
41 Link - flap connecting
42 Air distribution box
43 Heater switch } later
44 Control panel } models
45 Control lever knob

of the fascia surround and from the underside of the surround, the two screws from the centre flange and the two from either end.

6 Carefully ease the surround forwards, unscrew the drive from the speedometer and lift out the surround and fascia panel assembly.

7 Unscrew the wing nuts from either side of the ashtray and from behind each air vent on either side of the fascia.

8 Remove each screw from the bottom flange of the fascia panel and the two screws which also retain the glovebox catch from above the glovebox.

9 Separate the fascia panel, complete with instruments and switches from the surround.

10 Refitting the fascia panel assembly is the reverse sequence to removal.

---

33 Heater and ventilation system - removal and replacement

Heater control assembly

1 For safety reasons, disconnect the battery.

2 Detach the connectors from the rear of the blower switch.

3 Release the outer casing of both control cables from their clamps.

4 Disconnect the inner wires from their operating levers. It should be noted that there are three types of attachment:

a) A loop on the end of the inner wire which hooks over each lever pin.

b) The wire is threaded through a hole in each lever pin and then coiled round them.

c) The end of the wire is bent at a right-angle and passes through a hole in the end of each operating lever.

5 Undo and remove the securing screws and detach the heater control and panel assembly from beneath the parcel tray.

6 Refitting the heater control assembly is the reverse sequence to removal.

Heater unit assembly

1 For safety reasons, disconnect the battery.

2 Refer to Chapter 2, and drain the cooling system.

3 Refer to Chapter 11, and remove the steering column assembly.

4 Remove the parcel shelf complete with heater control assembly. It will be necessary to disconnect the control cables and switches as described in the previous Section.

Instructions for removal of the parcel shelf will be found in Section 31.

5 Disconnect the water hoses from the heater unit working inside the car.

6 Remove the demister tubes.

7 Detach the electrical connectors and bulb holder from the rear of the heater.

8 Undo and remove the screws that secure the heater assembly to the bulkhead.

9 Carefully remove the heater unit from the bulkhead. Do not tip excessively otherwise water will flow out of the heater matrix pipes and damage the carpeting.

10 Refitting the heater unit is the reverse sequence to removal. If an air lock is suspected once the system has been refilled with water, remove the radiator filler cap, detach the return pipe from the bottom hose and temporarily extend it to the radiator filler neck. Plug the return connection of the bottom hose, start the engine and run it until the flow of water into the radiator is free of bubbles. Remake the normal hose connections.

Water valve

1 Detach the control cable outer casing from its clamp and detach the inner wire from its trunnion.

2 The water valve and its gasket may now be removed from the engine.

3 Refitting the water valve is the reverse sequence to removal.

---

34 Heater unit assembly - dismantling and reassembly

---

1 Remove the heater unit, as described in Section 33.

2 Undo and remove the three screws, the earth wire and the electrical feed wire and lift away the motor from the heater casing.

3 If it is necessary to remove the fan, undo and remove the central nut so releasing the split collar around the centre of the fan and pull the fan from the motor spindle.

4 If the motor is faulty it cannot be repaired so a new motor will be required.

5 To remove the left-hand endplate slide the matrix from the heater casing. There are two clips on both endplates holding the matrix in place when it is assembled.

6 To inspect the air flaps remove the screws securing the air distribution boxes to the heater casing.

7 Check to see that both flaps are free to pivot and that the interconnecting link is operating correctly and has not become detached.

8 Reassembling the heater unit assembly is the reverse sequence to removal.

---

35 Rear subframe - removal and replacement

---

1 Take the car to your local BLMC garage for the hydrolastic suspension system to be depressurised. Drive the car home slowly (no faster than 30 mph).

2 Place the car in gear and then remove the rear hub caps, and loosen the wheel nuts.

3 Jack-up the rear of the car and place chocks or stands under the body in front of the subframe. Interpose a length of wood between the stands to spread the load across the underside of the floor.

4 Take out the floor in the boot and remove the two rubber plugs in the body floor panel which give access to the suspension displacer units.

5 Undo the hoses leading into the displacer units at their unions, and plug the open ends to keep out dirt.

6 Undo the nuts and bolts holding the exhaust pipe and silencer in place and remove them from under the car.

7 Undo the brake pipe union on the front crossmember of the subframe. Plug the open ends of the pipe to prevent total loss of the hydraulic fluid.

8 Take off the floor plate at the bottom of the handbrake lever and undo the cables from the trunnion. Pull the cables out from underneath the car so they are free from the body.

9 Take out the rear seat, and the rear seat squab. This exposes two rubber plugs in the floor. Remove them to give access to two of the mounting points.

10 Place a load spreader under the front and rear subframe crossmembers, and take the weight of the subframe in the centre of the load spreader with a jack.

11 Undo all the bolts, set screws, and nuts holding the mounting brackets to both the body and the subframe.

12 Replacement is a straightforward reversal of the removal sequence, but the following two points should be noted:

a) Do not fully tighten any of the mounting bracket bolts until all the bolts are in place. Tighten the bolts on each bracket a little in turn to ensure no distortion of the rubber mountings takes place.

b) The brakes must be bled before the car is driven to the local BLMC garage for pressurisation and trimming of the suspension.

Metric conversion tables

Inches	Decimals	Millimetres	Millimetres to Inches		Inches to Millimetres	
			mm	Inches	Inches	mm
1/64	0.015625	0.3969	0.01	0.00039	0.001	0.0254
1/32	0.03125	0.7937	0.02	0.00079	0.002	0.0508
3/64	0.046875	1.1906	0.03	0.00118	0.003	0.0762
1/16	0.0625	1.5875	0.04	0.00157	0.004	0.1016
5/64	0.078125	1.9844	0.05	0.00197	0.005	0.1270
3/32	0.09375	2.3812	0.06	0.00236	0.006	0.1524
7/64	0.109375	2.7781	0.07	0.00276	0.007	0.1778
1/8	0.125	3.1750	0.08	0.00315	0.008	0.2032
9/64	0.140625	3.5719	0.09	0.00354	0.009	0.2286
5/32	0.15625	3.9687	0.1	0.00394	0.01	0.254
11/64	0.171875	4.3656	0.2	0.00787	0.02	0.508
3/16	0.1875	4.7625	0.3	0.1181	0.03	0.762
13/64	0.203125	5.1594	0.4	0.01575	0.04	1.016
7/32	0.21875	5.5562	0.5	0.01969	0.05	1.270
15/64	0.234275	5.9531	0.6	0.02362	0.06	1.524
1/4	0.25	6.3500	0.7	0.02756	0.07	1.778
17/64	0.265625	6.7469	0.8	0.3150	0.08	2.032
9/32	0.28125	7.1437	0.9	0.03543	0.09	2.286
19/64	0.296875	7.5406	1	0.03937	0.1	2.54
5/16	0.3125	7.9375	2	0.07874	0.2	5.08
21/64	0.328125	8.3344	3	0.11811	0.3	7.62
11/32	0.34375	8.7312	4	0.15748	0.4	10.16
23/64	0.359375	9.1281	5	0.19685	0.5	12.70
3/8	0.375	9.5250	6	0.23622	0.6	15.24
25/64	0.390625	9.9219	7	0.27559	0.7	17.78
13/32	0.40625	10.3187	8	0.31496	0.8	20.32
27/64	0.421875	10.7156	9	0.35433	0.9	22.86
7/16	0.4375	11.1125	10	0.39270	1	25.4
29/64	0.453125	11.5094	11	0.43307	2	50.8
15/32	0.46875	11.9062	12	0.47244	3	76.2
31/64	0.484375	12.3031	13	0.51181	4	101.6
1/2	0.5	12.7000	14	0.55118	5	127.0
33/64	0.515625	13.0969	15	0.59055	6	152.4
17/32	0.53125	13.4937	16	0.62992	7	177.8
35/64	0.546875	13.8906	17	0.66929	8	203.2
9/16	0.5625	14.2875	18	0.70866	9	228.6
37/64	0.578125	14.6844	19	0.74803	10	254.0
19/32	0.59375	15.0812	20	0.78740	11	279.4
39/64	0.609375	15.4781	21	0.82677	12	304.8
5/8	0.625	15.8750	22	0.86614	13	330.2
41/64	0.640625	16.2719	23	0.90551	14	355.6
21/32	0.65625	16.6687	24	0.94488	15	381.0
43/64	0.671875	17.0656	25	0.98425	16	406.4
11/16	0.6875	17.4625	26	1.02362	17	431.8
45/64	0.703125	17.8594	27	1.06299	18	457.2
23/32	0.71875	18.2562	28	1.10236	19	482.6
47/64	0.734375	18.6531	29	1.14173	20	508.0
3/4	0.75	19.0500	30	1.18110	21	533.4
49/64	0.765625	19.4469	31	1.22047	22	558.8
25/32	0.78125	19.8437	32	1.25984	23	584.2
51/64	0.796875	20.2406	33	1.29921	24	609.6
13/16	0.8125	20.6375	34	1.33858	25	635.0
53/64	0.828125	21.0344	35	1.37795	26	660.4
27/32	0.84375	21.4312	36	1.41732	27	685.8
55/64	0.859375	21.8281	37	1.4567	28	711.2
7/8	0.875	22.2250	38	1.4961	29	736.6
57/64	0.890625	22.6219	39	1.5354	30	762.0
29/32	0.90625	23.0187	40	1.5748	31	787.4
59/64	0.921875	23.4156	41	1.6142	32	812.8
15/16	0.9375	23.8125	42	1.6535	33	838.2
61/64	0.953125	24.2094	43	1.6929	34	863.6
31/32	0.96875	24.6062	44	1.7323	35	889.0
63/64	0.984375	25.0031	45	1.7717	46	1168.4

1   Imperial gallon = 8 Imp pints = 1.16 US gallons = 277.42 cu in = 4.5459 litres

1   US gallon = 4 US quarts = 0.862 Imp gallon = 231 cu in = 3.785 litres

1   Litre = 0.2199 Imp gallon = 0.2642 US gallon = 61.0253 cu in = 1000 cc

Miles to Kilometres		Kilometres to Miles	
1	1.61	1	0.62
2	3.22	2	1.24
3	4.83	3	1.86
4	6.44	4	2.49
5	8.05	5	3.11
6	9.66	6	3.73
7	11.27	7	4.35
8	12.88	8	4.97
9	14.48	9	5.59
10	16.09	10	6.21
20	32.19	20	12.43
30	48.28	30	18.64
40	64.37	40	24.85
50	80.47	50	31.07
60	96.56	60	37.28
70	112.65	70	43.50
80	128.75	80	49.71
90	144.84	90	55.92
100	160.93	100	62.14

lb f ft to Kg f m		Kg f m to lb f ft		lb f/in^2 : Kg f/cm^2		Kg f/cm^2 : lb f/in^2	
1	0.138	1	7.233	1	0.07	1	14.22
2	0.276	2	14.466	2	0.14	2	28.50
3	0.414	3	21.699	3	0.21	3	42.67
4	0.553	4	28.932	4	0.28	4	56.89
5	0.691	5	36.165	5	0.35	5	71.12
6	0.829	6	43.398	6	0.42	6	85.34
7	0.967	7	50.631	7	0.49	7	99.56
8	1.106	8	57.864	8	0.56	8	113.79
9	1.244	9	65.097	9	0.63	9	128.00
10	1.382	10	62.330	10	0.70	10	142.23
20	2.765	20	144.660	20	1.41	20	284.47
30	4.147	30	216.990	30	2.11	30	426.70

Index

Printed by
J. H. HAYNES & Co. Ltd
Sparkford Yeovil Somerset
ENGLAND